THE MAKING OF AMERICAN DEMOCRACY
VOLUME ONE

☆

The Making of

AMERICAN

DEMOCRACY

READINGS AND DOCUMENTS

49289

EDITED BY

RAY ALLEN BILLINGTON

William Smith Mason Professor of History
Northwestern University

BERT JAMES LOEWENBERG

Professor of American History
Sarah Lawrence College

SAMUEL HUGH BROCKUNIER

Professor of History
Wesleyan University

DAVID S. SPARKS

Associate Professor of History
University of Maryland

VOLUME ONE
REVISED EDITION

HOLT, RINEHART AND WINSTON · NEW YORK

Preface to the Revised Edition

In revising this book a major effort has been made to emphasize and reflect the rapidly changing world about us. In the decade since the first edition of this work appeared, the face of the world has been radically altered. At home we have struggled to adjust to spreading suburbias with their bulging schools and overworked highways. The growing demands for new schools, better roads, and additional shopping centers have brought enormous changes in the political, economic, and social fabric of American life. Abroad, we have had to face changes wrought by an age of thermonuclear warheads and intercontinental missiles, changes complicated and sharpened by the onrushing tide of Asian and African nationalism. In addition, man's new ventures into outer space have implications for us that we are still trying to understand. The new edition of this book reflects these changes in several ways.

The chapters in Volume II dealing with the 1930s and 1940s have been completely revised. In addition, three entirely new chapters have been added to cover the 1950s and the current scene. The earlier chapters in the volume have not been neglected, each one having been thoroughly pruned and reshaped.

The revision of Volume I has been only a little less extensive. Approximately one third of the volume is entirely new. Chapters on social and economic developments have been added, and the Civil War chapter is substantially new. The remaining two thirds of the readings and documents have been reorganized.

The two principles that have guided the selection of new documents or readings have been, first, relevance to significant developments in the American heritage and, second, intrinsic interest for undergraduate students. Where controversial matters have been treated, a conscientious effort has been made to present the several sides of the question.

Many teachers and students will find the arrangement of the materials suitable to a "problem" approach to the American past; others will prefer to use the readings and documents as a supplement to a textbook on the subject.

While all three editors of the original edition have contributed to the revision, particular mention should be made of Professor Brockunier's constant interest and assistance, and Professor Loewenberg's helpful cooperation. Thanks are also due Professors William Hanchett of San Diego State College, Robert Kelley of the University of California, Santa Barbara, and Kenneth O'Brien of Colgate University, whose suggestions are an integral part of this revision. The contribution of Phyllis Bate Sparks has been the *sine qua non* of the entire effort.

David S. Sparks

January 1962

Preface to the First Edition

The purpose of this book is to present a continuous documentary account of American history. The sequence of chapters and topics centers attention on critical periods in the nation's growth. The connective tissue of narrative introductions provides an integrated account of major trends and relates the documentary excerpts to their larger social context. It is hoped that such a book, weaving documents into a narrative of general history, will be more significant and useful than an ordinary compilation of readings.

In view of the broadening historical horizon and the growth of interest in social, economic, and intellectual history, the editors have sought not only to include "standard" documents, but to balance them with other types of materials. The readings range from public and official documents to contemporary impressions and eye-witness accounts, contemporary statements of critical problems and ideas, and modern evaluations.

The documents are reproduced as originally written. Necessarily, excisions have been made, in order to delete extraneous material and to make room for additional documents. All omissions are indicated by ellipses. A few minor changes in punctuation and abbreviation have been made in the interest of clarity and uniformity.

The Constitution of the United States, including the Bill of Rights and all subsequent amendments, has been included as an appendix in both volumes; the Declaration of Independence, which appears as a document in the first volume, has also been included as an appendix in the second.

The editors wish to acknowledge special indebtedness to the following: to Professor Chester M. Destler for his several readings and many suggestions, as well as for his aid in obtaining documents; to Professors Edwin B. Coddington, Gilbert C. Fite, James B. Hedges, and Rodman W. Paul for their readings and helpful suggestions; and to Mr. Edward Lurie for his aid in checking various documents.

R.A.B.
B.J.L.
S.H.B.

February 1950

Contents

III
LAND, LABOR, LIFE, AND TRADE IN THE AMERICAN COLONIES

Land

Labor

Life

Trade

Restraints on Trade

IV
THE AGE OF REVOLUTION

Clash of Authority and Liberty

Preface to Revolution

Drifting toward Independence

The War for Independence

V
THE CONSTITUTION AND CONSERVATISM

The Problems of Victory

Constitutional Mechanics

The Rise of Political Parties

VI
ADOLESCENT NATIONALISM

The Foundations of American Foreign Policy

Self-Conscious Americans

The Enlightenment Deepens

VII
JEFFERSONIAN REPUBLICANISM

The Jeffersonian Philosophy

Foreign Affairs under Jefferson and Madison

The War of 1812

VIII
THE FLOWERING OF NATIONALISM

Sectional Specialization

Government Aid and Regional Interests

Constitutional Powers and Vested Rights

Slavery and Sectional Compromise

A National Foreign Policy

IX
THE CHALLENGE OF SECTIONALISM

The Democratic Spirit

Jackson and the Sectional Challenge

The Government and the Economy

Slavery and Sectionalism

X
THE TRIUMPH OF DEMOCRATIC REFORM

The Goals of Social Reform

Ideals of Economic Democracy

Crusade for the Equality of Women

The Religious Search for Utopia

Blueprints for Social Reform

XI
SECTIONALISM AND EXPANSION

Manifest Destiny

The Expansion Westward

The Mexican Campaign

Expansion and Slavery

XII
DRIFTING TOWARD DISUNION

The Debate is Renewed

The Division Widens

XIII
CIVIL WAR

The Breakdown of the Democratic Process

The Lines are Drawn

The Sound of Battle

War Echoes

The Greater Conflict

The Falling Curtain

XIV
ROAD TO REUNION

The Unresolved Conflict

The Fourteenth Amendment

The Critical Year

The Issue of White Supremacy

The Legacy of Reconstruction

The Rule of the Stalwarts

The Transit of European Civilization

The discovery of America was no accident. By the end of the fifteenth century all Europe desperately needed room for expansion, both commercial and physical. During four centuries European wealth had been drained eastward to purchase exotic Oriental goods from the Moslem traders of the Levant. Money shortages brought hard times. The spices and gems secured from Levantine middlemen were brought by caravan or ship from distant China and Japan. Why not establish a direct trade with the Far East, thus circumventing the Moslems whose high charges kept the Continent in poverty?

HOW THE NEW WORLD LOOKED TO EUROPEANS

1

The pioneers in this quest were merchants of the new national states fringing the Atlantic: Portugal, Spain, France, and England. Portugal led the way when Bartholomeo Diaz in 1486 rounded the southern tip of Africa to find the road to the Orient lying open before him. Spain hurried into action as soon as Moorish invaders from Africa were driven from her soil; six months after the last enemy stronghold at Granada fell, the Spanish monarchs, Ferdinand and Isabella, dispatched Christopher Columbus, a Genoese navigator, to explore the only other feasible route to the East. Upon his return, Columbus reported promptly to the king and queen. To Luis de Sant'Angel, an official of the royal court of Spain, Columbus wrote of what he had seen and done. It was through this letter, written within weeks of his return and soon circulating throughout the continent, that Europeans generally learned of Columbus' adventures:[1]

SIR: As I know that you will have pleasure from the great victory which our Lord hath given me in my voyage, I write you this, by which you shall know that in thirty-three days I passed over to the Indies with the fleet which the most illustrious King and Queen, our Lords, gave me; where I found very many islands peopled with inhabitants beyond number. And, of them all, I have taken possession for their Highnesses, with proclamation and the royal standard displayed; and I was not gainsaid. To the first which I found, I gave the name San Salvador, in commemoration of His High Majesty, who marvellously hath given all this: the Indians call it Guanaham. The second I named the Island of Santa Maria de Concepcion, the third Ferrandina, the fourth, Fair Island, the fifth La Isla Juana; and so for each one a new name. When I reached Juana, I followed its coast westwardly, and found it so large that I thought it might be mainland, the province of Cathay. And as I did not thus find any towns and villages on the sea-coast, save small hamlets with the people whereof I could not get speech, because they all fled away forthwith, I went on further in the same direction, thinking I should not miss of great cities or towns. And at the end of many leagues, seeing that there was no change, and that the coast was bearing me northwards, whereunto my desire was contrary, since the winter was already confronting us, I formed the purpose of mak-

[1] Bernard Quaritch, *The Spanish Letter of Columbus to Luis de Sant'Angel . . .* (London, 1893), pp. 10–18.

ing from thence to the South, and as the wind also blew against me, I determined not to wait for other weather and turned back as far as a port agreed upon; from which I sent two men into the country to learn if there were a king, or any great cities. They travelled for three days, and found innumerable small villages and a numberless population, but nought of ruling authority; wherefore they returned. I understood sufficiently from other Indians whom I had already taken, that this land, in its continuousness, was an island; and so I followed its coast eastwardly for a hundred and seven leagues as far as where it terminated; from which headland I saw another island to the east, eighteen leagues distant from this, to which I at once gave the name La Spañola. And I proceeded thither, and followed the northern coast, as with La Juana, eastwardly for a hundred and eighty-eight great leagues in a direct easterly course, as with La Juana. The which, and all the others, are most fertile to an excessive degree, and this extremely so. In it, there are many havens on the sea-coast, incomparable with any others that I know in Christendom, and plenty of rivers so good and great that it is a marvel. The lands thereof are high, and in it are very many ranges of hills, and the island of Tenerife, all most beautiful in most lofty mountains incomparably beyond a thousand shapes, and all accessible, and full of trees of a thousand kinds, so lofty that they seem to reach the sky. And I am assured that they never lose their foliage; as may be imagined, since I saw them as green and as beautiful as they are in Spain during May. And some of them were in flower, some in fruit, some in another stage according to their kind. And the nightingale was singing, and other birds of a thousand sorts, in the month of November, there where I was going. There are palm-trees of six or eight species, wondrous to see for their beautiful variety; but so are the other trees, and fruits, and plants therein. There are wonderful pine-groves, and very large plains of verdure, and there is honey, and many kinds of birds, and many various fruits. In the earth there are many mines of metals; and there is a population of incalculable number. Española is a marvel; the mountains and hills, and plains, and fields, and the soil, so beautiful and rich for planting and sowing, for breeding cattle of all sorts, for building of towns and villages. There could be no believing, without seeing, such harbors as are here, as well as the many and great rivers, and excellent waters, most of which contain gold. In the trees and fruits and plants, there are great diversities from those of Juana. In this, there are many spiceries, and great mines of gold and other metals. The people of this island, and of all the others that I have found and seen, or not seen, all go naked, men and women, just as their mothers bring them forth; although some women cover a single place with the leaf of a plant, or a cotton something which they make for that purpose. They have no iron or steel, nor any weapons; nor are they fit thereunto; not because they be not a well-formed people and of fair stature, but that they are most wondrously timorous. They have no other weapons than the stems of reeds in their seeding state, on the end of which they fix little sharpened stakes. Even these, they dare not use; for many times has it happened that I sent two or three men ashore to some village to parley, and countless numbers of them sallied forth, but as soon as they saw those approach, they fled away in such wise that even a father would not wait for his son. And this was not because any hurt had ever been done to any of them:—on the contrary, at every headland where I have gone and been able to hold speech with them, I gave them of everything which I had, as well cloth as many other things, without accepting aught therefor; —but such they are, incurably timid. It is true that since they have become more assured, and are losing that terror, they are artless and generous with what they have, to such a degree as no one would believe but him who had seen it. Of anything they have, if it be asked for, they never say no, but do rather invite the person to accept it, and show as much lovingness as though they would give their hearts. And whether it be a thing of value, or one of little worth, they are straightways content with whatsoever trifle of whatsoever kind may be given them in return for it. I forbade that anything so worthless as fragments of broken platters, and pieces of broken glass, and strap buckles, should be given them; although when they were able to get such things, they seemed to think they had the best jewel in the world, for it was the hap of a sailor to get, in exchange for a strap, gold to the weight of two and a half castellanos, and others much more for other things of far less value; while for new blancas they gave everything they had, even though it were [the worth of] two or three gold castellanos, or one or two arrobas of spun cotton. They took even pieces of broken barrel hoops, and gave whatever they had, like senseless brutes; insomuch that it seemed to me bad. I forbade it, and I gave gratuitously a thousand useful things that I carried, in order that they may conceive affection, and furthermore may become Christians; for they are inclined to the love and service of their Highnesses and of all the Castilian nation, and they strive to combine in giving us things which they have in abundance, and of which we are in need. And they knew no sect, nor idolatry; save that they all believe that power and goodness are in the sky, and they believed very firmly that I, with these ships and crews, came from the sky; and in such opinion, they received me at every place where I landed, after they had lost their terror. And this comes not because they are ignorant: on the contrary, they are men of very subtle wit, who navigate all those seas, and who give a marvellously good account of everything, but because they never saw men wearing clothes nor the like of our ships. And as soon as I arrived in the Indies, in the first island that I found, I took some of them by force, to the intent that they should learn [our speech] and give me information of what there was in those parts. And so it was, that very soon they understood [us] and we them, what by speech or what by signs; and those [Indians]

have been of much service. To this day I carry them [with me] who are still of the opinion that I come from Heaven [as appears] from much conversation which they have had with me. And they were the first to proclaim it wherever I arrived; and the others went running from house to house and to the neighboring villages, with loud cries of "Come! come to see the people from Heaven!" Then, as soon as their minds were reassured about us, every one came, men as well as women, so that there remained none behind, big or little; and they all brought something to eat and drink, which they gave with wondrous lovingness. They have in all the islands very many *canoas,* after the manner of rowing-galleys, some larger, some smaller; and a good many are larger than a galley of eighteen benches. They are not so wide, because they are made of a single log of timber, but a galley could not keep up with them in rowing, for their motion is a thing beyond belief. And with these, they navigate through all those islands, which are numberless, and ply their traffic. I have seen some of those *canoas* with seventy and eighty men in them, each one with his oar. In all those islands, I saw not much diversity in the looks of the people, nor in their manners and language; but they all understand each other, which is a thing of singular advantage for what I hope their Highnesses will decide upon, for converting them to our holy faith, unto which they are well disposed. I have already told how I had gone a hundred and seven leagues, in a straight line from West to East, along the seacoast of the Island of Juana; according to which itinerary, I can declare that that island is larger than England and Scotland combined; as, over and above those hundred and seven leagues, there remain for me, on the western side, two provinces whereto I did not go—one of which they call Avan, where the people are born with tails—which provinces cannot be less in length than fifty or sixty leagues, according to what may be understood from the Indians with me, who know all the islands. This other, Española, has a greater circumference than the whole of Spain from Col[ibre in Catal]unya, by the sea-coast, as far as Fuente Ravia in Biscay; since, along one of its four sides, I went for a hundred and eighty-eight great leagues in a straight line from west to east. This is [a land] to be desired,—and once seen, never to be relinquished—in which (although, indeed, I have taken possession of them all for their Highnesses, and all are more richly endowed than I have skill and power to say, and I hold them all in the name of their Highnesses who can dispose thereof as much and as completely as of the kingdoms of Castile) in this Española, in the place most suitable and best for its proximity to the gold mines, and for traffic with the mainland both on this side and with that over there belonging to the Great Can, where there will be great commerce and profit, I took possession of a large town which I named the city of Navidad. And I have made fortification there, and a fort (which by this time will have been completely finished) and I have left therein men enough for such a purpose, with arms and artillery, and provisions for more than a year, and a boat, and a [man who is] master of all seacraft for making others; and great friendship with the king of that land, to such a degree that he prided himself on calling and holding me as his brother. And even though his mind might change towards attacking those men, neither he nor his people know what arms are, and go naked. As I have already said, they are the most timorous creatures there are in the world, so that the men who remain there are alone sufficient to destroy all that land, and the island is without personal danger for them if they know how to behave themselves. It seems to me that in all those islands, the men are all content with a single wife; and to their chief or king they give as many as twenty. The women, it appears to me, do more work than the men. Nor have I been able to learn whether they held personal property, for it seemed to me that whatever one had, they all took share of, especially of eatable things. Down to the present, I have not found in those islands any monstrous men, as many expected, but on the contrary all the people are very comely; nor are they black like those in Guinea, but have flowing hair; and they are not begotten where there is an excessive violence of the rays of the sun. It is true that the sun is there very strong, although it is twenty-six degrees distant from the equinoctial line. In those islands, where there are lofty mountains, the cold was very keen there, this winter; but they endure it by being accustomed thereto, and by the help of the meats which they eat with many and inordinately hot spices. Thus I have not found, nor had any information of monsters, except of an island which is here the second in the approach to the Indies, which is inhabited by a people whom, in all the islands, they regard as very ferocious, who eat human flesh. These have many canoes with which they run through all the islands of India, and plunder and take as much as they can. They are no more ill-shapen than the others, but have the custom of wearing their hair long, like women; and they use bows and arrows of the same reed stems, with a point of wood at the top, for lack of iron which they have not. Amongst those other tribes who are excessively cowardly, these are ferocious; but I hold them as nothing more than the others. These are they who have to do with the women of Matinino—which is the first island that is encountered in the passage from Spain to the Indies—in which there are no men. Those women practise no female usages, but have bows and arrows of reed such as above mentioned; and they arm and cover themselves with plates of copper of which they have much. In another island, which they assure me is larger than Española, the people have no hair. In this there is incalculable gold; and concerning these and the rest I bring Indians with me as witnesses. And in conclusion, to speak only of what has been done in this voyage, which has been so hastily performed, their Highnesses may see that I shall give them as much gold as they may need, with very little aid which their Highnesses will give me; spices and cotton at once, as much as their High-nesses will order to be shipped, and as much as they shall order to be shipped of mastic,— which till now has never been found except in Greece, in the island of Xio, and the Seignory sells it for what it likes; and aloes-wood as much as they shall order to be shipped; and slaves as many as they shall order to be shipped,—and these shall be from idolators. And I believe that I have discovered rhubarb and cinnamon, and I shall find that the men whom I am leaving there will have discovered a thousand other things of value; as I made no delay at any point, so long as the wind gave me an opportunity of sailing, except only in the town of Navidad till I had left things safely arranged and well established. And in truth I should have done much more if the ships had served me as well as might reasonably have been expected. This is enough; and [thanks to] Eternal God our Lord who gives, to all those who walk His way, victory over things which seem impossible; and this was signally one such, for although men have talked or written of those lands, it was all by conjecture, without confirmation from eyesight, amounting only to this much that the hearers for the most part listened and judged that there was more fable in it than anything actual, however trifling. Since thus our Redeemer has given to our most illustrious King and Queen, and to their famous kingdoms, this victory in so high a matter, Christendom should have rejoicing therein and make great festivals, and give solemn thanks to the Holy Trinity for the great exaltation they shall have by the conversion of so many peoples to our holy faith; and next for the temporal benefit which will bring hither refreshment and profit, not only to Spain, but to all Christians. This briefly, in accordance with the facts. Dated, on the caravel, off the Canary Islands, the 15 February of the year 1493.

At your command,

THE ADMIRAL

Postscript Which Came Within the Letter

After having written this letter, and being in the sea of Castile, there rose upon me so much wind, South and Southeast, that it has caused me to lighten the vessels; however, I ran hither to-day into this port of Lisbon, which was the greatest wonder in the world; where I decided to write to their Highnesses. I have always found the seasons like May in all the Indies, whither I passed in thirty-three days, and returned in twenty-eight, but that these storms have delayed me twenty-three days running about this sea. All the seamen say here that there never has been so bad a winter, nor so many ship-wrecks.

Dated the 14th of March.

2

Francis Drake sailed from Plymouth, England on November 15, 1577. His course took him south along the east coast of South America. After a leisurely voyage, he sailed into the Pacific through the Straits of Magellan. Plundering the Spanish as he moved northward, Drake finally decided the best way home to England lay north and west across the Pacific Ocean, through the Indian Ocean, and around Africa. He was on the threshold of this high adventure when he visited the California coast in the spring of 1577. This account is attributed to Francis Pretty:[2]

From Guatulco we departed the day following, viz., April 16, [1579] setting our course directly into the sea, whereon we sayled 500 leagues in longitude, to get a wind: and betweene that and June 3, 1400 leagues in all, till we came into 42 deg. of North latitude, where in the night following we found such alteration of heate, into extreame and nipping cold, that our men in generall did grievously complaine thereof, some of them feeling their healths much impaired thereby; neither was it that this chanced in the night alone, but the day following carried with it not onely the markes, but the stings and force of the night going before, to the greatest admiration of us all; for besides that the pinching and biting aire

---

[2] Richard Hakluyt, *The Principall Navigations . . . of the English Nation* (1589 ed.). (In Part 3, six leaves inserted between pp. 643 and 644.)

was nothing altered, the very roapes of our ship were stiffe, and the raine which fell was an unnatural congealed and frozen substance, so that we seemed rather to be in the frozen Zone then any way so neere unto the sun, or these hotter climates. . . .

The next day [June 18, 1579], after our comming to anchor in the aforesaid harbour, [Drake's Bay, about 30 miles north of San Francisco] the people of the countrey shewed themselves, sending off a man with great expedition to us in a canow. Who being yet but a little from the shoare, and a great way from our ship, spake to us continually as he came rowing on. And at last at a reasonable distance staying himselfe, he began more solemnely a long and tedious oration, after his manner: using in the deliverie thereof many gestures and signes, moving his hands, turning his head and body many wayes; and after his oration ended, with great shew of reverence and submission returned backe to shoare againe. He shortly came againe the second time in like manner, and so the third time, when he brought with him (as a present from the rest) a bunch of feathers, much like the feathers of a blacke crow, very neatly and artificially gathered upon a string, and drawne together into a round bundle; being verie cleane and finely cut, and bearing in length an equall proportion one with another; a speciall cognizance (as wee afterwards observed) which they that guard their kings person weare on their heads. With this also he brought a little basket made of rushes, and filled with an herbe which they called *Tabáh* [possibly tobacco]. Both which being tyed to a short rodde, he cast into our boate. Our Generall intended to have recompenced him immediatly with many good things he would have bestowed on him; but entring into the boate to deliver the same, he could not be drawne to receive them by any meanes, save one hat, which being cast into the water out of the ship, he tooke up (refusing utterly to meddle with any other thing, though it were upon a board put off unto him) and so presently made his returne. After which time our boate could row no

way, but wondring at us as at gods, they would follow the same with admiration. . . .

To the intent, therefore, that this peace which they themselves so willingly sought might, without any cause of the breach thereof on our part given, be continued, and that wee might with more safety and expedition end our businesses in quiet, our Generall, with all his company, used all meanes possible gently to intreate them, bestowing upon each of them liberally good and necessary things to cover their nakedness; withall signifying unto them we were no Gods, but men, and had neede of such things to cover our owne shame; teaching them to use them to the same ends, for which cause also wee did eate and drinke in their presence, giving them to understand that without that wee could not live, and therefore were but men as well as they.

Notwithstanding nothing could perswade them, nor remove that opinion which they had conceived of us, that wee should be Gods.

In recompence of those things which they had received of us, as shirts, linnen cloth, etc., they bestowed upon our Generall, and diverse of our company, diverse things, as feathers, cawles of networke, the quivers of their arrowes, made of fawne skins, and the very skins of beasts that their women wore upon their bodies. Having thus had their fill of this times visiting and beholding of us, they departed with joy to their houses, which houses are digged round within the earth, and have from the uppermost brimmes of the circle clefts of wood set up, and joined close together at the top, like our spires on the steeple of a Church; which being covered with earth, suffer no water to enter, and are very warme; the doore in the most part of them performes the office also of a chimney to let out the smoake: its made in bignesse and fashion like to an ordinary scuttle in a ship, and standing slopewise: their beds are the hard ground, onely with rushes strewed upon it, and lying round about the house, have their fire in the middest, which by reason that the house is but low vaulted, round, and close, giveth a marvelous reflexion to their bodies to heate the same.

Their men for the most part goe naked; the women take a kinde of bulrushes, and kembing it after the manner of hemp, make themselves thereof a loose garment, which being knitte about their middles, hanges downe about their hippes, and so affordes to them a covering of that which nature teaches should be hidden; about their shoulders they weare also the skin of a deere, with the haire upon it. They are very obedient to their husbands, and exceeding ready in all services; yet of themselves offring to do nothing, without the consents or being called of the men. . . .

After that our necessary businesses were well dispatched, our Generall, with his gentlemen and many of his company, made a journy up into the land, to see the manner of their dwelling, and to be the better acquainted with the nature and commodities of the country. There houses were all such as we have formerly described, and being many of them in one place, made severall villages here and there. The inland we found to be farre different from the shoare, a goodly country, and fruitfull soyle, stored with many blessings fit for the use of man: infinite was the company of very large and fat Deere which there we sawe by thousands, as we supposed, in a heard; besides a multitude of a strange kinde of Conies, by farre exceeding them in number: their heads and bodies, in which they resemble other Conies, are but small; his tayle, like the tayle of a Rat, exceeding longe; and his feet like the pawes of a Want or moale; under his chinne, on either side, he hath a bagge, into which he gathereth his meate, when he hath filled his belly abroade, that he may with it, either feed his young, or feed himselfe when he lists not to travaile from his burrough; the people eate their bodies, and make great account of their skinnes, for their kings holidaies coate was made of them.

This country our Generall named *Albion*, and that for two causes; the one in respect of the white bancks and cliffes, which lie to-

ward the sea; the other, that it might have some affinity, even in name also, with our own country, which was sometimes so called.

3

When Sir Walter Raleigh was granted a patent authorizing him to "discover, search, finde out and view such remote, heathen, and barbarous lands, countries, and territories, not actually possessed by any Christian prince," he promptly fitted out an expedition for a preliminary survey of portions of the North American coast. Captain Arthur Barlowe, master of one of the two vessels sent out by Raleigh in 1584, wrote the following description of what was found. The account was first written as a report to Sir Walter:[3]

The 27 day of Aprill, in the yeere of our redemption 1584, we departed the West of England, with two barkes well furnished with men and victuals, having received our last and perfect directions by your letters, confirming the former instructions, and commandements delivered by your selfe at our leaving the river of Thames. . . .

The tenth of May we arrived at the Canaries, and the tenth of June in this present yeere, we were fallen with the Islands of the West Indies, keeping a more Southeasterly course then was needefull, because wee doubted that the current of the Bay of Mexico, disbogging betweene the Cape of Florida and Havana, had bene of greater force then afterwardes we found it to bee. At which Islands we found the ayre very unwholsome, and our men grew for the most part ill disposed; so that having refreshed our selves with sweet water, and fresh victuall, we departed the twelfth day of our arrivall there. . . .

The second of July, we found shole water, wher we smelt so sweet, and so strong a smel, as if we had bene in the midst of some delicate garden abounding with all kinde of odoriferous flowers, by which we were assured, that the land could not be farre distant: and keeping good watch, and bearing

---

[3] Edmund Goldsmid (ed.), *The Voyages of the English Nation to America, Collected by Richard Hakluyt* (Edinburgh, 1889), II, 282–293.

but slacke saile, the fourth of the same moneth we arrived upon the coast, which we supposed to be a continent and firme lande, and we sayled along the same a hundred and twentie English miles before we could finde any entrance, or river issuing into the Sea. The first that appeared unto us, we entred, though not without some difficultie, and cast anker about three harquebuz-shot within the havens mouth, on the left hand of the same: and after thankes given to God for our safe arrivall thither, we manned our boats, and went to view the land next adjoyning, and to take possession of the same, in the right of the Queenes most excellent Majestie, as rightfull Queene, and Princesse of the same, and after delivered the same over to your use, according to her Majesties grant, and letters patents, under her Highnesse great seale. Which being performed, according to the ceremonies used in such enterprises, we viewed the land about us, being, whereas we first landed, very sandie and low towards the waters side, but so full of grapes, as the very beating and surge of the sea overflowed them, of which we found such plentie, as well there as in all places else, both on the sand and on the greene soile on the hills, as in the plaines, as well on every little shrubbe, as also climing towardes the tops of high Cedars, that I thinke in all the world the like abundance is not to be found: and my selfe having seene those parts of Europe that most abound, find such difference as were incredible to be written. . . .

This lande lay stretching it selfe to the West, which after wee found to bee but an Island of twentie miles long, and not above six miles broade. . . .

This Island had many goodly woodes full of Deere, Conies, Hares, and Fowle, even in the middest of Summer in incredible abundance. The woodes are not such as you finde in Bohemia, Moscovia, or Hercynia, barren and fruitles, but the highest and reddest Cedars of the world, farre bettering the Ceders of the Açores, of the Indies, or Lybanus, Pynes, Cypres, Sassaphras, the Len-

tisk, or the tree that beareth the Masticke . . . We remained by the side of this Island two whole dayes before we saw any people of the Countrey: the third day we espied one small boate rowing towardes us having in it three persons: this boat came to the Island side, foure harquebuz-shot from our shippes, and there two of the people remaining, the third came along the shoreside towards us, and wee being then all within boord, he walked up and downe upon the point of the land next unto us: then the Master and the Pilot of the Admirall, Simon Ferdinando, and the Captaine Philip Amadas, my selfe, and others rowed to the land, whose comming this fellow attended, never making any shewe of feare or doubt. And after he had spoken of many things not understood by us, we brought him with his owne good liking, aboord the ships, and gave him a shirt, a hat and some other things, and made him taste of our wine, and our meat, which he liked very wel: and after having viewed both barks, he departed, and went to his owne boat againe, which hee had left in a little Cove or Creeke adjoyning: as soone as hee was two bow shoot into the water, he fell to fishing, and in lesse then halfe an houre, he had laden his boate as deepe, as it could swimme, with which hee came againe to the point of the lande, and there he divided his fish into two parts, pointing one part to the ship, and the other to the pinnesse; which, after he had (as much as he might) requited the former benefites received, departed out of our sight.

The next day there came unto us divers boates, and in one of them the Kings brother, accompanied with fortie or fiftie men, very handsome and goodly people, and in their behaviour as mannerly and civill as any of Europe. His name was Granganimeo, and the king is called Wingina, the countrey Wingandacoa and now by her Majestie Virginia. The maner of his comming was in this sort: hee left his boates altogether as the first man did a little from the shippes by the shore, and came along to the place over against the ships, followed with fortie men.

When he came to the place his servants spread a long matte upon the ground, on which he sate downe, and at the other ende of the matte foure others of his companie did the like, the rest of his men stood round about him, somewhat a farre off: when we came to the shore to him with our weapons, hee never mooved from his place, nor any of the other foure, nor never mistrusted any harme to be offred from us, but sitting still he beckoned us to come and sit by him, which we performed: and being set hee made all signes of joy and welcome, striking on his head and his breast, and afterwardes on ours, to shew wee were all one, smiling and making shewe the best he could of all love, and familiaritie. After hee had made a long speech unto us, wee presented him with divers things which hee received very joyfully, and thankefully. None of the companie durst speake one worde all the time: only the foure which were at the other ende, spake one in the others eare very softly. . . .

A day or two after this, we fell to trading with them, exchanging some things that we had, for Chamoys, Buffe, and Deere skinnes: when we shewed him all our packet of merchandize, of all things that he sawe, a bright tinne dish most pleased him, which hee presently tooke up and clapt it before his breast, and after made a hole in the brimme thereof and hung it about his necke, making signes that it would defende him against his enemies arrowes: for those people maintaine a deadly and terrible warre, with the people and King adjoyning. We exchanged our tinne dish for twentie skinnes, woorth twentie Crownes, or twentie Nobles: and a copper kettle for fiftie skins woorth fiftie Crownes. They offered us good exchange for our hatchets, and axes, and for knives and would have given any thing for swordes: but wee would not depart with any. After two or three dayes the Kings brother came aboord the shippes, and dranke wine, and eat of our meat and of our bread, and liked exceedingly thereof: and after a fewe days overpassed, he brought his wife with him to the ships, his daughter and two or three children: his wife was very well favoured, of meane stature, and very bashfull: shee had on her backe a long cloake of leather, with the furre side next to her body, and before her a piece of the same: about her forehead shee had a bande of white Corall, and so had her husband many times: in her eares shee had bracelets of pearles hanging downe to her middle, (whereof wee delivered your worship a little bracelet) and those were of the bignes of good pease. The rest of her women of the better sort had pendants of copper hanging in either eare, and some of the children of the kings brother and other noble men, have five or sixe in either eare: he himselfe had upon his head a broad plate of golde, or copper, for being unpolished we knew not what mettall it should be, neither would he by any meanes suffer us to take it off his head, but feeling it, it would bow very easily. His apparell was as his wives, onely the women weare their haire long on both sides, and the men but on one. They are of colour yellowish, and their hair black for the most part, and yet we saw children that had very fine aburne and chestnut coloured haire.

WHY THEY DECIDED TO COME

4

The New World was England's opportunity. To the rising merchant class overseas colonies offered economic opportunity; to zealous Protestants they offered a bulwark against Catholic Spain and France; to the poor they promised salvation—salvation from overcrowded farms, from oppressive political institutions, from burdensome church duties, and from starvation. The enclosure of fields for sheep growing, for example, which converted thousands of peasants into beggars and vagabonds was movingly portrayed by the Reverend William Harrison in a great Elizabethan cooperative work, Holinshed's Chronicles:[4]

---

[4] William Harrison, "An Historicall Description of the Iland of Britaine; with a Briefe Rehersall of the Nature and Qualities of the People of England," *Holinshed's Chronicles of England, Scotland, and Ireland* (London, 1807 ed.), II, bk. 2, pp. 307–308.

There is no common-wealth at this daie in Europe, wherein there is not great store of poore people, and those necessarilie to be relieued by the welthier sort, which otherwise would starue and come to vtter confusion. With vs the poore is commonlie diuided into thrée sorts, so that some are poore by impotencie, as the fatherlesse child, the aged, blind and lame, and the diseased person that is iudged to be incurable: the second are poore by casualtie, as the wounded souldier, the decaied house-holder, and the sicke person visited with grieuous and painefull diseases: the third consisteth of thriftlesse poore, as the riotour that hath consumed all, the vagabund that will abide no where, but runneth vp and downe from place to place (as it were séeking worke and finding none) and finallie the roge and strumpet which are not possible to be diuided in sunder, but runne too and fro ouer all the realme, chéefelie kéeping the champaine soiles in summer to auoid the scorching heat, and the woodland grounds in winter to eschew the blustering winds.

For the first two sorts, that is to saie, the poore by impotencie, and the poore by casualtie, which are the true poore in deed, and for whome the word dooth bind vs to make some dailie prouision: there is order taken through out euerie parish in the realme, that weekelie collection shall be made for their helpe and sustentation, to the end they should not scatter aboard, and by begging here and there annoie both towne and countrie. Authoritie also is giuen vnto the iustices in euerie countie, and great penalties appointed for such as make default, to sée that the intent of the statute in this behalfe be trulie executed, according to the purpose and meaning of the same, so that these two sorts are sufficientlie prouided for: and such as can liue within the limits of their allowance (as each one will doo that is godlie and well disposed) may well forbeare to rome and range about. But if they refuse to be supported by this benefit of the law, and will rather indeuour by going to and fro to mainteine their idle trades, then are they

adiudged to be parcell of the third sort, and so in stéed of courteous refreshing at home, are often corrected with sharpe execution, and whip of iustice abroad. Manie there are, which notwithstanding the rigor of the lawes prouided in that behalfe, yéeld rather with this libertie (as they call it) to be dailie vnder the feare and terrour of the whip, than by abiding where they were borne or bred, to be prouided for by the deuotion of the parishes. I found not long since a note of these latter sort, the effect whereof insueth. Idle beggers are such either through other mens occasion, or through their owne default. By other mens occasion (as one waie for example) when some couetous man, such I meane as haue the cast or right veine, dailie to make beggers inough wherby to pester the land, espieng a further commoditie in their commons, holds, and tenures, dooth find such meanes as thereby to wipe manie out of their occupiengs, and turne the same vnto his priuate gaines. Herevpon it followeth, that although the wise and better minded, doo either forsake the realme for altogether, and seeke to liue in other countries, as France, Germanie, Barbarie, India, Moscouria, and verie Calecute, complaining of no roome to be left for them at home, doo so behaue themselues that they are worthilie to be accompted among the second sort: yet the greater part commonlie having nothing to staie vpon are wilfull, and therevpon doo either prooue idle beggers, or else continue starke théeues till the gallowes doo eat them vp, which is a lamentable case. Certes in some mans iudgements these things are but trifles, and not worthie the regarding. Some also doo grudge at the great increase of people in these daies, thinking a necessarie brood of cattell farre better than a superfluous augmentation of mankind. But I can liken such men best of all vnto the pope and the diuell, who practise the hinderance of the furniture of the number of the elect to their vttermost, to the end the authoritie of the one vpon earth, the deferring of the locking vp of the other in euerlasting chaines, and the great gaines of the first may continue and indure the longer. But if it should come to passe that any forren inuasion should be made, which the Lord God forbid for his mercies sake! then should these men find that a wall of men is farre better than stackes of corne and bags of monie, and complaine of the want when it is too late to séeke remedie. The like occasion caused the Romans to de-uise their law Agraria: but the rich not lik-ing of it, and the couetous vtterlie condemn-ing it as rigorous and vnprofitable, neuer ceased to practise disturbance till it was quite abolished.

5

The upper classes hoped these conditions could be remedied by draining away the excess population, for without such a palliative a danger-ous social upheaval might occur. They listened eagerly to propagandists of expansion who, in language reminiscent of a modern patent-medi-cine salesman, assured them that colonies would cure all of England's ills. Of these empire pro-moters, by far the greatest was Richard Hakluyt, who not only collected records of the principal voyages but in the Discourse on Western Plant-ing *(1584) persuasively listed the benefits that would accrue to England after expansion:*[5]

It is well worthe the observation to see and consider what the like voyadges of dis-coverye and plantinge in the Easte and Weste Indies hath wroughte in the king-domes of Portingale and Spayne, . . . by these, their newe discoveries, they have so many honest wayes to set them on worke, as they rather wante men then meanes to ym-ploye them. But wee, for all the statutes that hitherto can be devised, . . . cannot deliver our commonwealthe from multitudes of loy-terers and idle vagabondes. Truthe it is, that throughe our longe peace and seldome sicknes (twoo singuler blessinges of Almightie God) wee are growen more populous than ever heretofore; so that nowe there are of every arte and science so many, that they can hardly lyve one by another, nay rather they

are readie to eate upp one another; . . . and often fall to pilferinge and thevinge and other lewdnes, . . . yf this voyadge were put in execution, these pety theves mighte be condempned for certen yeres in the westerne partes, especially in Newefounde lande, in sawinge and fellinge of tymber . . . in burn-inge of the firres and pine trees to make pitche, tarr, rosen, and sope ashes; in beat-inge and workinge of hempe for cordage; and, in the more southerne partes, in setting them to worke in mynes . . . in plantinge of suger canes . . . in dressinge of vines whereof there is greate aboundaunce of wyne. . . .

In somme, this enterprice will mynister matter for all sortes and states of men to worke upon; . . . an Englishe gentleman, Capitaine Muffett, whoe is nowe in Fraunce, tolde . . . that when he was in Spaine, pris-oner, not longe since, he hearde the threas-urer of the West Indies say, that there was no suche way to hinder his master, as to plante upon the coaste nere unto Florida. . . . And entringe into the consideration of the way how this Phillippe may be abased, I meane firste to begynne with the West In-dies, as there to laye a chefe foundation for his overthrowe. And like as the foundation of the strongest holde undermyned and re-moved, the mightiest and strongest walles fall flatt to the earthe; so this prince, spoiled or intercepted for a while of his treasure, oc-casion by lacke of the same is geven that all his territories in Europe oute of Spaine slide from him, and the Moores enter into Spaine it selfe, and the people revolte in every forrein territorie of his, and cutt the throates of the proude hatefull Spaniardes, their governours. . . . And therefore wee are to understande that Phillippe rather governeth in the West Indies by opinion, then by mighte; . . . as in truthe the Spaniarde ys very weake there. . . . If you touche him in the Indies, you touche the apple of his eye; for take away his treas-ure, which is *neruus belli,* and which he hath almoste oute of his West Indies, his olde bandes of souldiers will soone be dis-solved, his purposes defeated, his power and strengthe diminished, his pride abated, and

[5] Richard Hakluyt, "A Discourse on Western Planting," Maine Historical Society, Collections, 2d ser., *Documentary History of the State of Maine* (Cambridge, 1877), II, 36–41.

his tyranie utterly suppressed. . . . A BREFE collection of certaine reasons to induce her Majestie and the state to take in hande the westerne voyadge and the plantinge there. . . .

2. The passage thither and home is neither to longe nor to shorte, but easie, and to be made twise in the yere.

3. The passage cutteth not nere the trade of any prince, nor nere any of their contries or territories, and is a safe passage, and not easie to be annoyed by prince or potentate whatsoever.

4. The passage is to be perfourmed at all times of the yere. . . .

6. This enterprise may staye the Spanishe Kinge from flowinge over all the face of that waste firme of America, . . . Howe easie a matter may yt be to this realme, swarminge at this day with valiant youthes, . . . to be lordes of all those sees, and to spoile Phillipps Indian navye, and to deprive him of yerely passage of his treasure into Europe, and consequently to abate the pride of Spaine and of the supporter of the greate Antechriste of Rome, and to pull him downe in equallitie to his neighbour princes, and consequently to cutt of the common mischefes that come to all Europe by the peculiar aboundaunce of his Indian Treasure, and thiss withoute difficultie. . . .

16. Wee shall be plantinge there inlarge the glory of the gospell, and from England plante sincere religion, and provide a safe and a sure place to receave people from all partes of the worlde that are forced to flee for the truthe of Gods worde. . . .

20. Many men of excellent wittes and of divers singuler giftes, overthrowen by suertishippe, by sea, or by some folly of youthe, that are not able to live in England, may there by raised againe, and doe their contrie goodd service; . . .

21. Many souldiers and servitours, in the ende of the warres, . . . may there be unladen, to the commin profite and quiet of this realme. . . .

22. The frye of the wandringe beggars of England, that growe upp ydly, and hurtfull

and burdenous to this realme, may there be unladen, better bredd upp, and may people waste contries to the home and forreine benefite, and to their owne more happy state.

6

A very different set of motives impelled the Pilgrim Fathers to seek refuge in the New World. The official history of these simple folk was written by their long-time governor, William Bradford. His account of their ardent faith and remarkable resourcefulness in the face of incredible hardships is a major classic of American history. After their departure from English soil, the Pilgrims spent eleven to twelve years in the Dutch towns of Amsterdam and Leyden. In the following passage, Bradford discusses the "reasons and causes of their removal" from Holland:[6]

After they had lived in this city about some eleven or twelve years (which is the more observable being the whole time of that famous truce between that state and the Spaniards) and sundry of them were taken away by death and many others began to be well stricken in years (the grave mistress of Experience having taught them many things), those prudent governors with sundry of the sagest members began both deeply to apprehend their present dangers and wisely to foresee the future and think of timely remedy. In the agitation of their thoughts, and much discourse of things hereabout, at length they began to incline to this conclusion: of removal to some other place. Not out of any newfangledness or other such like giddy humor by which men are oftentimes transported to their great hurt and danger, but for sundry weighty and solid reasons, some of the chief of which I will here briefly touch.

And first, they saw and found by experience the hardness of the place and country to be such as few in comparison would come to them, and fewer that would bide it out and continue with them. For many that came to them, and many more that desired to be

---

6 William Bradford, *Of Plymouth Plantation, 1620–1647* (Samuel E. Morison, ed., New York, 1959), pp. 23–27. Reprinted with the kind permission of the publishers, Alfred A. Knopf, Inc.

with them, could not endure that great labour and hard fare, with other inconveniences which they underwent and were contented with. But though they loved their persons, approved their cause and honoured their sufferings, yet they left them as it were weeping, as Orpah did her mother-in-law Naomi, or as those Romans did Cato in Utica who desired to be excused and borne with, though they could not all be Catos. For many, though they desired to enjoy the ordinances of God in their purity and the liberty of the gospel with them, yet (alas) they admitted of bondage with danger of conscience, rather than to endure these hardships. Yea, some preferred and chose the prisons in England rather than this liberty in Holland with these afflictions. But it was thought that if a better and easier place of living could be had, it would draw many and take away these discouragements. Yea, their pastor would often say that many of those who both wrote and preached now against them, if they were in a place where they might have liberty and live comfortably, they would then practice as they did.

Secondly. They saw that though the people generally bore all these difficulties very cheerfully and with a resolute courage, being in the best and strength of their years; yet old age began to steal on many of them; and their great and continual labours, with other crosses and sorrows, hastened it before the time. So as it was not only probably thought, but apparently seen, that within a few years more they would be in danger to scatter, by necessities pressing them, or sink under their burdens, or both. And therefore according to the divine proverb, that a wise man seeth the plague when it cometh, and hideth himself, Proverbs xxii. 3, so they like skillful and beaten soldiers were fearful either to be entrapped or surrounded by their enemies so as they should neither be able to fight nor fly. And therefore thought it better to dislodge betimes to some place of better advantage and less danger, if any such could be found.

Thirdly. As necessity was a taskmaster over them so they were forced to be such, not only to their servants but in a sort to their dearest children, the which as it did not a little wound the tender hearts of many a loving father and mother, so it produced likewise sundry sad and sorrowful effects. For many of their children that were of best dispositions and gracious inclinations, having learned to bear the yoke in their youth and willing to bear part of their parents' burden, were oftentimes so oppressed with their heavy labours that though their minds were free and willing, yet their bodies bowed under the weight of the same, and became decrepit in their early youth, the vigour of nature being consumed in the very bud as it were. But that which was more lamentable, and of all sorrows most heavy to be borne, was that many of their children, by these occasions and the great licentiousness of youth in that country, and the manifold temptations of the place, were drawn away by evil examples into extravagant and dangerous courses, getting the reins off their necks and departing from their parents. Some became soldiers, others took upon them far voyages by sea, and others some worse courses tending to dissoluteness and the danger of their souls, to the great grief of their parents and dishonour of God. So that they saw their posterity would be in danger to degenerate and be corrupted.

Lastly (and which was not least), a great hope and inward zeal they had of laying some good foundation, or at least to make some way thereunto, for the propagating and advancing the gospel of the kingdom of Christ in those remote parts of the world; yea, though they should be but even as stepping-stones unto others for the performing of so great a work.

These and some other like reasons moved them to undertake this resolution of their removal; the which they afterward prosecuted with so great difficulties, as by the sequel will appear.

The place they had thoughts on was some of those vast and unpeopled countries of America, which are fruitful and fit for habitation, being devoid of all civil inhabitants, where there are only savage and brutish men which range up and down, little otherwise than the wild beasts of the same. This proposition being made public and coming to the scanning of all, it raised many variable opinions amongst men and caused many fears and doubts amongst themselves. Some, from their reasons and hopes conceived, laboured to stir up and encourage the rest to undertake and prosecute the same; others again, out of their fears, objected against it and sought to divert from it; alleging many things, and those neither unreasonable nor unprobable; as that it was a great design and subject to many unconceivable perils and dangers; as, besides the casualties of the sea (which none can be freed from), the length of the voyage was such as the weak bodies of women and other persons worn out with age and travail (as many of them were) could never be able to endure. And yet if they should, the miseries of the land which they should be exposed unto, would be too hard to be borne and likely, some or all of them together, to consume and utterly to ruinate them. For there they should be liable to famine and nakedness and the want, in a manner, of all things. The change of air, diet and drinking of water would infect their bodies with sore sicknesses and grievous diseases. And also those which should escape or overcome these difficulties should yet be in continual danger of the savage people, who are cruel, barbarous and most treacherous, being most furious in their rage and merciless where they overcome; not being content only to kill and take away life, but delight to torment men in the most bloody manner that may be; flaying some alive with the shells of fishes, cutting off the members and joints of others by piece-meal and broiling on the coals, eat the collops of their flesh in their sight whilst they live, with other cruelties horrible to be related.

And surely it could not be thought but the very hearing of these things could not but move the very bowels of men to grate within them and make the weak to quake and trem-

ble. It was further objected that it would require greater sums of money to furnish such a voyage and to fit them with necessaries, than their consumed estates would amount to; and yet they must as well look to be seconded with supplies as presently to be transported. Also many precedents of ill success and lamentable miseries befallen others in the like designs were easy to be found, and not forgotten to be alleged; besides their own experience, in their former troubles and hardships in their removal into Holland, and how hard a thing it was for them to live in that strange place, though it was a neighbouring country and a civil and rich commonwealth.

It was answered, that all great and honourable actions are accompanied with great difficulties and must be both enterprised and overcome with answerable courages. It was granted the dangers were great, but not desperate. The difficulties were many, but not invincible. For though there were many of them likely, yet they were not certain, It might be sundry of the things feared might never befall; others by provident care and the use of good means might in a great measure be prevented; and all of them, through the help of God, by fortitude and patience, might either be borne or overcome. True it was that such attempts were not to be made and undertaken without good ground and reason, not rashly or lightly as many have done for curiosity or hope of gain, etc. But their condition was not ordinary, their ends were good and honourable, their calling lawful and urgent; and therefore they might expect the blessing of God in their proceeding. Yea, though they should lose their lives in this action, yet might they have comfort in the same and their endeavours would be honourable. They lived here but as men in exile and in a poor condition, and as great miseries might possibly befall them in this place; for the twelve years of truce were now out and there was nothing but beating of drums and preparing for war, the events whereof are always uncertain. The Spaniard might prove as cruel as the savages of America, and the famine and pestilence as sore here as there, and their liberty less to look out for remedy.

After many other particular things answered and alleged on both sides, it was fully concluded by the major part to put this design in execution and to prosecute it by the best means they could.

7

That the forces driving Puritans overseas were not exclusively religious was clearly demonstrated by John Winthrop, the middle-class Englishman who became the leader and first governor of the Massachusetts Bay Colony. His "Reasons" for leaving the homeland resembled those of countless other Britons who responded to economic and imperialistic as well as religious motives:[7]

1. It will be a service to the Church of great consequence to carry the Gospell into those parts of the world, to helpe on the comminge of the fullnesse of the Gentiles, & to raise a Bulworke against the kingdome of AnteChrist wch the Jesuites labour to reare up in those parts.

2. All other churches of Europe are brought to desolation, & o^r sinnes, for wch the Lord beginnes allreaddy to frowne upon us & to cutte us short, doe threatne evill times to be comminge upon us, & whoe knowes, but that God hath provided this place to be a refuge for many whome he meanes to save out of the generall callamity, & seeinge the Church hath noe place lefte to flie into but the wildernesse, what better worke can there be, then to goe & provide tabernacles & foode for her against she comes thether:

3. This Land growes weary of her Inhabitants, soe as man, whoe is the most pretious of all creatures, is here more vile & base then the earth we treade upon, & of lesse prise among us then an horse or a sheepe: masters are forced by authority to entertaine servants, parents to maintaine there owne children, all townes complaine of the burthen of theire poore, though we have taken up

---

[7] R. C. Winthrop, *Life and Letters of John Winthrop* (Boston, 1864), I, 309–311.

many unnessisarie yea unlawfull trades to maintaine them, & we use the authoritie of the Law to hinder the increase of o^r people, as by urginge the Statute against Cottages, & inmates, & thus it is come to passe, that children, servants & neighboures, especially if they be poore, are compted the greatest burthens, wch if thinges weare right would be the cheifest earthly blessinges.

4. The whole earth is the Lords garden & he hath given it to the Sonnes of men wth a gen^l Comission: Gen: 1:28: increase & multiplie, & replenish the earth & subdue it, wch was againe renewed to Noah: the end is double & naturall, that man might enjoy the fruits of the earth, & God might have his due glory from the creature: why then should we stand striving here for places of habitation, etc. (many men spending as much labour & coste to recover or keepe sometimes an acre or twoe of Land, as would procure them many & as good or better in another Countrie) & in the meane time suffer a whole Continent as fruitfull & convenient for the use of man to lie waste wthout any improvement?

5. We are growne to that height of Intemperance in all excesse of Riott, as noe mans estate allmost will suffice to keepe saile wth his aequalls: & he whoe failes herein, must live in scorne & contempt. Hence it comes that all artes & Trades are carried in that deceiptfull & unrighteous course, as it is allmost impossible for a good & upright man to maintayne his charge & live comfortablie in any of them.

6. The ffountaines of Learning & Religion are soe corrupted as (besides the unsupportable charge of there education) most children (even the best witts & of fairest hopes) are perverted, corrupted, & utterlie overthrowne by the multitude of evill examples & the licentious governm^t of those seminaries, where men straine at knatts & swallowe camells, use all severity for mainetaynance of cappes & other accomplyments, but suffer all ruffianlike fashions & disorder in manners to passe uncontrolled.

7. What can be a better worke, & more

honorable & worthy a Christian then to helpe raise & supporte a particular Church while it is in the Infancy, & to ioyne his forces wth such a company of faithfull people, as by a timely assistance may growe stronge & prosper, & for wante of it may be put to great hazard, if not wholly ruined.

8. If any such as are knowne to be Godly, & live in wealth & prosperity here, shall forsake all this, to ioyne themselves wth this Church & to runne an hazard wth them of an hard & meane condition, it will be an example of great use both for removinge the scandall of worldly & sinister respects wch is cast upon the Adventurers; to give more life to the faith of Gods people, in their praiers for the Plantation; & to incorrage others to ioyne the more willingly in it.

9. It appeares to be a worke of God for the good of his Church, in that he hath disposed the hartes of soe many of his wise & faithfull servants, both ministers & others, not onely to approve of the enterprise but to interest themselves in it, some in their persons & estates, other by their serious advise & helpe otherwise, & all by their praiers for the welfare of it. Amos 3: the Lord revealeth his secreat to his servants and prophetts, it is likely he hath some great worke in hand wch he hath revealed to his prophetts among us, whom he hath stirred up to encourage his servants to this Plantation, for he doth not use to seduce his people by his owne prophetts, but comitte that office to the ministrie of false prophetts & lieing spiritts.

8

Something over a hundred years later, the same combination of motives was at work, producing a continued expansion in the English colonial effort. In 1733 an anonymous author attempted to enlist support for the colony of Georgia in the following "Brief Account." Undoubtedly written at the behest of James Oglethorpe and his fellow trustees, the text bears the unmistakable stamp of an early day real-estate speculator:[8]

---

[8] Peter Force, *Tracts and Other Papers* . . . (Washington, 1836), I, 4–6.

In *America* there are fertile lands sufficient to subsist all the useless Poor in *England,* and distressed Protestants in Europe; yet Thousands starve for want of mere sustenance. The distance makes it difficult to get thither. The same want that renders men useless here, prevents their paying their passage; and if others pay it for 'em, they become servants, or rather slaves for years to those who have defrayed the expense. Therefore, money for passage is necessary, but is not the only want; for if people were set down in America, and the land before them, they must cut down trees, build houses, fortify towns, dig and sow the land before they can get in a harvest; and till then, they must be provided with food, and kept together, that they may be assistant to each other for their natural support and protection. . . .

FROM THE CHARTER.—His Majesty having taken into his consideration, the miserable circumstances of many of his own poor subjects, ready to perish for want: as likewise the distresses of many poor foreigners, who would take refuge here from persecution; and having a Princely regard to the great danger the southern frontiers of South Carolina are exposed to, by reason of the small number of white inhabitants there, hath, out of his Fatherly compassion towards his subjects, been graciously pleased to grant a charter for incorporating a number of gentlemen by the name of *The Trustees for establishing the Colony of Georgia in America.* They are impowered to collect benefactions; and lay them out in cloathing, arming, sending over, and supporting colonies of the poor, whether subjects or foreigners, in Georgia. And his Majesty farther grants all his lands between the rivers *Savannah and Alatamaha,* which he erects into a Province by the name of GEORGIA, unto the Trustees, in trust for the poor, and for the better support of the Colony. At the desire of the Gentlemen, there are clauses in the Charter, restraining them and their successors from receiving any salary, fee, perquisite, or profit, whatsoever, by or from this undertaking; and also from receiving any grant of lands within the said district, to themselves, or in trust for them. There are farther clauses granting to the Trustees proper powers for establishing and governing the Colony, and liberty of conscience to all who shall settle there.

The Trustees intend to relieve such unfortunate persons as cannot subsist here, and establish them in an orderly manner, so as to form a well regulated town. As far as their fund goes, they will defray the charge of their passage to Georgia; give them necessaries, cattle, land, and subsistence, till such time as they can build their houses and clear some of their land. They rely for success, first on the goodness of Providence, next on the compassionate disposition of the people of England; and, they doubt not, that much will be spared from luxury, and superfluous expenses, by generous tempers, when such an opportunity is offered them by the giving of £20 to provide for a man or woman, or £10 to a child for ever. . . .

By such a Colony, many families, who would otherwise starve, will be provided for, and made masters of houses and lands; the people in Great Britain to whom these necessitous families were a burthen, will be relieved; numbers of manufacturers will be here employed, for supplying them with clothes, working tools, and other necessaries; and by giving refuge to the distressed Saltzburghers, and other persecuted Protestants, the power of Britain, as a reward for its hospitality, will be encreased by the addition of so many religious and industrious subjects.

The Colony of *Georgia* lying about the same latitude with part of *China, Persia, Palestine,* and the *Madeiras,* it is highly probable that when hereafter it shall be well-peopled and rightly cultivated, ENGLAND may be supplied from thence with raw Silk, Wine, Oil, Dyes, Drugs, and many other materials for manufactures, which she is obliged to purchase from Southern countries. As towns are established and grow populous along the rivers Savannah and Alatamaha, they will make such a barrier as will render the southern frontier of the British Colonies on the Continent of America, safe from Indian and other enemies.

All human affairs are so subject to chance, that there is no answering for events; yet from reason and the nature of things, it may be concluded, that the riches and also the number of the inhabitants in *Great Britain* will be increased, by importing at a cheap rate from this new Colony, the materials requisite for carrying on in Britain several manufactures. For our Manufacturers will be encouraged to marry and multiply, when they find themselves in circumstances to provide for their families, which must necessarily be the happy effect of the increase and cheapness of our materials of those Manufactures, which at present we purchase with our money from foreign countries, at dear rates; and also many people will find employment here, on account of such farther demands by the people of this Colony, for those manufactures which are made for the produce of our own country; and, as has been justly observed, the people will always abound where there is full employment for them.

CHRISTIANITY will be extended by the execution of this design; since, the good discipline established by the Society, will reform the manners of those miserable objects, who shall be by them subsided; and the example of a whole Colony, who shall behave in a just, moral, and religious manner, will contribute greatly towards the conversion of the Indians, and taking off the prejudices received from the profligate lives of such who have scarce any thing of Christianity but the name.

9

Stephen Vincent Benét, a recent American poet, wrote an ode to America, Western Star, *in which he describes the promptings of the European settlers:*[9]

[9] From *Western Star* by Stephen Vincent Benét, pp. 20–22. Holt, Rinehart and Winston, Inc. Copyright, 1943, by Rosemary Carr Benét. Reprinted by permission of Brandt & Brandt.

Gather them up, the bright and drowning
stars,
And with them gather, too,
The clay, the iron, and the knotted rope,
The disinherited, the dispossessed,
The hinds of the midland, eaten by the
squire's sheep,
The outcast yeoman, driven to tramp the
roads,
The sturdy beggars, roving from town to
town,
Workless, hopeless, harried by law and State,
The men who lived on nettles in Merry Eng-
land,
The men of the blackened years
When dog's meat was a dainty in Lincoln-
shire,
(Have you heard the news from Virginia?)
The poor, the restless, the striving, the broken
knights,
The cast-off soldiers, bitter as their own scars,
The younger sons without office or hope of
land,
Glover and cooper, mercer and cordwainer,
("Have you heard the news from Virginia?
Have you heard?
Wat swears he'll go, for the gold lies heaped
on the ground
And Ralph, the hatter, is ready as any man.
I keep my shop but my shop doth not keep
me.
Shall I give such chances the go-by and walk
the roads?
I am no hind to scratch in the earth for
bread.
Nay, a stocking-weaver I, and of good re-
pute
Though lately dogged by mischances. They'll
need such men.
Have you heard the news from Virginia?")
Gather the waifs of the London parishes,
The half-starved boys, the sparrows of Lon-
don streets,
The ones we caught before they could cut a
purse,
And bind them out and send them across the
sea.
("They will live or die but at least we are
rid of them.

We'll pick the likeliest ones. Boy, what's your
name?
Good lad. You sail in *The Fortune*. The fool
looks mazed.
Well, give him a wash and see he is fitted
out.
We'll settle his master later.")
                        Oh, spread the news,
The news of golden Virginia across the sea,
And let it sink in the hearts of the strange,
plain men
Already at odds with government and
church,
The men who read their Bibles late in the
night,
Dissenter and nonconformist and Puritan,
Let it go to Scrooby and stop at the pesthouse
there,
Let it go to the little meeting at Austerfield.
(We must worship God as we choose. We
must worship God
Though King and law and bishop stand in
the way.
It is far, in the North, and they will not
touch us here,
Yet I hear they mean to harry the sheep of
God
And His elect must be steadfast. I hear a
sound
Like the first, faint roll of thunder, but it is
far.
It is very far away.
Have you heard the news of Virginia?
                        Friend, I have heard
The burning news of the elections of God,
The comfortable word, the clear promise
sealed,
My heart is shaken with grace to my heart's
root.
I have prayed and wrestled and drunk at the
living fount
And God walks with me, guiding me with
His hand.
What matter your little news and your tinsel
world?)

Have you heard the news of Virginia? Have
you heard
The news, the news of Virginia?

PLANTING THE COLONIES

10

Whether for love of God or gold, of liberty or empire, those who came to America came to fulfill a dream. One of the earliest settlers of Jamestown, George Percy, communicates a sense of this excitement and hope in the pages of his diary:[10]

The six and twentieth day of April about foure a clocke in the morning, wee descried the Land of Virginia: the same day we entred into the Bay of Chesupioc directly, without any let or hindrance; there wee landed and discovered a little way, but wee could find nothing worth the speaking of, but faire meddowes and goodly tall Trees, with such Fresh-waters running through the woods, as I was almost ravished at the first sight thereof.

At night, when wee were going aboard, there came the Savages creeping upon all foure, from the Hills, like Beares, with their bowes in their mouthes, charged us very desperately in the faces, hurt Captaine Gabrille Archer in both his hands, and a sayler in two places of the body very dangerous. After they had spent their arrowes, and felt the sharpnesse of our shot, they retired in to the woods with a great noise, and so left us. . . .

Wee rowed over to a point of Land, where wee found a channell and sounded six, eight, ten, twelve fathom: which put us in good Comfort. Therefore we named that point of Land, Cape Comfort.

The nine and twentieth day we set up a Crosse at Chesupioc Bay, and named that place Cape Henry. . . .

The twelfth day we went backe to our ships, and discovered a point of Land, called Archers Hope, which was sufficient with a little labour to defend our selves against any Enemy. The soile was good and fruitfull, with

excellent good timber. There are also great store of Vines in bignesse of a mans thigh running up to the tops of the trees in great abundance. We also did see many squirrels, Conies, Black Birds with crimson wings, and divers other fowles and birds of divers and sundrie colours of crimson, watchet, yellow, greene, murry, and divers other hewes naturally without any art using.

We found store of Turkie nests and many egges. If it had not beene disliked, because the ship could not ride neere the shoare, we had setled there to all the Colonies contentment.

The thirteenth day we came to our seating place in Paspihas Countrey some eight miles from the point of Land, which I made mention before: where our shippes doe lie so neere the shoare that they are moored to the trees in six fathom water.

The fourteenth day we landed all our men which were set to worke about the fortification, and others some to watch and ward as it was convenient. . . .

The foure and twentieth day wee set up a Crosse at the head of this River, naming it Kings River, where we proclaimed James, King of England, to have the most right unto it. When wee had finished and set up our Crosse, we shipt our men and made for James Fort. By the way wee came to Pohatans Towne where the Captaine went on shore, suffering none to goe with him; hee presented the Commander of this place with a Hatchet which hee tooke joyfully, and was well pleased. . . .

The fifteenth day of June we had built and finished our Fort, which was triangle-wise, having three bulwarkes at every corner like a halfe moone, and foure or five pieces of artillerie mounted in them. We had made our selves sufficiently strong for these Savages, we had also sowne most of our Corne on two mountaines; it sprang a mans height from the ground. This countrey is a fruitfull soile, bearing many goodly and fruitfull trees, as mulberries, cherries, walnuts, ceders, cypresse, sassafras, and vines in great abundance.

---

[10] George Percy, "A Discourse of the Plantation of the Southerne Colonie in Virginia," in Samuel Purchas, *Purchas His Pilgrims* (Glasgow, 1906 ed.), XVIII, 405–416.

11

Failure frequently splintered the hopes of the early settlers. Many knew a "starving time." The remarkable Governor Bradford ascribed distress to a combination of bad planning, the wilderness, and sheer bad luck. There were also in each company men and women who were something less than saintly. The following selection is taken from his Of Plymouth Plantation:[11]

But that which was most sad and lamentable was, that in two or three months' time half of their company died, especially in January and February, being the depth of winter, and wanting houses and other comforts; being infected with the scurvy and other diseases which this long voyage and their inaccommodate condition had brought upon them. So as there died some times two or three of a day in the foresaid time, that of 100 and odd persons, scarce fifty remained. And of these, in the time of most distress, there was but six or seven sound persons who to their great commendations, be it spoken, spared no pains night nor day, but with abundance of toil and hazard of their own health, fetched them wood, made them fires, dressed them meat, made their beds, washed their loathsome clothes, clothed and unclothed them. In a word, did all the homely and necessary offices for them which dainty and queasy stomachs cannot endure to hear named; and all this willingly and cheerfully, without any grudging in the least, showing herein their true love unto their friends and brethren; a rare example and worthy to be remembered. Two of these seven were Mr. William Brewster, their reverend Elder, and Myles Standish, their Captain and military commander, unto whom myself and many others were much beholden in our low and sick condition. And yet the Lord so upheld these persons as in this general calamity they were not at all infected with sickness or lameness. And what I have said of these I may say of many others who died in this

general visitation, and others yet living; that whilst they had health, yea, or any strength continuing, they were not wanting to any that had need of them. And I doubt not but their recompense is with the Lord.

But I may not here pass by another remarkable passage not to be forgotten. As this calamity fell among the passengers that were to be left here to plant, and were hasted ashore and made to drink water that the seamen might have the more beer, and one in his sickness desiring but a small can of beer, it was answered that if he were their own father, he should have none. The disease began to fall amongst them also, so as almost half of their company died before they went away, and many of their officers and lustiest men, as the boatswain, gunner, three quartermasters, the cook and others. At which the Master was something strucken and sent to the sick ashore and told the Governor he should send for beer for them that had need of it, though he drunk water homeward bound.

But now amongst his company there was far another kind of carriage in this misery than amongst the passengers. For they that before had been boon companions in drinking and jollity in the time of their health and welfare, began now to desert one another in this calamity, saying they would not hazard their lives for them, they should be infected by coming to help them in their cabins; and so, after they came to lie by it, would do little or nothing for them but, "if they died, let them die." But such of the passengers as were yet aboard showed them what mercy they could, which made some of their hearts relent, as the boatswain (and some others) who was a proud young man and would often curse and scoff at the passengers. But when he grew weak, they had compassion on him and helped him; then he confessed he did not deserve it at their hands, he had abused them in word and deed. "Oh!" (saith he) "you, I now see, show your love like Christians indeed one to another, but we let one another lie and die like dogs." Another lay cursing his wife, saying if it had not

---

[11] William Bradford, *Of Plymouth Plantation, 1620–1647* (Samuel E. Morison, ed., New York, 1959), pp. 77–79. Reprinted by kind permission of the publishers, Alfred A. Knopf, Inc.

been for her he had never come this unlucky
voyage, and anon cursing his fellows, saying
he had done this and that for some of them;
he had spent so much and so much amongst
them, and they were now weary of him and
did not help him, having need. Another gave
his companion all he had, if he died, to help
him in his weakness; he went and got a little
spice and made him a mess of meat once or
twice. And because he died not so soon as
he expected, he went amongst his fellows and
swore the rogue would cozen him, he would
see him choked before he made him any
more meat; and yet the poor fellow died
before morning.

12

The eighteenth century augmented the pre-
dominantly English stock that characterized the
first migration. One group of settlers came from
northern Ireland. A second came from the Ger-
man Rhine, which had been devastated by war
and famine. Between 1709 and 1763 almost a
quarter of a million Germans spread themselves
across the back country from New York to Vir-
ginia, seeking cheap interior lands where they
could begin life anew. Their struggles amidst
the frontier poverty of a strange land were de-
scribed in a 1720 petition to the crown praying
for aid:[12]

That, In the year 1709. The Palatines, &
other Germans, being invited to come into
England about Four Thousand of them were
sent into New York in America, of whom
about 1700 Died on Board, or at their landing in that Province, by unavoidable sickness

That before they went on Board, they
were promised, those remaining alive should
have forty acres of Land, & Five pounds
sterling p^r Head, besides Cloths, Tools,
Utensils & other necessaries, to Husbandry
to be given at their arrival in America

That on their landing their they were
quartered in Tents, & divided into six companies, having each a Captain of their own
Nation, with a promise of an allowance of

[12] E. B. O'Callaghan (ed.), *Documents Relative*
to the Colonial History of the State of New York
(Albany, 1855), V, 553–555.

fifteen Pounds per annum to each commander

That afterwards they were removed on
Lands belonging to Mr Livingstone, where
they erected small Houses for shelter during
the winter season

That in the Spring following they were
ordered into the woods, to make Pitch &
Tar, where they lived about two years; But
the country not being fit to raise any considerable quantity of Naval Stores, They
were commanded to Build, to clear & improve the ground, belonging to a private
person

That the Indians hav^g yielded to Her late
Ma^{ty} of pious memory a small Tract of Land
called Schorie for the use of the Palatines,
they in fifteen days cleared a way of fifteen
miles through the woods & settled fifty Families therein

That in the following Spring the remainder
of the said Palatines joined the said fifty
families so settled therein Schorie

But that country being too small for their
encreasing families, they were constrained to
purchase some Neighbouring Land of the
Indians for which they were to give Three
hund^d pieces of Eight

And having built small Houses, & Hutts
there about one year after the said purchase
some gentlemen of Albani, declared to the
Palatines, that themselves having purchas^d
the said countrie of Schorie of the Govr of
New York they would not permit them to
live there, unless an agreement were also
made with those of Albany; But that the
Palatines having refused to enter into such
an agreement, A Sheriff & some officers were
sent from Albany to seize one of their Captains, who being upon his Guard; The Indians were animated against the Palatines;
but these found means to appease the Savages by giving them what they would of
their own substance.

That in the year 1717 the Governour of
New York having summoned the Palatines
to appear at Albani, some of them being
deputed went thither accordingly, where they
were told, that unless they did agree with

the Gentlemen of Albany, the Governor expected an order from England to transport them to another place, And that he would send twelve men to view their works & improvements to appraise the same & then to give them the value thereof in money

But this not being done the Palatines to the number of about three Thousand, have continued to manure & to sew the Land that they might not be starved for want of Corn & food

For which manuring the Gentlemen of Albani have put in prison one man and one woman, & will not release them, unless they have suffic[t] security of One Hundred Crowns for the former

Now in order that the Palatines may be preserved in the said Land of Schorie, which they have purchased of the Indians, or that they may be so settled in an adjoining Tract of Land, as to raise a necessary subsistance for themselves & their families, they have sent into England Three Persons one of whom is since dead humbly to lay their Case before His Maj[ty], not doubting but that in consideration of the Hardships they have suffered for want of a secure settlement, His Majestys Ministers and Council will compassionate those His faithful Subjects;

Who, in the first year after their arrival willingly and cheerfully sent Three Hundred men to the expedition against Canada, & afterwards to the Asistance of Albani which was threatened by the French and Indians, for which service they have never received One Penny tho' they were upon the Establishment of New York or New Jersey nor had they received one Penny of the five pounds per head promised at their going on board from England Neither have their commanders received anything of the allowance of fifteen pounds per Annum, and tho' the arms they had given them at the Canada expedition which were by special order from Her late Majesty, to be left in their possession, have been taken from them, yet they are still ready to fight against all the enemies of His Mat[y] & those countrys whenever there shall be occasion to shew

their hearty endeav[rs] for the prosperity of their generous Benefactors in England as well as in America

Therefore they hope from the Justice of the Right Hônble the Lords Commissioners of Trade and Plantations, to whom their Petition to their Excellencies the Lords Justices has been referred That they shall be so supported by their Lordships Report, as to be represented fit objects to be secured in the Land they now do inhabit or in some near adjoining lands remaining in the right of the Crown in the said Province of New York

13

The second group to come to America was from northern Ireland. Thousands of lowland Scots who lived in the wilds of Ulster began migrating to America in the early eighteenth century after repressive economic and religious laws drove them from their farms; like the Palatines they sought homes in the interior where land was cheap. One of these immigrants, Robert Witherspoon, wrote a vivid account of the trials of adjustment:[13]

We landed in Charleston three weeks before Christmas. We found the inhabitants very kind. We staid in town until after Christmas, and were put on board of an open boat, with tools and a year's provisions, and one still-mill. They allowed each hand upwards of sixteen, one axe, one broad hoe, and one narrow hoe. Our provisions were Indian corn, rice, wheaten flour, beef, pork, rum, and salt. We were much distressed in this part of our passage. As it was the dead of winter, we were exposed to the inclemency of the weather day and night; and (which added to the grief of all pious persons on board) the atheistical and blasphemous mouths of our Patroons and the other hands. They brought us up as far as Potatoe Ferry and turned us on shore, where we lay in Samuel Commander's barn for some time, and the boat wrought her way up to "the

---

[13] Quoted in Charles A. Hanna, *The Scotch-Irish* (New York, 1902), II, 26–28. Reprinted by permission of the publishers, G. P. Putnam's Sons.

King's Tree," with the goods and provisions, which is the first boat that I believe ever came up so high before.

While we lay at Mr. Commander's, our men came up in order to get dirt houses to take their families to. They brought some few horses with them. What help they could get from the few inhabitants in order to carry the children and other necessaries up they availed themselves of. As the woods were full of water, and most severe frosts, it was very severe on women and children. We set out in the morning; and some got no further that day than Mr. McDonald's and some as far as Mr. Plowden's; some to James Armstrong's, and some to Uncle William James's. . . . Their little cabins were as full that night as they could hold, and the next day every one made the best they could to their own place, which was the first day of February, 1735. My father had brought on shipboard four children, viz.: David, Robert, John, and Sarah. Sarah died in Charleston, and was the first buried at the Scotch Meeting House graveyard. When we came to the Bluff, my mother and we children were still in expectation that we were coming to an agreeable place. But when we arrived and saw nothing but a wilderness, and instead of a fine timbered house, nothing but a mean dirt house, our spirits quite sank; and what added to our trouble, our pilot we had with us from Uncle William James's left us when we came in sight of the place.

My father gave us all the comfort he could by telling us we would get all those trees cut down, and in a short time there would be plenty of inhabitants, so that we could see from house to house. While we were at this, our fire we brought from Bog Swamp went out. Father had heard, that up the river-swamp was the "King's Tree," although there was no path, neither did he know the distance. Yet he followed up the swamp until he came to the branch, and by that found Roger Gordon's. We watched him as far as the trees would let us see, and returned to our dolorous hut, expecting never

to see him or any human person more. But after some time he returned and brought fire. We were soon comforted, but evening coming on, the wolves began to howl on all sides. We then feared being devoured by wild beasts, having neither gun nor dog nor any door to our house. Howbeit we set to and gathered fuel, and made on a good fire, and so passed the first night. The next day being a clear warm morning, we began to stir about, but about mid-day there rose a cloud southwest attended with a high wind, thunder and lightning. The rain quickly penetrated through between the poles and brought down the sand that covered them over, which seemed to threaten to bury us alive. The lightning and claps were very awful and lasted a good space of time. I do not remember to have seen a much severer gust than that was. I believe we all sincerely wished ourselves again at Belfast. But this fright was soon over and the evening cleared up, comfortable and warm.

The boat that brought up the goods arrived at "the King's Tree." People were much oppressed in bringing their things, as there was no house there. They were obliged to toil hard, and had no other way but to convey their beds, clothing, chests, provisions, tools, pots, etc., on their backs. And at that time there were few or no roads and every family had to travel the best way they could, which was here double distance to some, for they had to follow swamps and branches for their guides for some time.

After a season, some men got such a knowledge of the woods as to "blaze" paths, so the people soon found out to follow "blazes" from place to place. As the winter season was far advanced, the time to prepare for planting was very short. Yet people were very strong and healthy, all that could do anything wrought diligently, and continued clearing and planting as long as the season would admit, so that they made provision for the ensuing year. As they had but few beasts, a little served them, and as the range was good, they had no need of feeding creatures for some years.

I remember that among the first things my father brought from the boat was his gun, which was one of Queen Anne's muskets. He had it loaded with swan-shot. One morning when we were at breakfast, there was a "travelling 'possum" on his way, passing by the door: my mother screamed out saying, "There is a great bear!" Mother and we children hid ourselves behind some barrels and a chest, at the other end of our hut, whilst father got his gun, and steadied it upon the fork that held up that end of the house, and shot the animal about the hinder parts, which caused the poor opossum to grin and open its mouth in a frightful manner. Father was in haste to give it a second bout, but the shot being mislaid in a hurry, could not be found. We were penned up for some time. Father at length ventured out and killed it with a pale.

Another source of alarm was the Indians. When they came to hunt in the spring, they were in great numbers in all places like the Egyptian locusts, but they were not hurtful. We had a great deal of trouble and hardships in our first settling, but the few inhabitants continued still in health and strength. Yet we were oppressed with fears, on divers accounts, especially of being massacred by the Indians, or bitten by snakes, or torn by wild beasts, or being lost and perishing in the woods. Of this last calamity there were three instances.

About the end of August, 1736, my uncle Robert arrived here. The ship he came in was called *New Built*. She was a ship of great burden, and brought many passengers. They chiefly came up here, and, obliged to travel by land, they had money given them by the public instead of provisions. Our second crop was in the ground when they came. As it was in the warm season, they were much fatigued in coming up, and many were taken with the fever and ague. Some died with that disorder, and many after the ague had ceased grew dropsical and died. About this time people began to form into societies, and sent to Ireland for a minister. One came named Robert Heron. He stayed three years, and then returned to Ireland.

14

"White's Relation," justly famous, is one of a series of reports by Jesuit priests to the superior-general of the Society of Jesus in Rome. The full title of this report, written in 1634, is A Relation of The Colony of the Lord Baron of Baltimore, in Maryland, near Virginia; A Narrative of the Voyage to Maryland, *by Father Andrew White:[14]*

At length, sailing from this, we reached what they call Point Comfort, in Virginia, on the 27th of February, full of fear lest the English inhabitants, to whom our plantation is very objectionable, should plot some evil against us. Letters, however, which we brought from the King and the Chancellor of the Exchequer to the Governor of these regions, served to conciliate their minds, and to obtain those things which were useful to us. For the Governor of Virginia hoped, by this kindness to us, to recover the more easily from the royal treasury a great amount of money due to him. . . .

After a kind entertainment for eight or nine days, making sail on the 3d of March, and carried into the Chesapeake bay, we bent our course to the north, that we might reach the Potomac river. The Chesapeake bay, ten leagues broad, and four, five, six, and even seven fathoms deep, flows gently between its shores; it abounds in fish when the season of the year is favorable. A more beautiful body of water you can scarcely find. It is inferior, however, to the Potomac, to which we gave the name of St. Gregory.

Having now arrived at the wished for country, we appointed names as occasion served. And, indeed, the point which is at the south we consecrated under the title of St. Gregory; designating the northern point, we consecrated it to St. Michael, in honor of all the angels. A larger or more beautiful river I have never seen. The Thames, compared with it, can scarcely be considered a rivulet. It is not rendered impure by marshes, but on each bank of solid earth rise beautiful groves of trees, not choked up with an undergrowth of brambles and bushes, but as if

---

[14] Peter Force, *Tracts and Other Papers. . .* (Washington, 1836), IV, 18–22.

laid out by the hand, in a manner so open, that you might freely drive a four horse chariot in the midst of the trees.

At the very mouth of the river we beheld the natives armed. That night fires were kindled through the whole region, and since so large a ship had never been seen by them, messengers were sent every where to announce "that a canoe as large as an island had brought as many men as there was trees in the woods." We proceeded, however, to the Heron islands, so called from the immense flocks of birds of this kind.

The first which presented itself we called by the name of St. Clement's, the second St. Catharine's, the third St. Cecilia's. We landed first at St. Clement's, to which access is difficult, except by fording, because of the shelving nature of the shore. Here the young women, who had landed for the purpose of washing, were nearly drowned by the upsetting of the boat—a great portion also of my linen being lost—no trifling misfortune in these parts.

This island abounds in cedar, sassafras, and the herbs and flowers for making salads of every kind, with the nut of a wild tree which bears a very hard nut, in a thick shell, with a kernel very small but remarkably pleasant. However, since it was only four hundred acres in extent, it did not appear to be a sufficiently large location for a new settlement. Nevertheless, a place was sought for building a fort to prohibit foreigners from the trade of the river, and to protect our boundaries, for that is the narrowest crossing of the river. . . .

From St. Clement's, having proceeded about nine leagues towards the north, we entered the mouth of a river, to which we gave the name of St. George. This river, in a course from south to north, runs about twenty miles before it is freed from its salt taste—not unlike the Thames. Two bays appeared at its mouth, capable of containing three hundred ships of the largest class. One of the bays we consecrated to St. George; the other bay, more inland, to the blessed Virgin Mary. The left bank of the river was the residence of King Yoacomico. We landed on the

right, and having advanced about a thousand paces from the shore, we gave the name of St. Mary's to the intended city; and that we might avoid all appearance of injury and of hostility, having paid in exchange axes, hatchets, hoes, and some yards of cloth, we bought from the King thirty miles of his territory, which part now goes by the name of Augusta Carolina. . . .

The natives are of tall and comely stature, of a skin by nature somewhat tawny, which they make more hideous by daubing, for the most part, with red paint mixed with oil, to keep away the musquitoes; in this, intent more on their comfort than their beauty. They smear their faces also with other colors; from the nose upwards, seagreen, downwards, reddish, or the contrary, in a manner truly disgusting and terrific. And since they are without beard almost to the end of life, they make the representation of beard with paint, a line of various colors being drawn from the tip of the lips to the ears. They encourage the growth of the hair, which is generally black, and bind it with a fillet when brought round in a fashionable style to the left ear, something which is held in estimation by them, being added by way of ornament. Some bear upon their forehead the representation of a fish in copper. They encircle their necks with glass beads strung upon a thread, after the manner of chains. These beads, however, begin to be more common with them, and less useful for traffic.

They are generally dressed in deerskin, or like kind of covering, which flows behind after the manner of a cloak, and are girded about the middle with an apron; in other respects they are naked. Boys and girls who have not reached the age of puberty, run about without any covering whatever. The soles of their feet are as hard as horn; they tread upon thorns and thistles without injury. Their weapons are bows and arrows two cubits long, pointed with buck horn or a piece of sharpened flintstone. They direct these with so much skill that at a distance, they can shoot a sparrow through the middle. And in order to practise themselves for skill they throw up a thong on high, and transfix it by an arrow impelled by a bowstring before it falls to the ground. They cannot strike an object situated at a distance from them, on account of not using a well strung bow. By means of these arms they live, and daily through the fields and woods, hunt squirrels, partridges, guinea-hens, and wild beasts; for of all these there is great plenty, though we, ourselves, do not venture as yet to provide food by hunting, through fear of falling into an ambuscade. They live in huts of an oblong, oval form, built nine or ten feet high. Into these huts light is admitted from above, by a window, a cubit in extent; it serves also for removing the smoke; for they kindle a fire in the middle of the floor and sleep around the fire. The kings, however, and principal men have, as it were, their private apartments and bed, four posts being driven into the earth and poles placed on them to receive the bed. One of these huts has been allotted to me and my companions, in which we are accommodated sufficiently well for the time being, until more commodious edifices shall be built. This is the first chapel in Maryland, which was built, however, by the Indians. The next voyage, if God prosper our undertaking, we shall not be destitute of the things which are found necessary in other houses.

15

With something of the character of history as well as the tone of promotional literature, the following anonymous description of the beginnings of Georgia guarantees its accuracy as "attested upon oath in the Court of Savannah on November 10, 1740":[15]

The Province of *Georgia* lies from the most Northern Stream of the River *Savannah* (the Mouth of which is in the Latitude of 32 Deg.) along the Sea-coast, to the most Southern Stream of the *Alatamha* (the Mouth of which is 30½ Deg.) and Westward from the Heads of the said Rivers, respectively in direct Lines to the South Seas. . . .
The Town of *Savannah* was laid out, and

---

[15] *Ibid.,* I, 1–12 *passim.*

began to be built, in which are now 142 Houses, and good habitable Huts. The Soil in general, when cleared, is productive of *Indian* Corn, Rice, Peas, Potatoes, Pumpions, Melons, and many other Kinds of Gourds, in great Quantities; Wheat, Oats, Barley, and other *European* Grains, 'tis found by divers Experiments, may be propagated in many Parts (more especially in the Uplands toward *Augusta*) with Success. Mulberry-Trees and Vines agree exceeding well with the Soil and Climate, and so does the Annual Cotton, whereof large Quantities have been raised; and it is much planted: But the Cotton, which in some Parts is perennial, dies here in the Winter; which nevertheless the Annual is not inferior to in Goodness, but requires more Trouble in cleansing from the Seed. Cattle, Hogs, Poultry, and Fruit-Trees of most Kinds, have increased even beyond Imagination.

Ships of about three hundred Tons can come up to the Town, where the Worm (which is the Plague of the *American* Seas) does not eat; and the River is navigable for large Boats, as far as the Town of *Augusta,* which lies in the Latitude of 33 D. 5 M. and is 250 Miles distant from *Savannah* by Water; small Boats can go 300 Miles further, to the *Cherokees.*

There is already a considerable Trade in the River; and there is in this Town a Court-House, a Gaol, a Store-House, a large House for receiving the *Indians,* a Wharf or Bridge, a Guard-House, and some other publick Buildings; a publick Garden of ten Acres cleared, fenced, and planted with Orange-Trees, Mulberry-Trees, Vines, some Olives, which thrive very well, Peaches, Apples, and etc. . . .

As the Boundaries of the Colony are now known, together with the Climate, and Manner of Agriculture, more might be done henceforward in one Year, than could in several Years before we attained to that Knowledge; but our People are weak, being decreased, by great Numbers having been decoyed away to other Colonies: Many having taken to Idleness, upon shutting up the Store went away; but those who stayed, and

now remain are still a Body of the most valuable People, that find Means to live comfortably, some by their Trades, some by
Planting, and raising live Stock, and some by
their Labour, either by Land or Water; and
one of those remaining, are worth three that
left us, for such Work: And if an Embarka-
tion was to come in with the next Year, it
would be of great Service to the Colony, the
Saltzburghers wishing for more of their
Countrymen, and having been very industrious.

The Persons sent from *England* on the
Charity were of the Unfortunate, many of
whom have by their Industry proved that
they deserved better, and have thriven;
many also shewed they were brought into
those Misfortunes by their own Faults; and
when those who quitted their own Country
to avoid Labour, saw Labour stand before
their Eyes in *Georgia,* they were easily persuaded to live in *Carolina* by Cunning,
rather than work: This has been a great
Misfortune also upon many Persons, who
brought over Servants indented to serve
them, for a certain Number of Years, who
being picked up in the Streets of *London,* or
some such Manner, their Masters found them
unfit for Labour, and many of them took
such Opportunities as they could get, to
desert and fly into *Carolina,* where they
could be protected.

THE SIGNIFICANCE

16

*Louis B. Wright, a perceptive modern scholar,
makes it clear that the motives which impelled
several generations of Englishmen to cross the
ocean were exceedingly complex:*[16]

The motives which first sent Englishmen
overseas to seek homes in the unfriendly
forests of Virginia and New England were
as complex as the society which had devel-

[16] Louis B. Wright, *The Atlantic Frontier, Colonial
American Civilization* [1607–1763] (Ithaca, 1947),
pp. 43–48. Reprinted with the kind permission of
the author.

oped in England by the end of the first third
of the seventeenth century, a society whose
qualities would largely determine the nature
of American culture for generations to come.
If England had ever been homogeneous in
social structure and mental attitude, that
condition was long since past. The tendency
of society all through the Tudor and Stuart
periods was to develop differences, to produce a spirit of individualism, sometimes to
break into separate fractions. Although this
quality was implicit in the very thesis of
the Protestant's independent and individual
relation to God, religion was not the only
explanation of the diversity of attitudes in
the seventeenth century. Almost as important
was the Renaissance educational heritage
emphasizing the cultivation of the individual
personality. Politically, socially, and intellectually, Englishmen were growing constantly
more individualistic—and more independent.
The air tingled with an electrical restlessness
felt in all of England. Few communities were
so isolated that they did not react to changes
taking place in their fluid world. The atmosphere of the age stimulated men to take
speculative risks. They were not afraid to
adventure their persons, their purses, their
minds, and even their immortal souls in pursuit of ends deemed good. For many men—
and women—for one reason or another, this
pursuit led across the stormy waters of the
Atlantic.

The sheer spirit of adventure must not be
overlooked in accounting for the impulse
that drove Englishmen overseas. Since the
great days of buccaneering, the New World
had been a land of romantic fascination.
During the peaceful years of James' reign,
youths whose fathers might have signed on
the "Golden Hind" to raid the Spanish Main
had to find other outlets for their energies.
The more prosaic business of joining a colonial enterprise was not without its appeal.
Many a youth went to Virginia or New
England for no other reason than to escape
a humdrum life at home. What proportion of
settlers, old and young, consisted of this type
of adventurer we can never know, but on

every English and American frontier they have always been numerous.

Much has been made of religious persecution as a cause of English migrations overseas. No one can deny that religious reasons were strong with certain groups, but we have overemphasized English persecution as a motive. So firmly fixed is this idea that we have created a popular legend that English America was peopled by refugees, fleeing for their lives and liberties, who set about establishing the principles of toleration when they reached these shores. In reality there was much less active persecution under the first two Stuarts than we have been led to believe, and the refugees, like most people in the seventeenth century, had no patience with toleration. The very fact that religious quarrels were so rife, repression so difficult, and conformity so ill-enforced argues the lack of violent religious persecution. The truth is that England enjoyed, even under the relatively severe exertions of Archbishop Laud, more freedom of conscience than any country in Europe except Holland. But Protestantism, which had no rigid Inquisition to hold heretics in check, inevitably produced sectaries to whom any restraint was anathema. Ecclesiastical authorities under both James I and his successor silenced some preachers for violating their oaths to conform to the Anglican ritual. An occasional sectary landed in jail for what was regarded as disorderly conduct in failing to observe the established religious decorum. But regulations which English dissenters hated as oppression would have seemed to an Italian or a Spaniard of that day a fantastic dream of license, if not of freedom.

Annoyance of nonconforming folk there was in abundance, and to independent spirits persistent annoyance became tyranny and persecution. Objections to regulation were sufficient indeed to induce many earnest souls to leave England for Holland or the New World where they hoped, usually in vain, to worship undisturbed by schismatics within the fold and oppressors without. Officially the government encouraged emigrants for religious reasons to settle in the dominions beyond the seas, and it is worthy of note that the government rarely pursued them with objectionable regulations. In time both Protestant and Catholic dissidents would find refuge under the British flag in America.

The most impelling single motive which induced emigrants to leave England was the desire for land and all that the possession of broad acres implied. Land hunger frequently was joined with other considerations —the lure of adventure, the desire for religious freedom, or any number of a multitude of frustrations at home—but the emigrant's brightest dream was the vision of becoming a landed proprietor. Even the poorest servant, who sold himself into a four-years' bondage to pay his passage, had a hope of ultimately settling upon a piece of ground which he would own in fee simple.

Americans, brought up in a country where anyone for a modest sum can purchase at least a small farm or a building lot, have difficulty comprehending the value which the seventeenth-century Englishman, of whatever degree, placed upon the possession of land. Most English soil was tightly held; and for such land as could be bought, the demand was great. Younger sons of the gentry, left without landed estates under the law of primogeniture, purchased holdings when they could. Rich merchants and tradesmen with money to invest eagerly sought country estates, the symbol of social prestige. Under the dual stimulation of inflation and an ever-increasing demand, land prices rose during the first half of the seventeenth-century until only the well-to-do could buy, at exorbitant rates, desirable country property.

The scarcity of purchasable land and the throngs of unemployed wanderers in Jacobean England gave rise to a popular notion that the country was over-populated and required an outlet for its surplus people. An island which today supports a population of more than forty-one million can scarcely have been burdened with less than five million souls, but the shifts in the balance between agriculture and industry had temporarily displaced many farmers and other laborers, who gave the impression of an excess of indigent people. Periodic financial depressions, notably between 1619 and 1624, also magnified the indications of impending calamity and convinced observers that settlements overseas were the only solution of acute—and permanent—unemployment.

Propagandists outdid themselves in commending the establishment of colonies in America. Poets, ballad writers, pamphleteers, and preachers took up the theme. Verily in North America Eden might be rediscovered. The fertility of the soil exceeded that in the valleys of the Nile or Euphrates. Every plant needful and pleasant flourished there. Fish, fowl, and beasts of the field seemed especially created for man's pleasure and profit. The climate was benign and the air wholesome. "Many that have been weak and sickly in old England, by coming hither have been thoroughly healed and grown healthful and strong," wrote the Reverend Francis Higginson from Massachusetts in 1630. Such was the softness of the air that he himself, who had "not gone without a cap for many years together, neither durst leave off the same, have now cast away my cap and do wear none at all in the day time." Though Higginson, ironically, died of tuberculosis within a year, his words must have encouraged prospective emigrants.

Preachers and other writers pointed out that colonization overseas would be a stroke for both God and King—as well as a direct profit to the individual settler. By taking the gospel message to heathen Indians, colonists would win the favor of the Almighty. By establishing outposts in America against England's enemies, they would perform a patriotic service. The new settlements would consume the goods of English merchants, furnish a ready supply of commodities useful to the mother country, and provide homes and farms for every needy person. This doctrine rang from press and pulpit.

One of the most persuasive books on colonization—one now almost forgotten—came from the pen of the Reverend Richard Eburne, vicar of Henstridge in Somerset, who published in 1624 *A Plain Pathway to Plantations,* commending in particular a settlement in Newfoundland and advocating in general a program of expansion overseas. Although the depression which had been responsible for considerable unemployment in the previous five years was really caused by a constriction of credit by the merchants and money-lenders of London, Eburne interpreted it as a result of luxury, extravagance, and sloth induced by an era of peace and prosperity. Life in the colonies would correct the tendency to idleness which had been growing, he believed, and restore to Englishmen their former virtues of diligence and thrift. The standard of living had improved, especially for urban and industrial groups, and Eburne remarked, quite correctly, that "Englishmen above many others are worst able to live with a little." To his countrymen, who had become accustomed to the good things of this world, the author held out the hope of renewed prosperity, combined with wholesome virtue, in the plantations across the sea.

The ordinary Englishman's refusal to be content with a little, as Eburne hints, resulted in a great stir of action during times of depression. The fundamental health of the economic system rather than its decay explains the vigor of emigrants who went abroad to carry a little of England with them. "Imagine all that to be England where English men, where English people, you with them, and they with you, do dwell," admonished Richard Eburne, anticipating Rupert Brooke by three centuries. "And it be the people that makes the land English, not the land the people. So you may find England, and an happy England, too, where now is, as I may say, no land." When times got hard, seventeenth-century citizens were too virile to accept distress supinely; they were men of action, with minds of their own, willing and able to make another England, improved and happier, in realms that waited their conquest.

Whether discontent was caused by grievances against the religious establishment, distress in the pocketbook, or plain restlessness, the Englishman, like his descendant in nineteenth-century America, had a remedy. He could begin a new life in a frontier society to the west, where he would carry his dream of a better world.

17

Michel Guillaume Jean de Crèvecœur was among the first, but scarcely the last, to attempt to answer the question, What is an American? A French-born aristocrat, Crèvecœur spent the years from 1765 to 1780 farming in Orange County, New York. With the special insight of a detached observer, Crèvecœur describes the American character from the perspective of the end of the colonial period:[17]

What then is the American, this new man? He is either an European, or the descendant of an European; hence that strange mixture of blood, which you will find in no other country. I could point out to you a man, whose grandfather was an Englishman, whose wife was Dutch, whose son married a French woman, and whose present four sons have now four wives of different nations. *He* is an American, who, leaving behind him all his ancient prejudices and manners, receives new ones from the new mode of life he has embraced, the new government he obeys, and the new rank he holds. He becomes an American by being received in the broad lap of our great *Alma Mater*. Here

[17] Jean de Crèvecœur, *Letters from an American Farmer* (London, 1912 ed.), pp. 43–44.

individuals of all nations are melted into a new race of men, whose labours and posterity will one day cause great change in the world. Americans are the western pilgrims, who are carrying along with them that great mass of arts, sciences, vigour, and industry, which began long since in the east; they will finish the great circle. The Americans were once scattered all over Europe; here they are incorporated into one of the finest systems of population which has ever appeared, and which will hereafter become distinct by the power of the different climates they inhabit. The American ought therefore to love this country much better than that wherein either he or his forefathers were born. Here the rewards of his industry follow with equal steps the progress of his labour; his labour is founded on the basis of nature, *self-interest;* can it want a stronger allurement? Wives and children, who before in vain demanded of him a morsel of bread, now, fat and frolicsome, gladly help their father to clear those fields whence exuberant crops are to arise to feed and to clothe them all; without any part being claimed, either by a despotic prince, a rich abbot, or a mighty lord. Here religion demands but little of him; a small voluntary salary to the minister, and gratitude to God; can he refuse these? The American is a new man, who acts upon new principles; he must therefore entertain new ideas, and form new opinions. From involuntary idleness, servile dependance, penury, and useless labour, he has passed to toils of a very different nature, rewarded by ample subsistence.—This is an American.

The Colonial Mind

Two centuries of colonial life equipped the American people intellectually for independence. Medieval notions—the inevitability of the *status quo*, the doctrine of complete obedience to authority, and the theological indifference to secular life —were dissolved by the new and stimulating ideas of the Enlightenment. Society, like the universe, was governed by natural forces rather than by divine decree; hence man could better himself by improving the environment in which he lived. He could, moreover, demand that rulers protect his natural right to life, liberty, and happiness.

THE IDEAS THEY BROUGHT WITH THEM

1

Belief in the supernatural was a basic assumption which most Englishmen brought to the New World, particularly to New England. The New England colonists were a devout people, reared on an undiluted diet of Calvinistic doctrine. They accepted the concept of a wrathful Deity who governed the universe with absolute sovereignty and admitted to His celestial abode only a few carefully selected souls whose salvation had been predestined since the death of Christ. In this atmosphere supernatural occurences were daily events. None was more faithful to the spirit of orthodoxy than Increase Mather, as his An Essay for the Recording of Illustrious Providences *(1684) attests. Mather was no simple superstitious bigot; he completed his studies with honors at Trinity College in Dublin, served as pastor of Boston's North Church, presided over the destinies of Harvard College between 1685 and 1701, and was recognized on two continents as a brilliant student of science and theology. His description of a bewitched house reflects his faith in a Puritan God whose power was manifest in ways awesome and strange:*[1]

In the Year 1679, the house of William Morse, in Newberry in New-England, was

[1] Increase Mather, *Remarkable Providences, Illustrative of the Early Days of American Colonization* (London, 1856 ed.), pp. 101–104.

strangely disquieted by a dæmon. After those troubles began, he did, by the advice of friends, write down the particulars of those unusual accidents. And the account which he giveth thereof is as followeth:——

On December 3, in the night time, he and his wife heard a noise upon the roof of their house, as if sticks and stones had been thrown against it with great violence; whereupon he rose out of his bed, but could see nothing. Locking the doors fast, he returned to bed again. About midnight they heard an hog making a great noise in the house, so that the man rose again, and found a great hog in the house, the door being shut, but upon the opening of the door it ran out.

On December 8. in the morning, there were five great stones and bricks by an invisible hand thrown in at the west end of the house while the mans wife was making the bed; the bedstead was lifted up from the floor, and the bedstaff flung out of the window, and a cat was hurled at her; a long staff danced up and down in the chimney; a burnt brick, and a piece of a weather-board were thrown in at the window, the man at his going to bed put out his lamp, but in the morning found that the saveall of it was taken away, and yet it was unaccountably brought into its former place. On the same day, the long staff, but now spoken of, was

31

hang'd up by a line, and swung to and fro; the man's wife laid it in the fire, but she could not hold it there, inasmuch as it would forcibly fly out; yet after much ado with joynt strength they made it to burn. A shingle flew from the window, though no body near it; many sticks came in at the same place, only one of these was so scragged that it could enter the hole but a little way, whereupon the man pusht it out; a great rail likewise was thrust in at the window, so as to break the glass.

At another time an iron crook that was hanged on a nail, violently flew up and down; also a chair flew about, and at last lighted on the table where victuals stood ready for them to eat, and was likely to spoil all, only by a nimble catching they saved some of their meal with the loss of the rest and the overturning of their table.

People were sometimes barricado'd out of doors, when as yet there was no body to do it; and a chest was removed from place to place, no hand touching it. Their keys being tied together, one was taken from the rest, and the remaining two would fly about making a loud noise by knocking against each other. But the greatest part of this devils feats were his mischievous ones, wherein indeed he was sometimes antick enough too, and therein the chief sufferers were, the man and his wife, and his grand-son. The man especially had his share in these diabolical molestations. For one while they could not eat their suppers quietly, but had the ashes on the hearth before their eyes thrown into their victuals; yea, and upon their heads and clothes, insomuch that they were forced up into their chamber, and yet they had no rest there; for one of the man's shoes being left below, it was filled with ashes and coals, and thrown up after them. Their light was beaten out, and they being laid in their bed with their little boy between them, a great stone (from the floor of the loft) weighing above three pounds was thrown upon the mans stomach, and he turning it down upon the floor; it was once more thrown upon him. A box, and a board were likewise thrown

upon them all; and a bag of hops was taken out of their chest, therewith they were beaten, till some of the hops were scattered on the floor, where the bag was then laid and left.

In another evening, when they sat by the fire, the ashes were so whirled at them, that they could neither eat their meat, nor endure the house. A peel struck the man in the face. An apron hanging by the fire, was flung upon it, and singed before they could snatch it off. The man being at prayer with his family, a beesom gave him a blow on his head behind, and fell down before his face.

On another day, when they were winnowing of barley, some hard dirt was thrown in, hitting the man on the head, and both the man and his wife on the back; and when they had made themselves clean, they essayed to fill their half bushel; but the foul corn was in spite of them often cast in amongst the clean, and the man being divers times thus abused was forced to give over what he was about.

On January 23 (in particular) the man had an iron pin twice thrown at him, and his inkhorn was taken away from him while he was writing, and when by all his seeking it he could not find it, at last he saw it drop out of the air, down by the fire. A piece of leather was twice thrown at him; and a shoe was laid upon his shoulder, which he catching at, was suddenly rapt from him. An handful of ashes was thrown at his face, and upon his clothes; and the shoe was then clapt upon his head, and upon it he clapt his hand, holding it so fast, that somewhat unseen pulled him with it backward on the floor.

On the next day at night, as they were going to bed, a lost ladder was thrown against the door, and their light put out; and when the man was a bed, he was beaten with an heavy pair of leather breeches, and pull'd by the hair of his head and beard, pinched and scratched, and his bed-board was taken away from him. Yet more: in the next night, when the man was likewise a bed, his bed-board did rise out of its place, notwithstanding his putting forth all his strength to keep it in; one of his awls was brought out of the next room into his bed, and did prick him; the clothes wherewith he hoped to save his head from blows were violently pluckt from thence. Within a night or two after, the man and his wife received both of them a blow upon their heads, but it was so dark that they could not see the stone which gave it. The man had his cap pulled off from his head while he sat by the fire.

2

Despite an intellectual environment of supernaturalism, Puritanism fostered a vigorous intellectual life. Education (to train literate congregations and intelligent ministers), literature (to glorify a jealous Deity), and newspapers (to mold public opinion in the patterns of orthodoxy) flourished in the New England colonies long before other colonists initiated similar departures from medieval practice. An educational system was established by the Massachusetts General Court in 1647, requiring each town to maintain an elementary school and each larger community a grammar school where youths could be prepared to enter "ye University," or Harvard:[2]

It being one chiefe &iect of y^t ould deluder, Satan, to keepe men from the knowledge of ye Scriptures; as in form^r times by keeping y^m in an unknowne tongue, so in these latt^r times by pswading from ye use of tongues, y^t so at least ye true sence & meaning of ye originall might be clouded by false glosses of saint seeming deceivers, y^t learning may not be buried in ye grave of o^r fath^{rs} in ye church & commonwealth, the Lord assisting o^r endeavo^{r}s,—

It is therefore ord^{r}ed, y^t ev^{r}y towneship in this iurisdiction, aft^r ye Lord hath increased y^m number to 50 houshold^{rs}, shall then forthwth appoint one wthin their towne to teach all such children as shall resort to him to write & reade, whose wages shall be paid eith^r by ye parents or mast^{rs} of such children, or by ye inhabitants in gen^{r}all, by way of supply, as ye maior p̃t of those y^t ord^r ye prudentials ye twone shall appoint; &vided, those y^t send their children be not oppressed by paying much more y^n they can have y^m taught for in oth^r townes; & it is furth^r ordered, y^t where any towne shall increase to ye numb^r of 100 families or household^{rs}, they shall set up a gram͞er schoole, ye m^r thereof being able to instruct youth so farr as they may be fitted for ye university, &vided, y^t if any towne neglect ye pformance hereof above one yeare, y^t every such towne shall pay 5£ to ye next schoole till they shall pforme this order.

3

The schools fostered by this law took pains to implant in young minds a knowledge of the "three Rs" as well as the Puritan faith. For half a century following its enactment in 1690 a principal educational instrument was The New-England Primer, *an elementary text that remained unchallenged in popularity until after the Revolution. Calvinistic doctrine crammed its grim pages in the rhymed alphabet through which young New Englanders "learned their letters" and their creed:*[3]

In *Adam's* Fall
We sinned all.

Thy Life to mend
This *Book* attend.

The *Cat* doth play
And after slay.

A *Dog* will bite
The Thief at night.

An *Eagle's* flight
Is out of sight.

The Idle *Fool,*
Is whipt at School.

As runs the *Glass*
Man's Life doth pass.

---

[2] *Records of the Governor and Company of the Massachusetts Bay in New England* (Boston, 1853), II, 203.

[3] *The New-England Primer.* Reprinted in Paul Leicester Ford, *The New-England Primer* (New York, 1897), pp. 65–68, 80.

My *Book* and *Heart*
Shall never part.

Job feels the rod
Yet blesses GOD.

Our KING the good
No man of blood.

The *Lion* bold
The *Lamb* doth hold.

The *Moon* gives light
In time of night.

Nightingales sing
In Time of Spring.

The *Royal Oak*
    it was the Tree
That sav'd His
    Royal Majestie.

Peter denies
His Lord and cries.

Queen *Esther* comes
    in Royal State
To save the JEWS
    from dismal Fate.

Rachel doth mourn
For her first born.

Samuel anoints
Whom God appoints.

Time cuts down all
Both great and small.

Uriah's beauteous Wife
Made *David* seek his life.

Whales in the Sea
God's Voice obey.

Xerxes the great did die
And so must you & I.

Youth forward slips
Death soonest nips.

Zacheus he
Did climb the Tree
His Lord to see.

Verses

I in the Burying Place may see
    Graves Shorter there than I;
From Death's Arrest no Age is free,
    Young Children too may die;
My God, may such an awful Sight,
    Awakening be to me!
Oh! that by early Grace I might
    For Death prepared be.

Good Children Must

Fear God all Day,   Love Christ alway
Parents obey,   In Secret Pray,
No False thing Say,   Mind little Play,
By no Sin stray,   Make no delay,
            In doing Good.

Awake, arise, behold thou hast
Thy Life a Leaf, thy Breath a Blast;
At Night lye down prepar'd to have
Thy sleep, thy death, thy bed, thy grave.

Learn These Four Lines by Heart

Have communion with few.
Be Intimate with ONE.
Deal justly with all.
Speak Evil of none.

4

Harvard topped the Puritan educational pyramid, the first college in English America. The opening of this important institution in 1636 was described in a promotion pamphlet, New Englands First Fruits, *which was printed in London in 1643:*[4]

After God had carried us safe to *New England,* and wee had builded our houses, provided necessaries for our liveli-hood,

---

[4] *New Englands First Fruits* (London, 1643). Reprinted in Samuel E. Morison, *The Founding of Harvard College* (Cambridge, 1935), pp. 432–433.

rear'd convenient places for Gods worship, and setled the Civill Government: One of the next things we longed for, and looked after was to advance *Learning* and perpetuate it to Posterity; dreading to leave an illiterate Ministery to the Churches, when our present Ministers shall lie in the Dust. And as wee were thinking and consulting how to effect this great Work, it pleased God to stir up the heart of one Mr. *Harvard* (a godly Gentleman, and a lover of Learning, there living amongst us) to give the one halfe of his Estate (it being in all about 1700. l.) towards the erecting of a Colledge: and all his Library: after him another gave 300. l. others after them cast in more, and the publique hand of the State added the rest: the Colledge was, by common consent, appointed to be at *Cambridge,* (a place very pleasant and accommodate) and is called (according to the name of the first founder) *Harvard Colledge.*

The Edifice is very faire and comely within and without, having in it a spacious Hall; (where they daily meet at Commons, Lectures) Exercises, and a large Library with some Bookes to it, the gifts of diverse of our friends, their Chambers and studies also fitted for, and possessed by the Students, and all other roomes of Office necessary and convenient, with all needfull Offices thereto belonging: And by the side of the Colledge a faire *Grammar* Schoole, for the training up of young Schollars, and fitting of them for Academicall Learning, that still as they are judged ripe, they may be received into the Colledge of this Schoole: Master *Corlet* is the Mr., who hath very well approved himselfe for his abilities, dexterity and painfulnesse in teaching and education of the youth under him.

Over the Colledge is master *Dunster* placed, as President, a learned conscionable and industrious man, who hath so trained up, his Pupills in the tongues and Arts, and so seasoned them with the principles of Divinity and Christianity, that we have to our great comfort, (and in truth) beyond our hopes, beheld their progress in Learning and godli-

nesse also; the former of these hath appeared in their publique declamations in *Latine* and *Greeke,* and Disputations Logicall and Philosophicall, which they have beene wonted (besides their ordinary Exercises in the Colledge-Hall) in the audience of the Magistrates, Ministers, and other Schollars, for the probation of their growth in Learning, upon set dayes, constantly once every moneth to make and uphold: The latter hath been manifested in sundry of them, by the savoury breathings of their Spirits in their godly conversation. Insomuch that we are confident, if these early blossomes may be cherished and warmed with the influence of the friends of Learning, and lovers of this pious worke, they will by the help of God, come to happy maturity in a short time.

Over the Colledge are twelve Overseers chosen by the generall Court, six of them are of the Magistrates, the other six of the Ministers, who are to promote the best good of it and (having a power of influence into all persons in it) are to see that every one be diligent and proficient in his proper place.

5

Not only did schools and universities train Puritans to fill the pulpits and churches, they also taught so many people to read that newspapers flourished in New England far earlier than in the other colonies. Benjamin Harris, a wandering English printer, launched the first when, on September 25, 1690, he distributed the first (and only) issue of America's pioneer paper with this bold announcement:[5]

PUBLICK
OCCURRENCES
Both FORREIGN and DOMESTICK

Boston, Thursday *Sept. 25th.* 1690.

It is designed, that the Countrey shall be furnished once a month (or if any Glut of Occurrences happen, oftener,) with an Account of such considerable things as have arrived unto our Notice.

---

[5] The first issue of *Publick Occurrences* is photographically reproduced in Frank L. Mott, *American Journalism* (New York, 1941), p. 10.

In order thereunto, the Publisher will take what pains he can to obtain a Faithful Relation of all such things; and will particularly make himself beholden to such Persons in Boston whom he Knows to have been for their own use the diligent Observers of such matters.

That which is herein proposed, is, First, That Memorable Occurrents of Divine Providence may not be neglected or forgotten, as they too often are. Secondly, That people every where may better understand the Circumstances of Publique Affairs, both abroad and at home; which may not only direct their Thoughts at all times, but at some times also to assist their Businesses and Negotiations.

Thirdly, That some thing may be done towards the Curing, or at least the Charming of that Spirit of Lying, which prevails amongst us, wherefore nothing shall be entered, but what we have reason to believe is true, repairing to the best fountains for our Information. And where there appears any material mistake in any thing that is collected, it shall be corrected in the next.

Moreover, the Publisher of these Occurrences is willing to engage, that whereas, there are many False Reports, maliciously made, and spread among us, if any well-minded person will be at the pains to trace any such false Report so far as to find out and Convict the First Raiser of it, he will in this Paper (unless just Advice be given to the contrary) expose the Name of such person, as A malicious Raiser of a false Report. It is suppos'd that none will dislike this Proposal, but such as intend to be guilty of so villanous a Crime.

PURITAN INTOLERANCE

6

Since devotion alone led to salvation, the Puritans were disdainful of all other sects. Zeal inspired intolerance; nonbelievers were disciples of the Devil who must be kept from contaminating God's faithful by conversion, banishment, or even extermination. This point of view was admirably summarized by Nathaniel Ward, pastor of the church at Ipswich, in a famous attack on freedom of conscience, The Simple Cobbler of Aggawam in America *(1647):*[6]

If the devill might have his free option, I beleeve he would ask nothing else, but liberty to enfranchize all false Religions, and to embondage the true; nor should hee need: It is much to be feared, that laxe Tolerations upon State-pretences and planting necessities, will be the next subtle Stratagem he will spread to distate the Truth of God and supplant the peace of the Churches. Tolerations in things tolerable, exquisitely drawn out by the lines of the Scripture, and pensill of the Spirit, are the sacred favours of Truth, the due latitudes of Love, the faire Compartiments of Christian fraternity: but irregular dispensations, dealth forth by the facilities of men, are the frontiers of error, the redoubts of Schisme, the perillous irritaments of carnall and spirituall enmity.

My heart hath naturally detested foure things: The standing of the Apocrypha in the Bible; Forrainers dwelling in my Countrey, to crowd out native Subjects into the corners of the Earth; Alchymized coines; Tolerations of divers Religions, or of one Religion in segregant shapes: He that willingly assents to the last, if he examines his heart by daylight, his conscience will tell him, he is either an Atheist, or an Heretique, or an Hypocrite, or at best a captive to some Lust: Polypiety is the greatest impiety in the world. True Religion is *Ignis probationis,* which doth *congregare homogenea & segregare heterogenea.*

Not to tolerate things meerly indifferent to weak consciences, argues a conscience too strong: pressed uniformity in these, causes much disunity: To tolerate more than indifferents, is not to deale indifferently with God: He that doth it, takes his Scepter out of his hand, and bids him stand by. The power of all Religion and Ordinances, lies in their purity: their purity in their simplicity:

---

[6] Nathaniel Ward, *The Simple Cobbler of Aggawam in America* (Lawrence C. Wroth, ed., New York, 1937), pp. 4–6.

then are mixtures pernicious. I lived in a City, where a Papist preached in one Church, a Lutheran in another, a Calvinist in a third; a Lutheran one part of the day, a Calvinist the other, in the same Pulpit: the Religion of that place was but motly and meagre, their affections Leopard-like.

If the whole Creature should conspire to doe the Creator a mischiefe, or offer him an insolency, it would be in nothing more, than in erecting untruths against his Truth, or by sophisticating his Truths with humane medley's: the removing of some one iota in Scripture, may draw out all the life, and traverse all the Truth of the whole Bible: but to authorise an untruth, by a Toleration of State, is to build a Sconce against the walls of heaven, to batter God out of his Chaire: To tell a practicall lye, is a great sinne, but yet transient; but to set up a Theoricall untruth, is to warrant every lye that lyes from its root to the top of every branch it hath.

7

In practice, Puritan intolerance was expressed in bitter attacks on dissenters bold enough to enter New England. The most troublesome were the Quakers, who began arriving in 1656 with missionary ambitions. When jail and lashings failed to halt their invasion, the death penalty was finally decreed for all who refused to stay banished. Quaker sufferings are portrayed in a memorial to the king prepared by one of their members, Edward Burrough, in 1660:[7]

2. Twelve Strangers in that Country, but free-born of this Nation, received twenty three Whippings, the most of them being with a Whip *of three Cords*, with *Knots at the ends*, and laid on with as much strength as they could be by the Arm of their Executioner, the stripes amounting to *Three hundred and seventy*.

3. Eighteen Inhabitants of the Country, being free-born *English*, received twenty three Whippings, the stripes amounting to two hundred and fifty.

4. Sixty four Imprisonments of the Lords People, for their obedience to his Will, amounting to Five hundred and nineteen weeks, much of it being *very cold weather*, and the Inhabitants kept in Prison *in harvest time*, which was very much to their losse; besides many more Imprisoned, of which time we cannot give a just account.

5. Two beaten with Pitched Ropes, the blows amounting to an hundred thirty nine, by which one of them was brought near unto death, much of his body being beat like unto a jelly, and one of their own Doctors, a Member of their Church, who saw him, said, *It would be a Miracle if ever he recovered, he expected the flesh should rot off the bones;* who afterwards was banished upon pain of death. There are many Witnesses of this there.

6. Also, an Innocent man, an Inhabitant of *Boston*, they banished from his Wife and Children, and put to seek a habitation in the Winter; and in case he returned again, he was to be kept Prisoner during his life: and for returning again, he was put in Prison, and hath been now a Prisoner above a year.

7. Twenty five Banishments, upon the penalties of being whipt, or having their Ears cut; or branded in the Hand, if they returned.

8. Fines laid upon the Inhabitants for meeting together, and edifying one another, as the Saints ever did; and for refusing to swear, it being contrary to Christ's Command, amounting to about a Thousand pound, besides what they have done since, that we have not heard of; many Families, in which there are many Children, are almost ruined, by these unmerciful proceedings.

9. Five kept *Fifteen dayes* (in all) *without food*, and *Fifty eight* dayes shut up close by the Jaylor, and had none that he knew of; and from some of them he stopt up the windows, hindring them from convenient air.

10. One laid Neck and Heels in Irons for *sixteen hours*.

11. One very deeply burnt in the right hand *with the letter* H. after he had been whipt with above *Thirty stripes*.

[7] Edward Burrough, *A Declaration of the Sad and Great Persecution and Martyrdom . . . of the Quakers, in New-England* (London, c. 1660), pp. 17–20.

12. One chained the most part of Twenty dayes to a Logg of wood in an open Prison in the Winter-time.

13. Five Appeals to *England,* denied at *Boston.*

14. Three had their right Ears cut by the Hangman in the Prison, the Door being barred, and not a Friend suffered to be present while it was doing, though some much desired it.

15. One of the Inhabitants of *Salem,* who since is banished upon pain of Death, *had one half of his House and Land seized on while he was in Prison,* a month before he knew of it.

16. At a General Court in *Boston,* they made an Order, That those who had not wherewithal to answer the Fines that were laid upon them (for their Consciences) should be sold for Bond-men, and Bond-women to Barbados, Virginia, or any of the English Plantations.

17. Eighteen of the People of God were at several times banished upon pain of Death, six of them were their own Inhabitants, two of which being very aged people, and well known among their Neighbours to be of honest Conversations, being Banished from their Houses and Families, and put upon Travelling and other hardships, soon ended their dayes; whose Death we can do no less than charge upon the Rulers of *Boston,* they being the occasion of it.

18. Also three of the Servants of the Lord they put to Death, all of them for obedience to the Truth, in the Testimony of it against the wicked Rulers and Laws at *Boston.*

19. And since they have banished four more, *upon pain of Death;* and twenty four of the Inhabitants of *Salem* were presented, and more Fines called for, and their Goods seized on, to the value of Forty pounds, for meeting together in the fear of God, and some for *refusing to swear.*

These things (O King) from time to time have we patiently suffered, and not for the transgression of any Just or Righteous Law, either pertaining to the Worship of God, or the Civil Government of *England,* but simply and barely for our Consciences to God, of which we can more at large give Thee (or whom thou mayest order) a full Account (if Thou wilt let us have admission to Thee, who are *Banished upon pain of Death,* and have had *our Ears cut,* who are, some of us, in *England* attending upon Thee) both of the *Causes of our Sufferings,* and *the Manner* of their disorderly and illegal Proceeding against us; Who begun with Immodesty, went on in Inhumanity and Cruelty, and were not satisfied until they had the Blood of three of the Martyrs of JESUS: Revenge for all which we do not seek, but lay them before Thee, considering Thou hast been well acquainted with Sufferings, and so mayest the better consider them that suffer, and mayest for the future restrain the Violence of these Rulers of *New-England,* having Power in Thy hands; they being but the Children of the Family, of which Thou art Chief Ruler; Who have in divers of their Proceedings forfeited their Patent; as upon a strict Inquiry in many particulars will appear.

And this, O King, we are assured of, that in time to come it will not repent Thee, if by a *Close Rebuke* Thou stoppest the Bloody Proceedings of these Bloody Persetutors; for in so doing, Thou wilt engage the hearts of many honest People unto Thee, both there and here; and for such Works of Mercy, the Blessing is obtained, and shewing it, is the way to prosper.

8

Intolerance of dissent not only governed the Puritan attitude toward others but shaped attitudes toward themselves. Within the borders of the wilderness Zion every man was his brother's keeper—or tried to be. Deviation from the norm was at once a crime against society and God; all were expected to conform to rigid rules of conduct laid down by the clergy. Often these decrees were incorporated into "Blue Laws" by magistrates; on other occasions they were contained in advice from ministers. A letter from the eminent divine, John Cotton, to one of his flock is typical:[8]

---

[8] John Cotton to R. Levett, Massachusetts Historical Society, *Collections* (Boston, 1843), 2d ser., X, 183–184.

Carding I take to be unlawful, and containing in it a lottery, at least in the shuffling and cutting and dealing. And a lottery also it is to choose Valentines in that sort you mention. Where man and his action is only causa per accidens of an event (as in carding and in choise of Valentines) God is the only and immediate cause per se. Now to appeal to him and his immediate providence for dispensing these ludicra, seemeth to me a taking of God's name in vain.

Dancing (yea though mixt) I would not simply condemn. For I see two sorts of mixt dancings in use with God's people in the Old Testament, the one religious, Exod. xv. 20, 21, the other civil, tending to the praise of conquerors, as the former of God, 1 Sam. xviii. 6, 7. Only lascivious dancing to wanton ditties, and in amorous gestures and wanton dalliances, especially after great feasts, I would bear witness against, as a great flabella libidinis.

9

The lash of Puritan intolerance fell heaviest upon witches—men and women who were thought to have sold themselves to the Devil in return for wealth or supernatural powers. These miserable unfortunates were systematically hunted down throughout the sixteenth and seventeenth centuries in America as in Europe; the epidemic that brought notoriety to Salem as the witch city of America was only a minor episode in the tragic history of a great world illusion. The Salem story began in 1692 when Tituba, a half-crazed old slave belonging to the local minister, was accused of bewitching a number of the town children. Nineteen persons were hanged and one was pressed to death before the episode ended. The trial of Tituba by a panel of learned judges marks a low point in colonial judicial history:[9]

SALEM VILLAGE, March 1st 1691

Titiba an Indian woman brought before vs by Const Joseph Herrick of Salem vpon Suspition of witchcraft by her committed according to ye complaint of Jos. Hutcheson and Thomas Putnam &c of Salem Village as appears p warrant granted Salem 29 ffebry

---

[9] William E. Woodward (comp.), *Records of Salem Witchcraft* (Roxbury, Mass., 1864), I, 11–48. Ezekiel Cheevers recorded the Tituba trial.

169½ Titiba vpon examination and after some deny all acknowledged ye matter of fact according to her examination giuen in more fully will appeare, and who also charged Sarah Good and Sarah Osburne with ye same. . . .

(H) Titibe whan evil spirit have you familiarity with.

(T) none.

(H) why do you hurt these children.

(T) I do not hurt them,

(H) who is it then.

(T) the devil for ought I know.

(H) Did you never see the devil.

(T) The devil came to me and bid me serve him.

(H) Who have you seen.

(T) Four women sometimes hurt the children.

(H) Who were they.

(T) Goode Osburn and Sarah Good and I doe not know who the other were. Sarah Good and Osburne would have me hurt the children but I would not she further saith there was a tale man of Boston that she did see.

(H) when did you see them.

(T) Last night at Boston.

(H) what did they say to you.

[T] they said hurt the children

(H) and did you hurt them

(T) no there is 4 women and one man they hurt the children and they lay upon me and they tell me if I will not hurt the children they will hurt me.

(H) but did you not hurt them

(T) yes, but I will hurt them no more.

(H) are you not sorry you did hurt them.

(T) yes.

(H) and why then doe you hurt them.

(T) they say hurt children or wee will doe worse to you.

(H) what have you seen.

[T] an man come to me and say serve me.

(H) what service.

(T) hurt the children and last night there was an appearance that said kill the children and if I would no go on hurting the children they would do worse to me.

(H) what is this appearance you see.

(T) Sometimes it is like a hog and some-times like a great dog, this appearance shee saith shee did see 4 times.

(H) what did it say to you

(T) it s the black dog said serve me but I said I am afraid he said if I did not he would doe worse to me.

(H) what did you say to it.

(T) I will serve you no longer. then he said he would hurt me and then he looked like a man and threatens to hurt me, shee said that this man had a yellow bird that kept with him and he told me he had more pretty things that he would give me if I would serve him.

(H) what were these pretty things.

(T) he did not show me them.

(H) what also have you seen

(T) two rats, a red rat and a black rat.

(H) what did they say to you.

(T) they said serve me.

(H) when did you see them.

(T) last night and they said serve me, but I said I would not

(H) what service.

(T) shee said hurt the children.

(H) did you not pinch Elizabeth Hub-bard this morning

(T) the man brought her to me and made me pinch her

(H) why did you goe to Thomas Putnams last night and hurt his child.

(T) they pull and hall me and make me goe

(H) and what would have you doe.

[T] Kill her with a knif.

Left. Fuller and others said at this time when the child saw these persons and was tormented by them that she did complayn of a knife, that they would have her cut her head off with a knife.

(H) how did you go

(T) we ride upon stickes and are there presently.

(H) doe you goe through the trees or over them.

(T) we see nothing but are there presently.

[H] why did you not tell your master.

[T] I was afraid they said they would cut of my head if I told.

[H] would you not have hurt others if you cold.

[T] They said they would hurt others but they could not

[H] what attendants hath Sarah Good.

[T] a yellow bird and shee would have given me one

[H] what meate did she give it

[T] it did suck her between her fingers.

[H] did not you hurt Mr Currins child

[T] goode good and goode Osburn told that they did hurt Mr Currens child and would have had me hurt him two, but I did not.

[H] what hath Sarah Osburn.

[T] yellow dog, shee had a thing with a head like a woman with 2 legges, and wings. Abigail Williams that lives with her Uncle Parris said that she did see the same crea-ture, and it turned into the shape of Goode Osburn.

[H] what else have you seen with Osburn.

[T] another thing, hairy it goes upright like a man it hath only 2 leggs.

[H] did you not see Sarah Good upon Elizabeth Hubbard, last Saterday.

[T] I did see her set a wolfe upon her to afflict her, the persons with this maid did say that she did complain of a wolfe.

T. shee further saith that shee saw a cat with good at another time.

[H] What cloathes doth the man go in

[T] he goes in black clouthes a tal man with white hair I thinke

[H] How doth the woman go

[T] in a white whood and a black whood with a top knot

[H] doe you see who it is that torments these children now.

[T] yes it is Goode Good, shee hurts them in her own shape

[H] and who is it that hurts them now.

[T] I am blind now. I cannot see.

PURITANS AND THE AMERICAN HERITAGE

10

Calvin and his Puritan followers believed that ordinary mortals were incapable of self-rule; the clergy alone could lead men in the footsteps of God. In Puritan eyes the best government was an oligarchy controlled by ministers and a few obedient civic leaders. The Reverend John Cotton, a prominent Puritan colonizer, offers a spirited defense of theocracy in A Discource about Civil Government in a New Plantation whose Design is Religion:[10]

Q. *Whether a new Plantation, where all or the most considerable part of free Planters profess their purpose and desire of securing to themselves and to their posterity the pure and peaceable enjoyment of Christ's Ordinances; Whether, I say, such Planters are bound in laying the Foundations of Church and Civil State, to take order, that all the free Burgesses be such as are in fellowship of the Church or Churches which are, or may be gathered according to Christ; and that those free Burgesses have the only power of chusing from among themselves Civil Magistrates, and men to be intrusted with transacting all publick Affairs of Importance, according to the rules and directions of Scripture?* . . .

Theocratie, *or to make the Lord God our Governour,* (a) *is the best Form of Government in a Christian Commonwealth, and which men that are free to chuse (as in new Plantations they are) ought to establish. The Form of Government described in the true stating of the Question is* Theocratic, *or that wherein we make the Lord God our Governour. Therefore that Form of Government which is described in the true stating of the Question, is the best Form of Government in a Christian Common-wealth, and which men that are free to chuse (as in new Plantations they are) ought to establish. The* Proposition

is clear of it self. The Assumption I prove thus:

That Form of Government where 1. *The people that have the power of chusing their Governours are in Covenant with God* (b): 2. *Wherein the men chosen by them are godly men, and fitted with a spirit of Government* (c): 3. *In which the Laws they rule by are the Laws of God* (d): 4. *Wherein Laws are executed, Inheritances allotted, and civil differences are composed, according to Gods appointment* (e): 5. *In which men of God are consulted with in all hard cases, and in matters of Religion* (f), is the Form which was received and established among the people of *Israel* whil'st the Lord God was their Governour, as the places of Scripture alleged shew; and is the very same with that which we plead for, as will appear to him that shall examine the true stating of the Question. The Conclusion follows necessarily.

That Form of Government which giveth unto Christ his due preheminence, is the best Form of Government in a Christian Common-wealth, and which men that are free to chuse (as in new Plantations they are) ought to establish. The Form of Government described in the true stating of the Question, is that which giveth unto Christ his due preheminence. Therefore the Form of Government which is described in the true stating of the Question, is the best Form of Government in a Christian Commonwealth, and which men that are free to chuse (as in new Plantations they are) ought to establish.

The Proposition is proved out of two places of Scripture, *Col.* I. 15. *to* 19, with *Eph.* I. 21, 22. From which Texts it doth appear, that it is a prehemi[ne]nce due to Christ, that all things, and all Governments in the world, should serve to Christs ends, for the welfare of the Church whereof he is the Head. For 1. In relation to God, he hath this by Right of Primogeniture, as he is *the first-born, and so Heir of all things, higher then the Kings of the earth.* 2. In relation to the World, it is said, *All things were made by him, and for him, and do consist in him,* and therefore it is a preheminence due to

---

[10] John Cotton, *A Discourse about Civil Government in a New Plantation whose Design is Religion* (Cambridge, 1663), pp. 14–17. This essay was written earlier, but was first published in 1663. It has been falsely ascribed to John Davenport.

him, that they all serve him. 3. In relation to the Church, it is said, *He hath made all things subject under his feet, and hath given him over all things to be Head of the Church, that in all things he might have the preheminence.* And indeed that he upholdeth the Creatures, and the Order that is in them, it is for his Churches sake; when that is once compleat, the world shall soon be at an end. And if you reade the stories of the great Monarchies that have been, and judge of them by Scripture-light, you will finde they stood or fell, according as God purposed to make use of them about some service to be done about his Church. So that the onely considerable part for which the world standeth at this day, is the Church: and therefore it is a Preheminence due to Christ, that his Headship over the Church should be exalted and acknowledged, and served by all. In which respect also the Title of *The first-born* is given to the Members of the Church, and they are called *The first-fruits of his Creatures,* to shew both their preheminence above others, and that they are fittest to serve to Gods ends.

The Assumption (*That the Form of Government described in the true stating of the Question, doth give unto Christ his due preheminence*) will easily be granted by those that shall consider what Civil Magistrates and Rulers in the Commonwealth those are, who are fittest to serve to Christ's ends for the good and welfare of his Church; which will be evident from two places of Scripture: First, in *Psa.* 2. 10, 11, 12 you have a description of those that are fitted to order Civil Affairs in their Magistracy to Christ's ends; they are such as are not onely wise and learned in matters of Religion, but also do reduce their knowledge into practice: they *Worship the Lord in fear;* and not only so, but *Kiss the Son,* which was a solemn & outward *Profession of love* (a), and *of Subjection* (b), and *of Religious Worship* (c), and so fitly serveth to express their joyning themselves to the Church of Christ. Secondly, in *Isa.* 49. 23. it is promised to the Church, that *Kings and Queens shall be their nursing-fathers and nursing-mothers,* and therefore it is added, *They shall worship with their faces to the earth, and lick up the dust of thy feet;* which is a proverbial expression of their voluntary humbling of themselves to Christ in his Ordinances, (taken from the manner of the *Persians,* in declaring their Subjection to their Emperour (d), which the Apostle calls *a voluntary submission to the Gospel* (e), which is the spirit of the Members of the Churches of Christ. And for this Reason it is, that the Lord, when he moulded a Communion among his own People, wherein all Civil Administrations should serve to holy ends, he described the men to whom that Trust should be committed, by certain Properties, which also qualified them for fellowship in Church-Ordinances, as *Men of ability and power over their own affections* (f); secondly, *fearing God, Truly Religious, Men of Courage, hating Covetousness, men of Wisdom, men of understanding, and men known* or approved of *among the people of God, & chosen by the Lord from among their Brethren,* & not a stranger, which is no Brother: the most of which concurre to describe Church-members in a Church rightly gathered and ordered, who are also in respect of their union with Christ, and fellowship together, called *Brethren* frequently in the New Testament, wherein the equity of that Rule is established to us. Object. *Christ will have his due Preheminence, though the Civil Rulers oppose him, and persecute the Churches, as in* Rome: *Therefore it is not necessary that this course be taken in Civil Affairs to establish Christs Preheminence.* Ans. The Question is of a Christian Commonwealth that should willingly subject themselves to Christ, not of a Heathen State that shall perforce be subdued unto Christ. It is concerning what Gods people being free should chuse, not what his enemies are compell'd unto.

11

Attempts to assess Puritan contributions to American life and thought have evoked scholarly controversies only slightly less heated than the controversies dividing Puritans in colonial New England. That Puritans profoundly influenced American ideas and institutions there can be no doubt, but there are wide differences of opinion on the meaning and consequences of Puritanism. Samuel Eliot Morison, a noted student of Puritan culture, seeks to correct the modern image of the Puritan:[11]

Who were these puritans, and what did they propose to do? They were a party in the Church of England that arose in Elizabeth's reign with the purpose of carrying out the Protestant reformation to its logical conclusion, to base the English Church both in doctrine and discipline on the firm foundation of Sacred Scripture; or in the words of Cartwright, to restore the primitive, apostolic church "pure and unspotted" by human accretions or inventions. Religion should permeate every phase of living. Man belonged to God alone: his only purpose in life was to enhance God's glory and do God's will, and every variety of human activity, every sort of human conduct, presumably unpleasing to God, must be discouraged if not suppressed.

English puritanism, though essentially a religious movement, had its political and economic aspects. In their search for the original pattern of the Christian Church in the apostolic age, the puritan leaders did not agree. They were divided into the Presbyterians, who thought that the primitive church was governed by a series of representative assemblies or synods; and the Congregationalists, who insisted that there never had been a unified church, only churches: each individual congregation should be a democracy of the "visible saints," of those admitted to full communion upon satisfactory evidence that they were God's elect. New England was founded by Congregationalists, the more democratic wing; and the latent democratic principle in their polity proved,

humorously enough, an exceptionally heavy cross for the autocratically inclined parsons to carry. But whether Congregational or Presbyterian in its polity, puritanism appealed to the average Englishman's anticlericalism. It gave the layman a larger part in the local church than he had enjoyed since the Roman emperors became Christian.

Puritanism also had its economic side. . . . In New England, certainly, the Church was no respecter of persons, and the spectacle of Robert Keayne, the profiteering merchant of Boston, having to stand up in meeting and take a tongue-lashing from the Reverend John Cotton for infringing the puritan code of business ethics, would have warmed the heart of any modern radical. . . . Puritanism was unascetic; it came to terms with this world. Under the medieval church you could only approach perfection (short of Heaven) by withdrawing from this world and entering the priesthood or a monastic order. But puritanism taught that a man could serve God quite as effectually in his chosen calling as by entering the sacred ministry; that a farmer or merchant who conducted his business according to Christian ethics was more agreeable in the sight of God than one who withdrew from the world and escaped his social responsibilities by a celibate or monastic life. This doctrine of the calling, that you could serve God by nobly fulfilling a function determined by the conditions of this world, and thus prove your right to an easy place in the next world, was probably the main reason why puritanism appealed to the rising middle class, the nascent capitalists of the sixteenth and seventeenth centuries. Puritanism was essentially a middle-class movement. It was far too exigent in its moral demands ever to be popular with earthy-minded peasants, or with the nobility and the very rich, who saw no point in having money if you could not spend it as you liked.

In its attitude toward love, puritanism had more in common with Judaism than with medieval Christianity or Jesuit piety. Puritanism did not hold with asceticism or celibacy. The clergy married young and often; their church

---

[11] Samuel E. Morison, *The Intellectual Life of Colonial New England* (New York University Press, 1956), pp. 8–12, 24–25. Copyright 1956 by New York University. Reprinted by permission of the publisher.

offered no monastic retreat for men who were too much troubled by women. Milton's invocation "Hail, wedded love!" in *Paradise Lost* expresses the puritan ideal very neatly; and William Ames, the puritan casuist, implies in his *de Conscientia* that women have a right to expect something more from their husbands than mere duty. "Increase and multiply," the oldest of God's commands, was one that the puritans particularly enjoyed obeying—or some of us would not be here. Continence was a moral ideal on which due weight was laid; abstinence was not a superior virtue confounded with chastity but was in conflict with the purpose of creation. Married men who came out to New England were bluntly told to send for their wives or return to them. It was easier to obtain a divorce in New England in the seventeenth century than in old England; for the puritans, having laid such store on wedded love, wished every marriage to be a success.

On its intellectual side, which mainly concerns us, puritanism was an enemy to that genial glorification of the natural man with all his instincts and appetites that characterized the Renaissance and the great Elizabethans. Shakespeare's

What a piece of work is man! how noble in reason! how infinite in faculties! in form and moving how express and admirable! in action how like an angel! in apprehension how like a god!

is the antithesis of puritanism, which taught that natural man was wholly vile, corrupt, and prone to evil; that he could do no good without God's assistance; that he thoroughly deserved to broil in hell for all eternity, and would do so if he did not grasp the hand of grace proffered him by a merciful God through Jesus Christ. . . .

The puritans, like the Jews, regarded this earth and humanity as a divine enterprise, the management of which was God's major interest; they were God's people and their God was a living God, always thought of as intensely concerned with the actions and characters of people and nations. Each individual was a necessary item in a significant and divinely ordered cosmos. God has a personal interest in me, and has appointed work for me to do. If I am incapable of receiving his grace, it is unfortunate; but if that is God's will, who am I to complain? Yet while there's life, there's hope; and at any time before death my risen Lord may whisper in my heart that I am of the blessed ones elected by his Father to salvation.

It is generally supposed that puritanism hampered intellectual and artistic activity; and there is some truth in this charge. Puritanism banned three forms in which the English excelled: the drama, religious music, and erotic poetry. Just why it banned the drama is still a matter of debate among the professors. Was it that the drama was supposed to lead to immorality, or because it amused people too much? Or simply because a number of the church fathers, like Chrysostom, had thundered against the pagan drama of their day? Whatever the reason, the puritan war on the theatre was hideously successful. There is no stranger phenomenon in literature than the swift rise of the English drama to a high zenith between 1580 and 1611, with Marlowe and Shakespeare; and its equally swift decline a few years after the death of Shakespeare. But it was not the puritans alone who killed the theatre. Their theological enemies, Bishop Laud and the high churchmen, were equally responsible. James I liked a good show as much as anyone and, as long as he reigned, the English theatre had court patronage; but Bishop Laud took charge of the conscience of Charles I, and discouraged the King from patronizing the drama as an object unworthy of a Christian monarch's support. Deprived both of middle-class and court patronage, the English theatre had no audience left but the sort that attends burlesque shows today; and the English theatre became not much better than burlesque shows. . . .

Although puritanism had nothing against music as such, the puritans injured music by taking it out of the churches. Religious exercises were stripped down to the bare rudiments of the days when early Christians met in secret, and would not have dared to play the organ, even if an organ had been available. Consequently instrumental music, like the other beautiful incidents with which the medieval church had enriched religious expression, was done away with for want of scriptural sanction, and because it was supposed to make the worshiper dreamy. . . .

It is not, then, correct to judge the puritans, as many writers have done, by the fanatical pamphlets of William Prynne, the Martin Marprelate tracts, and the writings of Richard Baxter. When in power they soon learned that no layman, however sincerely religious, could be expected to give all his waking moments to thoughts of God; that he must be given opportunity for earning a living, and for reasonable recreation, or, as they called it, "seasonable merriment." There was much opportunity for love and laughter in colonial New England, though not as much as there should have been. Thus, the puritans forbade the observance of Christmas, because of the pagan revelry that merry England had inflicted on the day of Christ's Nativity; but they established Thanksgiving Day which took its place; and now we have both Thanksgiving Day and Christmas. They abolished May Day, which in Elizabethan England was far from being the innocent school-children's holiday that it is now; but instead they got two holidays in spring and early summer: election day and the college commencement, which soon took on the character of a Flemish kermis. They attempted to regulate the liquor traffic; but they never attempted or even suggested a complete prohibition of all alcoholic beverages. Indeed, it might be agreed that puritan restrictions on purely physical enjoyment tended to stimulate intellectual life; that a good many people who in England would have lingered in a tavern, carousing and singing songs, stayed at home and wrote prose and poetry, or argued over the fine points of the last sermon and picked flaws in their parson's theology!

12

Alan Simpson, a modern scholar of English origin, defines Puritan virtues in relation to politics, education, and morality. The following

comments are parts of an extended comparison between Puritanism in old and New England:[12]

Let us return to the Puritan's impact on politics. Among his virtues I would list:

1. *His contribution to our system of limited government.*—The original Puritans had a genuine basis for their distrust of arbitrary power in addition to their experience of arbitrary government. They thought that man was too sinful to be trusted with too much power. They were likely to make an exception of the saint, but, once saints were prevented from ruling, they had kept their conviction that nobody else should be trusted. The Puritan tradition, with its everlasting insistence that only God is worthy of worship, is one insurance among Anglo-Saxon people that the state has no claim to worship. Fortunately, there are many other securities, but no one will undervalue the stubbornness of this one. They have defended, in season and out of season, the right to preach, to criticize, and to judge. . . .

2. *His contribution to self-government— to the development of initiative and self-reliance in the body of the community.*—The Puritan pilgrimage has been a perpetual pilgrimage in self-help. The significance of the dissenting chapel as a training ground for working-class leadership in English history has often been emphasized, and much the same services have been performed by the free church tradition in America. Nor should we forget, in the nineteenth century as in the seventeenth, the direct transfer from church affairs to political affairs of certain techniques of action. The political meeting of the nineteenth century owes an obvious, if not wholly healthy, debt to the camp meeting of the revivalist preacher.

3. *His contribution to education.*—The most anti-intellectual Puritan has been obliged to master at least one book—and that a great one. The most intellectual Puritans, in their desire to promote saving knowledge, have thrown up academy after

[12] Reprinted from *Puritanism in Old and New England* by Alan Simpson, pp. 111–114, by permission of The University of Chicago Press. Copyright 1955 by The University of Chicago.

academy, college after college, until their influence has been writ large over the history of education in England and America.

4. *His contribution to morality.*—The Puritan code has its repellent features, but it is no bad thing to have habits of honesty, sobriety, responsibility, and hard work impressed on a community. It seems probable that the acquisitive energy of the nineteenth century would have created far more havoc than it did without the restraining influence of this evangelical spirit.

Finally, there is the contribution which Puritanism within the religious tradition of Anglo-Saxon peoples, has made to " the class peace." Almost the worst thing that can happen to the politics of a modern society is to have them polarized around social classes. Any force which works across these divisions, and either conceals or cements them, has a permanent claim on our gratitude.

As the limitations of Puritanism have been sufficiently stressed in these essays, I shall quote only one passage which seems to sum them up. I might have chosen for censure the *cri de cœur* of the nonconformist conscience in nineteenth-century English politics as it appears in the protest of the famous preacher Hugh Price Hughes: "What is morally wrong can never be politically right." Instead, I shall take a passage from an American sermon called "Puritan Principles and the Modern World," which was delivered in 1897:

"Puritanism stands for reality; for character; for clean living as a condition of public service; for recognition of responsibility to God; for the supremacy of the spirit. When Oliver Cromwell entered Parliament in 1653, and said, pointing to one member, 'There sits a taker of bribes'; to another. 'There sits a man whose religion is a farce'; to another, using the hardest name possible, which I soften, 'There sits a man whose personal conduct is impure and foul'; and then in the name of Almighty God broke up the Parliament, he was the impersonation of Puritanism; and for one, I wish he would rise from his grave and in the same spirit enter some

of our halls of legislation, both state and national."

That passage, with its conviction that righteousness ought to prevail, with its tendency to make the Puritan's own moral character a test of political fitness, and with its pressure to turn politics, which ought to be the art of reconciliation, into a moral crusade, reminds us of the darkest blot on his political record.

13

Ralph Barton Perry, a Harvard philosopher, undertakes to assess the connections between Puritanism and democracy in America in a book published in 1944:[13]

Puritanism and democracy, under these or other names, form a substantial part of the heritage of Americans. The chief source of spiritual nourishment for any nation must be its own past, perpetually rediscovered and renewed. A nation which negates its tradition loses its historic identity and wantonly destroys its chief source of spiritual vitality; a nation which merely reaffirms its tradition grows stagnant and corrupt. . . .

Puritanism springs from the very core of the personal conscience—the sense of duty, the sense of responsibility, the sense of guilt, and the repentant longing for forgiveness. No man, if he grows to maturity, escapes these experiences. Every man, sooner or later, feels himself rightly exiled from paradise and looks for a return. Puritanism is the elaboration of this theme, and the inculcation of its stern implications; some things are better than other things, and the discovery of the best is of paramount importance; the order of better and worse does not coincide with the natural order of strength among human motives, and if a man is to cleave to the best he must therefore overcome the second-best, until its subordination shall have become his second nature; the best prescribes rules of action, to be scrupulously observed;

---

[13] Ralph Barton Perry, *Puritanism and Democracy* (New York, 1944), pp. 627–630. Reprinted with the permission of the publishers, the Vanguard Press, Inc. Copyright, the Vanguard Press, Inc.

judged by the standard of the best, human life is a record of tragic and ignominious failure, and the recognition of this failure is the condition of its redemption; to live well requires the forging of a will which is stronger than any natural appetite; the reorganization of the natural individual under the authority of his moral faculties constitutes personality, which is the essence of man as distinguished from his fellow animals; society, in proportion as it is human, is an association of persons in which mutual respect is mingled with solicitude and a sense of common responsibility; there is hope of salvation both for the person and for mankind, and indomitable perserverance in the moral struggle alone gives cosmic dignity to the human race. . . .

But there are certain ingredients in which the puritan mixture is deficient, or which it omits altogether. For lack of these things even the good ingredients lose their flavor, and the dish is bitter to the taste. The puritan saw a limited truth, and what he saw was distorted because of what he failed to see. This distorted puritanism consists of a narrow preoccupation with morality, to the exclusion of the graciousness and the beauty of life; a pharisaical emphasis on the letter of the rule at the expense of its spirit; evil imagination, prudishness, and canting humility; a hard repression of all spontaneities and natural impulses, resulting in the masking of real motives by virtuous and edifying pretension; a morbid habit of introspection; censoriousness; hardness, intolerance, and an aversion to joy, especially the joy of other people; obsequious submission to a cruel and despotic God, and through preoccupation with the moral law a neglect of those aspects which nature and the universe present to the senses, the affections, and the reason.

Democracy, like puritanism, has its perennial spring in the moral consciousness. It expresses man's spontaneous interests and sociability as setting limits to discipline and as constituting its only ultimate justification. It insists that man's natural faculties shall be freely developed, in order that they may serve as the guide and the sanction of life. It conceives the values of life in terms of the desires and the felt satisfactions of concrete individuals, and concedes to these individuals the right to be both the exponents and the guarantors of their own interests. The purpose of institutions is to be found in the material and the spiritual profit of individuals as judged by these individuals themselves; and the beneficence of institutions is therefore measured by the degree of freedom which is provided within their framework. Democracy expresses the social consciousness in the most naïve sense, as an awareness of the plurality and the otherness of individuals; and in the most humane sense, as feeling of kind, compassion for the unfortunate, and appreciation of those higher relationships which are founded on modesty, respect, and mutually enhancing differences. Man derives dignity from his inalienable capacity for joy and suffering, from his capacity for self-determination, and from his tragic but faithful and agelong effort to live and to live better through intelligence and co-operation. . . .

Historic democracy has suffered ill repute owing to its exaggerations and defects. Through its failure to recognize the forces of unreason it has misconstrued human nature and has underestimated the power of its enemies. It has failed to probe the depths of human interdependence and solidarity, and has confused public good with self-interest. It has seemed to forget that a government must govern, and that government implies obedience. It has confused liberty with anarchy. Through its anxiety to emphasize the equal dignity and rights of men, it has neglected their inequalities of native endowment and of achievement. Like that democracy which the ancients held in disesteem, it has been an exponent of vulgarity rather than of eminence. Through neglect of the economic sphere of life, it has allowed its name to be used as a cloak for greed and exploitation. In both the political and the economic fields, it has been too easily satisfied with the nominal rather than the real, and so has exposed itself to the charge of sentimentalism. Intoxicated by its early successes, it was too ready to assume that its triumph was written in the stars, and that progress and universal peace were guaranteed merely because they were reasonable and good. Hence democracy was unprepared to meet the shock of disillusionment, and is now as inclined to the excesses of despair as once it was to the excesses of hope. . . .

Puritanism and democracy are in a measure coincident and allied, and where this is the case, they are subject to the same errors. Thus they are both individualistic—in their conception of the good, and in their conception of human faculties. They both affirm the same Occidental, Christian code of justice, compassion, and personal dignity. But they both exaggerate the self-sufficiency of the individual. Both underestimate the intricacies of human relations—as between individuals, classes, or nations. They have as yet found no cure for either domestic exploitation or external war, and their failure has been due not only to ignorance but to infidelity. They suffer both from senility and from corruption.

But if puritanism and democracy reinforce one another's truths and aggravate one another's errors, they also serve to correct and complement one another's limitations. Puritanism is the exponent of the harsh necessities of the moral life. Morality is essentially the imposing of a form of personal integrity and of social justice upon the natural life of man. But morality has no justification except in terms of that very natural life to which it does violence. Personal integrity is justified by the fuller play which it gives to spontaneity, and social justice by the room which it gives to personal self-expression. Puritanism sees that life must be curtailed, to which democracy adds "in order that it may abound." As puritanism stresses the sinfulness of Adam after the fall, so democracy stresses his innocence before. Puritanism supplies the pessimistic realization of man's present predicament, democracy the optimistic affirmation of his hopes and possibilities.

THE ENLIGHTENMENT IN EUROPE AND AMERICA

14

Despite the efforts of seventeenth-century liberals, the colonists might not have emerged so rapidly from the heritage of the Middle Ages had it not been for the stimulating influence of the Enlightenment in Europe. The Enlightenment began in the sixteenth century; scientists initiated the assault on the stoutest bastion of medievalism: the belief that the earth, as man's habitation, was placed by God in the center of the universe. The Polish scholar who challenged this basic premise was Nikolaus Copernicus. Commentarioulus (Little Commentary) contained the essence of the epoch-making hypothesis that he later elaborated in his book On The Revolutions of the Heavenly Bodies *(1543):*[14]

Our ancestors assumed, I observe, a large number of celestial spheres for this reason especially, to explain the apparent motion of the planets by the principle of regularity. For they thought it altogether absurd that a heavenly body, which is a perfect sphere, should not always move uniformly. They saw that by connecting and combining regular motions in various ways they could make any body appear to move to any position.

Callippus and Eudoxus, who endeavored to solve the problem by the use of concentric spheres, were unable to account for all the planetary movements; they had to explain not merely the apparent revolutions of the planets but also the fact that these bodies appear to us sometimes to mount higher in the heavens, sometimes to descend; and this fact is incompatible with the principle of concentricity. Therefore it seemed better to employ eccentrics and epicycles, a system which most scholars finally accepted.

Yet the planetary theories of Ptolemy and most other astronomers, although consistent with the numerical data, seemed likewise to present no small difficulty. For these theories were not adequate unless certain equants were also conceived; it then appeared that a planet moved with uniform velocity neither

---

[14] Reprinted from *Three Copernican Treatises,* pp. 57–59, translated and edited by Edward Rosen. Copyright by Columbia University Press, 1939.

on its deferent nor about the center of its epicycle. Hence a system of this sort seemed neither sufficiently absolute nor sufficiently pleasing to the mind.

Having become aware of these defects, I often considered whether there could perhaps be found a more reasonable arrangement of circles, from which every apparent inequality would be derived and in which everything would move uniformly about its proper center, as the rule of absolute motion requires. After I had addressed myself to this very difficult and almost insoluble problem, the suggestion at length came to me how it could be solved with fewer and much simpler constructions than were formerly used, if some assumptions (which are called axioms) were granted me. They follow in this order.

Assumptions

1. There is no one center of all the celestial circles or spheres.

2. The center of the earth is not the center of the universe, but only of gravity and of the lunar sphere.

3. All the spheres revolve about the sun as their mid-point, and therefore the sun is the center of the universe. . . .

4. The ratio of the earth's distance from the sun to the height of the firmament is so much smaller than the ratio of the earth's radius to its distance from the sun that the distance from the earth to the sun is imperceptible in comparison with the height of the firmament.

5. Whatever motion appears in the firmament arises not from any motion of the firmament, but from the earth's motion. The earth together with its circumjacent elements performs a complete rotation on its fixed poles in a daily motion, while the firmament and highest heaven abide unchanged.

6. What appear to us as motions of the sun arise not from its motion but from the motion of the earth and our sphere, with which we revolve about the sun like any other planet. The earth has, then, more than one motion.

7. The apparent retrograde and direct motion of the planets arises not from their motion but from the earth's. The motion of the earth alone, therefore, suffices to explain so many apparent inequalities in the heavens.

Having set forth these assumptions, I shall endeavor briefly to show how uniformity of the motions can be saved in a systematic way. However, I have thought it well, for the sake of brevity, to omit from this sketch mathematical demonstrations, reserving these for my larger work. But in the explanation of the circles I shall set down here the lengths of the radii; and from these the reader who is not unacquainted with mathematics will readily perceive how closely this arrangement of circles agrees with the numerical data and observations.

Accordingly, let no one suppose that I have gratuitously asserted, with the Pythagoreans, the motion of the earth; strong proof will be found in my exposition of the circles. For the principal arguments by which the natural philosophers attempt to establish the immobility of the earth rest for the most part on the appearances; it is particularly such arguments that collapse here, since I treat the earth's immobility as due to an appearance.

15

Later scientific discoveries not only substantiated the Copernican theory but added the startling concept that the universe was governed by natural laws rather than by the direct and constant intervention of the Deity. Scholars reasoned that laws of nature also shaped the conduct of man. If this was the case, each man owed his character to the environment in which he was reared, rather than to any direct act of God. Philosophers of the Enlightenment reached a point which premised revolution in social thought: men could improve themselves by improving society! One of the most influential was John Locke, an English philosopher, whose Essay Concerning Human Understanding *(1690) argued against innate ideas and for the continuing progress of mankind through his own efforts:*[15]

---

[15] John Locke, *The Works of John Locke* (London, 1823 ed.), pp. 82–84.

1. *Idea is the object of thinking.*—Every man being conscious to himself that he thinks, and that which his mind is applied about whilst thinking being the ideas that are there, it is past doubt that men have in their mind several ideas, such as are those expressed by the words whiteness, hardness, sweetness, thinking, motion, man, elephant, army, drunkenness, and others: it is in the first place then to be inquired, How he comes by them? I know it is a received doctrine, that men have native ideas and original characters stamped upon their minds in their very first being. This opinion I have at large examined already; and, I suppose, what I have said in the foregoing book will be much more easily admitted, when I have shown whence the understanding may get all the ideas it has, and by what ways and degrees they may come into the mind; for which I shall appeal to everyone's own observation and experience.

2. *All ideas come from sensation or reflection.*—Let us then suppose the mind to be, as we say, white paper, void of all characters, without any ideas; how comes it to be furnished? Whence comes it by that vast store, which the busy and boundless fancy of man has painted on it with an almost endless variety? Whence has it all the materials of reason and knowledge? To this I answer, in one word, from experience. In that all our knowledge is founded, and from that it ultimately derives itself. Our observation, employed either about external sensible objects, or about the internal operations of our minds, perceived and reflected on by ourselves, is that which supplies our understandings with all the materials of thinking. These two are the fountains of knowledge, from whence all the ideas we have, or can naturally have, do spring.

3. *The object of sensation one source of ideas.*—First, our senses, conversant about particular sensible objects, do convey into the mind several distinct perceptions of things, according to those various ways wherein those objects do affect them; and thus we come by those ideas we have of yellow, white, heat, cold, soft, hard, bitter, sweet, and all those which we call sensible qualities; which when I say the senses convey into the mind, I mean, they from external objects convey into the mind what produces there those perceptions. This great source of most of the ideas we have, depending wholly upon our senses, and derived by them to the understanding, I call *sensation.*

4. *The operations of our minds the other source of them.*—Secondly, the other fountain, from which experience furnisheth the understanding with ideas, is the perception of the operations of our own minds within us, as it is employed about the ideas it has got; which operations when the soul comes to reflect on and consider, do furnish the understanding with another set of ideas which could not be had from things without; and such are perception, thinking, doubting, believing, reasoning, knowing, willing, and all the different actings of our own minds; which we, being conscious of, and observing in ourselves, do from these receive into our understandings as distinct ideas, as we do from bodies affecting our senses. This source of ideas every man has wholly in himself; and though it be not sense as having nothing to do with external objects, yet it is very like it, and might properly enough be called *internal sense.* But as I call the other sensation, so I call this *reflection,* the ideas it affords being such only as the mind gets by reflecting on its own operations within itself. By reflection, then, in the following part of this discourse, I would be understood to mean that notice which the mind takes of its own operations, and the manner of them, by reason whereof there come to be ideas of these operations in the understanding. These two, I say, viz., external material things as the objects of sensation, and the operations of our own minds within as the objects of reflection, are, to me, the only originals from whence all our ideas take their beginnings. The term *operations* here, I use in a large sense, as comprehending not barely the actions of the mind about its ideas,

but some sort of passions arising sometimes from them, such as is the satisfaction or uneasiness arising from any thought.

5. *All our ideas are of the one or the other of these.*—The understanding seems to me not to have the least glimmering of any ideas which it doth not receive from one of these two. *External objects* furnish the mind with the ideas of sensible qualities, which are all those different perceptions they produce in us; and *the mind* furnishes the understanding with ideas of its own operations.

These, when we have taken a full survey of them, and their several modes, [combinations, and relations,] we shall find to contain all our whole stock of ideas; and that we have nothing in our minds which did not come in one of these two ways. Let anyone examine his own thoughts, and thoroughly search into his understanding, and then let him tell me, whether all the original ideas he has there, are any other than of the objects of his senses, or of the operations of his mind considered as objects of his reflection; and how great a mass of knowledge soever he imagines to be lodged there, he will, upon taking a strict view, see that he has not any idea in his mind but what one of these two have imprinted, though perhaps with infinite variety compounded and enlarged by the understanding.

16

Such concepts were soon applied to special spheres of human action by other European disciples of the Enlightenment. Jean Jacques Rousseau, a French political theorist, argued in the Social Contract *(1762) that all men could expect from their rulers protection for their natural rights to life, liberty, and property, and that any violation of these rights by a king justified revolution:[16]*

Man is born free; and everywhere he is in chains. One thinks himself the master of others, and still remains a greater slave than they. How did this change come about? I

_____
[16] Jean Jacques Rousseau, *The Social Contract and Discourses* (G. D. H. Cole, ed., Everyman's Library, London, 1913), pp. 5–6, 14–16, 18–19.

do not know. What can make it legitimate? That question I think I can answer.

If I took into account only force, and the effects derived from it, I should say: "As long as a people is compelled to obey, and obeys, it does well; as soon as it can shake off the yoke, and shakes it off, it does still better; for, regaining its liberty by the same right as took it away, either it is justified in resuming it, or there was no justification for those who took it away." But the social order is a sacred right which is the basis of all other rights. . . .

I suppose men to have reached the point at which the obstacles in the way of their preservation in the state of nature show their power of resistance to be greater than the resources at the disposal of each individual for his maintenance in that state. That primitive condition can then subsist no longer; and the human race would perish unless it changed its manner of existence.

But, as men cannot engender new forces, but only unite and direct existing ones, they have no other means of preserving themselves than the formation, by aggregation, of a sum of forces great enough to overcome the resistance. These they have to bring into play by means of a single motive power, and cause to act in concert.

This sum of forces can arise only where several persons come together: but, as the force and liberty of each man are the chief instruments of his self-preservation, how can he pledge them without harming his own interests, and neglecting the care he owes to himself? This difficulty, in its bearing on my present subject, may be stated in the following terms—

"The problem is to find a form of association which will defend and protect with the whole common force the person and goods of each associate, and in which each, while uniting himself with all, may still obey himself alone, and remain as free as before." This is the fundamental problem of which the *Social Contract* provides the solution.

The clauses of this contract are so determined by the nature of the act that the slightest modification would make them vain and ineffective; so that, although they have perhaps never been formally set forth, they are everywhere the same and everywhere tacitly admitted and recognised, until, on the violation of the social compact, each regains his original rights and resumes his natural liberty, while losing the conventional liberty in favour of which he renounced it.

These clauses, properly understood, may be reduced to one—the total alienation of each associate, together with all his rights, to the whole community; for, in the first place, as each gives himself absolutely, the conditions are the same for all; and, this being so, no one has any interest in making them burdensome to others.

Moreover, the alienation being without reserve, the union is as perfect as it can be, and no associate has anything more to demand: for, if the individuals retained certain rights, as there would be no common superior to decide between them and the public, each, being on one point his own judge, would ask to be so on all; the state of nature would thus continue, and the association would necessarily become inoperative or tyrannical.

Finally, each man, in giving himself to all, gives himself to nobody; and as there is no associate over whom he does not acquire the same right as he yields others over himself, he gains an equivalent for everything he loses, and an increase of force for the preservation of what he has.

If then we discard from the social compact what is not of its essence, we shall find that it reduces itself to the following terms—

"*Each of us puts his person and all his power in common under the supreme direction of the general will, and, in our corporate capacity, we receive each member as an indivisible part of the whole.*"

At once, in place of the individual personality of each contracting party, this act of association creates a moral and collective body, composed of as many members as the assembly contains votes, and receiving from this act its unity, its common identity, its life and its will. This public person, so formed by the union of all other persons, formerly took the name of *city,* and now takes that of *Republic* or *body politic;* it is called by its members *State* when passive, *Sovereign* when active, and *Power* when compared with others like itself. Those who are associated in it take collectively the name of *people,* and severally are called *citizens,* as sharing in the sovereign power, and *subjects,* as being under the laws of the State. But these terms are often confused and taken one for another: it is enough to know how to distinguish them when they are being used with precision. . . .

The passage from the state of nature to the civil state produces a very remarkable change in man, by substituting justice for instinct in his conduct, and giving his actions the morality they had formerly lacked. Then only, when the voice of duty takes the place of physical impulses and right of appetite, does man, who so far had considered only himself, find that he is forced to act on different principles, and to consult his reason before listening to his inclinations. Although, in this state, he deprives himself of some advantages which he got from nature, he gains in return others so great, his faculties are so stimulated and developed, his ideas so extended, his feelings so ennobled, and his whole soul so uplifted, that, did not the abuses of this new condition often degrade him below that which he left, he would be bound to bless continually the happy moment which took him from it for ever, and, instead of a stupid and unimaginative animal, made him an intelligent being and a man.

Let us draw up the whole account in terms easily commensurable. What man loses by the social contract is his natural liberty and an unlimited right to everything he tries to get and succeeds in getting; what he gains is civil liberty and the proprietorship of all he possesses. If we are to avoid mistake in weighing one against the other, we must clearly distinguish natural liberty, which is bounded only by the strength of the individual, from civil liberty, which is limited by the general will; and possession, which is merely the effect of force or the right of the first occupier, from property, which can be founded only on a positive title.

We might, over and above all this, add, to what man acquires in the civil state, moral liberty, which alone makes him truly master of himself; for the mere impulse of appetite is slavery, while obedience to a law which we prescribe to ourselves is liberty. But I have already said too much on this head, and the philosophical meaning of the word liberty does not now concern us.

17

Building on the theoretical foundations of Copernicus, Locke, Rousseau, and others, a few English colonists in the New World sought to promote tolerance and liberty in the everyday affairs of men. Roger Williams summed up his advanced ideas on tolerance and democracy in his well-known work, The Bloudy Tenent *(1644):*[17]

Peace. The next distinction concerneth the manner of persons holding forth the aforesaid practices not only the waightier duties of the Law, but points of doctrine and worship less principall:—

"Some," saith he [John Cotton] "hold them forth in a meek and peaceable way; some with such arrogance and impetuousness, as of itself tendeth to the disturbance of civil peace."

Truth. In the examination of this distinction we shall discuss,

First, what is civil peace, (wherein we shall vindicate thy name the better),

Secondly, what it is to hold forth a doctrine or practice in this impetuousness or arrogancy.

First, for civil peace, what is it but *pax civitatis,* the peace of the city, whether an *English* city, Scotch, or Irish city, or further abroad, French, Spanish, Turkish city, &c.

Thus it pleased the Father of lights to define it, Jer. xxix 7. *Pray for the peace of the city;* which peace of the city, or citizens, so compacted in a civil way of union may be entire, unbroken, safe, &c., notwithstanding so many thousands of God's people the Jews, were there in bondage, and would neither be constrained to the worship of the city Babel, nor restrained from so much of the worship of the true God as they then could practice, as is plain in the practice of the three worthies, Shadrach, Misach, and Abednego, as also of Daniel, Dan. & iii Dan. vi.—the peace of the City or Kingdom, being a far different peace from the peace of the religion, or spiritual worship, maintained and professed of the citizens. This peace of their worship which worship also in some cities being various being a false peace, God's people were and ought to be Non-comformitants, not daring either to be restrained from the true, or constrained to false worship, and yet without breach of the civil or city peace, properly so called.

Peace. Hence it is that so many glorious and flourishing cities of the world maintain their civil peace; yea, the very Americans and wildest pagans keep the peace of their towns or cities, though neither in one nor the other can any man prove a true Church of God in those places, and consequently no spiritual and heavenly peace. The peace *spiritual,* whether true or false, being of a higher and far different nature from the peace of the place or people, being merely and essentially civil and human.

Truth. Oh! how lost are the sons of men in this point! To illustrate this:—The church, or company of worshippers, whether true or false, is like unto a body or college of physitians in a city; like unto a corporation, society, or company of East-India or Turkey merchants, or any other society or company in London; which companies may hold their courts, keep their records, hold disputations, and in matters concerning their society may dissent, divide, or breake into schisms and factions, sue and implead each other at the law, yea, wholly break up and dissolve into pieces and nothing, and yet the peace of the city not be in the least measure impaired or disturbed; because the essence or being of the city, and so the well being and peace

---

[17] Roger Williams, *The Bloudy Tenent of Persecution* (London, 1848 ed.), pp. 45–47, 214–215.

thereof, is essentially distinct from those particular societies; the city courts, city laws, city punishments distinct from theirs. The city was before them, and stands absolute and entire when such a corporation or society is taken down. For instance further, The city or Civil state of Ephesus was essentially distinct from the worship of Diana in the city, or of the whole city. Again, the church of Christ in Ephesus, which were God's people, converted and called out from the worship of that city unto Christianity or worship of God in Christ was distinct from both.

Now suppose that God remove the candlestick from Ephesus, yea, though the whole worship of the city of Ephesus should be altered, yet, if men be true and honestly ingenuous to city covenants, combinations and principles, all this might be without the least impeachment or infringement of the peace of the city of Ephesus.

Thus in the city of Smyrna was the city itself or civil estate one thing, The spiritual or religious state of Smyrna, another: The church of Christ in Smyrna, distinct from them both. And the synagogue of the Jews, whether literally Jews, as some think, or mystically, false Christians, as others, called the synagogue of Satan, Rev., ii., distinct from all these. And notwithstanding these spiritual oppositions in point of worship and religion, yet hear we not the least noise—nor need we, if men keep but the bond of civility of any civil breach, or breach of civil peace amongst them; and to persecute God's people there for religion, that only was a breach of civility itself. . . .

From this Grant I infer . . . that the sovereign, original, and foundation of civil power, lies in the people—. . . . And if so, that a people may erect and establish what form of government seems to them most meet for their civil condition. It is evident that such governments as are by them erected and established, have no more power, nor for no longer time, than the civil power or people consenting and agreeing, shall betrust them with. This is clear not only in reason, but in the experience of all commonweals, where the people are not deprived of their natural freedom by the power of tyrants.

18

The code of laws devised by Williams and adopted by the Rhode Island legislature in 1647 was based on Roger Williams's democratic faith. The new code swept away such relics of aristocracy as inheritance laws that kept large estates intact, assumed the equality of all before the law, and allowed no mitigation of penalties in favor of the wellborn. A modern historian finds in this enlightened legal code a humanitarianism rare in the seventeenth century:[18]

A frontier humanism infusing the new body of laws gave token of the inner springs of the levelling spirit. Rhode Island people, unencumbered by the old discipline of church and state and believing with Williams . . . in the gospel of common brotherhood and the power of reason among the mass of men, were moving toward a new social psychology. Logic based on an abundance of land and a scarcity of settlers strengthened a doctrine of man that made human worth the basic determinant. Population was sparse and man precious, and the refugees of the colony were imbued with Williams' vision of an asylum from brutality and a haven where the destitute could find friendliness and opportunity. This spirit of hospitality dictated the omission of the usual "Stranger" law such as that of the Massachusetts code which forbade towns or individuals to allow habitation to newcomers or convey land to them except by consent of a member of the oligarchy. The same humanist spirit led Williams and his fellow lawmakers to abolish imprisonment for debt. In an age which everywhere treated an insolvent like a criminal, they provided that if a debtor agreed to a "course" of payments, "he shall not be sent to prison, there to lye languishing to no

---

[18] Samuel Hugh Brockunier, *The Irrepressible Democrat—Roger Williams* (New York, 1940), pp. 175–177. Copyright 1940, The Ronald Press Company.

man's advantage." Frontier humanism ran counter to long penal servitude or the dire resort of capital punishment. For riots the code provided imprisonment for two weeks or a month: "Such long times of imprisonments mentioned in the Statute, 2 Hen. v. 8, suits not the constitution of our place." Largely abolishing the many score death penalties of the English penal code, Rhode Island lawmakers listed only nine crimes as capital. Even in this slender list the death penalty was not always mandatory and in the case of burglary sweeping exceptions were made, including the mentally deficient, children, and "poore persons that steale for Hunger," who were to receive mild punishment. Barbarous colonial legislation providing brutal punishment or death for a servant who struck a master or a child who struck a parent found scarcely a faint echo in the Rhode Island stipulation that such offenders be sent for a short time "to the House of Correction." Inspired by a belief in the regeneracy of man and freedom of the will, Rhode Island leaders recoiled from corporal punishment, bodily mutilation, and the cruelty of a law of vengeance and framed a humane legal code, seeking to reduce crime by clemency coupled with correction and encouragement of reform of the individual culprit. Only once did they specify punishment by whipping; and only for a thief guilty twice of grand larceny did they stipulate the branding iron—a penalty abolished nine years later when Williams was president. Other than this they abandoned the innumerable harsh physical punishments, tortures, brandings, and mutilations which dotted the penal codes of the time.

The new psychology exemplified in the humane and equalitarian character of the code leavened laws touching manners and morals and placed high esteem upon social freedom and personal liberty. Bred to Puritan and English *mores*, the "come-outers" of Rhode Island could not condone a free and easy morality, and Williams, their chief philosopher and spokesman, acknowledged it a duty of the state to promote "civility."

Secular officials, he contended, should be authorized to restrain "scandalous offenders" lest society lapse into a "wilderness of life and manners," but such regulations should conform "to the Nature and Constitution" of the nation or people and not to a biblical or rigorous absolute standard. In this spirit the code of 1647 duly followed English statutes in prohibiting sex crimes, fraud, slander, assault and battery and regulating tippling and gaming in public houses. With a striking modernity these enactments largely avoided the medieval and Puritan confusion of sin and crime and exhibited more confidence in the conscience of the citizen than in scarlet letters, stocks, whipping post, and hangman's noose. For "false witness" or perjury, punishable in Massachusetts and Connecticut by death, the Rhode Island penalty was the pillory. The laws against adultery and fornication were mild as compared with the Hebraic laws of neighboring colonies and included no alphabetic badges of shame. Tippling was permissible for twice as long as in Massachusetts and drunkenness cost the offender half as much—without the Bay colony's sterner threat of ten stripes or imprisonment for repeaters. The code makers recommended hot heads convicted as "Common Scoulds" to the sobering effect of the ducking stool, but with few exceptions stocks, pillory, and ignominious punishments were noteworthy for their absence. No law against idleness nor sumptuary legislation sought to compel thrift or impose "seemly" fashions of dress and adornment on persons of low estate. On the whole Rhode Islanders respected a man's private life and their laws had little of the sweeping assortment of minute regulations of daily conduct and threats of public shame by which sleuths of God in orthodox colonies prodded saints and knocked down sinners.

19

Maryland provides an example of tolerance similar to that of Roger Williams's Rhode Island in the Act of Toleration of 1649, written by Lord Baltimore to ensure equal treatment for

Catholics in a predominantly Protestant colony:[19]

And whereas the inforceing of the conscience in matters of Religion hath frequently fallen out to be of dangerous Consequence in those commonwealthes where it hath been practised, And for the more quiett and peaceable governmt of this Province, and the better to preserve mutuall Love and amity amongst the Inhabitants thereof. Be it Therefore also by the Lord Proprietary with the advise and consent of this Assembly Ordeyned and enacted (except as in this present Act is before Declared and sett forth) that noe person or persons whatsoever within this Province, or the Islands, Parts, Harbors, Creekes, or havens thereunto belonging, professing to believe in Jesus Christ, shall from henceforth bee any waies troubled, Molested or discountenanced for or in respect of his or her religion nor in the free exercise thereof within this Province or the Islands thereunto belonging nor any way compelled to the beleife or exercise of any other Religion against his or her consent, soe as they be not unfaithfull to the Lord Proprietary, or molest or conspire against the civill Government established or to bee established in this Province under him or his heires. And that all and every person and persons that shall presume Contrary to this Act and the true intent and meaning thereof directly or indirectly either in person or estate wilfully to wrong disturbe trouble or molest any person whatsoever within this Province professing to beleive in Jesus Christ for or in respect of his or her religion, or the free exercise thereof, with this Province . . . that such person or persons soe offending shall be compelled to pay trebble damages to the party soe wronged . . . and for every such offence shall also forfeit 20 s. sterling.

20

Likewise fortunate in its leadership was Pennsylvania. William Penn, benevolent Quaker and sincere humanitarian, believed as did Roger Williams in freedom of conscience, democratic institutions, and the equality of mankind. Granted the colony of Pennsylvania in 1681, he set up a liberal frame of government that proved workable until hostile rulers interfered. When his lands were restored to him, Penn drew up the Charter of Liberties (1701), one of the most forward-looking documents of the colonial era:[20]

Because no People can be truly happy, though under the greatest Enjoyment of Civil Liberties, if abridged of the Freedom of the Consciences, as to their Religious Profession and Worship: And Almighty God being the only Lord of Conscience, Father of Lights and Spirits; and the Author as well as Object of all divine Knowledge, Faith and Worship, who only doth enlighten the Minds, and persuade and convince the Understandings of People, I do hereby grant and declare, That no Person or Persons, inhabiting in this province or Territories, who shall confess and acknowledge One almighty God, the Creator, Upholder and Ruler of the World; and profess him or themselves obliged to live quietly under the Civil Government, shall be in any Case molested or prejudiced, in his or their Person or Estate, because of his or their conscientious Persuasion or Practice, nor be compelled to frequent or maintain any religious Worship, Place or Ministry, contrary to his or their Mind, or to do or suffer any other Act or Thing, contrary to their religious persuasions.

And that all Persons who also profess to believe in Jesus Christ, the Saviour of the World, shall be capable (notwithstanding their other Persuasions and Practices in Point of Conscience and Religion) to serve this Government in any Capacity, both legislatively and executively, he or they solemnly promising, when lawfully required, Allegiance to the King as Sovereign, and Fidelity to the Proprietary and Governor, and taking the Attests as now established by the Law

[19] Archives of Maryland (Baltimore, 1883), I, 246.

[20] Francis N. Thorpe (ed.), The Federal and State Constitutions, Colonial Charters and other organic laws of the States, Territories, and Colonies now or heretofore forming the United States of America (Washington, 1909), V, 3077–3080.

made at *New-Castle*, in the Year *One Thousand and Seven Hundred*, entitled, *An Act directing the Attests of several Officers and Ministers*, as now amended and confirmed this present Assembly.

II. For the well governing of this Province and Territories, there shall be an Assembly yearly chosen, by the Freemen thereof, to consist of *Four* Persons out of each County, of most Note for Virtue, Wisdom and Ability, . . . Which Assembly shall have Power to chuse a Speaker and other their Officers; and shall be Judges of the Qualifications and Elections of their own Members; sit upon their own Adjournments; appoint Committees; prepare Bills in order to pass into Laws; impeach Criminals, and redress Grievances; and shall have all other Powers and Privileges of an Assembly, according to the Rights of the free-born Subjects of *England*, and as is usual in any of the King's Plantations in *America*. . . .

III. That the Freemen in each respective County, at the Time and Place of Meeting for Electing their Representatives to serve in Assembly, may as often as there shall be Occasion, chuse a double Number of Persons to present to the Governor for Sheriffs and Coroners to serve for *Three* Years, if so long they behave themselves well; out of which respective Elections and Presentments, the Governor shall nominate and commissionate one for each of the said Officers, the *Third* Day after such Presentment, or else the *First* named in such Presentment, for each Office as aforesaid, shall stand and serve in that Office for the Time before respectively limited; and in Case of Death or Default, such Vacancies shall be supplied by the Governor, to serve to the End of the said Term. . . .

And that the Justices of the respective Counties shall or may nominate and present to the Governor *Three* Persons, to serve for Clerk of the Peace for the said County, when there is a Vacancy, one of which the Governor shall commissionate within *Ten* Days after such Presentment, or else the *First* nominated shall serve in the said Office during good Behavior.

IV. That the Laws of this Government shall be in this Stile, viz. *By the Governor, with the Consent and Approbation of the Freemen in General Assembly met;* and shall be, after Confirmation by the Governor, forthwith recorded in the Rolls Office, and kept at *Philadelphia*, unless the Governor and Assembly shall agree to appoint another place.

V. That all Criminals shall have the same Privileges of Witnesses and Council as their Prosecutors.

VI. That no Person or Persons shall or may, at any Time hereafter, be obliged to answer any Complaint, Matter or Thing whatsoever, relating to Property, before the Governor and Council, or in any other Place, but in ordinary Course of Justice, unless Appeals thereunto shall be hereafter by Law appointed. . . .

VIII. But because the Happiness of Mankind depends so much upon the Enjoying of Liberty of their Consciences as aforesaid, I do hereby solemnly declare, promise and grant, for me, my Heirs and Assigns, That the *First* Article of this Charter relating to Liberty of Conscience, and every Part and Clause therein, according to the true Intent and Meaning thereof, shall be kept and remain, without any Alteration, inviolably for ever.

And Lastly, I the said *William Penn*, Proprietary and Governor of the Province of *Pensilvania*, and Territories thereunto belonging, for myself, my Heirs and Assigns have solemnly declared, granted and confirmed, and do hereby solemnly declare, grant and confirm, That neither I, my Heirs or Assigns, shall procure or do any Thing or Things whereby the Liberties in this Charter contained and expressed, nor any Part thereof, shall be infringed or broken: And if any thing shall be procured or done, by any Person or Persons, contrary to these Presents, it shall be held of no Force or Effect.

21

Enlightenment doctrines found ready reception in America, for experimentation was almost a day-by-day occurrence and progress a universal hope. Moreover, colonial scholars contributed significantly to the expansion of knowledge upon which the Enlightenment rested. Outstanding was Benjamin Franklin, whose study of electricity elevated him to a front rank among the world's scientists. One of his many contributions was an analysis of the Leyden jar which, according to one of his biographers, stamped him a "master experimenter." Franklin describes his experiment in a letter written to Peter Collinson of London in 1748:[21]

16. The whole force of the bottle, and power of giving a shock, is in the GLASS IT-SELF; the non-electrics in contact with the two surfaces, serving only to *give* and *receive* to and from the several parts of the glass; that is, to give on one side, and take away from the other.

17. This was discovered here in the following manner: Purposing to analyze the electrified bottle, in order to find wherein its strength lay, we placed it on glass, and drew out the cork and wire which for that purpose had been loosely put in. Then taking the bottle in one hand, and bringing a finger of the other near its mouth, a strong spark came from the water, and the shock was as violent as if the wire had remained in it, which shewed that the force did not lie in the wire. Then to find if it resided in the water, being crouded into and condensed in it, as confin'd by the glass, which had been our former opinion, we electrified the bottle again, and placing it on glass, drew out the wire and cork as before; then taking up the bottle, we decanted all its water into an empty bottle, which likewise stood on glass; and taking up that other bottle, we expected, if the force resided in the water, to find a shock from it; but there was none. We judged then that it must either be lost in decanting, or remain in the first bottle. The latter we found to be true; for that bottle on trial gave the shock, though filled up as it stood with fresh unelectrified water from a tea-pot. ——— To find, then, whether glass had this

property merely as glass, or whether the form contributed any thing to it; we took a pane of sash-glass, and laying it on the hand, placed a plate of lead on its upper surface; then electrified that plate, and bringing a finger to it, there was a spark and shock. We then took two plates of lead of equal dimensions, but less than the glass by two inches every way, and electrified the glass between them, by electrifying the uppermost lead; then separated the glass from the lead, in doing which, what little fire might be in the lead was taken out, and the glass being touched in the electrified parts with a finger, afforded only very small pricking sparks, but a great number of them might be taken from different places. Then dextrously placing it again between the leaden plates, and compleating a circle between the two surfaces, a violent shock ensued. ——— Which demonstrated the power to reside in glass as glass, and that the non-electrics in contact served only, like the armature of a loadstone, to unite the force of the several parts, and bring them at once to any point desired: it being the property of a non-electric, that the whole body instantly receives or gives what electrical fire is given to or taken from any one of its parts.

22

The late Carl Becker, a twentieth-century historian, spent a good portion of his life evaluating the eighteenth-century Enlightenment. The Philosophes *he assesses in the selection below include the familiar French thinkers Montesquieu, Voltaire, Rousseau, Diderot; the well-known Englishmen Locke, Hume, Bolingbroke, Adam Smith; and the Germans Goethe, Lessing, Herder. Benjamin Franklin and Thomas Jefferson illustrates that the Enlightenment had crossed the Atlantic. The excerpt below is from Becker's best known book,* The Heavenly City of the Eighteenth-Century Philosophers:[22]

We are accustomed to think of the eighteenth century as essentially modern in its

---

[21] I. Bernard Cohen (ed.), *Benjamin Franklin's Experiments* (Cambridge, 1941), pp. 191–192.

[22] Carl Becker, *The Heavenly City of the Eighteenth-Century Philosophers* (New Haven, 1932), pp. 29–31. Reprinted with the kind permission of the publisher, the Yale University Press.

temper. Certainly, the *Philosophes* themselves made a great point of having renounced the superstition and hocus-pocus
of medieval Christian thought, and we have
usually been willing to take them at their
word. Surely, we say, the eighteenth century
was pre-eminently the age of reason, surely
the *Philosophes* were a skeptical lot, atheists
in effect if not by profession, addicted to science and the scientific method, always out
to crush the infamous, valiant defenders of
liberty, equality, fraternity, freedom of
speech, and what you will. All very true.
And yet I think the *Philosophes* were nearer
the Middle Ages, less emancipated from
the preconceptions of medieval Christian
thought, than they quite realized or we have
commonly supposed. If we have done them
more (or is it less?) than justice in giving
them a good modern character, the reason is
that they speak a familiar language. We read
Voltaire more readily than Dante, and follow
an argument by Hume more easily than one
by Thomas Aquinas. But I think our appreciation is of the surface more than of the
fundamentals of their thought. We agree
with them more readily when they are witty
and cynical than when they are wholly serious. Their negations rather than their affirm-
ations enable us to treat them as kindred
spirits.

But, if we examine the foundations of their
faith, we find that at every turn the *Philosophes* betray their debt to medieval thought
without being aware of it. They denounced
Christian philosophy, but rather too much,
after the manner of those who are but half-
emancipated from the "superstitions" they
scorn. They had put off the fear of God, but
maintained a respectful attitude toward the
Deity. They ridiculed the idea that the universe had been created in six days, but still
believed it to be a beautifully articulated
machine designed by the Supreme Being
according to a rational plan as an abiding
place for mankind. The Garden of Eden was
for them a myth, no doubt, but they looked
enviously back to the golden age of Roman
virtue, or across the waters to the unspoiled
innocence of an Arcadian civilization that
flourished in Pennsylvania. They renounced
the authority of church and Bible, but exhibited a naïve faith in the authority of nature and reason. They scorned metaphysics,
but were proud to be called philosophers.
They dismantled heaven, somewhat prema-
turely it seems, since they retained their
faith in the immortality of the soul. They
courageously discussed atheism, but not before the servants. They defended toleration
valiantly, but could with difficulty tolerate
priests. They denied that miracles ever happened, but believed in the perfectibility of
the human race. We feel that these Philosophers were at once too credulous and too
skeptical. They were the victims of common
sense. In spite of their rationalism and their
humane sympathies, in spite of their aversion
to hocus-pocus and enthusiasm and dim per-
spectives, in spite of their eager skepticism,
their engaging cynicism, their brave youthful blasphemies and talk of hanging the last
king in the entrails of the last priest—in
spite of all of it, there is more of Christian
philosophy in the writings of the *Philosophes*
than has yet been dreamt of in our histories.

Land, Labor, Life, and Trade
in the American Colonies

During the colonial period of American history, the European settler met the wilderness on its own terms. Some survived the experience, some did not. The wilderness was a tough and implacable foe. The chronic shortage of labor and capital in the colonies was overcome by making the land and natural resources supply the larger portion of the costs of production. Shortage of land and labor tied the colonies to Europe more firmly than the laws of kings and parliaments, for only in Europe could the colonists recruit additional labor and find markets for their surplus products. Between 1607 and 1775, European settlers converted a wilderness into a highly productive economy capable, as later events demonstrated, of sustaining revolution and independence. It was a remarkable achievement.

LAND

1

Peter Kalm, a Swedish naturalist, traveled widely in North America in 1748. His description of the American land and its people was widely read in England, Germany, and Holland, as well as in his native Sweden:[1]

September 21st, [Philadelphia, 1748]
In the afternoon, I rode with Mr. Cock to his country seat, about nine miles from the town, to the north-west.

The country on both sides of the road was covered with a great forest. The trees were all with annual leaves, I did not see a single fir or pine. . . . The ground ceased to be so even as it was before, and began to look more like the English ground, diversified with hills and vallies. We found neither

mountains nor great stones, and the wood was so much thinned, and the ground so uniformly even, that we could see a great way between the trees, under which we rode without any inconvenience, for there were no bushes to stop us. . . .

As we went on in the wood, we continually saw, at moderate distances, little fields which had been cleared of the wood. Each of these was a farm. These farms were commonly very pretty, and a walk of trees frequently led from them to the high-road. The houses were all built of brick, or the stone which is here commonly met with. Every countryman, even though he were the poorest peasant, had an orchard with apples, peaches, chestnuts, walnuts, cherries, quinces, and such fruits, and sometimes we saw the vines climbing along them. The vallies were frequently provided with little brooks which contained a crystal stream. The corn, on the sides of the road, was almost all mown, and no other grain besides maize and buckwheat was standing. The former was to be met with

[1] Peter Kalm, "Kalm's Travels in North America," in John Pinkerton (ed.), *A General Collection of the Best and Most Interesting Voyages and Travels in All Parts of the World* (London, 1812), XIII, 405–406.

near such farm, in greater or lesser quantities; it grew very well and to a great length, the stalks being from six to ten feet high; and covered with fine green leaves. Buckwheat likewise was not very uncommon, and in some places the people were beginning to reap it.

October 11th, [1748]

Agriculture was in a very bad state hereabouts. When a person had bought a piece of land, which perhaps had never been ploughed since the creation, he cut down part of the wood, tore up the roots, ploughed the ground, sowed corn on it, and the first time got a plentiful crop. But the same land being tilled for several years successively without being manured, it at last must of course lose its fertility. Its possessor therefore leaves it fallow, and proceeds to another part of this ground, which he treats in the same manner. Thus he goes on till he has changed a great part of his possessions into corn-fields, and by that means deprives the ground of its fertility. He then returns to the first field, which now is pretty well recovered; this he again tills as long as it will afford him a good crop, but when its fertility is exhausted, he leaves it fallow again, and proceeds to the rest as before.

It being customary here to let the cattle go about the fields and in the woods both day and night, the people cannot collect much dung for manure, but by leaving the land fallow for several years together, a great quantity of weeds spring up in it, and get such strength, that it requires a considerable time to extirpate them. From hence it likewise comes, that the corn is always so much mixed with weeds. The great richness of the soil, which the first European colonists found here, and which had never been ploughed before, has given rise to this neglect of agriculture, which is still observed by many of the inhabitants.

2

The anonymous author of the volumes on American Husbandry, *published in England in 1775, was one of many European travelers who* *comment upon the slipshod methods of the colonial farmer and display more understanding of the seemingly wasteful procedures than many of his contemporaries:*[2]

The products of North Carolina are rice, tobacco, indigo, cotton, wheat, peas, beans, Indian corn, and all sorts of roots, especially potatoes. Rice is not so much cultivated here as in South Carolina: but in the latter they raise no tobacco, whereas in North Carolina it is one of their chief articles. It grows in the northerly parts of the province, on the frontiers of Virginia, from which colony it is exported. Indigo grows very well in the province, particularly in the southern parts, and proves a most profitable branch of culture. Cotton does very well, and the sort is so excellent, that it is much to be wished they had made a greater progress in it. The greatest articles of their produce which is exported are tar, pitch, turpentine, and every species of lumber, in astonishing quantities. . . .

Notwithstanding these great advantages, there are very few people in North Carolina; this has been owing to several causes: there were obstructions in settling it, which occasioned some to leave the country, and a general idea was spread to its disadvantage; but the principal evil was the want of ports, of which there was not one good one in all North Carolina: the river Pedee falls into the sea at Winyaw, which is in South Carolina, and that has prevented an exportation of products from thence of the growth of North Carolina. And this want of good ports, and a trading town, has checked the culture of rice a good deal; but it has had another effect, which may probably prove a great advantage; it has driven the new settlers back into the country, and thrown them very much into common husbandry. . . .

It is this common husbandry which deserves our attention particularly, since in many respects it is different from that of any other part of America.

---

[2] Anon., *American Husbandry* (London, 1775), I, *passim.*

The two great circumstances which give the farmers of North Carolina such a superiority over those of most other colonies, are, first, the plenty of land; and, secondly, the vast herds of cattle kept by the planters. The want of ports, as I said, kept numbers from settling here, and this made the land of less value, consequently every settler got large grants; and, falling to the business of breeding cattle, their herds became so great, that the profit from them alone is exceeding great. It is not an uncommon thing to see one man the master of from 300 to 1200, and even to 2000 cows, bulls, oxen, and young cattle; hogs also in prodigious numbers. Their management is to let them run loose in the woods all day, and to bring them up at night by the sound of a horn; some times, particularly in winter, they keep them during the night in inclosures, giving them a little food, and letting the cows and sows to the calves and pigs; this makes them come home the more regularly. Such herds of cattle and swine are to be found in no other colonies; and when this is better settled, they will not be so common here; for at present the woods are all in common, and people's property has no other boundary or distinction than marks cut in trees, so that the cattle have an unbounded range; but when the country becomes more cultivated, estates will be surrounded by enclosures, and consequently the numbers of cattle kept by the planters will be proportioned to their own lands only.

It may easily be supposed that these vast flocks of cattle might be of surprising consequence in the raising of manure, were the planters as attentive as they ought to be to this essential object: they might by this means cultivate indigo and tobacco to greater advantage than their neighbours; some few make a good use of the advantage, but more of them are drawn from it by the plenty of rich land, which they run over, as in the northern colonies, till it is exhausted, and then take fresh, relying on such a change, instead of making the most of their manure, which would add infinitely to their profit. . . .

The mode of common husbandry here is to break up a piece of wood land, a work very easily done, from the trees standing at good distances from each other; this they sow with Indian corn for several years successively, till it will yield large crops no longer: they get at first fourscore or an hundred bushel an acre, but sixty or seventy are common: when the land is pretty well exhausted they sow it with peas or beans one year, of which they will get thirty or forty bushels per acre; and afterwards sow it with wheat for two or three years: it will yield good crops of this grain when it would bear Indian corn no longer, which shews how excellent the land must be. . . .

In this system of crops they change the land as fast as it wears out, clearing fresh pieces of wood land, exhausting them in succession; after which they leave them to the spontaneous growth. It is not here as in the northern colonies, that weeds come first and then grass; the climate is so hot, that, except on the rich moist lands, any sort of grass is scarce; but the fallow in a few years becomes a forest, for no climate seems more congenial to the production of quick growing trees. If the planter does not return to cultivate the land again, as may probably be the case, from the plenty of fresh, it presently becomes such a wood as the rest of the country is; and woods are here the pasture of the cattle, which is excellent for hogs, because they get quantities of mast and fruit; but for cattle is much inferior to pastures and meadows.

3

George Alsop was an indentured servant for two years on the plantation of a Mr. Thomas Stockett in Baltimore County, Maryland. His pamphlet, "A Character of the Province of Maryland," from which the following selection is taken, was published in London in 1666. Apparently it was written at the request of Lord Baltimore in an effort to induce more people from the English lower classes to come to Maryland as bonded servants:[3]

---

[3] George Alsop, *A Character of the Province of Maryland* (London, 1666), pp. 67–69. Reprinted in Maryland Historical Society, *Maryland Fund Publications*, no. 15 (Baltimore, 1880), pp. 475–477.

Tobacco is the only solid Staple Commodity of this Province: The use of it was first found out by the Indians many Ages agoe, and transferr'd into Christendom by that great Discoverer of America Columbus. It's generally made by all the Inhabitants of this Province, and between the months of March and April they sow the seed (which is much small than Mustard-seed) in small beds and patches digg'd up and made so by art, and about May the Plants commonly appear green in those beds: In June they are transplanted from their beds, and set in little hillocks in distant rowes, dug up for the same purpose; some twice or thrice they are weeded, and succoured from their illegitimate Leaves that would be peeping out from the body of the Stalk. They top the several Plants as they find occasion in their predominating rankness: About the middle of September they cut the Tobacco down, and carry it into houses, (made for that purpose) to bring it to its purity: And after it has attained, by a convenient attendance upon time, to its perfection, it is then tyed up in bundles, and packt into Hogs-heads, and then laid by for the Trade.

Between November and January there arrives in this Province Shipping to the number of twenty sail and upwards, all Merchantmen loaden with Commodities to Trafique and dispose of, trucking with the Planter for Silks, Hollands, Serges, and Broad-clothes, with other necessary Goods, priz'd at such and such rates as shall be judg'd on is fair and legal, for Tobacco at so much the pound, and advantage on both sides considered; the Planter for his work, and the Merchant for adventuring himself and his Commodity into so far a Country: Thus is the Trade on both sides drove on with a fair and honest Decorum.

The Inhabitants of this Province are seldom or never put to the affrightment of being robb'd of their money, nor to dirty their Fingers by telling of vast sums: They have more bags to carry Corn, then Coyn; and though they want, but why should I call that a want which is only a necessary miss? the very ef-fects of the dirt of this Province affords as great a profit to the general Inhabitant, as the Gold of Peru doth to the straight-breecht Commonalty of the Spaniard.

Our Shops and Exchanges of Mary-land, are the Merchants Store-houses, where with few words and protestations Goods are bought and delivered; not like those Shop-keepers Boys in London, that continually cry, What do ye lack Sir? What d'ye buy? yelping with so wide a mouth, as if some Apothecary had hired their mouths to stand open to catch Gnats and Vagabond Flyes in.

Tobacco is the current Coyn of Mary-land, and will sooner purchase Commodities from the Merchant, then money. I must confess the New-England men that trade into this Province, had rather have fat Pork for their Goods, then Tobacco or Furrs, which I conceive is, because their bodies being fast bound up with the cords of restringent Zeal, they are fain to make use of the lineaments of this Non-Canaanite creature physically to loosen them; for a bit of a pound upon a two-peny Rye load, according to the original Receipt, will bring the costiv'st red-ear'd Zealot in some three hours time to a fine stool, if methodically observed.

Medera-Wines, Sugars, Salt, Wickar-Chairs, and Tin Candlesticks, is the most of the Commodities they bring in: They arrive in Mary-land about September, being most of them Ketches and Barkes, and such small Vessels, and those dispersing themselves into several small Creeks of this Province, to sell and dispose of their Commodities, where they know the Market is most fit for their small Adventures.

4

Among the principal products of colonial Carolina were rice, indigo, and naval stores. The following description of the cultivation and proc-essing of rice and indigo was written for a London audience in 1761 by the governor of South Carolina, James Glen:[4]

[4] Governor James Glen, A Description of South Carolina; Containing Many Curious and Interesting Particulars Relating to the Civil, Natural, and Commercial History of that Colony. . . . (London, 1761), pp. 6–10.

The best land for *Rice* is a wet, deep, miry Soil; such as is generally to be found in *Cypress* Swamps; or a black greasy Mould with a Clay Foundation; but the very best Lands may be meliorated by laying them under Water at proper Seasons.

Good Crops are produced even the first Year, when the Surface of the Earth appears in Some Degree covered with the Trunks and Branches of Trees: the proper Months for sowing *Rice* are *March, April,* and *May;* the Method is, to plant it in Trenches or Rows made with a Hoe, about Three Inches deep; the Land must be kept pretty clear from Weeds; and at the latter End of *August* or the beginning of *September,* it will be fit to be reaped.

Rice is not the worse for being a little green when cut; they let it remain in the Stubble till dry, which will be in about Two or Three Days, if the Weather be favourable, and then they house or put it in large Stacks.

Afterwards it is threshed with a Flail, and then winnowed, which was formerly a very tedious Operation, but is now performed with great Ease, by a very simple Machine, a Wind-fan, but lately used here, and a prodigious Improvement.

The next Part of the Process is grinding, which is done in small Mills made of Wood, of about Two Feet in Diameter: it is then winnowed again, and afterwards put into a Mortar made of Wood, sufficient to contain from half a Bushel to a Bushel, where it is beat with a Pestle of a Size suitable to the Mortar and to the Strength of the Person who is to pound it; this is done to free the *Rice* from a thick Skin, and is the most laborious Part of the Work.

It is then sifted from the Flour and Dust, made by the pounding; and afterwards by a Wire-Sieve called a Market-Sieve, it is separated from the broken and small *Rice,* which fits it for the Barrels in which it is carried to Market.

They reckon Thirty *Slaves* a proper Number for a *Rice-Plantation,* and to be tended with one Overseer; these, in favourable Seasons and on good Land, will produce a surprizing Quantity of *Rice;* . . . each good working Hand employed in a *Rice-Plantation* makes four Barrels and a Half of *Rice,* each Barrel weighing Five Hundred Pounds Weight neat; besides a sufficient Quantity of Provisions of all Kinds, for the *Slaves, Horses, Cattle,* and *Poultry* of the Plantation, for the ensuing Year. . . .

Indigo is of several Sorts; what we have gone mostly upon, is, the Sort generally cultivated in the *Sugar-Islands,* which requires a high loose Soil, tolerably rich, and is an annual Plant; . . .

An Acre of good Land may produce about Eighty Pounds weight of good *Indigo;* and one Slave may manage two Acres and upwards, and raise Provisions besides, and have all the Winter Months to saw *Lumber* and be otherwise employed in: but as much of the Land hitherto used for *Indigo* is improper, I am persuaded that not above Thirty Pounds weight, of good *Indigo per Acre,* can be expected from the Land at present cultivated: . . .

But I cannot leave this Subject without observing, how conveniently and profitably, as to the Charge of Labour, both *Indigo* and *Rice* may be managed by the same Persons; for the Labour attending *Indigo* being over in the Summer Months, those who were employed in it may afterwards manufacture *Rice,* in the ensuing Part of the Year, when it becomes most laborious; and after doing all this, they will have some Time to spare for sawing *Lumber,* and making *Hogshead* and other *Staves,* to supply the *Sugar-Colonies.*

5

An important element in the colonial economy of North and South Carolina was the production of naval stores. Governor Glen presents a graphic account of obtaining and processing the various resins:[5]

Concerning the Extraction, Preparation, Etc. of Turpentine, Tar, Pitch, Oil of Turpentine, *and* Rosin.

---

[5] *Ibid.,* pp. 70–72.

The Five Sorts of Commodities known by these Names, are all extracted from a Species of *Pine-Tree,* called the *Pitch-Pine;* and may rather be said to be one and the same Thing under different Modes of Preparation, than Five differing Sorts of Commodities, because they are all included in the Gum Resin of the *Pine-Tree.*

Turpentine is the Gum in a liquid State, extracted by Incision and the Heat of the Sun, while the Tree is growing.

Oil of Turpentine is obtained by the Distillation of *Turpentine.*

Rosin is the Residuum, or Remainder, of such *Turpentine,* after the Oil is distilled from it.

Tar is the Gum in a liquid State, but forced out by a proper degree of confined Fire Heat, after the Tree is cut down, split in Pieces, and dried.

Pitch is the solid Part of *Tar,* separated from the liquid Part by boiling.

Turpentine is obtained by cutting Channels in the standing green Trees, so as to meet in a Point at the Foot of the Tree, where a Box of several Pieces of Board are fitted to receive it: the Channels are cut as high as a Man can reach with an Axe, and the Bark is peeled off from those Parts of the Tree which are exposed to the Sun, that the Heat of it may more easily draw out the *Turpentine.*

The Process of extracting the *Tar* is as followeth:—First, they prepare a circular Floor of Clay, declining a little towards the Centre; from which there is laid a Pipe of Wood, extending near horizontally, Two Feet without the Circumference, and so let into the Ground that its upper Side is near level with the Floor: at the outer End of the Pipe they dig a Hole large enough to hold the Barrels for the Tar, which when forced out of the Wood, naturally runs to the Centre of the Floor, as the lowest Part, and from thence along the Pipe into the Barrels: these Matters being first prepared, they raise upon that Clay Floor a large Pile of dry *Pine-wood,* split in Pieces, and inclose the whole Pile with a Wall of Earth, leaving only a little

Hole at the Top, where the Fire is to be kindled; and when that is done, so that the inclosed Wood begins to burn, the whole is stopped up with Earth; to the End that there may not be any Flame, but only Heat sufficient to force the *Tar* out of the Wood and make it run down to the Floor: they temper the Heat as they think proper, by thrusting a Stick through the Earth, and letting the Air in, at as many Places as they find necessary.

LABOR

6

The chronic labor shortage in the colonies was met in a variety of ways. One method used in many colonies was the indenturing of a servant who was then called a "redemptioner." Gottlieb Mittelberger was a German schoolmaster who came to Pennsylvania in 1750. He later returned home and describes to a German audience the terms and conditions of this form of contract labor:[6]

Both in Rotterdam and in Amsterdam the people are packed densely, like herrings so to say, in the large sea vessels. One person receives a place of scarcely 2 feet width and 6 feet length in the bedstead, while many a ship carries four to six hundred souls; not to mention the innumerable implements, tools, provisions, water-barrels and other things which likewise occupy much space.

On account of contrary winds it takes the ships sometimes 2, 3 and 4 weeks to make the trip from Holland to Kaupp [Cowes] in England. But when the wind is good, they get there in 8 days or even sooner. Everything is examined there and the custom-duties paid, whence it comes that the ships ride there 8, 10 to 14 days and even longer at anchor, till they have taken in their full cargoes. During that time every one is compelled to spend his last remaining money and to consume his little stock of provisions

---

6 Gottlieb Mittelberger, *Journey to Pennsylvania in the Year 1750 and Return to Germany in the Year 1754* (Philadelphia, 1898), pp. 19–20, 22, 24.

which had been reserved for the sea; so that most passengers, finding themselves on the ocean where they would be in greater need of them, must greatly suffer from hunger and want. Many suffer want already on the water between Holland and Old England.

When the ships have for the last time weighed their anchors near the city of Kaupp [Cowes] in Old England, the real misery begins with the long voyage. For from there the ships, unless they have good wind, must often sail 8, 9, 10 to 12 weeks before they reach Philadelphia. But even with the best wind the voyage lasts 7 weeks.

But during the voyage there is on board these ships terrible misery, stench, fumes, horror, vomiting, many kinds of seasickness, fever, dysentery, headache, heat, constipation, boils, scurvy, cancer, mouth-rot, and the like, all of which come from old and sharply salted food and meat, also from very bad and foul water, so that many die miserably.

Add to this want of provisions, hunger, thirst, frost, heat, dampness, anxiety, want, afflictions and lamentations, together with other trouble, as c. v. the lice abound so frightfully, especially on sick people, that they can be scraped off the body. The misery reaches the climax when a gale rages for 2 or 3 nights and days, so that every one believes that the ship will go to the bottom with all human beings on board. In such a visitation the people cry and pray most piteously. . . .

Many sigh and cry, "Oh, that I were at home again, and if I had to lie in my pig-sty!" Or they say: "O God, if I only had a piece of good bread, or a good fresh drop of water." Many people whimper, sigh and cry piteously for their homes; most of them get home-sick. Many hundred people necessarily die and perish in such misery and must be cast into the sea, which drives their relatives or those who persuaded them to undertake the journey, to such despair that it is almost impossible to pacify and console them. In a word, the sighing and crying and lamenting on board the ship continues night and day so as to cause the hearts even of the most hardened to bleed when they hear it. . . .

At length, when, after a long and tedious voyage, the ships come in sight of land, so that the promontories can be seen, which the people were so eager and anxious to see, all creep from below on deck to see the land from afar, and they weep for joy, and pray and sing, thanking and praising God. The sight of the land makes the people on board the ship, especially the sick and the half-dead, alive again, so that their hearts leap within them; they shout and rejoice, and are content to bear their misery in patience, in the hope that they may soon reach the land in safety. But alas!

When the ships have landed at Philadelphia after their long voyage, no one is permitted to leave them except those who pay for their passage or can give good security; the others, who cannot pay, must remain on board the ships till they are purchased, and are released from the ships by their purchasers. The sick always fare the worst, for the healthy are naturally preferred and purchased first; and so the sick and wretched must often remain on board in front of the city for 2 or 3 weeks, and frequently die, whereas many a one, if he could pay his debt and were permitted to leave the ship immediately, might recover and remain alive. . . .

The sale of human beings in the market on board the ship is carried on thus: Every day Englishmen, Dutchmen and High-German people come from the city of Philadelphia and other places, in part from a great distance, say 20, 30, or 40 hours away, and go on board the newly arrived ship that has brought and offers for sale passengers from Europe, and select among the healthy persons such as they deem suitable for their business, and bargain with them how long they will serve for their passage money, which most of them are still in debt for. When they have come to an agreement, it happens that adult persons bind themselves in writing to serve 3, 4, 5 or 6 years for the amount due by them, according to their age and strength. But very young people, from 10 to 15 years, must serve till they are 21 years old.

Many parents must sell and trade away their children like so many head of cattle; for if their children take the debt upon themselves, the parents can leave the ship free and unrestrained; but as the parents often do not know where and to what people their children are going, it often happens that such parents and children, after leaving the ship, do not see each other again for many years, perhaps no more in all their lives. . . .

It often happens that whole families, husband, wife, and children, are separated by being sold to different purchasers, especially when they have not paid any part of their passage money.

When a husband or wife has died at sea, when the ship has made more than half of her trip, the survivor must pay or serve not only for himself or herself, but also for the deceased.

When both parents have died over halfway at sea, their children, especially when they are young and have nothing to pawn or to pay, must stand for their own and their parents' passage, and serve till they are 21 years old. When one has served his or her term, he or she is entitled to a new suit of clothes at parting; and if it has been so stipulated, a man gets in addition a horse, a woman, a cow.

When a serf has an opportunity to marry in this country, he or she must pay for each year which he or she would have yet to serve, 5 to 6 pounds. But many a one who has thus purchased and paid for his bride, has subsequently repented his bargain, so that he would gladly have returned his exorbitantly dear ware, and lost the money besides.

If some one in this country runs away from his master, who has treated him harshly, he cannot get far. Good provision has been made for such cases, so that a runaway is soon recovered. He who detains or returns a deserter receives a good reward.

If such a runaway has been away from his master one day, he must serve for it as a punishment a week, for a week a month, and for a month half a year. But if the master will not keep the runaway after he has got him back,

he may sell him for so many years as he would have to serve him yet.

7

For the reasons outlined by Mittelberger and for others as well, indentured servants failed to meet the insatiable demand for labor in the colonies. Negro slaves were early resorted to and by 1700 exceeded the number of "redemptioners." Colonel E. Jennings, president of the Council of Virginia, addressed to the Lords of Trade in London the letter printed below:[7]

VIRGINIA *November ye 27th 1708 May it please yor Lordsps,*

It was the 11th of last moneth and the Fleet then sailed, before I had the honor to receive yor Lordships of the 15th of April concerning the Negro Trade Since which I have endeavoured by the means of the proper officers, and the information of the ancient Inhabitants, to answer Yo^r Lordps Commands, and in Order thereto have herewith sent yor Lordships an account of all the Negros imported into this Colony from the 24th of June 1699 to the 12th of October last past distinguishing those imported by the Royal African Company (679), and those by separate Traders (5928), wherein yor Lordships will perceive the latter have had much the greater Share. As to the particular Rates at which those Negros have been sold, they have been variable according to the different times of their coming in and the quality & ages of the Slaves, but the medium for men & women may be reckoned from 20 to 30 pounds a head for those sold by the Company & from 20 to 35 £ a head for the like kinds sold by the separate Traders, who in gen^l have sold theirs at a higher rate than the Company.

How the Country was supplyed with Negros before the Trade to Africa was laid open in the year 1698. I have endeavoured to Inform my Self from some ancient Inhabitants conversant in that Trade as well as by recollecting what hath happened in my own knowledge, & find that before the year 1680

---

[7] Col. Edmund Jennings to the Lords of Trade, November 27, 1708, in William L. Saunders (ed.), *Colonial Records of North Carolina*, I, 693–694.

what negros were brought to Virginia were imported generally from Barbados for it was very rare to have a Negro ship come to this Country directly from Africa since that time, and before the year 1698. the Trade of Negros became more frequent, tho not in any proportion to what it hath been of late, during which the African Company sent several Ships and others by their Licence (as I have been informed) having bought their Slaves of the Company brought them in hither for Sale, Among which I remember the late Alderman Jeffrys & Sr Jeffry Jeffrys were principally concerned, but all this time the price of the Negroes was currant from £18 to 25 per head for men and women & never exceeded that Rate. Whether the opening the Trade to Africa having created an Emulation between the Company and the Separate Traders which should outbid the other in the purchase of their Slaves there, or whether the dexterity of their Factors there in taking advantage of the prevailing humour of our Inhabitants for some years past of buying Negros even beyond their abilities, or the Concurrence of both, hath raised the Rates of Negros so extravagantly, I shall not pretend to determine but this I may venture to say that it will be much harder to lower the price again now tis raised unless there be the same Freedom of Trade continued as formerly for tho the Inhabitants of this Country in gen^l will not be so fond of purchasing Negros as of late being sensibly convinced of their Error which has in a manner ruined the Credit of the Country yet there will still be some that must, & others that will at any rate Venture to buy them, & if the Company alone have the management of the Trade, they'l find pretences enough to keep up the price if not to impose what higher rate they please, which the buyer must submit to, knowing he cannot be supplyed by any other hand. As for vessells trading directly from this place to the Coast of Africa I never knew of any nor is the same practicable this Country not being provided with Commoditys suitable for carrying on such a Trade. This is the best account I am able to give in Answer to yor

Lordships Commands, wherein if I have failed or mistaken in any point I beg yor Lordships favourable Construction thereof Since I can with truth assure your Lordships that no man hath a greater desire to serve yor Lordships than

My Lords
Your Lordships
most obedient servant
E. JENINGS

8

The lack of towns, markets, and money was both a cause and a consequence of the slow economic development of Virginia. This account discusses conditions in 1679:[8]

For want of Towns, Markets and Money, there is but little Encouragement for Tradesmen and Artificers, and therefore little Choice of them, and their Labour very dear in the Country. A Tradesman having no Opportunity of a Market, where he can buy Meat, Milk, Corn and all other things, must either make Corn, keep Cows, and raise Stocks himself: or must ride about the Country to buy Meat and Corn where he can find it; and then is puzzled to find Carriers, Drovers, Butchers, Salting (for he can't buy one Joynt or two) and a great many other Things, which there would be no Occasion for if there were Towns and Markets. Then a great deal of the Tradesman's Time being necessarily spent in going and coming to and from his Work, in dispersed Country Plantations, and his pay being generally in straggling Parcels of Tobacco, the Collection whereof costs about 10 per Cent. and the best of this Pay coming but once a Year, so that he cannot turn his Hand frequently with a small Stock, as Tradesmen do in England and Elsewhere, all this occasions the Dearth of all Tradesmen's Labour, and likewise the Discouragement, Scarcity and Insufficiency of Tradesmen.

---

[8] Anon., "An Account of Virginia," *Massachusetts Historical Society, Collections,* 1st ser. (1798), V, 128.

9

Peter Kalm, the Swedish naturalist, describes Negro slavery on the basis of observations made during his single trip to America in 1748:[9]

December 6th, [1748]

The negroes or blacks make the third kind. They are in a manner slaves; for when a negro is once bought, he is the purchaser's servant as long as he lives, unless he gives him to another, or makes him free. However, it is not in the power of the master to kill his negro for a fault, but he must leave it to the magistrates to proceed according to the laws. Formerly the negroes were brought over from Africa, and bought by almost every one who could afford it. The quakers alone scrupled to have slaves; but they are no longer so nice, and they have as many negroes as other people. However, many people cannot conquer the idea of its being contrary to the laws of Christianity to keep slaves. There are likewise several free negroes in town, who have been lucky enough to get a very zealous quaker for their master, who gave them their liberty, after they had faithfully served him for some time.

At present they seldom bring over any negroes to the English colonies, for those which were formerly brought thither, have multiplied considerably. In regard to their marriage, they proceed as follows: In case you have not only male but likewise female negroes, they must intermarry, and then the children are all your slaves; but if you possess a male negro only, and he has an inclination to marry a female belonging to a different master, you do not hinder your negro in so delicate a point; but it is no advantage to you, for the children belong to the master of the female; it is therefore advantageous to have negro-women. A man who kills his negro must suffer death for it: there is not however an example here of a white man's

having been executed on this account. A few years ago it happened that a master killed his slave; his friends and even the magistrates secretly advised him to leave the country, as otherwise they could not avoid taking him prisoner, and then he would be condemned to die according to the laws of the country, without any hopes of saving him. This lenity was employed towards him, that the negroes might not have the satisfaction of seeing a master executed for killing his slave; for this would lead them to all sorts of dangerous designs against their masters, and to value themselves too much. . . .

The price of negroes differs according to their age, health, and abilities. A full-grown negro costs from forty pounds and upwards to a hundred, of Pensylvania currency. A negro boy or girl, of two or three years old, can hardly be got for less than eight or fourteen pounds in Pensylvania currency. Not only the quakers, but likewise several christians of other denominations, sometimes let their negroes at liberty. This is done in the following manner: When a gentleman has a faithful negro, who has done him great services, he sometimes declares him independent at his death. This is however very expensive; for they are obliged to make a provision for the negro thus set at liberty, to afford him subsistence when he is grown old, that he may not be driven by necessity to wicked actions, or that he may be at any body's charge, for these free negroes become very lazy and indolent afterwards. But the children which the free negro has begot during his servitude, are all slaves, though their father be free. On the other hand, those negro children are free whose parents are at liberty.

10

John Josselyn, an Englishman who made two trips to New England, writes of his experiences and impressions of Maine in a book first published in London in 1675:[10]

---

[9] Peter Kalm, "Kalm's Travels in North America," in John Pinkerton (ed.), *A General Collection of the Best and Most Interesting Voyages and Travels in all Parts of the World* (London, 1812), XIII, 500–502.

[10] John Josselyn, "An Account of Two Voyages to New-England [1675]," in A. B. Hart (ed.), *American History Told by Contemporaries* (New York, 1896), I, 433–434.

The fishermen take yearly upon the coasts many hundred kentals of Cod, hake, haddock, polluck, etc. which they split, salt and dry at their stages, making three voyages in a year. When they share their fish (which is at the end of every voyage) they separate the best from the worst, the first they call Merchantable fish, being sound, full grown fish and well made up, which is known when it is clear like a Lanthorn horn and without spots; the second sort they call refuse fish, that is such as is salt burnt, spotted, rotten, and carelessly ordered: these they put off to the *Massachusets* Merchants. . . .

To every Shallop belong four fishermen, a Master or Steersman, a Midship-man, and a Foremast-man, and a shore man who washes it out of the salt and dries it upon hurdles pitcht upon stakes breast high and tends their Cookery; these often get in one voyage Eight or Nine pound a man for their shares, but it doth some of them little good, for the Merchant to increase his gains by putting off his Commodity in the midst of their voyages, and at the end thereof comes in with a walking Tavern, a Bark laden with the Legitimate bloud of the rich grape, which they bring from *Phial, Madera, Canaries,* with *Brandy, Rhum,* the *Barbadoes strong-water,* and *Tobacco,* coming ashore he gives them a Taster or two, which so charms them, that for no perswasions that their imployers can use will they go out to Sea, although fair and seasonable weather, for two or three days, nay sometimes a whole week till they are wearied with drinking, taking ashore two or three Hogsheads of *Wine* and *Rhum* to drink off when the Merchant is gone. If a man of quality chance to come where they are roystering and gulling in *Wine* with a dear felicity, he must be sociable and *Rolypoly* with them, taking off their liberal cups as freely, or else be gone, which is best for him. . . . When the day of payment comes, they may justly complain of their costly sin of drunkenness, for their shares will do no more than pay the reckoning; if they save a Kental or two to buy shooes and stockins, shirts and wastcoats with, 'tis well, other-

wayes they must enter into the Merchants books for such things as they stand in need of, becoming thereby the Merchants slaves, & when it riseth to a big sum are constrained to mortgage their plantation if they have any, the Merchant when the time is expired is sure to seize upon their plantation and stock of Cattle, turning them out of house and home, poor Creatures, to look out for a new habitation in some remote place where they begin the world again.

LIFE

11

Philip Vickers Fithian, an austere young Presbyterian theological student from Princeton, was tutor to the Carter family at Nomini Hall in Virginia during the year 1773–1774. Like many another northern boy, Fithian was charmed by the southland and its ways, although his Calvinistic background made him look with misgiving upon some of the diversions of the Virginia gentry:[11]

LETTER OF PHILIP V. FITHIAN TO THE REVEREND ENOCH GREEN, DECEMBER 1, 1773

I set out from home the 20th of Octr and arrived at the Hon: Robert Carters, of Nominy, in Westmorland County, the 28th I began to teach his children the first of November. He has two sons, and one Nephew; the oldest Son is turned of seventeen, and is reading Salust and the greek grammar; the others are about fourteen, and in english grammar and Arithmetic. He has besides five daughters which I am to teach english, the eldest is turned of fifteen, and is reading the spectator; she is employed two days in every week in learning to play the Forte-Piana, and Harpsicord—The others are smaller, and learning to read and spell. Mr Carter is one of the Councellors in the

---

11 Hunter D. Farish (ed.), *Journal & Letters of Philip Vickers Fithian, 1773–1774: A Plantation Tutor of the Old Dominion* (Williamsburg, 1943), pp. 34–35, 38–39. Reprinted by permission of the publisher, Colonial Williamsburg Incorporated.

general court at Williamsburg, and possest of as great, perhaps the clearest fortune according to the estimation of people here, of any man in Virginia: He seems to be a good scholar, even in classical learning, and is remarkable one in english grammar; and notwithstanding his rank, which in general seems to countenance indulgence to children, both himself and Mrs Carter have a manner of instructing and dealing with children far superior, I may say it with confidence, to any I have ever seen, in any place, or in any family. They keep them in perfect subjection to themselves, and never pass over an occasion of reproof; and I blush for many of my acquaintances when I say that the children are more kind and complaisant to the servants who constantly attend them than we are to our superiors in age and condition. Mr Carter has an overgrown library of Books of which he allows me the free use. It consists of a general collection of law books, all the Latin and Greek Classicks, vast number of Books on Divinity chiefly by writers who are of the established Religion; he has the works of almost all the late famous writers, as Locke, Addison, Young, Pope, Swift, Dryden, &c., in Short, Sir, to speak moderately, he has more than eight times your number—His eldest Son, who seems to be a Boy of genius and application is to be sent to Cambridge University, but I believe will go through a course either in Philadelphia or Princeton College first.

Journal

Monday 13. [December 1773]

Mr Carter is preparing for a Voyage in his Schooner, the Hariot, to the Eastern Shore in Maryland, for Oysters: there are of the party, Mr *Carter*, Captain *Walker* Colonel *Richd Lee*, & Mr *Lancelot Lee*. With Sailors to work the vessel—I observe it is a general custom on Sundays here, with Gentlemen to invite one another home to dine, after Church; and to consult about, determine their common business, either before or after Service—It is not the Custom for Gentlemen to go into Church til Service

is beginning, when they enter in a Body, in the same manner as they come out; I have known the Clerk to come out and call them in to prayers.—They stay also after the Service is over, usually as long, sometimes longer, than the Parson was preaching —Almost every Lady wears a red Cloak; and when they ride out they tye a white handkerchief over their Head and face, so that when I first came into Virginia, I was distress'd whenever I saw a Lady, for I thought She had the Tooth-Ach!—The People are extremely hospitable, and very polite both of which are most certainly universal Characteristics of the Gentlemen in Virginia —some swear bitterly, but the practise seems to be generally disapproved—I have heard that this Country is notorious for Gaming, however this be, I have not seen a Pack of *Cards,* nor a *Die,* since I left home, nor gaming nor Betting of any kind except at the Richmond-Race. Almost every Gentleman of Condition, keeps a Chariot and *Four;* many drive with six Horses—I observe that all the Merchants & shopkeepers in the Sphere of my acquaintance and I am told it is the Case through the Province, are young Scotch-men; Several of whom I know, as *Cunningham, Jennings, Hamilton, Blain;* —And it has been the custom heretofore to have all their Tutors and Schoolmasters from Scotland, tho' they begin to be willing to employ their own Country-men . . . Mr *Carter* is practising this Evening on the *Guittar* He begins with the *Trumpet Minuet.* He has a good Ear for Music; a vastly delicate Taste: and keeps good Instruments, he has here at Home a *Harpischord, Forte-Piano, Harmonica, Guitar, Violin,* & *German Flutes,* & at Williamsburg, has a good *Organ,* he himself also is indefatigable in the Practice.

12

Dr. Alexander Hamilton was a Scottish physician trained at the University of Edinburgh. He migrated to America and settled down to the practice of medicine in Annapolis, the provincial capital of Maryland. During the year 1744 he made a trip on horseback from Maryland to

Maine and back, for the purposes of "health and recreation." The following passages are from a journal he kept during this journey. They enable us to compare Philadelphia, New York, and Boston as they appeared to one pair of colonial eyes:[12]

PHILADELPHIA

I must make a few remarks before I leave this place. The people in generall are inquisitive concerning strangers. If they find one comes there upon the account of trade or traffic, they are fond of dealing with him and cheating him if they can. If he comes for pleasure or curiosity, they take little or no notice of him unless he be a person of more than ordinary rank; then they know as well as others how to fawn and cringe. Some persons there were inquisitive about the state of religion in Maryland. My common reply to such questions was that I studied their constitutions more than their consciences so knew something of the first but nothing of the latter.

They have in generall a bad notion of their neighboring province, Maryland, esteeming the people a sett of cunning sharpers; but my notion of the affair is that the Pensylvanians are not a whit inferior to them in the science of chicane, only their method of tricking is different. A Pensylvanian will tell a lye with a sanctified, solemn face; a Marylander, perhaps, will convey his fib in a volley of oaths; but the effect and point in view is the same tho' the manner of operating be different.

In this city one may live tollerably cheap as to the articles of eating and drinking, but European goods here are extravagantly dear. Even goods of their own manufacture such as linen, woolen, and leather bear a high price. Their government is a kind of anarchy (or no government), there being perpetual jarrs betwixt the two parts of the legislature.

But that is no strange thing, the ambition and avarice of a few men in both partys being the active springs in these dissentions and altercations, tho a specious story about the good and interest of the country is trumpt up by both; yet I would not be so severe as to say so of all in generall.

Mr. T[homa]s, the present gov[erno]r, I believe is an upright man and has the interest of the province really att heart, having done more for the good of that obstinate generation, the Quakers, than any of his predecessours have done. Neither are they so blind as not to see it, for he shares more of their respect than any of their former governours were wont to do.

There is polite conversation here among the better sort, among whom there is no scarcity of men of learning and good sense. The ladies, for the most part, keep att home and seldom appear in the streets, never in publick assemblies except att the churches or meetings; therefor I cannot with certainty enlarge upon their charms, having had little or no opportunity to see them either congregated or separate, but to be sure the Philadelphian dames are as handsome as their neighbours.

The staple of this province is bread, flower, and pork. They make no tobacco but a little for their own use. The country is generally plain and levell, fruitfull in grain and fruits, pretty well watered, and abounding in woods backward. It is upon the growing hand, more than any of the provinces of America. The Germans and High Dutch are of late become very numerous here.

NEW YORK

The people of New York att the first appearance of a stranger are seemingly civil and courteous, but this civility and complaisance soon relaxes if he be not either highly recommended or a good toaper. To drink stoutly with the Hungarian Club, who are all bumper men, is the readiest way for a stranger to recommend himself, and a sett among them are very fond of making a stranger drunk. To talk bawdy and to have

---

[12] Carl Bridenbaugh (ed.), *Gentleman's Progress, The Itinerarium of Dr. Alexander Hamilton, 1744* (Chapel Hill, 1948), pp. 28–30, 88–89, 144–146. Reprinted with the permission of the publisher, University of North Carolina Press.

a knack att punning passes among some there for good sterling wit. Govr. C[linto]n himself is a jolly toaper and gives good example and, for that one quality, is esteemed among these dons.

The staple of New York is bread flower and skins. It is a very rich place, but it is not so cheap living here as att Philadelphia. They have very bad water in the city, most of it being hard and brackish. Ever since the negroe conspiracy, certain people have been appointed to sell water in the streets, which they carry on a sledge in great casks and bring it from the best springs about the city, for it was when the negroes went for tea water that they held their caballs and consultations, and therefor they have a law now that no negroe shall be seen upon the streets without a lanthorn after dark.

In this city are a mayor, recorder, aldermen, and common council. The government is under the English law, but the chief places are possessed by Dutchmen, they composing the best part of the House of Assembly. The Dutch were the first settlers of this province, which is very large and extensive, the States of Holland having purchased the country of one Hudson who pretended first to have discovered it, but they att last exchanged it with the English for Saranam, and ever since there have been a great number of Dutch here, tho now their language and customs begin pretty much to wear out and would very soon die were it not for a parcell of Dutch domines here who, in the education of their children, endeavour to preserve the Dutch customs as much as possible. There is as much jarring here betwixt the powers of the legislature as in any of the other American provinces.

They have a diversion here, very common, which is the barbecuing of a turtle, to which sport the chief gentry in town commonly go once or twice a week.

There are a great many handsome women in this city. They appear much more in publick than att Philadelphia. It is customary here to ride thro the street in light chairs. When the ladys walk the streets in the day time, they commonly use umbrellas, prittily adorned with feathers and painted.

There are two coffee-houses in this city, and the northeren and southeren posts go and come here once a week. I was tired of nothing here but their excessive drinking, for in this place you may have the best of company and conversation as well as att Philadelphia.

BOSTON

I need scarce take notice that Boston is the largest town in North America, being much about the same extent as the city of Glasgow in Scotland and having much the same number of inhabitants, which is between 20 and 30 thousand. It is considerably larger than either Philadelphia or New York, but the streets are irregularly disposed, and, in generall, too narrow. The best street in the town is that which runs down towards the Long Wharff which goes by the name of King's Street. This town is a considerable place for shipping and carrys on a great trade in time of peace. There are now above 100 ships in the harbour besides a great number of small craft tho now, upon account of the war, the times are very dead. The people of this province chiefly follow farming and merchandise. Their staples are shipping, lumber, and fish. The government is so far democratic as that the election of the Governour's Council and the great officers is made by the members of the Lower House, or representatives of the people. Mr. Shirly, the present Governour, is a man of excellent sense and understanding and is very well respected there. He understands how to humour the people and, att the same time, acts for the interest of the Government. Boston is better fortified against an enimy than any port in North America, not only upon account of the strength of the Castle, but the narrow passage up into the harbour which is not above 160 foot wide in the channell att high water.

There are many different religions and perswasions here, but the chief sect is that of the Presbyterians. There are above 25 churches, chapells, and meetings in the town, but the Quakers here have but a small remnant, having been banished the province att the first settlement upon account of some disturbances they raised. The people here have lately been, and indeed are now, in great confusion and much infested with enthusiasm from the preaching of some fanaticks and New Light teachers, but now this humour begins to lessen. The people are generally more captivated with speculative than with practicall religion. It is not by half such a flagrant sin to cheat and cozen one's neighbour as it is to ride about for pleasure on the sabbath day or to neglect going to church and singing of psalms.

The middling sort of people here are to a degree dissingenuous and dissembling, which appears even in their common conversation in which their indirect and dubious answers to the plainest and fairest questions show their suspicions of one another. The better sort are polite, mannerly, and hospitable to strangers, such strangers, I mean, as come not to trade among them (for of them they are jealous). There is more hospitality and frankness showed here to strangers than either att York or at Philadelphia. And in the place there is abundance of men of learning and parts; so that one is att no loss for agreeable conversation nor for any sett of company he pleases. Assemblys of the gayer sort are frequent here; the gentlemen and ladys meeting almost every week att consorts of musick and balls. I was present att two or three such and saw as fine a ring of ladys, as good dancing, and heard musick as elegant as I had been witness to any where. I must take notice that this place abounds with pritty women who appear rather more abroad than they do att York and dress elegantly. They are, for the most part, free and affable as well as pritty. I saw not one prude while I was here.

13

*The Reverend Joseph Doddridge, an itinerant Methodist preacher, grew up on the frontier he describes in the selection below. In this account, Doddridge vividly pictures frontier con-*ditions *from Pennsylvania to Virginia in the years 1772–1774:*[13]

On the frontiers, and particularly amongst those who were much in the habit of hunting, and going on scouts, and campaigns, the dress of the men was partly Indian, and partly that of civilized nations.

The hunting shirt was universally worn. This was a kind of loose frock, reaching half way down the thighs, with large sleeves, open before, and so wide as to lap over a foot or more when belted. The cape was large, and sometimes handsomely fringed with a ravelled piece of cloth of a different colour from that of the hunting shirt itself. The bosom of this dress served as a wallet to hold a chunk of bread, cakes, jirk, tow for wiping the barrel of the rifle, or any other necessary for the hunter or warrior. The belt which was always tied behind answered several purposes, besides that of holding the dress together. In cold weather the mittens, and sometimes the bullet-bag occupied the front part of it. To the right side was suspended the tomahawk and to the left the scalping knife in its leathern sheath. The hunting shirt was generally made of linsey, sometimes of coarse linen, and a few of dressed deer skins. These last were very cold and uncomfortable in wet weather. The shirt and jacket were of the common fashion. A pair of drawers or breeches and leggings, were the dress of the thighs, and legs, a pair of mocassons answered for the feet much better than shoes. These were made of dressed deer skin. They were mostly made of a single piece with a gathering seam along the top of the foot, and another from the bottom of the heel, without gathers as high as the ankle joint or a little higher. Flaps were left on each side to reach some distance up the legs. These were nicely adapted to the ankles, and lower part of the leg by thongs of deer skin, so that no dust, gravel, or snow could get within the mocasson.

[13] Joseph Doddridge, *Notes on the Settlement and Indian Wars, of the Western Parts of Virginia and Pennsylvania* (Wellsburgh, Va., 1824), pp. 113–115, 134–137.

The mocassons in ordinary use cost but a few hours labour to make them. This was done by an instrument denominated a mocasson awl, which was made of the backspring of an old claspknife. This awl with its buckshorn handle was an appendage of every shot pouch strap, together with a roll of buckskin for mending the mocassons. This was the labour of almost every evening. They were sewed together and patched with deer skin thongs, or whangs as they were commonly called.

In cold weather the mocassons were well stuffed with deers hair, or dry leaves, so as to keep the feet comfortably warm; but in wet weather it was usually said that wearing them was "A decent way of going barefooted"; and such was the fact, owing to the spongy texture of the leather of which they were made.

Owing to the defective covering of the feet, more than to any other circumstance the greater number of our hunters and warriors were afflicted with the rheumatism in their limbs. Of this disease they were all apprehensive in cold or wet weather, and therefore always slept with their feet to the fire to prevent or cure it as well as they could. This practice unquestionably had a very salutary effect, and prevented many of them from becoming confirmed cripples in early life. . . .

I will proceed to state the usual manner of settling a young couple in the world.

A spot was selected on a piece of land of one of the parents, for their habitation. A day was appointed shortly after their marriage for commencing the work of building their cabin. The fatigue party consisted of choppers, whose business it was to fell the trees and cut them off at proper lengths. A man with a team for hauling them to the place, and arranging them, properly assorted, at the sides and ends of the building, a carpenter, if such he might be called, whose business it was to search the woods for a proper tree for making clapboards for the roof. The tree for the purpose must be straight grained and from three to four feet

in diameter. The boards were split four feet long, with a large frow, and as wide as the timber would allow. They were used without plaining or shaving. Another division were employed in getting puncheons for the floor of the cabin; this was done by splitting trees, about eighteen inches in diameter, and hewing the faces of them with a broad axe. They were half the length of the floor they were intended to make.

The materials for the cabin were mostly prepared on the first day and sometimes the foundation laid in the evening. The second day was allotted for the raising.

In the morning of the next day the neighbours collected for the raising. The first thing to be done was the election of four corner men, whose business it was to notch and place the logs. The rest of the company furnished them with the timbers. In the meantime the boards and puncheons were collecting for the floor and roof, so that by the time the cabin was a few rounds high the sleepers and floor began to be laid. The door was made by sawing or cutting the logs in one side so as to make an opening about three feet wide. This opening was secured by upright pieces of timber about three inches thick through which holes were bored into the ends of the logs for the purpose of pinning them fast. A similar opening, but wider, was made at the end for the chimney. This was built of logs and made large to admit of a back and jams of stone. At the square, two end logs projected a foot or eighteen inches beyond the wall to receive the butting poles, as they were called, against which the ends of the first row of clap boards was supported. The roof was formed by making the end logs shorter until a single log formed the comb of the roof, on these logs the clap boards were placed, the ranges of them laping some distance over those next below them and kept in their places by logs, placed at proper distances upon them.

The roof, and sometimes, the floor were finished on the same day of the raising. A third day was commonly spent by a few carpenters in leveling off the floor, making a clap board

door and a table. This last was made of a
split slab and supported by four round legs set
in auger holes. Some three-legged stools were
made in the same manner. Some pins stuck
in the logs at the back of the house supported
some clap boards which served for shelves
for the table furniture. A single fork, placed
with its lower end in a hole in the floor and
the upper end fastened to a joist served for
a bed stead, by placing a pole in the fork
with one end through a crack between the
logs of the wall. This front pole was crossed
by a shorter one within the fork, with its
outer end through another crack. From the
front pole, through a crack between the
logs of the end of the house, the boards
were put on which formed the bottom of the
bed. Some times other poles, were pinned to
the fork a little distance above these, for the
purpose of supporting the front and foot of
the bed, while the walls were the supports of
its back and head. A few pegs around the
wall for a display of the coats of the women,
and the hunting shirts of the men, and two
small forks or bucks horns to a joist for the
rifle and shot pouch, completed the carpenter work.

In the meantime masons were at work.
With the heart pieces of the timber of which
the clapboards were made, they made billets
for chunking up the cracks between the logs
of the cabin and chimney, a large bed of
mortar was made for daubing up those
cracks; a few stones formed the back and
jambs of the chimney.

The cabin being finished, the ceremony
of house warming took place, before the
young couple were permitted to move into it.

The house warming was a dance of a
whole night's continuance, made up of the
relations of the bride and groom, and their
neighbours. On the day following the young
couple took possession of their new mansion.

14

*Town life in Charleston, South Carolina, was
a good deal more pleasant and civilized than the
frontier conditions depicted by the Reverend
Doddridge. In some respects, however, it was
still somewhat primitive. Medical practice, for
example, decreed massive purges and heavy
bloodletting for almost every bodily ill. The
theory behind such treatment is outlined in the
following description of the kinds and causes of
diseases, written in 1763, by Dr. Milligan-
Johnston of Charleston:[14]*

The Diseases, that may be termed Epidemics, are either acute or chronic: The acute
Diseases may be subdivided into those of the
warm and those of the cold Seasons.

The first are Intermittents of all Kinds,
Fluxes, and Cholera Morbus: The Winter
Diseases are Pleurisies, Peripneumonies, and
Catarrhal Fevers.

The Chronic Diseases are Obstructions of
the Abdominal Viscera, Haemarrhoids, Rup-
tures, Worm-fevers, and what is called the
Lame Distemper.

Intermittents appear in different Forms,
such as Tertian, Double-tertian, Quotidian,
and Remitting Fevers; all which, however
they may vary in their Type, in different
Constitutions and other Circumstances, are,
nevertheless of the same nature, and proceed
from the same Cause, *viz.* Heat and Moisture. A principal Source of Humidity is from
the underground Water, which is always
near the Surface; and, as the Soil is light,
the Moisture easily transpires by the Heat
of the Sun loading the Air with Vapours,
even where no Water is visible. Another, and
more general Cause of the Humidity and
Corruption of the Atmosphere is from the
imperfect Ventilation, there being no Hills
to receive the Winds, or to direct them in
Streams upon the lower Grounds; hence the
Air is apt to stagnate, and the more so by
Reason of the great Quantities of Trees,
which not only confine but moisten the Air
by Transpiration from their Bodies and
Leaves: This is an excrementitious Moisture,
whose former salubrious Parts were spent in
the Nutrition of the Trees, Plants, and their
Efflorescencies; and the Remainder, being
perspirant, floats for a Time in the Air, till

14 Dr. George Milligan, *A Short Description of
the Province of South Carolina. . . .* (London,
1770), pp. 43–45.

the grosser Parts subside, and the finer rise higher.

The great Heat, in the Summer Time, conspires with the Moisture to relax the Solids, and dispose the Humours to Putrefaction; and, according to the various Degrees of Heat and Moisture of the Season, the Epidemics appear sooner or later, are of a longer or shorter Duration, and are attended with mild or alarming symptoms. The Summer Diseases begin commonly in *July*, and disappear about *Christmas*. In *Charles-town*, these Diseases are proportionably less frequent, and milder than in the Country; for here we are pretty clear of Trees, have a large Opening to the Sea, a Kind of Ventilation in the Streets, besides a Thousand culinary Fires in the hottest Season to dry the Air: In the Country they have none of those advantages, and the Inhabitants in general (being more careful to acquire splendid Fortunes, than to preserve their Healths) build their Houses near their Rice-Fields, or Indigo-Dams, where they must always keep stagnating Water.

15

If medical education at Edinburgh was primitive by later standards, Harvard schedules were no less so. But the seriousness with which the Puritan Fathers viewed education is amply revealed in this excerpt prepared for the guidance of students in 1641:[15]

3. The times and order of their Studies, unlesse experience shall shew cause to alter.

The second and third day of the weeke, read Lectures, as followeth.

To the first yeare at 8th. of the clock in the morning *Logick*, the first three quarters, *Physicks* the last quarter.

To the second yeare, at the 9th. houre, *Ethicks* and *Politicks*, at convenient distances of time.

To the third yeare at the 10th. *Arith-*

---

15 "New Englands First Fruits [1643]," in A. B. Hart (ed.), *American History Told by Contemporaries* (New York, 1896), I, 470–471.

metick and *Geometry*, the three first quarters, *Astronomy* the last.

Afternoone,

The first yeare disputes at the second houre.

The 2d. yeare at the 3d. houre.

The 3d. yeare at the 4th. every one in his Art.

The 4th. day reads Greeke.

To the first yeare the *Etymologie* and *Syntax* at the eigth houre.

To the 2d. at the 9th. houre, *Prosodia* and *Dialects.*

Afternoone.

The first yeare at 2d houre practice the precepts of *Grammar* in such Authors as have variety of words.

The 2d. yeare at 3d. houre practice in *Pöesy, Nonnus, Duport,* or the like.

The 3d. yeare perfect their *Theory* before noone, and exercise *Style, Composition, Imitation, Epitome,* both in Prose and Verse, afternoone.

The fifth day reads Hebrew, and the Easterne Tongues.

Grammar to the first yeare houre the 8th.

To the 2d. *Chaldee* at the 9th. houre.

To the 3d. *Syriack* at the 10th. houre.

Afternoone.

The first yeare practice in the Bible at the 2d. houre.

The 2d. in *Ezra* and *Daniel* at the 3d. houre.

The 3d. at the 4th. houre in *Trestius* New Testament.

The 6th. day reads Rhetorick to all at the 8th. houre.

Declamations at the 9th. So ordered that every Scholler may declaime once a moneth. The rest of the day *vacat Rhetoricis studiis.*

The 7th. day reads Divinity Catecheticall
at the 8th. houre, Common places
at the 9th. houre.

Afternoone.

The first houre reads history in the Winter,

The nature of plants in the Summer.

The summe of every Lecture shall be examined, before the new Lecture be read.

Every Schollar, that on proofe is found able to read the Originalls of the *Old* and *New Testament* in to the Latine tongue, and to resolve them *Logically;* withall being of godly life and conversation; And at any publick Act hath the Approbation of the Overseers and Master of the Colledge, is fit to be dignified with his first Degree.

Every Schollar that giveth up in writing a *System,* or *Synopsis,* or summe of *Logick,* Naturall and Morall *Philosophy, Arithmetick, Geometry* and *Astronomy:* and is ready to defend his *Theses* or positions: withall skilled in the Originalls as abovesaid: and of godly life & conversation: and so approved by the Overseers and Master of the Colledge, at any publique Act, is fit to be dignified with his 2d. Degree.

TRADE

16

William Gray, Jr., a highly successful merchant who helped make Salem, Massachusetts, one of the major trading centers of New England, wrote his brother-in-law, the master of a trading vessel, the following letter:[16]

CAPT. WILLIAM WARD,

The Brig Enterprise under your command being ready for sea, you will embrace the first opportunity and proceed for the Cape of Good Hope—upon your arrival sell such part of the cargo as you can to advantage which I suppose will be the Russia duck, coles and such other part of your cargo as

---

[16] William Gray to William Ward, August 10, 1792, in Edward Gray, *William Gray of Salem, Merchant* (Boston, 1914), pp. 13–16.

you think proper. I then advise you, if you can, to purchase about twenty hogsheads of brandy and from 60 to 80 hogsheads wine, such as is best calculated for the Isle of France market, some raisins and almonds, and then proceed for the Isle of France, then sell your cargo or such part as you think for my interest to sell, which I expect will be the whole, when you have sold if you can find any sugar, coffee, tea, Indigo, or cotton that will pay one hundred per cent profitt reckoning them to sell at the price you have at foot then I advise you to come back with such of those articles as you find will do best if you cannot find goods to answer to come home from the Isle of France, then I advise you to proceed for Calcutta in the Bay of Bengal, and there take sugar, saltpeters, Bandanno silk Handkerchiefs, or such other goods as you suppose will answer best in this market. If you have advise that nothing can be done to advantage at Calcutta then you may go to Canton if you can get a cargo of Black Wood, cheep, provided you can make out a stock of $20,000, exclusive of Black wood. When you arrive at Canton after selling your wood take on board as much Bohea tea, as the Brig will carry with some China ware, nankeens, some black sattins, and such other silks as you suppose will best answer. When you have compleated your business in the East Indies proceed directly to this port by such rout as you think safest, if you should come home in the winter it may be well to touch at St. Eustatia and then lay till the spring approaches, so that you may come on safer. I think it may be well to send your boat on shore of Triniti in Martinico where perhaps you will find letters from me. It will be best to sett your cooper at work as soon as you possibly can, and to agree for your wines and Brandies as soon as you can after you arrive, your cargo will sell for 10 or 20 per cent more to take wines and brandies than cash.

Notwithstanding what I have wrote I would have you sell your whole cargo at Good Hope if you can obtain 20 per cent advance and purchase sugars or any other goods that will pay fifty per cent profitt home, then proceed directly to this port. If you have opportunity to sell the Brig Enterprise and appurtanance at a price that you think will answer and can lay out the money to advantage, do it. She cost five thousand dollars and will be worth that surely when she returns, you will take into your calculations what freight she will make home what you must pay freight and what you can make profitt upon the proceeds of the Brig. . . .

Write me by all opportunities either to America or Europe. If to England, direct to the care of Messrs. Harrison Ansley & Co in London, if to Spain to Gardoqui & Co in Bilboa. If to France then to the care of Messrs. Lanchon & Co at L'Orient. If to Denmark to the care of Messrs. Ryberg & Co. at Copenhagen. If to Sweden then to the care of Mr. Thomas Erstein at Gottenburg. The port charges at Canton I suppose about three thousand dollars, at Calcutta the port charges are small. . . .

I further agree Captain Ward shall receive of the profitts that shall be made upon one hundred pound averaging my whole stock in this voyage at his return—as a further consideration of his services. In case you can obtain a credit to advantage and lay out the amount so as to pay me profitt you may take to the amount of six thousand dollars and draw upon me—payable either here or in London—and your bills shall meet due honour.

Wishing you Almight protection and a prosperous voyage

I am your Friend,

WILLIAM GRAY JR.

Salem 10 August 1792

17

Conditions in Virginia were not, as the comment below makes clear, conducive to the development of a large and prosperous business in marketing the primary product of the country, tobacco:[17]

The Merchants live the best of any in that Country, but yet are subject to great Inconveniences in the way of their Trade, which might be avoided if they had Towns, Markets and Money; For, first, they are obliged to sell upon Trust all the Year long, except just a little while when Tobacco is ready. 2. They likewise drive a pitiful retail Trade to serve every Man's little Occasions, being all, in Effect, but Country Chapmen, for want of Towns to be a Center of Trade and Business. 3. Besides the Charge of it they are necessitated to trust all their Concerns to their Receivers, who go about among the Planters that owe them Tobacco, and receive and mark it for them, which Receivers, if they want either Skill or Honesty it proves very fatal to the Merchant. 4. They are at the Charge of carting this Tobacco so mark'd and receiv'd, to convenient Landings; or if it lies not far from these Landings, they must trust to the Seamen for their careful rolling it on board of their Sloops and Shallops: and if the Seamen roll it in bad Weather, or in dirty Ways, it is exposed to a great deal of Damage. 5. It is a great while before the Ships can be loaded, their Freight lying at such a Distance, and being to be brought together in this scrambling manner. By Reason of this, it is an usual Thing with Ships to lye three or four Months in the Country, which might be dispatched in a Fortnight's Time, if the Tobacco were ready at certain Ports; and this inflames the Freight to almost double the Price of what it needed to be, if the Ships had a quick Dispatch.

18

An English mercantilist, Joshua Gee, provides a description of colonial trade as background for the argument that trade and industry ought to be regulated by the imperial government:[18]

CHAP. XV.

TRADE *BETWEEN* ENGLAND *AND* THE TOBACCO PLANTATIONS.

THE *Tobacco Plantations* take from *England* their Cloathing, Household Goods, Iron

---

[17] Anon., "An Account of Virginia," *Massachusetts Historical Society, Collections* (Boston, 1798), 1st Ser., V, 128–129.

[18] Joshua Gee, *The Trade and Navigation of Great Britain Considered: shewing increase in Riches, . . .* (London, 1731), pp. 22–25.

Manufactures of all Sorts, Saddles, Bridles, Brass and Copper Wares, and notwithstanding their dwelling among the Woods, they take their very Turner's Wares, and almost every Thing else that may be called the Manufacture of *England:* So that indeed it is a very great Number of People that are employed to provide a sufficient Supply of Goods for them.

ENGLAND takes from them not only what Tobacco we consume at Home, but very great Quantities for Re-exportation, which may properly be said to be the surest Way of enriching this Kingdom.

CHAP. XVI.

TRADE *BETWEEN* ENGLAND *AND* CAROLINA.

CAROLINA lies in as happy a Climate as any in the World, from 32 to 36 Degrees of *Northern* Latitude. The Soil is generally fertile: The Rice it produces is said to be the best in the World, and no Country affords better Silk than has been brought from thence, though for Want of sufficient Encouragement the Quantity imported is very small. . . . The Rice Trade, since it hath been made an enumerated Commodity, is under great Discouragement; for it cannot be sent directly to Portugal and Spain as formerly; and it will not bear the Charge of bringing home and Re-shipping, unless it be at a Time when the Crops in the Milanese and Egypt prove bad. . . .

CHAP. XVII.

TRADE *BETWEEN* ENGLAND *AND* PENSILVANIA.

PENSILVANIA within Forty Years has made wonderful Improvements; they have built a large and regular City, they have cleared great Tracts of Land, and raised very great Quantities of Wheat and other Provisions, and they have by Way of *Jamaica* beat out a very great Trade for their Corn and Provisions to the *Spanish West-Indies;* and if this Trade be properly nurs'd up, it may draw

the *Spanish* Coast very much to depend on us for a Supply of Flower, Bisket, etc. which may be of great Advantage to us.

It is already attended with that good Consequence, that it hath supplied them with Gold and Silver, which is frequently brought home by our trading Ships from thence, and has very much enlarged their Demands upon us for Broad-cloth, Kersies, Druggets, Serges, Stuffs, and Manufactures of all Sorts.

THEY supply the *Sugar Plantations* with Pipes and Barrel-Staves, and other Lumber, with Flower, Bisket, Port, etc. But this is not sufficient for their Cloathing, and therefore are forced to make something by their own Labour and Industry to answer that End.

CHAP. XVIII.

TRADE *BETWEEN* ENGLAND, NEW–JERSEY *AND* NEW–YORK

THE Provinces of *New-Jersey* and *New-York* produce much the same with *Pensilvania,* and their Traffic is much the same; we have what Money they can raise to buy our Manufactures for their Clothing, and what they further want, they are forced to manufacture for themselves as the aforesaid Colonies do.

CHAP. XIX.

TRADE *BETWEEN* ENGLAND *AND* NEW–ENGLAND.

NEW-ENGLAND takes from us all Sorts of Woollen Manufactures, Linnen, Haberdashery, etc. To raise Money to pay for what they take of us, they are forced to visit the *Spanish* Coasts, where they pick up any commodity they can trade for; They carry Lumber and Provisions to the Sugar Plantations, exchange Provision for Logwood with the Logwood Cutters at *Campeachey.* They send Pipe and Barrel-Staves and Fish to *Spain, Portugal,* and the *Streights.* They send Pitch, Tar and Turpentine to *England,* with some Skins: But all those Commodities fall very short of purchasing their Cloathing in *England;* and therfore what other Necessaries they want, they are forced to manufacture for themselves, as the aforementioned Colonies.

19

Peter Kalm gives a characteristically thorough account of the various aspects of the foreign trade of New York City in 1748:[19]

New York probably carries on a more extensive commerce than any town in the English North American provinces; at least it may be said to equal them; Boston and Philadelphia however come very near up to it. The trade of New York extends to many places; and it is said they send more ships from thence to London than they do from Philadelphia. They export to that capital all the various sorts of skins which they buy of the Indians, sugar, logwood, and other dying woods, rum, mahogany, and many other goods which are the produce of the West Indies; together with all the specie which they get in the course of trade. Every year they build several ships here, which are sent to London, and there sold; and of late years they have shipped a quantity of iron to England. In return for these, they import from London stuffs, and every other article of English growth or manufacture, together with all sorts of foreign goods. England, and especially London, profits immensely by its trade with the American colonies; for not only New York, but likewise all the other English towns on the continent, import so many articles from England, that all their specie, together with the goods which they get in other countries, must altogether go to Old England, in order to pay the amount, to which they are however insufficient. From hence it appears how much a well-regulated colony contributes to the increase and welfare of its mother country.

New York sends many ships to the West Indies, with flour, corn, biscuit, timber, tuns, boards, flesh, fish, butter, and other provisions; together with some of the new fruits that grow here. Many ships go to Boston in New England, with corn and flour; and take in exchange, flesh, butter, timber, different sorts of fish, and other articles, which they carry further to the West Indies. They now and then take rum from thence, which is distilled there in great quantities, and sell it here with a considerable advantage. Sometimes they send yachts with goods from New York to Philadelphia, and at other times yachts are sent from Philadelphia to New York, which is only done, as appears from the gazettes, because certain articles are cheaper at one place than at the other. They send ships to Ireland every year, laden with all kinds of West India goods, but especially with linseed, which is reaped in this province. I have been assured that in some years no less than ten ships have been sent to Ireland, laden with nothing but linseed, because it is said the flax in Ireland does not afford good seed; but probably the true reason is this; the people of Ireland, in order to have the better flax, make use of the plant before the seed is ripe, and therefore are obliged to send for foreign seed; and hence it becomes one of the chief articles in trade.

At this time a bushel of linseed is sold for eight shillings of New York currency, or exactly a piece of eight.

The goods which are shipped to the West Indies are sometimes paid for with ready money, and sometimes with West India goods, which are either first brought to New York, or immediately sent to England or Holland. If a ship does not chuse to take in West India goods in its return to New York, or if nobody will freight it, it often goes to Newcastle in England, to take in coals for ballast, which when brought home sell for a pretty good price. In many parts of the town coals are made use of, both for kitchen fires, and in rooms, because they are reckoned cheaper than wood, which at present costs thirty shillings of New York currency per fathom; of which measure I have before made mention. New York has likewise some intercourse with South Carolina; to which it

[19] Peter Kalm, "Kalm's Travels in North America," in John Pinkerton (ed.), *A General Collection of the Best and Most Interesting Voyages and Travels in all Parts of the World* (London, 1812), XIII, 458–459.

sends corn, flour, sugar, rum, and other goods, and takes rice in return, which is almost the only commodity exported from South Carolina.

The goods with which the province of New York trades are not very numerous. They chiefly export the skins of animals which are bought of the Indians about Oswego; great quantities of boards, coming for the most part from Albany; timber and ready-made lumber, from that part of the country which lies about the river Hudson; and lastly, wheat, flour, barley, oats, and other kinds of corn, which are brought from New Jersey and the cultivated parts of this province. I have seen yachts from New Brunswick, laden with wheat which lay loose on board, and with flour packed up in tuns; and also with great quantities of linseed. New York likewise exports some flesh and other provisions out of its own province, but they are very few; nor is the quantity of pease, which the people about Albany bring, much greater. Iron however may be had more plentifully, as it is found in several parts of this province, and is of a considerable goodness; but all the other products of this country are of little account.

Most of the wine, which is drank here and in the other colonies, is brought from the isle of Madeira, and is very strong and fiery.

No manufactures of note have as yet been established here; at present they get all manufactured goods, such as woollen and linen cloth, etc. from England, and especially from London.

The river Hudson is very convenient for the commerce of this city; as it is navigable for near an hundred and fifty English miles up the country, and falls into the bay not far from the town, on its western side. During eight months of the year this river is full of yachts, and other greater and lesser vessels, either going to New York or returning from thence, laden either with inland or foreign goods.

I cannot make a just estimate of the ships that annually come to this town or sail from it. But I have found, by the Pensylvania gazettes, that from the first of December in 1729, to the fifth of December in the next year, two hundred and eleven ships entered the port of New York, and two hundred and twenty-two cleared it; and since that time there has been a great increase of trade here.

RESTRAINTS ON TRADE

20

Restraints on trade in colonial America came from a variety of sources. The Puritans transplanted the European notion that both prices and wages ought to be set by the government. Robert Keayne, a Boston merchant, believed such principles had little relevance to colonial conditions. Keayne insisted upon selling imported goods at higher prices than those permitted by the General Court, which led to his trial and conviction in 1639 and a fine of £100. John Winthrop's comments reflect the state of Puritan economic thought:[20]

After the court had censured him, the church of Boston called him also in question, where (as before he had done in court) he did, with tears, acknowledge and bewail his covetous and corrupt heart, yet making some excuse for many of the particulars, which were charged upon him, as partly by pretence of ignorance of the true price of some wares, and chiefly by being misled by some false principles, as, 1. That, if a man lost in one commodity, he might help himself in the price of another. 2. That if, through want of skill or other occasion, his commodity cost him more than the price of the market in England, he might then sell it for more than the price of the market in New England, &c. These things gave occasion to Mr. Cotton, in his publick exercise the next lecture day, to lay open the errour of such false principles, and to give some rules of direction in the case.

Some false principles were these:

1. That a man might sell as dear as he can, and buy as cheap as he can.

---

[20] John Winthrop, *The History of New England from 1630 to 1649* (Boston, 1853), I, 313–317.

2. If a man lose by casualty of sea, &c. in some of his commodities, he may raise the price of the rest.

3. That he may sell as he bought, though he paid too dear, &c. and though the commodity be fallen, &c.

4. That, as a man may take the advantage of his own skill or ability, so he may of another's ignorance or necessity.

5. Where one gives time for payment, he is to take like recompense of one as of another.

The rules for trading were these:

1. A man may not sell above the current price, i.e. such a price as is usual in the time and place, and as another (who knows the worth of the commodity) would give for it, if he had occasion to use it; as that is called current money, which every man will take, &c.

2. When a man loseth in his commodity for want of skill, &c. he must look at it as his own fault or cross, and therefore must not lay it upon another.

3. Where a man loseth by casualty of sea, or, &c., it is a loss cast upon himself by providence, and he may not ease himself of it by casting it upon another; for so a man should seem to provide against all providences, &c. that he should never lose; but where there is a scarcity of the commodity, there men may raise their price; for now it is a hand of God upon the commodity, and not the person.

5. A man may not ask any more for his commodity than his selling price, as Ephron to Abraham, the land is worth thus much.

The causes being debated by the church, some were earnest to have him excommunicated; but the most thought an admonition would be sufficient. Mr. Cotton opened the causes, which required excommunication, out of that in 1 Cor. 5. 11. The point now in question was, whether these actions did declare him to be such a covetous person, &c. Upon which he showed, that it is neither the habit of covetousness, (which is in every man in some degree,) nor simply the act, that declares a man to be such but when it appears,

that a man sins against his conscience, or the very light of nature, and when it appears in a man's whole conversation. But Mr. Keaine did not appear to be such, but rather upon an errour in his judgment, being led by false principles; and, beside, he is otherwise liberal, as in his hospitality, and in church communion, &c. So, in the end, the church consented to an admonition.

21

Merchant Keayne was too much of a Puritan to accept these penalties without protest. He waited for revenge until his deathbed; then he penned a famous will, a lusty defense of his own conduct and a stirring protest against the economic restrictions of Massachusetts' rulers.[21]

I did not then, nor dare not now, go about to justify all my actions. I know God is righteous and does all upon just grounds, though men may mistake in their grounds and proceedings. Councils have erred and courts may err, and a faction may be too hard and outvote the better or more discerning part. I know the errors of my life; the failings in my trade and otherwise have been many. Therefore, from God it was most just; though it had been much more severe I dare not so open my mouth against it, nor never did, as I remember, but justify him. Yet I dare not say, nor did I ever think (so far as I can call to mind), that the censure was just and righteous from men. Was the price of a bridle, not for taking but only asking 2s. for it which cost here 20d., such a heinous sin, [such bridles] which have since been commonly sold and are still for 2s 6d. and 3s. or more, though worse in kind? . . .

Was the selling of 6-penny nails for 8d. per pound and 8-penny nails for 10d. per pound such a crying and oppressive sin? Though as I remember it was above two years before he that bought them paid me for them; and [they were] not paid for, if I forget not, when he made that quarreling

[21] *A Report of the Record Commissioners of the City of Boston* (Boston, 1856), Doc. No. 150, pp. 27–35.

exception and unrighteous complaint in the court against me (he then being of the court himself), as if I had altered and corrupted my book in adding more to the price than I had set down for them at first delivery. Which if I had set down 8d. for that after 2 years forbearance, which I would have sold for 7d. if he had paid me presently, I think it had been a more honest act in me than it was in him that promised, or at least pretended, to pay me presently, that he might get them at a lower price than a man could well live upon, and when he had got my goods into his hands to keep me 2 or 3 years without my money, and though all that while there was no fault found at the prices but when he could for shame keep the money no longer. Yet he will requite it with a censure in the court.

For my own part, as I did ever think it an ungodly act in him, so I do think in my conscience that it had been more just in the court to have censured him than me for this thing though this was the chief crime alleged and most powerfully carried against me and, [though] other things were drawn in to make this the more probable and to help to make up a censure, as some farthing skeins of thread, etc. . . .

Now I leave it to the world to judge, or any impartial man or any that hath understanding in trade, whether this was a just offense, or so crying a sin that I had such cause to be so penitent for (this being the chief [charge] and pressed on with so great aggravation by my opposers), except it should be that my actions innocent in themselves were so misconstrued and I knew not how to help myself. Especially considering it was no oppressive price, but usual with others at that time to sell the like so, and since, for almost half as much more frequently (as I think all know), and yet both given and taken without exception, or at least without public complaint. . . .

It is true that in any things wherein I might justly take shame or sorrow to myself God inclined my heart not to withstand it. For he that hides his sins shall not prosper,

but he that confesses and forsakes them shall find mercy. In many this [things] we sin all, and who can say his heart is clean. Yet, for the chief of the things that was most urged against me in court and for which the sentence [was] passed against me (as the gold buttons, the bridle, the nails, the falsifying of my books), I did justify and stand to maintain that they was evident mistakes and that I was wronged. . . . I had no cause of penitence or confession of guilt except it was for that I had been so used and reproached about them against all equity. But, if they should have cast me out of the church 20 times for this, I should have chosen it rather than to have confessed myself guilty, for the satisfaction of any, wherein I knew myself (better than anyone else did) to be innocent.

22

Another type of restraint of trade developed out of the trade itself. As in all new countries, currency was in short supply. Repeated colonial attempts to print paper money met with vetoes in the Privy Council, which was more interested in protecting British creditors than in improving colonial trade. A spirited defense of the colonial point of view was written in 1724 by Governor William Burnet of New York:[22]

I am very sensible of the disadvantage I lye under in writing upon this argument, and the misfortune it is to any cause to have already appeared in an odious light, as I am but too well convinced is the case of paper money Acts in the Plantations, by your Lordships last words in your letter of the 17th of June—*That Bills for encreasing of Paper money will meet with no encouragement*—I hope your Lordships will not think it presumption in me even after this declaration to endeavor to give you a more favorable opinion of such Acts and if I go too far in this, it is owing to the encouragement your Lordships have given me by receiving what I have offered on all occasions in so kind a

---

[22] E. B. O'Callaghan (ed.), *Documents Relative to the Colonial History of the State of New York* (Albany, 1855), V, 736–738.

manner and admitting the best constructions that my weak Reasoning will bear

I have already in my letter of the 12th of May last used several Arguments to justify the Paper Act in New Jersey, and therein I observed how well the Bills of New York keep up their credit and the reasons why they have not fall'n in value as those of Carolina and New England and that under a good regulation these Acts are both of Service to the Trade of the Plantations and of great Britain, for which that I may not repeat I beg leave to refer to my said letter of the 12th of May last and desire your Lordships would again take into your consideration when you are to determine your opinion on this present Act.—

But there are many things there only hinted at which I shall now lay before your Lordships and in which I shall cheifly argue from what is to be gathered from experience in Great Britain itself from observing the nature of credit and the events it has under gone, and in this I hope I may be the more patiently heard because what experience I have was purchased at no very cheap rate

Credit ought to be supported if it is possible, both by *reason* and *common opinion*. Reason tho ever so strong will not always do alone in the Beginning if common opinion is against it but it will carry all before it at the long run: Common opinion or humor will generally do for a time without reason nay, against it But then it is often attended with vast mischeif and danger—Of this we have a fatal Instance in the famous south Sea Scheme, which being left to common opinion without any restraint has produced the most terrible effects possible. If there had been a possitive Law, making all Bargains —for South Sea Stock above some fixed Price as 150. void and making it a legal tender at 100 all these mischeifs would have been avoided but this would have been called *compulsive Paper Credit,* yet because in Reason it is worth so much as long as the Nation stands and because the Parliament has always kept their engagements all clamors against this would soon have blown over and

no enemies would have been found to it but Brokers

To make this appear it is enough to prove, that at the bottom all the present voluntary credit stands upon this very foundation at last & no other

It is very certain that there is no proportion between the Specie & the great quantity of Bank Bills and Bankers Notes. commonly current who lend their notes on the several Branches of Government Securitys and seldom at a Rate under *par* very often above *par* When the Government is safe this would do when there is any danger, Common opinion pulls down her own work & Bankers break in abundance, and the Bank itself is put to Extremitys. An Instance of this I remember at the time of the Preston affair— The Bank would have broke in a few days, if the victory there had not happened as soon as it did

And the Reason was plainly this because when they had paid away all their Specie they had nothing left but Exchequer Notes, and such other Securitys to exchange for their remaining Bank Notes and these would have been at such a discount that they must have broke, and compounded for such Payment at the Best

Thus it is plain that the foundation in Reason of the credit of the Bank it self, not to speak of Private Goldsmiths is the Government Security remaining at *Par* and yet the Parliament is so good as to provide an interest on these Exchequer Bills, and to pay the Bank so much more per cent for circulation whereas in fact when foul weather comes the Bank is a Staff of Reed and must lean on the Government to prop itself up and so increase the load instead of easing it

And this humour keeps up the imaginary value, when there is no real accasion for it; all Government Securities being at the same time commonly above *par* But upon any ill News the like Humor beats down all voluntary credit, in the same manner as it does Exchequer Bills &c and really carries the General Discredit as much further than it ought as it had advanced credit beyond its reasonable bounds before and if once the Bank had broke, then all this would have appeared to a demonstration . . .

From all which I beg leave to conclude, that is not the names things get for the present but the real nature of them, that will be found to hold against all events & that in the instance of Paper money where it is regulated by just Laws and where the Publick have not acted contrary to them their credit is in reason better established than the credit of any private Persons or Society and that the method used to catch the common opinion of mankind by offering them their money when they please is nothing but a fashionable Bubble which People are every day sufferers by when a Banker breaks & that even the best founded Societys can not maintain their Credit when there is the Greatest need of them. But that all Credit finally centers in the Security of ye Governm^t

I take the liberty further to observe to your Lordships on how many occasions the Government of Great Britain has found it impracticable to raise all the money wanted within the year from whence all the present debts of the nation have arisen: The same necessity lyes often upon the Plantations where frequently a sum of ready money is wanted, which it would be intollerable Tax to raise at once, and therefore they are forced to imitate the Parliament at home, in anticipating upon remote funds. And as there is no Bank nor East India company nor even private subscribers capable of lending the Province the money they want at least without demanding the extravagant Interest of 8 Pr Cent which is the common Interest here, but would ruin the publick to pay since this is a Case there is no possible way left to make distant funds provide ready money, when it is necessarily wanted, but making paper Bills to be sunk by such funds. Without this Carolina would have been ruined by their Indian War Boston could not now support theirs nor could any of the Provinces have furnished such considerable Sums to the Expeditions against Canada Nor could at present any of the necessary repairs of this Fort be provided for, nor the arrears of the Revenue be discharged, which is done by this Act in a Tax to be levyed in 4 years nor indeed any publick Service readily and sufficiently effected

And I may add one thing more that this manner of compulsive credit does in fact keep up its value here and that it occasions much more Trade and business than would be without it and that more Specie is exported to England by reason of these Paper Bills than could be if there was no circulation but of Specie for which reason all the merchants here seem now well satisfied with it

23

Particularly upsetting to English merchants was the American habit of selling tobacco, fish, and cereals wherever prices were highest rather than within the confines of empire. The enormity of this crime is difficult to comprehend; the evolution of British colonial policy can be understood only against the background of the mercantilistic concepts which then governed economic action. These were outlined by a seventeenth-century economist, Thomas Mun, in England's Treasure by Forraign Trade *(1664):*[23]

The revenue or stock of a Kingdom by which it is provided of forraign wares is either *Natural* or *Artificial*. The Natural wealth is so much only as can be spared from our own use and necessities to be exported unto strangers. The Artificial consists in our manufactures and industrious trading with forraign commodities, concerning which I will set down such particulars as may serve for the cause we have in hand.

1. First, although this Realm be already exceeding rich by nature, yet might it be much encreased by laying the waste grounds (which are infinite) into such employments as should no way hinder the present revenues of other manured lands, but hereby to supply our selves and prevent the importations of Hemp, Flax, Cordage, Tobacco, and divers other things which now we fetch from strangers to our great impoverishing.

---

[23] Thomas Mun, *England's Treasure by Foreign Trade* (New York, 1903 ed.), pp. 9–12.

2. We may likewise diminish our importations, if we would soberly refrain from excessive consumption of forraign wares in our diet and rayment, with such often change of fashions as is used, so much the more to encrease the waste and charge; which vices at this present are more notorious amongst us than in former ages. Yet might they easily be amended by enforcing the observation of such good laws as are strictly practised in other Countries against the said excesses; where likewise by commanding their own manufactures to be used, they prevent the coming in of others, without prohibition, or offence to strangers in their mutual commerce.

3. In our exportations we must not only regard our own superfluities, but also we must consider our neighbours necessities, that so upon the wares which they cannot want, nor yet be furnished thereof elsewhere, we may (besides the vent of the Materials) gain so much of manufacture as we can, and also endeavour to sell them dear, so far forth as the high price cause not a less vent in the quantity. But the superfluity of our commodities which strangers use, and may also have the same from other Nations, or may abate their vent by the use of some such like wares from other places, and with little inconvenience; we must in this case strive to sell as cheap as possible we can, rather than to lose the utterance of such wares. For we have found of late years by good experience, that being able to sell our Cloth cheap in Turkey, we have greatly encreased the vent thereof, and the *Venetians* have lost as much in the utterance of theirs in those Countreys, because it is dearer. And on the other side a few years past, when by the excessive price of Wools our Cloth was exceeding dear, we lost at the least half our clothing for forraign parts, which since is no otherwise (well neer) recovered again than by the great fall of price for Wools and Cloth. We find that twenty five in the Hundred less in the price of these and some other Wares, to the loss of private mens revenues, may raise above fifty upon the hundred in

the quantity vented to the benefit of the publique. For when Cloth is dear, other Nations doe presently practise clothing, and we know they want neither art nor materials to this performance. But when by cheapness we drive them from this employment, and so in time obtain our dear price again, then do they also use their former remedy. So that by these alterations we learn, that it is in vain to expect a greater revenue of our wares than their condition will afford, but rather it concerns us to apply our endeavours to the times with care and diligence to help our selves the best we may, by making our cloth and other manufactures without deceit, which will encrease their estimation and use.

4. The value of our exportations likewise may be much advanced when we perform it ourselves in our own Ships, for then we get only not the price of our wares as they are worth here, but also the Merchants gains, the charges of ensurance, and fraight to carry them beyond the seas. As for example, if the *Italian* Merchants should come hither in their own shipping to fetch our Corn, our red Herrings or the like, in this case the Kingdom should have ordinarily but 25. s. for a quarter of Wheat, and 20. s. for a barrel of red herrings, whereas if we carry these wares ourselves into *Italy* upon the said rates, it is likely that wee shall obtain fifty shillings for the first, and forty shillings for the last, which is a great difference in the utterance or vent of the Kingdoms stock. And although it is true that the commerce ought to be free to strangers to bring in and carry out at their pleasure, yet nevertheless in many places the exportation of victuals and munition are either prohibited, or at least limited to be done onely by the people and Shipping of those places where they abound.

5. The frugal expending likewise of our own natural wealth might advance much yearly to be exported unto strangers; and if in our rayment we will be prodigal, yet let this be done with our own materials and manufactures, as Cloth, Lace, Imbroideries, Cutworks and the like, where the excess of

the rich may be the employment of the poor, whose labours notwithstanding of this kind, would be more profitable for the Commonwealth, if they were done to the use of Strangers.

6. The Fishing in his Majesties seas of *England, Scotland* and *Ireland* is our natural wealth, and would cost nothing but labour, which the *Dutch* bestow willingly, and thereby draw yearly a very great profit to themselves by serving many places of Christendom with our Fish, for which they return and supply their wants both of forraign Wares and Mony, besides the multitudes of Mariners and Shipping, which hereby are maintain'd, whereof a long discourse might be made to shew the particular manage of this important business. Our Fishing plantation likewise in *New-England, Virginia, Groenland,* the *Summer Islands* and the *New-found-land,* are of the like nature, affording much wealth and employments to maintain a great number of poor, and to encrease our decaying trade.

7. A Staple or Magazin for forraign Corn, Indico, Spices, Raw-silks, Cotton wool or any other commodity whatsoever, to be imported will encrease Shipping, Trade, Treasure, and the Kings customes, by exporting them again where need shall require, which course of Trading, hath been the chief means to raise *Venice, Genoa,* the *low-Countreys,* with some others; and for such a purpose *England* stands most commodiously, wanting nothing to this performance but our own diligence and endeavour.

24

But New England was developing a set of interests that did not fit into the pattern outlined by Mun. Producing few commodities that could be marketed directly in England, the Yankees were forced to sell their grain and fish in the West Indies, obtaining in return molasses, sugar, and gold. Technically commerce with the French and Spanish islands was restricted, especially after the Molasses Act of 1733 imposed heavy duties on imports from those countries. Yet New Englanders blithely continued to navigate between Boston, Santo Domingo, and Africa,

until any interference with the triangular trade would have upset the section's economy. Their stubborn insistence on the right to trade where they pleased was voiced by the Rhode Island legislature in 1764 in a "Remonstrance to the Board of Trade":[24]

The colony of Rhode Island included not a much larger extent of territory than about thirty miles square; and of this, a great part is a barren soil, not worth the expense of cultivation; the number of souls in it, amount to forty-eight thousand, of which the two seaport towns of Newport and Providence, contain near one-third. The colony hath no staple commodity for exportation, and does not raise provisions sufficient for its own consumption; yet, the goodness of its harbors, and its convenient situation for trade, agreeing with the spirit and industry of the people, hath in some measure supplied the deficiency of its natural produce, and provided the means of subsistence to its inhabitants.

By a moderate calculation, the quantity of British manufactures and other goods of every kind imported from Great Britain, and annually consumed in this colony, amount at least to £120,000, sterling, part of which is imported directly into the colony; but as remittances are more easily made to the neighbouring province of the Massachusetts Bay, Pennsylvania and New York, than to Great Britain, a considerable part is purchased from them.

This sum of £120,000, sterling, may be considered as a debt due from the colony, the payment of which is the great object of every branch of commerce, carried on by its inhabitants, and exercises the skill and invention of every trader.

The only articles produced in the colony, suitable for a remittance to Europe, consist of some flax seed and oil, and some few ships built for sale; the whole amounting to about £5,000, sterling, per annum. The other articles furnished by the colony for exportation, are some lumber, cheese and horses; the

---

[24] *Records of the Colony of Rhode Island and Providence Plantations, in New England* (Providence, 1861), VI, 379–380.

whole amount of all which together bears but a very inconsiderable proportion to the debt contracted for British goods. It can therefore be nothing but commerce which enables us to pay it.

As there is no commodity raised in the colony suitable for the European market, but the few articles aforementioned; and as the other goods raised for exportation, will answer at no market but in the West Indies, it necessarily follows that the trade thither must be the foundation of all our commerce; and it is undoubtedly true, that solely from the prosecution of this trade with the other branches that are pursued in consequence of it, arises the ability to pay for such quantities of British goods.

It appears from the custom house books, in Newport, that from January, 1763, to January, 1764, there were one hundred and eighty-four sail of vessels bound on foreign voyages; that is, to Europe, Africa and the West Indies; and three hundred and fifty-two sail of vessels employed in the coasting trade; that is, between Georgia and Newfoundland, inclusive; which, with the fishing vessels, are navigated by at least twenty-two hundred seamen.

Of these foreign vessels, about one hundred and fifty are annually employed in the West India trade, which import into this colony about fourteen thousand hogsheads of molasses; whereof, a quantity, not exceeding twenty-five hundred hogsheads, come from all the English islands together.

It is this quantity of molasses which serves as an engine in the hands of the merchant to effect the great purpose of paying for British manufactures; for part of it is exported to the Massachusetts Bay, to New York and Pennsylvania, to pay for British goods, for provisions and for many articles which compose our West India cargoes; and part to the other colonies, southward of these last mentioned, for such commodities as serve for a remittance immediately to Europe; such as rice, naval stores, &c., or such as are necessary to enable us to carry on our commerce; the remainder (besides what is consumed by the inhabitants) is distilled into rum, and exported to the coast of Africa; nor will this trade to Africa appear to be of little consequence, if the following account of it be considered.

Formerly, the negroes upon the coast were supplied with large quantities of French brandies; but in the year 1723, some merchants in this colony first introduced the use of rum there, which, from small beginnings soon increased to the consumption of several thousand hogsheads yearly; by which the French are deprived of the sale of an equal quantity of brandy; and as the demand for rum is annually increasing upon the coast, there is the greatest reason to think, that in a few years, if this trade be not discouraged, the sale of French brandies there will be entirely destroyed. This little colony, only, for more than thirty years past, has annually sent about eighteen sail of vessels to the coast, which have carried about eighteen hundred hogsheads of rum, together with a small quantity of provisions and some other articles, which have been sold for slaves, gold dust, elephants' teeth, camwood, &c. The slaves have been sold in the English islands, in Carolina and Virginia, for bills of exchange, and the other articles have been sent to Europe; and by this trade alone, remittances have been made from this colony to Great Britain, to the value of about £40,000, yearly; and this rum, carried to the coast, is so far from prejudicing the British trade thither, that it may be said rather to promote it; for as soon as our rum vessels arrive, they exchange away some of the rum with the traders from Britain, for a quantity of dry goods, with which each of them sort their cargoes to their mutual advantage.

Besides this method of remittance by the African trade, we often get bills of exchange from the Dutch colonies of Surinam, Barbice, &c.; and this happens when the sales of our cargoes amount to more than a sufficiency to load with molasses; so that, in this particular, a considerable benefit arises from the molasses trade, for these bills being paid in Holland, are the means of drawing from that republic so much cash yearly, into Great Britain, as these bills amount to.

From this deduction of the course of our trade, which is founded in exact truth, it appears that the whole trading stock of this colony, in its beginning, progress and end is uniformly directed to the payment of the debt contracted by the importation of British goods; and it also clearly appears, that without this trade, it would have been and always will be, utterly impossible for the inhabitants of this colony to subsist themselves, or to pay for any considerable quantity of British goods.

25

The economic facts of life as the colonists were coming to understand them ultimately received theoretical support from the ideas of the Enlightenment. The economic implications of the Enlightenment were emphasized by many scholars before they were given classic form by Adam Smith, the English economist, in The Wealth of Nations *(1776). Smith argued against the monopolies typical of his day and pleaded for a world in which the sole economic controls were provided by what he considered natural laws such as supply and demand:*[25]

As every individual . . . endeavours as much as he can both to employ his capital in the support of domestic industry, and so to direct that industry that its produce may be of the greatest value; every individual necessarily labours to render the annual revenue of the society as great as he can. He generally, indeed, neither intends to promote the public interest, nor knows how much he is promoting it. By preferring the support of domestic to that of foreign industry, he intends only his own security; and by directing that industry in such a manner as its produce may be of the greatest value, he intends only his own gain, and he is in this, as in many other cases, led by an invisible hand to promote an end which was no part of his intention. Nor is it always the worse for the society that it was no part of it. By

pursuing his own interest he frequently promotes that of the society more effectually than when he really intends to promote it. I have never known much good done by those who affected to trade for the public good. It is an affectation, indeed, not very common among merchants, and very few words need be employed in dissuading them from it.

What is the species of domestic industry which his capital can employ, and of which the produce is likely to be of the greatest value, every individual, it is evident, can, in his local situation, judge much better than any statesman or lawgiver can do for him. The statesman, who should attempt to direct private people in what manner they ought to employ their capitals, would not only load himself with a most unnecessary attention, but assume an authority which could safely be trusted, not only to no single person, but to no council or senate whatever, and which would nowhere be so dangerous as in the hands of a man who had folly and presumption enough to fancy himself fit to exercise it.

To give the monopoly of the home-market to the produce of domestic industry, in any particular art or manufacture, is in some measure to direct private people in what manner they ought to employ their capitals, and must, in almost all cases, be either a useless or a hurtful regulation. If the produce of domestic can be brought there as cheap as that of foreign industry, the regulation is evidently useless. If it cannot, it must generally be hurtful. It is the maxim of every prudent master of a family, never to attempt to make at home what it will cost him more to make than to buy. The taylor does not attempt to make his own shoes, but buys them of the shoemaker. The shoemaker does not attempt to make his own clothes, but employs a taylor. The farmer attempts to make neither the one nor the other, but employs those different artificers. All of them find it for their interest to employ their whole industry in a way in which they have some advantage over their neighbours, and to pur-

[25] Adam Smith, *The Wealth of Nations* (New York, 1937, The Modern Library ed.), pp. 423–463.

chase with a part of its produce, or what is the same thing, with the price of a part of it, whatever else they have occasion for.

What is prudence in the conduct of every private family, can scarce be folly in that of a great kingdom. If a foreign country can supply us with a commodity cheaper than we ourselves can make it, better buy it of them with some part of the produce of our own industry, employed in a way in which we have some advantage. The general industry of the country, being always in proportion to the capital which employs it, will not thereby be diminished, no more than that of the above-mentioned artificers; but only left to find out the way in which it can be employed with the greatest advantage. It is certainly not employed to the greatest advantage, when it is thus directed towards an object which it can buy cheaper than it can make. The value of its annual produce is certainly more or less diminished, when it is thus turned away from producing commodities evidently of more value than the commodity which it is directed to produce. According to the supposition, that commodity could be purchased from foreign countries cheaper than it can be made at home. It could, therefore, have been purchased with a part only of the commodities, or, what is the same thing, with a part only of the price of the commodities, which the industry employed by an equal capital would have produced at home, had it been left to follow its natural course. The industry of the country, therefore, is thus turned away from a more, to a less advantageous employment, and the exchangeable value of its annual produce, instead of being increased, according to the intention of the lawgiver, must necessarily be diminished by every such regulation. . . .

Nations have been taught that their interest consisted in beggaring all their neighbours. Each nation has been made to look with an invidious eye upon the prosperity of all the nations with which it trades, and to consider their gain as its own loss. Commerce, which ought naturally to be, among

nations, as among individuals, a bond of union and friendship, has become the most fertile source of discord and animosity. The capricious ambition of kings and ministers has not, during the present and the preceding century, been more fatal to the repose of Europe, than the impertinent jealousy of merchants and manufacturers. The violence and injustice of the rulers of mankind is an ancient evil, for which, I am afraid, the nature of human affairs can scarce admit of a remedy. But the mean rapacity, the monopolizing spirit of merchants and manufacturers, who neither are, nor ought to be, the rulers of mankind, though it cannot perhaps be corrected, may very easily be prevented from disturbing the tranquility of any body but themselves.

That it was the spirit of monopoly which originally both invented and propagated this doctrine, cannot be doubted; and they who first taught it were by no means such fools as they who believed it. In every country it always is and must be the interest of the great body of the people to buy whatever they want of those who sell it cheapest. The proposition is so very manifest, that it seems ridiculous to take any pains to prove it; nor could it ever have been called in question, had not the interested sophistry of merchants and manufacturers confounded the common sense of mankind. Their interest is, in this respect, directly opposite to that of the great body of the people. As it is the interest of the freemen of a corporation to hinder the rest of the inhabitants from employing any workmen but themselves, so it is the interest of the merchants and manufacturers of every country to secure to themselves the monopoly of the home market. Hence in Great Britain, and in most other European countries, the extraordinary duties upon almost all goods imported by alien merchants. Hence the high duties and prohibitions upon all those foreign manufactures which can come into competition with our own. Hence too the extraordinary restraints upon the importation of almost all sorts of goods from those countries with which the balance of trade is supposed to be disadvantageous; that is, from those against whom national animosity happens to be most violently inflamed.

The wealth of a neighbouring nation, however, though dangerous in war and politics, is certainly advantageous in trade. In a state of hostility it may enable our enemies to maintain fleets and armies superior to our own; but in a state of peace and commerce it must likewise enable them to exchange with us to a greater value, and to afford a better market, either for the immediate produce of our own industry, or for whatever is purchased with that produce. . . . The manufacturers of a rich nation, in the same manner, may no doubt be very dangerous rivals to those of their neighbours. This very competition, however, is advantageous to the great body of the people, who profit greatly besides by the good market which the great expence of such a nation affords them in every other way. . . . A nation that would enrich itself by foreign trade, is certainly most likely to do so when its neighbours are all rich, industrious, and commercial nations. . . . The modern maxims of foreign commerce, by aiming at the impoverishment of all our neighbours, so far as they are capable of producing their intended effect, tend to render that very commerce insignificant and contemptible. . . .

Consumption is the sole end and purpose of all production; and the interest of the producer ought to be attended to, only so far as it may be necessary for promoting that of the consumer. The maxim is so perfectly self-evident, that it would be absurd to attempt to prove it. But in the mercantile system, the interest of the consumer is almost constantly sacrificed to that of the producer; and it seems to consider production, and not consumption, as the ultimate end and object of all industry and commerce.

In the restraints upon the importation of all foreign commodities which can come into competition with those of our own growth, or manufacture, the interest of the home-consumer is evidently sacrificed to that of the producer. It is altogether for the benefit of the latter, that the former is obliged to pay that enhancement of price which this monopoly almost always occasions.

It is altogether for the benefit of the producer that bounties are granted upon the exportation of some of his productions. The home-consumer is obliged to pay, first, the tax which is necessary for paying the bounty, and secondly, the still greater tax which necessarily arises from the enhancement of the price of the commodity in the home market. . . .

But in the system of laws which has been established for the management of our American and West Indian colonies, the interest of the home-consumer has been sacrificed to that of the producer with a more extravagant profusion than in all our other commercial regulations. A great empire has been established for the sole purpose of raising up a nation of customers who should be obliged to buy from the shops of our different producers, all the goods with which these could supply them. For the sake of that little enhancement of price which this monopoly might afford our producers, the home-consumers have been burdened with the whole expence of maintaining and defending that empire. . . .

It cannot be very difficult to determine who have been the contrivers of this whole mercantile system; not the consumers, we may believe, whose interest has been entirely neglected; but the producers, whose interest has been so carefully attended to; and among this latter class our merchants and manufacturers have been by far the principal architects.

26

John R. Seeley, a late nineteenth-century British scholar, places the relations between the mother country and the colonies in a different historical perspective:[26]

It is the custom to describe the old colonies as sacrificed to the mother-country. We

[26] John R. Seeley, *The Expansion of England* (London, 1883), Course I, Lecture IV, pp. 76–80.

must be careful not to admit that statement without qualification. It is supposed for instance that the revolt of our own American colonies was provoked by the selfish treatment of our mother-country, which shackled their trade without rendering them any benefit in return for these restraints. This is far from being true. Between England and the American colonies there was a real interchange of services. England gave defence in return for trade-privileges. In the middle of the last century, at the time when the American quarrel began, it was perhaps rather the colonies than the mother-country that had fallen into arrear. We had been involved in two great wars mainly by our colonies, and the final breach was provoked not so much by the pressure of England upon the colonies as by that of the colonies upon England. If we imposed taxes upon them, it was to meet the debt which we had incurred in their behalf, and we saw with no unnatural bitterness that we had ourselves enabled our colonies to do without us, by destroying for their interest the French power in North America.

Still it was true of the old colonial system in general that it placed the colony in the position, not so much of a state in federation, as of a conquered state. Some theory of the kind is evidently implied in the language which is commonly used. We speak of the colonial *possessions* of England or of Spain. Now in what sense can one population be spoken of as the possession of another population? The expression almost seems to imply slavery, and at any rate it is utterly inappropriate, if it merely means that the one population is subject to the same Government as the other. At the bottom of it certainly was the idea that the colony was an estate which was to be worked for the benefit of the mother-country.

The relation of Spain to its colonies had become a type which other states kept before their eyes. A native population reduced to serfdom, in some parts driven to compulsory labour by caciques turned into state-officials, in other parts exterminated by overwork and then replaced by negroes; an imperious mother-country drawing from the colony a steady revenue, and ruling it through an artful mechanism of division, by which the settlers were held in check by the priesthood and by a serf-population treated paternally that it might be available for that purpose; such was the typical colonial system. It was wholly unfit to be a model to such a colony as New England, which paid no revenue, where there were neither subject Indians nor mines of gold and silver. Nevertheless governments could not afford to forget the precedent of profitable colonies, and I find Charles II. appealing to it in 1663. It became an established principle that a colony was a possession.

Now it is essentially barbaric that one community should be treated as the property of another and the fruits of its industry confiscated, not in return for benefits conferred, but by some absolute right whether of conquest or otherwise. Even where such a relation rests avowedly upon conquest it is too immoral to last long except in a barbarous state of manners. Thus for example we may have acquired India by conquest, but we cannot and do not hold it for our own pecuniary advantage. We draw no tribute from it; it is not to us a profitable investment; we should be ashamed to acknowledge that in governing it we in any way sacrificed its interest to our own. *A fortiori* then it is barbaric to apply such a theory to colonies, for it is to treat one's own countrymen, those with whom we have no concern at all except on the ground of kindred, as if they were conquered enemies, or rather in a way in which a civilized nation cannot treat even conquered enemies. And probably even in the old colonial system such a theory was not consciously and deliberately adopted. But since in the sixteenth century there was no scruple in applying it to conquered dependencies, and since the colonies of Spain were in a certain sense conquered dependencies, we can understand that unconsciously, unintentionally the barbaric principle crept into her colonial system, and that it lurked there and poisoned it in later times. We can understand too how the example of Spain and the precedents set by her influenced the other European States, Holland, France and England, which entered upon the career of colonisation a century later.

In the case of some of these States, for example France, the result of this theory was that the mother-country exercised an iron authority over her colonies. In Canada the French settlers were subject to a multitude of rigid regulations, from which they would have been free if they had remained in France. Nothing of the kind certainly can be said of the English colonies. They were subject to certain fixed restrictions in the matter of trade, but apart from these they were absolutely free. Carrying their nationality with them, they claimed everywhere the rights of Englishmen. It has been observed by Mr. Merivale that the old colonial system admitted no such thing as the modern Crown Colony, in which Englishmen are governed administratively without representative assemblies. In the old system assemblies were not formally instituted, but grew up of themselves, because it was the nature of Englishmen to assemble. Thus the old historian of the colonies, Hutchinson, writes under the year 1619, "This year a House of Burgesses *broke out* in Virginia." And assuredly the Home Government in those times did not sin by too much interference. So completely were the colonies left to themselves, that some of them, especially those of New England, were from the very beginning for the most practical purposes independent States. As early as 1665, only forty years after the first settlement and a hundred years before the Declaration of Independence, I find that Massachusetts did not regard itself as practically subject to England. "They say," writes a Commissioner, "that so long as they pay the fifth of all gold and silver, according to the terms of the Charter, they are not obliged to the King but by civility."

Thus our old colonial system was not practically at all tyrannous, and when the breach came the grievances of which the Americans complained, though perfectly real, were smaller than ever before or since led to such mighty consequences. The misfortune of that system was not that it interfered too much, but that such interference as it admitted was of an invidious kind. It claimed very little, but what it did claim was unjust. It gave unbounded liberty except in one department, namely trade, and in that department it interfered to fine the colonists for the benefit of the home traders. Now this was to put the mother-country in a false position. It put her forward as claiming to treat the colonies as a possession, as an estate to be worked for the benefit of those Englishmen who remained at home. No claim could be more invidious. If it was not quite the claim that a master makes upon a slave, it was at least similar to that which an absentee landlord makes upon tenants in whom he takes no further interest, and yet even the absentee landlord, if he gives nothing else, does at least give the use of land which was really his own. But what—a Massachusetts colonist might say—has England given to us that she should have this perpetual mortgage on our industry? The Charter of James I. allowed us the use of lands which James I. never saw and which did not belong to him, lands too which, without any Charter, we might perhaps have occupied ourselves without opposition.

27

A recent student of the question of imperial restraint on colonial trade argues with impressive evidence that the famous Acts of Trade and Navigation were not as burdensome upon the colonies as commonly supposed:[27]

Were the navigation and trade laws so generally burdensome upon the colonies as to interfere with their development, and thus produce general poverty and distress? Again the answer must be negative; just the oppo-

---

[27] Oliver M. Dickerson, *The Navigation Acts and the American Revolution* (Philadelphia, 1951), pp. 52–53, 55–56. Reprinted with the permission of the publisher, the University of Pennsylvania Press.

site condition existed. The colonies were prosperous and wages of labor were admittedly higher in the continental colonies than elsewhere in the world.

Population in continental America was doubling every twenty-five years, while in England it was scarcely doubling in a century. In fact the population of England seems to have doubled only once from 1066 to 1600, and again by about 1760, although a very marked increase in population was to characterize the reign of George III. In no other section of the world was there a white population expanding from natural increase so rapidly as in continental America. Marriages occurred early and families were large. The British colonies on the continent were attractive to emigrants, especially from the British Isles, and there are numerous references in the British periodicals, published in the decade, 1765 to 1775, to artisans of all kinds migrating to the new world.

Another measure of their prosperity was the expansion of trade that had occurred during the eighteenth century. Other evidences of wealth were the multiplying educational institutions, churches, newspapers, magazines, and other publications. Many of the finest specimens of colonial church architecture date from the period just before the Revolution.

The wealth acquired by American merchants and planters was a real cause of jealousy on the part of residents in the mother country. There had grown up in America a new race of untitled nobility with estates and palaces that compared favorably with the possessions of the titled classes in England. Their houses were not only well, but even luxuriously, furnished. Their consumption of British and European goods was not limited to necessities, but included luxuries of all kinds. The best evidence of this is the elaborate offerings of goods, including finery of all kinds for both men and women, found in the extensive advertisements in the newspapers of the time. The population of the seaboard was no longer clothed in homespun. Many men wore silk and velvet regularly.

Joseph Warren had on his usual silk waistcoat when he was killed at Bunker Hill.

One of the best tests of real prosperity is the rapidity with which a population can sink its public debts following a war. The French and Indian War had been a real world contest so far as the British Empire was concerned. Colonial exertion on the part of the northern colonists, especially, had been on a scale not unlike that of Canada and Australia in the last world war. Many of the colonies levied heavy taxes during the war, and came out with large debts. The total colonial debt according to Charles Lloyd, who prepared the statistical data for the Stamp Act, was £2,600,000. Yet this was sunk so rapidly that in 1765 it was estimated that only £767,000 remained, and the greater part of that would be sunk by 1767.

The estimate of the time within which the colonies could extinguish their remaining obligations was too optimistic; but past accomplishments made a profound impression upon people in England, who could not hope to reduce their own national debt to the level of 1754 in less than a generation.

The ability of the colonies to sink their heavy war debts at the rate of about twenty per cent a year was a startling performance to thoughtful Englishmen. . . .

British officers who served in America were struck by the vast real wealth here: the number of horses, cattle, hogs, farms, thriving cities, bountiful food supplies, and the lavish scale of living they found everywhere in the older parts of the country. Certainly they saw no evidences that the commercial system was reducing the Americans to poverty. On the contrary, they saw evidences of a people acquiring wealth and property more rapidly than elsewhere, with a vision of becoming the richest and most powerful nation in the world. The wealth and prosperity of the Americans was probably one of the causes of the Revolution. It excited both the envy and the fear of some British citizens, and led them to support the taxation policy. It also fired the imaginations of Americans, and led them to think and talk in terms of the vast empire that they conceived would develop here in the next century.

American and British writers prophesied that within half a century the population of the continental colonies and its resultant military and naval strength would exceed that of England. The realization of this fact was one of the reasons for the attempted imperial reorganization between 1763 and 1770, and was largely responsible for serious thinkers abandoning plans for a consolidated imperial legislature made up of representatives from the dependencies as well as the British Isles. Charles Lloyd, Grenville's chief financial lieutenant, urged in 1767 that force should be used to execute the taxation program because, if the Americans were not forced to submit to the authority of Parliament then, their growing strength would make any successful attempts in the future impossible.

No case can be made out for the Navigation Acts as a cause of the Revolution on the grounds that such laws were economically oppressive and were steadily reducing the Americans to a condition of hopeless poverty. It is true that evidences of hard times in the colonies may be found; but such conditions were periodic and were preceded and followed by other periods of overtrading, extravagance, and luxury. There was unquestionably high taxation in some of the colonies during and after the French and Indian War. In places there were price readjustments due to deflation and the termination of large governmental activities. Such conditions were not evenly distributed. There were times when merchants and newspaper publishers complained of slow collections; but such conditions can be found in any region where credit is easy, and they can also be found at times in even the most prosperous countries. The evidence indicates far less depression in the colonies than in the home country in the same years.

IV

The Age of Revolution

The Enlightenment prepared the Western world for revolution, and stirring events kept the Atlantic basin in turmoil during the waning years of the eighteenth century. In America, in France, and in Latin America, popular uprisings toppled monarchs from thrones or secured independence for colonial peoples. Each rebellion was motivated by the desire for greater liberty—liberty of political, economic, and social action which the philosophers of the Enlightenment proclaimed as every man's natural right. Arms alone could not achieve the coveted objective; if men were to live together they must submit to some degree of authority. How could authority be reconciled with freedom? The search for that magic formula precipitated the American colonists into revolution; victory involved them in a continuing search for solutions. The revolutionary generation explored the problems of government, of authority and freedom, of liberty and social control.

CLASH OF AUTHORITY AND LIBERTY

1

An extreme statement of the case for the divine right of kings to rule over their subjects is contained in a speech made by King James I to Parliament in 1609. It serves as a useful reminder of the vast changes that took place in the attitudes of men between that date and 1776:[1]

The state of monarchy is the supremest thing upon earth: for kings are not only God's lieutenants upon earth, and sit upon God's throne, but even by God himself they are called gods. . . .

Kings are justly called gods, for that they exercise a manner or resemblance of Divine power upon earth: for if you will consider the attributes of God, you shall see how they agree in the person of a king. God hath power to create, or destroy, make, or unmake at His pleasure, to give life, or send death, to judge all, and to be judged nor account-

able to none: to raise low things, and to make high things low at His pleasure, and to God are both soul and body due. And the like power have kings: they make and unmake their subjects: they have power of raising, and casting down: of life, and death: judges over all their subjects, and in all causes, and yet accountable to none but God only. They have power to exalt low things, and abase high things, and make of their subjects like men at the chess; a pawn to take a bishop or a knight, and to cry up, or down any of their subjects, as they do their money. And to the king is due both the affection of the soul and the service of the body of his subjects. . . .

But now in these our times we are to distinguish between the state of kings in their first original, and between the state of settled kings and monarchs that do at this time govern in civil kingdoms: for even as God, during the time of the Old Testament, spake by oracles, and wrought by miracles; yet how soon it pleased him to settle a church which was bought, and redeemed by the blood of his only son Christ, then was there

---

[1] James I, *Works* (London, 1616), pp. 529–531.

97

a cessation of both; He ever after governing His people and church within the limits of His revealed will. So in the first original of kings, whereof some had their beginning by conquest, and some by election of the people, their wills at that time served for law; yet how soon kingdoms began to be settled in civility and policy, then did kings set down their minds by laws, which are properly made by the king only; but at the rogation of the people, the king's grant being obtained thereunto. And so the king became to be *Lex loquens* [a speaking law], after a sort, binding himself by a double oath to the observation of the fundamental laws of his kingdom. . . . Therefore all kings that are not tyrants, or perjured, will be glad to bound themselves within the limits of their laws; and they that persuade them the contrary, are vipers, and pests, both against them and the Commonwealth. For it is a great difference between a king's government in a settled state, and what kings in their original power might do, . . . As for my part, I thank God, I have ever given good proof that I never had intention to the contrary; and I am sure to go to my grave with that reputation and comfort, that never king was in all his time more careful to have his laws duly observed, and himself to govern thereafter, than I.

I conclude then this point touching the power of kings, with this axiom of divinity, that as to dispute what God may do, is blasphemy; . . . so is it sedition in subjects, to dispute what a king may do in the height of his power; but just kings will ever be willing to declare what they will do, if they will not incur the curse of God. I will not be content that my power be disputed upon: but I shall ever be willing to make the reason appear of all my doings, and rule my actions according to my laws.

2

John Winthrop, following the logic of Calvin's theology, believed that magistrates were vested with divine authority. Winthrop, once under attack for his conduct while lieutenant governor of Massachusetts, lectured his fellow citizens and explained the divine rights of elected officials in a speech to the deputies in 1645:[2]

I am unwilling to stay you from your urgent affairs, yet give me leave (upon this special occasion) to speak a little more to this assembly. It may be of some good use, to inform and rectify the judgments of some of the people, and may prevent such distempers as have arisen amongst us. The great questions that have troubled the country, are about the authority of the magistrates and the liberty of the people. It is yourselves who have called us to this office, and being called by you, we have our authority from God, in way of an ordinance, such as hath the image of God eminently stamped upon it, the contempt and violation whereof hath been vindicated with examples of divine vengeance. I entreat you to consider, that when you choose magistrates, you take them from among yourselves, men subject to like passions as you are. Therefore when you see infirmities in us, you should reflect upon your own, and that would make you bear the more with us, and not be severe censurers of the failings of your magistrates, when you have continual experience of the like infirmities in yourselves and others.

We account him a good servant who breaks not his covenant. The covenant between you and us is the oath you have taken of us, which is to this purpose, that we shall govern you and judge your causes by the rules of God's laws and our own, according to our best skill. When you agree with a workman to build you a ship or house, etc., he undertakes as well for his skill as for his faithfulness, for it is his profession, and you pay him for both. But when you call one to be a magistrate, he doth not profess nor undertake to have sufficient skill for that office, nor can you furnish him with gifts, etc., therefore you must run the hazard of his skill and ability. But if he fail in faithfulness, which by his oath he is bound unto,

---

[2] John Winthrop, *The History of New England from 1630 to 1649* (Boston, 1853), II, 279–282.

that he must answer for. If it fall out that the case be clear to common apprehension, and the rule clear also, if he transgress here, the error is not in the skill, but in the evil of the will: it must be required of him. But if the case be doubtful, or the rule doubtful, to men of such understanding and parts as your magistrates are, if your magistrates should err here, yourselves must bear it.

3

Failure to solve the conflicting issues subsisting between concepts of liberty and authority is not surprising; English liberals had examined and debated the problem for centuries. At first they sought to achieve the goal by increasing parliamentary authority at the expense of the king. A climax was reached in the Glorious Revolution of 1688, which relegated the new monarchs, William and Mary, to a definitely subordinate role. The doctrine of parliamentary supremacy was expressed in a basic constitutional document emerging from the struggle, the Bill of Rights of 1689:[3]

1. That the pretended power of suspending laws, or the execution of laws, by regal authority, without consent of parliament, is illegal.

2. That the pretended power of dispensing with laws, or the execution of laws, by regal authority, as it hath been assumed and exercised of late, is illegal.

3. That the commission for erecting the late court of commissioners for ecclesiastical causes, and all other commissions and courts of like nature, are illegal and pernicious.

4. That levying money for or to the use of the crown by pretense of prerogative, without grant of parliament, for longer time or in other manner than the same is or shall be granted, is illegal.

5. That it is the right of the subjects to petition the king, and all commitments and prosecutions for such petitioning are illegal.

6. That the raising or keeping a standing army within the kingdom in time of peace, unless it be with consent of parliament, is against law.

7. That the subjects which are Protestants may have arms for their defense suitable to their conditions, and as allowed by law.

8. That election of members of parliament ought to be free.

9. That the freedom of speech, and debates or proceedings in parliament, ought not to be impeached or questioned in any court or place out of parliament.

10. That excessive bail ought not to be required, nor excessive fines imposed, nor cruel and unusual punishments inflicted.

11. That jurors ought to be duly impaneled and returned, and jurors which pass upon men in trials for high treason ought to be freeholders.

12. That all grants and promises of fines and forfeitures of particular persons before conviction are illegal and void.

13. And that for redress of all grievances, and for the amending, strengthening, and preserving of the laws, parliament ought to be held frequently.

And they do claim, demand, and insist upon all and singular the premises, as their undoubted rights and liberties; and that no declarations, judgments, doings, or proceedings, to the prejudice of the people in any of the said premises, ought in any wise to be drawn hereafter into consequence or example.

4

At times particular events in the American colonies mirrored the movement limiting absolutism and therefore the movement increasing greater individual and group freedom. One such memorable event occurred in 1735, when John Peter Zenger of New York, editor of the Weekly Journal, *was brought to trial for criticizing the tyrannical conduct of the governor. His lawyer, Andrew Hamilton of Philadelphia, admitted that his client had written the libelous remarks, then successfully urged the jury to agree with him that damning words were not "false, scandalous, and seditious." His plea became a landmark in the history of freedom of the press:[4]*

---

[3] Danby Pickering (ed.), *Statutes at Large* (Cambridge, 1764), IX, 68–69.

[4] John Peter Zenger, *The Trial of John Peter Zenger, of New-York, Printer* (London, 1765), pp. 42–46.

It is true in Times past it was a Crime to speak Truth, and in that terrible Court of Star-Chamber, many worthy and brave Men suffred for so doing; and yet even in that Court, and in those bad Times, a great and good Man durst say, what I hope will not be taken amiss of me to say in this Place, *to wit, the Practice of Informations for Libels is a Sword in the Hands of a wicked king and* [of] *an arrand Coward to cut down and destroy the innocent; the one cannot, because of his high station, and the other dares not, because of his Want of Courage, revenge himself in another Manner.*

Mr. ATTORNEY, Pray Mr. HAMILTON, have a Care what you say, don't go too far neither, I don't like those Liberties.

Mr. HAMILTON, Sure, Mr. Attorney, you won't make any Applications; all Men agree that we are governed by the best of Kings, and I cannot see the Meaning of Mr. Attorney's Caution. . . . May it please Your Honour, I was saying, That notwithstanding all the Duty and Reverence claimed by Mr. Attorney to Men in Authority, they are not exempt from observing the Rules of common Justice, either in their private or publick Capacities; the Laws of our Mother Country know no Exception. . . .

I hope to be pardon'd, Sir, for my Zeal upon this Occasion: It is an old and wise Caution, *That when our Neighbour's House is on Fire, We ought to take Care of our own.* For tho', blessed be God, I live in a Government where Liberty is well understood, and freely enjoy'd; yet Experience has shewn us all (I'm sure it has to me) that a bad Precedent in one Government, is soon set up for an Authority in another; and therefore I cannot but think it mine, and every Honest Man's Duty, that (while we pay all due Obedience to Men in Authority) we ought at the same Time to be upon our Guard against Power, wherever we apprehend that it may effect Ourselves or our Fellow-Subjects.

I am truly very unequal to such an Undertaking on many Accounts. And you see I labour under the Weight of many Years, and am born down with great Infirmities of Body; yet Old and Weak as I am, I should think it my Duty, if required, to go to the utmost Part of the land, where my Service cou'd be of any Use in assisting to quench the flame of Prosecutions upon Informations, set on Foot by the Government, to deprive a People of the Right of Remonstrating (and complaining too) of the arbitrary Attempts of Men in Power. Men who injure and oppress the People under their Administration provoke them to cry out and complain; and then make that very Complaint the foundation for new Oppressions and Prosecutions. . . . But to conclude; the Question before the Court and you, Gentlemen of the Jury, is not of small nor private Concern, it is not the Cause of a poor Printer, nor of *New York* alone, which you are now trying; No! It may in its Consequence, affect every Freeman that lives under a British Government on the Main of *America.* It is the best Cause. It is the Cause of Liberty; and I make no Doubt but your upright Conduct, this Day, will not only entitle you to the Love and Esteem of your Fellow-Citizens; but every Man, who prefers Freedom to a Life of Slavery, will bless and honour You, as Men who have baffled the Attempt of Tyranny; and by an impartial and uncorrupt Verdict, have laid a noble Foundation for securing to ourselves, our Posterity, and our Neighbours, That to which Nature and the Laws of our Country have given us a Right,—the Liberty—both of exposing and opposing arbitrary Power (in these Parts of the World, at least) by speaking and writing Truth.

5

Enlightenment doctrines permeated the American mind and prepared the way for revolution. Ministers and editors, particularly in New England, repeatedly told their audiences that resistance was justified whenever a ruler violated their natural rights to freedom of expression, freedom of worship, freedom of political action, and freedom of trade. Typical of these messages, later regarded by English officials as inflammatory, was a sermon preached by Jonathan Mayhew, pastor of the West Church in Boston, in January 1750:[5]

[5] John W. Thornton, *The Pulpit in the American Revolution* (Boston, 1860), pp. 83–88.

If we calmly consider the nature of the thing itself, nothing can well be imagined more directly contrary to common sense than to suppose that millions of people should be subjected to the arbitrary, precarious pleasure of one single man,—who has naturally no superiority over them in point of authority,—so that their estates, and everything that is valuable in life, and even their lives also, shall be absolutely at his disposal, if he happens to be wanton and capricious enough to demand them. What unprejudiced man can think that God made *all* to be thus subservient to the lawless pleasure and frenzy of *one*, so that it shall always be a sin to resist him? Nothing but the most plain and express revelation from heaven could make a sober, impartial man believe such a monstrous, unaccountable doctrine; and, indeed, the thing itself appears so shocking, so out of all proportion, that it may be questioned whether all the miracles that ever were wrought could make it credible that this doctrine really came from God. At present there is not the least syllable in Scripture which gives any countenance to it. The hereditary, indefeasible, divine right of kings, and the doctrine of non-resistance, which is built upon the supposition of such a right, are altogether as fabulous and chimerical as transubstantiation, or any of the most absurd reveries of ancient or modern visionaries. These notions are fetched neither from divine revelation nor human reason; and, if they are derived from neither of those sources, it is not much matter from whence they come or whither they go. Only it is a pity that such doctrines should be propagated in society, to raise factions and rebellions, as we see they have, in fact, been, both in the last and in the present reign. . . .

A people, really oppressed in a great degree by their sovereign, cannot well be insensible when they are so oppressed; and such a people—if I may alude to an ancient fable—have, like the hesperian fruit, a dragon for their protector and guardian. Nor would they have any reason to mourn if some Hercules should appear to dispatch him. For a nation thus abused to rise unani-

mously and resist their prince, even to the dethroning him, is not criminal, but a reasonable way of vindicating their liberties and just rights: it is making use of the means, and the only means, which God has put into their power for mutual and self defence. And it would be highly criminal in them not to make use of this means. It would be stupid tameness and unaccountable folly for whole nations to suffer *one* unreasonable, ambitious, and cruel man to wanton and riot in their misery. And in such a case, it would, of the two, be more rational to suppose that they that did not resist, than that they who did, would receive to themselves damnation.

PREFACE TO REVOLUTION

6

The victory of England over France in 1763 left a huge war debt and immensely increased responsibilities. These additional responsibilities were centered primarily in America, where a hostile French and Indian population constituted a threat of the renewal of war. The English need for revenue was real and immediate. Since much of the money would be spent in the defense of British territory in America, it seemed proper that a part of it should be collected there. When the "Sugar Act" was passed in 1764, George Grenville announced his intention of asking Parliament to enact a Stamp Act. He also expressed a willingness to permit the colonies to forestall a stamp tax by making it either unnecessary or undesirable. In the following year, there was considerable discussion of a stamp tax in London and in the colonies. Charles Garth, an agent for South Carolina, composed the following letter in London, June 5, 1764, addressed to the Committee of Correspondence of the South Carolina Assembly:[6]

Since I wrote last, the several Agents for the Colonies in America have had a meeting to consider of the steps proper on their part to be taken, in consequence of the Stamp Bill being postpon'd to the next Sessions of Parliament: in duty to our constitutents to procure the best intelligence possible and as a mark of respect for the candour shown in

---

[6] Charles Garth to Committee of Correspondence of the South Carolina Assembly, June 5, 1764, *The English Historical Review,* LIV (1939), 646–648.

not hurrying a measure so interesting to the subjects in America, we came to a resolution of waiting upon Mr. Grenville.

On the 17th of May we attended him, and after expressing our thanks for waving the intended bill in the last session, upon the principle of giving the Colonies the opportunity of knowing the intention of Government that they might be able to remit their several objections for the consideration of Parliament, we acquainted him with our wishes that he should be pleased to let us have copies of the Bill to transmit to America, in order that our respective constituents might have the whole, both substance and form under their deliberation, when they would be far better able to determine whether or how far, to approve or disapprove.—Mr. Grenville told us it was impossible for him to comply with our request, as the Bill was not yet thoroughly digested, and assured us that his motive for deferring it sprang from a desire of shewing his regard to the subjects in America, by previously consulting them on a measure, that if the principle upon which it was grounded should appear fair and just in itself, he believed could have the fewest objections of any that could be proposed:—the expence of maintaining, protecting and defending America, it was but natural for America to bear at a time when the revenue of the Mother Country stands in need of every relief and assistance to be had, in order to lessen and diminish as much as possible the immense load of debt upon the nation, that it may be able to exert itself upon every necessary occasion with that vigour, which the Colonies have happily experienced, and will at all times find essential to their immediate interest and wellfare. The method of raising this relief from America had employ'd much of his attention, from a desire of doing it by means the most easy and least exceptionable to the Colonies; the raising it within themselves and appropriating it would have been attended with very many difficulties even if it could be suppos'd that 26 colonies (including the Continent and West

India Islands) would all have adopted such a recommendation, and which in case of refusal to enforce the power of Parliament must have been had recourse to, whereas his intention by this delay was to have the sense of the Colonies themselves upon the matter, and if they could point out any system or plan as effectual and more easy to them, he was open to every proposition to be made from the Colonies, but when the subject had been fully considered by them upon its proper grounds and principles, and no other method should upon the whole be suggested so proper for America in general, it would be a satisfaction to him to carry it into the House with their concurrence and approbation. Objections of inability might possibly come from some Colonies, but, he believed, would have very little weight with Parliament; and with regard to the power of Parliament, the sense of the House of Commons had been sufficiently declaratory thereof, even if there had been no precedent of a revenue from America granted to the Crown by Act of Parliament, meaning the Act establishing a Post Office at New York.—We then took the liberty of asking him (upon supposition of concurrence in the Colonies to the mode) if he had either determined in his mind what things he should make subject to this Stamp Duty, and whether the stamps, to be directed, were to be as high as are by law imposed in Great Britain, or what proportion they would bear, as it seemed to us to be unreasonable that if stamps were to be as great as in England, they should be so high, the object of Government being nothing more than as it were a reimbursement for the expence annually incurred on account of the American Dominions, which £400,000 would amply satisfy, and towards raising the same the Duty Bill last Sessions must not be forgot, the Legislature having so appropriated the income that redounds to the revenue from the duties therein impos'd; Mr. Grenville believed upon the plan thought of the objects for the Stamp Duty would be as extensive, but what the rate of the stamps might be, was not determin'd, and added he should be very ready to consult with us before the meeting of Parliament thereon to receive any propositions we might in the mean time be instructed upon by our respective constituents with regard to these points, if our Assemblies should, as he could not doubt, upon a due consideration they would, transmit us instructions with their assent to the plan for levying this money in the American Dominions.

7

Jared Ingersoll, a Connecticut lawyer, had gone to London on business, commissioned by Connecticut to work against the proposed stamp tax. A letter to Governor Fitch neatly summarizes the argument in favor of the parliamentary power to impose such a tax on the colonies:[7]

The principal Attention has been to the Stamp bill that has been preparing to Lay before Parliament for taxing America. The Point of the Authority of Parliament to impose such Tax I found on my Arrival here was so fully and Universally yielded, that there was not the least hopes of making any impressions that way. Indeed it has appeared since that the House would not suffer to be brought in, nor would any one Member Undertake to Offer to the House, any Petition from the Colonies that held forth the Contrary of that Doctrine. I own I advised the Agents if possible to get that point Canvassed that so the Americans might at least have the Satisfaction of having the point Decided upon a full Debate, but I found it could not be done, and here before I proceed to acquaint you with the Steps that have been taken, in this Matter, I beg leave to give you a Summary of the Arguments which are made Use of in favour of such Authority.

The House of Commons, say they, is a branch of the supreme legislature of the Nation, & which in its Nature is supposed to represent, or rather to stand in the place of, the Commons, that is, of the great body of the people, who are below the dignity of peers; that this house of Commons Consists of a certain number of Men Chosen by certain people of certain places, which Electors, by the Way, they Insist, are not a tenth part of the people, and that the Laws, rules and Methods by which their number is ascertained have arose by degrees & from various Causes & Occasions, and that this house of Commons, therfore, is now fixt and ascertained & is a part of the Supreme unlimited power of the Nation, as in every State there must be some unlimited Power and Authority; and that when it is said they represent the Commons of England, it cannot mean that they do so because those Commons choose them, for in fact by far the greater part do not, but because by their Constitution they must themselves be Commoners, and not Peers, and so the Equals, or of the same Class of Subjects, with the Commons of the Kingdom. They further urge, that the only reason why America has not been heretofore taxed in the fullest Manner, has been merely on Account of their Infancy and Inability; that there have been, however, not wanting Instances of the Exercise of this Power, in the various regulations of the American trade, the Establishment of the post Office &c, and they deny any Distinction between what is called an internal & external Tax as to the point of the Authority imposing such taxes. And as to the Charters in the few provinces where there are any, they say, in the first place, the King cannot grant any that shall exempt them from the Authority of one of the branches of the great body of Legislation, and in the second place say the King has not done, or attempted to do it. In that of Pensilvania the Authority of Parliament to impose taxes is expressly mentioned & reserved; in ours tis said, our powers are generally such as are *According to the Course of other Corporations in England* (both which Instances by way of Sample were mentioned & referred to by Mr. Grenville in the House); in short they say a Power to tax is a necessary part of every Supreme Legislative Authority, and that if

---

[7] Jared Ingersoll to Thomas Fitch, February 11, 1765, *Papers of the New Haven Colony Historical Society,* IX (New Haven, Conn., 1918), 306–309.

they have not that Power over America, they have none, & then America is at once a Kingdom of itself.

On the other hand those who oppose the bill say, it is true the Parliament have a supreme unlimited Authority over every Part & Branch of the Kings dominions and as well over Ireland as any other place, yet we believe a British parliament will never think it prudent to tax Ireland. Tis true they say, that the Commons of England & of the british Empire are all represented in and by the house of Commons, but this representation is confessedly on all hands by Construction & Virtually only as to those who have no hand in choosing the representatives, and that the Effects of this implied Representation here & in America must be infinitely different in the Article of Taxation. Here in England the Member of Parliament is equally known to the Neighbour who elects & to him who does not; the Friendships, the Connections, the Influences are spread through the whole. If by any Mistake an Act of Parliament is made that prove injurious and hard the Member of Parliament here sees with his own Eyes and is moreover very accessible to the people, not only so, but the taxes are laid equally by one Rule and fall as well on the Member himself as on the people. But as to America, from the great distance in point of Situation, from the almost total unacquaintedness, Especially in the more northern Colonies, with the Members of Parliament, and they with them, or with the particular Ability & Circumstances of one another, from the Nature of this very tax laid upon others not Equally & in Common with ourselves, but with express purpose to Ease ourselves, we think, say they, that it will be only to lay a foundation of great Jealousy and Continual Uneasiness, and that to no purpose, as we already by the Regulations upon their trade draw from the Americans all that they can spare, at least they say this Step should not take place untill or unless the Americans are allowed to send Members to Parliament; for *who of you,* said Coll Barre Nobly in his Speech in the house upon this Occasion, *who of you reasoning upon this Subject feels warmly from the Heart* (putting his hand to his own breast) *for the Americans as they would for themselves or as you would for the people of your own native Country? . . .*

Thus I have given you, I think, the Substance of the Arguments on both sides of that great and important Question of the right & also of the Expediency of taxing America by Authority of Parliament.

8

Colonial resistance to the Stamp Act developed in several of the colonies. Probably the most widely known of the more famous incidents resulting from the opposition were the resolutions offered in the Virginia House of Burgesses in June of 1765 by Patrick Henry. Tradition says that Henry, when warned that his resolution constituted treason, retorted, "If this be treason, make the most of it." What was actually said and done remains obscure. Two of the three surviving contemporary accounts are given below: the first, from the pen of an anonymous French traveler; the second, written by Governor Francis Fauquier:[8]

May the 30th. Set out Early from halfway house in the Chair and broke fast at York, arived at williamsburg at 12, where I saw three Negroes hanging at the galous for haveing robed Mr. Waltho of 300 ps. I went immediately to the assembly which was seting, where I was entertained with very strong Debates Concerning Dutys that the parlement wants to lay on the american Colonys, which they Call or Stile stamp Dutys. Shortly after I Came in one of the members stood up and said he had read that in former times tarquin and Julus had their Brutus, Charles had his Cromwell, and he Did not Doubt but some good american would stand up, in favour of his Country, but (says he) in a more moderate manner, and was going to Continue, when the speaker of the house rose and Said, he, the

---

[8] Anon., "Journal of a French Traveller in the Colonies," *The American Historical Review,* XXVI (1921), 745–746. Reprinted with the kind permission of *The American Historical Review.*

last that stood up had spoke traison, and was sorey to see that not one of the members of the house was loyal Enough to stop him, before he had gone so far. upon which the Same member stood up again (his name is henery) and said that if he had afronted the speaker, or the house, he was ready to ask pardon, and he would shew his loyalty to his majesty King G. the third, at the Expence of the last Drop of his blood, but what he had said must be atributed to the Interest of his Countrys Dying liberty which he had at heart, and the heat of passion might have lead him to have said something more than he intended, but, again, if he said any thing wrong, he beged the speaker and the houses pardon. some other Members stood up and backed him, on which the afaire was droped.

May the 31th.   I returned to the assembly today, and heard very hot Debates stil about the Stamp Dutys. the whole house was for Entering resolves on the records but they Differed much with regard the Contents or purport therof. some were for shewing their resentment to the highest. one of the resolves that these proposed, was that any person that would offer to sustain that the parlement of Engl'd had a right to impose or lay any tax or Dutys whats'r on the american Colonys, without the Consent of the inhabitants therof, Should be looked upon as a traitor, and Deemed an Enemy to his Country. there were some others to the same purpose, and the majority was for Entring these resolves, upon which the Governor Disolved the assembly, which hinderd their proceeding.

9[9]

WILLIAMSBURG, *June 5th, 1765*

MY LORDS,

On *Saturday* the 1st instant I dissolved the Assembly after passing all the Bills, except one, which were ready for my assent. The four Resolutions which I have now the honor to inclose to your Lordships, will shew Your Lordships the reason of my conduct, and I hope justify it. I will relate the whole proceeding to your Lordships in as concise a manner as I am able.

On *Wednesday* the 29th of May, just at the end of the Session when most of the members had left the town, there being but 39 present out of 116 of which the House of Burgesses now consists, a motion was made to take into consideration the Stamp Act, a copy of which had crept into the House, and in a Committee of the whole House five resolutions were proposed and agreed to, all by very small majorities. On *Thursday* the 30th they were reported & agreed to by the House, the numbers being as before in the Committee; the greatest majority being 22 to 17; for the 5th Resolution, 20 to 19 only. On *Friday* the 31st there having happened a small alteration in the House there was an attempt to strike all the Resolutions off the Journals. The 5th which was thought the most offensive was accordingly struck off, but it did not succeed as to the other four. I am informed the gentlemen had two more resolutions in their pocket, but finding the difficulty they had in carrying the 5th which was by a single voice, and knowing them to be more virulent and inflammatory; they did not produce them. The most strenuous opposers of this rash heat were the late Speaker, the King's Attorney and Mr. *Wythe;* but they were overpowered by the young hot and giddy members. In the course of the debates I have heard that very indecent language was used by a Mr. *Henry* a young lawyer who had not been a month a Member of the House; who carried all the young Members with him; so that I hope I am authorised in saying there is cause at least to doubt whether this would have been the sense of the Colony if more of their Representatives had done their duty by attending to the end of the Session.

[9] J. P. Kennedy (ed.), *Journals of the House of Burgesses, 1761–1776* (Williamsburg, 1905–1907), I (1761–1765), lxvii.

10

The general resentment against the Stamp Act throughout the colonies is reflected in the indignant decrees of the Stamp Act Congress, which met in October 1765:[10]

I. That his Majesty's subjects in these colonies, owe the same allegiance to the Crown of Great-Britain, that is owing from his subjects born within the realm, and all due subordination to that august body the parliament of Great-Britain.

II. That his Majesty's liege subjects in these colonies, are entitled to all the inherent rights and liberties of his natural born subjects, within the kingdom of Great-Britain.

III. That it is inseparably essential to the freedom of a people, and the undoubted right of Englishmen, that no taxes be imposed on them but with their own consent, given personally, or by their representatives.

IV. That the people of these colonies are not, and, from their local circumstances cannot be, represented in the House of Commons in Great-Britain.

V. That the only representatives of the people of these colonies are persons chosen therein by themselves, and that no taxes ever have been, or can be constitutionally imposed on them, but by their respective legislature.

VI. That all supplies to the crown being free gifts of the people, it is unreasonable and inconsistent with the principles and spirit of the British constitution, for the people of Great-Britain to grant to his Majesty the property of the colonists.

VII. That trial by jury, is the inherent and invaluable right of every British subject in these colonies.

VIII. That, the late act of parliament, entitled *an act for granting and applying certain stamp-duties, and other duties, in the British colonies, and plantations in America,* Etc., by imposing taxes on the inhabitants of these colonies, and the said act, and several other acts, by extending the jurisdiction

of the courts of admiralty beyond its ancient limits, have a manifest tendency to subvert the rights and liberties of the colonists.

IX. That the duties imposed by several late acts of parliament, from the peculiar circumstances of these colonies, will be extremely burthensome and grievous; and from the scarcity of specie, the payment of them absolutely impracticable.

X. That as the profits of the trade of these colonies ultimately center in Great-Britain, to pay for the manufactures which they are obliged to take from thence, they eventually contribute very largely to all supplies granted there to the crown.

XI. That the restrictions imposed by several late acts of parliament on the trade of these colonies, will render them unable to purchase the manufactures of Great-Britain.

XII. That the increase, prosperity, and happiness of these colonies, depend on the full and free enjoyments of their rights and liberties, and an intercourse with Great-Britain mutually affectionate and advantageous.

XIII. That it is the rights of the British subjects in these colonies to petition the king, or either house of parliament.

Lastly, That it is the indispensable duty of these colonies, to the best of sovereigns, to the mother country, and to themselves, to endeavour by a loyal and dutiful address to his Majesty, and humble applications to both houses of parliament, to procure the repeal of the act for granting and applying certain stamp-duties, of all clauses of any other acts of parliament, whereby the jurisdiction of the admiralty is extended as aforesaid, and of the other late acts for the restriction of American commerce.

11

While the colonial upper classes protested through the provincial legislatures, the reaction of the lower classes was more direct. Societies such as the Sons of Liberty appeared and their leaders determined to defeat parliamentary will by mob pressure. The success of the Sons of

---

[10] *Authentic Account of the Proceedings of the Congress held at New-York, in MCCCLXV, on the Subject of the American Stamp Act* (London, 1767), pp. 5–8.

Liberty is described by Governor Fauquier in another letter to the Lords of Trade:[11]

WILLIAMSBURG, NOV. 3d, 1765

MY LORDS,

The present unhappy state of this Colony, will, to my great concern, oblige me to trouble Your Lordships with a long and very disagreeable letter. We were for some time in almost daily expectations of the arrival of Colonel Mercer with the Stamps for the use of this Colony, and rumours were industriously thrown out that at the time of the General Court parties would come down from most parts of the country to seize on and destroy all Stamped Papers. . . .

Very unluckily, Colonel Mercer arrived at the time this town was the fullest of Strangers. On Wednesday the 30th October he came up to town. I then thought proper to go to the Coffee house . . . that I might be an eye witness of what did really pass, and not receive it by relation from others. The mercantile people were all assembled as usual. The first word I heard was "One and all"; upon which, as at a word agreed on before between themselves, they all quitted the place to find Colonel Mercer at his Father's lodging where it was known he was. This concourse of people I should call a mob, did I not know that *it was chiefly if not altogether composed of gentlemen of property* in the Colony, some of them at the head of their respective Counties, *and the merchants of the country,* whether English, Scotch or Virginian; for few absented themselves. They met Colonel Mercer on the way, just at the Capitol: there they stopped and demanded of him an answer whether he would resign or act in this office as Distributor of the Stamps. He said it was an affair of great moment to him; he must consult his friends; and promised to give them an answer at 10 o'clock on Friday morning at that place. This did not satisfy them; and they followed

him to the Coffee house, in the porch of which I had seated myself with many of the Council and the Speaker, who had posted himself between the crowd and myself. We all received him with the greatest marks of welcome; with which, if one may be allowed to judge by their countenances, they were not well pleased, tho' they remained quiet and were silent. Now and then a voice was heard from the crowd that Friday was too late; the Act would take place, they would have an answer tomorrow. Several messages were brought to Mr. Mercer by the leading men of the crowd, to whom he constantly answered he had already given an answer and he would have no other extorted from him. After some little time a cry was heard, "let us rush in." Upon this we that were at the top of the [steps], knowing the advantage our situation gave us to repell those who should attempt to mount them, advanced to the edge of the Steps, of which number I was one. I immediately heard a cry, "See the Governor, take care of him." Those who before were pushing up the steps, immediately fell back, and left a small space between me and them. If your Lordships will not accuse me of vanity I would say that I believe this to be partly owing to the respect they bore to my character and partly to the love they bore to my person. After much entreaty of some of his friends, Mr. Mercer was, against his own inclination, prevailed upon to promise them an answer at the Capitol the next evening at five. The crowd did not yet disperse; it was growing dark, and I did not think it safe to have to leave Mr. Mercer behind me, so I again advanced to the edge of the steps and said aloud I believed no man there would do me any hurt, and turned to Mr. Mercer and told him if he would walk with me through the people I believed I could conduct him safe to my house; and we accordingly walked side by side through the thickest of the people, who did not molest us, tho' there was some little murmurs. By me thus taking him under my protection, I believe I saved him from being insulted at

---

[11] J. P. Kennedy (ed.), *Journals of the House of Burgesses, 1761–1776* (Williamsburg, 1905–1907), I (1761–1765), lxviii–lxxi.

least. When we got home we had much discourse on the subject. . . . He left me that night in a state of uncertainty what part he should act.

Accordingly Mr. Mercer appeared at the Capitol at 5, as he had promised. The number of people assembled there was much increased, by messengers having been sent into the neighborhood for that purpose. Colonel Mercer then read to them the answer which is printed in the Supplement of the Gazette, of which I enclose your Lordships a copy, to which I beg leave to refer. . . .

[Mercer offered to resign but the governor refused to accept the resignation.] If I accepted the resignation, I must appoint another, and I was well convinced I could not find one to accept of it, in those circumstances, which would render the office cheap. Besides if I left Mr. Mercer in possession of the place he would be always ready to distribute the Stamped papers, whenever peoples eyes should be opened and they should come to their senses, so as to receive them.

FRANCIS FAUQUIER

12

By September, 1765, every stamp agent save one had resigned; yet this alone was not enough to force Parliament to reconsider. More effective than mob action were economic boycotts that spread through the seaboard towns; everywhere merchants agreed to boycott English goods until the irksome measure was repealed. As commerce slackened and unemployment in Britain mounted, English merchants and manufacturers pressed Parliament to repeal a law becoming as distasteful to Englishmen as to Americans. London businessmen showered Parliament with petitions like the one presented on January 17, 1766:[12]

That the petitioners have been long concerned in carrying on the trade between this country and the *British* colonies on the continent of *North America;* and that they have annually exported very large quantities

---

[12] *The Debates and Proceedings of the British House of Commons* (London, 1772), VII, 100–103.

of *British* manufactures, consisting of woollen goods of all kinds, cottons, linens, hardware, shoes, household furniture, and almost without exception of every other species of goods manufactured in these kingdoms, besides other articles imported from abroad, chiefly purchased with our manufactures and with the produce of our colonies; by all which, many thousand manufacturers, seamen and labourers, had been employed, to the very great and increasing benefit of this nation; and that, in return for these exports, the petitioners have received from the colonies, rice, indigo, tobacco, naval stores, oil, whale fins, furs, and lately potash, with other commodities, besides remittances by bills of exchange and bullion, obtained by the colonists in payment for articles of their produce, not required for the *British* market, and therefore exported to other places; and that, from the nature of this trade, consisting of *British* manufactures exported, and of the import of raw materials from *America*, many of them used in our manufactures, and all of them tending to lessen our dependence on neighbouring states, it must be deemed of the highest importance in the commercial system of this nation; and that this commerce, so beneficial to the state, and so necessary for the support of multitudes, now lies under such difficulties and discouragements, that nothing less than its utter ruin was apprehended, without the immediate interposition of Parliament; and that, in consequence of the trade between the colonies and the mother country, as established and as permitted for many years, and of the experience which the petitioners have had of the readiness of the *Americans* to make their just remittances to the utmost of their real ability, they have been induced to make and venture such large exportations of *British* manufactures, as to leave the colonies indebted to the merchants of *Great Britain* in the sum of several millions sterling; and that now the colonists, when pressed for payment, appeal to past experience, in proof of their willingness; but declare it is not in their power, at present, to make good their engagements, alleging, that the taxes and restrictions laid upon them, and the extension of the jurisdiction of vice-admiralty courts established by some late acts of parliament, particularly by an act passed in the 4th year of his present Majesty, for granting certain duties in the *British* colonies and plantations in *America,* and by an act passed in the 5th year of his present Majesty, for granting and applying certain stamp duties, and other duties, in the *British* colonies and plantations in *America,* with several regulations and restraints, which, if founded in acts of Parliament for defined purposes, are represented to have been extended in such a manner as to disturb legal commerce and harass the fair trader, and to have so far interrupted the usual and former most fruitful branches of their commerce, restrained the sale of their produce, thrown the state of the several provinces into confusion, and brought on so great a number of actual bankruptcies, that the former opportunities and means of remittances and payments were utterly lost and taken from them; and that the petitioners were, by these unhappy events, reduced to the necessity of applying to the house, in order to secure themselves and their families from impending ruin; to prevent a multitude of manufacturers from becoming a burthen to the community, or else seeking their bread in other countries, to the irretrievable loss of this kingdom; and to preserve the strength of this nation intire, its commerce flourishing, the revenues increasing, our navigation, the bulwark of the kingdom, in a state of growth and extension, and the colonies, from inclination, duty, and interest, firmly attached to the mother country; and therefore praying the consideration of the premises, and entreating such relief, as to the house shall seem expedient.

13

In the end such protests forced the repeal of the Stamp Act, but colonial rejoicing was short-lived. In 1767, Parliament, still seeking revenue, enacted the Townshend Acts, which levied import duties on glass, red and white lead, paint-ers' colors, tea, and other items. Once more resistance stiffened. This time, however, the colonists faced a troublesome constitutional dilemma. The Stamp Act, they might argue, violated their natural right to be represented in the legislature which taxed them, but the Townshend Acts were simply trade-regulating measures of a sort often passed by Parliament. How could they deny England's right to impose such a law? A twentieth-century historian, Carl Becker, has examined their efforts to answer that question in his essay "The Spirit of '76," which records an imaginary conversation between Jeremiah Wynkoop, a wealthy but enlightened young aristocrat, and his conservative father-in-law, the crotchety old Nicholas Van Schoicken-dinck:[13]

It may strike my readers as odd that any one could have been surprised by anything Mr. Townshend took a notion to; but we were indeed not then as well aware of the man's essential frivolity as we have since become. I recall at all events that Mr. Wynkoop followed the proceedings in the House with amazement; and when we learned, one day in 1768, that Mr. Townshend had actually blarneyed the House into passing the Tea Act, the whole business struck Jeremiah as preposterous—"doubtless one of those deplorable jokes," I remember his saying, "which Mr. Townshend is fond of perpetrating when half drunk." I had some recollection that in the time of the Stamp Act troubles certain writers had hinted at a distinction between "internal" and "external" taxes; and Mr. Wynkoop admitted that some such distinction may have been made. But he said that for his part he thought little of such subtle distinctions, agreeing rather with Mr. Pitt that the real question was whether Parliament could "take money out of our pockets without our consent" by any tax whatsoever. There was, however, a difficulty in taking so advanced a position at that time, and as usual it was old Nicholas, always quick to perceive difficulties, who pointed it out.

[13] Carl Becker, "The Spirit of '76," in Carl Becker, J. M. Clark, and William E. Dodd, *The Spirit of '76 and Other Essays* (Washington, 1927), pp. 28–32. Reprinted by permission of The Brookings Institution, publishers.

"I fancy," old Nicholas had said, "that every act in regulation of trade takes money out of our pockets, but I don't imagine you have yet become so ardent a Son of Liberty as to deny Parliament the right of regulating our trade."

At that time we were all reading Mr. Dickinson's *Letters of a Pennsylvania Farmer*, and Mr. Wynkoop, who read everything, was able to meet that objection.

"The essential question," he said, "is whether an act of Parliament is laid primarily for the regulation of trade or for the raising of a revenue. If for the latter, it is a tax. The intention of the framers must decide, and there can be no question that the Tea Act is a tax since the framers expressly declare its purpose to be the raising of a revenue."

"A fine distinction, that! But it would be easy for the framers of an act to levy duties on imports with the real intention of raising a revenue, all the while professing loudly their intention of regulating trade. What then?"

"Americans would not be so easily deceived, sir. The nature of the Act would reveal the real intention clearly enough."

"Ha! You would determine the nature of an act by the intention of the framers, and the intention of the framers by the nature of the act. Excellent! That is the logic of your Pennsylvania Farmer. The New Englanders are still more advanced, I see. They are now saying that our rights are founded on a law of Nature, and God only knows what that is. God and Mr. Adams—it's the same thing, I dare say."

"The New Englanders are likely to be a little rash, sir, I think," Mr. Wynkoop admitted. "This argument of their Mr. Adams is complicated, and I fear too subtle to be easily followed. I'm not sure I understand it."

"Well, never mind. You will all understand it soon enough. First you say that Britain has no right to lay internal taxes. Then that she has no right to levy taxes of any sort. Next you will be saying that Parliament has no right of legislation for the colonies on any

matter whatsoever. And as you can't derive that from precedent you will derive it from the law of nature."

Mr. Wynkoop smiled at this outburst.

"I have no fear of its coming to that," he said. "The Tea Act is not really an act of Britain; it is Mr. Townshend's foolish hobby. A firm and sensible resistance on our part will effect its repeal. But if one could conceive Britain to be so blind as to push matters to extremes—well, I don't know. If it were really a choice between admitting that Parliament has a right of making all laws for us or denying that she has a right of making any laws for us, it would be a hard choice, but should we not be forced to choose the latter alternative? What other answer could we make?"

"You may well ask! What answer will you make when your precious Adams comes out with a declaration of independency from Great Britain?"

"Independence!" Mr. Wynkoop exclaimed. "Good God, sir, what an idea!"

And indeed, at that time, the idea of separation from Great Britain struck us all as fantastic.

14

This division among the upper classes was eventually to make one faction, represented by Jeremiah Wynkoop, into reluctant supporters of the Revolution while the other drifted toward Toryism. In 1767, however, they were still sufficiently united to present a solid front against the home country in seeking repeal of the Townshend Acts. Naturally nonimportation agreements were resorted to at once. Typical was one signed by Boston merchants in August, 1768:[14]

The merchants and traders in the town of Boston having taken into consideration the deplorable situation of the trade, and the many difficulties it at present labours under on account of the scarcity of money, which is daily increasing for want of the other re-

---

[14] *The Annual Register, or View of the History, Politicks, and Literature for the Year 1768* (London, 1768), pp. 235–236.

mittances to discharge our debts in Great Britain, and the large sums collected by the officers of the customs for duties on goods imported; the heavy taxes levied to discharge the debts contracted by the government in the late war; the embarrassments and restrictions laid on trade by several late acts of parliament; together with the bad success of our cod fishery this season, and the discouraging prospect of the whale fishery, by which our principal sources of remittance are like to be greatly diminished, and we thereby rendered unable to pay the debts we owe the merchants in Great Britain, and to continue the importation of goods from thence;

We, the subscribers, in order to relieve the trade under those discouragements, to promote industry, frugality, and economy, and to discourage luxury, and every kind of extravagance, do promise and engage to and with each other as follows:

First, That we will not send for or import from Great Britain, either upon our own account, or upon commission, this fall, any other goods than what are already ordered for the fall supply.

Secondly, That we will not send for or import any kind of goods or merchandize from Great Britain, either on our own account, or on commissions, or any otherwise, from the 1st of January 1769, to the 1st of January 1770, except salt, coals, fish-hooks and lines, hemp, and duck bar lead and shot, wool-cards and card-wire.

Thirdly, That we will not purchase of any factor, or others, any kind of goods imported from Great Britain, from January 1769, to January 1770.

Fourthly, That we will not import, on our own account, or on commissions, or purchase of any who shall import from any other colony in America, from January 1769, to January 1770, any tea, glass, paper, or other goods commonly imported from Great Britain.

Fifthly, That we will not, from and after the 1st of January 1769, import into this province any tea, paper, glass, or painters colours, until the act imposing duties on those articles shall be repealed.

15

Merchant pressure, combined with a belated realization that taxation of England's own exports was unwise, led to the repeal of all the Townshend Acts save that on tea in 1770. After three years of uninterrupted peace, Parliament blundered once more, this time with the Tea Act (1773). By this measure the East India Company was granted an exclusive right to market tea in the colonies; at the same time, to stimulate sales the import duty was lowered from seven to three pence a pound. Again colonial merchants, fearful for their own businesses should Parliament's authority to create monopolies go unchallenged, were thrown into an informal alliance with radical groups. Thus strengthened, the lower-class leaders swung into action. The New York Sons of Liberty expressed the sentiments of all patriots in resolutions adopted on December 15, 1773:[15]

To prevent a calamity which, of all others, is the most to be dreaded—slavery, and its terrible concomitants—we, the subscribers being influenced from a regard to liberty, and disposed to use all lawful endeavors in our power, to defeat the pernicious project, and to transmit to our posterity, those blessings of freedom which our ancestors have handed down to us; and to contribute to the support of the common liberties of America, which are in danger to be subverted, *do*, for those important purposes, agree to associate together, under the name and style of the *sons of New York*, and engage our honor to, and with each other, faithfully to observe and perform the following *resolutions, viz.*

1st. *Resolved*, That whoever shall aid, or abet, or in any manner assist in the introduction of tea, from any place whatsoever, into this colony, while it is subject, by a British act to parliament, to the payment of a duty, for the purpose of raising a revenue in America, he shall be deemed an enemy to the liberties of America.

2d. *Resolved*, That whoever shall be aiding, or assisting, in the landing, or carting, of such tea, from any ship or vessel, or shall hire any house, store-house, or cellar or any place

---

[15] Hezekiah Niles, *Principles and Acts of the Revolution in America* (New York, 1876; reprinted from the 1822 ed.), pp. 169–170.

whatsoever to deposit the tea, subject to a duty as aforesaid, he shall be deemed an enemy to the liberties of America.

3d. *Resolved,* That whoever shall sell, or buy, . . . tea, . . . or shall aid . . . in transporting such tea, . . . from this city, until the . . . revenue act shall be totally and clearly repealed, he shall be deemed an enemy to the liberties of America.

4th. *Resolved,* That whether the duties on tea, imposed by this act, be paid in Great Britain or in America, our liberties are equally affected.

5th. *Resolved,* That whoever shall transgress any of these resolutions, we will not deal with, or employ, or have any connection with him.

16

At New York, Philadelphia, and Charleston, the radicals were strong enough to stop the sale of tea, but in Boston a resolute governor refused to compromise. The result was the famous "tea party" of December 16, 1773, described by a contemporary letter writer:[16]

A general muster was assembled, from this and all yᵉ neighbouring towns, to the number of five or six thousand, at 10 o'clock Thursday morning in the Old South Meeting house, where they pass'd a *unanimous* vote that the *Tea* should go out of the *harbour* that afternoon, . . . when I found the moderator was just declaring the meeting to be *dissolv'd,* which caused another general shout, out doors and in, and three cheers. What with that, and the consequent noise of breaking up the meeting, you'd thought that the inhabitants of the infernal regions had broke loose. For my part, I went contentedly home and finish'd my tea, but was soon inform'd what was going forward: but still not crediting it without ocular demonstration, I went and was *satisfied.* They muster'd, I'm told, upon Fort Hill, to the number of about two hundred, and proceeded, two by two, to

Griffin's wharf, where Hall, Bruce, and Coffin lay, each with 114 chests of the *ill fated* article on board; . . . and before *nine* o'clock in yᵉ evening, every chest from on board the three vessels was knock'd to pieces and flung over yᵉ sides. They say the actors were *Indians* from *Narragansett.* Whether they were or not, to a transient observer they appear'd as *such,* being cloath'd in Blankets with the heads muffled, and copper color'd countenances, being each arm'd with a hatchet or axe, and pair pistols, nor was their *dialect* different from what I conceive these geniusses to *speak,* as their jargon was unintelligible to all but themselves. Not the least insult was offer'd to any person, save one Captain Conner . . . who had ript up the lining of his coat and waistcoat under the arms, and watching his opportunity had nearly fill'd 'em with tea, but being detected, was handled pretty roughly. They not only stripped him of his cloaths, but gave him a coat of mud, with a severe bruising into the bargain; and nothing but their utter aversion to make *any* disturbance prevented his being tar'd and feather'd.

DRIFTING TOWARD INDEPENDENCE

17

Conservative merchants, horrified at the destruction of property, deserted the radicals in large numbers. Conciliatory action by Parliament at this juncture might conceivably have ended revolutionary agitation, but as usual American patriots could count on the aid of inept politicians in London. During the spring of 1774 they hurriedly adopted the series of measures known to the colonists as the "Intolerable Acts"; these closed the port of Boston to all trade, altered the Massachusetts charter, decreed that royal officials accused of crimes be tried in England, and forced towns to quarter royal troops. The Boston Port Act of March 31, 1774, was most violently objected to:[17]

WHEREAS *dangerous commotions and insurrections have been fomented and raised in the town of Boston, in the province of*

---

16 Letter of John Andrews of Boston, Massachusetts Historical Society, *Proceedings,* 1864–1865 (Boston, 1866), pp. 325–326.

17 Danby Pickering (ed.), *Statutes at Large* (Cambridge, 1773), XXX, 336–337, 340.

Massachuset's Bay, in New England, by divers ill-affected persons, to the subversion of his Majesty's government, and to the utter destruction of the publick peace, and good order of the said town; in which commotions and insurrections certain valuable cargoes of teas, being the property of the East India Company, *and on board certain vessels lying within the bay or harbour of* Boston, *were seized and destroyed: And whereas, in the present condition of the said town and harbour, the commerce of his Majesty's subjects cannot be safely carried on there, nor the customs payable to his Majesty duly collected; and it is therefore expedient that the officers of his Majesty's customs should be forthwith removed from the said town: . . .* be it enacted . . . , That from and after the first day of *June,* one thousand seven hundred and seventy-four, it shall not be lawful for any person or persons whatsoever to lade put, or cause to procure to be laden or put, off or from any quay, wharf, or other place, within the said town of *Boston,* or in or upon any part of the shore of the bay, commonly called *The Harbour of Boston,* between a certain headland or point called *Nahant Point,* on the eastern side of the entrance into the said bay, and a certain other headland or point called *Alderton Point,* on the western side of the entrance into the said bay, or in or upon any island, creek, landing-place, bank, or other place, within the said bay or headlands, into any ship, vessel, lighter, boat, or bottom, any goods, wares, or merchandise whatsoever, to be transported or carried into any other country, province, or place whatsoever, or into any other part of the said province of the *Massachuset's Bay,* in *New England;* or to take up, discharge, or lay on land, . . . within the said town, or in or upon any of the places aforesaid, out of any boat, . . . any goods, wares, or merchandise whatsoever, to be brought from any other country, province, or place, or any other part of the said province of the *Massachuset's Bay* in *New England,* upon pain of the forfeiture of the said goods, . . .

X. Provided also, and it is hereby declared and enacted, That nothing herein contained shall extend, or be construed, to enable his Majesty to appoint such port, harbour, creeks, quays, wharfs, places, or officers, in the said town of *Boston,* or in the said bay or islands, until it shall sufficiently appear to his Majesty that full satisfaction hath been made by or on behalf of the inhabitants of the said town of *Boston* to the united company of merchants of *England* trading to the *East Indies,* for the damage sustained by the said company by the destruction of their goods sent to the said town of *Boston,* on board certain ships or vessels as aforesaid; and until it shall be certified to his Majesty, in council, by the governor, or lieutenant governor, of the said province, that reasonable satisfaction hath been made to the officers of his Majesty's revenue, and others, who suffered by the riots and insurrections above mentioned, in the months of *November* and *December,* in the year one thousand seven hundred and seventy-three, and in the month of *January,* in the year one thousand seven hundred and seventy-four.

18

Far worse than the defiant attitude of Boston, from the official point of view of the government, was the new unity that seemed now to mark American resistance. On May 27, 1774, Virginia suggested united action when the House of Burgesses issued a call for a Continental Congress; Massachusetts gave strong assent, and the other colonists soon fell into line. The result was the assembly of fifty-six delegates at Philadelphia in the late summer of 1774. John Adams, a representative from Massachusetts, confided his impressions of the first meeting to his diary:[18]

[Sept.] 5. Monday. At ten the delegates all met at the City Tavern, and walked to the Carpenters' Hall, where they took a view of the room, and of the chamber where is an excellent library; there is also a long entry where gentlemen may walk, and a convenient chamber opposite to the library. The

---

[18] Charles F. Adams (ed.), *The Works of John Adams* (Boston, 1851), II, 365–368.

general cry was, that this was a good room, and the question was put, whether we were satisfied with this room? and it passed in the affirmative. A very few were for the negative, and they were chiefly from Pennsylvania and New York. Then Mr. Lynch arose, and said there was a gentleman present who had presided with great dignity over a very respectable society, greatly to the advantage of Americans, and he therefore proposed that the Honorable Peyton Randolph, Esquire, one of the delegates from Virginia, and the late Speaker of their House of Burgesses, should be appointed Chairman, and he doubted not it would be unanimous.

The question was put, and he was unanimously chosen.

Mr. Randolph then took the chair, and the commissions of the delegates were all produced and read.

Then Mr. Lynch proposed that Mr. Charles Thomson, a gentleman of family, fortune, and character in this city, should be appointed Secretary, which was accordingly done without opposition, though Mr. Duane and Mr. Jay discovered at first an inclination to seek further.

Mr. Duane then moved that a committee should be appointed to prepare regulations for this Congress. Several gentlemen objected.

I then arose and asked leave of the President to request of the gentleman from New York an explanation, and that he would point out some particular regulations which he had in his mind. He mentioned particularly the method of voting, whether it should be by Colonies, or by the poll, or by interests.

Mr. Henry then rose, and said this was the first General Congress which had ever happened; that no former Congress could be a precedent; that we should have occasion for more general congresses, and therefore that a precedent ought to be established now; that it would be great injustice if a little Colony should have the same weight in the councils of America as a great one, and therefore he was for a committee.

Major Sullivan [New Hampshire] ob-

served that a little Colony had its all at stake as well as a great one. . . .

Mr. HENRY. Government is dissolved. Fleets and armies and the present state of things show that government is dissolved. Where are your landmarks, your boundaries of Colonies? We are in a state of nature, sir. . . .

The distinctions between Virginians, Pennsylvanians, New Yorkers, and New Englanders, are no more. I am not a Virginian, but an American.

Slaves are to be thrown out of the question, and if the freemen can be represented according to their numbers, I am satisfied.

Mr. LYNCH. I differ in one point from the gentleman from Virginia, that is, in thinking that numbers only ought to determine the weight of Colonies. I think that property ought to be considered, and that it ought to be a compound of numbers and property that should determine the weight of the Colonies.

I think it cannot be now settled.

19

The Irishman Edmund Burke, who had risen to great prominence in Parliament, distrusted an exclusive emphasis on questions of abstract rights and abstract sovereignty. In one of the greatest speeches of his career he reminded the Commons that the American question dealt with concrete and immediate problems. Burke's brilliant speech, "On Conciliation With the Colonies" (1775), then mattered little, for Burke lost the subsequent vote by 78 to 270. But American advocates of constitutional reform learned they had an ally in the House of Commons:[19]

I am sensible, Sir, that all which I have asserted in my detail is admitted in the gross, but that quite a different conclusion is drawn from it. America, gentlemen say, is a noble object,—it is an object well worth fighting for. Certainly it is, if fighting a people be the best way of gaining them. Gentlemen in this respect will be led to their choice of means by their complexions and their habits. Those who understand the military art will of course have some predilection

[19] Edmund Burke, *The Works of Edmund Burke* (New York, 1859), I, 28.

for it. Those who wield the thunder of the state may have more confidence in the efficacy of arms. But I confess, possibly for want of this knowledge, my opinion is much more in favor of prudent management than of force,—considering force not as an odious, but a feeble instrument, for preserving a people so numerous, so active, so growing, so spirited as this, in a profitable and subordinate connection with us.

First, Sir, permit me to observe, that the use of force alone is but *temporary*. It may subdue for a moment; but it does not remove the necessity of subduing again; and a nation is not governed which is perpetually to be conquered.

My next objection is its *uncertainty*. Terror is not always the effect of force, and an armament is not a victory. If you do not succeed, you are without resource: for, conciliation failing, force remains; but, force failing, no further hope of reconciliation is left. Power and authority are sometimes bought by kindness; but they can never be begged as alms by an impoverished and defeated violence.

A further objection to force is, that you *impair the object* by your very endeavors to preserve it. The thing you fought for is not the thing which you recover, but depreciated, sunk, wasted, and consumed in the contest. Nothing less will content me than *whole America*. I do not choose to consume its strength along with our own; because in all parts it is the British strength that I consume. I do not choose to be caught by a foreign enemy at the end of this exhausting conflict, and still less in the midst of it. I may escape, but I can make no insurance against such an event. Let me add, that I do not choose wholly to break the American spirit; because it is the spirit that has made the country.

Lastly, we have no sort of *experience* in favor of force as an instrument in the rule of our colonies. Their growth and their utility has been owing to methods altogether different. Our ancient indulgence has been said to be pursued to a fault. It may be so; but we know, if feeling is evidence, that our

fault was more tolerable than our attempt to mend it, and our sin far more salutary than our penitence.

20

Many participated in the fateful events in Massachusetts on April 19, 1775. A British expedition under Colonel Francis Smith was ordered to march to Lexington and Concord. One of the few who wrote down what he saw that day was the author of the following account. That he was a British officer is certain, and his name was probably Lieutenant John Barker of the King's Own:[20]

ACCOUNT PRESUMABLY BY
LIEUTENANT JOHN BARKER
OF THE KING'S OWN.

1775, April 19th. Last night between 10 and 11 o'clock all the Grenadiers and Light Infantry of the Army, making about 600 Men (under the command of Lt. Col. Smith of the 10th and Major Pitcairn of the Marines), embarked and were landed upon the opposite shore on Cambridge Marsh; few of the Commanding Officers knew what expedition we were going upon. After getting over the marsh, where we were wet up to the knees, we were halted in a dirty road and stood there till two o'clock in the morning, waiting for provisions to be brought from the boats and divided, and which most of the Men threw away, having carried some with 'em. At 2 o'clock we began our March by wading through a very long ford up to our Middles. After going a few miles we took 3 or 4 People who were going off to give intelligence; about 5 miles on this side of a Town called Lexington, which lay in our road, we heard there were some hundreds of People collected together intending to oppose us and stop our going on. At 5 o'clock we arrived there and saw a number of People, I believe between 2 and 300, formed in a Common in the middle of the Town. We still continued advancing, keeping prepared against an attack tho' without intending to attack them; but

---

[20] R. H. Dana, Jr. (ed.), "Diary of a British Officer," *Atlantic Monthly*, XXXIX (April 1877), 398–400.

on our coming near them they fired one or two shots, upon which our Men without any orders rushed in upon them, fired and put 'em to flight; several of them were killed, we cou'd not tell how many, because they were got behind Walls and into the Woods. We had a Man of the 10th light Infantry wounded, nobody else hurt. We then formed on the Common, but with some difficulty, the men were so wild they cou'd hear no orders; We waited a considerable time there, and at length proceeded on our way to Concord, which we then learnt was our destination, in order to destroy a Magazine of Stores collected there. We met with no interruption 'till within a mile or two of the Town, where the Country People had occupied a hill which commanded the road; The light Infantry were orderd away to the right and ascended the height in one line, upon which the Yankies quitted it without firing, which they did likewise for one or two more successively. They then crossed the River beyond the Town, and we marchd into the Town after taking possession of a Hill with a Liberty Pole on it and a flag flying, which was cut down; the Yankies had the Hill but left it to us; we expected they wou'd have made a stand there, but they did not chuse it. While the Grenadiers remained in the Town, destroying 3 pieces of Cannon, several Gun Carriages, and about 100 barrels of flour, with Harness and other things, the Light Companies were detached beyond the River to examine some Houses for more stores; 1 of these Compys. was left at the Bridge, another on some distance from it, and another on a hill ¼ of a mile from that; the other 3 went forward 2 or 3 miles to seek for some Cannon which had been there but had been taken away that morning. During this time the People were gathering together in great numbers, and, taking advantage of our scatter'd disposition, seemed as if they were going to cut off the communication with the Bridge, upon which the two Companies joined and went to the Bridge to support that Company. The three Compys. drew up in the road the far side the Bridge and the Rebels on the Hill

above, cover'd by a Wall; in that situation they remained a long time, very near an hour, the three Companies expecting to be attacked by the Rebels, who were about 1000 strong. Captn. Lawrie, who commanded these three companies, sent to Colo. Smith begging he would send more Troops to his Assistance and informing him of his situation; the Colo. order'd 2 or 3 Compys. but put himself at their head, by which means stopt 'em from being time enough, for being a very fat heavy Man he would not have reached the bridge in half an hour, tho' it was not half a mile to it; In the mean time the Rebels marched into the Road and were coming down upon us when Capt. L made his Men retire to this side the Bridge (which by the bye he ought to have done at first, and then he would have had time to make a good disposition, but at this time he had not, for the Rebels were got so near him that his people were obliged to form the best way they cou'd); as soon as they were over the Bridge the three companies got one behind the other so that only the front one cou'd fire; the Rebels when they got near the Bridge halted and fronted, filling the road from the top to the bottom. The fire soon began from a dropping shot on our side, when they and the front Company fired almost at the same instant, there being nobody to support the front Compy. The others not firing, the whole were forced to quit the Bridge and return toward Concord; some of the Grenadiers met 'em in the road and then advanced to meet the Rebels, who had got this side the Bridge and on a good height, but seeing the manoeuvre they thought proper to retire again over the Bridge; the whole then went into Concord, drew up in the Town and waited for the 3 Companies that were gone on, which arrived in about an hour; 4 officers of 8 who were at the Bridge were wounded; 3 men killed; 1 Sergt. and several Men wounded; after getting as good conveniences for the wounded as we cou'd, and having done the business we were sent upon We set out upon our return; before the whole had quitted the Town we were fired on from Houses and behind Trees, and before we had gone ½ miles we were fired on from all sides, but mostly from the Rear, where People had hid themselves in houses till we had passed, and then fired; the country was an amazing strong one, full of Hills, Woods, stone Walls, etc., which the Rebels did not fail to take advantage of, for they were all lined with People who kept an incessant fire upon us, as we did too upon them, but not with the same advantage, for they were so concealed there was hardly any seeing them; in this way we marched between 9 and 10 miles, their numbers increasing from all parts, while ours was reduced by deaths, wounds and fatigue; and we were totally surrounded with such an incessant fire as it's impossible to conceive; our ammunition was likewise near expended. In this critical situation we perceived the 1st Brigade coming to our assitance: it consisted of the 4th, 23rd and 47th Regts, and the Battalion of Marines, with two field pieces, 6-pounders; we had been flattered ever since the morning with expectations of the Brigade coming out, but at this time had given up all hopes of it, as it was so late. I since heard it was owing to a mistake of the orders, or the Brigade would have been with us 2 hours sooner. As soon as the Rebels saw this reinforcement, and tasted the field pieces, they retired, and we formed on a rising ground and rested ourselves a little while, which was extremely necessary for our Men, who were almost exhausted with fatigue: In about ½ an hour we marched again, and, some of the Brigade taking the flanking parties, we marched pretty quiet for about 2 miles; they then began to pepper us again from the same sort of places, but at rather a greater distance. We were now obliged to force almost every house in the road, for the Rebels had taken possession of them and galled us exceedingly; but they suffered for their temerity, for all that were found in the houses were put to death. When we got to Menotomy there was a very heavy fire; after that we took the short cut into the Charles Town road, very luckily for us too, for the

Rebels, thinking we should endeavour to return by Cambridge, had broken down the Bridge and had a great number of men to line the road and to receive us there. However, we threw them and went on to Charles Town without any great interruption. We got there between 7 and 8 o'clock at night, took possession of the hill above the town, and waited for the Boats to carry us over, which came sometime after; the Rebels did not chuse to follow us to the Hill, as they must have fought us on open ground and that they did not like. The Piquets of the Army were sent over to Charles Town and 200 of the 64th to keep that ground; they threw up a work to secure themselves, and we embarked and got home very late in the night. . . .

Thus ended this Expedition, which from the beginning to end was as ill planned and ill executed as it was possible to be.

21

The subsequent (and misnamed) battle of Bunker Hill also had its quota of eyewitnesses. One of the livelier descriptions of that affair comes from a diary kept by a corporal in the Massachusetts militia, Amos Farnsworth:[21]

Friday june. 16.   Nothing Done in ye forenoon in the afternoon we had orders to be redy to march At Six Agreable to Orders our Regiment Preadid and about Sun-set we was Drawn up and herd Prayers: And about Dusk Marched for Bunkers hill; under Command of our own Col Prescott. jest before we turned out of ye rode to go up Bunkers-Hill; Charlestown we was halted; And about Sixty men was taken out of our batallion to go into Charlestown; I being one of them: Capt Nutten heded us Down to ye town house; we Sot our Centres by yᵉ waterside; the most of us got in the town house But had orders not to Shut our eyes Our Men marched to Bunker-Hill And begun thair intrenchment And Careed it on with

[21] "Diary of Amos Farnsworth," Massachusetts Historical Society, *Proceedings,* 2d ser., XII (1897–1899), 83–84.

the utmost Viger all Night, Early in the Morning I joined them

Saturday June ye 17. the Enemy appeared to be much Alarmed on Saturday Morning when thay discovered Our operations and immediately began a heavy Cannonading from a batery on Corps-Hill Boston and from the Ships in ye Harbour. we with little loss Continued to Carry on our works till 1 o'Clock when we Discovered a large Body of the Enemy Crossing Charles-River from Boston. thay landed on a Pointed of land about a Mile Eastward of our Intrenchment And immediately disposed thair army for an attack previous to which thay Set fire to the town of Charlestown. It is supposed that the Enemy intended to attack us under the Cover of the Smoke from the burning Houses, the Wind favouring them in Such a Design; While on the other side their Army was extending Northward towards Mistick-River with an apparant Design of surrounding our Men in the Works, And of cutting of any Assistance intended for our Relief. Thay ware however in some Measure, counteracted in this Design, and Drew their Army into closer Order. As the Enemy approached, Our men was not only Exposed to the Attack of a very numerous Musketry but to the heavy Fire of the Battery on Corps-Hill, 4 or 5 Men of War, Several Armed Boats or Floating Batteries in Mistick-River, and a number of Field pieces. Notwithstanding we within the intrenchment, and at a Breast Work without, sustained the Enemy's Arracks with [g]reat Bravery and Resolution, kiled and wounded great Numbers, and repulsed them several times; and after bearing, for about 2 Hours, as severe and heavy a Fire as perhaps ever was known, and many having fired away all their Ammunition, and having no Reinforsement: althoe thare was a great Boddy of Men nie By: we ware overpowered by Numbers and obliged to leave the Intrenchment retreating about Sunset, to a small Distance over Charlestown Neck. N.B. I Did not leave the Intrenchment untill the Enemy got in I then Retreated ten or

Fifteen rods, then I receved a wound in my rite arm the bawl going through a little below my Elbow breaking the little shel Bone Another bawl struk my Back taking of a piece of Skin about as big as a Penny But I got to Cambridge that night. the Town of Charlestown supposed to contain about 300 Dwelling-Houses, a great Number of which were large and elegant, besides 150 or 200 other Buildings, are almost all laid in ashes by the Barbarity and wanton Cruelty of that infernal Villain Thomas Gage.

22

Calm might yet have been restored to the troubled colonies, for few dared speak of independence; they treasured their liberties, not separation from Britain. Instead, an inept Parliament and an obstinate king were apparently more concerned with chastisement than analysis. The result was a rapid shift in American sentiment. Bloodshed at Lexington and Concord convinced many that separation had at last to be considered as a serious possibility; thousands of others were converted by the pamphlet Common Sense. *This inflammatory document, which circulated more than a hundred thousand copies in the months following its publication in January, 1776, was the work of an English liberal, Thomas Paine, who had come to America to aid the revolution. Its final paragraphs contained a passionate indictment of all tyranny:*[22]

But where, say some, is the king of America? I'll tell you, Friend, he reigns above, and doth not make havoc of mankind like the royal brute of Great Britain. Yet that we may not appear to be defective even in earthly honours, let a day be solemnly set apart for proclaiming the charter; let it be brought forth placed on the divine law, the Word of God; let a crown be placed thereon, by which the world may know, that so far as we approve of monarchy, that in America the law is king. For as in absolute governments the king is law, so in free countries the law ought to be king; and there ought to be no other. But lest any ill use should after-

---

[22] Philip S. Foner (ed.), *The Complete Writings of Thomas Paine* (New York, 1945), I, 29–31, 46.

wards arise, let the crown at the conclusion of the ceremony be demolished, and scattered among the People whose right it is.

A government of our own is our natural right: and when a man seriously reflects on the precariousness of human affairs, he will become convinced, that it is infinitely wiser and safer, to form a constitution of our own, in a cool deliberate manner, while we have it in our power, than to trust such an interesting event to time and chance. If we omit it now, some Massanello may hereafter arise, who laying hold of popular disquietudes, may collect together the desperate and the discontented, and by assuming to themselves the powers of government, may sweep away the liberties of the continent like a deluge. Should the government of America return again into the hands of Britain, the tottering situation of things will be a temptation for some desperate adventurer to try his fortune; and in such a case, what relief can Britain give? Ere she could hear the news, the fatal business might be done; and ourselves suffering like the wretched Britons under the oppression of the conqueror. Ye that oppose independance now, ye know not what ye do; ye are opening a door to eternal tyranny, by keeping vacant the seat of government. There are thousands, and tens of thousands, who would think it glorious to expel from the continent, that barbarous and hellish power, which hath stirred up the Indians and the Negroes to destroy us; the cruelty hath a double guilt, it is dealing brutally by us, and treacherously by them.

To talk of friendship with those in whom our reason forbids us to have faith, and our affections wounded thro' a thousand pores instruct us to detest, is madness and folly. Every day wears out the little remains of kindred between us and them; and can there be any reason to hope, that as the relationship expires, the affection will increase, or that we shall agree better when we have ten times more and greater concerns to quarrel over than ever?

Ye that tell us of harmony and reconcilia-tion, can ye restore to us the time that is past? Can ye give to prostitution its former innocence? Neither can ye reconcile Britain and America. The last cord now is broken, the people of England are presenting addresses against us. These are injuries which nature cannot forgive; she would cease to be nature if she did. As well can the lover forgive the ravisher of his mistress, as the continent forgive the murders of Britain. The Almighty hath implanted in us these unextinguishable feelings for good and wise purposes. They are the guardians of his image in our hearts. They distinguish us from the herd of common animals. The social compact would dissolve, and justice be extirpated from the earth, or have only a casual existence were we callous to the touches of affection. The robber and the murderer would often escape unpunished, did not the injuries which our tempers sustain, provoke us into justice.

O! ye that love mankind! Ye that dare oppose not only the tyranny but the tyrant, stand forth! Every spot of the old world is overrun with oppression. Freedom hath been hunted round the globe. Asia and Africa have long expelled her. Europe regards her like a stranger, and England hath given her warning to depart. O! receive the fugitive, and prepare in time an asylum for mankind.

On these grounds I rest the matter. And as no offer hath yet been made to refute the doctrine contained in the former editions of this pamphlet, it is a negative proof that either the doctrine cannot be refuted, or that the party in favour of it are too numerous to be opposed. WHEREFORE, instead of gazing at each other, with suspicious or doubtful curiosity, let each of us hold out to his neighbour the hearty hand of friendship, and united in drawing a line, which, like an act of oblivion, shall bury in forgetfulness every former dissension. Let the names of Whig and Tory be extinct; and let none other be heard among us, than those of a *good citizen, an open and resolute friend,* and *a virtuous supporter of the* RIGHTS OF

MANKIND, *and of the* FREE AND INDEPENDENT STATES OF AMERICA.

23

By June, 1776, opinion had reached a stage to welcome action. Richard Henry Lee, a Virginia delegate to the Continental Congress, on June 7 moved the resolutions that committed the colonies to go their separate way. For the next month Congress debated Lee's resolutions while a committee labored over the declaration that would almost certainly be called for. Finally, on July 2, they were adopted; two days later the immortal document from Jefferson's pen was accepted by Congress:[23]

In Congress, July 4, 1776,

The unanimous Declaration of the thirteen United States of America.

When in the Course of human events, it becomes necessary for one people to dissolve the political bands which have connected them with another, and to assume among the Powers of the earth, the separate and equal station to which the Laws of Nature and of Nature's God entitle them, a decent respect to the opinions of mankind requires that they should declare the causes which impel them to the separation.

We hold these truths to be self-evident, that all men are created equal, that they are endowed by their Creator with certain unalienable Rights, that among these are Life, Liberty and the pursuit of Happiness. That to secure these rights, Governments are instituted among Men, deriving their just Powers from the consent of the governed. That, whenever any Form of Government becomes destructive of these ends, it is the Right of the People to alter or to abolish it, and to institute new Government, laying its foundation on such Principles and organizing its Powers in such form, as to them shall seem most likely to effect their Safety and Happiness. Prudence, indeed, will dictate that Governments long established should not be changed for light and

transient causes; and accordingly, all experience hath shewn, that mankind are more disposed to suffer, while evils are sufferable, than to right themselves by abolishing the forms to which they are accustomed. But when a long train of abuses and usurpations, pursuing invariably the same Object, evinces a design to reduce them under absolute Despotism, it is their right, it is their duty, to throw off such Government, and to provide new Guards for their future security. Such has been the patient sufferance of these Colonies; and such is now the necessity which constrains them to alter their former Systems of Government. The history of the present King of Great Britain is a history of repeated injuries and usurpations, all having in direct object the establishment of an absolute Tyranny over these States. To prove this, let Facts be submitted to a candid world.

He has refused his Assent to Laws, the most wholesome and necessary for the public good.

He has forbidden his Governors to pass Laws of immediate and pressing importance, unless suspended in their operation till his Assent should be obtained; and when so suspended, he has utterly neglected to attend to them.

He has refused to pass other Laws for the accommodation of large districts of People, unless those People would relinquish the right of Representation in the legislature, a right inestimable to them and formidable to tyrants only.

He has called together legislative bodies at places unusual, uncomfortable, and distant from the depository of their Public Records, for the sole Purpose of fatiguing them into compliance with his measures.

He has dissolved Representative Houses repeatedly, for opposing with manly firmness, his invasions on the rights of the People.

He has refused for a long time, after such dissolutions, to cause others to be elected; whereby the Legislative Powers, incapable of Annihilation, have returned to the People

[23] Worthington C. Ford, *et al.* (eds.), *Journals of the Continental Congress, 1774–1789* (Washington, 1906), V, 510–515.

at large for their exercise; the State remaining in the mean time exposed to all the dangers of invasion from without, and convulsions within.

He has endeavoured to prevent the Population of these States; for that purpose obstructing the Laws of Naturalization for Foreigners; refusing to pass others to encourage their migration hither, and raising the conditions of new Appropriations of Lands.

He has obstructed the Administration of Justice, by refusing his Assent to Laws for establishing Judiciary Powers.

He has made Judges dependent on his Will alone, for the tenure of their offices, and the amount and payment of their salaries.

He has erected a multitude of New Offices, and sent hither swarms of Officers to harass our People, and eat out their substance.

He has kept among us, in times of Peace, Standing Armies without the Consent of our legislatures.

He has affected to render the Military independent of and superior to the Civil Power.

He has combined with others to subject us to a jurisdiction foreign to our constitution, and unacknowledged by our laws; giving his Assent to their Acts of pretended Legislation:

For quartering large bodies of armed troops among us:

For protecting them, by a mock Trial, from Punishment for any Murders which they should commit on the Inhabitants of these States:

For cutting off our Trade with all parts of the world:

For imposing taxes on us without our Consent:

For depriving us in many cases, of the benefits of Trial by Jury:

For transporting us beyond Seas to be tried for pretended offences:

For abolishing the free System of English Laws in a neighbouring province, establishing therein an Arbitrary government, and enlarging its Boundaries so as to render it

at once an example and fit instrument for introducing the same absolute rule into these Colonies:

For taking away our Charters, abolishing our most valuable Laws, and altering fundamentally the Forms of our Governments:

For suspending our own Legislatures, and declaring themselves invested with Power to legislate for us in all cases whatsoever.

He has abdicated Government here, by declaring us out of his Protection and waging War against us.

He has plundered our seas, ravaged our Coasts, burnt our towns, and destroyed the Lives of our People.

He is at this Time transporting large armies of foreign Mercenaries to compleat the works of death, desolation and tyranny, already begun with circumstances of Cruelty and perfidy scarcely paralleled in the most barbarous ages, and totally unworthy the Head of a civilized nation.

He has constrained our fellow Citizens taken Captive on the high Seas to bear Arms against their Country, to become the executioners of their friends and Brethren, or to fall themselves by their Hands.

He has excited domestic insurrections amongst us, and has endeavoured to bring on the inhabitants of our frontiers, the merciless Indian Savages, whose known rule of warfare, is an undistinguished destruction of all ages, sexes and conditions.

In every stage of these Oppressions We have Petitioned for Redress in the most humble terms: Our repeated Petitions have been answered only by repeated injury. A Prince, whose character is thus marked by every act which may define a Tyrant, is unfit to be the ruler of a free People.

Nor have We been wanting in attention to our Brittish brethren. We have warned them from time to time of attempts by their legislature to extend an unwarrantable jurisdiction over us. We have reminded them of the circumstances of our emigration and settlement here. We have appealed to their native justice and magnanimity, and we have conjured them by the ties of our common kindred, to disavow these usurpations, which, would inevitably interrupt our connections and correspondence. They too have been deaf to the voice of justice and of consanguinity. We must, therefore, acquiesce in the necessity, which denounces our Separation, and hold them, as we hold the rest of mankind, Enemies in War, in Peace Friends.

WE, THEREFORE, the REPRESENTATIVES of the *UNITED STATES OF AMERICA*, in GENERAL CONGRESS, Assembled, appealing to the Supreme Judge of the world for the rectitude of our intentions, DO, in the Name, and by Authority of the good People of these Colonies, solemnly PUBLISH and DECLARE, That these United Colonies are, and of Right ought to be *FREE AND INDEPENDENT STATES;* that they are Absolved from all Allegiance to the British Crown, and that all political connexion between them and the State of Great Britain, is and ought to be totally dissolved; and that as FREE and INDEPENDENT STATES, they have full Power to levy War, conclude Peace, contract Alliances, establish Commerce, and to do all other Acts and Things which INDEPENDENT STATES may of right do. AND for the support of this Declaration, with a firm reliance on the protection of Divine Providence, we mutually pledge to each other our Lives, our Fortunes and our sacred Honour.

24

Bold though it was, the Declaration would have been still bolder had Thomas Jefferson had his democratic way. Among the paragraphs deleted by conservative pressure was one condemning slavery:[24]

He has waged cruel war against human nature itself, violating its most sacred rights of life & liberty in the persons of a distant people who never offended him, captivating & carrying them into slavery in another hemisphere, or to incur miserable death in their

transportation thither. This piratical warfare, the opprobrium of *infidel* powers, is the warfare of the *Christian* King of Great Britain, determined to keep open a market where MEN should be bought & sold, he has prostituted his negative for suppressing every legislative attempt to prohibit or to restrain this execrable commerce: and that this assemblage of horrors might want no fact of distinguished die, he is now exciting those very people to rise in arms among us, and to purchase that liberty of which *he* has deprived them by murdering the people upon whom *he* also obtruded them: thus paying off former crimes committed against the *liberties* of one people, with crimes which he urges them to commit against the *lives* of another.

25

The Declaration proclaimed colonial independence; it also brought the colonists face to face with the problems of freedom. What manner of government would best secure those natural rights which, they believed, had been threatened by England? They first tried to answer this question in the several state constitutions drafted to replace the colonial charters. Most of these documents contained a "Bill of Rights" designed to protect individuals from arbitrary authority. Of these the most influential was that of Virginia, which was adopted June 12, 1776:[25]

SECTION 1. That all men are by nature equally free and independent, and have certain inherent rights, of which, when they enter into a state of society, they cannot by any compact deprive or divest their posterity; namely, the enjoyment of life and liberty, with the means of acquiring and possessing property, and pursuing and obtaining happiness and safety.

SEC. 2. That all power is vested in, and consequently derived from, the people; that magistrates are their trustees and servants, and at all times amenable to them.

---

[24] Facsimile of original is in Walter Goetz (ed.), *Propylaen Weltgeschichte* (Berlin, 1929–1933), VI, 464–465.

[25] Francis N. Thorpe (ed.), *The Federal and State Constitutions, Colonial Charters, and other organic laws of the States, Territories, and Colonies now or heretofore forming the United States of America* (Washington, 1909), VII, 3813–3814.

SEC. 3. That government is, or ought to be, instituted for the common benefit, protection, and security of the people, nation, or community; of all the various modes and forms of government, that is best which is capable of producing the greatest degree of happiness and safety, and is most effectually secured against the danger of maladministration; and that, when any government shall be found inadequate or contrary to these purposes, a majority of the community hath an indubitable, inalienable, and indefeasible right to reform, alter, or abolish it, in such manner as shall be judged most conducive to the public weal.

SEC. 4. That no man, or set of men, are entitled to exclusive or separate emoluments or privileges from the community, but in consideration of public services; which, not being descendible, neither ought the offices of magistrate, legislator, or judge to be hereditary.

SEC. 5. That the legislative and executive powers of the State should be separate and distinct from the judiciary; and that the members of the two first may be restrained from oppression, by feeling and participating the burdens of the people, they should, at fixed periods, be reduced to a private station, return into that body from which they were originally taken, and the vacancies be supplied by frequent, certain, and regular elections, in which all, or any part of the former members, to be again eligible, or ineligible, as the laws shall direct.

SEC. 6. That elections of members to serve as representatives of the people, in assembly, ought to be free; and that all men, having sufficient evidence of permanent common interest with, and attachment to the community, have the right of suffrage, and cannot be taxed or deprived of their property for public uses, without their own consent, or that of their representatives so elected, nor bound by any law to which they have not, in like manner, assembled, for the public good.

SEC. 7. That all power of suspending laws, or the execution of laws, by any authority, without consent of the representatives of the people, is injurious to their rights, and ought not to be exercised.

SEC. 8. That in all capital or criminal prosecutions a man hath a right to demand the cause and nature of his accusation, to be confronted with the accusers and witnesses, to call for evidence in his favour, and to a speedy trial by an impartial jury of twelve men of his vicinage, without whose unanimous consent he cannot be found guilty; nor can he be compelled to give evidence against himself; that no man be deprived of his liberty, except by the law of the land or the judgment of his peers.

SEC. 9. That excessive bail ought not to be required, nor excessive fines imposed, nor cruel and unusual punishments inflicted.

SEC. 10. That general warrants, whereby an officer or messenger may be commanded to search suspected places without evidence of a fact committed, or to seize any person or persons not named, or whose offence is not particularly described and supported by evidence, are grievous and oppressive, and ought not to be granted.

SEC. 11. That in controversies respecting property, and in suits between man and man, the ancient trial by jury is preferable to any other, and ought to be held sacred.

SEC. 12. That the freedom of the press is one of the great bulwarks of liberty, and can never be restrained but by despotic governments.

SEC. 13. That a well-regulated militia, composed of the body of the people trained to arms, is the proper, natural and safe defence of a free State; that standing armies in time of peace should be avoided as dangerous to liberty; and that in all cases the military should be under strict subordination to, and governed by, the civil power.

SEC. 14. That the people have a right to uniform government; and, therefore, that no government separate from, or independent of the government of Virginia, ought to be erected or established within the limits thereof.

SEC. 15. That no free government, or the

blessings of liberty, can be preserved to any people, but by a firm adherence to justice, moderation, temperance, frugality, and virtue, and by frequent recurrence to fundamental principles.

SEC. 16. That religion, or the duty which we owe to our Creator, and the manner of discharging it, can be directed only by reason and conviction, not by force or violence; and therefore all men are equally entitled to the free exercise of religion, according to the dictates of conscience; and that it is the mutual duty of all to practise Christian forbearance, love, and charity towards each other.

THE WAR FOR INDEPENDENCE

26

Faith in the principles of individual freedom and democracy helped sustain the Americans during the trying years of the Revolution. No one better understood the need for a sustaining faith than Thomas Paine, the liberal pamphleteer whose Common Sense *had helped turn the tide toward independence. When, in the early years of the war, he sensed a slackening of popular zeal, he set out to rekindle the democratic spirit by publishing another remarkable pamphlet.* The American Crisis, *appearing during the troubled days of 1776 and 1777 when the colonial cause seemed hopeless, did much to rally public sentiment behind George Washington's leadership:*[26]

These are the times that try men's souls. The summer soldier and the sunshine patriot will, in this crisis, shrink from the service of their country; but he that stands it *now*, deserves the love and thanks of man and woman. Tyranny, like hell, is not easily conquered; yet we have this consolation with us, that the harder the conflict, the more glorious the triumph. What we obtain too cheap, we esteem too lightly: it is dearness only that gives every thing its value. Heaven knows how to put a proper price upon its

[26] Philip S. Foner (ed.), *The Complete Writings of Thomas Paine* (New York, 1945), I, 50–51, 53–54.

goods; and it would be strange indeed if so celestial an article as FREEDOM should not be highly rated. Britain, with an army to enforce her tyranny, has declared that she has a right (*not only to* TAX) but "to BIND *us in* CASES WHATSOEVER," and if being *bound in that manner*, is not slavery, then there is not such a thing as slavery upon earth. Even the expression is impious; for so unlimited a power can belong only to God.

Whether the independence of the continent was declared too soon, or delayed too long, I will not now enter into as an argument; my own simple opinion is, that had it been eight months earlier, it would have been much better. We did not make a proper use of last winter, neither could we, while we were in a dependent state. However, the fault, if it were one, was all our own; we have none to blame but ourselves. But no great deal is lost yet. All that Howe has been doing for this month past, is rather a ravage than a conquest, which the spirit of the Jerseys, a year ago, would have quickly repulsed, and which time and a little resolution will soon recover.

I have as little superstition in me as any man living, but my secret opinion has ever been, and still is, that God Almighty will not give up a people to military destruction, or leave them unsupportedly to perish, who have so earnestly and so repeatedly sought to avoid the calamities of war, by every decent method which wisdom could invent. Neither have I so much of the infidel in me, as to suppose that He has relinquished the government of the world, and given us up to the care of devils; and as I do not, I cannot see on what grounds the king of Britain can look up to heaven for help against us: a common murderer, a highwayman, or a housebreaker, has as good a pretence as he.

'Tis surprising to see how rapidly a panic will sometimes run through a country. All nations and ages have been subject to them. Britain has trembled like an ague at the report of a French fleet of flat bottomed boats; and in the fourteenth century the whole English army, after ravaging the kingdom of France, was driven back like men petrified with fear; and this brave exploit was performed by a few broken forces collected and headed by a woman, Joan of Arc. Would that heaven might inspire some Jersey maid to spirit up her countrymen, and save her fair fellow sufferers from ravage and ravishment! Yet panics, in some cases, have their uses; they produce as much good as hurt. Their duration is always short; the mind soon grows through them, and acquires a firmer habit than before. But their peculiar advantage is, that they are the touchstones of sincerity and hypocrisy, and bring things and men to light, which might otherwise have lain forever undiscovered. In fact, they have the same effect on secret traitors, which an imaginary apparition would have upon a private murderer. They sift out the hidden thoughts of man, and hold them up in public to the world. Many a disguised Tory has lately shown his head, that shall penitentially solemnize with curses the day on which Howe arrived upon the Delaware. . . .

I shall conclude this paper with some miscellaneous remarks on the state of our affairs; and shall begin with asking the following question, Why is it that the enemy have left the New England provinces, and made these middle ones the seat of war? The answer is easy: New England is not infested with Tories, and we are. I have been tender in raising the cry against these men, and used numberless arguments to show them their danger, but it will not do to sacrifice a world either to their folly or their baseness. The period is now arrived, in which either they or we must change our sentiments, or one or both must fall. And what is a Tory? Good God! what is he? I should not be afraid to go with a hundred whigs against a thousand Tories, were they to attempt to get into arms. Every Tory is a coward; for servile, slavish, self-interested fear is the foundation of Toryism; and a man under such influence, though he may be cruel, never can be brave.

But, before the line of irrecoverable separation be drawn between us, let us reason the matter together: Your conduct is an invitation to the enemy, yet not one in a thousand of you has heart enough to join him. Howe is as much deceived by you as the American cause is injured by you. He expects you will all take up arms, and flock to his standard, with muskets on your shoulders. Your opinions are of no use to him, unless you support him personally, for 'tis soldiers, and not Tories, that he wants.

I once felt all that kind of anger, which a man ought to feel, against the mean principles that are held by the Tories: a noted one, who kept a tavern at Amboy, was standing at his door, with as pretty a child in his hand, about eight or nine years old, as ever I saw, and after speaking his mind as freely as he thought was prudent, finished with this unfatherly expression, *"Well! give me peace in my day."* Not a man lives on the continent but fully believes that a separation must some time or other finally take place, and a generous parent should have said, *"If there must be trouble, let it be in my day, that my child may have peace";* and this single reflection, well applied, is sufficient to awaken every man to duty. Not a place upon earth might be so happy as America. Her situation is remote from all the wrangling world, and she has nothing to do but to trade with them. A man can distinguish himself between temper and principle, and I am as confident, as I am that God governs the world, that America will never be happy till she gets clear of foreign dominion. Wars, without ceasing, will break out till that period arrives, and the continent must in the end be conqueror; for though the flame of liberty may sometimes cease to shine, the coal can never expire.

27

The selection of Virginia militiaman George Washington to lead the growing colonial forces encamped in the environs of Boston in the summer of 1775 was a stroke of either genius or luck for which Americans may well be thankful. The conditions confronting Washington were deplorable. Occasional bursts of despondency are quite understandable. Such an outburst occurs in a letter to a remote cousin, Lund Washington, written August 20, 1775:[27]

TO LUND WASHINGTON

Camp at Cambridge, *August 20, 1775*

The People of this government have obtained a Character which they by no means deserved; their officers generally speaking are the most indifferent kind of People I ever saw. I have already broke one Colo. and five Captains for Cowardice and for drawing more Pay and Provisions than they had Men in their Companies; there is two more Colos. now under arrest, and to be tried for the same offences; in short they are by no means such Troops, in any respect, as you are led to believe of them from the accts. which are published, but I need not make myself Enemies among them by this declaration, although it is consistent with truth. I dare say the Men would fight very well (if properly Officered) although they are an exceeding dirty and nasty people; had they been properly conducted at Bunkers Hill . . . or those that were there properly supported, the Regulars would have met with a shameful defeat, and a much more considerable loss than they did. . . ; it was for their behaviour on that occasion that the above Officers were broke, for I never spared one that was accused of Cowardice but brot 'em to immediate Tryal.

28

Dr. James Thacher witnessed the stirring events at Yorktown when General Washington's perseverance finally resulted in the surrender of Lord Cornwallis in 1781:[28]

JOURNAL OF DR. JAMES THACHER

[*October*] *19th.*—This is to us a most glorious day, but to the English, one of bitter chagrin and disappointment. Preparations are now making to receive as captives that vindicative, haughty commander and that victorious army, who, by their robberies and murders, have so long been a scourge to our brethren of the Southern states. Being on horseback, I anticipate a full share of satisfaction in viewing the various movements in the interesting scene.

The stipulated terms of capitulation are similar to those granted to General Lincoln at Charleston the last year. The captive troops are to march out with shouldered arms, colors cased and drums beating a British or German march, and to ground their arms at a place assigned for the purpose. The officers are allowed their side-arms and private property, and the generals and such officers as desire it are to go on parole to England or New York. The marines and seamen of the king's ships are prisoners of war to the navy of France; and the land forces to the United States. All military and artillery stores to be delivered up unimpaired. The royal prisoners to be sent into the interior of Virginia, Maryland and Pennsylvania in regiments, to have rations allowed them equal to the American soldiers, and to have their officers near them. Lord Cornwallis to man and despatch the *Bonetta* sloop-of-war with despatches to Sir Henry Clinton at New York without being searched, the vessel to be returned and the hands accounted for.

At about twelve o'clock, the combined army was arranged and drawn up in two lines extending more than a mile in length. The Americans were drawn up in a line on the right side of the road, and the French occupied the left. At the head of the former, the great American commander, mounted on his noble courser, took his station, attended by his aids. At the head of the latter was posted the excellent Count Rochambeau and his suite. The French troops, in complete uniform, displayed a martial and noble appearance; their bands of music, of which the timbrel formed a part, is a delightful novelty and produced while marching to the ground

---

[27] George Washington to Lund Washington, August 20, 1775, in John C. Fitzpatrick (ed.), *The Writings of George Washington* (Washington, 1931), III, 433.

[28] James Thacher, M.D., *A Military Journal During the American Revolutionary War, from 1775 to 1783* (Boston, 1723), pp. 345–348.

a most enchanting effect. The Americans, though not all in uniform, nor their dress so neat, yet exhibited an erect, soldierly air, and every countenance beamed with satisfaction and joy. The concourse of spectators from the country was prodigious, in point of numbers was probably equal to the military, but universal silence and order prevailed.

It was about two o'clock when the captive army advanced through the line formed for their reception. Every eye was prepared to gaze on Lord Cornwallis, the object of peculiar interest and solicitude; but he disappointed our anxious expectations; pretending indisposition, he made General O'Hara his substitute as the leader of his army. This officer was followed by the conquered troops in a slow and solemn step, with shouldered arms, colors cased and drums beating a British march. Having arrived at the head of the line, General O'Hara, elegantly mounted, advanced to his excellency the commander-in-chief, taking off his hat, and apologized for the non-appearance of Earl Cornwallis. With his usual dignity and politeness, his excellency pointed to Major-General Lincoln for directions, by whom the British army was conducted into a spacious field, where it was intended they should ground their arms.

The royal troops, while marching through the line formed by the allied army, exhibited a decent and neat appearance, as respects arms and clothing, for their commander opened his store and directed every soldier to be furnished with a new suit complete, prior to the capitulation. But in their line of march we remarked a disorderly and unsoldierly conduct, their step was irregular and their ranks frequently broken.

But it was in the field, when they came to the last act of the drama, that the spirit and pride of the British soldier was put to the severest test: here their mortification could not be concealed. Some of the platoon officers appeared to be exceedingly chagrined when giving the word "*ground arms*," and I am a witness that they performed this duty in a very unofficer-like manner; and that many of the soldiers manifested a *sullen*

temper, throwing their arms on the pile with violence, as if determined to render them useless. This irregularity, however, was checked by the authority of General Lincoln. After having grounded their arms and divested themselves of their accoutrements, the captive troops were conducted back to Yorktown and guarded by our troops till they could be removed to the place of their destination.

The British troops that were stationed at Gloucester surrendered at the same time and in the same manner to the command of the Duke de Luzerne [Lauzun].

This must be a very interesting and gratifying transaction to General Lincoln, who, having himself been obliged to surrender an army to a haughty foe the last year, has now assigned him the pleasing duty of giving laws to a conquered army in return, and of reflecting that the terms which were imposed on him are adopted as a basis of the surrender in the present instance. It is a very gratifying circumstance that every degree of harmony, confidence and friendly intercourse subsisted between the American and French troops during the campaign—no contest, except an emulous spirit to excel in exploits and enterprise against the common enemy, and a desire to be celebrated in the annals of history for an ardent love of great and heroic actions.

We are not to be surprised that the pride of the British officers is humbled on this occasion, as they have always entertained an exalted opinion of their own military prowess and affected to view the Americans as a contemptible, undisciplined rabble. But there is no display of magnanimity when a great commander shrinks from the inevitable misfortunes of war; and when it is considered that Lord Cornwallis has frequently appeared in splendid triumph at the head of his army, by which he is almost *adored*, we conceive it incumbent on him cheerfully to participate in their misfortunes and degradations, however humiliating; but it is said he gives himself up entirely to vexation and despair.

29

In Edmund Burke's speech, "On Conciliation with the Colonies," there is a prophetic note. Burke anticipates many subsequent explanations of the colonial drive toward independence. He similarly understood the sentiment of the American people:[29]

In this character of the Americans a love of freedom is the predominating feature which marks and distinguishes the whole: and as an ardent is always a jealous affection, your colonies become suspicious, restive, and untractable, whenever they see the least attempt to wrest from them by force, or shuffle from them by chicane, what they think the only advantage worth living for. This fierce spirit of liberty is stronger in the English colonies, probably, than in any other people of the earth, and this from a great variety of powerful causes; which, to understand the true temper of their minds, and the direction which this spirit takes, it will not be amiss to lay open somewhat more largely.

First, the people of the colonies are descendants of Englishmen. England, Sir, is a nation which still, I hope, respects, and formerly, adored, her freedom. The colonists emigrated from you when this part of your character was most predominant; and they took this bias and direction the moment they parted from your hands. They are therefore not only devoted to liberty, but to liberty according to English ideas and on English principles. Abstract liberty, like other mere abstractions, is not to be found. Liberty inheres in some sensible object; and every nation has formed to itself some favorite point, which by way of eminence becomes the criterion of their happiness. It happened, you know, Sir, that the great contests for freedom in this country were from the earliest times chiefly upon the question of taxing. Most of the contests in the ancient commonwealths turned primarily on the right of election of magistrates, or on the balance among the several orders of the state. The

question of money was not with them so immediate. But in England it was otherwise. On this point of taxes the ablest pens and most eloquent tongues have been exercised, the greatest spirits have acted and suffered . . . The colonies draw from you, as with their life-blood, these ideas and principles. Their love of liberty, as with you, fixed and attached on this specific point of taxing. Liberty might be safe or might be endangered in twenty other particulars without their being much pleased or alarmed. Here they felt its pulse; and as they found that beat, they thought themselves sick or sound. I do not say whether they were right or wrong in applying your general arguments to their own case. It is not easy, indeed, to make a monopoly of theorems and corollaries. The fact is, that they did thus apply those general arguments; and your mode of governing them, whether through lenity or indolence, through wisdom or mistake, confirmed them in the imagination, that they, as well as you, had an interest in these common principles.

They were further confirmed in this pleasing error by the form of their provincial legislative assemblies. Their governments are popular in an high degree: some are merely popular; in all, the popular representative is the most weighty; and this share of the people in their ordinary government never fails to inspire them with lofty sentiments, and with a strong aversion from whatever tends to deprive them of their chief importance.

If anything were wanting to this necessary operation of the form of government, religion would have given it a complete effect. Religion, always a principle of energy, in this new people is no way worn out or impaired; and their mode of professing it is also one main cause of this free spirit. The people are Protestants, and of that kind which is the most adverse to all implicit submission of mind and opinion. This is a persuasion not only favorable to liberty, but built upon it. I do not think, Sir, that the reason of this averseness in the dissenting churches from all that looks like absolute

---

[29] Edmund Burke, *The Works of Edmund Burke* (New York, 1859), I, 28–29.

government is so much to be sought in their religious tenets as in their history. Every one knows that the Roman Catholic religion is at least coeval with most of the governments where it prevails, that it has generally gone hand in hand with them, and received great favor and every kind of support from authority. The Church of England, too, was formed from her cradle under the nursing care of regular government. But the dissenting interests have sprung up in direct opposition to all the ordinary powers of the world, and could justify that opposition only on a strong claim to natural liberty. Their very existence depended on the powerful and unremitted assertion of that claim. All Protestantism, even the most cold and passive, is a sort of dissent. But the religion most prevalent in our northern colonies is a refinement on the principle of resistance: it is the dissidence of dissent, and the protestantism of the Protestant religion. This religion, under a variety of denominations agreeing in nothing but in the communion of the spirit of liberty, is predominant in most of the northern provinces, where the Church of England, notwithstanding its legal rights, is in reality no more than a sort of private sect, not composing, most probably, the tenth of the people. The colonists left England when this spirit was high, and in the emigrants was the highest of all; and even the stream of foreigners which has been constantly flowing into these colonies has, for the greatest part, been composed of dissenters from the establishments of their several countries, and have brought with them a temper and character far from alien to that of the people with whom they mixed.

Sir, I can perceive, by their manner, that some gentlemen object to the latitude of this description, because in the southern colonies the Church of England forms a large body and has a regular establishment. It is certainly true. There is, however, a circumstance attending these colonies, which, in my opinion, fully counterbalances this difference, and makes the spirit of liberty still more high and haughty than in those to the northward.

It is, that in Virginia and the Carolinas they have a vast multitude of slaves. Where this is the case in any part of the world, those who are free are by far the most proud and jealous of their freedom. Freedom is to them not only an enjoyment, but a kind of rank and privilege. Not seeing there, that freedom, as in countries where it is a common blessing, and as broad and general as the air, may be united with much abject toil, with great misery, with all the exterior of servitude, liberty looks, amongst them, like something that is more noble and liberal. I do not mean, Sir, to commend the superior morality of this sentiment, which has at least as much pride as virtue in it; but I cannot alter the nature of man. The fact is so; and these people of the southern colonies are much more strongly, and with an higher and more stubborn spirit, attached to liberty, than those to the northward. . . .

Permit me, Sir, to add another circumstance in our colonies, which contributes no mean part towards the growth and effect of this untractable spirit: I mean their education. In no country, perhaps, in the world is the law so general a study. The profession itself is numerous and powerful, and in most provinces it takes the lead. The greater number of the deputies sent to the Congress were lawyers. But all who read, and most do read, endeavor to obtain some smattering in that science. I have been told by an eminent bookseller, that in no branch of his business, after tracts of popular devotion, were so many books as those on the law exported to the plantations. The colonists have now fallen into the way of printing them for their own use. I hear that they have sold nearly as many of Blackstone's "Commentaries" in America as in England. General Gage marks out this disposition very particularly in a letter on your table. He states, that all the people in his government are lawyers, or smatterers in law. . . . This study renders men acute, inquisitive, dexterous, prompt in attack, ready in defence, full of resources. In other countries, the people, more simple, and of a less mercurial cast, judge of an ill principle in government only by an actual grievance; here they anticipate the evil, and judge of the pressure of the grievance by the badness of the principle. They augur misgovernment at a distance, and snuff the approach of tyranny in every tained breeze.

The last cause of this disobedient spirit in the colonies is hardly less powerful than the rest, as it is not merely moral, but laid deep in the natural constitution of things. Three thousand miles of ocean lie between you and them. No contrivance can prevent the effect of this distance in weakening government. Seas roll, and months pass, between the order and the execution; and the want of a speedy explanation of a single point is enough to defeat an whole system. You have, indeed, winged ministers of vengeance, who carry your bolts in their pounces to the remotest verge of the sea: but there a power steps in, that limits the arrogance of raging passions and furious elements, and says, "So far shalt thou go, and no farther." Who are you, that should fret and rage, and bite the chains of Nature? Nothing worse happens to you than does to all nations who have extensive empire; and it happens in all the forms into which empire can be thrown. In large bodies, the circulation of power must be less vigorous at the extremities. Nature has said it. The Turk cannot govern Egypt,

and Arabia, and Kurdistan, as he governs Thrace; nor has he the same dominion in Crimea and Algiers which he has at Brusa and Smyrna. Despotism itself is obliged to truck and huckster. The Sultan gets such obedience as he can. He governs with a loose rein, that he may govern at all; and the whole of the force and vigor of his authority in his centre is derived from a prudent relaxation in all his borders. Spain, in her provinces, is perhaps not so well obeyed as you are in yours. She complies, too; she submits; she watches times. This is the immutable condition, the eternal law, of extensive and detached empire.

Then, Sir, from these six capital sources, of descent, of form of government, of religion in the northern provinces, of manners in the southern, of education, of the remoteness of situation from the first mover of government,—from all these causes a fierce spirit of liberty has grown up. It has grown with the growth of the people in your colonies, and increased with the increase of their wealth: a spirit, that, unhappily meeting with an exercise of power in England, which, however lawful, is not reconcilable to any ideas of liberty, much less with theirs, has kindled this flame that is ready to consume us.

The Constitution and Conservatism

The problem of reconciling liberty and order and of finding the proper distribution of power between the center and the parts of the body politic which had plagued the British now plagued the Americans as well. These fundamental governmental problems were attacked immediately upon the adoption of the Declaration of Independence. From then until 1781, the delgates to the various sessions of the Second Continental Congress wrestled, whenever the more pressing demands for war legislation allowed, with the problems of creating a national government. Many distrusted a strong central government. That tyranny and centralization were indissolubly linked seemed one of the plainest lessons of history; that popular liberties could best be preserved by dispersing power seemed equally plain. Accordingly, the eighteenth-century expedient was to lodge control in local governments. On the other hand, the central authority must be strong enough to provide for an efficient national administration. A compromise between these two requirements was embodied in the Articles of Confederation.

THE PROBLEMS OF VICTORY

1

The Articles of Confederation, ratified in 1781 after long delays, provided the framework for a new central government. But the Articles were severely challenged by the problems posed by liquidating a war, a task more difficult than beginning one:[1]

ARTICLE I. The Stile of this confederacy shall be "The United States of America."

ART. II. Each state retains its sovereignty, freedom and independence, and every Power, Jurisdiction and right, which is not by this confederation expressly delegated to the United States, in Congress assembled.

ART. III. The said states hereby severally enter into a firm league of friendship with each other, for their common defence, the security of their Liberties, and their mutual and general welfare, binding themselves to

assist each other, against all force offered to, or attacks made upon them, or any of them, on account of religion, sovereignty, trade, or any other pretence whatever. . . .

ART. V. For the more convenient management of the general interests of the united states, delegates shall be annually appointed in such manner as the legislature of each state shall direct, to meet in Congress on the first Monday in November, in every year, with a power reserved to each state, to recal its delegates, or any of them, at any time within the year, and to send others in their stead, for the remainder of the Year.

No state shall be represented in Congress by less than two, nor by more than seven Members; and no person shall be capable of being a delegate for more than three years in any term of six years; nor shall any person, being a delegate, be capable of holding any office under the united states, for which he, or another for his benefit receives any salary, fees or emolument of any kind.

Each state shall maintain its own delegates in a meeting of the states, and while

---

[1] James D. Richardson (comp.), *A Compilation of the Messages and Papers of the Presidents, 1789–1897* (Washington, 1897), I, 9–16.

they act as members of the committee of the states.

In determining questions in the united states, in Congress assembled, each state shall have one vote.

Freedom of speech and debate in Congress shall not be impeached or questioned in any Court, or place out of Congress, and the members of congress shall be protected in their persons from arrests and imprisonments, during the time of their going to and from, and attendance on congress, except for treason, felony, or breach of the peace. . . .

ART. VIII. All charges of war, and all other expences that shall be incurred for the common defence or general welfare, and allowed by the united states in congress assembled, shall be defrayed out of a common treasury, which shall be supplied by the several states, in proportion to the value of all land within each state, granted to or surveyed for any Person, as such land and the buildings and improvements thereon shall be estimated according to such mode as the united states in congress assembled, shall from time to time direct and appoint. The taxes for paying that proportion shall be laid and levied by the authority and direction of the legislatures of the several states within the time agreed upon by the united states in congress assembled.

ART. IX. The united states in congress assembled, shall have the sole and exclusive right and power of determining on peace and war, except in the cases mentioned in the sixth article—of sending and receiving ambassadors—entering into treaties and alliances, provided that no treaty of commerce shall be made whereby the legislative power of the respective states shall be restrained from imposing such imposts and duties on foreigners, as their own people are subjected to, or from prohibiting the exportation or importation of any species of goods or commodities whatsoever—of establishing rules for deciding in all cases, what captures on land or water shall be legal, and in what manner prizes taken by land or naval forces in the service of the united states shall be

divided or appropriated.—of granting letters of marque and reprisal in times of peace—appointing courts for the trial of piracies and felonies committed on the high seas and establishing courts for receiving and determining finally appeals in all cases of captures, provided that no member of congress shall be appointed a judge of any of the said courts.

The united states in congress assembled shall also be the last resort on appeal in all disputes and differences now subsisting or that hereafter may arise between two or more states concerning boundary, jurisdiction or any other cause whatever; which authority shall always be exercised in the manner following. Whenever the legislative or executive authority or lawful agent of any state in controversy with another shall present a petition to congress, stating the matter in question and praying for a hearing, notice thereof shall be given by order of congress to the legislative or executive authority of the other state in controversy, and a day assigned for the appearance of the parties by their lawful agents, who shall then be directed to appoint by joint consent, commissioners or judges to constitute a court for hearing and determining the matter in question: but if they cannot agree, congress shall name three persons out of each of the united states, and from the list of such persons each party shall alternately strike out one, the petitioners beginning, until the number shall be reduced to thirteen; and from that number not less than seven, nor more than nine names as congress shall direct, shall in the presence of congress be drawn out by lot, and the persons whose names shall be so drawn or any five of them, shall be commissioners or judges, to hear and finally determine the controversy, so always as a major part of the judges who shall hear the cause shall agree in the determination: and if either party shall neglect to attend at the day appointed, without shewing reasons, which congress shall judge sufficient, or being present shall refuse to strike, the congress shall proceed to nominate three persons out of each state, and the secretary of congress shall strike in behalf of such party absent or refusing; and the judgment and sentence of the court to be appointed, in the manner before prescribed, shall be final and conclusive; and if any of the parties shall refuse to submit to the authority of such court, or to appear to defend their claim or cause, the court shall nevertheless proceed to pronounce sentence, or judgment, which shall in like manner be final and decisive, the judgment or sentence and other proceedings being in either case transmitted to congress, and lodged among the acts of congress for the security of the parties concerned: provided that every commissioner, before he sits in judgment, shall take an oath to be administered by one of the judges of the supreme or superior court of the state, where the cause shall be tried, "well and truly to hear and determine the matter in question, according to the best of his judgment, without favour, affection or hope of reward:" provided also that no state shall be deprived of territory for the benefit of the united states.

All controversies concerning the private right of soil claimed under different grants of two or more states, whose jurisdictions as they may respect such lands, and the states which passed such grants are adjusted, the said grants or either of them being at the same time claimed to have originated antecedent to such settlement of jurisdiction, shall on the petition of either party to the congress of the united states, be finally determined as near as may be in the same manner as is before prescribed for deciding disputes respecting territorial jurisdiction between different states.

The united states in congress assembled shall also have the sole and exclusive right and power of regulating the alloy and value of coin struck by their own authority, or by that of the respective states—fixing the standard of weights and measures throughout the united states.—regulating the trade and managing all affairs with the Indians, not members of any of the states, provided that the legislative right of any state within its own

limits be not infringed or violated—establishing and regulating post-offices from one state to another, throughout all the united states, and exacting such postage on the papers passing thro' the same as may be requisite to defray the expences of the said office—appointing all officers of the land forces, in the service of the united states, excepting regimental officers.—appointing all the officers of the naval forces, and commissioning all officers whatever in the service of the united states—making rules for the government and regulation of the said land and naval forces, and directing their operations.

The united states in congress assembled shall have authority to appoint a committee, to sit in the recess of congress, to be denominated "A Committee of the States," and to consist of one delegate from each state; and to appoint such other committees and civil officers as may be necessary for managing the general affairs of the united states under their direction—to appoint one of their number to preside, provided that no person be allowed to serve in the office of president more than one year in any term of three years; to ascertain the necessary sums of Money to be raised for the service of the united states, and to appropriate and apply the same for defraying the public expences —to borrow money, or emit bills on the credit of the united states, transmitting every half year to the respective states an account of the sums of money so borrowed or emitted,—to build and equip a navy—to agree upon the number of land forces, and to make requisitions from each state for its quota, in proportion to the number of white inhabitants in such state; which requisition shall be binding, and thereupon the legislature of each state shall appoint the regimental officers, raise the men and cloath, arm and equip them in a soldier like manner, at the expence of the united states, and the officers and men so cloathed, armed and equipped shall march to the place appointed, and within the time agreed on by the united states in congress assembled: but if the united states in congress assembled shall, on consideration of circumstances judge proper that any state should not raise men, or should raise a smaller number than its quota, and that any other state should raise a greater number of men than the quota thereof, such extra number shall be raised, officered, cloathed, armed and equipped in the same manner as the quota of such state, unless the legislature of such state shall judge that such extra number cannot be safely spared out of the same, in which case they shall raise officer, cloath, arm and equip as many of such extra number as they judge can be safely spared. And the officers and men so cloathed, armed and equipped, shall march to the place appointed, and within the time agreed on by the united states in congress assembled.

The united states in congress assembled shall never engage in a war, nor grant letters of marque and reprisal in time of peace, nor enter into any treaties or alliances, nor coin money, nor regulate the value thereof, nor ascertain the sums and expences necessary for the defence and welfare of the united states, or any of them, nor emit bills, nor borrow money on the credit of the united states, nor appropriate money, nor agree upon the number of vessels of war, to be built or purchased, or the number of land or sea forces to be raised, nor appoint a commander in chief of the army or navy, unless nine states assent to the same: nor shall a question on any other point, except for adjourning from day to day be determined, unless by the votes of a majority of the united states in congress assembled.

The congress of the united states shall have power to adjourn to any time within the year, and to any place within the united states, so that no period of adjournment be for a longer duration than the space of six Months, and shall publish the Journal of their proceedings monthly, except such parts thereof relating to treaties, alliances or military operations as in their judgment require secrecy; and the yeas and nays of the delegates of each state on any question shall be entered on the Journal, when it is desired by any delegate; and the delegates of a state, or any of them, at his or their request shall be furnished with a transcript of the said Journal, except such parts as are above excepted, to lay before the legislatures of the several states.

2

The Articles of Confederation, although marking a distinct step forward in the theory of federal government, were far from satisfactory to all groups. Nevertheless, the Confederation Congress adopted two monumental ordinances. The first, the Ordinance of 1785, set up an efficient method for the division and sale of the public domain:[2]

The Surveyors, as they are respectively qualified, shall proceed to divide the said territory into townships of six miles square, by lines running due north and south, and others crossing these at right angles, as near as may be, unless where the boundaries of the late Indian purchases may render the same impracticable, . . .

The first line, running due north and south as aforesaid, shall begin on the river Ohio, at a point that shall be found to be due north from the western termination of a line, which has been run as the southern boundary of the state of Pennsylvania; and the first line, running east and west, shall begin at the same point, and shall extend throughout the whole territory. Provided, that nothing herein shall be construed, as fixing the western boundary of the state of Pennsylvania. The geographer shall designate the townships, or fractional parts of townships, by numbers progressively from south to north; always beginning each range with number one; and the ranges shall be distinguished by their progressive numbers to the westward. The first range, extending from the Ohio to the lake Erie, being marked number

---

[2] Worthington C. Ford, *et al.* (eds.), *Journals of the Continental Congress, 1774–1789* (Washington, 1933), XXVIII, 375–378.

one. The Geographer shall personally attend to the running of the first east and west line; and shall take the latitude of the extremes of the first north and south line, and of the mouths of the principal rivers. . . .

The parts of the townships respectively, shall be marked by subdivisions into lots of one mile square, or 640 acres, in the same direction as the external lines, and numbered from 1 to 36; always beginning the succeeding range of the lots with the number next to that with which the preceding one concluded. . . .

The board of treasury shall transmit a copy of the original plats, previously noting thereon the townships and fractional parts ⸱of townships, which shall have fallen to the several states, by the distribution aforesaid, to the Commissioners of the loan office of the several states, who, after giving notice . . . shall proceed to sell the townships or fractional parts of townships, at public vendue, in the following manner, viz.: The township, or fractional part of a township, N. 1, in the first range, shall be sold entire; and N. 2, in the same range, by lots; and thus in alternate order through the whole of the first range . . . provided, that none of the lands, within the said territory, be sold under the price of one dollar the acre, to be paid in specie, or loan office certificates, reduced to specie value, by the scale of depreciation, or certificates of liquidated debts of the United States, including interest, besides the expense of the survey and other charges thereon, which are hereby rated at thirty six dollars the township, . . . on failure of which payment the said lands shall again be offered for sale.

There shall be reserved for the United States out of every township the four lots being numbered 8, 11, 26, 29, and out of every fractional part of a township, so many lots of the same numbers as shall be found thereon, for future sale. There shall be reserved the lot N. 16, of every township, for the maintenance of public schools within the said township; also one third part of all gold, silver, lead and copper mines, to be sold, or otherwise disposed of as Congress shall hereafter direct.

3

The Ordinance of 1787 was even more far reaching. The lands north of the Ohio and east of the Mississippi were to be divided into from three to five territories which would go through a process of political evolution as their population increased until they were admitted into the Union as states. During the probationary stage they were to be administered by a governor named by Congress, but:[3]

So soon as there shall be five thousand free male inhabitants of full age in the district, upon giving proof thereof to the governor, they shall receive authority, with time and place, to elect representatives from their counties or townships to represent them in the general assembly, *Provided,* That, for every five hundred free male inhabitants, there shall be one representative, and so on progressively with the number of free male inhabitants shall the right of representation increase, until the number of representatives shall amount to twenty five; after which, the number and proportion of representatives shall be regulated by the legislature; *Provided,* That no person be eligible or qualified to act as a representative unless he shall have been a citizen of one of the United States three years, and be a resident in the district, or unless he shall have resided in the district three years; and, in either case, shall likewise hold in his own right, in fee simple, two hundred acres of land within the same; *Provided, also,* That a freehold in fifty acres of land in the district having been a citizen of one of the states, and being resident in the district or the like freehold and two years residence in the district, shall be necessary to qualify a man as an elector of a representative.

The representatives thus elected, shall serve for the term of two years; and, in case of the death of a representative, or removal from office, the governor shall issue a writ

---

[3] *Ibid.,* (1936), XXXII, 337–339.

to the county or township for which he was a member, to elect another in his stead, to serve for the residue of the term.

The general assembly or legislature shall consist of the governor, legislative council, and a house of representatives. The legislative council shall consist of five members, to continue in Office five years, unless sooner removed by Congress any three of whom to be a quorum and the members of the Councill shall be nominated and appointed in the following manner, to wit; As soon as representatives shall be elected, the Governor shall appoint a time and place for them to meet together, and when met they shall nominate ten persons residents in the district and each possessed of a freehold in five hundred acres of Land and return their names to Congress; five of whom Congress shall appoint and commission to serve as aforesaid; and whenever a vacancy shall happen in the council, by death or removal from office, the house of representatives shall nominate two persons qualified as aforesaid, for each vacancy, and return their names to Congress, one of whom Congress shall appoint and commission for the residue of the term, and every five years, four months at least before the expiration of the time of service of the Members of Council, the said house shall nominate ten persons, qualified as aforesaid, and return their names to Congress, five of whom Congress shall appoint and commission to serve as Members of the council five years, unless sooner removed. And the Governor, legislative council, and house of representatives, shall have authority to make laws in all cases, for the good government of the district, not repugnant to the principles and Articles in this Ordinance established and declared. And all bills having passed by a majority in the house, and by a majority in the council, shall be referred to the Governor for his assent; but no bill or legislative Act whatever, shall be of any force without his assent. The governor shall have power to convene, prorogue, and dissolve the general assembly, when in his opinion, it shall be expedient.

4

In addition, the Northwest Ordinance contained a Bill of Rights which guaranteed the frontiersmen against governmental tyranny:[4]

It is hereby ordained and declared by the authority aforesaid, That the following articles shall be considered as Articles of compact between the Original States and the people and States in the said territory and forever remain unalterable, unless by common consent, *to wit,*

Article the First. No person demeaning himself in a peaceable and orderly manner shall ever be molested on account of his mode of worship or religious sentiments in the said territory.

Article the Second. The Inhabitants of the said territory shall always be entitled to the benefits of the writ of habeas corpus, and of the trial by Jury; of a proportionate representation of the people in the legislature, and of judicial proceedings according to the course of the common law; all persons shall be bailable, unless for capital offences, where the proof shall be evident or the presumption great; all fines shall be moderate; and no cruel or unusual punishments shall be inflicted; no man shall be deprived of his liberty or property, but by the judgment of his peers or the law of the land; and, should the public exigencies make it necessary for the common preservation to take any persons property, or to demand his particular services, full compensation shall be made for the same; and in the just preservation of rights and property it is understood and declared; that no law ought ever to be made, or have force in the said territory, that shall in any manner whatever, interfere with or affect private contracts or engagements, bona fide, and without fraud previously formed.

Article the Third. Religion, morality, *and knowledge being necessary to good government and the happiness of mankind,* Schools and the means of education shall forever be encouraged. The utmost good faith shall al-

---

[4] *Ibid.,* pp. 339–343.

ways be observed towards the Indians, their lands and property shall never be taken from them without their consent; and, in their property, rights, and liberty, they shall never be invaded or disturbed, unless in just and lawful wars authorized by Congress; but laws founded in justice and humanity shall from time to time be made, for preventing wrongs being done to them, and for preserving peace and friendship with them.

Article the Fourth. The said territory, and the States which may be formed therein, shall forever remain a part of this Confederacy of the United States of America, subject to the Articles of Confederation, and to such alterations therein as shall be constitutionally made; and to all the Acts and Ordinances of the United States in Congress assembled, conformable thereto. The inhabitants and settlers in the said territory, shall be subject to pay a part of the federal debts contracted or to be contracted, and a proportional part of the expences of Government, to be apportioned on them by Congress, according to the same common rule and measure by which apportionments thereof shall be made on the other States; and the taxes for paying their proportion shall be laid and levied by the authority and direction of the legislatures of the district or districts or new States, as in the original States, within the time agreed upon by the United States in Congress assembled. The legislatures of those districts or new States, shall never interfere with the primary disposal of the Soil by the United States in Congress assembled, nor with any regulations Congress may find necessary for securing the title in such soil to the bona fide purchasers. No tax shall be imposed on lands the property of the United States; and in no case shall non resident proprietors be taxed higher than residents. The navigable waters leading into the Mississippi and St. Lawrence, and the carrying places between the same shall be common highways and forever free, as well to the Inhabitants of the said territory as to the Citizens of the United States, and those of any other States that may be admitted into the Con-

federacy, without any tax, impost or duty therefor. . . .

Article the Sixth. *There shall be neither Slavery nor involuntary Servitude in the said territory otherwise than in the punishment of crimes, whereof the party shall have been duly convicted;* Provided, always, *That any person escaping into the same, from whom labor or service is lawfully claimed in any one of the original States, such fugitive may be lawfully reclaimed and conveyed to the person claiming his or her labor or service as aforesaid.*

5

The Ordinance of 1787 assured the preservation of the Union by guaranteeing eventual political equality to the territories and attested to the adequacy of the central government under the Articles of Confederation. Yet the Articles had weaknesses. That Congress lacked power over the states or over individuals sufficient to keep the ship of state on an even keel became clear when a serious depression gripped the country between 1785 and 1787; the national government could neither aid the poor nor force the states to act. Therefore in some states, where unsympathetic aristocrats controlled the legislatures, the lower classes attempted to take matters into their own hands. In Massachusetts they found a leader in the person of Daniel Shays, who organized a march on Boston in a vain effort to secure help by force. Their grievances were movingly voiced by one of Shays' rebels in a letter to the Hampshire Herald *in December 1786:*[5]

To the Printer of the Hampshire Herald.
Sir,

It has some how or other fallen to my lot to be employed in a more conspicuous manner than some others of my fellow citizens, in stepping forth on defence of the rights and privileges of the people, more especially of the county of Hampshire.

Therefore, upon the desire of the people now at arms, I take this method to publish to the world of mankind in general, particu-

---

[5] George R. Minot, *The History of the Insurrections in Massachusetts* (Boston, 1810 ed.), pp. 84–86.

larly the people of this Commonwealth, some of the principal grievances we complain of, . . .

In the first place, I must refer you to a draught of grievances drawn up by a committee of the people, now at arms, under the signature of Daniel Gray, chairman, which is heartily approved of; some others also are here added, viz.

1st. The General Court, for certain obvious reasons, must be removed out of the town of Boston.

2d. A revision of the constitution is absolutely necessary.

3d. All kinds of governmental securities, now on interest, that have been bought of the original owners for two shillings, three shillings, four shillings, and the highest for six shillings and eight pence on the pound, and have received more interest than the principal cost the speculator who purchased them—that if justice was done, we verily believe, nay positively know, it would save this Commonwealth thousands of pounds.

4th. Let the lands belonging to this Commonwealth, at the eastward, be sold at the best advantage to pay the remainder of our domestick debt.

5th. Let the monies arising from impost and excise be appropriated to discharge the foreign debt.

6th. Let that act, passed by the General Court last June by a small majority of only seven, called the Supplementary Aid, for twenty five years to come, be repealed.

7th. The total abolition of the Inferiour Court of Common Pleas and General Sessions of the Peace.

8th. Deputy Sheriffs totally set aside, as a useless set of officers in the community; and Constables who are really necessary, be empowered to do the duty, by which means a large swarm of lawyers will be banished from their wonted haunts, who have been more damage to the people at large, especially the common farmers, than the savage beasts of prey.

To this I boldly sign my proper name, as a hearty well-wisher to the real rights of the people.

THOMAS GROVER

Worcester, Dec. 7, 1786

6

Shays' Rebellion had its counterpart elsewhere, and legislation to aid debtors in states where the lower classes controlled the legislature helped convince conservatives that the Articles were inadequate. The merchant class and government leaders agreed that a strong central government was needed to keep "mobocracy" in check. A Brown University senior, in an address delivered in 1786, sums up the point of view of the merchants:[6]

It is allowed by all good Politicians that no form of government was ever better calculated to preserve the rights of mankind and make the subjects happy than that of Great Britain.

It joins the two extreams of Monarchy and Democracy and forms that Glorious ballance of Power which checks Usurpation and Tyranny in the throne and equally checks the Power in the hands of the people: which when left without restraint: like a Conflagration consumes the body from whence it originates.

As for the right of Taxation Claimed by the British Parliament even admitting of it to take place with all force yet when Great Britain should have found by experience how much it impeded the Growth and population of these Colonies, and of Consequence injured the Interest and happiness of the whole nation it is unreasonable to think 'tis folly to suppose that this pretended right would have been long in force.

It has been found by experience; it appears evident from the nature of governments that Republics can never flourish or answer the end of Society; but only in Countries of Small extent—

---

[6] Robert E. Moody (ed.), "Oratorical Afterthoughts on American Independence," *New England Quarterly*, VIII (September, 1935), 415–417. Reprinted by permission of the *New England Quarterly*.

This vast Continent is too widely extended to form a Republican government;

It is too unwieldly and unconnected to form a strict Union of Consequence its political Countenance must be weak and sickly Buisiness can never be transacted with despatch, or in Season; and it is next to impossible to accomplish any matters relating to the whole Secrecy and expedition so necessary in war are impractible. The Enemy will know our designs before we can carry them into execution; and while we are making the necessary preparation, it will either anticipate the blow or be prepaired for the attack We have heard much said in favour of the Glorious Liberty we have obtained by independence.

But let us stop a moment and count the Cost of this boasted aquisition—England before the American Revolution stood in the same Relationship to us as a Parent does to his child.

She was honourable amoung the nations; and like the Lionness in the forest her voice protected her young where ever it went.

Her Arm she extended over these Colonies and when our savage enemies invaded us She sent her veteran troops Commanded by some of the greatest Generals Europe ever boasted; who United with Americas Sons drove our enemies from our borders; and with their blood: bought us the victory! These were the most flourishing most happy days America ever saw.

But that fatal hour in which the Sword of Civil war was drawn: this pleasing Scene was changed—Consternation and distress sat on every Countenance; Fifty thousand souls fell victims to this Cruel war. Our Towns and lands were laid waste.

Our Fathers, Brothers, and Children in thousands fell around us; and our Breavest youth in the gay morn of Life armed at the rising hopes and pleasing prospects of future Glory were Cut off by untimely Death. Where ere we turned our Eyes we saw the breathless Corse; The Din of war Lamentation and sorrow Continually sounded in our

Ears: and the virgin Distress echoed in the evning gales. To these we must now subjoin the flood of Luxury and vice introduced by this unnatural war: vices which have Corrupted our former honest simple manners, and will soon fix us down in abject Slavery; and ripen us for heavens severest Judgment. Add to these immence debt foreign and domestic; into which this we are plunged; The Interest of which thus early in the morn of Independency is [*blank*] per Annum. Here then is a Sacrifice of Life Virtue and property; to gain what? An imaginary Liberty! Are we more free than we use to be? We enjoyed formerly all the Liberty Consistent with good government. What has since been aded is but Licentiousness.

Let us next view our present Situation of affairs. From a stagnation of buisness during the war we have run into an excess of Trade and thereby [strip] ourselves of nearly all our Circulating medium.—

America is in debts for millions more than She has money to pay; while her Commerce (which is almost the only way of surplying a Country situated like ours, with money and is the strongest bond of Union between Nations) is decreased in proportion to the scarcity of money.

Thus we are without money, Trade, and parmenent Alliances—Our repeated Attempts to surply the Defficiency of money by a paper Currency have destroyed our national Faith at home and abroad: and ruined thousands of our worthy Citizens—

The large extent of each State together with their Different manners and Customs fills them with Jealousies and animosities towards each other and prevent their vesting Congress as a head with that Power which is absolutely necessary in all governments But little regarde is paid to our Laws:

Our public pentioners are more numerous now than ever they were under the British Administration.

Our agriculture and manufactures are neglected while we revel in all the Luxuries of foreign Countries.

7

George Washington spoke for conservative governmental leaders in a panicky letter written to Henry Lee:[7]

The picture which you have exhibited . . . of the commotions and temper of numerous bodies in the eastern States, are equally to be lamented and deprecated. They exhibit a melancholy proof of what our transatlantic foe has predicted; and of another thing perhaps, which is still more to be regretted, and is yet more unaccountable, that mankind, when left to themselves, are unfit for their own government. I am mortified beyond expression when I view the clouds that have spread over the brightest morn that ever dawned upon any country. In a word, I am lost in amazement when I behold what intrigue, the interested views of desperate characters, ignorance, and jealousy of the minor part, are capable of effecting, as a scourge on the major part of our fellow citizens of the Union; for it is hardly to be supposed, that the great body of the people, though they will not act, can be so short-sighted or enveloped in darkness, as not to see rays of distant sun through all this mist of intoxication and folly.

You talk, my good Sir, of employing influence to appease the present tumults in Massachusetts. I know not where that influence is to be found, or, if attainable, that it would be a proper remedy for the disorders. *Influence* is no *government.* Let us have one by which our loves, liberties, and properties will be secured, or let us know the worst at once. Under these impressions, my humble opinion is, that there is a call for decision. Know precisely what the insurgents aim at. If they have *real* grievances, redress them if possible; or acknowledge the justice of them, and your inability to do it in the present moment. If they have not, employ the force of government against them at once. If this is inadequate, *all* will be convinced, that the

superstructure is bad, or wants support. To be more exposed in the eyes of the world, and more contemptible than we already are, is hardly possible. To delay one or the other of these, is to exasperate . . . or to give confidence, and will add to their numbers; for, like snow-balls, such bodies increase by every moment unless there is something in the way to obstruct and crumble them before the weight is too great and irresistible. . . .

CONSTITUTIONAL MECHANICS

8

For thirteen years after Shays' Rebellion articulate American political thought became increasingly conservative. Men alarmed over the security of their property, and those who desired greater unity in the conduct of foreign affairs demanded a central government much stronger than the decentralized government existing under the Articles of Confederation. The conservative trend materialized when the fifty-five men who were to frame the Constitution assembled at Philadelphia in the spring of 1787. The radicals of Revolutionary fame were absent; in their places were substantial men of property whose personal and class inclinations were toward a strong minority-controlled government. Yet they were fully aware that they could not obtain the complete satisfaction of their interests without a commitment to local and agrarian interests. In the following letter written to his son, George Mason, a delegate to the Constitutional Convention from Virginia, suggests something of the mood of the delegates on the eve of this memorable meeting:[8]

PHILADELPHIA, *May 20, 1787.*
Upon our arrival here on Thursday evening, seventeenth May, I found only the States of Virginia and Pennsylvania fully represented; and there are at this time only five—New York, the two Carolinas, and the two before mentioned. All the States, Rhode Island excepted, have made their appointments; but the members drop in slowly; some of the deputies from the Eastern States are here, but none of them have yet a suffi-

---

[7] John C. Fitzpatrick (ed.), *The Writings of George Washington* (Washington, 1939), XXIX, 33–34.

[8] George Mason to his son, George, May 20, 1787, in Kate M. Rowland, *The Life of George Mason* (New York, 1892), II, 100–102.

cient representation, and it will probably be several days before the Convention will be authorized to proceed to business. The expectations and hopes of all the Union centre in this Convention. God grant that we may be able to concert effectual means of preserving our country from the evils which threaten us.

The Virginia deputies (who are all here) meet and confer together two or three hours every day, in order to form a proper correspondence of sentiments; and for form's sake, to see what new deputies are arrived, and to grow into some acquaintance with each other, we regularly meet every day at three o'clock. These and some occasional conversations with the deputies of different States, and with some of the general officers of the late army (who are here upon a general meeting of the Cincinnati), are the only opportunities I have hitherto had of forming any opinion upon the great subject of our mission, and, consequently, a very imperfect and indecisive one. Yet, upon the great principles of it, I have reason to hope there will be greater unanimity and less opposition, except from the little States, than was at first apprehended. The most prevalent idea in the principal States seems to be a total alteration of the present federal system, and substituting a great national council or parliament, consisting of two branches of the legislature, founded upon the principles of equal proportionate representation, with full legislative powers upon all the subjects of the Union; and an executive: and to make the several State legislatures subordinate to the national, by giving the latter the power of a negative upon all such laws as they shall judge contrary to the interest of the federal Union. It is easy to foresee that there will be much difficulty in organizing a government upon this great scale, and at the same time reserving to the State legislatures a sufficient portion of power for promoting and securing the prosperity and happiness of their respective citizens; yet with a proper degree of coolness, liberality and candor (very rare commodities by the bye), I doubt

not but it may be effected. There are among a variety some very eccentric opinions upon this great subject; and what is a very extraordinary phenomenon, we are likely to find the republicans, on this occasion issue from the Southern and Middle States, and the anti-republicans from the Eastern; however extraordinary this may at first seem, it may, I think be accounted for from a very common and natural impulse of the human mind. Men disappointed in expectations too hastily and sanguinely formed, tired and disgusted with the unexpected evils they have experienced, and anxious to remove them as far as possible, are very apt to run into the opposite extreme; and the people of the Eastern States, setting out with more republican principles, have consequently been more disappointed than we have been.

We found travelling very expensive—from eight to nine dollars per day. In this city the living is cheap. We are at the old *Indian Queen* in Fourth Street, where we are very well accommodated, have a good room to ourselves, and are charged only twenty-five Pennsylvania currency per day, including our servants and horses, exclusive of club in liquors and extra charges; so that I hope I shall be able to defray my expenses with my public allowance, and more than that I do not wish.

9

When the framers of the Constitution had assembled, several of the delegates had already prepared tentative plans, and on these the ultimate document was based. One such plan, the Large State or Virginia Plan, went far toward creating a national government much stronger than that of the Articles of Confederation:[9]

1. *Resolved.* That the articles of Confederation ought to be so corrected & enlarged as to acomplish the objects proposed by their institution; namely "common defence, security of liberty and general welfare."

2. *Resolved therefore,* That the rights of

---

[9] Max Farrand (ed.), *The Records of the Federal Convention of 1787* (New Haven, 1911), I, 20–22.

suffrage in the National Legislature ought to be proportioned to the Quotas of contribution, or to the number of free inhabitants, as the one or the other rule may seem best in different cases.

3. *Resolved,* That the National Legislature ought to consist of two branches.

4. *Resolved,* That the members of the first branch of the National Legislature ought to be elected by the people of the several States every   for the terms of   ; to be of the age of   years at least, to receive liberal stipends by which they may be compensated for the devotion of their time to public service, to be ineligible to any office established by a particular State, or under the authority of the United States, except those peculiarly belonging to the functions of the first branch, during the term of service, and for the space of   after its expiration; to be incapable of reelection for the space of   after the expiration of their term of service, and to be subject to recall.

5. *Resolved,* That the members of the second branch of the National Legislature ought to be elected by those of the first, out of a proper number of persons nominated by the individual Legislatures, to be of the age of   years at least; to hold their offices for a term sufficient to ensure their independency; to receive liberal stipends, by which they may be compensated for the devotion of their time to public service; and to be ineligible to any office established by a particular State, or under the authority of the United States, except those peculiarly belonging to the functions of the second branch, during the term of service, and for the space of   after the expiration thereof.

6. *Resolved,* That each branch ought to possess the right of originating Acts; that the National Legislature ought to be impowered to enjoy the Legislative Rights vested in Congress by the Confederation & moreover to legislate in all cases to which the separate States are incompetent, or in which the harmony of the United States may be interrupted by the exercise of individual Legislation; to negative all laws passed by the several States, contravening in the opinion of the National Legislature the articles of Union; and to call forth the force of the Union agst. any member of the Union failing in its duty under the articles thereof.

7. *Resolved,* That a National Executive be instituted; to be chosen by the National Legislature for the term of   years; to receive punctually, at stated times, a fixed compensation for the services rendered, in which no increase or diminution shall be made so as to affect the Magistracy, existing at the time of the increase or diminution, and to be ineligible a second time; and that besides a general authority to execute the National laws, it ought to enjoy the Executive rights vested in Congress by the Confederation.

8. *Resolved,* That the Executive and a convenient number of the National Judiciary, ought to compose a Council on revision with authority to examine every act of the National Legislature before it shall operate, & every act of a particular Legislature before a Negative thereon shall be final; and that the dissent of the said Council shall amount to a rejection, unless the Act of the National Legislature be passed again, or that of a particular Legislature be again negatived by   of the members of each branch.

9. *Resolved,* That a National Judiciary be established to consist of one or more supreme tribunals, and of inferior tribunals to be chosen by the National Legislature, to hold their offices during good behaviour; and to receive punctually at stated times fixed compensation for their services, in which no increase or diminution shall be made so as to affect the persons actually in office at the time of such increase or diminution. That the jurisdiction of the inferior tribunals shall be to hear and determine in the first instance, and of the supreme tribunal to hear & determine in the dernier resort, all piracies & felonies on the high seas, captures from an enemy; cases in which foreigners or citizens of other States applying to such jurisdictions may be interested, or which respect the collection of the National revenue; impeachments of any National officers, and questions

which may involve the national peace and harmony.

10. *Resolved,* That provision ought to be made for the admission of States lawfully arising within the limits of the United States, whether from a voluntary junction of Government & Territory or otherwise, with the consent of a number of voices in the National legislature less than the whole.

11. *Resolved,* That a Republican Government & the territory of each State, except in the instance of a voluntary junction of Government & territory, ought to be guaranteed by the United States to each State.

12. *Resolved,* That provision ought to be made for the continuance of Congress and their authorities and privileges, until a given day after the reform of the articles of Union shall be adopted, and for the completion of all their engagements.

13. *Resolved,* That provision ought to be made for the amendment of the Articles of Union whensoever it shall seem necessary, and that the assent of the National Legislature ought not to be required thereto.

14. *Resolved,* That the Legislative Executive & Judiciary powers within the several States ought to be bound by oath to support the articles of Union.

15. *Resolved,* That the amendments which shall be offered to the Confederation, by the Convention ought at a proper time, or times, after the approbation of Congress to be submitted to an assembly or assemblies of Representatives, recommended by the several Legislatures to be expressly chosen by the people, to consider & decide thereon.

10

The Virginia Plan failed to provide an acceptable arrangement for state-national relations. Its proposal for a Council to "examine every act . . . of a particular legislature before a Negative thereon shall be final" would have aroused states rights opposition, just as would the provision that Congress have power to "negative all laws passed by the several States" contrary to the Constitution. The delegates turned instead to the so-called New Jersey Plan, which suggested in its sixth article a

more disguised national principle later adopted as the "supreme law of the land clause":[10]

6. *Resd,* That all Acts of the U. States in Cong. made by virtue & in pursuance of the powers hereby & by the articles of confederation vested in them, and all Treaties made & ratified under the authority of the U. States shall be the supreme law of the respective States so far north as those Acts or Treaties shall relate to the said States or their Citizens, and that the Judiciary of the several States shall be bound thereby in their decisions, any thing in the respective laws of the Individual States to the contrary notwithstanding, and that if any State, or any body of men in any State shall oppose or prevent ye carrying into execution such acts or treaties, the federal Executive shall be authorized to call forth the power of the Confederated States, or so much thereof as may be necessary to enforce and compel an obedience to such Acts or an observance of such Treaties.

11

The temper of the delegates was shown in the long debate over these plans. Some, embittered by their experiences during the "Critical Period," held with Hamilton that the people should be denied participation in the new government; others sincerely advocated democracy or held that popular concessions were needed to win support. These divisions were highlighted during the debate on means of selecting members of the House of Representatives:[11]

In committee of the whole on Mr. Randolph's propositions.

The 3d Resolution "that the National Legislature ought to consist of two branches" was agreed to without debate or dissent, except that of Pennsylvania, given probably from complaisance to Doctor Franklin, who was understood to be partial to a single House of legislation.

Resolution 4, first clause "that the members of the first branch of the National Leg-

---

10 *Ibid.,* I, 245.
11 *Ibid.,* I, 47–50.

islature ought to be elected by the people of the several States" being taken up,

Mr. SHERMAN [Conn.] opposed the election by the people. insisting that it ought to be by the State Legislatures. The people, he said, immediately should have as little to do as may be about the government. They want information, and are constantly liable to be misled.

Mr. GERRY [Mass.]. The evils we experience flow from the excess of democracy. The people do not want virtue, but are the dupes of pretended patriots. In Massachusetts it had been fully confirmed by experience that they are daily misled into the most baneful measures and opinions by the false reports circulated by designing men, and which no one on the spot can refute. One principal evil arises from the want of due provision for those employed in the administration of government. It would seem to be a maxim of democracy to starve the public servants. He mentioned the popular clamour in Massachusetts for the reduction of salaries and the attack made on that of the Governor, though secured by the spirit of the Constitution itself. He had he said been too republican heretofore: he was still however republican, but had been taught by experience the danger of the levilling spirit.

Mr. MASON [Va.] argued strongly for an election of the larger branch by the people. It was to be the grand depository of the democratic principle of the Government. It was, so to speak, to be our House of Commons. It ought to know and sympathise with every part of the community; and ought therefore to be taken not only from different parts of the whole republic, but also from different districts of the larger members of it, which had in several instances, particularly in Virginia, different interests and views arising from difference of produce, of habits, etc., etc. He admitted that we had been too democratic, but was afraid we should incautiously run into the opposite extreme. We ought to attend to the rights of every class of the people. He had often wondered at the indifference of the superior classes of society

to this dictate of humanity and policy; considering that however affluent their circumstances, or elevated their situations might be, the course of a few years not only might but certainly would distribute their posterity throughout the lowest classes of society. Every selfish motive, therefore, every family attachment, ought to recommend such a system of policy as would provide no less carefully for the rights and happiness of the lowest than of the highest orders of citizens.

Mr. WILSON [Penn.] contended strenuously for drawing the most numerous branch of the Legislature immediately from the people. He was for raising the federal pyramid to a considerable altitude, and for that reason wished to give it as broad a basis as possible. No government could long subsist without the confidence of the people. In a republican government this confidence was peculiarly essential. He also thought it wrong to increase the weight of the State Legislatures by making them the electors of the National Legislature. All interference between the general and local governments should be obviated as much as possible. On examination it would be found that the opposition of States to federal measures had proceded much more from the officers of the States than from the people at large.

Mr. MADISON considered the popular election of one branch of the National Legislature as essential to every plan of free government. He observed that in some of the States one branch of the Legislature was composed of men already removed from the people by an intervening body of electors. That if the first branch of the general legislature should be elected by the State Legislatures, the second branch elected by the first, the Executive by the second together with the first; and other appointments again made for subordinate purposes by the Executive, the people would be lost sight of altogether; and the necessary sympathy between them and their rulers and officers, too little felt. He was an advocate for the policy of refining the popular appointments by successive filtrations, but thought it might be pushed too far. He wished the expedient to be resorted to only in the appointment of the second branch of the Legislature, and in the executive and judiciary branches of the government. He thought, too, that the great fabric to be raised would be more stable and durable, if it should rest on the solid foundation of the people themselves, than if it should stand merely on the pillars of the Legislatures.

Mr. GERRY did not like the election by the people. The maxims taken from the British Constitution were often fallacious when applied to our situation which was extremely different. Experience he said had shewn that the State legislatures drawn immediately from the people did not always possess their confidence. He had no objection, however, to an election by the people, if it were so qualified that men of honor and character might not be unwilling to be joined in the appointments. He seemed to think the people might nominate a certain number out of which the State legislatures should be bound to choose.

Mr. BUTLER [S. C.] thought an election by the people an impracticable mode.

On the question for an election of the first branch of the National Legislature by the people:

Mass. ay. Conn. div. N. Y. ay. N. J. no. Penn. ay. Del. div. Va. ay. N. C. ay. S. C. no. Geo. ay.

CONSTITUTION OF THE UNITED STATES

12

The conflicting objectives of diverse groups and divisive sectional antagonisms has frequently obscured the substantial agreement of the constitution makers of 1787. Disagreements about federal-state relations were real and issues of representation were vital. But these were actually disagreements of detail. The Founding Fathers wished to supplant the Articles of Confederation and to create a national government with powers adequate to the needs they regarded as essential to the safety and security of the

nation. The document framed in Philadelphia met their goals:[12]

We the people of the United States in order to form a more perfect union, establish justice, insure domestic tranquillity, provide for the common defence, promote the general welfare and secure the blessings of liberty to ourselves and our posterity, do ordain and establish this CONSTITUTION for the United States of America.

ARTICLE I

Section 1. All legislative powers herein granted shall be vested in a Congress of the United States, which shall consist of a Senate and House of Representatives.

Section 2. The House of Representatives shall be composed of members chosen every second year by the people of the several States, and the electors in each State shall have the qualifications requisite for electors of the most numerous branch of the State Legislature.

No person shall be a Representative who shall not have attained to the age of twenty-five years, and been seven years a citizen of the United States, and who shall not when elected, be an inhabitant of that State in which he shall be chosen.

Representatives and direct taxes shall be apportioned among the several States which may be included within this Union, according to their respective numbers, which shall be determined by adding to the whole number of free persons, including those bound to service for a term of years, and excluding Indians not taxed, three fifths of all other persons. The actual enumeration shall be made within three years after the first meeting of the Congress of the United States, and within every subsequent term of ten years, in such manner as they shall by law direct. The number of Representatives shall not

---

[12] Jonathan Elliot, *The Debates in the Several Conventions on the Adoption of the Federal Constitution* (1836), 1–21, "copied and carefully compared with the original in the Department of State. Punctuation, paragraphs, and capital letters, same as said original."

exceed one for every thirty thousand, but each State shall have at least one Representative; and until such enumeration shall be made, the State of *New Hampshire* shall be entitled to choose three, *Massachusetts* eight, *Rhode Island* and *Providence Plantations* one, *Connecticut* five, *New York* six, *New Jersey* four, *Pennsylvania* eight, *Delaware* one, *Maryland* six, *Virginia* ten, *North Carolina* five, *South Carolina* five, and *Georgia* three.

When vacancies happen in the representation from any State, the Executive authority thereof shall issue writs of election to fill such vacancies.

The House of Representatives shall choose their Speaker and other officers; and shall have the sole power of impeachment.

Section 3. The Senate of the United States shall be composed of two Senators from each State, chosen by the Legislature thereof, for six years; and each Senator shall have one vote.

Immediately after they shall be assembled in consequence of the first election, they shall be divided as equally as may be, into three classes. The seats of the Senators of the first class shall be vacated at the expiration of the second year, of the second class at the expiration of the fourth year, and of the third class at the expiration of the sixth year, so that one third may be chosen every second year; and if vacancies happen by resignation or otherwise, during the recess of the Legislature of any State, the executive thereof may make temporary appointments, until the next meeting of the Legislature, which shall then fill such vacancies.

No person shall be a Senator who shall not have attained to the age of thirty years, and been nine years a citizen of the United States, and who shall not, when elected, be an inhabitant of that State for which he shall be chosen.

The Vice President of the United States shall be President of the Senate, but shall have no vote unless they be equally divided.

The Senate shall choose their other officers, and also a President protempore, in the absence of the Vice President or when he shall exercise the office of President of the United States.

The Senate shall have the sole power to try all impeachments: when sitting for that purpose, they shall be on oath or affirmation. When the President of the United States is tried the Chief Justice shall preside: and no person shall be convicted without the concurrence of two-thirds of the members present.

Judgment in cases of impeachment shall not extend farther than to removal from office, and disqualification to hold and enjoy any office of honor, trust, or profit under the United States: but the party convicted shall nevertheless be liable and subject to indictment, trial, judgment and punishment, according to law.

Section 4. The times, places and manner of holding elections for Senators and Representatives, shall be prescribed in each State by the legislature thereof; but the Congress may at any time by law make or alter such regulations, except as to the places of choosing Senators.

The Congress shall assemble at least once in every year, and such meeting shall be on the first Monday in December unless they shall by law appoint a different day.

Section 5. Each House shall be the judge of the elections, returns and qualifications of its own members, and a majority of each shall constitute a quorum to do business; but a smaller number may adjourn from day to day, and may be authorized to compel the attendance of absent members, in such manner, and under such penalties as each House may provide.

Each House may determine the rules of its proceedings, punish its members for disorderly behavior, and, with the concurrence of two thirds, expel a member.

Each House shall keep a journal of its proceedings, and from time to time publish the same, excepting such parts as may in their judgment require Secrecy; and the yeas and nays of the members of either House on any question shall, at the desire of one-fifth of those present, be entered on the journal.

Neither House, during the Session of Congress, shall, without the consent of the other, adjourn for more than three days, nor to any other place than that in which the two Houses shall be sitting.

Section 6. The Senators and Representatives shall receive a compensation for their services, to be ascertained by law, and paid out of the Treasury of the United States. They shall in all cases except treason, felony and breach of the peace, be privileged from arrest during their attendance at the session of their respective Houses, and in going to and returning from the same; and for any speech or debate in either House, they shall not be questioned in any other place.

No Senator or Representative shall, during the time for which he was elected, be appointed to any civil office under the authority of the United States, which shall have been created, or the emoluments whereof shall have been increased during such time: and no person holding any office under the United States shall be a member of either House during his continuance in office.

Section 7. All bills for raising revenue shall originate in the House of Representatives; but the Senate may propose, or concur with, amendments, as on other bills.

Every bill which shall have passed the House of Representatives, and the Senate, shall, before it become a law, be presented to the President of the United States; if he approve he shall sign it, but if not he shall return it, with his objections to that House in which it shall have originated, who shall enter the objections at large on their journal, and proceed to reconsider it. If after such reconsideration two thirds of that House shall agree to pass the bill, it shall be sent, together with the objections, to the other House, by which it shall likewise be reconsidered, and if approved by two thirds of that House, it shall become a law. But in all such cases the votes of both Houses shall be determined by yeas and nays, and the names of the persons voting for and against the bill shall be entered on the journal of each House respectively. If any bill shall not be returned by the President within ten days (Sundays excepted,) after it shall have been presented to him, the same shall be a law, in like manner as if he had signed it, unless the Congress by their adjournment prevent its return, in which case it shall not be a law.

Every order, resolution, or vote to which the concurrence of the Senate and House of Representatives may be necessary (except on a question of adjournment) shall be presented to the President of the United States; and before the same shall take effect, shall be approved by him, or, being disapproved by him, shall be repassed by two-thirds of the Senate and House of Representatives, according to the rules and limitations prescribed in the case of a bill.

Section 8. The Congress shall have power To lay and collect taxes, duties, imposts and excises, to pay the debts and provide for the common defence and general welfare of the United States; but all duties, imposts and excises shall be uniform throughout the United States;

To borrow money on the credit of the United States;

To regulate commerce with foreign nations, and among the several States, and with the Indian tribes;

To establish an uniform rule of naturalization, and uniform laws on the subject of bankruptcies throughout the United States;

To coin money, regulate the value thereof, and of foreign coin, and fix the standard of weights and measures;

To provide for the punishment of counterfeiting the securities and current coin of the United States;

To establish post offices and post roads;

To promote the progress of science and useful arts, by securing for limited times to authors and inventors the exclusive right to their respective writings and discoveries;

To constitute tribunals inferior to the supreme court;

To define and punish piracies and felonies committed on the high seas and offences against the law of nations;

To declare war, grant letters of marque and reprisal, and make rules concerning captures on land and water;

To raise and support armies, but no appropriation of money to that use shall be for a longer term than two years;

To provide and maintain a navy;

To make rules for the government and regulation of the land and naval forces;

To provide for calling forth the militia to execute the laws of the Union, suppress insurrections and repel invasions;

To provide for organizing, arming and disciplining, the militia, and for governing such part of them as may be employed in the service of the United States, reserving to the States respectively, the appointment of the officers, and the authority of training the militia according to the discipline prescribed by Congress;

To exercise exclusive legislation in all cases whatsoever over such district (not exceeding ten miles square) as may, by cession of particular States, and the acceptance of Congress, become the seat of the government of the United States, and to exercise like authority over all places purchased by the consent of the Legislature of the State in which the same shall be, for the erection of forts, magazines, arsenals, dockyards, and other needful buildings;—And

To make all laws which shall be necessary and proper for carrying into execution the foregoing powers, and all other powers vested by this constitution in the government of the United States, or in any department or officer thereof.

Section 9. The migration or importation of such persons as any of the States now existing shall think proper to admit, shall not be prohibited by the Congress prior to the year eighteen hundred and eight, but a tax or duty may be imposed on such importation, not exceeding ten dollars for each person.

The privilege of the writ of *Habeas Corpus* shall not be suspended, unless when in cases of rebellion or invasion the public safety may require it.

No bill of attainder or ex post facto law shall be passed.

No capitation, or other direct, tax shall be laid, unless in proportion to the census or enumeration herein before directed to be taken.

No tax or duty shall be laid on articles exported from any State.

No preference shall be given by any regulation of commerce or revenue to the ports of one State over those of another: nor shall vessels bound to, or from, one State, be obliged to enter, clear, or pay duties in another.

No money shall be drawn from the Treasury, but in consequence of appropriations made by law; and a regular statement and account of the receipts and expenditures of all public money shall be published from time to time.

No title of nobility shall be granted by the United States and no person holding any office of profit or trust under them, shall, without the consent of the Congress, accept of any present, emolument, office, or title, of any kind whatever, from any king, prince, or foreign State.

Section 10. No State shall enter into any treaty, alliance, or confederation; grant letters of marque and reprisal; coin money, emit bills of credit; make any thing but gold and silver coin a tender in payment of debts; pass any bill of attainder, ex post facto law; or law impairing the obligation of contracts; or grant any title of nobility.

No State shall, without the consent of the Congress, lay any imposts or duties on imports or exports, except what may be absolutely necessary for executing its inspection laws: and the net produce of all duties and imposts, laid by any State on imports or exports, shall be for the use of the Treasury of the United States; and all such laws shall be subject to the revision and control of the Congress.

No State shall, without the consent of Congress, lay any duty of tonnage, keep troops, or ships of war in time of peace, enter into any agreement or compact with another State, or with a foreign power, or engage in war, unless actually invaded, or in such imminent danger as will not admit of delay.

ARTICLE II

Section 1. The executive power shall be vested in a President of the United States of America. He shall hold his office during the term of four years, and, together with the Vice-President, chosen for the same term, be elected as follows:

Each State shall appoint, in such manner as the Legislature thereof may direct, a number of electors equal to the whole number of Senators and Representatives to which the State may be entitled in the Congress; but no Senator or Representative, or person holding office of trust or profit under the United States, shall be appointed an elector.

The electors shall meet in their respective States, and vote by ballot for two persons, of whom one at least shall not be an inhabitant of the same State with themselves. And they shall make a list of all the persons voted for, and of the number of votes for each; which list they shall sign and certify, and transmit sealed to the seat of the government of the United States, directed to the President of the Senate. The President of the Senate shall, in the presence of the Senate and House of Representatives, open all the certificates, and the votes shall then be counted. The person having the greatest number of votes shall be the President, if such number be a majority of the whole number of electors appointed; and if there be more than one who have such majority, and have an equal number of votes, then the House of Representatives shall immediately choose by ballot one of them for President; and if no person have a majority, then from the five highest on the list the said House shall, in like manner, choose the President. But in choosing the President, the votes shall be taken by States, the representation from each State having one vote; a quorum for this purpose shall consist of a member or members from two-thirds of the States, and a majority of all the States shall be necessary to a choice. In every case, after the choice of the President, the person having the greatest number of votes of the electors shall be the Vice-President. But if there should remain two or more who have equal votes, the Senate shall choose from them by ballot the Vice-President.

The Congress may determine the time of choosing the electors, and the day on which they shall give their votes; which day shall be the same throughout the United States.

No person except a natural born citizen, or a citizen of the United States, at the time of the adoption of this constitution, shall be eligible to the office of President; neither shall any person be eligible to that office who shall not have attained to the age of thirty-five years, and been fourteen years a resident within the United States.

In case of the removal of the President from office, or of his death, resignation or inability to discharge the powers and duties of the said office, the same shall devolve on the Vice-President, and the Congress may by law provide for the case of removal, death, resignation or inability, both of the President and Vice-President, declaring what officer shall then act as President, and such officer shall act accordingly, until the disability be removed, or a President shall be elected.

The President shall, at stated times, receive for his services, a compensation, which shall neither be increased nor diminished during the period for which he shall have been elected, and he shall not receive within that period any other emolument from the United States, or any of them.

Before he enter on the execution of his office, he shall take the following oath or affirmation: *"I do solemnly swear (or affirm) that I will faithfully execute the office of President of the United States, and will, to the best of my ability, preserve, protect, and defend the Constitution of the United States."*

Section 2. The President shall be commander in chief of the army and navy of the United States, and of the militia of the several States, when called into the actual service of the United States; he may require the opinion, in writing, of the principal officer in each of the executive departments, upon any subject relating to the duties of their respective offices; and he shall have power to grant reprieves and pardons for offences against the United States, except in cases of impeachment.

He shall have power, by and with the advice and consent of the Senate, to make treaties, provided two-thirds of the Senators present concur; and he shall nominate, and by and with the advice and consent of the Senate, shall appoint ambassadors, other public ministers and consuls, judges of the supreme court, and all other officers of the United States, whose appointments are not herein otherwise provided for, and which shall be established by law: But the Congress may by law vest the appointment of such inferior officers as they think proper, in the President alone, in the courts of law, or in the heads of departments.

The President shall have power to fill up all vacancies that may happen during the recess of the Senate, by granting commissions which shall expire at the end of their next session.

Section 3. He shall from time to time give to the Congress information of the state of the Union, and recommend to their consideration such measures as he shall judge necessary and expedient; he may, on extraordinary occasions, convene both Houses, or either of them, and, in case of disagreement between them, with respect to the time of adjournment, he may adjourn them to such time as he shall think proper; he shall receive ambassadors and other public ministers; he shall take care that the laws be faithfully executed, and shall commission all the officers of the United States.

Section 4. The President, Vice-President and all civil officers of the United States, shall be removed from office on impeachment for, and conviction of, treason, bribery, or other high crimes and misdemeanors.

ARTICLE III

Section 1. The judicial power of the United States shall be vested in one Supreme Court, and in such inferior courts as the Congress

may from time to time ordain and establish. The judges, both of the supreme and inferior courts, shall hold their offices during good behaviour, and shall, at stated times, receive for their services, a compensation, which shall not be diminished during their continuance in office.

Section 2. The judicial power shall extend to all cases in law and equity, arising under this constitution, the laws of the United States, and the treaties made, or which shall be made, under their authority; to all cases—affecting ambassadors, other public ministers, and consuls;—to all cases of admiralty and maritime jurisdiction;—to controversies to which the United States shall be a party;—to controversies between two or more States;—between a State and citizens of another State;—between citizens of different States;—between citizens of the same State, claiming lands under grants of different States, and between a State or the citizens thereof, and foreign States, citizens or subjects.

In all cases affecting ambassadors, other public ministers and consuls, and those in which a State shall be party, the supreme court shall have original jurisdiction. In all the other cases before-mentioned, the supreme court shall have appellate jurisdiction, both as to law and fact, with such exceptions, and under such regulations, as the Congress shall make.

The trial of all crimes, except in cases of impeachment, shall be by jury; and such trial shall be held in the State where the said crimes shall have been committed; but when not committed within any State, the trial shall be at such place or places as the Congress may by law have directed.

Section 3. Treason against the United States, shall consist only in levying war against them, or in adhering to their enemies, giving them aid and comfort. No person shall be convicted of treason, unless on the testimony of two witnesses to the same overt act, or on confession in open court.

The Congress shall have power to declare the punishment of treason, but no attainder of treason shall work corruption of blood, or forfeiture except during the life of the person attainted.

ARTICLE IV

Section 1. Full faith and credit shall be given in each State to the public acts, records, and judicial proceedings of every other State. And the Congress may by general laws prescribe the manner in which such acts, records, and proceedings shall be proved, and the effect thereof.

Section 2. The citizens of each State shall be entitled to all the privileges and immunities of citizens in the several States.

A person charged in any State with treason, felony, or other crime, who shall flee from justice, and be found in another State, shall on demand of the executive authority of the State from which he fled, be delivered up, to be removed to the State having jurisdiction of the crime.

No person held to service or labor in one State, under the laws thereof, escaping into another, shall, in consequence of any law or regulation therein, be discharged from such service or labor, but shall be delivered up on claim of the party to whom such service or labor may be due.

Section 3. New States may be admitted by the Congress into this Union; but no new State shall be formed or erected within the jurisdiction of any other State; nor any State be formed by the junction of two or more States, or parts of States, without the consent of the Legislature of the States concerned as well as of the Congress.

The Congress shall have power to dispose of and make all needful rules and regulations respecting the territory or other property belonging to the United States; and nothing in this constitution shall be so construed as to prejudice any claims of the United States, or of any particular State.

Section 4. The United States shall guaranty to every State in this Union a republican form of government, and shall protect each of them against invasion; and on application of the legislature, or of the executive (when the legislature cannot be convened) against domestic violence.

ARTICLE V

The Congress, whenever two-thirds of both Houses shall deem it necessary, shall propose amendments to this constitution, or, on the application of the legislatures of two-thirds of the several States, shall call a convention for proposing amendments, which in either case, shall be valid to all intents and purposes, as part of this constitution, when ratified by the legislatures of three-fourths of the several States, or by conventions in three-fourths thereof, as the one or the other mode of ratification may be proposed by the Congress; provided, that no amendment, which may be made prior to the year one thousand eight hundred and eight, shall in any manner affect the first and fourth clauses in the ninth section of the first article; and that no State, without its consent, shall be deprived of its equal suffrage in the Senate.

ARTICLE VI

All debts contracted and engagements entered into, before the adoption of this constitution, shall be as valid against the United States under this constitution as under the confederation.

This constitution, and the laws of the United States which shall be made in pursuance thereof; and all treaties made, or which shall be made, under the authority of the United States, shall be the supreme law of the land; and the judges in every state shall be bound thereby, any thing in the constitution or laws of any State to the contrary notwithstanding.

The Senators and Representatives before mentioned, and the members of the several State legislatures, and all executive and judicial officers, both of the United States and of the several States shall be bound by oath or affirmation, to support this constitution: but no religious test shall ever be required as a qualification to any office or public trust under the United States.

ARTICLE VII

The ratification of the conventions of nine states, shall be sufficient for the establishment of this constitution between the States so ratifying the same.

Done in convention by the unanimous consent of the States present the seventeenth day of September in the year of our Lord one thousand seven hundred and eighty-seven and of the independence of the United States of America the twelfth.

13

The Constitution makers agreed that the new frame of government should become operative when ratified by conventions in nine of the states. The choice of delegates to these bodies occasioned the first national political campaign in American history. On one side were the opponents of the Constitution: small farmers, workers, and artisans, who feared a centralized government that seemed to incorporate so little of real democracy. They constituted the majority of the population, but their strength was minimized largely because they were disorganized and unprepared. In this situation they resorted to exaggeration and intimidation, methods that are described by a disgusted Federalist from the back country of North Carolina:[13]

The week previous to the election, I was riding in company with Major Murfee . . . and a Dr. Garvey, a warm-hearted and energetic Irishman, several miles in the interior from Winton, where we noticed a paper pasted upon a tree, which read as follows: "Notice!—On Wednesday next, at three o'clock, all persons desirous of hearing the new Constitution explained, by Elder B——t, are requested to attend his church in the Woodlands, 17th March, 1788." The time appointed was only two days previous to the election.

We felt indignant, at what we deemed an insidious attempt to deceive the community; and determined to be present, in order to counteract his movement. On our arrival we found a horse hitched to every

---

[13] Winslow C. Watson, *Men and Times of the Revolution* (New York, 1856), pp. 262–264.

tree about the church, and the interior of the building crowded. We pressed our way into seats, a little distance from the pulpit. B——t had been some time at his nefarious work, explaining the Constitution to suit his unhallowed purposes. He frequently cast a suspicious and disconcerted eye upon our pew. He then began to explain the object of the ten miles square, as the contemplated seat of the Government. "This, my friends," said the preacher, "will be walled in or fortified. Here an army of 50,000, or, perhaps, 100,000 men, will be finally embodied, and will sally forth, and enslave the people, who will be gradually disarmed." This absurd assumption set our blood in fermentation, strongly excited already by party feeling. We consulted a moment, and agreed to possess ourselves of the seat directly under the pulpit, and make an effort to discuss the subject, or break up the meeting. We arose together, Garvey with the Constitution in his hand, supported by Murfee on his right, and myself on his left. Garvey turned towards B——t, and said, in a loud voice:—

"Sir, as to the ten miles square, you are" —here he was interrupted by a general movement and buz, which instantly swelled into a perfect uproar. At this crisis we were in a most critical situation, and only saved from violence by the personal popularity of Murfee, who was universally beloved. We were glad to pass out with the torrent, gain our horses, and be off. We however attained our object—the meeting was dissolved.

The next day Garvey and myself planned and executed a caricature; and as it was a new exhibition among the people, we hoped it would have a good effect at the polls. A clergyman was represented in a pulpit, dressed in his bands, with a label proceeding from his mouth, having this inscription:— "And lo, he brayeth!" This we committed to some resolute fellows, with instructions to post it up at the door of the court-house, on the opening of the polls; they engaging to defend and protect it. Some of B——t's friends stung to the quick by the sarcasm, attempted to pull it down. Our gallant band defended it. A general battle ensued. This obstructed, as we desired, the voting. Candles were lighted in the court-house; these were extinguished in the melée, and both parties, in great confusion, were left in the dark, literally as well as politically. I embraced the opportunity of taking *French leave*. B——t gained the election, to our great annoyance, and the Constitution was rejected for that year, by North-Carolina.

14

In June 1788 the Virginia ratification convention gathered in Richmond. The following exchange, with George Mason and Patrick Henry opposed by John Marshall, illustrates the battle in Virginia for amendments to the Constitution that would protect the freedom of the individual against the coercive power of a centralized government:[14]

Mr. GEORGE MASON . . . When the people of Virginia formed their government, they reserved certain great powers in the bill of rights. They would not trust their own citizens, who had a similarity of interest with themselves, and who had frequent and intimate communication with them. They would not trust their own fellow-citizens, I say, with the exercise of those great powers reserved in the bill of rights. Do we not, by this system, give up a great part of the rights, reserved by the bill of rights, to those who have no fellow-feeling for the people —to a government where the representatives will have no communication with the people? I say, then, there are great and important powers, which were not transferred to the state government, given up to the general government by this Constitution.

Let us advert to the 6th article. It expressly declares, that "this Constitution, and the laws of the United States which shall be made in persuance thereof, and all treaties made, or which shall be made, under the authority of the United States, shall be the supreme law of

the land, and the judges in every state shall be bound thereby; any thing in the Constitution or laws of any state to the contrary notwithstanding." Now, sir, if the laws and Constitution of the general government, as expressly said, be paramount to those of any state, are not those rights with which we were afraid to trust our own citizens annulled and given up to the general government? The bill of rights is a part of our own Constitution. The judges are obliged to take notice of the laws of the general government; consequently, the rights secured by our bill of rights are given up. If they are not given up, where are they secured? By implication! Let gentlemen show that they are secured in a plain, direct, unequivocal manner. It is not in their power. Then where is the security? Where is the barrier drawn between the government and the rights of the citizens, as secured in our own state government? These rights are given up in that paper; but I trust that this Convention will never give them up, but will take pains to secure them to the latest posterity. If a check be necessary in our own state government, it is much more so in a government where our representatives are to be at the distance of a thousand miles from us, without any responsibility.

We wish only our rights to be secured. We must have such amendments as will secure the liberties and happiness of the people on a plain, simple construction, not on a doubtful ground. We wish to give the government sufficient energy, on real republican principles; but we wish to withhold such powers as are not absolutely necessary in themselves, but are extremely dangerous. We wish to shut the door against corruption in that place where it is most dangerous—to secure against the corruption of our own representatives. We ask such amendments as will point out what powers are reserved to the state governments, and clearly discriminate between them and those which are given to the general government, so as to prevent future disputes and clashing of interests. Grant us amendments like these,

---

[14] Jonathan Elliot, ed., *Debates in the Several State Conventions on the Adoption of the Federal Constitution* . . . (Phila., 1863 ed.), III, 265, 271, 445, 447–449, 552, 554, 561.

and we will cheerfully, with our hands and hearts, unite with those who advocate it, and we will do every thing we can to support and carry it into execution.

Mr. HENRY. Mr. Chairman, the necessity of a bill of rights appears to me to be greater in this government than ever it was in any government before. I have observed already, that the sense of the European nations, and particularly Great Britain, is against the construction of rights being retained which are not expressly relinquished. I repeat, that all nations have adopted this construction—that all rights not expressly and unequivocally reserved to the people are impliedly and incidentally relinquished to rulers, as necessarily inseparable from the delegated powers. It is so in Great Britain; for every possible right, which is not reserved to the people by some express provision or compact, is within the king's prerogative. It is so in that country which is said to be in such full possession of freedom. It is so in Spain, Germany, and other parts of the world. Let us consider the sentiments which have been entertained by the people of America on this subject. At the revolution, it must be admitted that it was their sense to set down those great rights which ought, in all countries, to be held inviolable and sacred. Virginia did so, we all remember. She made a compact to reserve, expressly, certain rights.

When fortified with full, adequate, and abundant representation, was she satisfied with that representation? No. She most cautiously and guardedly reserved and secured those invaluable, inestimable rights and privileges, which no people, inspired with the least glow of patriotic liberty, ever did, or ever can, abandon. She is called upon now to abandon them, and dissolve that compact which secured them to her. She is called upon to accede to another compact, which most infallibly supersedes and annihilates her present one. Will she do it? This is the question. If you intend to reserve your unalienable rights, you must have the most express stipulation; for, if implication be al-

lowed, you are ousted of those rights. If the people do not think it necessary to reserve them, they will be supposed to be given up. How were the congressional rights defined when the people of America united by a confederacy to defend their liberties and rights against the tyrannical attempts of Great Britain? The states were not then contented with implied reservation. No, Mr. Chairman. It was expressly declared in our Confederation that every right was retained by the states, respectively, which was not given up to the government of the United States. But there is no such thing here. You, therefore, by a natural and unavoidable implication, give up your rights to the general government.

Congress, from their general powers, may fully go into business of human legislation. They may legislate, in criminal cases, from treason to the lowest offence—petty larceny. They may define crimes and prescribe punishments. In the definition of crimes, I trust they will be directed by what wise representatives ought to be governed by. But when we come to punishments, no latitude ought to be left, nor dependence put on the virtue of representatives. What says our bill of rights?—"that excessive bail ought not to be required, nor excessive fines imposed, nor cruel and unusual punishments inflicted." Are you not, therefore, now calling on those gentlemen who are to compose Congress, to prescribe trials and define punishments without this control? Will they find sentiments there similar to this bill of rights? You let them loose; you do more—you depart from the genius of your country. That paper tells you that the trial of crimes shall be by jury, and held in the state where the crime shall have been committed. Under this extensive provision, they may proceed in a manner extremely dangerous to liberty: a person accused may be carried from one extremity of the state to another, and be tried, not by an impartial jury of the vicinage, acquainted with his character and the circumstances of the fact, but by a jury unacquainted with both, and who may be biased against him.

Is not this sufficient to alarm men? How different is this from the immemorial practice of your British ancestors, and your own!

In this business of legislation, your members of Congress will loose the restriction of not imposing excessive fines, demanding excessive bail, and inflicting cruel and unusual punishments. These are prohibited by your declaration of rights. What has distinguished our ancestors?—That they would not admit of tortures, or cruel and barbarous punishments. But Congress may introduce the practice of the civil law, in preference to that of the common law. They may introduce the practice of France, Spain, and Germany—of torturing, to extort a confession of the crime. They will say that they might as well draw examples from those countries as from Great Britain, and they will tell you that there is such a necessity of strengthening the arm of government, that they must have a criminal equity, and extort confession by torture, in order to punish with still more relentless severity. We are then lost and undone. And can any man think it troublesome, when we can, by a small inference, prevent our rights from being lost? If you will, like the Virginian government, give them knowledge of the extent of the rights retained by the people, and the powers of themselves, they will, if they be honest men, thank you for it. Will they not wish to go on sure grounds? But if you leave them otherwise, they will not know how to proceed; and, being in a state of uncertainty, they will assume rather than give up powers by implication.

A bill of rights may be summed up in a few words. What do they tell us?—That our rights are reserved. Why not say so? Is it because it will consume too much paper? Gentlemen's reasoning against a bill of rights does not satisfy me. Without saying which has the right side, it remains doubtful. A bill of rights is a favorite thing with the Virginians and the people of the other states likewise. It may be their prejudice, but the government ought to suit their geniuses; otherwise, its operation will be unhappy. A bill of rights, even if its necessity be doubtful, will exclude the possibility of dispute; and, with great submission, I think the best way is to have no dispute. In the present Constitution, they are restrained from issuing general warrants to search suspected places, or seize persons not named, without evidence of the commission of a fact, &c. There was certainly some celestial influence governing those who deliberated on that Constitution; for they have, with the most cautious and enlightened circumspection, guarded those indefeasible rights which ought ever to be held sacred! The officers of Congress may come upon you now, fortified with all the terrors of paramount federal authority. Excisemen may come in multitudes; for the limitation of their numbers no man knows. They may, unless the general government be restrained by a bill of rights, or some similar restriction, go into your cellars and rooms, and search, ransack, and measure, every thing you eat, drink, and wear. They ought to be restrained within proper bounds. With respect to the freedom of the press, I need say nothing; for it is hoped that the gentlemen who shall compose Congress will take care to infringe as little as possible the rights of human nature. This will result from their integrity. They should, from prudence, abstain from violating the rights of their constituents. They are not, however, expressly restrained. But whether they will intermeddle with that palladium of our liberties or not, I leave you to determine.

Mr. JOHN MARSHALL . . . Gentlemen have gone on an idea that the federal courts will not determine the causes which may come before them with the same fairness and impartiality with which other courts decide. What are the reasons of this supposition? Do they draw them from the manner in which the judges are chosen, or the tenure of their office? What is it that makes us trust our judges? Their independence in office, and manner of appointment. Are not the judges of the federal court chosen with as much wisdom as the judges of the state governments? Are they not equally, if not more independent? If so, shall we not conclude that they will decide with equal impartiality and candor?

To what quarter will you look for protection from an infringement on the Constitution, if you will not give the power to the judiciary? There is no other body that can afford such a protection. But the honorable member objects to it, because he says that the officers of the government will be screened from merited punishment by the federal judiciary. The federal sheriff, says he, will go into a poor man's house and beat him, or abuse his family, and the federal court will protect him. Does any gentleman believe this? Is it necessary that the officers will commit a trespass on the property or persons of those with whom they are to transact business? Will such great insults on the people of this country be allowable? Were a law made to authorize them, it would be void. The injured man would trust to a tribunal in his neighborhood. To such a tribunal he would apply for redress, and get it. There is no reason to fear that he would not meet that justice there which his country will be ever willing to maintain.

We are satisfied with the provision made in this country on the subject of trial by jury. Does our Constitution direct trials to be by jury? It is required in our bill of rights, which is not a part of the Constitution. Does any security arise from hence? The bill of rights is merely recommendatory. Were it otherwise, the consequence would be that many laws which are found convenient would be unconstitutional. What does the government before you say? Does it exclude the legislature from giving a trial by jury in civil cases? If it does not forbid its exclusion, it is on the same footing on which your state government stands now. The legislature of Virginia does not give a trial by jury where it is not necessary, but gives it wherever it is thought expedient. The federal legislature will do so too, as it is formed on the same principles.

15

The defenders of the Constitution were just as ably represented. This was especially the case in New York, where three of its leading proponents, Alexander Hamilton, John Jay, and James Madison, penned a series of remarkable arguments in its favor. Published originally in newspapers, these Federalist Papers *became a political classic. Any excerpts from them obscure the comprehensive defense of the Constitution, yet Essay No. 10, written by James Madison, is a notable example of political reasoning in the eighteenth century:*[15]

Among the numerous advantages promised by a well constructed union, none deserves to be more accurately developed than its tendency to break and control the violence of faction. The friend of popular governments, never finds himself so much alarmed for their character and fate, as when he contemplates their propensity to this dangerous vice. He will not fail therefore to set a due value on any plan which, without violating the principles to which he is attached, provides a proper cure for it. The instability, injustice and confusion introduced into the public councils, have in truth been the mortal diseases under which popular governments have everywhere perished; as they continue to be the favorite and fruitful topics from which the adversaries to liberty derive their most specious declamations. The valuable improvements made by the American constitutions on the popular models, both ancient and modern, cannot certainly be too much admired; but it would be an unwarrantable partiality, to contend that they have as effectually obviated the danger on this side as was wished and expected. Complaints are every where heard from our most considerate and virtuous citizens, equally the friends of public and private faith, and of public and personal liberty; that our governments are too unstable; that the public good is disregarded in the conflicts of rival parties; and that measures are too often decided, not according to the rules of justice,

---

[15] *The Federalist* (New York, 1799), I, 52–61.

and the rights of the minor party; but by the superior force of an interested and overbearing majority. However anxiously we may wish that these complaints had no foundation, the evidence of known facts will not permit us to deny that they are in some degree true. It will be found indeed, on a candid review of our situation, that some of the distresses under which we labor have been erroneously charged on the operation of our governments; but it will be found at the same time, that other causes will not alone account for many of our heaviest misfortunes; and, particularly, for that prevailing and increasing distrust of public engagements, and alarm for private rights, which are echoed from one end of the continent to the other. These must be chiefly, if not wholly, effects of the unsteadiness and injustice, with which a factious spirit has tainted our public administration.

By a faction I understand a number of citizens, whether amounting to a majority or minority of the whole, who are united and actuated by some common impulse of passion, or of interest, adverse to the rights of other citizens, or to the permanent and aggregate interests of the community.

There are two methods of curing the mischiefs of faction: The one, by removing its causes; the other, by controlling its effects.

There are again two methods of removing the causes of faction: The one, by destroying the liberty which is essential to its existence; the other, by giving to every citizen the same opinions, the same passions, and the same interests.

It could never be more truly said than of the first remedy, that it is worse than the disease. Liberty is to faction, what air is to fire, an ailment without which it instantly expires. But it could not be less folly to abolish liberty, which is essential to political life, because it nourishes faction, than it would be to wish the annihilation of air, which is essential to animal life because it imparts to fire its destructive agency.

The second expedient is as impracticable as the first would be unwise. As long as the reason of man continues fallible, and he is at liberty to exercise it, different opinions will be formed. As long as the connection subsists between his reason and his self-love, his opinions and his passions will have a reciprocal influence on each other; and the former will be objects to which the latter will attach themselves. The diversity in the faculties of men from which the rights of property originate, is not less an insuperable obstacle to an uniformity of interests. The protection of these faculties is the first object of government. From the protection of different and unequal faculties of acquiring property, the possession of different degrees and kinds of property immediately results: And from the influence of these on the sentiments and views of the respective proprietors ensues a division of the society into different interests and parties.

The latent causes of faction are thus sown in the nature of man; and we see them everywhere brought into different degrees of activity, according to the different circumstances of civil society. A zeal for different opinions concerning religion, concerning government, and many other points, as well of speculation as of practice; an attachment to different leaders ambitiously contending for pre-eminence and power; or to persons of other descriptions whose fortunes have been interesting to the human passions, have in turn divided mankind into parties, inflamed them with mutual animosity, and rendered them much more disposed to vex and oppress each other, than to co-operate for their common good. So strong is this propensity of mankind to fall into mutual animosities, that where no substantial occasion presents itself, the most frivolous and fanciful distinctions have been sufficient to kindle their unfriendly passions, and excite their most violent conflicts. But the most common and durable source of factions, has been the various and unequal distribution of property. Those who hold, and those who are without property, have ever formed distinct interests in society. Those who are creditors, and those who are debtors, fall under a like discrimination. A landed interest, a manufacturing interest, a mercantile interest, a moneyed interest, with many lesser interests, grow up of necessity in civilized nations, and divide them into different classes, actuated by different sentiments and views. The regulation of these various and interfering interests forms the principal task of modern legislation, and involves the spirit of party and faction in the necessary and ordinary operations of government.

No man is allowed to be a judge in his own cause; because his interest would certainly bias his judgment, and, not improbably, corrupt his integrity. With equal, nay with greater reason, a body of men, are unfit to be both judges and parties, at the same time; yet, what are many of the most important acts of legislation, but so many judicial determinations, not indeed concerning the rights of single persons, but concerning the rights of large bodies of citizens; and what are the different classes of legislators, but advocates and parties to the causes which they determine? Is a law proposed concerning private debts? it is a question to which the creditors are parties on one side, and the debtors on the other. Justice ought to hold the balance between them. Yet the parties are and must be themselves the judges; and the most numerous party, or, in other words, the most powerful faction must be expected to prevail. Shall domestic manufactures be encouraged, and in what degree, by restrictions on foreign manufactures? Are questions which would be differently decided by the landed and the manufacturing classes; and probably by neither, with a sole regard to justice and the public good. The apportionment of taxes on the various descriptions of property, is an act which seems to require the most exact impartiality, yet there is perhaps no legislative act in which greater opportunity and temptation are given to a predominant party, to trample on the rules

of justice. Every shilling with which they overburden the inferior number is a shilling saved to their own pockets.

It is in vain to say, that enlightened statesmen will be able to adjust these clashing interests and render them all subservient to the public good. Enlightened statesmen will not always be at the helm: Nor, in many cases, can such an adjustment be made at all, without taking into view indirect and remote considerations, which will rarely prevail over the immediate interest which one party may find in disregarding the rights of another, or the good of the whole.

The inference to which we are brought, is, that the *causes* of faction cannot be removed; and that relief is only to be sought in the means of controlling its *effects*.

If a faction consists of less than a majority, relief is supplied by the republican principle, which enables the majority to defeat its sinister views by regular vote: It may clog the administration, it may convulse the society; but it will be unable to execute and mask its violence under the forms of the constitution. When a majority is included in a faction, the form of popular government on the other hand enables it to sacrifice to its ruling passion or interest, both the public good and the rights of other citizens. To secure the public good, and private rights against the danger of such a faction, and at the same time to preserve the spirit and the form of popular government, is then the great object to which our inquiries are directed. Let me add that it is the great desideratum, by which alone this form of government can be rescued from the opprobrium under which it has so long labored, and be recommended to the esteem and adoption of mankind.

By what means is this object attainable? Evidently by one of two only. Either the existence of the same passion or interest in a majority at the same time, must be prevented; or the majority, having such coexistent passion or interest, must be rendered, by their number and local situation, unable to concert and carry into effect schemes of oppression. If the impulse and the opportunity be suffered to coincide, we well know that neither moral nor religious motives can be relied on as an adequate control. They are not found to be such on the injustice and violence of individuals, and lose their efficacy in proportion to the number combined together; that is, in proportion as their efficacy becomes needful.

From this view of the subject, it may be concluded that a pure democracy, by which I mean a society consisting of a small number of citizens, who assemble and administer the government in person, can admit of no cure for the mischiefs of faction. A common passion or interest will, in almost every case, be felt by a majority of the whole; a communication and concert results from the form of government itself; and there is nothing to check the inducements to sacrifice the weaker party, or an obnoxious individual. Hence it is that such democracies have ever been spectacles of turbulence and contention; have ever been found incompatible with personal security, or the rights of property; and have in general been as short in their lives, as they have been violent in their deaths.—Theoretic politicians, who have patronized this species of government, have erroneously supposed, that by reducing mankind to a perfect equality in their political rights, they would, at the same time, be perfectly equalized, and assimilated in their possessions, their opinions, and their passions.

A republic, by which I mean a government in which the scheme of representation takes place, opens a different prospect, and promises the cure for which we are seeking. Let us examine the points in which it varies from pure democracy, and we shall comprehend both the nature of the cure, and the efficacy which it must derive from the union.

The two great points of difference between a democracy and a republic, are first, the delegation of the government, in the latter, to a small number of citizens elected by the rest; secondly, the greater number of citizens,

and greater sphere of country, over which the latter may be extended.

The effect of the first difference is, on the one hand, to refine and enlarge the public views, by passing them through the medium of a chosen body of citizens, whose wisdom may best discern the true interest of their country, and whose patriotism and love of justice, will be least likely to sacrifice it to temporary of partial considerations. Under such a regulation, it may well happen that the public voice pronounced by the representatives of the people, will be more consonant to the public good, than if pronounced by the people themselves, convened for the purpose. On the other hand, the effect may be inverted. Men of factious tempers, of local prejudices, or of sinister designs, may by intrigue, by corruption, or by other means, first obtain the suffrages, and then betray the interests of the people. The question resulting is, whether small or extensive republics are most favorable to the election of proper guardians of the public weal; and it is clearly decided in favor of the latter by two obvious considerations.

In the first place, it is to be remarked that, however small the republic may be, the representatives must be raised to a certain number, in order to guard against the cabals of a few; and that, however large it may be, they must be limited to a certain number, in order to guard against the confusion of a multitude. Hence the number of representatives in the two cases not being in proportion to that of the constituents, and being proportionally greatest in the small republic, it follows, that if the proportion of fit characters be not less in the large than in the small republic, the former will present a greater option, and consequently a greater probability of a fit choice.

In the next place, as each representative will be chosen by a greater number of citizens in the large than in the small republic, it will be more difficult for unworthy candidates to practise with success the vicious arts, by which elections are too often carried; and the suffrages of the people, being more free, will be more likely to centre in men who possess the most attractive merit, and the most diffusive and established characters.

It must be confessed, that in this, as in most other cases, there is a mean, on both sides of which inconveniences will be found to lie. By enlarging too much the number of electors, you render the representative too little acquainted with all their local circumstances and lesser interests; as by reducing it too much, you render him unduly attached to these, and too little fit to comprehend and pursue great and national objects. The federal constitution forms a happy combination in this respect; the great and aggregate interests being referred to the national, the local and particular to the state legislatures.

The other point of difference is, the greater number of citizens and extent of territory which may be brought within the compass of republican, than of democratic government; and it is this circumstance principally which renders factious combinations less to be dreaded in the former, than in the latter. The smaller the society, the fewer probably will be the distinct parties and interests composing it; the fewer the distinct parties and interests, the more frequently will a majority be found of the same party; and the smaller the number of individuals composing a majority, and the smaller the compass within which they are placed, the more easily will they concert and execute their plans of oppression. Extend the sphere, and you take in a greater variety of parties and interests; you make it less probable that a majority of the whole will have a common motive to invade the rights of other citizens; or if such a common motive exists, it will be more difficult for all who feel it to discover their own strength, and to act in unison with each other. Besides other impediments, it may be remarked that where there is a consciousness of unjust or dishonorable purposes, communication is always checked by distrust, in proportion to the number whose concurrence is necessary.

Hence it clearly appears, that the same advantage, which a republic has over a democracy, in controlling the effects of faction, is enjoyed by a large over a small republic—is enjoyed by the union over the states composing it. Does the advantage consist in the substitution of representatives, whose enlightened views and virtuous sentiments render them superior to local prejudices, and to schemes of injustice? It will not be denied, that the representation of the union will be most likely to possess these requisite endowments. Does it consist in the greater security afforded by a greater variety of parties, against the event of any one party being able to outnumber and oppress the rest? In an equal degree does the encreased variety of parties, comprised within the union, encrease this security. Does it, in fine, consist in the greater obstacles opposed to the concert and accomplishment of the secret wishes of an unjust and interested majority? Here, again, the extent of the union gives it the most palpable advantage.

The influence of factious leaders may kindle a flame within their particular states, but will be unable to spread a general conflagration through the other states: A religious sect, may degenerate into a political faction in a part of the confederacy; but the variety of sects dispersed over the entire face of it, must secure the national councils against any danger from that source: A rage for paper money, for an abolition of debts, for an equal division of property, or for any other improper or wicked project, will be less apt to pervade the whole body of the union, than a particular member of it; in the same proportion as such a malady is more likely to taint a particular country or district, than an entire State.

In the extent and proper structure of the union, therefore, we behold a republican remedy for the diseases most incident to republican government. And according to the degree of pleasure and pride, we feel in being republicans, ought to be our zeal in cherishing the spirit, and supporting the character of federalists.

16

James Madison's forecast of the role of political parties, or "factions" as they were then called, in the democratization of American government stamps him as a master seer. A modern scholar, E. E. Schattschneider, makes this clear in his careful analysis of Madison's essay and of the impact of parties on the Constitution:[16]

American parties are important in view of their accomplishments. It can be said justly that they have transformed the American Constitution. They have substantially abolished the electoral college, created a plebiscitary presidency, and contributed powerfully to the extraconstitutional growth of that office. As a result of the efforts of the political parties the President of the United States today receives a mandate to govern the nation and is responsible for the safety and welfare of the Republic. The parties have greatly simplified the most complex system of government in the world, and we may be certain that the work of reconstruction will continue as long as the party system endures. More important than all other changes the parties have wrought in the system of government is the fact that they have democratized it. They took over an eighteenth-century constitution and made it function to satisfy the needs of modern democracy in ways not contemplated by the authors. As the political entrepreneurs who have mobilized and organized the dynamic forces of American public life, these parties have presided over the transformation of the government of the United States from a small experiment in republicanism to the most powerful regime on earth, vastly more liberal and democratic than it was in 1789. They have supervised or adapted themselves to the conquest of a continent, the transformation of the economic system, the absorption of the

---

[16] E. E. Schattschneider, *Party Government*, pp. 2, 6–9. Copyright, 1942, by E. E. Schattschneider. Reprinted by permission Holt, Rinehart, and Winston, publishers.

largest immigrant population in the history of the world, a series of great economic crises, and the rise of the modern administrative state, to mention only a few of the developments in which the parties have participated. . . .

. . . The theory of the Constitution, inherited from the time of the Glorious Revolution in England, was legalistic and preparty in its assumptions. Great reliance was placed in a system of separation of powers, a legalistic concept of government incompatible with a satisfactory system of party government. No place was made for the parties in the system, party government was not clearly foreseen or well understood, government by parties was thought to be impossible or impracticable and was feared and regarded as something to be avoided. The Founding Fathers knew intuitively that party competition, if given a chance, would upset their calculations.

Consequently, the Convention at Philadelphia produced a constitution with a dual attitude: it was proparty in one sense and antiparty in another. The authors of the Constitution refused to suppress the parties by destroying the fundamental liberties in which parties originate. They or their immediate successors accepted amendments that guaranteed civil rights and thus established a system of party tolerance, i.e., the right to agitate and to organize. This is the proparty aspect of the system. On the other hand, the authors of the Constitution set up an elaborate division and balance of powers within an intricate governmental structure designed to make parties ineffective. It was hoped that the parties would lose and exhaust themselves in futile attempts to fight their way through the labyrinthine framework of the government, much as an attacking army is expected to spend itself against the defensive works of a fortress. This is the antiparty part of the constitutional scheme. To quote Madison, the "great object" of the Constitution was "to preserve the public good and private rights against the danger of such a faction [party] and at the same time to preserve the spirit and form of popular government."

In Madison's mind the difference between an autocracy and a free republic seems to have been largely a matter of the precise point at which parties are stopped by the government. In an autocracy parties are controlled (suppressed) at the source; in a republic parties are tolerated but are invited to strangle themselves in the machinery of government. The result in either case is much the same; sooner or later the government checks the parties but *never do the parties control the government.* Madison was perfectly definite and unmistakable in his disapproval of party government as distinguished from party tolerance. In the opinion of Madison, parties were intrinsically bad, and the sole issue for discussion was the means by which bad parties might be prevented from becoming dangerous. What never seems to have occurred to the authors of the Constitution, however, is that parties might be *used* as beneficent instruments of popular government. It is at this point that the distinction between the modern and the antique is made.

The offspring of this combination of ideas was a constitutional system having conflicting tendencies. The Constitution made the rise of parties inevitable yet was incompatible with party government. The scheme, in spite of its subtlety, involved a miscalculation. Political parties refused to be content with the role assigned to them. The vigor and enterprise of the parties have therefore made American political history the story of the unhappy marriage of the parties and the Constitution, a remarkable variation of the case of the irresistible force and the immovable object, which in this instance have been compelled to live together in a permanent partnership.

Nearly the whole of the constitutional theory on the subject of political parties can be studied in capsule form in Number 10 of the *Federalist Papers,* written by James Madison. The ideas in this little essay deserve examination in detail. Madison's argument . . . is part of his defense of the separation of powers. He justifies the system by stating a famous argument against democracy, the supposed tendency of majorities to become tyrannical. In the course of this argument Madison makes his celebrated analysis of the origins of parties and the economic basis of politics; that is, he argues that the rise of parties in a free system of politics is inevitable. He then demonstrates that parties ("factions") are inherently oppressive and must be frustrated by an elaborate system of separation of powers if liberty is not to become self-destructive. Almost immediately, however, he turns his attention to a second argument, his famous defense of "large republics," i.e., federalism. This argument is indubitably one of the principal claims of James Madison to immortality. With rare prescience he saw the multiplicity of interests in a modern national state and demonstrated that, as a consequence of the multiplicity of interests, no one of them is likely to win a majority. The advantage of a large republic, a federal republic, is that the diversity of interests in a large community is greater than it is in a small community and, consequently, the danger that a tyrannical majority, composed of a single interest, will be able to oppress the whole community is correspondingly diminished. This analysis might still be used as an introduction to the study of political parties. Considering the fact that Madison, though a veteran of factional politics in Virginia, had never seen a modern party in action when he wrote his essay, his insight was remarkable. What is more amazing, however, is that the second argument destroys the first. Madison's defense of federalism annihiliates his defense of the separation of powers. If the multiplicity of interests in a large republic makes tyrannical majorities impossible, the principal theoretical prop of the separation of powers has been demolished.

17

While James Madison underlined the ways in which the proposed Constitution would combat the pernicious effects of faction, Alexander Hamilton was attempting to quiet the growing demand for a "bill of rights." In The Federalist, *No. 84, he argued that such guarantees as many of the Antifederalists were demanding, were as needless as they were dangerous:*[17]

TO THE PEOPLE OF THE STATE OF NEW YORK:

In the course of the foregoing review of the Constitution, I have taken notice of, and endeavored to answer most of the objections which have appeared against it. . . .

The most considerable of the remaining objections is that the plan of the convention contains no bill of rights. Among other answers given to this, it has been upon different occasions remarked that the constitutions of several of the States are in a similar predicament. I add that New York is of the number. And yet the opposers of the new system, in this State, who profess an unlimited admiration for its constitution, are among the most intemperate partisans of a bill of rights. To justify their zeal in this matter, they allege two things; one is that, though the constitution of New York has no bill of rights prefixed to it, yet it contains, in the body of it, various provisions in favor of particular privileges and rights, which, in substance, amount to the same thing; the other is, that the Constitution adopts, in their full extent, the common and statute law of Great Britain, by which many other rights, not expressed in it, are equally secured. . . .

It has been several times truly remarked that bills of rights are, in their origin, stipulations between kings and their subjects, abridgments of prerogative in favor of privilege, reservations of rights not surrendered to the prince. Such was MAGNA CHARTA, obtained by the barons, sword in hand, from King John. Such were the subsequent confirmations of that charter by succeeding princes. Such was the *Petition of Right* assented to by Charles I, in the beginning of his reign. Such, also, was the Declaration of Right presented by the Lords and Commons

to the Prince of Orange in 1688, and afterwards thrown into the form of an act of parliament called the Bill of Rights. It is evident, therefore, that according to their primitive signification, they have no application to constitutions, professedly founded upon the power of the people, and executed by their immediate representatives and servants. Here, in strictness, the people surrender nothing; and as they retain every thing they have no need of particular reservations. "WE, THE PEOPLE of the United States, to secure the blessings of liberty to ourselves and our posterity, do *ordain* and *establish* this Constitution for the United States of America." Here is a better recognition of popular rights, than volumes of those aphorisms which make the principal figure in several of our State bills of rights, and which would sound much better in a treatise of ethics than in a constitution of government. . . .

I go further, and affirm that bills of rights, in the sense and to the extent in which they are contended for, are not only unnecessary in the proposed Constitution, but would even be dangerous. They would contain various exceptions to powers not granted; and, on this very account, would afford a colorable pretext to claim more than were granted. For why declare that things shall not be done which there is no power to do? Why, for instance, should it be said that the liberty of the press shall not be restrained, when no power is given by which restrictions may be imposed? I will not contend that such a provision would confer a regulating power; but it is evident that it would furnish, to men disposed to usurp, a plausible pretence for claiming that power. They might urge with a semblance of reason, that the Constitution ought not to be charged with the absurdity of providing against the abuse of an authority which was not given, and that the provision against restraining the liberty of the press afforded a clear implication, that a power to prescribe proper regulations concerning it was intended to be vested in the national government. This may serve as a

---

[17] *The Federalist* (New York, 1799), II, 344–349.

specimen of the numerous handles which would be given to the doctrine of constructive powers, by the indulgence of an injudicious zeal for bills of rights.

THE RISE OF POLITICAL PARTIES

18

The deep-seated divisions marking the ratification contest were immediately apparent in the new government of President George Washington that took office in the spring of 1789. On one side was the agrarian-debtor class, which hoped to democratize the Constitution by weakening the central government: on the other the merchant-planter-creditor class, which planned to assure property protection by strengthening the authority of Congress over the states and the people alike. The gulf between these two factions became clear when the first House of Representatives began debating the mass of amendments to the Constitution, all proposed by the states during the ratification process, which eventually became the Bill of Rights. Liberals favoring the amendments insisted they were "delegates" of the people and hence bound to obey the popular will; conservatives held that congressmen were "representatives" of the people entitled to follow their personal predilections in doing what was best for the masses:[18]

Mr. TUCKER . . . noticed that the most material part proposed by those States [Virginia and North Carolina] was omitted, which was, a declaration that the people should have a right to instruct their representatives. He would move to have those words inserted. . . .

Mr. TUCKER then moved to insert these words, "to instruct their Representatives."

Mr. HARTLEY. . . . if, by misconduct, they forfeit it, their constituents have the power of leaving them out at the expiration of that time—thus they are answerable for the part they have taken in measures that may be contrary to the general wish.

Representation is the principle of our Government; the people ought to have confidence in the honor and integrity of those

they send forward to transact their business; their right to instruct them is a problematical subject. We have seen it attended with bad consequences, both in England and America. . . .

Can it be supposed that the inhabitants of a single district in a State, are better informed with respect to the general interests of the Union, than a select body assembled from every part? Can it be supposed that a part will be more desirous of promoting the good of the whole than the whole will of the part? . . . . Mr. MADISON. I think the committee acted prudently in omitting to insert these words in the report they have brought forward; . . . My idea of the sovereignty of the people is, that the people can change the constitution if they please; but while the constitution exists, they must conform themselves to its dictates. But I do not believe that the inhabitants of any district can speak the voice of the people; so far from it, their ideas may contradict the sense of the whole people; hence the consequence that instructions are binding on the representative is of a doubtful, if not of a dangerous nature. . . .

Mr. VINING. . . . The gentleman last up [Gerry] has insinuated a reflection upon the committee for not reporting all the amendments proposed by some of the State conventions. I can assign a reason for this. The committee conceived some of them superfluous or dangerous, and found many of them so contradictory that it was impossible to make any thing of them; and this is a circumstance the gentleman cannot pretend ignorance of. . . . As to the business of instruction, I look upon it inconsistent with the general good. Suppose our constituents were to instruct us to make paper money; no gentleman pretends to say it would be unconstitutional, yet every honest mind must shudder at the thought. . . .

Mr. GERRY. . . . The gentleman from Maryland [Stone] had said that the amendment would change the nature of the Government, and make it a democracy. Now he had always heard that it was a democracy; but perhaps he was misled, and the honor-

---

[18] *Annals of Congress*, 1st Cong., 1st Sess., 760–765 (1789).

able gentleman was right in distinguishing it by some other appellation; perhaps an aristocracy was a term better adapted to it.

Mr. SEDGWICK. . . . The sovereignty, the independence, and the rights of the States are intended to be guarded by the Senate; . . . . Mr. PAGE . . . all power vests in the people of the United States; it is, therefore, a Government of the people, a democracy. If it were consistent with the peace and tranquillity of the inhabitants, every freeman would have a right to come and give his vote upon the law; but, inasmuch as this cannot be done, by reason of the extent of territory, and some other causes, the people have agreed that their representatives shall exercise a part of their authority. To pretend to refuse them the power of instructing their agents, appears to me to deny them a right. One gentleman asks how the instructions are to be collected. . . . Another gentleman asks if they were to instruct us to make paper money, what we would do. I would tell them, said he, it was unconstitutional; alter that, and we will consider on the point. . . .

Mr. WADSWORTH. . . . The honorable gentleman who was up last says, if he were instructed to make paper money, he would tell his constituents it was unconstitutional. I believe that is not the case, for this body would have a right to make paper money; but if my constituents were to instruct me to vote for such a measure, I would disobey them, let the consequence be what it would.

Mr. MADISON. . . . I appeal to the gentlemen who have heard the voice of their country, to those who have attended the debates of the State conventions, whether the amendments now proposed are not those most strenuously required by the opponents to the constitution? It was wished that some security should be given for those great and essential rights which they had been taught to believe were in danger. I concurred, in the convention of Virginia, with those gentlemen, so far as to agree to a declaration of those rights which corresponded with my own judgment, and the other alterations which I had the honor to bring forward be-

fore the present Congress. I appeal to the gentlemen on this floor who are desirous of amending the constitution, whether these proposed are not compatible with what are required by our constituents?

19

The upshot of the debate over the amendments was the adoption of the first ten amendments, declared in force December 15, 1791, which were quickly labelled a "Bill of Rights":[19]

THE BILL OF RIGHTS
1791

AMENDMENTS

ARTICLE I

Congress shall make no law respecting an establishment of religion, or prohibiting the free exercise thereof; or abridging the freedom of speech, or of the press; or the right of the people peaceably to assemble, and to petition the government for a redress of grievances.

ARTICLE II

A well-regulated militia being necessary to the security of a free State, the right of the people to keep and bear arms shall not be infringed.

ARTICLE III

No soldier shall, in time of peace, be quartered in any house without the consent of the owner, nor in time of war but in a manner to be prescribed by law.

ARTICLE IV

The right of the people to be secure in their persons, houses, papers, and effects, against unreasonable searches and seizures, shall not be violated; and no warrants shall issue but upon probable cause, supported by oath or affirmation, and particularly describing the place to be searched and the persons or things to be seized.

[19] Office of Education, United States Department of the Interior, 1935.

ARTICLE V

No person shall be held to answer for a capital or otherwise infamous crime, unless on a presentment or indictment of a grand jury, except in cases arising in the land or naval forces, or in the militia when in actual service, in time of war or public danger; nor shall any person be subject, for the same offence, to be twice put in jeopardy of life or limb, nor shall be compelled in any criminal case to be a witness against himself; nor be deprived of life, liberty, or property, without due process of law; nor shall private property be taken for public use without just compensation.

ARTICLE VI

In all criminal prosecutions the accused shall enjoy the right to a speedy and public trial, by an impartial jury of the State and district wherein the crime shall have been committed, which district shall have been previously ascertained by law; and to be informed of the nature and cause of the accusation; to be confronted with the witnesses against him; to have compulsory process for obtaining witnesses in his favor; and have the assistance of counsel for his defence.

ARTICLE VII

In suits at common law, where the value in controversy shall exceed twenty dollars, the right of trial by jury shall be preserved; and no fact tried by a jury shall be otherwise reëxamined in any court of the United States, than according to the rules of the common law.

ARTICLE VIII

Excessive bail shall not be required, nor excessive fines imposed, nor cruel and unusual punishments inflicted.

ARTICLE IX

The enumeration in the Constitution of certain rights shall not be construed to deny or disparage others retained by the people.

ARTICLE X

The powers not delegated to the United States by the Constitution, nor prohibited by it to the States, are reserved to the States respectively, or to the people.

20

The conservatives, or Federalists as they styled themselves, were particularly well represented in the first Senate. Using their dominance there, they set out to make the central government into an authoritarian body capable of inflicting the will of the few on the many. One device employed was the invention of elaborate ceremonials which would, it was hoped, impress the people with the austerity of office and the need for obedience. A cynical observer of these ludicrous attempts was Senator William Maclay of Pennsylvania, a staunch democrat who despised aristocracy as heartily as he did frivolity. One passage in the Journal *kept by Senator Maclay describes the inauguration of the first President in 1789:*[20]

30th April, Thursday.—This is a great, important day. Goddess of etiquette, assist me while I describe it. The Senate stood adjourned to half after eleven o'clock. About ten dressed in my best clothes; went for Mr. Morris' lodgings, but met his son, who told me that his father would not be in town until Saturday. Turned into the Hall. The crowd already great. The Senate met. The Vice-President rose in the most solemn manner. This son of *Adam* seemed impressed with deeper gravity, yet what shall I think of him? He often, in the midst of his most important airs—I believe when he is at loss for expressions (and this he often is, wrapped up, I suppose, in the contemplation of his own importance)—suffers an unmeaning kind of vacant laugh to escape him. This was the case to-day, and really to me bore the air of ridiculing the farce he was acting. "Gentlemen, I wish for the direction of the Senate. The President will, I suppose, address the Congress. How shall I behave?

---

[20] *The Journal of William Maclay, United States Senator from Pennsylvania, 1789–1791,* with an introduction by Charles A. Beard, pp. 6–9. Copyright 1927 by Albert and Charles Boni, Inc.

How shall we receive it? Shall it be standing or sitting?"

Here followed a considerable deal of talk from him which I could make nothing of. Mr. Lee began with the House of Commons (as is usual with him), then the House of Lords, then the King, and then back again. The result of his information was, that the Lords sat and the Commons stood on the delivery of the King's speech. Mr. Izard got up and told how often he had been in the Houses of Parliament. He said a great deal of what he had seen there. [He] made, however, this sagacious discovery, that the Commons stood because they had no seats to sit on, being arrived at the bar of the House of Lords. It was discovered after some time that the King sat, too, and had his robes and crown on.

Mr. Adams got up again and said he had been very often indeed at the Parliament on those occasions, but there always was such a crowd, and *ladies along*, that for his part he could not say how it was. Mr. Carrol got up to declare that he thought it of no consequence how it was in Great Britain; they were no rule to us, etc. But all at once the Secretary, who had been out, whispered to the Chair that the Clerk from the Representatives was at the door with a communication. Gentlemen of the Senate, how shall he be received? A silly kind of resolution of the committee on that business had been laid on the table some days ago. The amount of it was that each House should communicate to the other what and how they chose; it concluded, however, something in this way: That everything should be done with all the *propriety* that was *proper*. The question was, Shall this be adopted, that we may know how to receive the Clerk? It was objected [that] this will throw no light on the subject; it will leave you where you are. Mr. Lee brought the House of Commons before us again. He reprobated the rule; declared that the Clerk should not come within the bar of the House; that the proper mode was for the Sergeant-at-Arms, with the mace on his shoulder, to meet the Clerk at the

door and receive his communication; we are not, however, provided for this ceremonious way of doing business, having neither mace nor sergeant nor Masters in Chancery, who carry down bills from the English Lords.

Mr. Izard got up and labored unintelligibly to show the great distinction between a communication and a delivery of a thing, but he was not minded. Mr. Elsworth showed plainly enough that if the Clerk was not permitted to deliver the communication, the Speaker might as well send it inclosed. Repeated accounts came [that] the Speaker and Representatives were at the door. Confusion ensued; the members left their seats. Mr. Read rose and called the attention of the Senate to the neglect that had been shown Mr. Thompson, late Secretary. Mr. Lee rose to answer him, but I could not hear one word he said. The Speaker was introduced, followed by the Representatives. Here we sat an hour and ten minutes before the President arrived—this delay was owing to Lee, Izard, and Dalton, who had stayed with us while the Speaker came in, instead of going to attend the President. The President advanced between the Senate and Representatives, bowing to each. He was placed in the chair by the Vice-President; the Senate with their president on the right, the Speaker and the Representatives on his left. The Vice-Presdent rose and addressed a short sentence to him. The import of it was that he should now take the oath of office as President. He seemed to have forgot half what he was to say, for he made a dead pause and stood for some time, to appearance, in a vacant mood. He finished with a formal bow, and the President was conducted out of the middle window into the gallery, and the oath was administered by the Chancellor. Notice that the business done was communicated to the crowd by proclamation, etc., who gave three cheers, and repeated it on the President's bowing to them.

As the company returned into the Senate chamber, the President took the chair and the Senators and Representatives their seats. He rose, and all arose also, and addressed them (see the address). This great man was agitated and embarrassed more than ever he was by the leveled cannon or pointed musket. He trembled, and several times could scarce make out to read, though it must be supposed he had often read it before. He put part of the fingers of his left hand into the side of what I think the tailors call the fall of the breeches [corresponding to the modern side-pocket], changing the paper into his left [right] hand. After some time he then did the same with some of the fingers of his right hand. When he came to the words *all the world,* he made a flourish with his right hand, which left rather an ungainly impression. I sincerely, for my part, wished all set ceremony in the hands of the dancing-masters, and that this first of men had read off his address in the plainest manner, without ever taking his eyes from the paper, for I felt hurt that he was not first in everything. He was dressed in deep brown, with metal buttons, with an eagle on them. white stockings, a bag, and sword.

From the hall there was a grand procession to Saint Paul's Church, where prayers were said by the Bishop. The procession was well conducted and without accident, as far as I have heard. The militia were all under arms, lined the street near the church, made a good figure, and behaved well.

The Senate returned to their chamber after service, formed, and took up the address. Our Vice-President called it *his most gracious speech.* I can not approve of this. A committee was appointed on it—Johnson, Carroll, Patterson. Adjourned. In the evening there were grand fireworks. The Spanish Ambassador's house was adorned with transparent paintings; the French Minister's house was illuminated, and had some transparent pieces; the Hall was grandly illuminated, and after all this the people went to bed.

21

With the great sarcasm of which he was master, Senator Maclay recounted the debate over presidential titles:[21]

---

[21] *Ibid.,* pp. 22–25.

May 8th. . . . "Excellency" was moved for as a title by Mr. Izard. It was withdrawn by Mr. Izard, and "highness" with some prefatory word, proposed by Mr. Lee. Now long harangues were made in favor of this title. "Elective" was placed before. It was insisted that such a dignified title would add greatly to the weight and authority of the Government both at home and abroad. I declared myself totally of a different opinion; that at present it was impossible to add to the respect entertained for General Washington; that if you gave him the title of any foreign prince or potentate, a belief would follow that the manners of that prince and his modes of government would be adopted by the President. (Mr. Lee had, just before I got up, read over a list of the titles of all the princes and potentates of the earth, marking where the word "highness" occurred. The Grand Turk had it, all the princes of Germany had [it], sons and daughters of crown heads, etc.) That particularly "elective highness," which sounded nearly like "electoral highness," would have a most ungrateful sound to many thousands of industrious citizens who had fled from German oppression; that "highness" was part of the title of a prince or princes of the blood, and was often given to dukes; that it was degrading our President to place him on a par with any prince of any blood in Europe, nor was there one of them that could enter the list of true glory with him.

But I will minute no more. The debate lasted till half after three o'clock, and it ended in appointing a committee to consider of a title to be given to the President. This whole silly business is the work of Mr. Adams and Mr. Lee; Izard follows Lee, and the New England men, who always herd together, follow Mr. Adams. Mr. Thompson says this used to be the case in the old Congress. I had, to be sure, the greatest share in this debate, and must now have completely sold (no, sold is a bad word, for I have got nothing for it) every particle of court favor, for a court our House seems determined on, and to run into all the fooleries, fopperies,

fineries, and pomp of royal etiquette; and all
this for Mr. Adams.

May 9th.—Attended the Hall at ten o'clock
to go on the Judicial Committee. Met many
of the members. I know not the motive, but
I never was received with more familiarity,
nor quite so much, before by the members.
Elsworth in particular seemed to show a
kind of fondness. The Judicial Committee
did no business. Senate formed. It took a
long time to correct the minutes. Otis keeps
them miserably. At length the committee
came in and reported a title—*His Highness
the President of the United States of America
and Protector of the Rights of the Same.* Mr.
Few had spoken a word or two with me,
and signified his unwillingness to do anything hastily. He got up and spoke a great
deal against hasty measures. He did not
pointedly move for postponement, but it
amounted nearly to it. The Clerk of the
other House in the mean time appeared at
the bar and announced the adoption of the
report of the Joint Committee (rejecting
titles).

22

*Alexander Hamilton's ambitions to remake the
"frail and worthless fabric" of the Constitution,
as he termed it, into an instrument for strongly
centralized national control were more serious.
As Washington's secretary of the treasury he
was in an admirable position to do so; in restoring the national economy he could help
create the "government with energy" that was
his ideal. His suggestions were embodied in a
series of "financial reports" which, although
ostensibly designed to strengthen national credit,
were all aimed at the larger objective of increasing central power. For example, he urged
Congress to charter a national bank. Hamilton
argued that although the legislature had no
specific constitutional authority to do so, the
right could be inferred from its undisputed
power to levy taxes and to coin and to borrow
money. A bank, he insisted, was a "necessary
and proper" means of managing the fiscal policies of the country. Hamilton was, of course,
aware that acceptance of this proposition would
vastly broaden the powers of the central government. When the measure was submitted to
President Washington he had sufficient doubts
of its constitutionality to ask Thomas Jefferson,*
*his secretary of state, to prepare an opinion.
Jefferson's argument against the bank is a
concise statement of the "strict construction" attitude toward the Constitution (1791):*[22]

I consider the foundation of the Constitution as laid on this ground: that "all
powers not delegated to the United States,
by the Constitution, nor prohibited by it
to the states, are reserved to the states, or
to the people." [XIIth amendment.] To take
a single step beyond the boundaries thus
specially drawn around the powers of Congress, is to take possession of a boundless
field of power, no longer susceptible of any
definition.

The incorporation of a bank, and the
powers assumed by this bill, have not, in
my opinion, been delegated to the United
States by the Constitution.

I. They are not among the powers specially enumerated: For these are:

1st. A power to lay taxes for the purpose
of paying the debts of the United States;
but no debt is paid by this bill, nor any tax
laid. Were it a bill to raise money, its organization in the Senate would condemn it
by the Constitution.

2d. To "borrow money." But this bill
neither borrows money nor insures the bor-
rowing of it. The proprietors of the bank
will be just as free as any other money holders, to lend or not to lend their money to
the public. The operation proposed in the
bill, first to lend them two millions, and then
borrow them back again, cannot change the
nature of the latter act, which will still be
a payment, and not a loan, call it by what
name you please.

3d. To "regulate commerce with foreign
nations, and among the States, and with the
Indian tribes." To erect a bank, and to regulate commerce, are very different acts. He
who erects a bank creates a subject of commerce in its bills; so does he who makes a
bushel of wheat, or digs a dollar out of the
mines; yet neither of these persons regulates

---

[22] Albert Bergh (ed.), *The Writings of Thomas
Jefferson* (Washington, 1905), III, 146–152.

commerce thereby. To make a thing which may be bought and sold, is not to prescribe regulations for buying and selling. Besides, if this were an exercise of the power of regulating commerce, it would be void, as extending as much to the internal commerce of every State, as to its external. For the power given to Congress by the Constitution does not extend to the internal regulation of the commerce of a State . . . which remain exclusively with its own legislature; but to its external commerce only, that is to say, its commerce with another State, or with foreign nations, or with the Indian tribes. Accordingly, the bill does not propose the measure as a regulation of trade, but as "productive of considerable advantage to trade." Still less are these powers covered by any other of the special enumerations.

II. Nor are they within either of the general phrases, which are the two following:—

1. To lay taxes to provide for the general welfare of the United States, that is to say, "to lay taxes for *the purpose* of providing for the general welfare." For the laying of taxes is the *power*, and the general welfare the *purpose* for which the power is to be exercised. They are not to lay taxes *ad libitum, for any purpose they please;* but only to *pay the debts, or provide for the welfare, of the Union.* In like manner, they are not *to do anything they please,* to provide for the general welfare, but only *to lay taxes* for that purpose. To consider the latter phrase, not as describing the purpose of the first, but as giving a distinct and independent power to do any act they please which might be for the good of the Union, would render all the preceding and subsequent enumerations of power completely useless.

It would reduce the whole instrument to a single phrase, that of instituting a Congress with power to do whatever would be for the good of the United States; and, as they would be the sole judges of the good or evil, it would be also a power to do whatever evil they pleased.

It is an established rule of construction, where a phrase will bear either of two meanings, to give it that which will allow some meaning to the other parts of the instrument, and not that which will render all the others useless. Certainly no such universal power was meant to be given them. It was intended to lace them up straitly within the enumerated powers, and those without which, as means, these powers could not be carried into effect. It is known that the very power now proposed *as a means* was rejected *as an end* by the Convention which formed the Constitution. A proposition was made to them, to authorize Congress to open canals, and an amendatory one to empower them to incorporate. But the whole was rejected, and one of the reasons of objection urged in debate was, that they then would have a power to erect a bank, which would render great cities, where there were prejudices and jealousies on that subject, adverse to the reception of the Constitution.

2. The second general phrase is, "to make all laws *necessary* and proper for carrying into execution the enumerated powers." But they can all be carried into execution without a bank. A bank, therefore, is not *necessary*, and consequently not authorized by this phrase.

It has been much urged that a bank will give great facility or convenience in the collection of taxes. Suppose this were true: yet the Constitution allows only the means which are "necessary," not those which are merely "convenient," for effecting the enumerated powers. If such a latitude of construction be allowed to this phrase as to give any nonenumerated power, it will go to every one, for there is no one which ingenuity may not torture into a *convenience,* in some instance *or other,* to *some one* of so long a list of enumerated powers. It would swallow up all the delegated powers, and reduce the whole to one phrase, as before observed. Therefore it was that the Constitution restrained them to the *necessary* means, that is to say, to those means without which the grant of the power would be nugatory. . . .

Perhaps, indeed bank bills may be a more

convenient vehicle than treasury orders. But a little *difference* in the degree of *convenience,* cannot constitute the necessity which the Constitution makes the ground for assuming any non-enumerated power. . . .

Can it be thought that the Constitution intended that, for a shade or two of *convenience,* more or less, Congress should be authorized to break down the most ancient and fundamental laws of the several states such as those against Mortmain, the laws of Alienage, the rules of descent, the acts of distribution, the laws of escheat and forfeiture, the laws of monopoly? Nothing but a necessity invincible by other means, can justify such a prostitution of laws, which constitute the pillars of our whole system of jurisprudence. Will Congress be too straitlaced to carry the Constitution into honest effect, unless they may pass over the foundation-laws of the state governments, for the slightest convenience of theirs?

The negative of the President is the shield provided by the Constitution to protect against the invasions of the legislature: 1. The right of the Executive. 2. Of the Judiciary. 3. Of the States and State Legislatures. The present is the case of a right remaining exclusively with the States, and consequently one of those intended by the Constitution to be placed under his protection.

23

Jefferson's argument was presented to Hamilton for rebuttal. His reply became the bible of the "loose construction" view of the Constitution, a reasoned statement of the doctrine of implied powers:[23]

In entering upon the argument it ought to be premised that the objections of the Secretary of State and the Attorney-General are founded on a general denial of the authority of the United States to erect corporations. The latter, indeed, expressly admits, that if there be anything in the bill which is

not warranted by the Constitution, it is the clause of incorporation.

Now it appears to the Secretary of the Treasury that this *general principle is inherent* in the very *definition* of government, and *essential* to every step of the progress to be made by that of the United States, namely: That every power vested in a government is in its nature *sovereign,* and includes, by *force* of the *term* a right to employ all the *means* requisite and fairly applicable to the attainment of the ends of such power, and which are not precluded by restrictions and exceptions specified in the Constitution, or not immoral, or not contrary to the *essential ends* of political society. . . .

If it would be necessary to bring proof to a proposition so clear, as that which affirms that the powers of the federal government, as to *its objects,* were sovereign, there is a clause of the Constitution which would be decisive. It is that which declares that the Constitution, and the laws of the United States made in pursuance of it, . . . shall be the *supreme law of the land.* The power which can create a *supreme law of the land,* in *any case,* is doubtless *sovereign* as to such case.

This general and indisputable principle puts at once an end to the *abstract* question, whether the United States have power to erect a *corporation;* that is to say, to give a *legal* or *artificial capacity* to one or more persons, distinct from the *natural.* For it is unquestionably incident to *sovereign power* to erect corporations, and consequently to *that* of the United States, in *relation* to the *objects* intrusted to the management of the government. The difference is this: where the authority of the government is general, it can create corporations in *all cases;* where it is confined to certain branches of legislation, it can create corporations *only* in those cases. . . .

It is not denied that there are *implied* as well as *express powers,* and that the *former* are as effectually delegated as the *latter.* And for the sake of accuracy it shall be men-

---

[23] Henry C. Lodge (ed.), *The Works of Alexander Hamilton* (New York, 1885), III, 180–182, 184–190, 192.

tioned, that there is another class of powers, which may be properly denominated *resulting powers*. It will not be doubted, that if the United States should make a conquest of any of the territories of its neighbours, they would possess sovereign jurisdiction over the conquered territory. This would be rather a result, from the whole mass of the powers of the government, and from the nature of political society, than a consequence of either of the powers specially enumerated. . . .

To return: It is conceded that *implied powers* are to be considered as delegated equally with *express ones*. Then it follows, that as a power of erecting a corporation may as well be *implied* as any other thing, it may as well be employed as an *instrument* or *mean* of carrying into execution any of the specified powers, as any other *instrument* or *mean* whatever. The only question must be, in this, as in every other case, whether the mean to be employed, or in this instance, the corporation to be erected, has a natural relation to any of the acknowledged objects or lawful ends of the government. Thus a corporation may not be erected by Congress for superintending the police of the city of Philadelphia, because they are not authorized to *regulate* the *police* of that city. But one may be erected in relation to the collection of taxes, or to the trade with foreign countries, or to the trade between the States, or with the Indian tribes; because it is the province of the federal government to *regulate* those objects and because it is incident to a general *sovereign* or *legislative* power to *regulate* a thing, to employ all the means which relate to its regulation to the best and greatest advantage. . . .

Through this mode of reasoning respecting the right of employing all the means requisite to the execution of the specified powers of the government, it is objected, that none but necessary and proper means are to be employed; and the Secretary of State maintains, that no means are to be considered as *necessary* but those without

which the grant of the power would be *nugatory*. . . .

It is essential to the being of the national government, that so erroneous a conception of the meaning of the word *necessary* should be exploded.

It is certain, that neither the grammatical nor popular sense of the term requires that construction. According to both, *necessary* often means no more than *needful, requisite, incidental, useful*, or *conducive to*. . . . And it is the true one in which it is to be understood as used in the Constitution. The whole turn of the clause containing it indicates, that it was the intent of the Convention, by that clause, to give a liberal latitude to the exercise of the specified powers. The expressions have peculiar comprehensiveness. They are "to make all *laws* necessary and proper for *carrying into execution* the *foregoing powers*, and *all other powers*, vested by the Constitution in the *government* of the United States, or in any *department* or *officer* thereof."

To understand the word as the Secretary of State does, would be to depart from its obvious and popular sense, and to give it a restrictive operation, an idea never before entertained. It would be to give it the same force as if the word *absolutely* or *indispensably* had been prefixed to it. . . .

The *degree* in which a measure is necessary, can never be a *test* of the legal right to adopt it; that must be a matter of opinion, and can only be a *test* of expediency. The *relation* between the *measure* and the *end;* between the *nature* of the *means* employed towards the execution of a power, and the object of that power, must be the criterion of constitutionality, not the more or less of *necessity* or *utility*. . . .

This restrictive interpretation of the word *necessary* is also contrary to this sound maxim of construction; namely, that the powers contained in a constitution of government, especially those which concern the general administration of the affairs of a country, its finances, trade, defence etc., ought to be construed liberally in advancement of the public good. . . . The means by which national exigencies are to be provided for, national inconveniences obviated, national prosperity promoted, are of such infinite variety, extent, and complexity, that there must of necessity be great latitude of discretion in the selection and application of those means. Hence, consequently, the necessity and propriety of exercising the authorities intrusted to a government on principles of liberal construction. . . .

But the doctrine which is contended for is not chargeable with the consequences imputed to it. It does not affirm that the National Government is sovereign in all respects, but that it is sovereign to a certain extent;—that is, to the extent of the objects of its specified powers.

It leaves, therefore, a criterion of what is constitutional and of what is not so. This criterion is the *end*, to which the measure relates as a *means*. If the *end* be clearly comprehended within any of the specified powers, and if the measure have an obvious relation to that *end*, and is not forbidden by any particular provision of the Constitution, it may safely be deemed to come within the compass of the national authority. There is also this further criterion, which may materially assist the decision: Does the proposed measure abridge a preexisting right of any State or of any individual? If it does not, there is a strong presumption in favor of its constitutionality, and slighter relations to any declared object of the Constitution may be permitted to turn the scale.

24

Convinced that the welfare of society depended upon a government of wealth, culture, and education, the Federalists carried on an intensive campaign in behalf of property. Among the many converts to this point of view was the Revolutionary liberal John Adams. A Defense of the Constitutions of Government of the United States of America (1788), although written just before Washington took office, illustrates Federalist distrust of democracy as well as Adams' political change of heart:[24]

Property is surely a right of mankind as really as liberty. Perhaps, at first, prejudice, habit, shame or fear, principle or religion, would restrain the poor from attacking the rich, and the idle from usurping on the industrious; but the time would not be long before courage and enterprise would come, and pretexts be invented by degrees, to countenance the majority in dividing all the property among them, or at least, in sharing it equally with its present possessors. Debts would be abolished first; taxes laid heavy on the rich, and not at all on the others; and at last a downright equal division of every thing be demanded, and voted. What would be the consequence of this? The idle, the vicious, the intemperate, would rush into the utmost extravagance of debauchery, sell and spend all their share, and then demand a new division of those who purchased from them. The moment the idea is admitted into society, that property is not as sacred as the laws of God, and that there is not a force of law and public justice to protect it, anarchy and tyranny commence. If "Thou shalt not covet," and "Thou shalt not steal," were not commandments of Heaven, they must be made inviolable precepts in every society, before it can be civilized or made free. . . .

There is in every nation and people under heaven a large proportion of persons who take no rational and prudent precautions to preserve what they have, much less to acquire more. Indolence is the natural character of man, to such a degree that nothing but the necessities of hunger, thirst, and other wants equally pressing, can stimulate him to action, until education is introduced in civilized societies, and the strongest motives of ambition to excel in arts, trades, and professions, are established in the minds of all men. Until this emulation is introduced,

[24] Charles F. Adams (ed.), *The Works of John Adams* (Boston, 1851), VI, 8–9, 65–66.

the lazy savage holds property in too little estimation to give himself trouble for the preservation or acquisition of it. In societies the most cultivated and polished, vanity, fashion, and folly prevail over every thought of ways to preserve their own. They seem rather to study what means of luxury, dissipation, and extravagance they can invent to get rid of it. . . .

It is agreed that "the end of all government is the good and ease of the people, in a secure enjoyment of their rights, without oppression"; but it must be remembered, that the rich are *people* as well as the poor; that they have rights as well as others; that they have as clear and as *sacred* a right to their large property as others have to theirs which is smaller; that oppression to them is as possible and as wicked as to others; that stealing, robbing, cheating, are the same crimes and sins, whether committed against them or others. The rich, therefore, ought to have an effectual barrier in the constitution against being robbed, plundered, and murdered, as well as the poor; and this can never be without an independent senate. The poor should have a bulwark against the same dangers and oppressions; and this can never be without a house of representatives of the people. But neither the rich nor the poor can be defended by their respective guardians in the constitution, without an executive power, vested with a negative [veto], equal to either, to hold the balance even between them, and decide when they cannot agree. If it is asked, When will this negative be used? it may be answered, Perhaps never. The known existence of it will prevent all occasion to exercise it; but if it has not a being, the want of it will be felt every day. If it has not been used in England for a long time past, it by no means follows that there have not been occasions when it might have been employed with propriety. But one thing is very certain, that there have been many occasions since the Revolution [of 1688], when the constitution would have been overturned if the negative had not been an indubitable prerogative of the crown.

It is agreed that the people are "most sensible of their own burdens; and being once put into a capacity and freedom of acting, are the most likely to provide remedies for their own relief." For this reason they are an essential branch of the legislature, and have a negative on all laws, an absolute control over every grant of money, and an unlimited right to accuse their enemies before an impartial tribunal. Thus far they are most sensible of their burdens, and are most likely to provide remedies. But it is affirmed that they are not only incapable of managing the executive power, but would be instantly corrupted by it in such numbers, as would destroy the integrity of all elections. It is denied that the legislative power can be wholly intrusted in their hands with a moment's safety. The poor and the vicious would instantly rob the rich and virtuous, spend their plunder in debauchery, or confer it upon some idol, who would become the despot; or, to speak more intelligibly, if not more accurately, some of the rich, by debauching the vicious to their corrupt interest, would plunder the virtuous, and become more rich, until they acquired all the property, or a balance of property and of power, in their own hands, and domineered as despots in an oligarchy.

Adolescent Nationalism

Two compelling goals shaped American thought during the postrevolutionary years: a patriotic desire to create a distinctive culture and a powerful urge to fulfill the democratic promise of the Declaration of Independence. The struggle for liberty and equality continued unceasingly even during the years of Federalist domination. Reformers injected rationalistic concepts into religion, agitated for schools to train the population for political responsibility, and initiated crusades against archaic legal practices that oppressed the poor. All Americans, upper and lower classes alike, shared in the nationalistic fervor that prompted the cultural strivings of the postrevolutionary era. A popular consciousness of the unique American governmental system—which, patriots all agreed, was vastly superior to the effete aristocracies of Europe—frequently appeared as national arrogance bolstered by a belief that Americans were a people apart. Drawn from many lands by a migration process that sifted out the complacent, smiled on by a bountiful nature that provided infinite opportunities for development, they seemingly stood on the threshold of a period of growth unparalleled in history.

THE FOUNDATIONS OF AMERICAN FOREIGN POLICY

1

American independence was in one sense a by-product of the great imperial struggle in which England and most of the rest of Europe were involved. During the early years of American nationhood, years coinciding with national weakness, Europe was far too immersed in concerns of its own to interfere in American affairs. Consequently, America was protected from interference. Marcus Cunliffe, a contemporary British student of American civilization, makes some cogent observations on this point:[1]

In 1789, and immediately afterward, the countries of Europe were too engrossed in the affairs of their own continent to devote more than secondary attention to the United States. The great nations, in population, wealth, commerce, and military prowess,

were France and Britain. Spain had declined, but she too was reckoned as a major power, still the mistress of a vast overseas empire. Russia, though a remote enigma, was a significant factor in world diplomacy. So were Austria and Prussia. In between these and the mass of petty principalities there were other states—Portugal, Denmark, the Netherlands—that were by no means negligible.

This is not to say that Europeans were unaware of the rest of the world, but that they were accustomed to think of it as an extension of Europe and Europe's problems. A sea fight in the Indian Ocean or the Caribbean, or a clash between mixed forces of whites and Indians in the forest wilderness of North America, was still in essence a European encounter.

How did the United States fit into the scheme? To both Britain and France, America represented a group of former colonies. True, these colonies had secured their independence, thanks to French aid. But their revolutionary war had been only part of a

---

[1] Reprinted from *The Nation Takes Shape: 1789–1837* by Marcus Cunliffe, pp. 40–44, by the permission of the University of Chicago Press. Copyright 1959 by The University of Chicago.

larger conflict between Great Britain and most of the rest of Europe. Britain had lost on the American mainland yet won nearly everywhere else. She consoled herself for the defection of the thirteen colonies by reflecting that she still retained enormous territories to the north, in what had been French Canada, as well as valuable possessions in the West Indies; that the thirteen colonies were good riddance; that they would come to a bad end in their lawless, disunited, republican way; and that in any case their cultural and economic ties were still mainly with the mother country, so that American independence would be largely an illusion. Thus, the merchant shipping of Europe, for reasons that now seem incomprehensible, paid regular blackmail to the pirate nests of North Africa. American vessels in the Mediterranean formerly had been "protected" under these arrangements, as being within the British Empire. Now they had to pay their own way; and, failing to do so, they were suffering severely at the hands of Algerian pirates.

There was of course an element of pique in the British attitude to the United States—though some Englishmen were well disposed. Defeat had been humiliating; disdain and dislike were bound to follow. The new nation had never paid the debts to Britain recognized in the peace treaty of 1783. In turn the British had not settled American claims for compensation for slaves carried off during the Revolution. Moreover, the British, maintaining close connections with the Indian tribes of the back country and keenly interested in the profitable fur trade of the region, had ignored their treaty obligation to withdraw from the forts on American territory at Michilimackinac, Detroit, and elsewhere. The British commander at Fort Niagara even refused to allow American visitors to view the famous falls, and as late as 1794 the British established a further fortified trading post at the Maumee rapids, sixty miles into American territory from Detroit. Though the United States had her diplomatic representatives abroad (mere ministers, of inferior status to ambassadors), Britain did not trouble to send a properly accredited minister to the United States until 1791.

As for France, here too a certain coolness was observable. In the years from 1783 to 1789 the French had misgivings at the republican specter they had raised up in the New World. Nor, when all the mutual congratulations and some treaty recriminations died down after 1783, could the French forget that the war had cost them much in treasure, that the United States owed them a sizable sum, and that their own flag had until recently flown over much of North America. Thomas Jefferson, American minister to France in 1785–89, was unpleasantly conscious of the equivocal status of the United States, treated in the French court with strained politeness, as if it were a distant relative of doubtful morality. "We are," he said, "the lowest and most obscure of the whole diplomatic tribe." After the French Revolution broke out in 1789, the Franco-American link became emotionally stronger; ideologically, the infant nation could be regarded as father to the ancient one.

In Spain there was no such transformation. Monarchist Spain would give no encouragement to republicanism, especially since her own American colonies might emulate the example of the United States. Worse, the United States was contiguous with the Spanish Floridas and with Spanish Louisiana. Who could guarantee their survival—not to mention that of Cuba, Mexico, or the other Spanish possessions that stretched in a thinly held arc beyond the frontiers of the United States, all the way from Oregon and California to the Caribbean and the Orinoco? It was bad enough to confront the British in North America, still less agreeable to have to deal with the aggressive backwoodsmen of an aggressive new people. Spain had closed the Mississippi to American navigation; as American settlements continued to increase, far upriver in the Ohio Valley, she rightly feared for the future.

America, then, appeared to European diplomatists in 1789 as an awkward but junior interloper. None wholeheartedly wished her well; each had special grounds for hoping that the United States would run into difficulties.

The American reaction to Europe was bound up with her feeling about the nature and prospects of the Union. There was considerable distrust of Britain, heightened by British intrigues—real or imagined—in the frontier regions. There was growing indignation among westerners at what they interpreted as Spanish intransigence. There was a strong if inchoate belief that the United States was a special case among the nations of the world; the first popular republic, the first independent state in the American hemisphere, the first collection of European colonies to repudiate all allegiances. There was also widespread sympathy for France in the early years of its revolution.

These were only attitudes, not statements of policy. A statement was not called for until 1793; yet the controversy it initiated was to offer lengthy and heated proof that the United States was a vulnerable union, still feeling her way amid what Washington in his Farewell Address of 1796 was to call "our mutual cares, labors, and dangers." The problem was acute in the spring of 1793. Republican France, invaded by enemies, ousted them in a tremendous accession of nationalist energy and then proceeded to declare war upon Britain, Austria, Prussia, Sardinia, and the Netherlands. The President, after consulting his advisers, issued a proclamation of neutrality, and America was able to adhere to the policy embodied in it for nearly twenty years.

2

During the Washington and Adams administrations the rift between the parties was widened by controversies over foreign affairs. This was particularly the case after 1793, when the United States was confronted by the struggle between revolutionary France and England. Jeffersonians insisted that the French be given all aid short of war; Federalists openly sided with Britain and condemned the "anarchy and atheism" of the French Revolution. When President Washington decided to steer a neutral course, a Jeffersonian letter writer excoriated the President for refusing to recognize America's role as a proponent of world-wide democracy:[2]

In countries where *the people* have little or no share in the government, (as in Great Britain for instance) it is not uncommon for the executive to act in direct opposition to the *will of the nation.* It is to be hoped that the practice of apeing the absurd and tyrannical systems of Britain, though already carried to an alarming extent in this country, will never proceed so far, as to induce our executive to try the vain experiment of officially opposing the *national will.* An attempt of this kind, at present, would be scouted with deserved contempt, and bring ruin on its author; and such must continue to be the case, unless government shall be able to establish so much corrupt influence as, with the aid of bayonet-logic, will be sufficient to support it, in defiance of the people.

Had you, Sir, before you ventured to issue a proclamation which appears to have given much uneasiness, consulted the *general* sentiments of your fellow-citizens, you would have found them, from one extremity of the Union to the other, firmly attached to the cause of France. You would not have found them disposed to consider it as a "duty" to forget their debt of gratitude to the French nation; or to view with unconcern, the magnanimous efforts of a faithful ally, to baffle the infernal projects of those despots who have confederated for the purpose of crushing her infant liberty. Neither would you have found them so far divested of the feelings of men, as to treat with "impartiality," and equal "friendship," those tigers, who so lately deluged our country with the blood of thousands, and the men who generously flew to her rescue and became her deliverers. No, Sir—had even no written treaty existed between France and

---

[2] The letter, signed "Veritas," appeared in the *National Gazette* (Philadelphia), June 5, 1793. Jefferson, when charged with being the writer, denied authorship.

the United States, still would the strongest ties of amity have united the people of both nations; still would the republican citizens of America have regarded Frenchmen, contending for liberty, as their brethren; still would they have sympathized with them in their misfortunes, and have exulted in their success. Such, unquestionably, is the disposition of the generality of the people of the United States with respect to the French revolution. To such a people it would have been a pleasing circumstance, to have been able to discover in the proclamation a recognition of the treaties with France. That so little attention has been paid to the clamours which have arisen on this subject, in various parts of the Union, is to be lamented by every friend to the general government. Had you, Sir, considered the importance of retaining your popularity, you would, perhaps, have listened to the murmurs of the citizens; and have *deigned* to give them such explanations as might appear necessary to clear up the doubts which yet distract their minds. If this would have been *descending too far*, the secretary might have been authorized to satisfy the doubts or correct the mistakes of the people.

It ought never to be forgotten by our magistrates, that popular opinion is the basis of our government; and that when any public measure is not well understood, it would be by no means degrading to the authors of that measure, however exalted their station, to explain. Let me intreat you, Sir, to deal candidly with the people; and, without loss of time, to remove their anxiety, by informing them whether it is intended that the treaties with France are to be observed or not.

I am aware, Sir, that some court satellites may have deceived you, with respect to the sentiments of your fellow citizens. The first magistrate of a country, whether he be called a king or a president, seldom knows the real state of the nation, particularly if he be so much buoyed up by official importance, as to think it beneath his dignity to mix occasionally with the people. Let me caution you,

Sir, to beware that you do not view the state of the public mind, at this critical moment, through a fallacious medium. Let not the little buzz of the aristocratic few, and their contemptible minions, of speculators, tories, and British emissaries, be mistaken for the exalted and general voice of the American people. The spirit of 1776 is again roused; and soon shall the mushroom-lordlings of the day, the enemies of American as well as French liberty, be taught that American whigs of 1776, will not suffer French patriots of 1792, to be vilified with impunity, by the common enemies of both.

3

Washington's Farewell Address is probably the most widely quoted and least understood public statement General Washington ever made:[3]

UNITED STATES, *September 17, 1796.*
FRIENDS AND FELLOW-CITIZENS:

The period for a new election of a citizen to administer the Executive Government of the United States being not far distant, and the time actually arrived when your thoughts must be employed in designating the person who is to be clothed with that important trust, it appears to me proper, especially as it may conduce to a more distinct expression of the public voice, that I should now apprise you of the resolution I have formed to decline being considered among the number of those out of whom a choice is to be made. . . .

Here, perhaps, I ought to stop. But a solicitude for your welfare which can not end with my life, and the apprehension of danger natural to that solicitude, urge me on an occasion like the present to offer to your solemn contemplation and to recommend to your frequent review some sentiments which are the result of much reflection, of no inconsiderable observation, and which appear to me all important to the permanency of your felicity as a people. . . .

[3] James D. Richardson (comp.), A *Compilation of the Messages and Papers of the Presidents, 1789–1902* (Washington, 1903), I, 213–224, *passim.*

To the efficacy and permanency of your union a government for the whole is indispensable. No alliances, however strict, between the parts can be an adequate substitute. They must inevitably experience the infractions and interruptions which all alliances in all times have experienced. Sensible of this momentous truth, you have improved upon your first essay by the adoption of a Constitution of Government better calculated than your former for an intimate union and for the efficacious management of your common concerns. This Government, the offspring of our own choice, uninfluenced and unawed, adopted upon full investigation and mature deliberation, completely free in its principles, in the distribution of its powers, uniting security with energy, and containing within itself a provision for its own amendment, has a just claim to your confidence and your support. Respect for its authority, compliance with its laws, acquiescence in its measures, are duties enjoined by the fundamental maxims of true liberty. The basis of our political systems is the right of the people to make and to alter their constitutions of government. But the constitution which at any time exists till changed by an explicit and authentic act of the whole people is sacredly obligatory upon all. The very idea of the power and the right of the people to establish government presupposes the duty of every individual to obey the established government. . . .

I have already intimated to you the danger of parties in the State, with particular reference to the founding of them on geographical discriminations. Let me now take a more comprehensive view, and warn you in the most solemn manner against the baneful effects of the spirit of party generally.

This spirit, unfortunately, is inseparable from our nature, having its root in the strongest passions of the human mind. It exists under different shapes in all governments, more or less stifled, controlled, or repressed; but in those of the popular form it is seen in its greatest rankness and is truly their worst enemy. . . .

It serves always to distract the public councils and enfeeble the public administration. It agitates the community with ill-founded jealousies and false alarms; kindles the animosity of one part against another; foments occasionally riot and insurrection. It opens the door to foreign influence and corruption, which find a facilitated access to the government itself through the channels of party passion. Thus the policy and the will of one country are subjected to the policy and will of another. . . .

Observe good faith and justice toward all nations. Cultivate peace and harmony with all. Religion and morality enjoin this conduct. And can it be that good policy does not equally enjoin it? It will be worthy of a free, enlightened, and at no distant period a great nation to give to mankind the magnanimous and too novel example of a people always guided by an exalted justice and benevolence. . . .

In the execution of such a plan nothing is more essential than that permanent, inveterate antipathies against particular nations and passionate attachments for others should be excluded, and that in place of them just and amicable feelings toward all should be cultivated. The nation which indulges toward another an habitual hatred or an habitual fondness is in some degree a slave. It is a slave to its animosity or to its affection, either of which is sufficient to lead it astray from its duty and its interest. . . .

So, likewise, a passionate attachment of one nation for another produces a variety of evils. Sympathy for the favorite nation, facilitating the illusion of an imaginary common interest in cases where no real common interest exists, and infusing into one the enmities of the other, betrays the former into a participation in the quarrels and wars of the latter without adequate inducement or justification. . . .

The great rule of conduct for us in regard to foreign nations is, in extending our commercial relations to have with them as little *political* connection as possible. So far as we have already formed engagements let them be fulfilled with perfect good faith. Here let us stop.

Europe has a set of primary interests which to us have none or a very remote relation. Hence she must be engaged in frequent controversies, the causes of which are essentially foreign to our concerns. Hence, therefore, it must be unwise in us to implicate ourselves by artificial ties in the ordinary vicissitudes of her politics or the ordinary combinations and collisions of her friendships or enmities. . . .

It is our true policy to steer clear of permanent alliances with any portion of the foreign world, so far, I mean, as we are now at liberty to do it; for let me not be understood as capable of patronizing infidelity to existing engagements. I hold the maxim no less applicable to public than to private affairs that honesty is always the best policy. I repeat, therefore, let those engagements be observed in their genuine sense. But in my opinion it is unnecessary and would be unwise to extend them.

Taking care always to keep ourselves by suitable establishments on a respectable defensive posture, we may safely trust to temporary alliances for extraordinary emergencies.

4

The political implications of the Washington valedictory have been analyzed by an acute student of American foreign policy. His analysis first appeared in 1957 and is excerpted below:[4]

When in 1789 George Washington became the nation's first president the French alliance was the cornerstone of American foreign policy. It largely had made possible American independence and had established American foreign policy orientation. At the end of Washington's second term, in fact as he prepared his farewell to public life, the

[4] Alexander DeConde, "Washington's Farewell, the French Alliance, and the Election of 1796," *Mississippi Valley Historical Review*, XLIII (March 1957), 641, 648–650. Reprinted with the permission of the author, Alexander DeConde, and the publisher, The Mississippi Valley Historical Association.

life-giving alliance was practically dead and the United States was virtually at war with France. Why, in eight formative years, did such a drastic reversal in foreign policy take place? A full answer to this question would be long and complex; yet by looking closely at the election of 1796 and by reviewing the Farewell Address in its political context we may find a partial answer as to how the alliance received its mortal wound. We may also find additional reason for revising the traditional interpretation of the Farewell Address as a wise, timeless, and unbiased warning to the nation. . . .

Once the decision to retire was made, Washington turned to Hamilton, as usual, for advice. When, he asked, would be the best time for publication of his farewell to the nation? Hamilton, with his eye on the coming election, advised that the public announcement be held off as long as possible. "The proper period now for your declaration," wrote Hamilton, "seems to be *Two months* before the time for the Meeting of the Electors. This will be sufficient. The parties will in the meantime electioneer conditionally, that is to say, *if you decline;* for a serious opposition to you will I think hardly be risked."

Three months before the gathering of electors Washington announced to the nation his intention to retire. Although in 1792 he had planned a valedictory to the nation and James Madison had drafted one, the September, 1796 version, in which Hamilton's hand was prominent, became a piece of partisan politics directed specifically against Republicans and Francophiles who had made Washington's last years miserable. At the time, it was recognized for what it was: a political manifesto, a campaign document. The 1792 version, drawn up before popular passions had been stirred by war in Europe, did not, for example, stress politics nor did it touch on foreign affairs. In the 1796 version partisan politics and foreign affairs were central.

Washington's specific target in foreign affairs, heartily seconded by Hamilton, was the alliance with France. He struck at Adet's partisan activities, at French meddling in

American politics (while passing over British meddling), and at the allegedly dangerous implications of the French alliance. Washington told Hamilton that had it not been for the status of "party disputes" and of foreign affairs he would not have considered it necessary to revise his valedictory. He was convinced that a warning to the nation was necessary to combat foreign (French) intrigue "in the internal concerns of our country." It is indeed easy "to foresee," he warned, "that it may involve us in disputes and finally in War, to fulfill political alliances." This was the crux of the matter; Washington believed that the French alliance was no longer an asset to the country.

Washington's valedictory trumpeted the Federalist answer to Republican accusations that the administration had sold the country to the British; it countered the antiadministration furor over the Jay Treaty; it was a justification and defense of his policies. As such it was designed and as such it became the opening blast in the presidential campaign, contrived to prevent the election of Thomas Jefferson. The Farewell laid the basis for Federalist strategy of using Washington's great prestige to appeal to patriotism, as against the evil of foreign machinations, to make "Federalist" and "patriot" synonyms in the minds of the electorate. Under the banner of patriotism the Farewell spearheaded the attack on the opposition party and on French diplomacy.

In the address Washington opened with the announcement that he would not be a candidate for a third term and then stressed the advantages of union and the evils of political parties. Having in mind, undoubtedly, the French Republic, he advised against "a passionate attachment of one Nation for another." Such "sympathy for the favourite nation," he warned, leads to wars and quarrels "without adequate inducement or justification." Then followed the oft-quoted "Great rule of Conduct" that with foreign nations we should have "as little *political* connection as possible." While stressing fidelity to "already formed engagements," he announced that " 'tis our true policy to steer

clear of permanent Alliances with any portion of the foreign world." Washington deplored the growth of political opposition, chastised the public for its attachment to France, and concluded with a defense of his foreign policy, particularly his much criticized policy of neutrality which was based on the Proclamation of April 22, 1793. He called this the "index" to his plan or policy.

Although cloaked in phrases of universal or timeless application, the objectives of the address were practical, immediate, and partisan. Men often attempt to rationalize their partisan political views in pronouncements studded with timeless patriotic appeals; so it was with Washington and Hamilton. The valedictory bore directly on the coming election, on the French alliance, and on the status of Franco-American relations in general.

While expressed cogently and linked forever with Washington's name, the main ideas and foreign policy principles of the Farewell were not unique with either Hamilton or Washington. They were prevalent Federalist ideas on current foreign policy and politics, and can be found expressed in various ways in the polemical literature of the time. The concept of no entanglement with Europe, for instance, was a common one among Federalists and others. More often than not it was a universalized reaction against a specific annoyance—the French alliance. Stated as non-involvement with Europe an attack against the alliance had great psychological appeal. In time this specific meaning was lost and only the generalization remained.

5

The Jeffersonians, like the Federalists, reached for timeless symbols of liberty and freedom in their efforts to curb the growing nationalism, or what they called the "consolidation," of the Federalists. When the latter passed the Alien and Sedition Acts, the Republicans responded with the Kentucky and Virginia Resolutions. The latter were written by Jefferson and adopted by the Kentucky legislature in 1799 in the form reprinted below:[5]

---

[5] Paul L. Ford (ed.), *The Works of Thomas Jefferson* (New York, 1905), VIII, 458–461.

I. *Resolved,* that the several States composing the United States of America, are not united on the principle of unlimited submission to their general government; but that by compact under the style and title of a Constitution for the United States and of amendments thereto, they constituted a general government for special purposes, delegated to that government certain definite powers, reserving each State to itself, the residuary mass of right to their own self-government; and that whensoever the general government assumes undelegated powers, its acts are unauthoritative, void, and of no force: That to this compact each State acceded as a State, and is an integral party, its co-States forming, as to itself, the other party: That the government created by this compact was not made the exclusive or final judge of the extent of the powers delegated to itself; since that would have made its discretion, and not the Constitution, the measure of its powers; but that as in all other cases of compact among parties having no common Judge, *each party has an equal right to judge for itself, as well of infractions as of the mode and measure of redress.*

6

The winds of political doctrine that swirled around the Alien and Sedition Acts, and the subsequent Virginia and Kentucky Resolutions, expelled John Adams out of the presidency after but a single term in office. His rejection wounded him deeply. In 1815, when the pain had subsided, he wrote a letter to an old friend and fellow Federalist, James Lloyd, the senator from Massachusetts, in which he tried to summarize the accomplishments of his single administration:[6]

QUINCY, *March 31, 1815*
I cannot repent of my "strong character." Whether I have one or not, I know not. I am not conscious of any character stronger than common. If I have such a nature, it was given me. I shall neither be rewarded

nor punished for it. For all my foibles, strong or weak, I hold myself responsible to God and man. I hope to be forgiven for what I humbly acknowledge I cannot justify, and not be too severely censured for what, in my circumstances, *"humana parum cavet natura."* I did not humble France, nor have the combined efforts of emperors and kings humbled her, and, I hope, she never will be humbled below Austria, Russia, or England. But I humbled the French Directory as much as all Europe has humbled Bonaparte. I purchased navy yards, which would now sell for double their cost with compound interest. I built frigates, manned a navy, and selected officers with great anxiety and care, who perfectly protected our commerce, and gained virgin victories against the French, and who afterwards acquired such laurels in the Mediterranean, and who have lately emblazoned themselves and their country with a naval glory, which I tremble to think of. God forbid that American naval power should ever be such a scourge to the human race as that of Great Britain has been! I was engaged in the most earnest, sedulous, and, I must own, expensive exertions to preserve peace with the Indians, and prepare them for agriculture and civilization, through the whole of my administration. I had the inexpressible satisfaction of complete success. Not a hatchet was lifted in my time; and the single battle of Tippecanoe has since cost the United States a hundred times more money than it cost me to maintain universal and perpetual peace. I finished the demarcation of limits, and settled all controversies with Spain. I made the composition with England, for all the old Virginia debts, and all the other American debts, the most snarling, angry, thorny, *scabreux* negotiation that ever mortal ambassador, king, prince, emperor, or president was ever plagued with. I say I made it, and so I did, though the treaty was not ratified till Jefferson came in. My labors were indefatigable to compose all difficulties and settle all controversies with all nations, civilized and savage. And I had complete and perfect suc-

---

[6] John Adams to James Lloyd, March 31, 1815. Reprinted with the kind permission of the Massachusetts Historical Society.

cess, and left my country at peace with all the world, upon terms consistent with the honor and interest of the United States, and with all our relations with other nations, and all our obligations by the law of nations or by treaties. This is so true that no nation or individual ever uttered a complaint of injury, insult, or offence. I had suppressed an insurrection in Pennsylvania, and effectually humbled and punished the insurgents; not by assembling an army of militia from three or four States, and marching in all the pride, pomp, and circumstances of war, at an expense of millions, but silently, without noise, and at a trifling expense....

As I am not now writing a history of my administration, I will sum up all I have to say in a few words. I left my country in peace and harmony with all the world, and after all my "extravagant expenses" and "wanton waste of public money," I left navy yards, fortifications, frigates, timber, naval stores, manufactories of cannon and arms, and a treasury full of five millions of dollars. This was all done step by step, against perpetual oppositions, clamors and reproaches, such as no other President ever had to encounter, and with a more feeble, divided, and incapable support than has ever fallen to the lot of any administration before or since. For this I was turned out of office, degraded and disgraced by my country; and I was glad of it. I felt no disgrace, because I felt no remorse. It has given me fourteen of the happiest years of my life; and I am certain I could not have lasted one year more in that station, shackled in the chains of that arbitrary faction.

SELF–CONSCIOUS AMERICANS

7

Of major importance in explaining the American spirit of nationalism is the impact of the Revolution itself. This struggle not only welded a divergent people together but indoctrinated them with a sense of high national destiny. This cultural nationalism was expressed in many

ways. Thomas Jefferson, although spiritually a cosmopolitan, was so affected by the pervasive atmosphere of patriotism that even he reflected the current trend. Writing to a friend in 1785, he argued that the youthful colleges of America were superior to the ancient universities of Europe:[7]

DEAR SIR,—I should sooner have answered the paragraph in your letter, of September the 19th, respecting the best seminary for the education of youth in Europe, but that it was necessary for me to make inquiries on the subject. The result of these has been, to consider the competition as resting between Geneva and Rome. They are equally cheap, and probably equal in the course of education pursued. The advantage of Geneva is, that students acquire there the habit of speaking French. The advantages of Rome are, the acquiring a local knowledge of a spot so classical and so celebrated; the acquiring the true pronunciation of the Latin language; a just taste in the fine arts, more particularly those of painting, sculpture, architecture, and music; a familiarity with those objects and processes of agriculture which experience has shown best adapted to a climate like ours; and lastly, the advantage of a fine climate for health. It is probable, too, that by being boarded in a French family, the habit of speaking that language may be obtained. I do not count on any advantage to be derived, in Geneva, from a familiar acquaintance with the principles of that government. The late revolution has rendered it a tyrannical aristocracy, more likely to give ill than good ideas to an American. I think the balance in favor of Rome. Pisa is sometimes spoken of as a place of education. But it does not offer the first and third of the advantages of Rome. But why send an American youth to Europe for education? What are the objects of an useful American education? Classical knowledge, modern languages, chiefly French, Spanish,

---

[7] Thomas Jefferson to J. Bannister, Jr., October 15, 1785, in Albert E. Bergh (ed.), *The Writings of Thomas Jefferson* (Washington, 1905), V, 185–188.

and Italian; Mathematics, Natural philosophy, Natural history, Civil history, and Ethics. In Natural philosophy, I mean to include Chemistry and Agriculture, and in Natural history, to include Botany, as well as the other branches of those departments. It is true that the habit of speaking the modern languages cannot be so well acquired in America; but every other article can be as well acquired at William and Mary college, as at any place in Europe. When college education is done with, and a young man is to prepare himself for public life, he must cast his eyes (for America) either on Law or Physics. For the former, where can he apply so advantageously as to Mr. Wythe? For the latter, he must come to Europe: the medical class of students, therefore, is the only one which need come to Europe. Let us view the disadvantages of sending a youth to Europe. To enumerate them all, would require a volume. I will select a few. If he goes to England, he learns drinking, horse racing, and boxing. These are the peculiarities of English education. The following circumstances are common to education in that, and the other countries of Europe. He acquires a fondness for European luxury and dissipation, and a contempt for the simplicity of his own country; he is fascinated with the privileges of the European aristocrats, and sees, with abhorrence, the lovely equality which the poor enjoy with the rich, in his own country; he contracts a partiality for aristocracy or monarchy; he forms foreign friendships which will never be useful to him, and loses the seasons of life for forming, in his own country, those friendships which, of all others, are the most faithful and permanent; he is led, by the strongest of all the human passions, into a spirit for female intrigue, destructive of his own and others' happiness, or a passion for whores, destructive of his health, and, in both cases, learns to consider fidelity to the marriage bed as an ungentlemanly practice, and inconsistent with happiness; he recollects the voluptuary dress and arts of the European women, and pities and despises the chaste affections and simplicity of those of his own country; he retains, through life, a fond recollection, and a hankering after those places, which were the scenes of his first pleasures and of his first connections; he returns to his own country, a foreigner, unacquainted with the practices of domestic economy, necessary to preserve him from ruin, speaking and writing his native tongue as a foreigner, and therefore unqualified to obtain those distinctions, which eloquence of the pen and tongue ensures in a free country; for I would observe to you, that what is called style in writing or speaking is formed very early in life, while the imagination is warm, and impressions are permanent. I am of opinion, that there never was an instance of a man's writing or speaking his native tongue with elegance, who passed from fifteen to twenty years of age out of the country where it was spoken. Thus, no instance exists of a person's writing two languages perfectly. That will always appear to be his native language, which was most familiar to him in his youth. It appears to me, then, that an American, coming to Europe for education, loses his in knowledge, in his morals, in his health, in his habits, and in his happiness. I had entertained only doubts on this head before I came to Europe: what I see and hear, since I came here, proves more than I had even suspected. Cast your eye over America: who are the men of learning, of most eloquence, most beloved by their countrymen and most trusted and promoted by them? They are those who have been educated among them, and whose manners, morals, and habits, are perfectly homogeneous with those of the country.

Did you expect by so short a question, to draw such a sermon on yourself? I dare say you did not. But the consequences of foreign education are alarming to me, as an American. I sin, therefore, through zeal, whenever I enter on the subject. You are sufficiently American to pardon me for it. Let me hear of your health, and be assured of the esteem with which I am, dear Sir, your friend and servant.

8

*Others, less urbane than the polished Jeffer-
son, resented the continued use of a language
that had originated in hated England. The more
hotheaded of this tribe proposed that a new
language—Hebrew or German—be adopted;
others found solace in the belief that they were
not really speaking English, but American. A
French traveler, the Marquis de Chastellux, who
visited the United States between 1780 and
1782, notes this tendency with amusement:*[8]

At the beginning, they thought that their
language was universal in Europe; but if
they owed this opinion to a faulty education, to a kind of national pride, this same
pride had to suffer when they recalled (and
this happened often) that the language of
their country was that of their oppressors.
And so they would avoid such expressions as
"You speak English well," "You understand
English easily." I have often heard them say,
"You speak American well," "American is not
hard to learn." They went even further; it
was seriously proposed to introduce a new
language, and some people wanted, for public convenience, to substitute Hebrew for
English—they would have had it taught in
the schools, and it would have served for all
public documents. It will be imagined that
this plan was not accepted, but one can at
least grasp the fact that the aversion of the
Americans for the English could not show
itself in a more emphatic fashion.

9

*One patriot determined to translate the vision
of a distinctive American language into reality.
Noah Webster, Connecticut-born educator and
editor, realizing that the spoken languages of
the United States and Britain had diverged in
the 150 years of the colonial period, proposed
recasting his country's written language to conform to the oral. Insisting upon the need of
language reform to secure cultural independence
from Europe, he urged adoption of phonetic
spelling and simplified grammatical forms to*

*create a native-American mother "tung." Web-
ster's life-long devotion to his project resulted
in his monumental* American Dictionary of the
English Language *(1828), but long before this
appeared,* An Essay on the Necessity, Advantages and Practicability of Reforming the Mode
of Spelling . . . *(1789) outlined the changes that
he planned to make:*[9]

The advantages to be derived from these
alterations are numerous, great and permanent.

1. The simplicity of the orthography
would facilitate the learning of the language. It is now the work of years for children to learn to spell; and after all, the business is rarely accomplished. A few men, who
are bred to some business that requires constant exercise in writing, finally learn to spell
most words without hesitation; but most
people remain, all their lives, imperfect
masters of spelling, and liable to make mistakes, whenever they take up a pen to write
a short note. Nay, many people, even of
education and fashion, never attempt to
write a letter, without frequently consulting
a dictionary.

But with the proposed orthography, a
child would learn to spell, without trouble,
in a very short time, and the orthography
being very regular, he would ever afterwards
find it difficult to make a mistake. It would,
in that case, be as difficult to spell *wrong*
as it is now to spell *right*.

Besides this advantage, foreigners would
be able to acquire the pronunciation of English, which is now so difficult and embarrass-
ing that they are either wholly discouraged
on the first attempt, or obliged, after many
years' labor, to rest contented with an imperfect knowledge of the subject.

2. A correct orthography would render the
pronunciation of the language as uniform as
the spelling in books. A general uniformity
thro the United States would be the event

---

[8] Robert Withington (ed.), "The Marquis de
Chastellux on Language and Peace," *New England
Quarterly,* XVI (June 1943), 316–319. Reprinted
by permission of the *New England Quarterly.*

[9] Noah Webster, *An Essay on the Necessity, Advantages and Practicability of Reforming the Mode
of Spelling, and of Rendering the Orthography
Correspondent to the Pronunciation* (1789). Reprinted in *Old South Leaflets,* VIII, no. 196 (Boston,
n.d.), pp. 4–6.

of such a reformation as I am here recommending. All persons, of every rank, would speak with some degree of precision and uniformity. Such a uniformity in these states is very desirable; it would remove prejudice, and conciliate mutual affection and respect.

3. Such a reform would diminish the number of letters about one sixteenth or eighteenth. This would save a page in eighteen; and a saving of an eighteenth in the expense of books, is an advantage that should not be overlooked.

4. But a capital advantage of this reform in these states would be, that it would make a difference between the English orthography and the American. This will startle those who have not attended to the subject; but I am confident that such an event is an object of vast political consequence. For the alteration, however small, would encourage the publication of books in our own country. It would render it, in some measure, necessary that all books should be printed in America. The English would never copy our orthography for their own use; and consequently the same impressions of books would not answer for both countries. The inhabitants of the present generation would read the English impressions; but posterity, being taught a different spelling, would prefer the American orthography.

Besides this, a *national language* is a band of *national union*. Every engine should be employed to render the people of this country *national;* to call their attachments home to their own country; and to inspire them with the pride of national character. However they may boast of independence, and the freedom of their government, yet their *opinions* are not sufficiently independent; an astonishing respect for the arts and literature of their parent country, and a blind imitation of its manners, are still prevalent among the Americans. Thus an habitual respect for another country, deserved indeed and once laudable, turns their attention from their own interests, and prevents their respecting themselves.

10

So contagious was the patriotic fervor, many churchmen were infected. National churches, able to shape their own creeds and name their own clergy, became the ideal of both laymen and ministers. That this objective was secured by most of the Protestant denominations is easy to understand; that even leaders of the most international of all churches, the Roman Catholic, felt the same urge is tribute to the spirit of the day. This was evident in a letter written in 1785 by John Carroll, the first bishop of the Roman Catholic Church in the United States:[10]

Our objections to it [the ordering of American Catholic ecclesiastical affairs from Rome] are—1st. We conceive our situation no longer as that of missioners; and the Ecclesiastical constitution here no longer as that of a mission. By acquiring civil and religious rights in common with other Christians, we are become a national Catholic Clergy; Colleges are now erecting for giving general and liberal education; these Colleges are open, both to masters and scholars of every religious denomination; and as we have every reason to believe, that amongst the youth trained in these different Colleges, there will be frequently some inclined to the Ecclesiastical State, we Catholics propose instituting a Seminary to form them to the virtues of their future state, and to instruct them in Divinity. Thus we shall in a few years, with the blessing of providence, be able to supply this country with labourers in the Lord's vineyard, and keep up a succession, if we are indulged in a Bishop. We are not in immediate want of one, and it will be more agreeable to many of my Brethren not to have any yet appointed; but whenever the time for it comes, we conceive that it will be more advantageous to Religion and less liable to give offence that he be an ordinary Bishop, and not a Vicar-Apostolic, and be chosen and presented to his Holiness by the American Cath. Clergy. For two reasons we think it improper to be subject

---

[10] Peter Guilday, *The Life and Times of John Carroll* (New York, 1922), pp. 208–210.

in our Ecclesiastical government to the Propaganda: the first is, that not being missioners,
we conceive ourselves, not a proper object
of their institutions; and the second is, that
tho' our free and tolerant forms of Government (in Virginia, Maryland, and Pennsylvania) admit us to equal civil rights with
other Christians, yet the leading men in our
respective States often express a jealousy of
any foreign jurisdiction; and surely will be
more offended about submitting to it in matters not essential to our faith. I hope they
will never object to our depending on the
Pope in things purely spiritual; but I am
sure there are men, at least in this State, who
would blow up a flame of animosity against
us, if they suspected that we were to be so
much under the government of any Con-
g[regatio]n at Rome, as to receive our Superior from it, commissioned only during
their good will; and that this Superior was
restricted from employing any Clergyman
here, but such as that Congregation should
direct. I dread so much the consequences of
its being known that this last direction was
ever given, that I have not thought it proper
to mention it to several of my Brethren.

11

*While grammarians and churchmen yielded
to the patriotic fever, historians felt the urge to
magnify the virtues of their country and its
heroes. Dozens of books bristling with extravagant statements and prideful epics wove such
a fabric of untruth about the Revolutionary
period that scholars have been trying to un-
ravel it ever since. Of these self-appointed glori-
fiers, none was more popular than the Reverend
Mason L. Weems, a renegade Anglican who
peddled books along the Atlantic coast for many
years before becoming an author himself. The
Life and Memorable Actions of George Washington (1800), a fictionalized biography that went
through forty editions, immortalized Weems and
dehumanized Washington. In the fifth edition
appeared for the first time a classic of American
folklore: the story of George, the hatchet, and
the cherry tree:[11]*

---

[11] Mason L. Weems, *The Life of George Washington* (Philadelphia, 1892 ed.), pp. 14–16.

Never did the wise Ulysses take more
pains with his beloved Telemachus, than
did Mr. Washington with George, to inspire
him with an early love of truth. "Truth,
George," said he "is the loveliest quality of
youth. I would ride fifty miles, my son, to
see the little boy whose heart is so honest,
and his lips so pure, that we may depend on
every word he says. O how lovely does such
a child appear in the eyes of every body!
his parents doat on him. His relations glory
in him. They are constantly praising him to
their children, whom they beg to imitate
him. They are often sending for him to visit
them; and receive him, when he comes, with
as much joy as if he were a little angel, come
to set pretty examples to their children.

"But, Oh! how different, George, is the
case with the boy who is so given to lying,
that nobody can believe a word he says! He
is looked at with aversion wherever he goes,
and parents dread to see him come among
their children. Oh, George! my son! rather
than see you come to this pass, dear as you
are to my heart, gladly would I assist to
nail you up in your little coffin, and follow
you to your grave. Hard, indeed, would it be
to me to give up my son, whose little feet
are always so ready to run about with me,
and whose fondly looking eyes, and sweet
prattle make so large a part of my happiness.
But still I would give him up, rather than
see him a common liar."

"Pa," said George very seriously, "do I
ever tell lies?"

"No, George, I thank God you do not, my
son; and I rejoice in the hope you never will.
At least, you shall never, from me, have
cause to be guilty of so shameful a thing.
Many parents, indeed, even compel their
children to this vile practice, by barbarously
beating them for every little fault: hence, on
the next offence, the little terrified creature
slips out a lie! just to escape the rod. But as
to yourself George, you know I have always
told you, and now tell you again, that, whenever by accident, you do anything wrong,
which must often be the case, as you are but

a poor little boy yet, without experience or knowledge, you must never tell a falsehood to conceal it; but come bravely up, my son, like a little man, and tell me of it: and, instead of beating you, George, I will but the more honour, and love you for it, my dear."

This, you'll say, was sowing good seed! —Yes, it was: and the crop, thank God, was, as I believe it ever will be, where a man acts the true parent, that is, the Guardian Angel, by his child.

The following anecdote is a case in point. It is too valuable to be lost, and too true to be doubted; for it was communicated to me by the same excellent lady to whom I am indebted for the last.

"When George," said she, "was about six years old, he was made the wealthy master of a hatchet! of which, like most little boys, he was immoderately fond; and was constantly going about chopping every thing that came in his way. One day, in the garden, where he often amused himself hacking his mother's pea-sticks, he unluckily tried the edge of his hatchet on the body of a beautiful young English cherry-tree, which he barked so terribly, that I don't believe the tree ever got the better of it. The next morning the old gentleman, finding out what had befallen his tree, which, by the by, was a great favourite, came into the house; and with much warmth asked for the mischievous author, declaring at the same time, that he would not have taken five guineas for his tree. Nobody could tell him any thing about it. Presently George and his hatchet made their appearance. 'George,' said his father, 'do you know who killed that beautiful little cherry tree yonder in the garden?' This was a tough question, and George staggered under it for a moment; but quickly recovered himself: and looking at his father, with the sweet face of youth brightened with the inexpressible charm of all-conquering truth, he bravely cried out, 'I can't tell a lie, Pa; you know I can't tell a lie. I did cut it with my hatchet.'—'Run to my arms, you dearest boy,' cried his father in transports, 'run to my arms, glad am I, George, that you killed my tree;

for you have paid me for it a thousand fold. Such an act of heroism in my son is more worth than a thousand trees, though blossomed with silver, and their fruits of purest gold.'"

It was in this way by interesting at once both his heart and head, that Mr. Washington conducted George with great ease and pleasure along the happy paths of virtue.

THE ENLIGHTENMENT DEEPENS

12

Zeal for democracy was reflected not only in the military triumphs that in 1783 ended the war, but in the social reforms undertaken even while the Revolution was in progress. To the lower classes the turbulent times and the exodus of the conservative Tories offered opportunities to fulfill the promise of the Declaration of Independence. The established church, aristocratic inheritance laws, slavery, and other archaic practices were attacked. The democratic surge was particularly noticeable in the South, partly because the relics of aristocracy were more firmly rooted there than in the North, partly because of the influence of such enlightened leaders as Thomas Jefferson. Jefferson's particular object was to secure freedom of conscience for men of all faiths. He explains his animosity toward an established church in his Notes on Virginia *(1782):*[12]

The error seems not sufficiently eradicated, that the operations of the mind, as well as the acts of the body, are subject to the coercion of the laws. But our rulers can have authority over such natural rights only as we have submitted to them. The rights of conscience we never submitted, we could not submit. We are answerable for them to our God. The legitimate powers of government extend to such acts only as are injurious to others. But it does me no injury for my neighbour to say there are twenty gods, or no god. It neither picks my pocket nor breaks my leg. If it be said, his testimony in a court of justice cannot be relied on, reject it then, and be the stigma on him.

---

[12] Thomas Jefferson, *Notes on the State of Virginia* (Trenton, 1803), pp. 307–310.

Constraint may make him worse by making him a hypocrite, but it will never make him a truer man. It may fix him obstinately in his errors, but will not cure them. Reason and free enquiry are the only effectual agents against error. Give a loose to them, they will support the true religion, by bringing every false one to their tribunal to the test of their investigation. They are the natural enemies of error, and of error only. Had not the Roman government permitted free enquiry, Christianity could never have been introduced. Had not free enquiry been indulged, at the aera of the reformation, the corruptions of Christianity could not have been purged away. If it be restrained now, the present corruptions will be protected, and new ones encouraged.

13

One of the most effective and most controversial propagandists for rationalism in religion was the Revolutionary radical Thomas Paine. His book on The Age of Reason *(1796) was an impassioned plea for deism. Paine begins the volume with a brief statement of his own faith:*[13]

I believe in one God, and no more; and I hope for happiness beyond this life.

I believe in the equality of man, and I believe that religious duties consist in doing justice, loving mercy, and endeavouring to make our fellow-creatures happy.

But, lest it should be supposed that I believe many other things in addition to these, I shall, in the progress of this work, declare the things I do not believe, and my reasons for not believing them.

I do not believe in the creed professed by the Jewish church, by the Roman church, by the Greek church, by the Turkish church, by the Protestant church, nor by any church that I know of. My own mind is my own church.

All national institutions of churches, whether Jewish, Christian, or Turkish, appear to me no other than human inventions

set up to terrify and enslave mankind, and monopolize power and profit.

I do not mean by this declaration to condemn those who believe otherwise; they have the same right to their belief as I have to mine. But it is necessary to the happiness of man, that he be mentally faithful to himself. Infidelity does not consist in believing, or in disbelieving; it consists in professing to believe what he does not believe.

It is impossible to calculate the moral mischief, if I may so express it, that mental lying has produced in society. When a man has so far corrupted and prostituted the chastity of his mind as to subscribe his professional belief to things he does not believe he has prepared himself for the commission of every other crime.

He takes up the trade of a priest for the sake of gain, and in order to qualify himself for that trade he begins with a perjury. Can we conceive anything more destructive to morality than this?

Soon after I had published the pamphlet "Common Sense," in America, I saw the exceeding probability that a revolution in the system of government would be followed by a revolution in the system of religion. The adulterous connection of church and state, wherever it had taken place, whether Jewish, Christian, or Turkish, had so effectually prohibited, by pains and penalties, every discussion upon established creeds, and upon first principles of religion, that until the system of government should be changed, those subjects could not be brought fairly and openly before the world; but that whenever this should be done, a revolution in the system of religion would follow. Human inventions and priest-craft would be detected; and man would return to the pure, unmixed, and unadulterated belief of one God, and no more.

14

The revolt against religious orthodoxy was only one aspect of the broadening Enlightenment. No less typical was the desire to improve mankind through education. With the colonial school system shattered by the war, the time

---

[13] Philip S. Foner (ed.), *The Complete Writings of Thomas Paine* (New York, 1945), I, 464–465.

seemed ripe to establish a broad-based educational structure to give all youth an equal chance for development, regardless of economic status. This could be achieved, reformers argued, only through state-supported schools offering free education to all who were mentally qualified. Thomas Jefferson prepared the plans for such a program; Virginia, he proposed, should be divided into school districts ("hundreds") containing free primary schools for all children, and into larger areas with "grammer schools" for the best qualified graduates of the elementary schools, chosen by competitive examination. Although conservative opposition and an economic depression prevented the adoption of Jefferson's plan when it was introduced in 1779, his enlightened concepts served as a model for later reformers:[14]

SECTION I. Whereas it appeareth that however certain forms of government are better calculated than others to protect individuals in the free exercise of their natural rights, and are at the same time themselves better guarded against degeneracy, yet experience hath shewn, that even under the best forms, those entrusted with power have, in time, and by slow operations, perverted it into tyranny; and it is believed that the most effectual means of preventing this would be, to illuminate, as far as practicable, the minds of the people at large, and more especially to give them knowledge of those facts, which history exhibiteth, that, possessed thereby of the experience of other ages and countries, they may be enabled to know ambition under all its shapes, and prompt to exert their natural powers to defeat its purposes; And whereas it is generally true that that people will be happiest whose laws are best, and are best administered, and that laws will be wisely formed, and honestly administered, in proportion as those who form and administer them are wise and honest; whence it becomes expedient for promoting the public happiness that those persons, whom nature hath endowed with genius and virtue, should be rendered by liberal education worthy to receive, and able to guard the sacred deposit of the rights and liberties of their fellow citi-

zens, and that they should be called to that charge without regard to wealth, birth or other accidental condition or circumstance; but the indigence of the greater number disabling them from so educating, at their own expence, those of their children whom nature hath fitly formed and disposed to become useful instruments for the public, it is better that such should be sought for and educated at the common expence of all, than that the happiness of all should be confined to the weak or wicked: . . .

SEC. VI. At every of those schools shall be taught reading, writing, and common arithmetick, and the books which shall be used therein for instructing the children to read shall be such as will at the same time make them acquainted with Graecian, Roman, English, and American history. At these schools all the free children, male and female, resident within the respective hundred, shall be intitled to receive tuition gratis, for the term of three years, and as much longer, at their private expence, as their parents, guardians, or friends shall think proper.

SEC. VII. Over every ten of these schools (or such other number nearest thereto, as the number of hundreds in the county will admit, without fractional divisions) an overseer shall be appointed annually by the Aldermen at their first meeting, eminent for his learning, integrity, and fidelity to the commonwealth, whose business and duty it shall be, from time to time, to appoint a teacher to each school, who shall give assurance of fidelity to the commonwealth, and to remove him as he shall see cause; to visit every school once in every half year at the least; to examine the scholars; see that any general plan of reading and instruction recommended by the visiters of William and Mary College shall be observed; and to superintend the conduct of the teacher in everything relative to his school.

SEC. VIII. Every teacher shall receive a salary of —— by the year, which, with the expences of building and repairing the school-houses, shall be provided in such

---

[14] Saul K. Padover (ed.), *The Complete Jefferson* (New York, 1943), pp. 1048–1054.

manner as other county expences are by law directed to be provided and shall also have his diet, lodging, and washing found him, to be levied in like manner, save only that such levy shall be on the inhabitants of each hundred for the board of their own teacher only. . . .

Sec. XVI. Every overseer of the hundred schools shall, in the month of September annually, after the most diligent and impartial examination and inquiry, appoint from among the boys who shall have been two years at the least at some one of the schools under his superintendence, and whose parents are too poor to give them farther education, someone of the best and most promising genius and disposition, to proceed to the grammer school of his district; which appointment shall be made in the court-house of the county, and on the court day for that month if fair, and if not, then on the next fair day, excluding Sunday, in the presence of the Aldermen, or two of them at the least, assembled on the bench for that purpose, the said overseer being previously sworn by them to make such appointment, without favor or affection, according to the best of his skill and judgment, and being interrogated by the Aldermen, either on their own motion, or on suggestions from the parents, guardians, friends, or teachers of the children, competitors for such appointment; which teachers the parents shall attend for the information of the Aldermen. On which interrogatories the said Aldermen, if they be not satisfied with the appointment proposed, shall have right to negative it; whereupon the said visiter may proceed to make a new appointment, and the said Aldermen again to interrogate and negative, and so toties quoties until an appointment be approved.

Sec. XVII. Every boy so appointed shall be authorized to proceed to the grammer school of his district, there to be educated and boarded during such time as is hereafter limited; and his quota of the expences of the house together with a compensation to the master or usher for his tuition, at the rate of twenty dollars by the year, shall be

paid by the Treasurer quarterly on warrant from the Auditors.

15

The supreme importance that Jefferson attached to this measure and the good that he expected it to accomplish were both revealed in a letter written to John Adams many years later:[15]

At the first session of our legislature after the Declaration of Independence, we passed a law abolishing entails. And this was followed by one abolishing the privilege of primogeniture, and dividing the lands of intestates equally among all their children, or other representatives. These laws, drawn by myself, laid the ax to the foot of pseudo-aristocracy. And had another which I prepared been adopted by the legislature, our work would have been complete. It was a bill for the more general diffusion of learning. This proposed to divide every county into wards of five or six miles square, like your townships; to establish in each ward a free school for reading, writing and common arithmetic; to provide for the annual selection of the best subjects from these schools, who might receive, at the public expense, a higher degree of education at a district school; and from these district schools to select a certain number of the most promising subjects, to be completed at an University, where all the useful sciences should be taught. Worth and genius would thus have been sought out from every condition of life, and completely prepared by education for defeating the competition of wealth and birth for public trusts. My proposition had, for a further object, to impart to these wards those portions of self-government for which they are best qualified, by confiding to them the care of their poor, their roads, police, elections, the nomination of jurors, administration of justice in small cases, ele-

15 Thomas Jefferson to John Adams, October 28, 1813, in Thomas Jefferson Randolph (ed.), *Memoir, Correspondence, and Miscellanies from the Papers of Thomas Jefferson* (Charlottesville, 1829), IV, 228–230.

mentary exercises of militia; in short, to have made them little republics, with a warden at the head of each, for all those concerns which, being under their eye, they would better manage than the larger republics of the county or State. A general call of ward meetings by their wardens on the same day through the State, would at any time produce the genuine sense of the people on any required point, and would enable the State to act in mass, as your people have so often done, and with so much effect by their town meetings. The law for religious freedom, which made a part of this system, having put down the aristocracy of the clergy, and restored to the citizen the freedom of the mind, and those of entails and descents nurturing an equality of condition among them, this on education would have raised the mass of the people to the high ground of moral respectability necessary to their own safety, and to orderly government; and would have completed the great object of qualifying them to select the veritable aristoi, for the trusts of government, to the exclusion of the pseudalists; and the same Theognis who has furnished the epigraphs of your two letters, assures us that ["good men, Curnus, have not yet destroyed a state"].

Although this law has not yet been acted on but in a small and inefficient degree, it is still considered as before the legislature, with other bills of the revised code, not yet taken up, and I have great hope that some patriotic spirit will, at a favorable moment, call it up, and make it the keystone of the arch of our government.

16

Another facet of the deepening Enlightenment in America was a rapidly developing social conscience. Goaded by shocking revelations of conditions in English prisons, Americans turned belatedly to their own mismanaged penal institutions. In Pennsylvania, where the heritage of Quaker humanitarianism was strong, the Society for Alleviating the Miseries of Public Prisons was formed in 1787, with the avowed purpose of shocking public opinion by revealing the inhuman conditions in the state's jails. Its an-nual reports so influenced legislators that improvements soon followed, although many years were to pass before prisons became reformatories rather than breeding grounds for crime:[16]

That in the article of clothing few complaints arise respecting the condemned criminals, but amongst the greater number confined in prison previous to trial, there frequently happen cases of great want, many of the prisoners being destitute of shirts and stockings and warm covering, partly owing to the length of time before trial, and partly to easy access, by various means, to spirituous liquors, for which their clothes are disposed of. Clothing distributed by the society to the apparently destitute, has, in many instances, been quickly exchanged for rum. No provision being made by law for relieving these distressed objects, or for preventing the abuses of charitable donations, it is at present an evil without a remedy, though it is conceived that a kind of prison dress might be adopted by law, and as easily preserved from sale as those of the convicts.

In the article of diet an allowance is made by law to the working criminals, and no complaints have come to the knowledge of the society on that head. To those who are committed for trial, the half of a four-penny loaf only is daily allowed, but no provision is made for persons who are committed as witnesses, amongst whom cases of great distress have appeared to the society. A stranger, accidently present at the commission of a criminal action, but without friends to enter security for his appearance as witness, is committed to jail, for the benefit of the community, and suffers more than the actual criminal, and what adds greatly to his grievance, he is afterwards detained for his fees; —and whilst on this subject, the committee would wish to suggest the very great hardship of a prisoner's being detained for his fees after being legally acquitted of the crime for which he had been committed.

---

[16] Robert Vaux, *Notices of the Original and Successive Attempts to Improve the Discipline of the Prison at Philadelphia, and to Reform the Criminal Code of Pennsylvania* (Philadelphia, 1826), pp. 26–28.

In cases where women are imprisoned, having a child, or children, at the breast, they have only the allowance of a single person, except what arises from the casual supplies of charity, to which the society have contributed, by a distribution to the most necessitous of both sexes, of upward of one hundred gallons of soup weekly during the last winter and spring.

With respect to lodging, it appears that no provision of any kind is made by law, the prisoners lying promiscuously on the floor, unless supplied by their friends. In some jails in England, mentioned by the humane Howard, they are accommodated with strong cribs, and supplied, at stated times, with clean straw. On the first institution of the society, in their visits to the jail, they found that men and women had general intercourse with each other, and it was afterwards discovered that they were locked up together in their rooms at night; but through the remonstrances of the committee on the impropriety of the practice, the women were, at length, removed into a different part of the prison—the apparent consequence of which was, that from the number of about thirty or forty, at first, in confinement, they have been reduced to four or five; for it was said to be a common practice for the women to procure themselves to be arrested for fictitious debts, in order to gain admission among the men—a constant and steady adherence to this mode of separation, the committee are of opinion, will be of great utility. The present mode of burning fuel in the rooms, in open chimneys, with the very scanty allowance, subjects the unhappy prisoners to great misery, in the severity of winters; if stoves could be introduced, this might be, in some measure, abated.

THE COUNTERREVOLUTIONARIES

17

These reforms in theology, education, and the law were watched with jaundiced eyes by members of the newly formed upper class that was created by the returning prosperity of the *1790s. Distrustful of the plain people, horrified by the democratic excesses of the French Revolution, and convinced that property would never be safe until the "rabble" was thoroughly curbed, these self-made aristocrats in the waning years of the eighteenth century instituted a vigorous campaign against the leveling tendencies of the Revolution and the Enlightenment, a campaign that lasted until the days of Jackson. The conservative philosophy was well expressed by James Kent, a Hamiltonian, who led the antidemocratic faction in the New York constitutional convention of 1821:*[17]

Now, sir, I wish to preserve our senate as the representative of the landed interest. I wish those who have an interest in the soil, to retain the exclusive possession of a branch in the legislature, as a strong hold in which they may find safety through all the vicissitudes which the state may be destined, in the course of Providence, to experience. I wish them to be always enabled to say that their freeholds cannot be taxed without their consent. The men of no property, together with the crowds of dependants connected with great manufacturing and commercial establishments, and the motley and undefinable population of crowded ports, may, perhaps, at some future day, under skilful management, predominate in the assembly, and yet we should be perfectly safe if no laws could pass without the free consent of the owners of the soil. That security we at present enjoy; and it is that security which I wish to retain.

The apprehended danger from the experiment of universal suffrage applied to the whole legislative department, is no dream of the imagination. It is too mighty an excitement for the moral constitution of men to endure. The tendency of universal suffrage, is to jeopardize the rights of property, and the principles of liberty. There is a constant tendency in human society, and the history of every age proves it; there is a tendency in

[17] Nathaniel H. Carter, William L. Stone, and Marcus T. C. Gould, *Reports of the Proceedings and Debates of the Convention of 1821, Assembled for the Purpose of Amending the Constitution of the State of New York* (Albany, 1821), pp. 220–222.

the poor to covet and to share the plunder of the rich; in the debtor to relax or avoid the obligation of contracts; in the majority to tyranize over the minority, and trample down their rights; in the indolent and the profligate, to cast the whole burthens of society upon the industrious and the virtuous; and *there is a tendency in ambitious and wicked men, to inflame these combustible materials.* It requires a vigilant government, and a firm administration of justice, to counteract that tendency. Thou shalt not covet; thou shalt not steal; are divine injunctions induced by this miserable depravity of our nature. Who can undertake to calculate with any precision, how many millions of people, this great state will contain in the course of this and the next century, and who can estimate the future extent and magnitude of our commercial ports? The disproportion between the men of property, and the men of no property, will be in every society in a ratio to its commerce, wealth, and population. We are no longer to remain plain and simple republics of farmers, like the New-England colonists, or the Dutch settlements on the Hudson. We are fast becoming a great nation, with great commerce, manufactures, population, wealth, luxuries, and with the vices and miseries that they engender. One seventh of the population of the city of Paris at this day subsists on charity, and one third of the inhabitants of that city die in the hospitals; what would become of such a city with universal suffrage? France has upwards of four, and England upwards of five millions of manufacturing and commercial labourers without property. Could these kingdoms sustain the weight of universal suffrage? The radicals in England, with the force of that mighty engine, would at once sweep away the property, the laws, and the liberties of that island like a deluge. . . .

The notion that every man that works a day on the road, or serves an idle hour in the militia, is entitled as of right to an equal participation in the whole power of the government, is most unreasonable, and has no foundation in justice. We had better at once discard from the report such a nominal test of merit. If such persons have an equal share in one branch of the legislature, it is surely as much as they can in justice or policy demand. Society is an association for the protection of property as well as of life, and the individual who contributes only one cent to the common stock, ought not to have the same power and influence in directing the property concerns of the partnership, as he who contributes his thousands. He will not have the same inducements to care, and diligence, and fidelity. His inducements and his temptation would be to divide the whole capital upon the principles of an agrarian law.

Liberty, rightly understood, is an inestimable blessing, but liberty without wisdom, and without justice, is no better than wild and savage licentiousness. The danger which we have hereafter to apprehend, is not the want, but the abuse, of liberty. We have to apprehend the oppression of minorities, and a disposition to encroach on private right—to disturb chartered privileges—and to weaken, degrade, and overawe the administration of justice; we have to apprehend the establishment of unequal, and consequently, unjust systems of taxation, and all the mischiefs of a crude and mutable legislation. A stable senate, exempted from the influence of universal suffrage, will powerfully check these dangerous propensities, and such a check becomes the more necessary, since this Convention has already determined to withdraw the watchful eye of the judicial department from the passage of laws.

18

Religious organization was a vital element of conservative strategy. Conscious of the connection between deism and democracy, and convinced that the "anarchy and atheism" of Revolutionary France went hand in hand, they advocated a return to orthodoxy as a means of keeping the majority quiescent. Although such organizations as the Christian Constitutional Society, proposed by Alexander Hamilton to restore respect for authority, never developed, the conservatives had their way nevertheless. For ministers, made eloquent by their mounting fear of French irreligion, found their congregations newly stirred in the middle 1790s. Encouraged by success, they redoubled their efforts until by 1800 a full-blown revival was sweeping the nation. All parts of the country were affected, but religious enthusiasm reached flood tide in the West, where isolated frontiersmen, brought together amidst the infectious tension of the "camp meeting," expressed their emotionalism in fantastic ways. One of the most successful evangelists, Reverend Peter Cartwright, describes such a scene in his Autobiography:[18]

From 1801 for years a blessed revival of religion spread through almost the entire inhabited parts of the West, Kentucky, Tennessee, the Carolinas, and many other parts, especially through the Cumberland country, which was so called from the Cumberland River, which headed and mouthed in Kentucky, but in its great bend circled south through Tennessee, near Nashville. The Presbyterians and Methodists in a great measure united in this work, met together, prayed together, and preached together.

In this revival originated our camp-meetings, and in both these denominations they were held every year, and, indeed, have been ever since, more or less. They would erect their camps with logs or frame them, and cover them with clapboards or shingles. They would also erect a shed, sufficiently large to protect five thousand people from wind and rain, and cover it with boards or shingles; build a large stand, seat the shed, and here they would collect together from forty to fifty miles around, sometimes further than that. Ten, twenty, and sometimes thirty ministers, of different denominations, would come together and preach night and day, four or five days together; and, indeed, I have known these camp-meetings to last three or four weeks, and great good resulted from them. I have seen more than a hundred sinners fall like dead men under one powerful sermon, and I have seen and heard more than five hundred Christians all shouting aloud the high praises of God at once; and

18 W. P. Strickland (ed.), *Autobiography of Peter Cartwright* (New York, 1857), pp. 45–46, 48–51.

I will venture to assert that many happy thousands were awakened and converted to God at these camp-meetings. Some sinners mocked, some of the old dry professors opposed, some of the old starched Presbyterian preachers preached against these exercises, but still the work went on and spread almost in every direction, gathering additional force, until our country seemed all coming home to God. . . .

In this revival, usually termed in the West the Cumberland revival, many joined the different Churches, especially the Methodist and Cumberland Presbyterians. The Baptists also came in for a share of the converts, but not to any great extent. Infidelity quailed before the mighty power of God, which was displayed among the people. Universalism was almost driven from the land. The Predestinarians of almost all sorts put forth a mighty effort to stop the work of God.

Just in the midst of our controversies on the subject of the powerful exercises among the people under preaching, a new exercise broke out among us, called the *jerks*, which was overwhelming in its effects upon the bodies and minds of the people. No matter whether they were saints or sinners, they would be taken under a warm song or sermon, and seized with a convulsive jerking all over, which they could not by any possibility avoid, and the more they resisted the more they jerked. If they would not strive against it and pray in good earnest, the jerking would usually abate. I have seen more than five hundred persons jerking at one time in my large congregations. Most usually persons taken with the jerks, to obtain relief, as they said, would rise up and dance. Some would run, but could not get away. Some would resist; on such the jerks were generally very severe.

To see those proud young gentlemen and young ladies, dressed in their silks, jewelry, and prunella, from top to toe, take the *jerks* would often excite my risibilities. The first jerk or so, you would see their fine bonnets, caps, and combs fly; and so sudden would be the jerking of the head that their long loose

hair would crack almost as loud as a wag-
oners whip.

At one of my appointments in 1804 there
was a very large congregation turned out to
hear the Kentucky boy, as they called me.
Among the rest there were two very finely-
dressed, fashionable young ladies, attended
by two brothers with loaded horsewhips. Although the house was large, it was crowded.
The two young ladies, coming in late, took
their seats near where I stood, and their two
brothers stood in the door. I was a little un-
well, and I had a phial of peppermint in my
pocket. Before I commenced preaching I
took out my phial and swallowed a little of
the peppermint. While I was preaching, the
congregation was melted into tears. The two
young gentlemen moved off to the yard
fence, and both the young ladies took the
jerks, and they were greatly mortified about
it. There was a great stir in the congregation.
Some wept, some shouted, and before our
meeting closed several were converted.

As I dismissed the assembly a man stepped
up to me, and warned me to be on my guard,
for he had heard the two brothers swear
they would horsewhip me when meeting
was out, for giving their sisters the jerks.
"Well," said I, "I'll see to that."

I went out and said to the young men that
I understood they intended to horsewhip
me for giving their sisters the jerks. One
replied that he did. I undertook to expostu-
late with him on the absurdity of the charge
against me, but he swore I need not deny
it; for he had seen me take out a phial, in
which I carried some truck that gave his
sister the jerks. As quick as thought it came
into my mind how I would get clear of my
whipping, and, jerking out the peppermint
phial, said I, "Yes; if I gave your sisters the
jerks I'll give them to you." In a moment I
saw he was scared. I moved toward him, he
backed, I advanced, and he wheeled and
ran, warning me not to come near him, or
he would kill me. It raised the laugh on him,
and I escaped my whipping. I had the pleasure, before the year was out, of seeing all
four soundly converted to God, and I took
them into the Church.

While I am on this subject I will relate a
very serious circumstance which I knew to
take place with a man who had the jerks at
a camp-meeting, on what was called the
Ridge, in William Magee's congregation.
There was a great work of religion in the
encampment. The jerks were very prevalent.
There was a company of drunken rowdies
who came to interrupt the meeting. These
rowdies were headed by a very large drinking man. They came with their bottles of
whisky in their pockets. This large man
cursed the jerks, and all religion. Shortly
afterward he took the jerks, and he started to
run, but he jerked so powerfully he could
not get away. He halted among some sap-
lings, and, although he was violently agitated, he took out his bottle of whisky, and
swore he would drink the damned jerks to
death; but he jerked at such a rate he could
not get the bottle to his mouth, though he
tried hard. At length he fetched a sudden
jerk, and the bottle struck a sapling and was
broken to pieces, and spilled his whisky on
the ground. There was a great crowd gathered round him, and when he lost his
whisky he became very much enraged, and
cursed and swore very profanely, his jerks
still increasing. At length he fetched a very
violent jerk, snapped his neck, fell, and soon
expired, with his mouth full of cursing and
bitterness.

I always looked upon the jerks as a judgment sent from God, first, to bring sinners to
repentance; and, secondly to show professors
that God could work with or without means,
and that he could work over and above
means, and do whatsoever seemeth him
good, to the glory of his grace and the salvation of the world.

19

*The wild enthusiasm demonstrated in such
activities continued to mount during the early
years of the nineteenth century; on both sides
of the Appalachians backsliders returned to the
fold, congregations increased, and church membership mounted. These gains, the champions
of orthodoxy resolved, should not be lost. To
forestall the return of postrevolutionary deism,
they busied themselves forming missionary so-*

*cieties, Bible societies, tract societies, and a host
of other organizations devoted to the ambitious
end of converting all Americans to a belief in
revealed Christianity. The spirit animating these
societies was reflected in "The Address of the
Executive Committee of the American Tract
Society to the Christian Public" issued by the
American Tract Society in 1816:*[19]

In making this presentation of their object
to the friends of the Redeemer in the United
States, and in venturing most respectfully to
urge the claims of this institution to general
patronage, the Committee feel that it is needless to exhibit, to any considerable extent,
the superior advantages of that method of
moral and religious instruction which is
pursued by the distribution of Tracts.
Though men are fallen by their iniquity, and
are to be recovered from their apostacy and
condemnation only through the redemption
that is in Christ Jesus, and by the renewing
of the Holy Ghost, yet does this method of
mercy most distinctly recognise the use of
means in the business of their salvation.
Next to the Bible and the living Ministry,
one of these means of light and salvation
will be found to be short, plain, striking, entertaining, and instructive *Tracts*, exhibiting
in writing some of the great and glorious
truths of the Gospel. "The Word of Truth"
is the great instrument of moral renovation.
He who scatters it, scatters the seed of the
Kingdom, and may look for the Harvest in
God's own good time and way. A Tract may
be perused at leisure; it may be consulted in
the hour of retirement and solitude; it can be
read in a little time; and though it may contain instruction important and weighty
enough for the consideration of the sage, and
yet simple enough to be accommodated to
the taste and intelligence of a child, may be
easily weighed and deposited in the memory. This method of instruction is peculiarly
calculated for the poor, and is especially demanded by the poor of an extended population. It is a method by which the blessings
of a religious education may, to no inconsiderable degree, be extended to the lower

ranks of society with peculiar facility, and
which, as a practical system, is already entitled to the claims of successful experiment.
It is a means of doing good which is level to
every capacity, and adapted to every condition. The man of low attainment in science, the mother, the child, the obscure in
the meanest condition, can give away a
Tract, and, perhaps, accompany it with a
word of advice or admonition, with as much
promise of success as a Missionary or an
Apostle. A Minister may distribute Tracts
among his people, and thus impress and extend his public instructions where impressions of his official duty would otherwise be
lost, or never extended; and in this way he
may double his usefulness, and devote two
lives to his Master's glory instead of one. The
teacher and the pupil, the parent and the
child, the master and the servant, may become to each other the most effectual preachers, by the distribution of Tracts. The traveller may scatter them along the roads and
throughout the inns and cottages; and in return, the inns and cottages may spread them
before the eye of the thoughtless traveller.
Merchants may distribute them to ship-
masters and ship-masters to seamen; men of
business may transmit them with every bale
of goods, to the remote corners of the land
and globe; and thus the infinitely important
truths of the Gospel—truths by which it is
the purpose of the God of Heaven to make
men "wise to salvation"—like the diffusive
light, may be emitted from numberless
sources, and in every direction. All this may
be done in the most inoffensive and inob-
trusive way; with no magisterial authority;
no claims of superior wisdom or goodness;
and no alarm to human pride or forward-
ness. All this may be done, too, with no loss
of time. "A Tract can be given away, and
God's blessing asked upon it, in a moment."
Aside from the influence of those institutions
which involve no expense at all, in no way
can so much probable good be effected at so
little expense, as by the distribution of
Tracts. A Tract which contains *ten pages* can
be published for a *single cent!* And when we
recollect how long a single Tract may be

[19] *Publications of the American Tract Society*
(New York, n.d.), pp. 1–12.

preserved, by how many individuals and families it may be read, and when read by them, to how many others it may be lent, it is difficult to conceive of a way in which more good can be accomplished by a very small amount of means. As an auxilliary to other means of doing good, the distribution of Tracts also holds a distinguished place. In how many sick chambers, in how many meetings of anxious inquiry, in how many circles of wealth and prosperity, of fashion, folly, and vice, may these faithful witnesses be left to testify what otherwise never would be told. The language of every Missionary Society, either Domestic or Foreign, is, "A Missionary without a supply of Tracts is unprovided for his work; the press is the grand medium of communication in all parts of the missionary world." A Missionary at *Sumatra* writes—"I am fully of opinion that, among all nations not accustomed to books, the distribution of small Tracts, written in an easy style, or of single Gospels, is much more likely to do good than that of larger works. This opinion is strengthened by the experience and observation of every day."

We live, fellow-citizens, at an eventful period of the world. The purposes of God's mercy appear to be rapidy unfolding, and rapidly and surely advancing toward their final issue. New scenes are already opening upon the world and upon the Church; and the "enterprise to be achieved is the conversion of the world to its Redeeming God and King." In this vast and arduous enterprise no portion of mankind are bound to feel a deeper interest than the people of these United States. The state of our country is one of unparalleled prosperity. At peace among ourselves and with all nations, our population is becoming "as the sand which is by the sea, in multitude." Our industry and wealth are giving this favoured people a high elevation in the catalogue of nations. The light of science and the arts is diffusing its influence through every part of our growing Republic. Our plans of internal improvement and public utility are raising our dignity and glory in the view of future ages; and our happy religion, born of God, descended from Heaven, and dwelling in undisturbed security in this Western World, has already exerted its efficient power in forming here a people for his praise. The Committee indulge the hope that great multitudes in this happy portion of the globe will enroll their names among the patrons of this institution and the benefactors of mankind. They know that the enterprise in which they are engaged is one which cannot prosper, unless the God of all the earth control and prosper it. They earnestly solicit an interest in your prayers as well as your benefactions. To them it is a delightful thought that the cause is God's, and dependent absolutely on him. *"Not by might nor by power, but by my Spirit, saith the Lord of Hosts!"* This is their motto. We cannot hope too much from God. In the name of God alone they begin and go forward, confiding always in that divine guidance and favour, which in all their toil shall be invoked by prayer, and in all their success be honoured with thanksgiving.

Jeffersonian Republicanism

Despite ambitious schemes and formal pronouncements, the Jeffersonian era was singularly barren of democratic accomplishment. Partly responsible was the conviction of Jefferson, and his successor James Madison, that the people were not yet sufficiently educated to administer public affairs wisely; until schools could be founded, governmental control should rest in the hands of the landed gentry whose agricultural interests were closely identified with those of the small farmers making up the bulk of the population. Partly to blame, too, was Jefferson's preoccupation with foreign affairs. Warfare in Europe during the Jefferson and Madison administrations so involved the United States that little attention was devoted to domestic reform.

THE JEFFERSONIAN PHILOSOPHY

1

Abigail Adams, wife of one president and mother of another, was an indefatigable letter writer. When the national capital was moved from Philadelphia to Washington during the final months of John Adams' administration, Mrs. Adams, who occupied the partially completed Executive Mansion for a few months, wrote a delightful description of her new home in a letter to her daughter Mrs. W. S. Smith, November 21, 1800:[1]

WASHINGTON, *21 November, 1800.*

I arrived here on Sunday last, and without meeting with any accident worth noticing, except losing ourselves when we left Baltimore, and going eight or nine miles on the Frederick road, by which means we were obliged to go the other eight through woods, where we wandered two hours without finding a guide, or the path. Fortunately, a straggling black came up with us, and we engaged him as a guide, to extricate us out of our difficulty; but woods are all you see, from Baltimore until you reach *the city*, which is only

so in name. Here and there is a small cot, without a glass window, interspersed amongst the forests, through which you travel miles without seeing any human being. In the city there are buildings enough, if they were compact and finished, to accommodate Congress and those attached to it; but as they are, and scattered as they are, I see no great comfort for them. The river, which runs up to Alexandria, is in full view of my window, and I see the vessels as they pass and repass. The house is upon a grand and superb scale, requiring about thirty servants to attend and keep the apartments in proper order, and perform the ordinary business of the house and stables; an establishment very well proportioned to the President's salary. The lighting the apartments, from the kitchen to parlours and chambers, is a tax indeed; and the fires we are obliged to keep to secure us from daily agues is another very cheering comfort. To assist us in this great castle, and render less attendance necessary, bells are wholly wanting, not one single one being hung through the whole house, and promises are all you can obtain. This is so great an inconvenience, that I know not what to do, or how to do. The ladies

---

[1] Abigail Adams, *Letters* (C. F. Adams ed., Boston, 1840), II, 239–242.

from Georgetown and in the city have many
of them visited me. Yesterday I returned
fifteen visits,—but such a place as Georgetown appears,—why, our Milton is more
beautiful. But no comparisons;—if they will
put me up some bells, and let me have wood
enough to keep fires, I design to be pleased.
I could content myself almost anywhere
three months; but, surrounded with forests,
can you believe that wood is not to be had,
because people cannot be found to cut and
cart it! Briesler entered into a contract with
a man to supply him with wood. A small
part, a few cords only, has he been able to
get. Most of that was expended to dry the
walls of the house before we came in, and
yesterday the man told him it was impossible
for him to procure it to be cut and carted.
He has had recourse to coals; but we cannot
get grates made and set. We have, indeed,
come into a *new country.*

You must keep all this to yourself, and,
when asked how I like it, say that I write
you the situation is beautiful, which is true.
The house is made habitable, but there is
not a single apartment finished, and all with-
inside, except the plastering, has been done
since Briesler came. We have not the least
fence, yard, or other convenience, without,
and the great unfinished audience-room I
make a drying-room of, to hang up the
clothes in. The principal stairs are not up,
and will not be this winter. Six chambers
are made comfortable; two are occupied by
the President and Mr. Shaw; two lower
rooms, one for a common parlour, and one
for a levee-room. Up stairs there is the oval
room, which is designed for the drawing-
room, and has the crimson furniture in it.
It is a very handsome room now; but, when
completed, it will be beautiful. If the twelve
years, in which this place has been considered
as the future seat of government, had been
improved, as they would have been if in New
England, very many of the present inconvenience would have been removed. It is a
beautiful spot, capable of every improvement, and, the more I view it, the more I
am delighted with it.

Since I sat down to write, I have been
called down to a servant from Mount Vernon, with a billet from Major Custis, and a
haunch of venison, and a kind, congratula-
tory letter from Mrs. Lewis, upon my arrival
in the city, with Mrs. Washington's love, inviting me to Mount Vernon, where, health
permitting, I will go, before I leave this
place.

The Senate is much behind-hand. No congress has yet been made. 'T is said ————
———— is on his way, but travels with so
many delicacies in his rear, that he cannot
get on fast, lest some of them should suffer.

Thomas comes in and says a House is
made; so to-morrow, though Saturday, the
President will meet them. Adieu, my dear.
Give my love to your brother, and tell him
he is ever present upon my mind.

2

*Early the following year, Abigail and her
husband moved out of the "great castle" to
make room for President Jefferson. The latter's
inaugural address of March 4, 1801, became a
cherished statement of the emerging tradition of
popular rule. He expressed his philosophy of
government: to elevate the common people until
they were capable of ruling themselves, in the
meantime protecting them from either political
or economic exploitation by the upper classes:*[2]

During the contest of opinion through
which we have passed, the animation of discussions and of exertions has sometimes worn
an aspect which might impose on strangers
unused to think freely and to speak and to
write what they think; but this being now
decided by the voice of the nation, announced according to the rules of the constitution, all will, of course, arrange themselves under the will of the law, and unite
in common efforts for the common good.
All too will bear in mind this sacred principle, that though the will of the majority
is in all cases to prevail, that will, to be
rightful, must be reasonable; that the mi-

---

[2] Thomas Jefferson, Inaugural Address, in Albert
E. Bergh (ed.), *The Writings of Thomas Jefferson*
(Washington, 1905), III, 317–323.

nority possess their equal rights, which equal laws must protect, and to violate would be oppression. Let us then, fellow citizens, unite with one heart and one mind. Let us restore to social intercourse that harmony and affection without which liberty and even life itself are but dreary things. And let us reflect that having banished from our land that religious intolerance under which mankind so long bled and suffered, we have yet gained little if we countenance a political intolerance as despotic, as wicked, and capable of as bitter and bloody persecutions. During the throes and convulsions of the ancient world, during the agonizing spasms of infuriated man, seeking through blood and slaughter his long-lost liberty, it was not wonderful that the agitation of the billows should reach even this distant and peaceful shore; that this should be more felt and feared by some and less by others; and should divide opinions as to measures of safety. But every difference of opinion is not a difference of principle. We have called by different names brethren of the same principle. We are all republicans —we are all federalists. If there be any among us who would wish to dissolve this Union, or to change its republican form, let them stand undisturbed as monuments of the safety with which error of opinion may be tolerated, where reason is left free to combat it. I know, indeed, that some honest men have feared that a republican government cannot be strong; that this government is not strong enough. But would the honest patriot, in the full tide of successful experiment, abandon a government which has so far kept us free and firm, on the theoretic and visionary fear that this government, the world's best hope, may by possibility want energy to preserve itself? I trust not. I believe this, on the contrary, the strongest government on earth. I believe it the only one where every man, at the call of the laws, would fly to the standard of the law, and would meet invasions of the public order as his own personal concern. Sometimes it is said that man cannot be trusted with the government of himself. Can he, then, be

trusted with the government of others? Or have we found angels in the form of kings to govern him? Let history answer this question.

Let us, then, pursue with courage and confidence our own federal and republican principles, our attachment to union and representative government. Kindly separated by nature and a wide ocean from the exterminating havoc of one quarter of the globe; too high-minded to endure the degradations of the others; possessing a chosen country, with room enough for our descendants to the hundredth and thousandth generation; entertaining a due sense of our equal right to the use of our own faculties, to the acquisitions of our industry, to honor and confidence from our fellow citizens, resulting not from birth but from our actions and their sense of them; enlightened by a benign religion, professed indeed and practiced in various forms yet all of them inculcating honesty, truth, temperance, gratitude, and the love of man; acknowledging and adoring an overruling Providence, which by all its dispensations proves that it delights in the happiness of man here and his greater happiness hereafter; with all these blessings, what more is necessary to make us a happy and prosperous people? Still one thing more, fellow citizens —a wise and frugal government, which shall restrain men from injuring one another, shall leave them otherwise free to regulate their own pursuits of industry and improvement, and shall not take from the mouth of labor the bread it has earned. This is the sum of good government; and this is necessary to close the circle of our felicities.

About to enter, fellow citizens, on the exercise of duties which comprehend everything dear and valuable to you, it is proper you should understand what I deem the essential principle of our government, and consequently those which ought to shape its administration. I will compress them in the narrowest compass they will bear, stating the general principle but not all its limitations. Equal and exact justice to all men of whatever state or persuasion, religious or

political; peace, commerce and honest friendship, with all nations—entangling alliances
with none; the support of the state governments in all their rights, as the most competent administrations for our domestic concerns, and the surest bulwarks against
anti-republican tendencies; the preservation
of the general government in its whole constitutional vigor, as the sheet anchor of our
peace at home and safety abroad; a jealous
care of the right of election by the people
—a mild and safe corrective of abuses which
are lopped by the sword of revolution where
peaceable remedies are unprovided; absolute
acquiescence in the decisions of the majority
—the vital principle of republics, from which
there is no appeal but to force, the vital
principle and immediate parent of despotism;
a well-disciplined militia—our best reliance
in peace and for the first moments of war,
till regulars may relieve them; the supremacy
of the civil over the military authority; economy in the public expense, that labor may
be lightly burdened; the honest payment of
our debts and sacred preservation of the
public faith; encouragement of agriculture,
and of commerce as its handmaid; the diffusion of information and arraignment of all
abuses at the bar of the public reason; freedom of religion, freedom of the press; freedom
of person, under the protection of the *habeas
corpus;* and trial by juries impartially selected—these principles form the bright con-
stellation which has gone before us, and
guided our steps through an age of revolution and reformation. The wisdom of our
sages and blood of our heroes have been devoted to their attainment. They should be the
creed of our political faith—the text of civil
instruction—the touchstone by which to try
the services of those we trust; and should
we wander from them in moments of error
or alarm, let us hasten to retrace our steps
and to regain the road which alone leads to
peace, liberty, and safety.

I repair then, fellow citizens, to the post
you have assigned me. With experience
enough in subordinate stations to know the
difficulties of this, the greatest of all, I have
learned to expect that it will rarely fall to
the lot of imperfect man to retire from this
station with the reputation and the favor
which bring him into it. Without pretensions
to that high confidence you reposed in our
first and greatest revolutionary character,
whose pre-eminent services had entitled him
to the first place in his country's love, and
had destined for him the fairest page in the
volume of faithful history, I ask so much
confidence only as may give firmness and
effect to the legal administration of your
affairs. I shall often go wrong through defect
of judgment. When right, I shall often be
thought wrong by those whose positions will
not command a view of the whole ground.
I ask your indulgence for my own errors,
which will never be intentional; and your
support against the errors of others who may
condemn what they would not, if seen in all
its parts. The approbation implied by your
suffrage is a great consolation to me for the
past; and my future solicitude will be to retain the good opinion of those who have
bestowed it in advance, to conciliate that of
others by doing them all the good in my
power, and to be instrumental to the happiness and freedom of all.

Relying then on the patronage of your
good will, I advance with obedience to the
work, ready to retire from it whenever you
become sensible how much better choice it
is in your power to make. And may that Infinite Power which rules the destinies of the
universe lead our councils to what is best,
and give them a favorable issue for your
peace and prosperity.

3

*An important part of the philosophy of gov-
ernment which Thomas Jefferson brought to the
presidency was embodied in the Statute of Religious Freedom which he had introduced into
the Virginia assembly in 1779. After a bitter and
protracted contest, it was adopted in 1786:*[3]

Well aware that Almighty God hath created the mind free; that all attempts to in-

---

[3] *Ibid.,* II, 300–303.

fluence it by temporal punishments or burdens, or by civil incapacitations, tend only
to beget habits of hypocrisy and meanness,
and are a departure from the plan of the
Holy author of our religion, who being Lord
of both body and mind, yet chose not to
propagate it by coercions on either, as was
in his Almighty power to do; that the impious
presumption of legislators and rulers, civil
as well as ecclesiastical, who being themselves but fallible and uninspired men, have
assumed dominion over the faith of others,
setting up their own opinions and modes of
thinking as the only true and infallible, and
as such endeavouring to impose them on
others, hath established and maintained false
religions over the greatest part of the world,
and through all time; that to compel a man
to furnish contributions of money for the
propagation of opinions which he disbelieves,
is sinful and tyrannical; that even the forcing
him to support this or that teacher of his own
religious persuasion, is depriving him of the
comfortable liberty of giving his contributions to the particular pastor whose morals
he would make his pattern, and whose powers he feels most persuasive to righteousness,
and is withdrawing from the ministry those
temporary rewards, which proceeding from
an approbation of their personal conduct,
are an additional incitement to earnest and
unremitting labours for the instruction of
mankind; that our civil rights have no dependence on our religious opinions, any more
than our opinions in physics or geometry;
that therefore the proscribing any citizen as
unworthy the public confidence by laying
upon him an incapacity of being called to
offices of trust and emolument, unless he
profess or renounce this or that religious
opinion, is depriving him injuriously of those
privileges and advantages to which in common with his fellow-citizens he has a natural
right; that it tends only to corrupt the principles of that religion it is meant to encourage, by bribing with a monopoly of
worldly honours and emoluments, those who
will externally profess and conform to it;
that though indeed these are criminal who

do not withstand such temptation, yet neither
are those innocent who lay the bait in their
way; that to suffer the civil magistrate to
intrude his powers into the field of opinion,
and to restrain the profession or propagation
of principles on supposition of their ill tendency, is a dangerous fallacy, which at once
destroys all religious liberty, because he being of course judge of that tendency will
make his opinions the rule of judgment, and
approve or condemn the sentiments of others
only as they shall square with or differ from
his own; that it is time enough for the rightful purposes of civil government, for its officers to interfere when principles break out
into overt acts against peace and good order;
and finally, that truth is great and will prevail if left to herself, that she is the proper
and sufficient antagonist to error, and has
nothing to fear from the conflict, unless by
human interposition disarmed of her natural
weapons, free argument and debate, errors
ceasing to be dangerous when it is permitted
freely to contradict them.

*Be it therefore enacted by the General
Assembly,* That no man shall be compelled
to frequent or support any religious worship,
place or ministry whatsoever, nor shall be
enforced, restrained, molested, or burthened
in his body or goods, nor shall otherwise
suffer on account of his religious opinions
or belief; but that all men shall be free to
profess, and by arguments to maintain, their
opinion in matters of religion, and that the
same shall in no wise diminish, enlarge or
affect their civil capacities.

And though we well know that this Assembly, elected by the people for the ordinary purposes of legislation only, have no
power to restrain the acts of succeeding Assemblies, constituted with powers equal to
our own, and that therefore to declare this
act to be irrevocable would be of no effect
in law, yet as we are free to declare, and do
declare, that the rights hereby asserted are
of the natural rights of mankind, and that if
any act shall hereafter be passed to repeal
the present, or to narrow its operation, such
act will be an infringement of natural right.

4

Significantly, Jefferson retained his faith in the contemporary generation long after he had retired from active participation in politics. His classic statement of this point of view is contained in a letter he wrote to his friend Samuel Kercheval in 1816:[4]

Some men look at constitutions with sanctimonious reverence, and deem them like the arc of the covenant, too sacred to be touched. They ascribe to the men of the preceding age a wisdom more than human, and suppose what they did to be beyond amendment. I knew that age well; I belonged to it, and labored with it. It deserved well of its country. It was very like the present, but without the experience of the present; and forty years of experience in government is worth a century of book-reading; and this they would say themselves, were they to rise from the dead. I am certainly not an advocate for frequent and untried changes in laws and constitutions. I think moderate imperfections had better be borne with; because, when once known, we accommodate ourselves to them, and find practical means of correcting their ill effects. But I know also, that laws and institutions must go hand in hand with the progress of the human mind. As that becomes more developed, more enlightened, as new discoveries are made, new truths disclosed, and manners and opinions change with the change of circumstances, institutions must advance also, and keep pace with the times. We might as well require a man to wear still the coat which fitted him when a boy, as civilized society to remain ever under the regimen of their barbarous ancestors. It is this preposterous idea which has lately deluged Europe in blood. Their monarchs, instead of wisely yielding to the gradual change of circumstances, of favoring progressive accommodation to progressive improvement, have clung to old abuses, entrenched themselves behind

steady habits, and obliged their subjects to seek through blood and violence rash and ruinous innovations, which, had they been referred to the peaceful deliberations and collected wisdom of the nation, would have been put into acceptable and salutary forms. Let us follow no such examples, nor weakly believe that one generation is not as capable as another of taking care of itself, and of ordering its own affairs. Let us, as our sister States have done, avail ourselves of our reason and experience, to correct the crude essays of our first and unexperienced, although wise, virtuous, and well-meaning councils. And lastly, let us provide in our constitution for its revision at stated periods. What these periods should be, nature herself indicates. By the European tables of mortality, of the adults living at any one moment of time, a majority will be dead in about nineteen years. At the end of that period, then, a new majority is come into place; or, in other words, a new generation. Each generation is as independent as the one preceding, as that was of all which had gone before. It has then, like them, a right to choose for itself the form of government it believes most promotive of its own happiness; consequently, to accommodate to the circumstances in which it finds itself, that received from its predecessors; and it is for the peace and good of mankind that a solemn opportunity of doing this every nineteen or twenty years, should be provided by the constitution; so that it may be handed on, with periodical repairs, from generation to generation, to the end of time, if anything human can so long endure. It is now forty years since the constitution of Virginia was formed. The same tables inform us, that, within that period, two-thirds of the adults then living are now dead. Have then the remaining third, even if they had the wish, the right to hold in obedience to their will, and to laws heretofore made by them, the other two-thirds, who, with themselves, compose the present mass of adults? If they have not, who has? The dead? But the dead have no rights. They are nothing; and nothing cannot own

---

[4] Thomas Jefferson to Samuel Kercheval, July 12, 1816, in Paul L. Ford (ed.), *The Works of Thomas Jefferson* (New York, 1905), XII, 11–14.

something. Where there is no substance, there can be no accident. This corporeal globe, and everything upon it, belong to its present corporeal inhabitants, during their generation. They alone have a right to direct what is the concern of themselves, alone, and to declare the law of that direction; and this declaration can only be made by their majority. That majority, then, has a right to depute representatives to a convention, and to make the constitution what they think will be the best for themselves.

5

In attempting to carry his theories into effect, Jefferson experienced his first rebuff at Federalist hands. They had entrenched themselves in the federal judicial system, hoping to use their control of the courts to frustrate any moves toward equalitarianism. To circumvent their attempt to deny the majority will, the Jeffersonians repealed a congressional judicial act that had been passed in the dying moments of John Adams' regime, thus depriving many minor judges of their offices. One of these Federalists, William Marbury, countered by asking the Supreme Court for a writ of mandamus to compel James Madison, the secretary of state, to deliver his commission to him. This was the origin of the famous case of Marbury v. Madison *(1803), which enshrined the doctrine of judicial review in American constitutional law. For Chief Justice John Marshall refused to grant the writ, holding that the section of the Judiciary Act of 1789 which authorized the court to do so was unconstitutional:*[5]

The question, whether an act repugnant to the constitution, can become the law of the land, is a question deeply interesting to the United States; but, happily not of an intricacy proportioned to its interest. It seems only necessary to recognize certain principles supposed to have been long and well established, to decide it.

That the people have an original right to establish for their future government such principles as, in their opinion, shall most conduce to their own happiness, is the basis on which the whole American fabric has been erected. The exercise of this original

right is a very great exertion, nor can it, nor ought it, to be frequently repeated. The principles therefore so established are deemed fundamental. And as the authority from which they proceed is supreme and can seldom act, they are designed to be permanent.

This original and supreme will organizes the government, and assigns to different departments their respective powers. It may either stop here, or establish certain limits not to be transcended by those departments.

The government of the United States is of the latter description. The powers of the legislature are defined and limited; and that those limits may not be mistaken, or forgotten, the constitution is written. To what purpose are powers limited, and to what purpose is that limitation committed to writing, if these limits may, at any time, be passed by those intended to be restrained? The distinction between a government with limited and unlimited powers is abolished, if those limits do not confine the persons on whom they are imposed, and if acts prohibited and acts allowed, are of equal obligation. It is a proposition too plain to be contested, that the constitution controls any legislative act repugnant to it; or, that the legislature may alter the constitution by an ordinary act.

Between these alternatives there is no middle ground. The constitution is either a superior paramount law, unchangeable by ordinary means, or it is on a level with ordinary legislative acts, and, like other acts, is alterable when the legislature shall please to alter it.

If the former part of the alternative be true, then a legislative act contrary to the constitution is not law: if the latter part be true, then written constitutions are absurd attempts, on the part of the people, to limit a power in its own nature illimitable.

Certainly all those who have framed written constitutions contemplate them as forming the fundamental and paramount law of the nation, and, consequently, the theory of every such government must be,

[5] I CRANCH 175–179.

that an act of the legislature, repugnant to the constitution, is void.

This theory is essentially attached to a written constitution, and, is consequently, to be considered, by this court, as one of the fundamental principles of our society. It is not therefore to be lost sight of in the further consideration of this subject.

If an act of the legislature, repugnant to the constitution, is void, does it, notwithstanding its invalidity, bind the courts and oblige them to give it effect? Or, in other words, though it be not law, does it constitute a rule as operative as if it was a law? This would be to overthrow in fact what was established in theory; and would seem, at first view, an absurdity too gross to be insisted on. It shall, however, receive a more attentive consideration.

It is emphatically the province and duty of the judicial department to say what the law is. Those who apply the rule to particular cases must of necessity expound and interpret that rule. If two laws conflict with each other, the courts must decide on the operation of each.

So if a law be in opposition to the constitution; if both the law and the constitution apply to a particular case, so that the court must either decide that case conformably to the law, disregarding the constitution; or conformably to the constitution, disregarding the law; the court must determine which of these conflicting rules governs the case. This is of the very essence of judicial duty.

If, then, the courts are to regard the constitution, and the constitution is superior to any ordinary act of the legislature, the constitution, and not such ordinary act, must govern the case to which they both apply.

Those, then, who controvert the principle that the constitution is to be considered, in court, as a paramount law, are reduced to the necessity of maintaining that courts must close their eyes on the constitution and see only the law.

This doctrine would subvert the very foundation of all written constitutions. It would declare that an act which, according to the principles and theory of our government, is entirely void, is yet, in practice, completely obligatory. It would declare that if the legislature shall do what is expressly forbidden, such act, notwithstanding the express prohibition, is in reality effectual. It would be giving to the legislature a practical and real omnipotence, with the same breath which professes to restrict their powers within narrow limits. It is prescribing limits, and declaring that those limits may be passed at pleasure.

That it thus reduces to nothing what we have deemed the greatest improvement on political institutions, a written constitution, would of itself be sufficient, in America, where written constitutions have been viewed with so much reverence, for rejecting the construction. But the peculiar expressions of the constitution of the United States furnish additional arguments in favor of its rejection.

The judicial power of the United States is extended to all cases arising under the constitution.

Could it be the intention of those who gave this power, to say that in using it the constitution should not be looked into? That a case arising under the constitution should be decided without examining the instrument under which it arises?

This is too extravagant to be maintained.

In some cases, then, the constitution must be looked into by the judges. And if they can open it at all, what part of it are they forbidden to read or to obey?

There are many other parts of the constitution which serve to illustrate this subject.

It is declared that "no tax or duty shall be laid on articles exported from any state." Suppose a duty on the export of cotton, of tobacco, or of flour; and a suit instituted to recover it. Ought judgment to be rendered in such a case? ought the judges to close their eyes on the constitution, and only see the law?

The constitution declares "that no bill of attainder or *ex post facto* law shall be passed."

If, however, such a bill should be passed,

and a person should be prosecuted under it; must the court condemn to death those victims whom the constitution endeavors to preserve?

"No person," says the constitution, "shall be convicted of treason unless on the testimony of two witnesses to the same overt act, or on confession in open court."

Here the language of the constitution is addressed especially to the courts. It prescribes, directly for them, a rule of evidence not to be departed from. If the legislature should change that rule, and declare *one* witness, or a confession, *out* of court, sufficient for conviction, must the constitutional principle yield to the legislative act?

From these, and many other selections which might be made, it is apparent that the framers of the constitution contemplated that instrument as a rule for the government of *courts*, as well as of the legislature.

Why otherwise does it direct the judges to take an oath to support it? This oath certainly applies in an especial manner to their conduct in their official character. How immoral to impose it on them if they were to be used as the instruments, and the knowing instruments, for violating what they swear to support!

The oath of office, too, imposed by the legislature, is completely demonstrative of the legislative opinion on this subject. It is in these words: "I do solemnly swear that I will administer justice without respect to persons, and do equal right to the poor and to the rich; and that I will faithfully and impartially discharge all the duties incumbent on me as   according to the best of my abilities and understanding, agreeably to *the constitution* and laws of the United States."

Why does a judge swear to discharge his duties agreeably to the constitution of the United States, if that constitution forms no rule for his government? if it is closed upon him, and cannot be inspected by him?

If such be the real state of things, this is worse than solemn mockery. To prescribe, or to take this oath, becomes equally a crime.

It is also not entirely unworthy of observa-tion, that in declaring what shall be the *supreme* law of the land, the *constitution* itself is first mentioned, and not the laws of the United States generally, but those only which shall be made in *pursuance* of the constitution, have that rank.

Thus, the particular phraseology of the constitution of the United States confirms and strengthens the principle, supposed to be essential to all written constitutions, that a law repugnant to the constitution is void; and that *courts*, as well as other departments, are bound by that instrument.

The rule must be discharged.

6

In letters to friends written in 1820 and 1822, Jefferson summarizes his views:[6]

You seem . . . to consider the judges as the ultimate arbiters of all constitutional questions; a very dangerous doctrine indeed, and one which would place us under the despotism of an oligarchy. Our judges are as honest as other men, and not more so. They have, with others, the same passions for party, for power, and the privilege of their corps. Their maxim is *"boni judicis est ampliare jurisdictionem,"* and their power the more dangerous as they are in office for life, and not responsible, as the other functionaries are, to the elective control. The Constitution has erected no such single tribunal, knowing that to whatever hands confided, with the corruptions of time and party, its members would become despots. It has more wisely made all the departments co-equal and co-sovereign within themselves. If the legislature fails to pass laws for a census, for paying the judges and other officers of government, for establishing a militia, for naturalization as prescribed by the Constitution, or if they fail to meet in congress, the judges cannot issue their mandamus to them; if the President fails to supply the place of a judge, to ap-

[6] Thomas Jefferson to William C. Jarvis, September 28, 1820, and to William T. Barry, July 2, 1822, in Albert E. Bergh (ed.), *The Writings of Thomas Jefferson* (Washington, 1905), XV, 277, 389–390.

point other civil or military officers, to issue requisite commissions, the judges cannot force him. They can issue their mandamus or distringas to no executive or legislative officer to enforce the fulfilment of their official duties, any more than the President or legislature may issue orders to the judges or their officers. Betrayed by English example, and unaware, as it should seem, of the control of our Constitution in this particular, they have at times overstepped their limit by undertakings to command executive officers in the discharge of their executive duties; but the Constitution, in keeping three departments distinct and independent, restrains the authority of the judges to judiciary organs, as it does the executive and legislative to executive and legislative organs. The judges certainly have more frequent occasion to act on constitutional questions, because the laws of *meum* and *tuum* and of criminal action, forming the great mass of the system of law, constitute their particular department. When the legislative or executive functionaries act unconstitutionally, they are responsible to the people in their elective capacity. The exemption of the judges from that is quite dangerous enough. I know no safe depository of the ultimate powers of the society but the people themselves; and if we think them not enlightened enough to exercise their control with a wholesome discretion, the remedy is not to take it from them, but to inform their discretion by education. This is the true corrective of abuses of constitutional power. Pardon me, Sir, for this difference of opinion. My personal interest in such questions is entirely extinct, but not my wishes for the longest possible continuance of our government on its pure principles; if the three powers maintain their mutual independence on each other it may last long, but not so if either can assume the authorities of the other.

We already see the power, installed for life, responsible to no authority, (for impeachment is not even a scare-crow,) advancing with a noiseless and steady pace to the great object of consolidation. The foundations are already deeply laid by their decisions, for the annihilation of constitutional State rights, and the removal of every check, every counterpoise to the ingulfing power of which themselves are to make a sovereign part. If ever this vast country is brought under a single government, it will be one of the most extensive corruption, indifferent and incapable of a wholesome care over so wide a spread of surface. This will not be borne, and you will have to choose between reformation and revolution. If I know the spirit of this country, the one or the other is inevitable. Before the canker is become inveterate, before its venom has reached so much of the body politic as to get beyond control, remedy should be applied. Let the future appointments of judges be for four or six years, and renewable by the President and Senate. This will bring their conduct, at regular periods, under revision and probation, and may keep them in equipoise between the general and special governments. We have erred in this point, by copying England, where certainly it is a good thing to have the judges independent of the king. But we have omitted to copy their caution also, which makes a judge removable on the address of both legislative Houses. That there should be public functionaries independent of the nation, whatever may be their demerit, is a solecism in a republic, of the first order of absurdity and inconsistency.

7

A recent scholar, Merrill Peterson, has attempted to trace the rise and fall of the reputation of Jefferson from his death to the present day. The summary below tells us a great deal about the Jeffersonian image, as well as a great deal about ourselves:[7]

The great man makes history—and is consumed by it. He swiftly becomes a symbol, perhaps many symbols, through which men

---

[7] Merrill Peterson, *The Jeffersonian Image in the American Mind* (New York, 1960), pp. 443–446. Reprinted with the kind permission of the publishers, the Oxford University Press.

of different persuasions and at different times seek to comprehend their experiences and state their purposes. Confusion and error, legend and myth, wish and aspiration transform the life that has thus been imaginatively extended in posterity. The process is never the same with any two individuals. George Washington, for example, was a demigod before he died, and forever after, with barely a shade of turning, the lonely and immutable monument of American glory. "He created his own silence whilst the others were obliged to await the hand of time." Andrew Jackson, to take another American instance, witnessed the creation of his own legend years before he became President. "The symbol for an age," as John William Ward has shown, Jackson was also encompassed by it. Thomas Jefferson presents a case altogether different from either of these, perhaps from any other known to history. When he died, Americans thought to shape his life and work into a symbol of the fabled republic. But Jefferson was not of an age, not limpid, not stereotyped, not a demigod. An ill-arranged cluster of meanings, rancorous, mercurial, fertile, the Jefferson Image was constantly evolving. Crudely unfinished at his death, his contract untransacted, Jefferson was fulfilled in the procession of the American mind. The templed god of an American faith in 1943 was, therefore, a different Jefferson from the one who lived in the remote spaces behind 1826.

The chronicle of his progress calls, in retrospect, for some final accounting of Jefferson's prodigious vigor and kaleidoscopic changeability. At the beginning was the man. He lived eighty-three years, helped to found a nation, reflected deeply, wrote voluminously, and plied himself at countless tasks. The image mirrored Jefferson's prodigality. In the vast corpus of his mind anyone could find things to arouse anger or sympathy, invite ridicule or admiration. He was a great rhetorician, one who lived on the spiritual capital of his words even more than on the tangible rewards of his work. "He walked through life pencil in hand." The written record of a life such as his could not be consistent in every detail. He willingly risked the hobgoblin "consistency," and risked too the vicious constructions which his regard for the amenities of human intercourse enabled his enemies to put on his thoughts. Their shifting contexts were easily ignored; Jefferson seemed to exist in a historical void. Men called him a philosopher, and demanded of him more thorough and timeless wisdom than he could supply. He never had the occasion, probably never the desire, to work out a systematic statement of his philosophy. So he appeared before posterity with his rich intellectual garments dangling and disarrayed. This was relatively inconsequential except in the main arena of his life and reputation, politics. His failure to codify political ideas and doctrines confused his followers, enabled fractional pseudo-Jeffersonians of various descriptions to cut his creed into pieces, and contributed, some thought disastrously, to the rule of expediency in American politics and the general collapse of the Jeffersonian polity. Whether or not this lack of a firm political code seriously weakened Jefferson's powers of resistance, there did seem to be a wide gap between his theories and his actions. His reputation suffered accordingly, but chiefly in quarters where it did not amount to much anyway. The loss was far more than offset by the gain. For just as Jefferson multiplied himself through the range and variety of his interests, he doubled, quite unconsciously of course, his political usefulness to the generations, simultaneously posing in himself the dilemmas they must face, by seeming to recommend one thing in theory and another thing in practice. The Louisiana Purchase offered the most striking instance of this curious doubling of Jefferson's significance, though numerous others may be recalled.

Which Jefferson Do You Quote? Clinton Rossiter asked in a recent magazine article. He counted seven different Jeffersons still being "batted around the political arena": Anti-Statist, States'-Righter, Isolationist, Agrarian, Rationalist, Civil Libertarian, Constitutional Democrat. And there had been, still were, several others. Of course, Rossiter had his own opinion as to the *real* Jefferson, and he decried the presence of Jefferson's flag on any craft other than his own. Jefferson had been so indiscriminately parceled out, Rossiter thought, "he may yet be classed as a long-winded trimmer, and be allowed to sink into disuse." And so he had been classed many times, but without sinking into disuse. "If he goes on belonging to everyone, he may end up belonging to no one." And yet it was precisely because Jefferson lent himself to everyone that he had been so useful, that he had been for generations after his death a political watchword, that his reputation was carried forward until, indeed, he belonged to everyone and no one.

While the man explains much, it cannot explain why posterity felt the need constantly to recall Jefferson to its experience. He could be quoted on every side of every question, it was often said; but why did men quote him? First, because among the nation's founders Jefferson was the most eloquent exponent of political ideals which were to be called democratic and which were to become virtually synonymous with the American ideal. Had his life not been enough, the circumstances of his death and the subsequent course of events assured his pre-eminence as a democratic symbol. As such, he was vociferously hated by some; but the symbol and the ideal were fortified by the massive power of public opinion. Second, because of the compelling sense of tradition in American politics. Politicians were the main carriers of Jefferson's reputation. Its history was determined to a very large extent by political events, and particularly by the fortunes of the Democratic party. The strange fascination with the nation's classic age, combined with the stereotyped images of the American conflict, kept alive the historical debate in which Jefferson figured as protagonist of democracy. Third, because Jefferson was implicated in the successive crises of the democratic experiment. American history sometimes seemed a protracted litigation, negotiations

and hearings, trials and appeals in endless number, on Jefferson. The major trial during the first period of his posthumous reputation turned on the ideological conflict between republicanism and democracy. It was practically decided, so far as it concerned the Union, by the Civil War. In the second period it turned more precisely on the conflict between the individualistic and anti-statist clauses of the Jeffersonian creed, on the one side, and the humanitarian and progressivist clauses, on the other side. The verdict in this case called for the subordination of the formal elements of doctrine and principle to the "spirit of Jefferson"—the New Deal solution to the dilemma. Finally, Jefferson summoned the imagination because he prefigured a civilization and furnished important clues to its ethos. When Americans outgrew the political hero, their interest quickened in the cultural hero. Difficult as it was to form Jefferson's varied qualities and activities into a single design, the cultural image best presented itself at Monticello, "portico facing the wilderness." Here was luminously preserved for the inspiration of men in search of their own cultural identity the two heritages discovered in Jefferson—pioneer and aristocrat, American and world-citizen, the values of nature and of civilization—which, fruitfully joined in him, signified the common heritage of America.

FOREIGN AFFAIRS UNDER JEFFERSON AND MADISON

8

Jefferson believed profoundly that the success of the American experiment required peace. He was, on the other hand, perfectly prepared to use the quarrels of Europe to win advantages for America—even at the risk of war. His letter to Robert R. Livingston, the American Minister in Paris, on the subject of New Orleans is suggestive of this attitude:[8]

---

[8] Thomas Jefferson to Robert R. Livingston, April 18, 1802, in Paul L. Ford (ed.), *The Works of Thomas Jefferson* (New York, 1905), IX, 364–367.

WASHINGTON, *April 18, 1802.*

The cession of Louisiana and the Floridas by Spain to France, works most sorely on the United States. On this subject the Secretary of State has written to you fully, yet I cannot forbear recurring to it personally, so deep is the impression it makes on my mind. It completely reverses all the political relations of the United States, and will form a new epoch in our political course. Of all nations of any consideration, France is the one which, hitherto, has offered the fewest points on which we could have any conflict of right, and the most points of a communion of interests. From these causes, we have ever looked to her as our *natural friend,* as one with which we never could have an occasion of difference. Her growth, therefore, we viewed as our own, her misfortunes ours. There is on the globe one single spot, the possessor of which is our natural and habitual enemy. It is New Orleans, through which the produce of three-eighths of our territory must pass to market, and from its fertility it will ere long yield more than half of our whole produce, and contain more than half of our inhabitants. France, placing herself in that door, assumes to us the attitude of defiance. Spain might have retained it quietly for years. Her pacific dispositions, her feeble state, would induce her to increase our facilities there, so that her possession of the place would be hardly felt by us, and it would not, perhaps, be very long before some circumstance might arise, which might make the cession of it to us the price of something of more worth to her. Not so can it ever be in the hands of France: the impetuosity of her temper, the energy and restlessness of her character, placed in a point of eternal friction with us, and our character, which, though quiet and loving peace and the pursuit of wealth, is high-minded, despising wealth in competition with insult or injury, enterprising and energetic as any nation on earth; these circumstances render it impossible that France and the United States can continue long friends, when they meet in so irritable a position. They, as well

as we, must be blind if they do not see this; and we must be very improvident if we do not begin to make arrangements on that hypothesis. The day that France takes possession of New Orleans, fixes the sentence which is to restrain her forever within her low-water mark. It seals the union of two nations, who, in conjunction, can maintain exclusive possession of the ocean. From that moment, we must marry ourselves to the British fleet and nation. We must turn all our attention to a maritime force, for which our resources place us on very high ground; and having formed and connected together a power which may render reinforcement of her settlements here impossible to France, make the first cannon which shall be fired in Europe the signal for the tearing up any settlement she may have made, and for holding the two continents of America in sequestration for the common purposes of the United British and American nations. This is not a state of things we seek or desire. It is one which this measure, if adopted by France, forces on us as necessarily, as any other cause, by the laws of nature, brings on its necessary effect.

9

Among the constructive acts of Jefferson's first administration, the most important was the purchase of Louisiana. That vast territory, lying west of the Mississippi, became a source of potential danger in 1800, when it passed from hapless Spain to aggressive France. Jefferson determined to secure at least a portion of the domain, although he probably could not have done so except for the collapse of Napoleon's dream of empire. When the Franco-English war was resumed in 1803, the French leader determined to sell lest his colony fall to the British navy. The unpopularity of his decision among his followers was amusingly described by Henry Adams, the nineteenth-century historian, who pictured the scene between Napoleon and his two brothers when the First Consul's determination became known:[9]

[9] Henry Adams, *History of the United States of America during the Administration of Thomas Jefferson* (New York, 1930 ed.), I, 34–36. Copyright 1889. Reprinted by permission of the publishers, Charles Scribner's Sons.

The next morning Lucien went to the Tuileries; by his brother's order he was admitted, and found Napoleon in his bath, the water of which was opaque with mixture of *eau de Cologne*. They talked for some time on indifferent matters. Lucien was timid, and dared not speak until Joseph came. Then Napoleon announced his decision to sell Louisiana, and invited Lucien to say what he thought of it.

"I flatter my self," replied Lucien, "that the Chambers will not give their consent."

"You flatter yourself!" repeated Napoleon in a tone of surprise; then murmuring in a lower voice, "that is precious, in truth!" (*c'est précieux, en vérité!*)

"And I too flatter myself, as I have already told the First Consul," cried Joseph.

"And what did I answer?" said Napoleon warmly, glaring from his bath at the two men.

"That you would do without the Chambers."

"Precisely! That is what I have taken the great liberty to tell Mr. Joseph, and what I now repeat to the Citizen Lucien,—begging him at the same time to give me his opinion about it, without taking into consideration his parental tenderness for his diplomatic conquest." Then, not satisfied with irony, he continued in a tone of exasperating contempt: "And now, gentlemen, think of it what you will; but both of you go into mourning about this affair,—you, Lucien, for the sale itself; you, Joseph, because I shall do without the consent of any one whomsoever. Do you understand?"

At this Joseph came close to the bath, and rejoined in a vehement tone: "And you will do well, my dear brother, not to expose your project to parliamentary discussion; for I declare to you that if necessary I will put myself first at the head of the opposition which will not fail to be made against you."

The First Consul burst into a peal of forced laughter, while Joseph, crimson with anger and almost stammering his words, went on: "Laugh, laugh, laugh, then! I will act up to my promise; and though I am not fond of mounting the tribune, this time you will see me there!"

Napoleon, half rising from the bath, rejoined in a serious tone: "You will have no need to lead the opposition, for I repeat that there will be no debate, for the reason that the project which has not the fortune to meet your approval, conceived by me, negotiated by me, shall be ratified and executed by me alone, do you comprehend?—by me, who laugh at your opposition!"

Hereupon Joseph wholly lost his self-control, and with flashing eyes shouted: "Good! I tell you, General, that you, I, and all of us, if you do what you threaten, may prepare ourselves soon to go and join the poor innocent devils whom you so legally, humanely, and especially with such justice, have transported to Sinnamary."

At this terrible rejoinder Napoleon half started up, crying out: "You are insolent! I ought—" then threw himself violently back in the bath with a force which sent a mass of perfumed water into Joseph's flushed face, drenching him and Lucien, who had the wit to quote, in a theatrical tone, the words which Virgil put into the mouth of Neptune reproving the waves—"*Quos ego . . .*"

Between the water and the wit the three Bonapartes recovered their tempers, while the valet who was present, overcome by fear, fainted and fell on the floor.

10

During Jefferson's second administration, national calm gave way to international turbulence. England and France, locked in a death struggle for control of the Continent, determined to starve each other into submission. Both combatants resolved to prevent American foodstuffs from reaching the enemy. They issued a series of decrees which eventually imposed blockades around most of the ports where United States shippers traded. France began the process with the Berlin Decree of November 21, 1806:[10]

ARTICLE 1. The British islands are declared in a state of blockade.

---

[10] *Annals of Congress*, 10th Cong. 2d Sess. XIX, 1750–1751 (1808–1809).

ART. 2. All commerce and correspondence with the British islands are prohibited. In consequence, letters or packets, addressed either to England, to an Englishman, or in the English language, shall not pass through the postoffice and shall be seized.

ART. 3. Every subject of England, of whatever rank and condition soever, who shall be found in the countries occupied by our troops, or by those of our allies, shall be made a prisoner of war.

ART. 4. All magazines, merchandise, or property whatsoever, belonging to a subject of England, shall be declared lawful prize.

ART. 5. The trade in English merchandise is forbidden; all merchandise belonging to England, or coming from its manufactories and colonies, is declared lawful prize.

ART. 6. One-half of the proceeds of the confiscation of the merchandise and property, declared good prize by the preceding articles, shall be applied to indemnify the merchants for the losses which they have suffered by the capture of merchant vessels by English cruisers.

ART. 7. No vessel coming directly from England, or from the English colonies, or having been there since the publication of the present decree, shall be received into any port.

ART. 8. Every vessel contravening the above clause, by means of a false declaration, shall be seized, and the vessel and cargo confiscated, as if they were English property.

ART. 9. Our Tribunal of Prizes at Paris is charged with the definitive adjudication of all the controversies, which may arise within our Empire, or in the countries occupied by the French army, relative to the execution of the present decree. Our Tribunal of Prizes at Milan shall be charged with the definitive adjudication of the said controversies, which may arise within the extent of our kingdom of Italy.

ART. 10. The present decree shall be communicated by our Minister of Exterior Relations, to the Kings of Spain, of Naples, of Holland, and of Etruria, and to our allies, whose subjects, like ours, are the victims of the injustice and the barbarism of the English maritime laws. Our Ministers of Exterior Relations, of War, of Marine, of Finances, our police, and our post masters general, are charged each, in what concerns him, with the execution of the present decree.

11

The English responded to Napoleon's threats by issuing a number of "Orders In Council" designed to blockade the European coast. The heavy losses suffered by American shippers in this war of decrees, and the galling English custom of impressing sailors from United States ships into service with the British navy, soon brought public opinion to a war fever. Anger reached a boiling point in June, 1807, when an American warship, the "Chesapeake," was forcibly stopped and searched by a British gunboat, the "Leopard." As the demand for war flamed, President Jefferson, whose hatred of warfare was transcended only by his love of democracy, cast frantically about for some means of bringing France and England to their senses without bloodshed. The result was the Embargo Act of December 22, 1807:[11]

Be it enacted . . . That an embargo be, and hereby is laid on all ships and vessels in the ports and places within the limits or jurisdiction of the United States, cleared or not cleared, bound to any foreign port or place; and that no clearance be furnished to any ship or vessel bound to such foreign port or place, except vessels under the immediate direction of the President of the United States: and that the President be authorized to give such instructions to the officers of the revenue, and of the navy and revenue cutters of the United States, as shall appear best adapted for carrying the same into full effect: *Provided,* that nothing herein contained shall be construed to prevent the departure of any foreign ship or vessel, either in ballast, or with the goods, wares and merchandise on board of such foreign ship or vessel, when notified of this act.

SECTION 2. . . . That during the continuance of this act, no registered, or sea letter

---

[11] U. S., *Statutes at Large,* II, 451–453.

vessel, having on board goods, wares and merchandise, shall be allowed to depart from one port of the United States to any other within the same, unless the master, owner, consignee or factor of such vessel shall first give bond, with one or more sureties to the collector of the district from which she is bound to depart, in a sum of double the value of the vessel and cargo, that the said goods, wares, or merchandise shall be relanded in some port of the United States, dangers of the seas excepted, which bond, and also a certificate from the collector where the same may be relanded, shall by the collector respectively be transmitted to the Secretary of the Treasury. All armed vessels possessing public commissions from any foreign power, are not to be considered as liable to the embargo laid by this act.

12

While the Embargo Act injured France and England, it injured New England merchants more. In March 1809, Congress repealed the Embargo Act and voted instead a milder Non-Intercourse Act. When the latter proved unenforceable, the Jeffersonians, still seeking a moral substitute for war through economic coercion, devised a method incorporated in Macon's Bill No. 2. This bill, in effect, offered the exclusive trade of the United States to either England or France in an effort to open trade with both. Napoleon made a pro forma acceptance of its terms, and President Madison again imposed a boycott on trade with England. The English suffered so intensely that, on June 16, 1812, they decided to reconsider; Parliament at once repealed all the "Orders In Council" to which Americans had objected. But before news of British concessions reached the United States, Congress declared war on England. Farmers, planters, and frontiersmen of the Mississippi Valley exerted pressures, which together with other factors, led to war. Ground down by a depression that they laid to Britain's interference with American trade, anxious to expand into lands owned by England or her Spanish ally, and suffering from an Indian war that was blamed on British agents, Westerners were convinced that both peace and prosperity depended on humbling English power. Of all these grievances, the Indian war was the most terrifyingly real. Actually its origin was traceable to the land-grabbing treaties forced on the red men

by William Henry Harrison, governor of the Northwest Territory. Native determination to resist encroachment on their lands may be observed in a dignified speech of their leader, the Shawnee chieftain Tecumseh, in 1809:[12]

Brother. I wish you to listen to me well— I wish to reply to you more explicitly, as I think you do not clearly understand what I before said to you I shall explain it again.

When we were first discover'd it was by the French who told us that they would adopt us as their children and gave us presents without asking anything in return but our considering them as our fathers. Since we have changed our fathers we find it different.

Brother. This is the manner that the treaty was made by us with the French. They gave us many presents and treated us well. They asked us for a small piece of country to live on which they were not to leave and continue to treat us as their children after some time the British and French come to quarrel the British were victorious yet the French promised to think of us as their child and if they ever could serve us to do it. Now my red children I know I was obliged to abandon you in disagreeable circumstances, but we have never ceased to look upon you and if we could now be of service to you we would still be your friends.

The next father we found was the British who told us that they would now be our fathers and treat us in the same manner as our former fathers the French—they would occupy the same land they did and not trouble us on ours; but would look on us as their children.

Brother. We were very glad to hear the British promise to treat us our fathers the French had done they began to treat us in the same way but at last they changed their good treatment by raising the Tomahawk against the Americans and put it into our hands, by which we have suffered the loss of a great many of our young men.

---

12 Logan B. Esarey (ed.), *Governors Messages and Letters*, Indiana Historical Society, *Collections* (Indianapolis, 1922), VII, 463–467.

Brother. Now we begin to discover the treachery of the British they never troubled us for our lands but they have done worse by inducing us to go to war. The Hurons have particularly suffered during the war and have at length become certain of it. They have told us that we must bury the British Tomahawk entirely that if we did not they (the B.) would ere long ask us to take it up.

You ought to know that after we agreed to bury the Tomahawk at Greenville we then found our new fathers in the Americans who told us they would treat us well, not like the British who gave us but a small piece of pork every day. I want now to remind you of the promises of the white people. You recollect that the time the Delawares lived near the white people (Americans) and satisfied with the promise of friendship and remained in security yet one of their town was surprised and the men women and children murdered.

The same promises were given to the Shawanese flags, were given to them and were told by the Americans that they were now the children of the Americans. Their flags will be as security for you if the white people intend to do you harm hold up your flags and no harm will be done you. This was at length practised and the consequence was that the person bearing the flag was murdered with others in their village. Now my Bro. after this conduct can you blame me for placing little confidence in the promises of our fathers the Americans.

Brother. Since the peace was made you have kill'd some of the Shawanese, Winebagoes Delawares and Miamies and you have taken our lands from us and I do not see how we can remain at peace with you if you continue to do so. You have given goods to the Kickapoos for the sale of their lands to you which has been the cause of many deaths amongst them. You have promised us assistance but I do not see that you have given us any.

You try to force the red people to do some injury. It is you that is pushing them on to do mischief. You endeavour to make de-

structions, you wish to prevent the Indians to do as we wish them to unite and let them consider their land as the common property of the whole you take tribes aside and advise them not to come into this measure and untill our design is accomplished we do not wish to accept of your invitation to go and visit the President.

The reason I tell you this is—You want by your distinctions of Indian tribes in allotting to each a particular track of land to make them to war with each other. You never see an Indian come and endeavour to make the white people do so. You are continually driving the red people when at last you will drive them into the great lake where they can't either stand or work.

Brother. You ought to know what you are doing with the Indians. Perhaps it is by direction of the President to make those distinctions. It is a very bad thing and we do not like it. Since my residence at Tippecanoe we have endeavoured to level all distinctions to destroy village chiefs by whom all mischief is done; it is they who sell our land to the Americans our object is to let all our affairs be transacted by Warriors.

Brother. This land that was sold and the goods that was given for it was only done by a few. The treaty was afterwards brought here and the Weas were induced to give their consent because of their small numbers. The treaty at Fort Wayne was made through the threats of Winamac but in future we are prepared to punish those chiefs who may come forward to propose to sell their land. If you continue to purchase of them it will produce war among the different tribes and at last I do not know what will be the consequences to the white people.

Brother. I was glad to hear your speech you said if we could show that the land was sold by persons that had no right to sell you would restore it, that that did sell did not own it it was *me*. These tribes set up a claim but the tribes with me will not agree to their claim, if the land is not restored to us you will soon see when we return to our homes how it will be settled. We shall have a great council at which all the tribes shall be present when we will show to those who sold that they had no right to see the claim they set up and we will know what will be done with those Chiefs that did sell the land to you. I am not alone in this determination it is the determination of all the warriors and red people that listen to me.

I now wish you to listen to me. If you do not it will appear as if you wished me to kill all the chiefs that sold you this land. I tell you so because I am authorised by all the tribes to do so. I am at the head of them all. I am a Warrior and all the Warriors will meet together in two or three moons from this. Then I will call for those chiefs that sold you that land and shall know what to do with them. If you do not restore the land you will have a hand in killing them.

Brother. Do not believe that I came here to get presents from you if you offer us anything we will not take it. By taking goods from you you will hereafter say that with them you purchased another piece of land from us. If we want anything we are able to buy it, from your traders. Since the land was sold to you no traders come among us. I now wish you would clear all the roads and let the traders come among us. Then perhaps some of our young men will occasionally call upon you to get their guns repaired. This is all the assistance we ask of you.

Brother. I should now be very glad to know immediately, what is your determination about the land also of the traders I have mentioned.

Brother. It has been the object of both myself and brother from the beginning to prevent the lands being sold should you not return the land, it will occasion us to call a great council that will meet at the Huron Village where the council fire has already been lighted. At which those who sold the land shall be call'd and shall suffer for their conduct.

Brother. I wish you would take pity on all the red people and do what I have requested. If you will not give up the land and do cross the boundary of your present settlement it will be very hard and produce great troubles among us. How can we have confidence in the white people when Jesus Christ came upon the earth you kill'd and nail'd him on a cross, you thought he was dead but you were mistaken. You have shaken among you and you laugh and make light of their worship.

13

Tecumseh's firm words failed to deter Harrison; land-grabbing continued until the harried Indians were left with no choice but the warpath. To Westerners, however, Indian recourse to war could be laid solely at the door of England, for they believed the natives were armed at the Canadian Fort Malden, then sent forth with flintlock and scalping knife to spread desolation along the frontier. The pioneers' attitude was expressed by one of their congressmen, young Henry Clay of Kentucky, who on February 22, 1810, demanded war with England as the only way to solve the West's problems:[13]

No man in the nation wants peace more than I; but I prefer the troubled ocean of war, demanded by the honor and independence of the country, with all its calamities and desolation, to the tranquil and putrescent pool of ignominious peace. If we can accommodate our differences with one of the belligerents only, I should prefer that one to be Britain; but if with neither, and we are forced into a selection of our enemy, then am I for war with Britain, because I believe her prior in aggression, and her injuries and insults to us were atrocious in character. I shall not attempt to exhibit an account between the belligerents of mercantile spoliations inflicted and menaced. On that point we have just cause of war with both. Britain stands pre-eminent in her outrage on us, by her violation of the sacred personal rights of American freemen, in the arbitrary and lawless imprisonment of our seamen, the attack on the Chesapeake—the murder, sir. I will not dwell on the long catalogue of our wrongs and disgrace, which has been

---

[13] *Annals of Congress*, 11th Cong., 1st Sess. 579–581 (1809–1810).

repeated until the sensibility of the nation is benumbed by the dishonorable detail.

But we are asked for the means of carrying on the war, and those who oppose it triumphantly appeal to the vacant vaults of the Treasury. With the unimpaired credit of the Government, invigorated by a faithful observance of public engagements, and a rapid extinction of the debt of the land, with the boundless territories in the West presenting a safe pledge for reimbursement of loans to any extent, is it not astonishing that despondency itself should disparage the resources of this country? You have, sir, I am credibly informed, in the city and vicinity of New Orleans alone, public property sufficient to extinguish the celebrated deficit in the Secretary's report. And are we to regard as nothing the patriotic offer so often made by the States, to spend their last cent, and risk their last drop of blood, in the preservation of our neutral privileges? Or, are we to be governed by the low, grovelling parsimony of the counting room, and to cast up the actual pence in the drawer before we assert our inestimable rights?

It is said, however, that no object is attainable by war with Great Britain. In its fortunes, we are to estimate not only the benefit to be derived to ourselves, but the injury to be done the enemy. The conquest of Canada is in your power. I trust I shall not be deemed presumptuous when I state that I verily believe that the militia of Kentucky are alone competent to place Montreal and Upper Canada at your feet. Is it nothing to the British nation; is it nothing to the pride of her Monarch, to have the last of the immense North American possessions held by him in the commencement of his reign wrested from his dominion? Is it nothing to us to extinguish the torch that lights up savage warfare? Is it nothing to acquire the entire fur trade connected with that country, and to destroy the temptation and the opportunity of violating your revenue and other laws?

War with Great Britain will deprive her of those supplies of raw materials and provisions which she now obtains from this country. It is alleged that the nonintercourse law, constantly evaded, is incapable of execution. War will be a nonintercourse, admitting of but partial elusion. The pressure upon her, contemplated by your restrictive laws, will then be completely realized. She will not have the game, as she will if you press this bill without an efficient system, entirely in her own hands. The enterprise and valor of our maritime brethren will participate in the spoils of capture.

Another effect of war will be, the reproduction and cherishing of a commercial spirit amongst us. Is there no danger that we shall become enervated by the spirit of avarice, unfortunately so predominant? I do not wish to see that diffusive military character, which, pervading the whole nation, might possibly eventuate in the aggrandizement of some ambitious chief, by prostrating the liberties of the country. But a certain portion of military ardor (and that is what I desire) is essential to the protection of the country. The withered arm and wrinkled brow of the illustrious founders of our freedom are melancholy indications that they will shortly be removed from us. Their deeds of glory and renown will then be felt only through the cold medium of the historic page. We shall want the presence and living example of a new race of heroes to supply their places, and to animate us to preserve inviolate what they achieved. Am I counting too much on the valor of my countrymen, when I indulge the hope, that if we are forced into war, the American hero now lives, who, upon the walls of Quebec, imitating his glorious example, will avenge the fall of the immortal Montgomery? But we shall, at least, gain the approbation of our own hearts. If we surrender without a struggle to maintain our rights, we forfeit the respect of the world and (what is worse) of ourselves.

14

The intensity of such pressure was more than President Madison could endure. On June 1,

1812, he sent an impassioned message to Congress demanding an immediate declaration of war against England:[14]

Without going back beyond the renewal in 1803 of the war in which Great Britain is engaged, and omitting unrepaired wrongs of inferior magnitude, the conduct of her Government presents a series of acts hostile to the United States as an independent and neutral nation.

British cruisers have been in the continued practice of violating the American flag on the great highway of nations, and of seizing and carrying off persons sailing under it, not in the exercise of a belligerent right founded on the law of nations against an enemy, but of a municipal prerogative over British subjects. British jurisdiction is thus extended to neutral vessels in a situation where no laws can operate but the law of nations and the laws of the country to which the vessels belong, and a self-redress is assumed which, if British subjects were wrongfully detained and alone concerned, is that substitution of force for a resort to the responsible sovereign which falls within the definition of war. . . .

The practice, hence, is so far from affecting British subjects alone that, under the pretext of searching for these, thousands of American citizens, under the safeguard of public law and of their national flag, have been torn from their country and from everything dear to them; have been dragged on board ships of war of a foreign nation, and exposed, under the severities of their discipline, to be exiled to the most distant and deadly climes, to risk their lives in the battles of their oppressors, and to be the melancholy instruments of taking away those of their own brethren.

Against this crying enormity, which Great Britain would be so prompt to avenge if committed against herself, the United States have in vain exhausted remonstrances and expostulations, and that no proof might be wanting of their conciliatory dispositions,

and no pretext left for a continuance of the practice, the British Government was formally assured of the readiness of the United States to enter into arrangements such as could not be rejected if the recovery of British subjects were the real and the sole object. The communication passed without effect. . . .

Under pretended blockades, without the presence of an adequate force and sometimes without the practicability of applying one, our commerce has been plundered in every sea, the great staples of our country have been cut off from their legitimate markets, and a destructive blow aimed at our agricultural and maritime interests. In aggravation of these predatory measures they have been considered as in force from the dates of their notification, a retrospective effect being thus added, as has been done in other important cases, to the unlawfulness of the course pursued. And to render the outrage the more signal these mock blockades have been reiterated and enforced in the face of official communications from the British Government declaring as the true definition of a legal blockade "that particular ports must be actually invested and previous warning given to vessels bound to them not to enter."

Not content with these occasional expedients for laying waste our neutral trade, the cabinet of Britain resorted at length to the sweeping system of blockades, under the name of orders in council, which has been molded and managed as might best suit its political views, its commercial jealousies, or the avidity of British cruisers. . . .

It has become, indeed, sufficiently certain that the commerce of the United States is to be sacrificed, not as interfering with the belligerent rights of Great Britain; not as supplying the wants of her enemies, which she herself supplies; but as interfering with the monopoly which she covets for her own commerce and navigation. She carries on a war against the lawful commerce of a friend that she may the better carry on a commerce with an enemy—a commerce polluted by the forgeries and perjuries which are for the

---

[14] James D. Richardson (comp.), *A Compilation of the Messages and Papers of the Presidents, 1789–1897* (Washington, 1897), I, 499–505.

most part the only passports by which it can succeed. . . .

In reviewing the conduct of Great Britain toward the United States our attention is necessarily drawn to the warfare just renewed by the savages on one of our extensive frontiers—a warfare which is known to spare neither age nor sex and to be distinguished by features peculiarly shocking to humanity. It is difficult to account for the activity and combinations which have for some time been developing themselves among tribes in constant intercourse with British traders and garrisons without connecting their hostility with that influence and without recollecting the authenticated examples of such interpositions heretofore furnished by the officers and agents of that Government.

Such is the spectacle of injuries and indignities which have been heaped on our country, and such the crisis which its unexampled forbearance and conciliatory efforts have not been able to avert. . . .

Our moderation and conciliation have had no other effect than to encourage perseverance and to enlarge pretensions. We behold our seafaring citizens still the daily victims of lawless violence, committed on the great common and highway of nations, even within sight of the country which owes them protection. We behold our vessels, freighted with the products of our soil and industry, or returning with the honest proceeds of them, wrested from their lawful destinations, confiscated by prize courts no longer the organs of public law but the instruments of arbitrary edicts, and their unfortunate crews dispersed and lost, or forced or inveigled in British ports into British fleets, whilst arguments are employed in support of these aggressions which have no foundation but in a principle equally supporting a claim to regulate our external commerce in all cases whatsoever.

We behold, in fine, on the side of Great Britain a state of war against the United States, and on the side of the United States a state of peace toward Great Britain.

Whether the United States shall continue passive under these progressive usurpations and these accumulating wrongs, or, opposing force to force in defense of their national rights, shall commit a just cause into the hands of the Almighty Disposer of Events, avoiding all connections which might entangle it in the contest or views of other powers, and preserving a constant readiness to concur in an honorable reëstablishment of peace and friendship, is a solemn question which the Constitution wisely confides to the legislative department of the Government. In recommending it to their early deliberations I am happy in the assurance that the decision will be worthy the enlightened and patriotic councils of a virtuous, a free, and a powerful nation.

15

Neither nation distinguished itself in the three years of war following Madison's dramatic message. American ships won a few valiant victories and American armies defeated the redcoats in a few battles, but the struggle ended with Canada still in British hands, Florida still occupied by Spain, the Atlantic as truly an English lake as in 1812, and the capitol at Washington burned. Even more disastrous was the wartime conduct of the New Englanders who, mindful of their ruined trade and distrustful of "radical" France, not only failed to support the war but expressed open disapproval of its prosecution in the Hartford Convention of December 15, 1814.[15]

Therefore resolved,

That it be and hereby is recommended to the legislatures of the several states represented in this Convention, to adopt all such measures as may be necessary effectually to protect the citizens of said states from the operation and effects of all acts which have been or may be passed by the Congress of the United States, which shall contain provisions, subjecting the militia or other citizens to forcible drafts, conscriptions, or impress-

---

[15] Theodore Dwight, *History of the Hartford Convention, with a Review of the Policy of the United States Government, which led to the War of 1812* (New York, 1835), pp. 368–370, 376–378.

ments, not authorized by the constitution of the United States.

Resolved, That it be and hereby is recommended to the said Legislatures, to authorize an immediate and earnest application to be made to the government of the United States, requesting their consent to some arrangement, whereby the said states may, separately or in concert, be empowered to assume upon themselves the defence of their territory against the enemy; and a reasonable portion of the taxes, collected within said States, may be paid into the respective treasuries thereof, and appropriated to the payment of the balance due said states, and to the future defence of the same. The amount so paid into the said treasuries to be credited, and the disbursements made as aforesaid to be charged to the United States.

Resolved, That it be, and hereby is, recommended to the legislatures of the aforesaid states, to pass laws (where it has not already been done) authorizing the governors or commanders-in-chief of their militia to make detachments from the same, or to form voluntary corps, as shall be most convenient and conformable to their constitutions, and to cause the same to be well armed, equipped, and disciplined, and held in readiness for service; and upon the request of the governor of either of the other states to employ the whole of such detachment or corps, as well as the regular forces of the state, or such part thereof as may be required and can be spared consistently with the safety of the state, in assisting the state, making such request to repel any invasion thereof which shall be made or attemped by the public enemy.

Resolved, That the following amendments of the constitution of the United States be recommended to the states represented as aforesaid, to be proposed by them for adoption by the state legislatures, and in such cases as may be deemed expedient by a convention chosen by the people of each state.

And it is further recommended, that the said states shall persevere in their efforts to obtain such amendments, until the same shall be effected.

First. Representatives and direct taxes shall be apportioned among the several states which may be included within this Union, according to their respective numbers of free persons, including those bound to serve for a term of years, and excluding Indians not taxed, and all other persons.

Second. No new state shall be admitted into the Union by Congress, in virtue of the power granted by the constitution, without the concurrence of two thirds of both houses.

Third. Congress shall not have power to lay any embargo on the ships or vessels of the citizens of the United States, in the ports or harbours thereof, for more than sixty days.

Fourth. Congress shall not have power, without the concurrence of two thirds of both houses, to interdict the commercial intercourse between the United States and any foreign nation, or the dependencies thereof.

Fifth. Congress shall not make or declare war, or authorize acts of hostility against any foreign nation, without the concurrence of two thirds of both houses, except such acts of hostility be in defence of the territories of the United States when actually invaded.

Sixth. No person who shall hereafter be naturalized, shall be eligible as a member of the senate or house of representatives of the United States, nor capable of holding any civil office under the authority of the United States.

Seventh. The same person shall not be elected president of the United States a second time; or shall the president be elected from the same state two terms in succession.

Resolved, That if the application of these states to the government of the United States, recommended in a foregoing resolution, should be unsuccessful and peace should not be concluded, and the defence of these states should be neglected, as it has since the commencement of the war, it will, in the opinion of this convention, be expedient for the legislatures of the several states to appoint delegates to another convention, to meet at Boston . . . with such powers and instructions as the exigency of a crisis so momentous may require.

THE WAR OF 1812

16

While a few New Englanders talked of disunion at Hartford, the British were making war. Cruising up and down the Chesapeake Bay, in what was called a "chicken-house" war, they took pot shots at likely plantation targets along the way. In August 1814, they landed on the lower Patuxent River, brushed aside a badly disorganized force of American militiamen at Bladensburg, and marched into Washington. President Madison and many government officials were forced to flee. The following account of the "conquest" of Washington was written by a British officer, George R. Gleig:[16]

While the two brigades which had been engaged, remained upon the field to recover their order, the third, which had formed the reserve, and was consequently unbroken, took the lead, and pushed forward at a rapid rate towards Washington.

As it was not the intention of the British government to attempt permanent conquests in this part of America; and as the General was well aware that, with a handful of men, he could not pretend to establish himself, for any length of time, in an enemy's capital, he determined to lay it under contribution, and to return quietly to the shipping. . . .

Such being the intention of General Ross, he did not march the troops immediately into the city, but halted them upon a plain in its immediate vicinity, whilst a flag of truce was sent in with terms. But whatever his proposal might have been, it was not so much as heard; for scarcely had the party bearing the flag entered the street, than they were fired upon from the windows of one of the houses, and the horse of the General himself,

---

[16] George Robert Gleig, *The Campaigns of the British Army at Washington and New Orleans in the Years 1814–1815*, 3d ed., (London, 1827), pp. 128–137.

who accompanied them, killed. . . . All thoughts of accommodation were instantly laid aside; the troops advanced forthwith into the town, and having first put to the sword all who were found in the house from which the shots were fired, and reduced it to ashes, they proceeded, without a moment's delay, to burn and destroy everything in the most distant degree connected with government. In this general devastation were included the Senate-house, the President's palace, an extensive dock-yard and arsenal, barracks for two or three thousand men, several large store-houses filled with naval and military stores, some hundreds of cannon of different descriptions, and nearly twenty thousand stand of small arms. There were also two or three public rope-works, which shared the same fate, a fine frigate pierced for sixty guns, and just ready to be launched, several gun-brigs and armed schooners, with a variety of gun-boats and small craft. The powder magazines were of course set on fire, and exploded with a tremendous crash, throwing down many houses in their vicinity, partly by pieces of the walls striking them, and partly by the concussion of the air; whilst quantities of shot, shell, and hand-grenades, which could not otherwise be rendered useless, were thrown into the river. . . .

Had the arm of vengeance been extended no farther, there would not have been room given for so much as a whisper of disapprobation. But, unfortunately, it did not stop there; a noble library, several printing offices, and all the national archives were likewise committed to the flames, which, though no doubt the property of government, might better have been spared. . . .

While the third brigade was thus employed, the rest of the army, having recalled its stragglers, and removed the wounded into Bladensburg, began its march towards Washington. Though the battle was ended by four o'clock, the sun had set before the different regiments were in a condition to move, consequently this short journey was performed in the dark. The work of destruction had also begun in the city, before they quitted their ground; and the blazing of houses, ships, and stores, the report of exploding magazines, and the crash of falling roofs, informed them, as they proceeded, of what was going forward. You can conceive nothing finer than the sight which met them as they drew near to the town. The sky was brilliantly illuminated by the different conflagrations; and a dark red light was thrown upon the road, sufficient to permit each man to view distinctly his comrade's face. . . .

I need scarcely observe, that the consternation of the inhabitants was complete, and that to them this was a night of terror. So confident had they been of the success of their troops, that few of them had dreamt of quitting their houses, or abandoning the city; nor was it till the fugitives from the battle began to rush in, filling every place as they came with dismay, that the President himself thought of providing for his safety. That gentleman, as I was credibly informed, had gone forth in the morning with the army, and had continued among his troops till the British forces began to make their appearance. Whether the sight of his enemies cooled his courage or not, I cannot say, but, according to my informer, no sooner was the glittering of our arms discernible, than he began to discover that his presence was more wanted in the senate than with the army; and having ridden through the ranks, and exhorted every man to do his duty, he hurried back to his own house, that he might prepare a feast for the entertainment of his officers, when they should return victorious. For the truth of these details, I will not be answerable; but this much I know, that the feast was actually prepared, though, instead of being devoured by American officers, it went to satisfy the less delicate appetites of a party of English soldiers. When the detachment, sent out to destroy Mr. Madison's house, entered his dining parlour, they found a dinner-table spread, and covers laid for forty guests. Several kinds of wine, in handsome cut-glass decanters, were cooling on the side-board; plate-holders stood by the fire-place, filled with dishes and plates; knives, forks and spoons, were arranged for immediate use; in short, every thing was ready for the entertainment of a ceremonious party. Such were the arrangements in the dining-room, whilst in the kitchen were others answerable to them in every respect. Spits, loaded with joints of various sorts, turned before the fire; pots, saucepans, and other culinary utensils, stood upon the grate; and all the other requisites for an elegant and substantial repast, were exactly in a state which indicated that they had been lately and precipitately abandoned.

You will readily imagine, that these preparations were beheld, by a party of hungry soldiers, with no indifferent eye. An elegant dinner, even though considerably overdressed, was a luxury to which few of them, at least for some time back, had been accustomed; and which, after the dangers and fatigues of the day, appeared peculiarly inviting. They sat down to it, therefore, not indeed in the most orderly manner, but with countenances which would not have disgraced a party of aldermen at a civic feast; and having satisfied their appetites with fewer complaints than would have probably escaped their rival *gourmands*, and partaken pretty freely of the wines, they finished by setting fire to the house which had so liberally entertained them. . . .

At day-break next morning, the light brigade moved into the city, while the reserve fell back to a height, about half a mile in the rear. Little, however, now remained to be done, because every thing marked out for destruction, was already consumed. Of the senate-house, the President's palace, the barracks, the dock-yard, &c. nothing could be seen, except heaps of smoking ruins; and even the bridge, a noble structure upwards a mile in length, was almost wholly demolished. There was, therefore, no farther occasion to scatter the troops, and they were accordingly kept together as much as possible on the Capitol hill.

17

American bungling at Bladensburg contrasted sharply with the achievement of an odd assortment of militia, townsmen, freedmen, and pirates who engaged British regulars under Sir Edward Packenham at New Orleans. The core of the American force consisted of Tennessee and Kentucky volunteers and Louisiana militia, led by General Andrew Jackson. Fought two weeks after a peace treaty had been signed in Ghent (December 24, 1814), the battle of New Orleans turned into a slaughter for the British. The description below is from an anonymous source, but the writer probably hailed from Kentucky:[17]

Col. Smiley, from Bardstown, was the first one who gave us orders to fire from our part of the line; and then, I reckon, there was a pretty considerable noise. There were also brass pieces on our right, the noisest kind of varmints, that began blaring away as hard as they could, while the heavy iron cannon, toward the river, and some thousands of small arms, joined in the chorus and made the ground shake under our feet. Directly after the firing began, Capt. Patterson, I think he was from Knox County, Kentucky, but an Irishman born, came running along. He jumped upon the brestwork and stooping a moment to look through the darkness as well as he could, he shouted with a broad North of Ireland brogue, "shoot low, boys! shoot low! rake them—rake them! They're comin' on their all fours!"

The official report said the action lasted two hours and five minutes, but it did not seem half that length of time to me. It was so dark that little could be seen, until just about the time the battle ceased. The morning dawned to be sure, but the smoke was so thick that every thing seemed to be covered up in it. Our men did not seem to apprehend any danger, but would load and fire as fast as they could, talking, swearing, and joking all the time. All ranks and sections were soon broken up. After the first shot, every one loaded and banged away on

his own hook. Henry Spillman did not load and fire quite so often as some of the rest, but every time he did fire he would go up to the brestwork, look over until he could see something to shoot at, and then take deliberate aim and crack away. Lieut. Ashby was as busy as a sailor and it was evident that the River Raisin was uppermost in his mind all the time. He kept dashing about and every now and then he would call out, with an oath, "We'll pay you now for the River Raisin! We'll give you something to remember the River Raisin!" When the British had come up to the opposite side of the brestwork, having no gun, he picked up an empty barrel and flung it at them. Then finding an iron bar, he jumped up on the works and hove that at them.

At one time I noticed, a little on our right, a curious kind of a chap named Ambrose Odd, one of Captain Higdon's company, and known among the men by the nickname of "Sukey," standing coolly on the top of the brestworks and peering into the darkness for something to shoot at. The balls were whistling around him and over our heads, as thick as hail, and Col. Slaughter coming along, ordered him to come down. The Colonel told him there was policy in war, and that he was exposing himself too much. Sukey turned around, holding up the flap of his old broad brimmed hat with one hand, to see who was speaking to him, and replied: "Oh! never mind Colonel—here's Sukey—I don't want to waste my powder, and I'd like to know how I can shoot until I see something?" Pretty soon after, Sukey got his eye on a red coat, and, no doubt, made a hole through it, for he took deliberate aim, fired and then coolly came down to load again.

During the action, a number of the Tennessee men got mixed with ours. One of them was killed about five or six yards from where I stood. I did not know his name. A ball passed through his head and he fell against Ensign Weller. I always thought, as did many others who were standing near, that he must have been accidently shot by some

---

17 Anon., "A Contemporary Account of the Battle of New Orleans," *The Louisiana Historical Quarterly,* IX (January 1926), 11–14.

of our own men. From the range of the British balls, they could hardly have passed over the brestwork without passing over our heads, unless we were standing very close to the works, which were a little over brest high, and five or six feet wide on the top. This man was standing a little back and rather behind Weller. After the battle, I could not see that any of the balls had struck the oak tree lower than ten or twelve feet from the ground. Above that height it was thickly peppered. This was the only man killed near where I was stationed.

It was near the close of the firing. About the time that I observed three or four men carrying his body away or directly after, there was a white flag raised on the opposite side of the brestwork and the firing ceased. . . .

When the smoke had cleared away and we could obtain a fair view of the field, it looked, at the first glance, like a sea of blood. It was not blood itself which gave it this appearance but the red coats in which the British soldiers were dressed. Straight out before our position, for about the width of space which we supposed had been occupied by the British column, the field was entirely covered with prostrate bodies. In some places they were laying in piles of several, one on top of the other. On either side, there was an interval more thinly sprinkled with the slain; and then two other dense rows, one near the levee and the other towards the swamp. About two hundred yards off, directly in front of our position, lay a large dapple gray horse, which we understood to have been Packenham's.

Something about half way between the body of the horse and our brestwork there was a very large pile of dead, and at this spot, as I was afterward told, Packenham had been killed; his horse having staggered off to a considerable distance before he fell. I have no doubt that I could have walked on the bodies from the edge of the ditch to where the horse was laying, without touching the ground. I did not notice any other horse on the field.

18

Scholars have long debated the causes of the War of 1812. In this debate a major contribution has been made by Professor Julius W. Pratt, the results of whose study are here summarized:[18]

The examination made in the course of this study reveals an ardent expansionist sentiment already at work along the whole southern and southwestern border, varying in scope from the relatively modest proposal for the annexation of the Floridas to the more visionary idea of seizing all the Spanish possessions on the continent of North America. The link between the designs of the Southwest and those of the Northwest was the existence of the alliance between Great Britain and Spain. It was widely assumed that war with Great Britain would mean war with Spain, and that thus expansion at the north and at the south would proceed *pari passu*.

The purposes of the present study have been: to examine the development in the Northwest of the demand for the conquest and annexation of Canada; to trace the rise in the South and Southwest of the plan to annex the Floridas and possibly Mexico; to discover the relations of these two proposals to each other and to the question of war with Great Britain; to determine the position of the executive branch of the United States government (especially of Madison and his Secretary of State, Monroe) toward the plans for expansion, north and south; and finally, to determine the causes for the failure, all along the line, of the expansionist hopes with which the war began.

The principal conclusions arrived at may be summarized as follows:

I. The belief that the United States would one day annex Canada had a continuous existence from the early days of the War of Independence to the War of 1812. From 1783 to about 1810 such annexation was thought of only as a matter for an indefinite future, the nation during those years having

---

[18] Julius W. Pratt, *Expansionists of 1812* (New York, 1925), pp. 11–14. Reprinted with the permission of the publishers, The Macmillan Company.

neither the strength, nor any sufficient motive, for taking Canada by force. The rise of Tecumseh, backed, as was universally believed, by the British, produced an urgent demand in the Northwest that the British be expelled from Canada. This demand was a factor of primary importance in bringing on the war.

II. The South was almost unanimous in its demand for the Floridas, for agrarian, commercial, and strategic reasons, and in the spring of 1812 appeared to be in a fair way to accomplish its purpose. In the Southwest, at the same time, there was a lively interest in Mexico, and a widely prevalent opinion that it was ready to fall into American hands.

III. Even within the Republican party, there was already a distinct sectional rift between North and South, and neither section was anxious to see the other increase its territory and population. But if both could gain at the same time, and in something like equal proportion, such objections would be obviated on both sides. There is good evidence that, before the declaration of war, northern and southern Republicans came to a definite understanding that the acquisition of Canada on the north was to be balanced by the annexation of the Floridas on the south. Thus the war began with a double-barrelled scheme of territorial aggrandizement.

IV. Both Madison and Monroe, especially the latter as Secretary of State, were wholly in sympathy with the proposal for annexing Florida. The invasion of East Florida by General Mathews in March and April, 1812, was effected with the full knowledge of the administration. Special circumstances forced the government to repudiate Matthews, but the territory he had taken from the Spanish was held for over a year, until Congress had twice refused to sanction the occupation. At the same time, Monroe's official correspondence shows that he never really desired or expected the annexation of Canada.

V. It appears that in the all round failure of the expansionist plans, sectional feeling played a larger part than is commonly supposed. The sectional bargain with which the war had begun broke down. Opposition from northern Republicans combined with Federalists forced the abandonment of East Florida. On the other hand, it is evident that in the utter failure of the efforts to take Canada, not only want of skill and preparation, but also a lack of enthusiasm on the part of the administration and of certain southern men in Congress played a part.

VI. Finally, in the expansionist program with which the war opened, we have the first general appearance of the idea which later received the name of "Manifest Destiny." Although enthusiasts like Jefferson had dreamed years before of a nation destined to embrace the continent, the date usually given for the dawn of "Manifest Destiny" is about 1830. Yet both in the Congressional debates of 1812 and in the contemporary press, particularly that of the Southwest, we find the idea repeatedly expressed. "Where is it written in the book of fate," asked the editor of the Nashville *Clarion* (April 28, 1812), "that the American republic shall not stretch her limits from the Capes of the Chesapeake to Nootka sound, from the isthmus of Panama to Hudson bay?" . . .

If we should locate on a map of the United States the homes of those men in Congress who were most outspoken for war and annexation, and plot from these points the line of maximum war and expansionist sentiment, we should find our line to be the circumference of a crescent with one end in New Hampshire and the other in Savannah, Georgia. . . . From end to end the crescent traversed frontier territory, bordering foreign soil, British or Spanish, or confronting dangerous Indian tribes among whom foreign influence was suspected and feared. And the men who came from these districts to Washington displayed many of the characteristic frontier traits. They had national patriotism, to the point sometimes of chauvinism, resenting with a new bitterness their country's wrongs and scorning the pacific measures hitherto used to repel them. They had unlimited faith in their country's future, believing its destined limits to be no less than the eastern and western oceans, the Gulf of Mexico and the "regions of eternal frost." Hence they were for a war which should at the same time defend the country's rights and expand its boundaries; they would punish British insults with the sword, wresting Canada from Great Britain and the residue of the Floridas from her weak ally, Spain.

Nothing could better demonstrate the frontier character of the war spirit than to observe its progressive decline as we pass from the rim of the crescent to its center at the national capital. Expansionist enthusiasm declined even more rapidly. . . .

As there were men from the border who opposed the war, and cared nothing for territorial expansion, so there were men from the older states and districts who warmly supported both. Macon of North Carolina and Matthew Clay of Virginia, and a considerable part of the Pennsylvania delegation showed unquestioned zeal for the war program and the annexation of Canada. In general, however, our thesis holds good—that enthusiasm for war and annexation was at its height at the periphery of the crescent, while faction flourished most luxuriantly near the center.

19

A. L. Burt finds Pratt's thesis deficient because adequate weight is not given to the western need for markets for agricultural surpluses:[19]

According to a thesis which has been widely accepted in recent years, we cannot understand why there was a War of 1812 unless we look inland. This thesis may be summarized as follows. The quarrel over neutral rights on the sea brought the United States to the verge of war with Britain but

[19] A. L. Burt, *The United States, Great Britain, and British North America from the Revolution to the Establishment of Peace after the War of 1812* (New Haven, 1940), pp. 305–316. Reprinted with the kind permission of the Carnegie Endowment for International Peace.

did not do more than that, for the maritime constituencies voted against war. The force that induced the last fatal step was largely, though not wholly, an urge to conquer Canada. This urge was chiefly inspired by the determination to uproot the British-Indian evil but was also compounded of the old jealousy of the British fur trade and a new lust for territorial expansion that anticipated "Manifest Destiny"; and it found abundant "righteous pretexts" in the maritime quarrel. "By the end of the spring of 1812, the whole frontier country from New Hampshire to Kentucky was insisting that the British must be expelled from Canada." But the people of the Northwest might have clamored in vain for war if they had not found fortuitous allies in the people of the South, who were likewise impatient to take Florida from Spain, the weak ally of Britain. This combination, which promised to preserve the balance between North and South by adding territory and population to both, brought on the war. . . .

Confirmation has also been found in the division of Congress on the war issue, "most of the navigating interests voting nay, and the interior, particularly the whole frontier in a great crescent from Vermont to Louisiana, voting aye," with "only a small majority for war."

There is more than one *non sequitur* in this argument. Does the voting of the maritime constituencies prove that neutral rights alone could not have produced the war? Their votes were divided, . . . and the division would have been more equal if it had truly reflected the opinions of the people. Nor should it be forgotten that this was the part of the country that stood to suffer most in a trial of strength with British sea power. Much more serious is another consideration which we have already seen. The American government had to champion the maritime interests not only in spite of their opposition but also because of their opposition. The commercial and shipping elements had been betraying the national honor. They would have sold neutral rights and the country's independence for selfish profit and sectional welfare.

The southern pressure for war is also misconstrued. Why should Americans want war with Britain in order to seize Florida? Part had already been taken without it, and the obstacle that seemed to stand in the way of getting the rest was the possibility of British intervention. Britain ruled the waves, and the waves nearly surrounded Florida. Moreover the administration's schemes for acquiring this weakly held Spanish possession were well under way long before the "War Hawks" flocked to the Twelfth Congress. The one reason why the South should welcome war with Britain to aid in getting Florida was to buy off sectional opposition within the United States by letting the North have its *quid pro quo* in Canada; but, as already suggested, this meant running the obvious danger of the means defeating the end. The reports of the debates in the *Annals of Congress* contain no suggestion of Florida's being a motive for war; but they do reveal another material motive which has attracted too little attention. It was a strong one.

The planters were being badly pinched. "Our cotton is reduced to seven cents, and our tobacco to nothing," cried old Robert Wright of Maryland in the House. He denied Randolph's assertion "that our own restrictive system has undone us," pointing out that re-

strictions on the export of these articles had ceased and if they had been the cause the effect should have ceased too. "The price of cotton depends on the demand for the manufactures of that article; the English-made cottons depend on the continental markets, from which the British manufactures are excluded. The price of tobacco never was materially varied by the consumption in England, but depended on the foreign demand from Great Britain, which, by their exclusion from the continent, is almost entirely arrested." The retaliatory system of the two great belligerents, he said, had ruined the market for these American staples, and since Napoleon had revoked his decrees the blame now rested on the British orders-in-council. Wright put his finger on the sore spot of the South. This was the one section of the country that was vitally dependent upon the markets controlled by Napoleon. It was not a commercial region; but its very life was tied up with commerce. Here was a further reason for championing the maritime interests in their own despite. Maritime New England would have deserted the planter South; and the rural North would have done the same thing, for it was attracted by the fabulous price of wheat in England and the market for provisions created by the Peninsular War.

The Flowering of Nationalism

Nationalism and conservatism, the twin forces that have dominated American life in every postwar era, dominated the years between the close of the War of 1812 and the inauguration of Andrew Jackson. Proud of their few military victories over mighty England, the American people responded to the nationalistic impulse. Moreover, the rise of industry and the growth of internal trade made them conscious of their economic self-sufficiency. Complacent, they watched approvingly as the national government extended its power at state expense, elevated upper-class concepts of social and economic decorum into law, and asserted its new-found strength by defying the rest of the world through the Monroe Doctrine. United, cocksure, absorbed in exploiting the limitless resources of the land, Americans felt secure and looked toward a future of continued harmony and prosperity.

SECTIONAL SPECIALIZATION

1

During and after the War of 1812, manufacturing developed rapidly in the Northeast, cotton culture in the South, and diversified agriculture in the West. An economic basis for nationalism was provided by the mutual interdependence that derived from sectional specialization; the Northeast clothed the West, the West fed the South, and the South provided the fibers for northeastern textile mills. Conservatism was also strengthened as a result of economic changes; the rising industrial class preached that the success of business would ultimately be reflected in the prosperity of every worker and farmer. A traveler in the Northeast during these years explains the growing emphasis on industry in that section:[1]

The Northern or New England States are endowed by nature with a mountainous and sterile soil, which but poorly rewards the labor of the husbandman. However, its wooded slopes, and tumbling streams, which fall into commodious harbors, early pointed out to the restless energy of the first settlers the direction in which their industry was to be employed. Ship-building and navigation at once became the leading industry, bringing with it more or less wealth. The harsh rule of the mother country forbade a manufacturing development, and that branch of industry had never got a footing in the colonies. The act of independence which opened up that field of employment, also provided, by freedom of intercourse, a large market for the sale of manufactures to the agricultural laborers of the more fertile fields of the Middle and Southern States. The genius of Northern industry was not slow in applying the capital earned in commerce to the prosecution of this branch of labor, and with every increase in numbers, and every extension of national territory, the New England States have had only a larger market for their wares, while the foreign competing supply has been restricted by high duties on imports. The mountain torrents of New England have become motors, by which annually improving machinery has been driven. These machines require only the attendance of females, but a few years since a non-producing class, to turn out immense quantities of tex-

[1] Thomas P. Kettell, *Southern Wealth and Northern Profits* (New York, 1860), pp. 51–52.

tile fabrics. In the hands of the male population, other branches of industry have multiplied, in a manner which shows the stimulant of an ever-increasing effective demand.

At about the time that New England became free to manufacture, the discoveries in navigation wrought that singular change in commerce by which Charleston, S.C., was no longer regarded as the nearest port to Europe, and New York assumed its proper position, as the central marine point. The commerce of the Middle States rapidly increased, and with that increase a larger demand for the manufactures of New England was created. When population spread west of the Alleghanies, and the annexation of Louisiana opened the Mississippi river to a market for Western produce, thus putting an end to that Western discontent, which had made separation from the East, and consolidation with the lower countries of the Mississippi for the sake of an outlet, imminent, a new demand for New England manufactures was felt, and this was further enhanced by the opening of the Erie canal. In later years, the vast foreign immigration, pouring over new lands opened up by railroads, has given a further stimulus to consumption; more, however, through the enormous sums of money sent in that direction to build railroads, than by any legitimate development of Western wealth.

2

Sectional specialization was even more evident in the South, where King Cotton apparently ruled after the War of 1812. By the 1820s every acre from the Atlantic to Texas that was fertile enough to support cotton plants yielded up bale on bale of snowy fibers, all earmarked for the mills of the Northeast or England. A traveler bound from Charleston to St. Louis pictures the emphasis on one-crop agriculture in a letter to the Georgia Courier:[2]

---

[2] *Georgia Courier*, October 11, 1827. Reprinted by permission of the publishers, The Arthur H. Clark Company, from *A Documentary History of American Industrial Society*, edited by John R. Commons and others (Cleveland, 1910), I, 284–285.

When I took my last walk along the wharves in Charleston, and saw them piled up with mountains of Cotton, and all your stores, ships, steam and canal boats, crammed with and groaning under, the weight of Cotton, I returned to the Planters' Hotel, where I found the four daily papers, as well as the conversation of the boarders, teeming with Cotton! Cotton!! Cotton!!! Thinks I to myself "I'll soon change this scene of cotton." But, alas! How easily deceived is short-sighted man! Well, I got into my gig and wormed my way up through Queen, Meeting, King, and St. Philip's-streets, dodging from side to side, to steer clear of the cotton waggons, and found a number on the other side, loaded with cotton, going to town. From this I continued on, meeting with little else than cotton fields, cotton gins, cotton waggons—but "the wide, the unbounded prospect lay before me!" I arrived in Augusta; and when I saw cotton waggons in Broad-street, I whistled! but said nothing!!! But this was not all; there was more than a dozen tow boats in the river, with more than a thousand bales of cotton on each; and several steam boats with still more. And you must know, that they have cotton warehouses there covering whole squares, all full of cotton; and some of the knowing ones told me, that there were then in the place from 40,000 to 50,000 bales. And Hamburg (as a negro said) was worser, according to its size; for it puzzled me to tell which was the largest, the piles of cotton or the houses. I now left Augusta; and overtook hordes of cotton planters from North Carolina, South Carolina, and Georgia, with large gangs of negroes, bound to Alabama, Mississippi and Louisiana; "where the cotton land is not worn out." Besides these, I overtook a number of empty cotton waggons, returning home, and a great many loaded with cotton going to Augusta. Two of these waggons meeting one day, directly opposite me, the following dialogue took place between the drivers—"What's cotton in Augusta?" says the one with a load.—"Cotton!" says the other. The enquirer supposing himself not to be understood, repeats "What's cotton in Augusta?" "It's cotton," says the other. "I know that," says the first, "but what is it?"—"Why," says the other, "I tell you its cotton! cotton is cotton! in Augusta, and every where else, that ever I heard of." "I know that as well as you," says the first, "but what does cotton bring in Augusta?" "Why, it brings nothing there, but everybody brings cotton." "Look here," says the first waggoner, with an oath, "you had better leave the State; for I'll be d—d if you don't know too much for Georgia."

3

Prior to 1815, internal commerce developed very slowly. Many of the frontier regions were without valuable products that could be exchanged for manufactured goods. Beginning with the War of 1812, and increasingly thereafter, internal trade expanded rapidly. Professor Guy S. Callender's comments help to explain why:[3]

The influence which rapidly changed all this was the introduction of cotton culture into the South and its extension after 1815 over the southwest. About the same time, also, there was a considerable extension of sugar culture in Louisiana, and tobacco culture in Kentucky and Tennessee. Here was a group of commodities almost as much in demand everywhere as the precious metals themselves, and having large value in small bulk so that they were able to bear the expense of land transportation for long distances over the poor roads of new settlements. The soil and climate of a vast region was peculiarly suited to the production of cotton, the demand for which was increasing at a prodigious rate. This region was covered by a network of navigable streams that could easily and cheaply float this valuable product to tide water. The timely application of steam power to navigation perfected a natural transportation system entirely ade-

quate for a community devoted to producing a few such commodities and exchanging them with the outside world. In this combination of favoring circumstances the southern half of the country possessed an economic prize beside which the more dramatic discovery of gold in California a generation later sinks into comparative insignificance. It provided the inhabitants of a large part of this section with the means of satisfying their wants by trade similar to that which the later gold discoveries furnished to a comparatively small number of people. It furnished to the settlers in the southwest both the staples they could easily produce and a market for those staples. Thus for the first time did the pioneer of the West possess the necessary conditions for rapid progress in the accumulation of wealth.

The effect of these economic advantages was not confined to the South. Very soon they were felt by every other section of the country. The great profit to be secured in the cultivation of cotton and sugar caused the people of South Carolina and the Gulf States to devote themselves chiefly to these industries and to neglect the other branches of agriculture. The gradual absorption of these industries by planters with slave labor increased this tendency, as the one advantage of that labor, viz., its capacity for being organized, could only be utilized in them. Mixed farming could not be profitably carried on by slaves in the South; hence the planters were glad to purchase their agricultural supplies, so far as possible, from other producers. The live stock could be driven overland to the plantations, and the great network of rivers with their flatboats and steamboats provided an easy means of transportation for other supplies. All kinds of produce, from such important products as pork, bacon, lard, beef, butter, cheese, corn, flour, and whiskey to such little ones as apples, cider, vinegar, soap, and candles, went down the Ohio and Mississippi in great quantities. This was the first important market which the farmers of Tennessee, Kentucky, and the northwest secured, and it

[3] Guy S. Callender, *Selections from the Economic History of the United States, 1765–1860, With Introductory Essays* (Boston, 1909), pp. 272–274. Reprinted by permission of the publishers, Ginn and Company.

wrought an improvement in their economic situation almost as remarkable as the introduction of cotton culture produced in the southwest.

The prosperity of the South and West now in turn influenced the East. The people of these sections were able for the first time to purchase freely from other communities. The commodities to satisfy their wants were partly imported from abroad, and partly produced in New England and the Middle States. Accordingly, both the commercial and manufacturing interests of this section were greatly stimulated. New York reached out with her Erie Canal to secure a larger share of the growing internal trade, and a keen rivalry sprang up among the commercial cities of the seaboard which has lasted to the present day. Manufactures also began now to feel the influence of that expanding home market which has played so great a part in their development ever since.

The growth of commercial cities and manufacturing towns in turn provided a home market for the northern farmers. This did not at first affect the northwest as Henry Clay and the protectionists of the time expected, for little western produce was sent east over the canals until after 1840. The farmers of the Middle States were, however, greatly benefited by the development of a home market in the manufacturing and commercial centers; and the numerous canals of this region brought them into close contact with it. In the early forties the northwest began to share in this advantage and sent increasing supplies of produce through the Erie Canal to New England. With the Irish famine and the repeal of the English Corn Laws, a foreign market for their grain and provisions also arose. From both these sources their means of purchasing eastern manufactures was greatly increased.

Finally, those sections of the older slave states which were not able to produce cotton, especially Maryland, Virginia, and North Carolina, were not left entirely unaffected by this great movement. In the first place they were able through the coasting trade

to share in supplying the commercial and manufacturing communities of the northeast with agricultural produce. Then the rapid extension of cotton culture into the southwest opened a profitable field for the employment of their surplus slave labor, which since the Revolution had been felt to be a burden upon them. The rise of an active internal slave trade transformed this burden into an economic resource. . . .

This account is sufficient to make clear the general character of internal commerce. Its basis was a territorial division of labor among the three great sections of the country resting upon foreign commerce. The South was able to devote itself chiefly to the production of a few staples, turning out a great surplus of them for export and depending upon the other two sections for much of its agricultural produce, nearly all of its manufactures, and to a large extent for the conduct of its commerce. Both its exports and imports were carried largely by northern shipping, went through northern ports, and was either actually in the hands of northern merchants or financed by northern capital. The northwest devoted itself chiefly to agriculture, depending at first entirely upon the South for its markets, but gradually acquiring after 1840 a home market in the northeast and a foreign one in Europe. New England and the Middle States were devoted principally to commerce and manufactures by which they were enabled to supply the needs of the other two sections, depending at first upon their own farmers for their agricultural supplies and later drawing them partly from the southern seaboard slave states and partly from the northwest, especially from the region about the Great Lakes.

GOVERNMENT AID AND REGIONAL INTERESTS

4

With each section of the nation concentrating on one type of economic enterprise, improved transportation suddenly became necessary; if New Englanders were to be fed, Westerners clothed, and Southerners provided with a market for their cotton, roads and canals must connect the three sections. The undertaking was so vast that the limited funds of either the states or private enterprise were inadequate; hence the federal government must act. That was the demand ringing through the halls of Congress in the postwar years, voiced especially by western and southern representatives. Of the Westerners, none was more outspoken than Henry Clay of Kentucky. His speech on internal improvements, delivered before the House of Representatives in January 1824, expresses the attitude of his section:[4]

But, Mr. Chairman, if there be any part of this Union more likely than all others to be benefited by the adoption of the . . . principle, regulating the public expenditure, it is the West. There is a perpetual drain from that embarrassed and highly distressed portion of our country, of its circulating medium to the East. There, but few and inconsiderable expenditures of the public money take place. There we have none of those public works, no magnificent edifices, forts, armories, arsenals, dockyards, &c. which more or less are to be found in every Atlantic State. In at least seven States beyond the Alleghany, not one solitary public work of this Government is to be found. If, by one of those awful and terrible dispensations of Providence, which sometimes occur, this Government should be unhappily annihilated, every where on the seaboard traces of its former existence would be found; whilst we should not have, in the West, a single monument remaining on which to pour out our affections and our regrets. Yet, Sir, we do not complain. No portion of your population is more loyal to the Union, than the hardy freemen of the West. Nothing can weaken or eradicate their ardent desire for its lasting preservation. None are more prompt to vindicate the interests and rights of the nation from all foreign aggression. Need I remind you of the glorious scenes in which they participated, during the late war —a war in which they had no peculiar or

direct interest, waged for no commerce, no seamen of theirs? But it was enough for them that it was a war demanded by the character and the honour of the nation. They did not stop to calculate its cost of blood, or of treasure. They flew to arms; they rushed down the valley of the Mississippi, with all the impetuosity of that noble river. They sought the enemy. They found him at the beach. They fought; they bled; they covered themselves and their country with immortal glory. They enthusiastically shared in all the transports occasioned by our victories, whether won on the ocean or on the land. They felt, with the keenest distress, whatever disaster befel us. No, Sir, I repeat it, neglect, injury itself, cannot alienate the affections of the West from this Government. They cling to it, as to their best, their greatest, their last hope. You may impoverish them, reduce them to ruin, by the mistakes of your policy, and you cannot drive them from you. They do not complain of the expenditure of the public money, where the public exigencies require its disbursement. But, I put it to your candour, if you ought not, by a generous and national policy, to mitigate, if not prevent, the evils resulting from the perpetual transfer of the circulating medium from the West to the East. One million and a half of dollars annually, is transferred for the public lands alone; and, almost every dollar goes, like him who goes to death—to a bourne from which no traveller returns. In ten years it will amount to fifteen millions; in twenty to——; but I will not pursue the appalling results of arithmetic. Gentlemen who believe that these vast sums are supplied by emigrants from the East, labor under great error. There was a time when the tide of emigration from the East bore along with it the means to effect the purchase of the public domain. But the time has, in a great measure, now stopped. And as population advances farther and farther West, it will entirely cease. The greatest migrating States in the Union, at this time, are Kentucky first, Ohio next, and Tennessee. The emigrants from those States carry with them,

---

[4] *Annals of Congress,* 18th Cong., 1st Sess. 1038–1042 (1824).

to the States and territories lying beyond them, the circulating medium, which, being invested in the purchase of the public land, is transmitted to the points where the wants of government require it. If this debilitating and exhausting process were inevitable, it must be borne with manly fortitude. But we think that a fit exertion of the powers of this Government would mitigate the evil. We believe that the Government incontestibly possesses the Constitutional power to execute such internal improvements as are called for by the good of the whole. And we appeal to your equity, to your parental regard, to your enlightened policy, to perform the high and beneficial trust thus sacredly reposed. I am sensible of the delicacy of the topic to which I have reluctantly adverted, in consequence of the observations of the honourable gentleman from Virginia. And I hope there will be no misconception of my motives in dwelling upon it. A wise and considerate government should anticipate and prevent, rather than wait for the operation of causes of discontent.

Let me ask, Mr. Chairman, what has this government done on the great subject of Internal Improvements, after so many years of its existence, and with such an inviting field before it? You have made the Cumberland road only. Gentlemen appear to me to have considered that a western road. They ought to recollect that not one stone has yet been broken, not one spade of earth has been yet removed in any Western State. The road begins in Maryland, and it terminates at Wheeling. It passes through the states of Maryland, Pennsylvania, and Virginia. All the direct benefit of the expenditure of the public money on that road, has accrued to those three States. Not one cent in any Western State. And yet we have had to beg, entreat, supplicate you, session after session, to grant the necessary appropriations to complete the road. I have myself toiled until my powers have been exhausted and prostrated, to prevail on you to make the grant. We were actuated to make these exertions for the sake of the collateral benefit only to the West;

that we might have a way by which we should be able to continue and maintain an affectionate intercourse with our friends and brethren—that we might have a way to reach the Capitol of our country, and to bring our councils, humble as they may be, to consult and mingle with yours in the advancement of the national prosperity. Yes, Sir, the Cumberland road has only reached the margin of a Western State; and, from some indications which have been given during this session, I should apprehend it would there pause for ever, if my confidence in you were not unbounded; if I had not before witnessed that appeals were never unsuccessful to your justice, to your magnanimity, to your fraternal affection.

But, Sir, the bill on your table is no Western bill. It is emphatically a national bill, comprehending all, looking to the interests of the whole. The people of the West never thought of, never desired, never asked, for a system exclusively for their benefit. The system contemplated by this bill looks to great national objects, and proposes the ultimate application to their accomplishment of the only means by which they can be effected, the means of the nation—means which, if they be withheld from such objects, the Union, I do most solemnly believe, of these now happy and promising States, may, at some distant (I trust a far, far distant) day, be endangered and shaken at its centre.

5

Equally insistent on government aid was young John C. Calhoun of South Carolina, later to become the leading opponent of extended federal power. His 1817 speech on behalf of internal improvements was as impassioned as any from the lips of nationalistic Westerners:[5]

We occupy a surface prodigiously great in proportion to our numbers. The common strength is brought to bear with great difficulty on the point that may be menaced by an enemy. It is our duty, then, as far as in the nature of things it can be effected, to

---

[5] *Ibid.,* 14th Cong., 2d Sess. 852–854 (1817).

counteract this weakness. Good roads and canals judiciously laid out, are the proper remedy. In the recent war, how much did we suffer for the want of them! Besides the tardiness and the consequential inefficacy of of our military movements, to what an increased expense was the country put for the article of transportation alone! In the event of another war, the saving in this particular would go far towards indemnifying us the expense of constructing the means of transportation.

It is not, however, in this respect only, that roads and canals add to the strength of the country. Our power of raising revenue, in war particularly, depends . . . mainly on them. In peace our revenue depends principally on the imposts; in war this source, in a great measure, fails, and internal taxes, to a great amount, become necessary. Unless the means of commercial intercourse are rendered much more perfect than they now are, we shall never be able in war to raise the necessary supplies. . . . The taxes are raised in every part of this extensive country, uniformly; but the expenditure must, in its nature, be principally confined to the scene of military operations. This drains the circulating medium from one part and accumulates it in another, and perhaps a very distant one. The result . . . is obvious. Unless it can return through the operation of trade, the parts from which the constant drain takes place must ultimately be impoverished. Commercial intercourse is the true remedy to this weakness; and the means by which that is to be effected, are roads, canals, and the coasting trade. On these, combined with domestic manufactures, does the moneyed capacity of this country, in war, depend. Without them, not only will we be unable to raise the necessary supplies, but the currency of the country must necessarily fall into the greatest disorder—such as we lately experienced.

But on this subject of national power, what . . . can be more important than a perfect unity in every part, in feelings and sentiments? And what can tend more powerfully to produce it, than overcoming the effects of distance? No country, enjoying freedom, ever occupied anything like as great an extent of country as this Republic. . . . and, what is most remarkable, such is the happy mould of our Government, so well are the State and general powers blended, that much of our political happiness draws its origin from the extent of our Republic. . . . Let it not, however, be forgotten, let it . . . be forever kept in mind that it exposes us to the greatest of all calamities, next to the loss of liberty, and even to that in its consequence—*disunion*. We are great, and rapidly . . . growing. This is our pride and danger—our weakness and our strength. Little . . . does he deserve to be intrusted with the liberties of this people, who does not raise his mind to these truths. We are under the most imperious obligation to counteract every tendency to disunion. The strongest of all cements is, undoubtedly, the wisdom, justice, and above all, the moderation of this House; yet the great subject on which we are now deliberating, in this respect, deserves the most serious consideration. Whatever . . . impedes the intercourse of the extremes with this, the centre of the Republic, weakens the Union. The more enlarged the sphere of commercial circulation, the more extended that of social intercourse; the more strongly are we bound together; the more inseparable are our destinies. Those who understand the human heart best, know how powerfully distance tends to break the sympathies of our nature. Nothing, not even dissimilarity of language, tends more to estrange man from man. Let us then . . . bind the Republic together with a perfect system of roads and canals. Let us conquer space. It is thus that the most distant parts of the Republic will be brought within a few days travel of the centre; it is thus that a citizen of the West will read the news of Boston still moist from the press. The mail and the press . . . are the nerves of the body politic. By them the slightest impression made on the most remote parts is communicated to the whole system; and the more perfect the means of transportation, the more rapid and true the vibration.

6

The nationalistic spirit of Clay and Webster was more than equalled by the attitudes of the new administration in Washington. President John Quincy Adams, in his first annual message to Congress, December 6, 1825, went far beyond rivers, harbors, roads, and canals:[6]

Upon this first occasion of addressing the Legislature of the Union, with which I have been honored, in presenting to their view the execution so far as it has been effected of the measures sanctioned by them for promoting the internal improvement of our country, I can not close the communication without recommending to their calm and persevering consideration the general principle in a more enlarged extent. The great object of the institution of civil government is the improvement of the condition of those who are parties to the social compact, and no government, in whatever form constituted, can accomplish the lawful ends of its institution but in proportion as it improves the condition of those over whom it is established. Roads and canals, by multiplying and facilitating the communications and intercourse between distant regions and multitudes of men, are among the most important means of improvement. But moral, political, intellectual improvement are duties assigned by the Author of Our Existence to social no less than to individual man. For the fulfillment of those duties governments are invested with power, and to the attainment of the end—the progressive improvement of the condition of the governed—the exercise of delegated powers is a duty as sacred and indispensable as the usurpation of powers not granted is criminal and odious. Among the first, perhaps the very first, instrument for the improvement of the condition of men is

6 James D. Richardson (comp.), *A Compilation of the Messages and Papers of Presidents, 1789–1902* (Washington, 1903), II, 311–314.

knowledge, and to the acquisition of much of the knowledge adapted to the wants, the comforts, and enjoyments of human life public institutions and seminaries of learning are essential. So convinced of this was the first of my predecessors in this office, now first in the memory, as, living, he was first in the hearts, of our countrymen, that once and again in his addresses to the Congresses with whom he cooperated in the public service he earnestly recommended the establishment of seminaries of learning, to prepare for all the emergencies of peace and war—a national university and a military academy. With respect to the latter, had he lived to the present day, in turning his eyes to the institution at West Point he would have enjoyed the gratification of his most earnest wishes; but in surveying the city which has been honored with his name he would have seen the spot of earth which he had destined and bequeathed to the use and benefit of his country as the site for an university still bare and barren.

In assuming her station among the civilized nations of the earth it would seem that our country had contracted the engagement to contribute her share of mind, of labor, and of expense to the improvement of those parts of knowledge which lie beyond the reach of individual acquisition, and particularly to geographical and astronomical science. Looking back to the history only of the half century since the declaration of our independence, and observing the generous emulation with which the Governments of France, Great Britain, and Russia have devoted the genius, the intelligence, the treasures of their respective nations to the common improvement of the species in these branches of science, is it not incumbent upon us to inquire whether we are not bound by obligations of a high and honorable character to contribute our portion of energy and exertion to the common stock? The voyages of discovery prosecuted in the course of that time at the expense of those nations have not only redounded to their glory, but to the improvement of human knowledge. We have been partakers of that improvement and owe for it a sacred debt, not only of gratitude, but of equal or proportional exertion in the same common cause. Of the cost of these undertakings, if the mere expenditures of outfit, equipment, and completion of the expeditions were to be considered the only charges, it would be unworthy of a great and generous nation to take a second thought. One hundred expeditions of circumnavigation like those of Cook and La Pérouse would not burden the exchequer of the nation fitting them out so much as the ways and means of defraying a single campaign in war. But if we take into the account the lives of those benefactors of mankind of which their services in the cause of their species were the purchase, how shall the cost of those heroic enterprises be estimated, and what compensation can be made to them or to their countries for them? Is it not by bearing them in affectionate remembrance? Is it not still more by imitating their example—by enabling countrymen of our own to pursue the same career and to hazard their lives in the same cause?

In inviting the attention of Congress to the subject of internal improvements upon a view thus enlarged it is not my design to recommend the equipment of an expedition for circumnavigating the globe for purposes of scientific research and inquiry. We have objects of useful investigation nearer home, and to which our cares may be more beneficially applied. The interior of our own territories has yet been very imperfectly explored. Our coasts along many degrees of latitude upon the shores of the Pacific Ocean, though much frequented by our spirited commercial navigators, have been barely visited by our public ships. The River of the West, first fully discovered and navigated by a countryman of our own, still bears the name of the ship in which he ascended its waters, and claims the protection of our armed national flag at its mouth. With the establishment of a military post there or at some other point of that coast, recommended by my

predecessor and already matured in the deliberations of the last Congress, I would suggest the expediency of connecting the equipment of a public ship for the exploration of the whole northwest coast of this continent.

The establishment of an uniform standard of weights and measures was one of the specific objects contemplated in the formation of our Constitution, and to fix that standard was one of the powers delegated by express terms in that instrument to Congress. The Governments of Great Britain and France have scarcely ceased to be occupied with inquiries and speculations on the same subject since the existence of our Constitution, and with them it has expanded into profound, laborious, and expensive researches into the figure of the earth and the comparative length of the pendulum vibrating seconds in various latitudes from the equator to the pole. These researches have resulted in the composition and publication of several works highly interesting to the cause of science. The experiments are yet in the process of performance. Some of them have recently been made on our own shores, within the walls of one of our own colleges, and partly by one of our own fellow-citizens. It would be honorable to our country if the sequel of the same experiments should be countenanced by the patronage of our Government, as they have hitherto been by those of France and Britain.

Connected with the establishment of an university, or separate from it, might be undertaken the erection of an astronomical observatory, with provision for the support of an astronomer, to be in constant attendance of observation upon the phenomena of the heavens, and for the periodical publication of his observations. It is with no feeling of pride as an American that the remark may be made that on the comparatively small territorial surface of Europe there are existing upward of 130 of these light-houses of the skies, while throughout the whole American hemisphere there is not one. If we reflect a moment upon the discoveries which in the last four centuries have been made in the physical constitution of the universe by the means of these buildings and of observers stationed in them, shall we doubt of their usefulness to every nation? And while scarcely a year passes over our heads without bringing some new astronomical discovery to light, which we must fain receive at second hand from Europe, are we not cutting ourselves off from the means of returning light for light while we have neither observatory nor observer upon our half of the globe and the earth revolves in perpetual darkness to our unsearching eyes?

7

Internal improvements of all kinds promised benefits to the whole nation, but the needs of the West were particularly acute. Professor Callender offers an explanation:[7]

In considering the way in which new settlements have been made and the conditions determining their economic and social progress, two circumstances appear to be of prime importance. The first is whether or no they possess markets for those commodities which their natural resources enable the settlers to easily produce. . . .

The second circumstance affecting the settlement of new territory is the extent to which the settlers are able to secure the cooperation of capital from older communities to assist them. This has played nearly as important a part in the settlement of new countries in recent times as the possession of markets. The nature of this influence and the extent to which it has changed the process of pioneering ought to be pointed out. Capital may cooperate in the settlement of new territory in several ways. First, it may supply stocks of commodities of all kinds to meet the immediate wants of settlers before they have had time to produce such forms of wealth as they require. These stocks are accumulated in the new country to some ex-

tent by merchants using their own capital, but much more through the agency of commercial credit extended to the local merchants by commercial houses in older communities. These stocks are sold to the settlers largely upon credit. Secondly, capital may provide transportation facilities to connect the settlers with the outside world and especially with those markets which are so necessary to their prosperity. This usually takes the form of organizing steamboat companies, improving the navigation of the streams, building important roads, and, above all, the construction of railroads. Finally, capital from older communities may provide loans of cash directly to the settlers which will enable them to procure by purchase either the various concrete forms of capital needed by them in their industries or that surplus of means of subsistence for the population which is the first step which every community must take in the accumulation of capital. The community must have something to live upon while it devotes its labor to the opening of roads, the clearing and improvement of lands, the building of saw and grist mills, and the creation of other forms of capital needed to carry on industry. This means of subsistence may be secured through the agency of loans negotiated by individuals, corporations, or governments in older communities. The population may live upon the proceeds of such loans while it creates capital of various kinds. . . .

The difference in the social and economic condition of a community of pioneers who have all their more pressing, immediate wants for either subsistence or implements of industry supplied to them in this way, and of one in which the settlers must secure these by the slow process of saving and accumulation, is very great. In the latter the settlers must make their own way into the wilderness, providing their own means of transportation, and carrying with them such supplies of subsistence as are needed until they have had time to produce others, and also such tools and utensils as are required to begin industries. They must then create by

[7] Guy S. Callender, *Selections from the Economic History of the United States, 1765–1860, With Introductory Essays* (Boston, 1909), pp. 598–600. Reprinted by permission of the publishers, Ginn and Company.

their own labor, while they provide subsistence for themselves and families, all the forms of concrete capital which a civilized community requires. Even when they possess markets for one or two staple commodities, easily produced and exchangeable for whatever forms of wealth they need, their progress must be slow. The rude life of the frontier must continue for a generation or more at least. Without this advantage of markets it may continue indefinitely, as it has done among the mountain population of our southern states.

The experience of a body of emigrants to a new country who have the cooperation of capital in the various ways explained above is very different from all this. They are transported quickly and easily to their new homes with little effort on their part beyond what is necessary to provide money to pay a small railway and steamer fare. There they find stocks of goods of all kinds accumulated and ready to be advanced to them on credit, while they produce some valuable crop for the market. Enterprising men with capital advanced from older communities stand ready to buy these products for cash and send them to the market. After a few years, when they have made improvements upon their land, they are able to secure loans on mortgage and thus to supply themselves with the means of developing their industries and rendering them as efficient as those of older communities. The typical frontier conditions, both economic and social, disappear within a few years and are never so rude as in the other community. It is clear that the application of capital to the settlement of new lands transforms completely the social process of pioneering.

CONSTITUTIONAL POWERS AND VESTED RIGHTS

8

As effective as internal improvements in fostering nationalism were the Supreme Court decisions of Chief Justice John Marshall. Momentous at the time were three lines of decisions,

forming precedents for the growth and objectives of judicial power. One was Marshall's precedent in Marbury v. Madison (1803), in which he deliberately strengthened the Supreme Court by defying Jeffersonian critics and asserting the right of the Court to review acts of Congress. Another was a series of decisions restricting the power of state legislatures to interfere with vested rights. The third was a group of decisions underwriting nationalism by upholding the power of Congress. A grim old Federalist, Marshall viewed the Court as a bulwark against the dangerous localizing tendencies of Jeffersonianism. Basic among decisions emphasizing national supremacy at the expense of state power were those in McCulloch v. Maryland (1819) and Gibbons v. Ogden (1824). The former concerned Maryland's right to tax the Second Bank of the United States. At issue were two questions: did Congress have the constitutional right to create a national bank, and did the states have the power to tax an instrument of the federal government? In answering the first, Marshall underscored the doctrine of implied powers; he dismissed the second with his famous phrase, "the power to tax is the power to destroy." Most pertinent were the sections of the decision dealing with congressional power:[8]

The first question made in this cause is, has Congress power to incorporate a bank?

It has been truly said, that this can scarcely be considered as an open question, entirely unprejudiced by the former proceedings of the nation respecting it. The principle now contested was introduced at a very early period of our history, has been recognized by many successive legislatures, and has been acted upon by the judicial department, in cases of peculiar delicacy, as a law of undoubted obligation. . . .

In discussing this question, the counsel for the State of Maryland have deemed it of some importance, in the construction of the constitution, to consider that instrument not as emanating from the people, but as the act of sovereign and independent States. The powers of the general government, it has been said, are delegated by the States, who alone are truly sovereign; and must be exercised in subordination to the States, who alone possess supreme dominion.

---

[8] 4 WHEATON 401–415, 420, 423.

It would be difficult to sustain this proposition. The convention which framed the constitution was, indeed, elected by the State legislatures. But the instrument, when it came from their hands, was a mere proposal, without obligation, or pretensions to it. It was reported to the then existing Congress of the United States, with a request that it might "be submitted to a convention of Delegates, chosen in each State by the people thereof, under the recommendation of its legislature, for their assent and ratification." This mode of proceeding was adopted; and by the Convention, by Congress, and by the State Legislatures, the instrument was submitted to the people. They acted upon it in the only manner in which they can act safely, effectively, and wisely, on such a subject, by assembling in Convention. It is true, they assembled in their several States—and where else should they have assembled? No political dreamer was ever wild enough to think of breaking down the lines which separate the States, and of compounding the American people into one common mass. Of consequence, when they act, they act in their States. But the measures they adopt do not, on that account, cease to be the measures of the people themselves, or become the measures of the State governments.

From these Conventions the constitution derives its whole authority. The government proceeds directly from the people; is "ordained and established" in the name of the people; and is declared to be ordained, "in order to form a more perfect union, establish justice, insure domestic tranquillity, and secure the blessings of liberty to themselves and to their posterity." The assent of the States, in their sovereign capacity, is implied in calling a Convention, and thus submitting that instrument to the people. But the people were at perfect liberty to accept or reject it; and their act was final. It required not the affirmance, and could not be negatived, by the State governments. The constitution, when thus adopted, was of complete obligation, and bound the State sovereignties. . . .

The government of the Union, then,

(whatever may be the influence of this fact on the case,) is, emphatically and truly a government of the people. In form and in substance it emanates from them. Its powers are granted by them, and are to be exercised directly on them, and for their benefit.

This government is acknowledged by all to be one of enumerated powers. The principle, that it can exercise only the powers granted to it, would seem too apparent to have required to be enforced by all those arguments which its enlightened friends, while it was depending before the people, found it necessary to urge. That principle is now universally admitted. But the question respecting the extent of the powers actually granted, is perpetually arising, and will probably continue to arise, as long as our system shall exist.

In discussing these questions, the conflicting powers of the general and State governments must be brought into view, and the supremacy of their respective laws, when they are in opposition, must be settled.

If any one proposition could command the universal assent of mankind, we might expect it would be this—that the government of the Union, though limited in its powers, is supreme within its sphere of action. This would seem to result necessarily from its nature. It is the government of all; its powers are delegated by all; it represents all, and acts for all. Though any one State may be willing to control its operations, no State is willing to allow others to control them. The nation, on those subjects on which it can act, must necessarily bind its component parts. But this question is not left to mere reason: the people have, in express terms, decided it, by saying, "this constitution, and the laws of the United States, which shall be made in pursuance thereof," "shall be the supreme law of the land," and by requiring that the members of the State legislatures, and the officers of the executive and judicial departments of the States, shall take the oath of fidelity to it.

The government of the United States, though limited in its powers, is supreme;

and its laws, when made in pursuance of the constitution, form the supreme law of the land, "any thing in the constitution or laws of any State to the contrary notwithstanding." . . .

Although, among the enumerated powers of government, we do not find the word "bank," or "incorporation," we find the great powers to lay and collect taxes; to borrow money; to regulate commerce; to declare and conduct a war; and to raise and support armies and navies. The sword and the purse, all the external relations, and no inconsiderable portion of the industry of the nation, are intrusted to its government. It can never be pretended that these vast powers draw after them others of inferior importance, merely because they are inferior. Such an idea can never be advanced. But it may with great reason be contended, that a government, entrusted with such ample powers, on the due execution of which the happiness and prosperity of the nation so vitally depends, must also be entrusted with ample means for their execution. The power being given, it is the interest of the nation to facilitate its execution. It can never be their interest, and cannot be presumed to have been their intention, to clog and embarrass its execution by withholding the most appropriate means. Throughout this vast republic, from the St. Croix to the Gulf of Mexico, from the Atlantic to the Pacific, revenue is to be collected and expended, armies are to be marched and supported. The exigencies of the nation may require, that the treasure raised in the north should be transported to the south, *that* raised in the east conveyed to the west, or that this order should be reversed. Is that construction of the constitution to be preferred which would render these operations difficult, hazardous, and expensive? Can we adopt that construction (unless the words imperiously require it,) which would impute to the framers of that instrument, when granting these powers for the public good, the intention of impeding their exercise by withholding a choice of means? If, indeed, such be the mandate of the constitution, we

have only to obey; but that instrument does not profess to enumerate the means by which the powers it confers may be executed; nor does it prohibit the creation of a corporation, if the existence of such a being be essential to the beneficial exercise of those powers. It is, then, the subject of fair inquiry, how far such means may be employed.

It is not denied, that the powers given to the government imply the ordinary means of execution. That, for example, of raising revenue and applying it to national purposes, is admitted to imply the power of conveying money from place to place, as the exigencies of the nation may require, and of employing the usual means of conveyance. But it is denied that the government has its choice of means, or that it may employ the most convenient means; if to employ them it be necessary to erect a corporation. . . .

The government which has a right to do an act, and has imposed on it the duty of performing that act, must, according to the dictates of reason, be allowed to select the means; and those who contend that it may not select any appropriate means, that one particular mode of effecting the object is excepted, take upon themselves the burden of establishing that exception. . . .

But the constitution of the United States has not left the right of Congress to employ the necessary means, for the execution of the powers conferred on the government, to general reasoning. To its enumeration of powers is added that of making "all laws which shall be necessary and proper, for carrying into execution the foregoing powers, and all other powers vested by this constitution, in the government of the United States, or in any department thereof."

The counsel for the State of Maryland have urged various arguments, to prove that this clause, though in terms a grant of power, is not so in effect; but is really restrictive of the general right, which might otherwise be implied, of selecting means of executing the enumerated powers. . . .

But the argument on which most reliance is to be placed, is drawn from the peculiar language of this clause. Congress is not empowered by it to make all laws, which may have relation to the powers conferred on the government, but such only as may be *"necessary and proper"* for carrying them into execution. The word *"necessary"* is considered as controlling the whole sentence, and as limiting the right to pass laws for the execution of the granted powers, to such as are indispensable, and without which the power would be nugatory. That it excludes the choice of means, and leaves to Congress, in each case, that only which is most direct and simple.

Is it true, that this is the sense in which the word "necessary" is always used? Does it always import an absolute physical necessity, so strong, that one thing, to which another may be termed necessary cannot exist without that other? We think it does not. If reference be had to its use, in the common affairs of the world, or in approved authors, we find that it frequently imports no more than that one thing is convenient, or useful, or essential to another. To employ the means necessary to an end, is generally understood as employing any means calculated to produce the end, and not as being confined to those single means, without which the end would be entirely unattainable. Such is the character of human language, that no word conveys to the mind, in all situations one single definite idea; and nothing is more common than to use words in a figurative sense. Almost all compositions contain words, which, taken in their rigorous sense, would convey a meaning different from that which is obviously intended. It is essential to just construction, that many words which import something excessive, should be understood in a more mitigated sense—in that sense which common usage justifies. The word "necessary" is of this description. It has not a fixed character peculiar to itself. It admits of all degrees of comparison; and is often connected with other words, which increase or diminish the impression the mind receives of the urgency it imports. A thing may be necessary, very necessary, absolutely or in-

dispensably necessary. To no mind would the same idea be conveyed, by these several phrases. . . . This word, then, like others, is used in various senses; and, in its construction, the subject, the context, the intention of the person using them, are all to be taken into view.

Let this be done in the case under consideration. The subject is the execution of those great powers on which the welfare of a nation essentially depends. It must have been the intention of those who gave these powers, to insure, as far as human prudence could insure, their beneficial execution. This could not be done by confiding the choice of means to such narrow limits as not to leave it in the power of Congress, to adopt any which might be appropriate, and which were conducive to the end. This provision is made in a constitution intended to endure for ages to come, and, consequently, to be adapted to the various *crises* of human affairs. To have prescribed the means by which government should, in all future time, execute its powers, would have been to change, entirely, the character of the instrument, and give it the properties of a legal code. It would have been an unwise attempt to provide, by immutable rules, for exigencies which, if foreseen at all, must have been seen dimly, and which can be best provided for as they occur. To have declared that the best means shall not be used, but those alone without which the power given would be nugatory, would have been to deprive the legislature of the capacity to avail itself of experience, to exercise its reason, and to accommodate its legislation to circumstances. . . .

The result of the most careful and attentive consideration bestowed upon this clause is, that if it does not enlarge, it cannot be construed to restrain the powers of Congress, or to impair the right of the legislature to exercise its best judgment in the section of measures to carry into execution the constitutional powers of the government. If no other motive for its insertion can be suggested, a sufficient one is found in the desire to legislate on that vast mass of incidental powers which must be involved in the constitution, if that instrument be not a splendid bauble.

We admit, as all must admit, that the powers of the government are limited, and that its limits are not to be transcended. But we think the sound construction of the constitution must allow to the national legislature that discretion, with respect to the means by which the powers it confers are to be carried into execution, which will enable that body to perform the high duties assigned to it, in the manner most beneficial to the people. Let the end be legitimate, let it be within the scope of the constitution, and all means which are appropriate, which are plainly adapted to that end, which are not prohibited, but consist with the letter and spirit of the constitution, are constitutional. . . .

After the most deliberate consideration, it is the unanimous and decided opinion of this court, that the act to incorporate the Bank of the United States is a law made in pursuance of the constitution, and is a part of the supreme law of the land.

9

Gibbons v. Ogden *involved the right of New York to grant a syndicate monopolistic control over steamboat transportation in the state's waters. Marshall ruled against a state-charted monopoly, holding that all "intercourse" was commerce within the meaning of the "commerce clause" of the Constitution. In defining the term broadly, the Chief Justice laid the basis for the extensive national control of economic activities in the twentieth century:*[9]

It has been contended by the counsel for the appellant, that, as the word "to regulate" implies in its nature, full power over the thing to be regulated, it excludes, necessarily, the action of all others that would perform the same operation on the same thing. That regulation is designed for the entire result, applying to those parts which remain as they were, as well as to those

[9] 9 WHEATON 209–211, 222, 240.

which are altered. It produces a uniform whole, which is as much disturbed and deranged by changing what the regulating power designs to leave untouched, as that on which it has operated.

There is great force in this argument, and the court is not satisfied that it has been refuted.

Since, however, in exercising the power of regulating their own purely internal affairs, whether of trading or police, the states may sometimes enact laws the validity of which depends on their interfering with, and being contrary to, an act of Congress passed in pursuance of the constitution, the court will enter upon the inquiry, whether the laws of New-York, as expounded by the highest tribunal of that State, have, in their application to this case, come into collision with an act of Congress, and deprived a citizen of a right to which that act entitles him. Should this collision exist, it will be immaterial whether those laws were passed in virtue of a concurrent power "to regulate commerce with foreign nations and among the several States," or, in virtue of a power to regulate their domestic trade and police. In one case and the other the acts of New-York must yield to the law of Congress; and the decision sustaining the privilege they confer, against a right given by a law of the Union, must be erroneous.

This opinion has been frequently expressed in this Court, and is founded, as well on the nature of the government as on the words of the constitution. In argument, however, it has been contended that if a law passed by a State, in the exercise of its acknowledged sovereignty, comes into conflict with a law passed by Congress in pursuance of the constitution, they affect the subject, and each other, like equal opposing powers.

But the framers of the constitution foresaw this state of things, and provided for it, by declaring the supremacy not only of itself, but of the laws made in pursuance of it. The nullity of any act, inconsistent with the constitution, is produced by the declaration that the constitution is supreme law. . . .

In every such case, the act of Congress, or the treaty, is supreme; and the law of the State, though enacted in the exercise of powers not controverted, must yield to it. . . .

Powerful and ingenious minds, taking as postulates, that the powers expressly granted to the government of the Union, are to be contracted by construction, into the narrowest possible compass, and that the original powers of the States are retained, if any possible construction will retain them, may, by a course of well digested, but refined and metaphysical reasoning, founded on these premises, explain away the constitution of our country, and leave it a magnificent structure indeed, to look at, but totally unfit for use. They may so entangle and perplex the understanding, as to obscure principles, which were before thought quite plain, and induce doubts where, if the mind were to pursue its own course, none would be perceived. In such a case, it is peculiarly necessary to recur to safe and fundamental principles, to sustain those principles, and, when sustained, to make them the tests of the arguments to be examined.

This Court is, therefore, of opinion, that the decree of the Court of New-York for the Trial of Impeachments and the Correction of Errors, affirming the decree of the Chancellor of that State, which perpetually enjoins the said Thomas Gibbons, the appellant, from navigating the waters of the State of New-York with the steam boats the Stoudinger and the Bellona, by steam or fire, is erroneous, and ought to be reversed, and the same is hereby reversed and annulled: and this Court doth further DIRECT, ORDER, and DECREE, that the bill of the said Aaron Ogden be dismissed, and the same is hereby dismissed accordingly.

10

Almost as important as the decisions in which Marshall broadly construed the powers of the federal government were those in which he stripped powers from the states. Notable was the case of Dartmouth College v. Woodward *(1819), which held that a corporation charter was a contract that could not be altered by the* *legislative agents of a subsequent popular majority. Thus was established a protection for property that gave the vested rights of chartered corporations an immunity from state regulation:*[10]

From this review of the charter, it appears, that Dartmouth College is an eleemosynary institution, incorporated for the purpose of perpetuating the application of the bounty of the donors, to the specified objects of that bounty; that its trustees or governors were originally named by the founder, and invested with the power of perpetuating themselves; that they are not public officers, nor is it a civil institution, participating in the administration of government; but a charity school, or a seminary of education, incorporated for the preservation of its property, and perpetual application of that property to the objects of its creation. . . .

According to the theory of the British constitution, their parliament is omnipotent. To annul corporate rights might give a shock to public opinion, which that government has chosen to avoid; but its power is not questioned. Had parliament, immediately after the emanation of this charter, and the execution of those conveyances which followed it, annulled the instrument, so that the living donors would have witnessed the disappointment of their hopes, the perfidy of the transaction would have been universally acknowledged. Yet then, as now, the donors would have had no interest in the property; then, as now, those who might be students would have had no rights to be violated; then, as now, it might be said that the trustees, in whom the rights of all were combined, possessed no private, individual beneficial interest in the property confided to their protection. Yet the contract would at that time have been deemed sacred by all. What has since occurred to strip it of its inviolability? Circumstances have not changed it. In reason, in justice, and in law, it is now what it was in 1769.

[10] 4 WHEATON 640–644, 649–654.

This is plainly a contract to which the donors, the trustees, and the crown (to whose rights and obligations New-Hampshire succeeds,) were the original parties. It is a contract made on a valuable consideration. It is a contract for the security and disposition of property. It is a contract, on the faith of which, real and personal estate has been conveyed to the corporation. It is then a contract within the letter of the constitution, and within its spirit also, unless the fact that the property is invested by the donors in trustees for the promotion of religion and education, for the benefit of persons who are perpetually changing, though the objects remain the same, shall create a particular exception, taking this case out of the prohibition contained in the constitution.

It is more than possible, that the preservation of rights of this description was not particularly in the view of the framers of the constitution, when the clause under consideration was introduced into that instrument. It is probable, that interferences of more frequent recurrence, to which the temptation was stronger, and of which the mischief was more extensive, constituted the great motive for imposing this restriction on the State legislatures. But although a particular and a rare case may not, in itself, be of sufficient magnitude to induce a rule, yet it must be governed by the rule, when established, unless some plain and strong reason for excluding it can be given. It is not enough to say, that this particular case was not in the mind of the Convention when the article was framed, nor of the American people, when it was adopted. It is necessary to go farther, and to say that, had this particular case been suggested, the language would have been so varied, as to exclude it, or it would have been made a special exception. The case being within the words of the rule, must be within its operation likewise, unless there be something in the literal construction so obviously absurd, or mischievous, or repugnant to the general spirit of the instrument, as to justify those who expound the constitution in making it an exception.

On what safe and intelligent ground can this exception stand? There is no expression in the constitution, no sentiment delivered by its contemporaneous expounders, which would justify us in making it. . . .

The opinion of the court, after mature deliberation, is, that this is a contract, the obligation of which cannot be impaired without violating the constitution of the United States. This opinion appears to us to be equally supported by reason, and by the former decisions of this court.

2. We next proceed to the inquiry whether its obligation has been impaired by those acts of the legislature of New Hampshire, to which the special verdict refers. . . .

The obligations then, which were created by the charter to Dartmouth College, were the same in the new that they had been in the old government. The power of the government was also the same. A repeal of this charter at any time prior to the adoption of the present constitution of the United States, would have been an extraordinary and unprecedented act of power, but one which could have been contested only by the restrictions upon the legislature to be found in the constitution of the state. But the consitution of the United States has imposed this additional limitation, that the legislature of a state shall pass no act "impairing the obligation of contracts."

It has been already stated that the act "to amend the charter and enlarge and improve the corporation of Dartmouth College," increases the number of trustees to twenty-one, gives the appointment of the additional members to the executive of the state, and creates a board of overseers, to consist of twenty-five persons, of whom twenty-one are also appointed by the executive of New Hampshire, who have power to inspect and control the most important acts of the trustees.

On the effect of this law, two opinions cannot be entertained. Between acting directly, and acting through the agency of trustees and overseers, no essential difference is perceived. The whole power of governing the college is transformed from trustees appointed according to the will of the founder, expressed in the charter, to the executive of New Hampshire. The management and application of the funds of this eleemosynary institution, which are placed by the donors in the hands of trustees named in the charter, and empowered to perpetuate themselves, are placed by this act under the control of the government of the state. The will of the state is substituted for the will of the donors, in every essential operation of the college. This is not an immaterial change. . . . This system is totally changed. The charter of 1769 exists no longer. It is reorganized; and reorganized in such a manner as to convert a literary institution, molded according to the will of its founders, and placed under the control of private literary men, into a machine entirely subservient to the will of government. This may be for the advantage of this college in particular, and may be for the advantage of literature in general; but it is not according to the will of the donors, and is subversive of that contract on the faith of which their property was given. . . .

It results from this opinion, that the acts of the legislature of New Hampshire, which are stated in the special verdict found in this cause, are repugnant to the constitution of the United States; and that the judgment on this special verdict ought to have been for the plaintiffs. The judgment of the State Court must, therefore, be reversed.

11

Marshall's insistence on "loose construction" and broad national authority allowed the United States to adjust itself to the changed conditions ushered in by the revolutions in economics of the late nineteenth century. Had he not been so insistent on elevating nationalism above localism, the Constitution would have been deprived of the elasticity that permitted it to function in a machine age. A student of modern life, Max
Lerner, analyzes the present-day impact of those decisions in his Ideas Are Weapons *(1939):[11]*

These decisions were part of the upswing of a rising capitalism. Through them Marshall sought to strengthen congressional jurisdiction over the two main lines of business expansion of the day—a national banking system and a national transportation system. In the early stages of industrial capitalism, the function of a central government was to ensure favorable conditions for the development of business enterprise.

Marshall here had the advantage of working with the course of history. He had vision enough to see that political power had to be coterminous with the scale of economic activity. He saw it only dimly, and it was obscured in his mind by a hatred of states' rights and of the common man, and by a protective obsession about the rights of property. But his historical meaning for us lies none the less in this dim insight of his. The position of his opponents, such as Jefferson and John Taylor, embodied an archaic economic vision, whatever the merits of their political views. They dreamed the Physiocratic dream of a society that was even then beyond recall—a republic of small farmers. They failed to see that technology was settling that question for them, and that the issue was now not between states' rights and national power, but between some form of control and no control at all. If, instead of following a policy of states'-rights obstructionism, they had come out frankly for national legislative control of the developing industrial system, Marshall's much vaunted nationalism would quickly have changed to a different tune. What it amounted to was aid and tolerance for business enterprise, both of them on a national scale.

As American capitalism developed, it was inevitable that the mere absence of restraint

---

[11] From *Ideas Are Weapons*, pp. 34–36, by Max Lerner, copyright 1939, by Max Lerner. Reprinted by permission of the Viking Press, Inc., New York.

over private property should no longer be adequate to resolve the deepening contradictions of economic life. In the search for new methods of economic control through the federal government, Marshall's judicial nationalism proved a memorable instrument. The Marshall technique of interpretation became a tradition that created new uses not only for the commerce power, but for the taxing and spending power of Congress as well. It is this technique which, since the eighteen-seventies, has formed one facet of judicial liberalism. And it was upon the continuation of this technique that the administration laid its hope for the New Deal legislation. Indeed, a very good case could have been made out, on the basis of continuous precedents since the Swift case in 1905, when the nature of our market economy had already become clear to some of the Justices, that all important business enterprise today is interstate commerce, that the whole industrial process is an unbroken chain flung out over a national market, and that every important link in that chain is therefore a link in interstate commerce.

But the important question, as we have since learned, is not whether the Court *could if it would* interpret the commerce clause broadly enough to validate legislative control of industry, but whether it *would if it could*. And to explain its unwillingness we have to go back to Marshall as surely as we do when we wish to explain its competence. Marshall's class interest took two forms in his own thinking: the doctrine of the vested rights of property and the doctrine of judicial nationalism. Each of these has given rise to a tradition that has been followed in the later history of the Court, the first principally by the conservatives, the second principally by the liberals. And it need scarcely be added that the dominant one has been not the broad interpretation of the Constitution in the interests of federal jurisdiction over industry, but the setting up of the Supreme Court as the guardian of the vested interests. In Marshall's thought, in the period of a rising capitalism, these

two streams could flow together smoothly and feed each other. But the movement of economic events has caused a deepening cleavage between them.

Today, in a period of capitalist crisis, to follow Marshall's vested-rights tradition means to entrench further the hegemony of Big Ownership; to follow his tradition of judicial nationalism means for a time to salvage capitalism, but to salvage it by stripping it of some of its powers; and, more important, it means to maintain tolerable standards of wages and working conditions. Today, even more than in Marshall's time, the issue is one between national control of business enterprise and no control at all. What the Court thus far has done has been to turn its back on everything in the Marshall tradition that was worth following, everything that was an abiding part of the campaign of history. And it has chosen to cling to that part of his tradition which was narrow, immediate, and actuated chiefly by a jealous and exclusive class interest.

SLAVERY AND SECTIONAL COMPROMISE

12

The writer of the following selection was Timothy Flint, a Massachusetts man who became a clergyman, an editor, and a novelist after his graduation from Harvard. His description, written in 1826, records impressions of life among the Louisiana sugar planters shortly after the War of 1812:[12]

The opulent planters of this state have many amiable traits of character. They are high-minded and hospitable, in an eminent degree. I have sojourned much among them, and have never experienced a more frank, dignified, and easy hospitality. . . . You enter without ceremony, call for what you wish, and intimate your wishes to the servants. In short you are made to feel yourself at home. This simple and noble hospitality

---

[12] Timothy Flint, *Recollections of the Last Ten Years* (Boston, 1826), pp. 335–337.

seems to be a general trait among these planters, for I have not yet called at a single house, where it has not been exercised towards me. Suppose the traveller to be a gentleman, to speak French, and to have letters to one respectable planter, it becomes an introduction to the settlement, and he will have no occasion for a tavern.

It results in some way from their condition, from their ample income, or perhaps as they would say, from the influence of slavery, that they are liberal in their feelings, as it respects expenditure, and are more reckless of the value of money, than any people that I have seen. The ladies no doubt have their tea-table, or rather their coffee-table scandal. But I confess, that I have seen less of that prying curiosity to look into the affairs of neighbours, and have heard less scandal here, than in other parts of the United States.

The luxury of the table is carried to a great extent among them. They are ample in their supply of wines, though Claret is generally drunk. Every family is provided with Claret, as we at the North are with cider. I have scarcely seen an instance of intoxication among the respectable planters. In drinking, the guests universally raise their glasses, and touch them together instead of a health. In the morning, before you rise, a cup of strong coffee is offered you. After the dessert at dinner, you are offered another. It is but very recently that the ladies have begun to drink tea. During the warm months, before you retire, it is the custom in many places for a black girl to take off your stockings, and perform the ancient ceremonial of washing the feet. . . .

An intelligent and instructed planter's family is certainly a delightful family in which to make a short sojourn, and they have many of the lesser virtues exercised in a way so peculiar, and appropriate to their modes of existence, as to impress you with all the freshness of novelty. Unhappily, as appertains to all earthly things, there is a dark ground to the picture. The men are "sudden and quick in quarrel." The dirk or the pistol

is always at hand. Fatal duels frequently occur. They are profane, and excessively addicted to gambling. This horrible vice, so intimately associated with so many others, prevails like an epidemic. Money gotten easily, and without labour, is easily lost. Betting and horse-racing are amusements eagerly pursued, and often times to the ruin of the parties. A Louisianian will forego any pleasure, to witness and bet at a horse-race. Even the ladies visit these amusements, and bet with the gentlemen.

13

Thomas E. Watson of Georgia was a different kind of planter. Living at the home of his Horton grandfather in the years before the Civil War, young Watson recalled that his people, though comfortably situated, were never given to display. Yet Horton owned eighty-one slaves. Fewer than four thousand slaveholders in the entire South owned as many:[13]

We Hortons were a family of middle-class farmers. We had never been anything else. We never expected to be anything else. Our condition was good enough for us. We had plenty of land. We had always had it. From the time that the original Horton came down into East Georgia, along with a Quaker Colony, from North Carolina, which took possession of a tract of forty thousand acres, we had occupied the comfortable position of local landowners.

The Hortons had grown tobacco on their farms until Eli Whitney, Jesse Bull, Nathan Lyons, Daniel Pratt, and several others, invented the cotton-gin. Then they began to grow cotton. But they never failed to make it their object to produce on the farm the necessary supplies: tobacco or cotton being merely the surplus crop, the "money" crop.

Yes: we had prospered: and had always been independent. We were not rich, you understand: just comfortable; with good farms, fat stock, and likely niggers. We owed no debts; we had a few hundred of dollars in pocket, ready for an emergency—such as

[13] Thomas E. Watson, *Bethany* (New York, 1904), pp. 3–10.

a request for a loan to some friend who might have got into a temporary "tight" by betting on the wrong horse, or by trying to make four queens beat a straight flush.

In such cases, the neighbor was welcome to the money. Perhaps he might give his "Promisserry" note for it. Oftener, he did not. To take a "Promisserry" note was considered very formal—if not exacting.

My grandfather owned some thirteen hundred acres of land, and his slaves, counting the children, numbered eighty-one. He was a man of few words, had no fondness for display, was well satisfied with his modest fortune; and in a quiet way took a pride in the fine appearance of his fields, fences, houses, mules, cows, hogs, and negroes. His face was rather stern, his eye somewhat severe, and his manner did not invite familiarity. Tall, square-framed, towering above other men, my grandfather filled me with awe. I used to wonder whether he was not a fair agricultural copy of General Washington.

The mansion in which we lived was a very modest affair. It did not, in the least, resemble a Grecian Temple which had been sent into exile, and which was striving, unsuccessfully, to look at ease among corn-cribs, cow-pens, horse-stables, pig-styes, chicken-houses, negro cabins, and worm-fenced cotton fields. It did not perch upon the top of the highest hill for miles around, and brow-beat the whole community with its arrogant self-assertion. No: ours was just a plain house and none too large, not built out of bricks brought over from England, but of timbers torn from the heart of the long-leaf Georgia pine.

The main body was made of logs hewed with the broad-axe, smoothed with the foot-adze, and joined powerfully at the ends—the four corners—by being interlocked into deep notches; upon these solid, heavy logs was laid, inside and out, a covering of plank: strong sleepers bore up the plank floor, stout rafters held the shingle roof. There you had the main body of the original house, which a partition, running from side to side nearest the western end, cut into two equal parts,

the smaller being a bedroom, the larger being the living room, where life on the homestead centered. Springing off from the main roof, other rafters reached downward to rest upon outer plates— forming a shed-roof; the half of this, being closed in with planks, made a shed room: the other half, left unenclosed, but floored, made a back piazza. Two stone chimneys, built outside, gave fireplaces to the living room and to the shed room.

A very unpretentious dwelling you will say, with but four rooms, counting the attic, to which one could climb by dark, corkscrew stairs: but it did not remain quite so small. After my grandfather had lived in it many years, and had built the fine, two-story barn over on the other side of the Big Road, it seemed high time that he should make some improvement in his dwelling. So it came to pass that two handsome rooms were built in the front of the west end of the old house, forming an "ell" thereto, and connected, by a piazza, to the front piazza of the original dwelling. These new rooms were filled with costly furniture, and were dedicated to the use of "company"—such visitors as might spend the night, or who were not of such familiar footing as to be received into the "living room" of the older house.

My grandfather remained faithful to the older house, spending his days and nights, Sundays and Mondays, winters and summers, in the big sitting room, where he welcomed friends, talked business with his overseer, read his newspapers, and made entries in his "account books."

14

Fanny Kemble was a famous English actress. During a tour of America, she met and married a wealthy Georgia planter, Pierce Butler. The newlyweds went to live on one of Butler's rice plantations on the Georgia coast. In a series of letters to an English friend, she writes about her new home:[14]

[14] Frances Anne Kemble, *Journal of a Residence on a Georgia Plantation in 1838–1839* (London, 1863), pp. 32–34.

[*The slave quarters*] These cabins consist of one room, about twelve feet by fifteen, with a couple of closets smaller and closer than the state-rooms of a ship, divided off from the main room and each other by rough wooden partitions, in which the inhabitants sleep. They have almost all of them a rude bedstead, with the gray moss of the forests for mattress, and filthy, pestilential-looking blankets for covering. Two families (sometimes eight and ten in numbers) reside in one of these huts which are mere wooden frames pinned, as it were, to the earth by a brick chimney outside, whose enormous aperture within pours down a flood of air, but little counteracted by the miserable spark of fire, which hardly sends an attenuated thread of lingering smoke up its huge throat. A wide ditch runs immediately at the back of these dwellings, which is filled and emptied daily by the tide. Attached to each hovel is a small scrap of ground for a garden, which, however, is for the most part untended and uncultivated. Such of these dwellings as I visited to-day were filthy and wretched in the extreme, and exhibited that most deplorable consequence of ignorance and an abject condition, the inability of the inhabitants to secure and improve even such pitiful comfort as might yet be achieved by them. Instead of the order, neatness, and ingenuity which might convert even these miserable hovels into tolerable residences, there was the careless, reckless, filthy indolence which even the brutes do not exhibit in their lairs and nests, and which seemed incapable of applying to the uses of existence the few miserable means of comfort yet within their reach. Firewood and shavings lay littered about the floors, while the half-naked children were cowering around two or three smouldering cinders. The moss with which the chinks and crannies of their ill-protected dwellings might have been stuffed was trailing in dirt and dust about the ground, while the back door of the huts, opening upon a most unsightly ditch, was left wide open for the fowls and ducks, which they are allowed to raise, to

travel in and out, increasing the filth of the cabin by what they brought and left in every direction. In the midst of the floor, or squatting round the cold hearth, would be four or five little children from four to ten years old, the latter all with babies in their arms, the care of the infants being taken from the mothers (who are driven afield as soon as they recover from child labor), and devolved upon these poor little nurses, as they are called, whose business it is to watch the infant, and carry it to its mother whenever it may require nourishment. To these hardly human little beings I addressed my remonstrances about the filth, cold, and unnecessary wretchedness of their room, bidding the elder boys and girls kindle up the fire, sweep the floor, and expel the poultry. For a long time my very words seem unintelligible to them, till, when I began to sweep and make up the fire, etc., they first fell to laughing, and then imitating me.

15

At one time it seemed as if the growing interdependence of the sections might be smothered by a conflict over national expansion. The crisis was surmounted by the famous Missouri Compromise, which interested the politicians more than the people. Thomas Jefferson, as politically sensitive as ever, despite his advancing age, was deeply disturbed by the dangers involved in slavery and expansion. His famous letter to the Massachusetts senator John Holmes, is quoted below. It was dated April 22, 1820:[15]

MONTICELLO, *April 22, 1820.*
I thank you, dear Sir, for the copy you have been so kind as to send me of the letter to your constituents on the Missouri question. It is a perfect justification to them. I had for a long time ceased to read newspapers, or pay any attention to public affairs, confident they were in good hands, and content to be a passenger in our bark to the shore from which I am not distant. But this momentous question, like a fire bell in the night, awakened and filled me with terror.

---

[15] Thomas Jefferson to John Holmes, April 22, 1820, in Paul L. Ford (ed.), *The Works of Thomas Jefferson* (New York, 1905), XII, 158–160.

I considered it at once as the knell of the Union. It is hushed, indeed, for the moment. But this is a reprieve only, not a final sentence. A geographical line, coinciding with a marked principle, moral and political, once conceived and held up to the angry passions of men, will never be obliterated; and every new irritation will mark it deeper and deeper. I can say, with conscious truth, that there is not a man on earth who would sacrifice more than I would to relieve us from this heavy reproach, in any *practicable* way. The cession of that kind of property, for so it is misnamed, is a bagatelle which would not cost me a second thought, if, in that way, a general emancipation and *expatriation* could be effected; and gradually, and with due sacrifices, I think it might be. But as it is, we have the wolf by the ears, and we can neither hold him, nor safely let him go. Justice is in one scale and self-preservation in the other. Of one thing I am certain, that as the passage of slaves from one State to another, would not make a slave of a single human being who would not be so without it, so their diffusion over a greater surface would make them individually happier, and proportionally facilitate the accomplishment of their emancipation, by dividing the burthen on a greater number of coadjutors. An abstinence too, from this act of power, would remove the jealousy excited by the undertaking of Congress to regulate the condition of the different descriptions of men composing a State. This certainly is the exclusive right of every State, which nothing in the constitution has taken from them and given to the General Government. Could Congress, for example, say, that the non-freemen of Connecticut shall be freemen, or that they shall not emigrate into any other State?

I regret that I am now to die in the belief that the useless sacrifice of themselves by the generation of 1776, to acquire self-government and happiness to their country, is to be thrown away by the unwise and unworthy passions of their sons, and that my only consolation is to be, that I live not to weep over it. If they would but dispassion-

ately weigh the blessings they will throw away, against an abstract principle more likely to be effected by union than by scission, they would pause before they would perpetrate this act of suicide on themselves, and of treason against the hopes of the world. To yourself, as the faithful advocate of the Union, I tender the offering of my high esteem and respect.

A NATIONAL FOREIGN POLICY

16

The fervor of nationalism helped Americans reach a peaceful settlement in the first conflict over slavery. It also helped shape American foreign policy, as suggested by the general acclaim accorded the Monroe Doctrine. The chain of events leading to this declaration began in 1823, when French armies invaded Spain, ostensibly to rescue the Spanish monarch from his rebellious subjects but actually, according to rumor, to help that nation reconquer its revolted Latin-American colonies. George Canning, the British foreign secretary, was horrified by this possibility, for England's merchants coveted South American markets long closed to them by Spain's mercantile system. Nor could he forestall the reconquest simply by recognizing the Latin-American republics; his conservative monarch, George IV, would have none of that. In this dilemma, Canning hit upon the idea of a joint Anglo-American declaration against outside interference in South America. He laid his proposal before Richard Rush, American minister to England:[16]

FOREIGN OFFICE, *Aug. 20, 1823*
Private and Confidential

MY DEAR SIR,—Before leaving Town I am desirous of bringing before you in a more distinct, but still in an unofficial and confidential shape, the question which we shortly discussed the last time that I had the pleasure of seeing you.

Is not the moment come when our Governments might understand each other as to the Spanish American Colonies? And if we can arrive at such an understanding, would

---

[16] George Canning to Richard Rush, August 20, 1823, in Massachusetts Historical Society, *Proceedings* (Boston, 1902), 2d ser., XV, 415–416.

it not be expedient for ourselves, and beneficial for all the world, that the principles of it should be clearly settled and plainly avowed?

For ourselves we have no disguise.

1. We conceive the recovery of the Colonies by Spain to be hopeless.

2. We conceive the question of the recognition of them, as Independent States, to be one of time and circumstances.

3. We are, however, by no means disposed to throw any impediment in the way of an arrangement between them and the mother country by amicable negotiations.

4. We aim not at the possession of any portion of them ourselves.

5. We could not see any portion of them transferred to any other Power, with indifference.

If these opinions and feelings are, as I firmly believe them to be, common to your Government with ours, why should we hesitate mutually to confide them to each other; and to declare them in the face of the world?

If there be any European Power which cherishes other projects, which looks to a forcible enterprise for reducing the colonies to subjugation, on the behalf or in the name of Spain; or which meditates the acquisition of any part of them to itself, by cession or by conquest; such a declaration on the part of your government and ours would be at once the most effectual and the least offensive mode of intimating our joint disapprobation of such projects.

It would at the same time put an end to all the jealousies of Spain with respect to her remaining Colonies, and to agitation which prevails in those Colonies, an agitation which it would be but humane to allay; being determined (as we are) not to profit by encouraging it.

Do you conceive that under the power which you have recently received, you are authorized to enter into negotiation and to sign any Convention upon this subject? Do you conceive, if that be not within your competence, you could exchange with me ministerial notes upon it?

Nothing could be more gratifying to me than to join with you in such a work, and, I am persuaded, there has seldom, in the history of the world, occurred an opportunity when so small an effort of two friendly Governments might produce so unequivocal a good and prevent such extensive calamities.

I shall be absent from London but three weeks at the utmost; but never so far distant but that I can receive and reply to any communication within three or four days.

I have the honor to be

My Dear Sir, with great respect and esteem

    Your obedient and faithful servant

        GEORGE CANNING

R. RUSH, Esqr.

17

Upon receipt of the British proposal, President Monroe asked the advice of his Cabinet and one or two elder statesmen. Jefferson's reply to the President's query came on October 24, 1823:[17]

October 24, 1823.

DEAR SIR,—The question presented by the letters you have sent me, is the most momentous which has ever been offered to my contemplation since that of Independence. That made us a nation, this sets our compass and points the course which we are to steer through the ocean of time opening on us. And never could we embark on it under circumstances more auspicious. Our first and fundamental maxim should be, never to entangle ourselves in the broils of Europe. Our second, never to suffer Europe to intermeddle with cis-Atlantic affairs. America, North and South, has a set of interests distinct from those of Europe, and peculiarly her own. She should therefore have a system of her own, separate and apart from that of Europe. While the last is laboring to become the domicil of despotism, our endeavor should surely be, to make our hemisphere that of freedom. One nation, most of all,

---

[17] Thomas Jefferson to James Monroe, October 24, 1823, in Paul L. Ford (ed.), *The Works of Thomas Jefferson* (New York, 1905), XII, 318–321.

could disturb us in this pursuit; she now offers to lead, aid, and accompany us in it. By acceding to her proposition, we detach her from the bands, bring her mighty weight into the scale of free government, and emancipate a continent at one stroke, which might otherwise linger long in doubt and difficulty. Great Britain is the nation which can do us the most harm of anyone, or all on earth; and with her on our side we need not fear the whole world. With her then, we should most sedulously cherish a cordial friendship; and nothing would tend more to knit our affections than to be fighting once more, side by side, in the same cause. Not that I would purchase even her amity at the price of taking part in her wars. But the war in which the present proposition might engage us, should that be its consequence, is not her war, but ours. Its object is to introduce and establish the American system, of keeping out of our land all foreign powers, of never permitting those of Europe to intermeddle with the affairs of our nations. It is to maintain our own principle, not to depart from it. And if, to facilitate this, we can effect a division in the body of the European powers, and draw over to our side its most powerful member, surely we should do it. But I am clearly of Mr. Canning's opinion, that it will prevent instead of provoking war. . . .

I could honestly, therefore, join in the declaration proposed, that we aim not at the acquisition of any of those possessions, that we will not stand in the way of any amicable arrangement between them and the mother country; but that we will oppose, with all our means, the forcible interposition of any other power, as auxiliary, stipendiary, or under any other form or pretext, and most especially, their transfer to any power by conquest, cession, or acquisition in any other way.

18

The American secretary of state, John Quincy Adams, urged an independent statement of policy. Knowing that England's navy could stop Franco-Spanish intervention, he feared that the British purpose was to stop the United States from acquiring Cuba or Texas. Won over by this argument, President Monroe decided to spurn Canning's proposal, issuing instead a warning to all the world that the Americas were closed to colonization by any outside power. The result was the famous Monroe Doctrine, which was embodied in his message to Congress on December 2, 1823:[18]

At the proposal of the Russian Imperial Government, made through the minister of the Emperor residing here, a full power and instructions have been transmitted to the minister of the United States at St. Petersburg to arrange by amicable negotiation the respective rights and interests of the two nations on the northwest coast of this continent. A similar proposal had been made by His Imperial Majesty to the Government of Great Britain, which has likewise been acceded to. The Government of the United States has been desirous by this friendly proceeding of manifesting the great value which they have invariably attached to the friendship of the Emperor and their solicitude to cultivate the best understanding with his Government. In the discussions to which this interest has given rise and in the arrangements by which they may terminate the occasion has been judged proper for asserting, as a principle in which the rights and interests of the United States are involved, that the American continents, by the free and independent condition which they have assumed and maintain, are henceforth not to be considered as subjects for future colonization by any European powers. . . .

It was stated at the commencement of the last session that a great effort was then making in Spain and Portugal to improve the condition of the people of those countries, and that it appeared to be conducted with extraordinary moderation. It need scarcely be remarked that the result has been so far very different from what was then antici-

[18] James D. Richardson (comp.), *A Compilation of the Messages and Papers of the Presidents, 1789–1897* (Washington, 1897), II, 209, 217–219.

pated. Of events in that quarter of the globe, with which we have so much intercourse and from which we derive our origin, we have always been anxious and interested spectators. The citizens of the United States cherish sentiments the most friendly in favor of the liberty and happiness of their fellow-men on that side of the Atlantic. In the wars of the European powers in matters relating to themselves we have never taken any part, nor does it comport with our policy so to do. It is only when our rights are invaded or seriously menaced that we resent injuries or make preparation for our defense. With the movements in this hemisphere we are of necessity more immediately connected, and by causes which must be obvious to all enlightened and impartial observers. The political system of the allied powers is essentially different in this respect from that of America. This difference proceeds from that which exists in their respective Governments; and to the defense of our own, which has been achieved by the loss of so much blood and treasure, and matured by the wisdom of their most enlightened citizens, and under which we have enjoyed unexampled felicity, this whole nation is devoted. We owe it, therefore, to candor and to the amicable relations existing between the United States and those powers to declare that we should consider any attempt on their part to extend their system to any portion of this hemisphere as dangerous to our peace and safety. With the existing colonies or dependencies of any European power we have not interfered and shall not interfere. But with the Governments who have declared their independence and maintained it, and whose independence we have, on great consideration and on just principles, acknowledged, we could not view any interposition for the purpose of oppressing them, or controlling in any other manner their destiny, by any European power in any other light than as the manifestation of an unfriendly disposition toward the United States. In the war between those new Governments and Spain we declared our neutrality at the time of their recognition, and to this we have adhered, and shall continue to adhere, provided no change shall occur which, in the judgment of the competent authorities of this Government, shall make a corresponding change on the part of the United States indispensable to their security.

The late events in Spain and Portugal shew that Europe is still unsettled. Of this important fact no stronger proof can be adduced than that the allied powers should have thought it proper, on any principle satisfactory to themselves, to have interposed by force in the internal concerns of Spain. To what extent such interposition may be carried, on the same principle, is a question in which all independent powers whose governments differ from theirs are interested, even those most remote, and surely none more so than the United States. Our policy in regard to Europe, which was adopted at an early stage of the wars which have so long agitated that quarter of the globe, nevertheless remains the same, which is, not to interfere in the internal concerns of any of its powers; to consider the government *de facto* as the legitimate government for us; to cultivate friendly relations with it, and to preserve those relations by a frank, firm, and manly policy, meeting in all instances the just claims of every power, submitting to injuries from none. But in regard to those continents circumstances are eminently and conspicuously different. It is impossible that the allied powers should extend their political system to any portion of either continent without endangering our peace and happiness; nor can anyone believe that our southern brethren, if left to themselves, would adopt it of their own accord. It is equally impossible, therefore, that we should behold such interposition in any form with indifference. If we look to the comparative strength and resources of Spain and those new Governments, and their distance from each other, it must be obvious that she can never subdue them. It is still the true policy of the United States to leave the parties to themselves, in the hope that other powers will pursue the same course.

19

Russian designs in the Pacific basin were a factor in the evolution of the Monroe Doctrine. Writing in the 1830s, Alexis de Tocqueville, an astute observer of America, foresaw a world polarized between Russia and America:[19]

There are at the present time two great nations in the world, which started from different points, but seem to tend towards the same end. I allude to the Russians and the Americans. Both of them have grown up unnoticed; and while the attention of mankind was directed elsewhere, they have suddenly placed themselves in the front rank among the nations, and the world learned their existence and their greatness at almost the same time.

All other nations seem to have nearly

---

[19] Alexis de Tocqueville, *Democracy in America*, Henry Reeve Text, revised by Francis Bowen (Cambridge, 1862), I, 558–559.

reached their natural limits, and they have only to maintain their power; but these are still in the act of growth. All the others have stopped, or continue to advance with extreme difficulty; these alone are proceeding with ease and celerity along a path to which no limit can be perceived. The American struggles against the obstacles that nature opposes to him; the adversaries of the Russian are men. The former combats the wilderness and savage life; the latter, civilization with all its arms. The conquests of the American are therefore gained by the plowshare; those of the Russian by the sword. The Anglo-American relies upon personal interest to accomplish his ends and gives free scope to the unguided strength and common sense of the people; the Russian centers all the authority of society in a single arm. The principal instrument of the former is freedom; of the latter, servitude. Their starting-point is different and their courses are not the same; yet each of them seems marked out by the will of Heaven to sway the destinies of half the globe.

The Challenge of Sectionalism

Andrew Jackson's election to the presidency in 1828 symbolized the dawning of a new day. For a generation democrats had chafed under the aristocratic rule of the National Republicans. Advocates of popular rule increased their political strength as industry coalesced eastern workers and migrations added thousands to the ranks of frontier farmers. In Jackson these elements recognized a leader, one trained in the rough-and-ready school of life rather than in the wily ways of statesmanship. They placed "Old Hickory" in the White House, happy to follow where he led.

THE DEMOCRATIC SPIRIT

1

Jackson's supporters were unrestrained in their enthusiasm. Conservatives were dismayed. The little people, they felt, now owned the country in as much as they owned Andrew Jackson. Jackson men swooped down upon Washington on a sunny March day when their "Andy" walked up Capitol Hill to be inaugurated. They cheered and shouted and made themselves thoroughly at home in the Executive Mansion. Society leaders grumbled "mobocracy" and talked of the dangers of a new reign of terror. A contemporary reports the scene of the inauguration:[1]

The day of the inauguration was one of the brightest and balmiest of the spring. An eye-witness shall describe to us the memorable scene:

"No one who was at Washington at the time of General Jackson's inauguration is likely to forget that period to the day of his death. To us, who had witnessed the quiet and orderly period of the Adams' administration, it seemed as if half the nation had rushed at once into the Capital. It was like the inundation of the northern barbarians into Rome, save that the tumultuous

[1] James Parton, *Life of Andrew Jackson* (New York, 1860), III, 169–171.

tide came in from a different point of the compass. The West and the South seemed to have precipitated themselves upon the North and overwhelmed it. . . . It appeared to me that every Jackson editor in the country was on the spot. They swarmed, especially in the lobbies of the House, an expectant host, a sort of Praetorian band, which, having borne in upon their shields their idolized leader, claimed the reward of the hard-fought contest. . . . On the morning of the inauguration, the vicinity of the Capital was like a great agitated sea; every avenue to the fateful spot was blocked up with people, ... Never can I forget the spectacle which presented itself on every side, nor the electrifying moment when the eager, expectant eyes of that vast and motley multitude caught sight of the tall and imposing form of their adored leader, as he came forth between the columns of the portico, the color of the whole mass changed, as if by miracle; all hats were off at once, and the dark tint which usually pervades a mixed map of men was turned, as by a magic wand, into the bright hue of ten thousand upturned and exultant human faces, radiant with sudden joy. The peal of shouting that arose rent the air, and seemed to shake the very ground. But when the Chief Justice took his place and commenced the brief ceremony of administering the oath of office, it quickly sank into comparative silence; and as the new President proceeded to read his inaugural address, the stillness gradually increased; but all efforts to hear him, beyond a brief space immediately around, were utterly vain. . . ."

The ceremony over, the President drove from the Capitol to the White House, followed soon by a great part of the crowd who had witnessed the inauguration. . . . A letter writer said: "A profusion of refreshments had been provided. Orange punch by barrels full was made, but as the waiters opened the door to bring it out, a rush would be made, the glasses broken, the pails of liquor upset, and the most painful confusion prevailed. To such a painful degree was this carried, that wine and ice-creams could not be brought out to the ladies, and tubs of punch were taken from the lower story into the garden, to lead off the crowd from the rooms. On such an occasion it was certainly difficult to keep any thing like order, but it was mortifying to see men, with boots heavy with mud, standing on the damask satin covered chairs, from their eagerness to get a sight of the President."

2

The new constitutions adopted by western states entering the Union between 1802 and 1828 institutionalized the aspirations of Jacksonian democrats. The constitution of Illinois (1818) limited executive authority and extended the suffrage to all white males:[2]

ARTICLE II

SECTION 1. The legislative authority of this State shall be vested in a general assembly, which shall consist in a senate and house of representatives, both to be elected by the people. . . .

SEC. 27. In all elections, all white male inhabitants above the age of twenty-one

years, having resided in the State six months next preceding the election, shall enjoy the right of an elector; but no person shall be entitled to vote except in the county or district in which he shall actually reside at the time of the election. . . .

ARTICLE III

SECTION 1. The executive power of the State shall be vested in a governor. . . .

SEC. 19. The governor for the time being, and the judges of the supreme court or a major part of them, together with the governor, shall be, and are hereby, constituted a council to revise all bills about to be passed into laws by the general assembly; and for that purpose shall assemble themselves from time to time when the general assembly shall be convened, for which nevertheless they shall not receive any salary or consideration under any pretence whatever; and all bills which have passed the senate and house of representatives shall, before they become laws, be presented to the said council for their revisal and consideration; and if, upon such revisal and consideration, it should appear improper to the said council or a majority of them, that the bill should become a law of this State, they shall return the same, together with their objections thereto, in writing, to the senate or house of representatives, (in whichsoever the same shall have originated), who shall enter the objections set down by the council at large in their minutes, and proceed to reconsider the said bill. But if, after such reconsideration, the said senate or house of representatives shall, notwithstanding the said objections, agree to pass the same by a majority of the whole number of members elected, it shall, together with the said objections, be sent to the other branch of the general assembly, where it shall also be reconsidered, and if approved by a majority of all the members elected, it shall become a law. If any bill shall not be returned within ten days after it shall have been presented, the same shall be a law, unless the general assembly shall by their adjournment, render a return

[2] Francis N. Thorpe (ed.), *The Federal and State Constitutions, Colonial Charters, and other organic laws of the States, Territories, and Colonies now or heretofore forming the United States of America* (Washington, 1909), II, 972–980.

of the said bill in ten days impracticable; in which case the said bill shall be returned on the first day of the meeting of the general assembly, after the expiration of the said ten days, or be a law.

3

Eastern workers were as insistent in demanding popular rule as western farmers. To laborers in the spawning mill towns of the Northeast the vote meant an opportunity to exact better working conditions, wages, and hours of labor from employers. The labor unions and working-men's parties that appeared in the late 1820s were all propaganda agencies for an enlarged democracy. The resolutions adopted by the national trade union convention that met in New York in August 1834 indicates the broad program of democratic reform desired by the workers:[3]

Be it resolved, That this Convention, deeply impressed with the conviction, that the primary causes of all the evils and difficulties with which the laboring classes are environed, can be traced to the want of a correct knowledge of their own value as producers, and the just estimate of their resources, would recommend, that such of the working class of these United States as have not already formed themselves into societies for the protection of their industry, do so forthwith, that they may by these means be enabled effectively to make common cause with their oppressed brethren, and the more speedily disseminate such knowledge as may be most conducive to their interests in their respective trades and arts, as well as their general interests as productive laborers.

Resolved, That this Convention view the systems of Education now in operation in these United States as destructive of that Equality which is predicated in the Declaration of Independence, because of their exclusive character in giving instruction to the wealthy few at the expense of the industrious many, fostering, by means of Colleges, Uni-

versities, Military or Naval Academies, &c., a professional Monopoly of Knowledge, thereby drawing a line of demarcation between the producers of all the wealth, and the other portions of society which subsist upon the fruits of the Working Man's industry.

Resolved, That this Convention do recommend to the various Trades Unions, that they take into serious consideration the importance of an Equal, Universal, Republican system of Education, and that they take such measures thereon as may to them be deemed advisable. . . .

Resolved, That the laws existing in portions of our country, under which Trades' Unions among mechanics for the maintenance of their rights, and the correction of abuses, are declared illegal Combinations, are a manifest violation of the Constitution of these United States, and an infringement of the lawful rights of every citizen: and this Convention do hereby urge upon the serious consideration of every laboring man the absolute necessity of their repeal.

Resolved, That as productive labor is the only legitimate source of wealth, and as the productive laborers have been deprived of the advantages of their labor by bad legislation, it behooves this portion of the community to regain and maintain, by correct legislation, what they have lost by inattention to their own best interests.

Resolved, That hereafter it should be the first as well as the last duty of every laborer, to inform himself on the subject of his equal rights and labor to promote the good of the whole community, rather than to confer privileges on a favored few.

4

As the common people of America grew in numbers and gained in strength, they directed their attack against the many remaining aristocratic residues in the social order. One objective was the property qualifications for voting that endured in some eastern states. One by one franchise laws were liberalized during the 1830s, until only Rhode Island clung to its outworn restrictions. There a popular rebellion, led by

---

[3] Reprinted by permission of the publishers, The Arthur H. Clark Company, from *A Documentary History of American Industrial Society,* edited by John R. Commons and others (Cleveland, 1910), VI, 206–209.

Thomas Dorr, was needed before conservatives opened the ballot box to all. The constitution drawn up by Dorr's People's party typifies the democratic gains made everywhere (1842):[4]

ARTICLE I

Declaration of Principles and Rights

1. In the spirit and in the words of ROGER WILLIAMS, the illustrious Founder of this State, and of his venerated associates, WE DECLARE, "that this government shall be a DEMOCRACY," or government of the PEOPLE, "by the major consent" of the same, "ONLY IN CIVIL THINGS." The will of the people shall be expressed by Representatives freely chosen, and returning at fixed periods to their constituents. This State shall be, and forever remain, as in the design of its founder, sacred to "SOUL LIBERTY," to the rights of conscience, to freedom of thought, of expression and of action, as hereinafter set forth and secured.

2. All men are created free and equal, and are endowed by their Creator with certain natural, inherent and inalienable Rights; among which are life, liberty, the acquisition of property, and the pursuit of happiness. Government cannot create or bestow these rights, which are the gift of God; but it is instituted for the stronger and surer defence of the same; that men may safely enjoy the rights of life and liberty, securely possess and transmit property, and, so far as laws avail, may be successful in the pursuit of happiness.

3. All political power and sovereignty are originally vested in, and of right belong to the PEOPLE. All free governments are founded in their authority, and are established for the greatest good of the whole number. The PEOPLE have therefore an inalienable and indefeasible right, in their original, sovereign and unlimited capacity, to ordain and institute government, and, in the same capacity, to alter, reform, or totally change the same, whenever their safety or happiness requires.

4. No favor or disfavor ought to be shown in legislation toward any man, or party, or society, or religious denomination. The laws should be made not for the good of the few, but of the many; and the burdens of the State ought to be fairly distributed among its citizens. . . .

ARTICLE II

Of Electors and the Right of Suffrage

1. Every white male citizen of the United States, of the age of twenty-one years, who has resided in this State for one year, and in any town, city, or district of the same for six months, next preceding the election at which he offers to vote, shall be an elector of all officers, who are elected, or may hereafter be made eligible by the People. But persons in the military, naval, or marine service of the United States shall not be considered as having such established residence, by being stationed in any garrison, barrack, or military place, in any town or city in this State.

2. Paupers and persons under guardianship, insane, or lunatic, are excluded from the electoral right; and the same shall be forfeited on conviction of bribery, forgery, perjury, theft, or other infamous crime, and shall not be restored unless by an act of the General Assembly.

3. No person, who is excluded from voting, for want of the qualification first named in section first of this article, shall be taxed, or be liable to do military duty; provided that nothing in said first article shall be so construed as to exempt from taxation any property or persons now liable to be taxed.

5

Popular demand for better educational facilities was no less vocal. Schooling alone could provide an answer to the conservative charge that the majority of the people were ill-equipped to govern. As the state would benefit in the end from an intelligent electorate, reformers reasoned the state should provide educational facilities. Labor unions and workingmen's parties agitated for what became a typically American institution, the free public school. Their argu-

---

[4] Quoted in Jacob Frieze, *A Concise History of the Efforts to Obtain an Extension of Suffrage in Rhode Island* (Providence, 1842), pp. 117–121.

ments appear in a report drafted in September 1829 by a committee of Philadelphia working-men:[5]

With the exception of this city and county, the city and incorporated borough of Lancaster, and the city of Pittsburgh, erected into "school districts" since 1818, it appears that the entire state is destitute of any provisions for public instruction, except those furnished by the enactment of 1809. This law requires the assessors of the several counties to ascertain and return the number of children whose parents are unable, through poverty, to educate them; and such children are permitted to be instructed at the most convenient schools at the expense of their respective counties.

The provisions of this act, however, are incomplete and frequently inoperative. . . . The funds, appropriated by the act, have, in some instances, been embezzled by fraudulent agents; and in others, partial returns of the children have been made, and some have been illegally and intentionally excluded from participating in the provisions of the law. From a parsimonious desire of saving the county funds, the cheapest, and consequently the most inefficient schools have been usually selected by the commissioners of the several counties.

The elementary schools throughout the state are irresponsible institutions, established by individuals, from mere motives of private speculation or gain, who are sometimes destitute of character, and frequently, of the requisite attainments and abilities. From the circumstance of the schools being the absolute property of individuals, no supervision or effectual control can be exercised over them; hence, ignorance, inattention, and even immorality, prevail to a lamentable extent among their teachers.

In some districts, no schools whatever ex-ist! No means whatever of acquiring education are resorted to; while ignorance, and its never failing consequence, crime, are found to prevail in these neglected spots, to a greater extent than in other more favored portions of the state. . . .

But the principles on which these "school districts" are founded, are yet, in the opinion of the committees, extremely defective and inefficient. Their leading feature is pauperism! They are confined exclusively to the children of the poor, while there are, perhaps, thousands of children whose parents are unable to afford for them, a good private education, yet whose standing, professions or connexions in society effectually exclude them from taking the benefit of a poor law. There are great numbers, even of the poorest parents, who hold a dependence on the public bounty to be incompatible with the rights and liberties of an American citizen, and whose deep and cherished consciousness of independence determines them rather to starve the intellect of their offspring, than submit to become the objects of public charity.

There are, also, many poor families, who are totally unable to maintain and clothe their children, while at the schools; and who are compelled to place them, at a very early age, at some kind of labor that may assist in supporting them, or to bind them out as apprentices. . . .

Another radical and glaring defect in the existing public school system is the very limited amount of instruction it affords, even to the comparatively small number of youth, who enjoy its benefits. It extends, in no case, further than a tolerable proficiency in reading, writing, and arithmetic, and sometimes to a slight acquaintance with geography. Besides these, the girls are taught a few simple branches of industry. . . .

The present public school system, limited as it is to three solitary school districts, makes no provision for the care and instruction of children under five years old. This class of children is numerous, especially among the poor, and it frequently happens

[5] *Working Man's Advocate,* March 6, 1830. Reprinted by permission of the publishers, The Arthur H. Clark Company, from *A Documentary History of American Industrial Society,* edited by John R. Commons and others (Cleveland, 1910), V, 94–107.

that the parents, or parent, (perhaps a widow) whose only resource for a livelihood is her needle or wash tub, is compelled to keep her elder children from the school to take charge of the younger ones, while her own hands are industriously employed in procuring a subsistence for them. . . .

An opinion is entertained by many good and wise persons, and supported to a considerable extent, by actual experiment, that proper schools for supplying a judicious infant training, would effectually prevent much of that vicious depravity of character which penal codes and punishments are vainly intended to counteract. Such schools would, at least, relieve, in a great measure, many indigent parents, from the care of children, which in many cases occupies as much of their time as would be necessary to earn the children a subsistence. They would also afford many youth an opportunity of participating in the benefits of the public schools, who otherwise must, of necessity, be detained from them.

From this view of the public instruction in Pennsylvania, it is manifest that, even in "the school districts," to say nothing of the remainder of the state, a very large proportion of youth are either partially or entirely destitute of education.

It is true the state is not without its colleges and universities, several of which have been fostered with liberal supplies from the public purse. Let it be observed, however, that the funds so applied, have been appropriated exclusively for the benefit of the wealthy, who are thereby enabled to procure a liberal education for their children, upon lower terms than it could otherwise be afforded them. . . .

The original element of despotism is a monopoly of talent, which consigns the multitude to comparative ignorance, and secures the balance of knowledge on the side of the rich and the rulers. . . .

In a republic, the people constitute the government, and by wielding its powers in accordance with the dictates, either of their intelligence or their ignorance; of their judgment or their caprices, are the makers and the rulers of their own good or evil destiny. They frame the laws and create the institutions, that promise their happiness or produce their destruction. If they be wise and intelligent, no laws but what are just and equal will receive their approbation, or be sustained by their suffrages. If they be ignorant and capricious, they will be deceived by mistaken or designing rulers, into the support of laws that are unequal and unjust.

It appears, therefore, to the committees that there can be no real liberty without a wide diffusion of real intelligence; that the members of a republic, should all be alike instructed in the nature and character of their equal rights and duties, as human beings, and as citizens; and that education, instead of being limited as in our public poor schools, to a simple acquaintance with words and cyphers, should tend, as far as possible, to the production of a just disposition, virtuous habits, and a rational self governing character.

The instruction afforded by common schools, . . . being only elementary, must, of necessity, produce a very limited development of the human faculties. It would indeed diminish, but could not destroy, the present injurious monopoly of talent. While the higher branches of literature and science remain accessible only to the children of the wealthy, there must still be a balance of knowledge, and with it a "balance of power," in the hands of the privileged few, the rich and the rulers.

Another radical defect in the best system of common schools yet established, will be found in its not being adapted to meet the wants and necessities of those who stand most in need of it. Very many of the poorest parents are totally unable to clothe and maintain their children while at school, and are compelled to employ their time, while yet very young, in aiding to procure a subsistence. . . .

The constitution of this state declares that "the legislature shall provide schools in which the poor may be taught gratis." If this signifies that the poor shall have an opportunity afforded for instruction, it must involve means equal to the end. The poverty of the poor must be no obstruction, otherwise the constitution is a dead letter—nay, worse, an insult on their unfortunate condition and feelings.

6

Massachusetts set up the first Board of Education in the United States in 1837 with the gifted Horace Mann as its secretary. Mann increased the number of schools, raised teachers' pay, lengthened the school year, and established normal schools, until every child in the state had an opportunity for a primary education. More importantly, his example was imitated everywhere, especially in New England where industrial wealth provided an economic foundation for an adequate school system. Mann's wide influence was partly due to his "annual reports," which served as guides to reformers in other states. In his report for 1845, Mann demonstrated simply but forcibly the connection between education and democracy:[6]

The great, the all-important, the only important question still remains: By what spirit are our schools animated? Do they cultivate the higher faculties in the nature of childhood,—its conscience, its benevolence, a reverence for whatever is true and sacred? or are they only developing, upon a grander scale, the lower instincts and selfish tendencies of the race,—the desires which prompt men to seek, and the powers which enable them to secure, sensual ends,—wealth, luxury, preferment,—irrespective of the well-being of others? Knowing, as we do, that the foundations of national greatness can be laid only in the industry, the integrity, and the spiritual elevation of the people, are we equally sure that our schools are forming the character of the rising generation upon the everlasting principles of duty and humanity? or, on the other hand, are they only stimulating the powers which lead to a base pride of intellect, which prompt to the os-

tentation instead of the reality of virtue, and which give augury that life is to be spent only in selfish competitions between those who should be brethren? Above all others, must the children of a republic be fitted for society as well as for themselves. As each citizen is to participate in the power of governing others, it is an essential preliminary that he should be imbued with a feeling for the wants, and a sense of the rights, of those whom he is to govern; because the power of governing others, if guided by no higher motive than our own gratification, is the distinctive attribute of oppression; an attribute whose nature and whose wickedness are the same, whether exercised by one who calls himself a republican, or by one born an irresponsible despot. In a government like ours, each individual must think of the welfare of the State, as well as of the welfare of his own family, and, therefore, of the children of others as well as his own. It becomes, then, a momentous question, whether the children in our schools are educated in reference to themselves and their private interests only, or with a regard to the great social duties and prerogatives that await them in after-life. Are they so educated, that, when they grow up, they will make better philanthropists and Christians, or only grander savages? For, however loftily the intellect of man may have been gifted, however skillfully it may have been trained, if it be not guided by a sense of justice, a love of mankind, and a devotion to duty, its possessor is only a more splendid, as he is a more dangerous, barbarian.

7

Tocqueville had had some reservations about the virtues of a system of universal suffrage:[7]

Many people in Europe are apt to believe without saying it, or to say without believing it, that one of the great advantages of universal suffrage is that it entrusts the direction of affairs to men who are worthy of

---

[6] M. T. P. Mann, *The Life and Works of Horace Mann* (Boston, 1891), IV, 3–4.

[7] Alexis de Tocqueville, *Democracy in America* (Cambridge, 1862), I, 253–256.

the public confidence. They admit that the people are unable to govern of themselves, but they aver that the people always wish the welfare of the state and instinctively designate those who are animated by the same good will and who are the most fit to wield the supreme authority. I confess that the observations I made in America by no means coincide with these opinions. On my arrival in the United States I was surprised to find so much distinguished talent among the subjects and so little among the heads of government. It is a constant fact that at the present day the ablest men in the United States are rarely placed at the head of affairs; and it must be acknowledged that such has been the result in proportion as democracy has outstepped all its former limits. The race of American statesmen has evidently dwindled most remarkably in the course of the last fifty years.

Several causes may be assigned for this phenomenon. It is impossible, after the most strenuous exertions, to raise the intelligence of the people above a certain level. Whatever may be the facilities of acquiring information, whatever may be the profusion of easy methods and cheap science, the human mind can never be instructed and developed without devoting considerable time to these objects.

The greater or lesser possibility of subsisting without labor is therefore the necessary boundary of intellectual improvement. This boundary is more remote in some countries and more restricted in others, but it must exist somewhere as long as the people are constrained to work in order to procure the means of subsistence; that is to say, as long as they continue to be the people. It is therefore quite as difficult to imagine a state in which all the citizens should be well informed as a state in which they should all be wealthy; these two difficulties are correlative. I readily admit that the mass of the citizens sincerely wish to promote the welfare of the country; nay, more, I even grant that the lower classes mix fewer considerations of personal interest with their patriotism than the higher orders; but it is always

more or less difficult for them to discern the best means of attaining the end which they sincerely desire. Long and patient observation and much acquired knowledge are requisite to form a just estimate of the character of a single individual. Men of the greatest genius often fail to do it, and can it be supposed that the vulgar will always succeed? The people have neither the time nor the means for an investigation of this kind. Their conclusions are hastily formed from a superficial inspection of the more prominent features of a question. Hence it often happens that mountebanks of all sorts are able to please the people, while their truest friends frequently fail to gain their confidence.

Moreover, the democracy not only lacks that soundness of judgment which is necessary to select men really deserving of their confidence, but often have not the desire or the inclination to find them out. It cannot be denied that democratic institutions strongly tend to promote the feeling of envy in the human heart; not so much because they afford to everyone the means of rising to the same level with others as because those means perpetually disappoint the persons who employ them. Democratic institutions awaken and foster a passion for equality which they can never entirely satisfy. This complete equality eludes the grasp of the people at the very moment when they think they have grasped it, and "flies," as Pascal says, "with an eternal flight"; the people are excited in the pursuit of an advantage, which is more precious because it is not sufficiently remote to be unknown or sufficiently near to be enjoyed. The lower orders are agitated by the chance of success, they are irritated by its uncertainty; and they pass from enthusiasm of pursuit to the exhaustion of ill success, and lastly to the acrimony of disappointment. Whatever transcends their own limitations appears to be an obstacle to their desires, and there is no superiority, however legitimate it may be, which is not irksome in their sight.

It has been supposed that the secret instinct which leads the lower orders to remove their superiors as much as possible from the direction of public affairs is peculiar to France. This is an error, however; the instinct to which I allude is not French, it is democratic; it may have been heightened by peculiar political circumstances, but it owes its origin to a higher cause.

In the United States the people do not hate the higher classes of society, but are not favorably inclined towards them and carefully exclude them from the exercise of authority. They do not fear distinguished talents, but are rarely fond of them. In general, everyone who rises without their aid seldom obtains their favor.

Whilst the natural instincts of democracy induce the people to reject distinguished citizens as their rulers, an instinct not less strong induces able men to retire from the political arena, in which it is so difficult to retain their independence, or to advance without becoming servile. This opinion has been candidly expressed by Chancellor Kent, who says, in speaking with high praise of that part of the Constitution which empowers the executive to nominate the judges: "It is indeed probable that the men who are best fitted to discharge the duties of this high office would have too much reserve in their manners, and too much austerity in their principles, for them to be returned by the majority at an election where universal suffrage is adopted." Such were the opinions which were printed without contradiction in America in the year 1830!

I hold it to be sufficiently demonstrated that universal suffrage is by no means a guarantee of the wisdom of the popular choice. Whatever its advantages may be, this is not one of them.

JACKSON AND THE SECTIONAL CHALLENGE

8

Andrew Jackson, emboldened by popular support, disregarded opposition, whether from the states, the courts, or the Congress. Jackson's confidence explains his forthright method in his handling of two touchy problems during his first administration: the Georgia Indian controversy *and the conflict between South Carolina and Congress. The first assumed national importance after Georgia attempted to expel the Cherokee Indians from their tribal lands in the western part of the state. The tribesmen, maintaining they were a separate nation under the protection of the federal government, carried their cause to the Supreme Court. Chief Justice John Marshall, in Worcester v. Georgia (1832), sided with the Indians, holding that Georgia did not have jurisdiction over them. Jackson, who as a frontiersman was sympathetic with Georgia, fumed at what he considered a violation of the popular will. Refusing to enforce the Supreme Court's decision, he stood aside while the Indians were forced to accept a heartless treaty binding them to move beyond the Mississippi. The "Memorial and Protest of the Cherokee Nation" laid before the Senate March 11, 1836, a moving plea for justice, was completely ignored:[8]*

It cannot be concealed that the situation of the Cherokees is peculiarly distressing. In adverting to that situation it is not done to arouse, at this late day, a useless sympathy, but only as matter of history, and from necessity in giving a fair and impartial illustration of their difficulties. It is well known to those who have paid any attention to their history for the last five years, that they have been contending for the faithful execution of treaties between their nation and the United States, and that their distresses have not been mitigated; their efforts seem to have increased their difficulties. It remains for them to seek an adjustment by treaty, and an equitable acknowledgment of their rights and claims, so far as circumstances will permit. For this purpose, this delegation has been deputed, as the proper organ of the Cherokee people, to settle, by treaty, their difficulties; and they wish, in sincerity, to have them settled, for the good, peace, and harmony of the whole nation. This desired end can only be attained by a contract with the constituted and acknowledged authorities of the Cherokee nation. If the difficulties are attempted to be arranged in any other way, it will not meet the wishes of the Cherokees, and their situation will be miserable

---

[8] H. R. Exec. Doc. No. 286, 24th Cong., 1st Sess., VII, 30–32.

beyond description, and their distresses augmented, for they will never agree to a treaty made with unauthorized individuals. Deal with them as friends, and suffer them to be relieved from their sorrows and difficulties by their own act, and whatever may be their situation in time to come, they will console themselves by the reflection, it is the dispensation of an all-wise Providence. The delegation are sure it cannot be the wish of the Senate of the United States to ratify and have enforced upon the unoffending Cherokee people, a treaty made without their authority, false upon its face, and against the known wishes of the nation. Such is the instrument submitted to your honorable body. For the truth of this statement, should the Senate require further proof, it can be obtained from numerous persons of unimpeachable integrity and veracity. But if it be the fate of the Cherokee people, and the decree has gone forth, that they must leave their homes and native land, and seek a new residence in the wilds of the far west, without their consent, let them be expelled and removed by an act of Congress, when they or their posterity, in after times, may have some claims upon the magnanimity of the American people. The delegation do solemnly declare, they would consider such an act preferable and more humane than the ratification and enforcement of a fraudulent treaty, false upon its face, and made without the consent of one of the professed contracting parties. The past history of the United States furnishes admonitions against the ratification of treaties made with unauthorized individuals. Resting upon the sacred rights of the Cherokee nation, so often recognised and solemnly guaranteed on the faith of treaties, the delegation now appeal to the sympathies, the honor, good faith, and magnanimity of the United States, to preserve and protect their nation from fraud, rapine, plunder, and destruction. They have now discharged their duty to themselves and to their unfortunate people, with that frankness that becomes the occasion. Their case is fairly before your honorable body, and the

destiny of the Cherokee people in the hands of the American Senate. We are all children of the same Great Parent, and bound to be kind to each other, without regard to the situation in which we may be placed. If an earthly parent have a child unfortunately weak and poor, how would he feel to see the brothers of that child abusing it for its misfortunes, insulting its feelings, exulting in their own superiority, curling the lip of scorn, with a significant cant of the head, at its earnest supplication for justice? Let every man's own heart give him the answer. You have before you that unfortunate child in the weak and dependent Cherokees. With hands elevated towards the throne of grace and mercy, we all supplicate, saying: Our brothers, is it true you will drive us from the land of our nativity, and from the tombs of our fathers and our mothers? We know you possess the power, but, by the tie that unites us yonder, we implore you to forbear. Our case is with you.

9

Jackson sided with Georgia in its defiance of the Supreme Court; yet when South Carolina challenged the authority of Congress, he was equally firm in upholding national authority. The controversy that led him into this apparently contradictory course originated when South Carolina, impelled by a growing distrust of protective tariffs which interfered with cotton exports, rebelled against the badly drawn Tariff of 1828. Its first protest was orderly; John C. Calhoun was commissioned to draw up a statement of grievances. In the South Carolina "Exposition" Calhoun argued that as Congress exceeded its constitutional authority by adopting protective tariffs, the states were not bound to obey. Its closing paragraphs lists the South's reasons for opposing protection:[9]

1st. *Because* the good people of this commonwealth believe that the powers of Congress were delegated to it in trust for the accomplishment of certain specified objects

9 Jonathan Elliot (ed.), *Debates in the Several State Conventions on the Adoption of the Federal Constitution* . . . (Philadelphia, 1836 ed.), IV, 580–582.

which limit and control them, and that every exercise of them for any other purposes, is a violation of the Constitution as unwarrantable as the undisguised assumption of substantive, independent powers not granted or expressly withheld.

2d. *Because* the power to lay duties on imports is, and in its very nature can be, only a means of effecting objects specified by the Constitution; since no free government, and least of all a government of enumerated powers, can of right impose any tax, any more than a penalty, which is not at once justified by public necessity, and clearly within the scope and purview of the social compact; and since the right of confining appropriations of the public money to such legitimate and constitutional objects is as essential to the liberty of the people as their unquestionable privilege to be taxed only by their consent.

3d. *Because* they believe that the tariff law passed by Congress at its last session, and all other acts of which the principal object is the protection of manufactures, or any other branch of domestic industry, if they be considered as the exercise of a power in Congress to tax the people at its own good will and pleasure, and to apply the money raised to objects not specified in the Constitution, is a violation of these fundamental principles, a breach of a well-defined trust, and a perversion of the high powers vested in the federal government for federal purposes only.

4th. *Because* such acts, considered in the light of a regulation of commerce, are equally liable to objection; since, although the power to regulate commerce may, like all other powers, be exercised so as to protect domestic manufactures, yet it is clearly distinguishable from a power to do so *eo nomine,* both in the nature of the thing and in the common acception of the terms; and because the confounding of them would lead to the most extravagant results, since the encouragement of domestic industry implies an absolute control over all the interests, resources, and pursuits of a people, and is con-

sistent with the idea of any other than a simple, consolidated government.

5th. *Because,* from the contemporaneous exposition of the Constitution in the numbers of the *Federalist,* (which is cited only because the Supreme Court has recognized its authority,) it is clear that the power to regulate commerce was considered by the Convention as only incidentally connected with the encouragement of agriculture and manufactures; and because the power of laying imposts and duties on imports was not understood to justify in any case, a prohibition of foreign commodities, except as a means of extending commerce, by coercing foreign nations to a fair reciprocity in their intercourse with us, or for some *bona fide* commercial purpose.

6th. *Because,* whilst the power to protect manufactures, is nowhere expressly granted to Congress, nor can be considered as necessary and proper to carry into effect any specified power, it seems to be expressly reserved to the states, by the 10th section of the 1st article of the Constitution.

7th. *Because* even admitting Congress to have a constitutional right to protect manufactures by the imposition of duties, or by regulations of commerce, designed principally for that purpose, yet a tariff of which the operation is grossly unequal and oppressive, is such an abuse of power as is incompatible with the principles of a free government and the great ends of civil society, justice, and equality of rights and protection.

8th. *Finally,* because South Carolina, from her climate, situation, and peculiar institutions, is, and must ever continue to be, wholly dependent upon agriculture and commerce, not only for her prosperity, but for her very existence as a state; because the valuable products of her soil—the blessings by which Divine Providence seems to have designed to compensate for the great disadvantages under which she suffers in other respects—are among the very few that can be cultivated with any profit by slave labor; and if, by the loss of her foreign commerce, these products should be confined to an inadequate market, the fate of this fertile state would be poverty and utter desolation; her citizens, in despair, would emigrate to more fortunate regions, and the whole frame and constitution of her civil policy be impaired and deranged, if not dissolved entirely.

Deeply impressed with these considerations, the representatives of the good people of this commonwealth, anxiously desiring to live in peace with their fellow-citizens, and to do all that in them lies to preserve and perpetuate the union of the states, and liberties of which it is the surest pledge, but feeling it to be their bounden duty to expose and resist all encroachments upon the true spirit of the Constitution, lest an apparent acquiescence in the system of protecting duties should be drawn into precedent—do, in the name of the commonwealth of South Carolina, claim to enter upon the Journal of the Senate their *protest* against it as unconstitutional, oppressive, and unjust.

10

Having issued this warning, South Carolina waited, hoping that Congress would capitulate. When another protective measure was passed in 1832, however, the state acted at once. A convention, meeting in November 1832, solemnly declared the tariffs of 1828 and 1832 "null, void, and no law, not binding upon this State, its officers or citizens":[10]

WHEREAS, The Congress of the United States, by various acts, purporting to be acts laying duties and imposts on foreign imports, but in reality intended for the protection of domestic manufactures, and the giving of bounties to classes and individuals engaged in particular employments, at the expense and to the injury and oppression of other classes and individuals, and by wholly exempting from taxation certain foreign commodities, such as are not produced or manufactured in the United States, to afford a pretext for imposing higher and excessive duties on articles similar to those intended to be protected, hath exceeded its just pow-

ers under the Constitution, which confers on it no authority to afford such protection, and hath violated the true meaning and intent of the Constitution, which provides for equality in imposing the burdens of taxation upon the several States and portions of the Confederacy. *And whereas,* the said Congress, exceeding its just power to impose taxes and collect revenue for the purpose of effecting and accomplishing the specific objects and purposes which the Constitution of the United States authorizes it to effect and accomplish, hath raised and collected unnecessary revenue for objects unauthorized by the Constitution—

We, therefore, the People of the State of South Carolina in Convention assembled, do Declare and Ordain, . . . That the several acts and parts of acts of the Congress of the United States, purporting to be laws for the imposing of duties and imposts on the importation of foreign commodities, . . . are unauthorized by the Constitution of the United States, and violate the true meaning and intent thereof, and are null, void, and no law, nor binding upon this State, its officers or citizens; and all promises, contracts, and obligations, made or entered into, or to be made or entered into, with purpose to secure the duties imposed by the said acts, and all judicial proceedings which shall be hereafter had in affirmance thereof, are and shall be held utterly null and void.

11

At the same time, the South Carolina leaders attempted to solicit support by issuing an "Address to the People of the United States," which both defended nullification and attacked protection:[11]

In resorting to this important measure, to which we have been impelled by the most sacred of all duties which a free people can owe, either to the memory of their ancestors or to the claims of their posterity, we feel that it is due to the intimate political relation which exists between South Carolina

---

10 Thomas Cooper (ed.), *Statutes at Large of South Carolina* (Columbia, S. C., 1836), I, 329–331.

11 *Ibid.,* pp. 346–349.

and the other States of this confederacy, that we should present a clear and distinct exposition of the principles on which we have acted, and of the causes by which we have been reluctantly constrained to assume this attitude of sovereign resistance in relation to the usurpations of the Federal Government. . . .

We hold, then, that on their separation from the Crown of Great Britain, the several colonies became free and independent States, each enjoying the separate and independent right of self government; and that no authority can be exercised over them or within their limits, but by their consent, respectively given as States. It is equally true, that the Constitution of the United States is a compact formed between the several States, acting as sovereign communities; that the government created by it is a joint agency of the States, appointed to execute the powers enumerated and granted by that instrument; that all its acts not intentionally authorized are of themselves essentially null and void, and that the States have the right, in the same sovereign capacity in which they adopted the Federal Constitution, to pronounce, in the last resort, authoritative judgment on the usurpations of the Federal Government, and to adopt such measures as they may deem necessary and expedient to arrest the operation of the unconstitutional acts of that Government, within their respective limits. Such we deem to be inherent rights of the States; rights, in the very nature of things, absolutely inseparable from sovereignty. Nor is the duty of a State, to arrest an unconstitutional and oppressive act of the Federal Government less imperative, than the right is incontestible. Each State, by ratifying the Federal Constitution, and becoming a member of the confederacy, contracted an obligation to "protect and defend" that instrument, as well by resisting the usurpations of the Federal Government, as by sustaining that government in the exercise of the powers actually conferred upon it. And the obligation of the oath which is imposed, under the Constitution, on every functionary of the

States to "preserve, protect, and defend" the Federal Constitution, as clearly comprehends the duty of protecting and defending it against the usurpations of the Federal Government, as that of protecting and defending it against violation in any other form or from any other quarter.

It is true, that in ratifying the Federal Constitution, the States placed a large and important portion of the rights of their citizens under the joint protection of all the States, with a view to their more effectual security; but it is not less true that they reserved a portion still larger and not less important under their own immediate guardianship, and in relation to which their original obligation to protect their citizens, from whatever quarter assailed, remains unchanged and undiminished.

12

Jackson responded by issuing a Proclamation that left no room for doubt about his determination to uphold the authority of the federal government:[12]

To preserve this bond of our political existence from destruction, to maintain inviolate this state of national honor and prosperity, and to justify the confidence my fellow-citizens have reposed in me, I, Andrew Jackson, President of the United States, have thought proper to issue this my proclamation, stating my views of the Constitution and laws applicable to the measures adopted by the convention of South Carolina and to the reasons they have put forth to sustain them, declaring the course which duty will require me to pursue, and, appealing to the understanding and patriotism of the people, warn them of the consequences that must inevitably result from an observance of the dictates of the convention. . . .

The ordinance is founded, not on the indefeasible right of resisting acts which are plainly unconstitutional and too oppressive

---

[12] J. D. Richardson (comp.), *A Compilation of the Messages and Papers of the Presidents, 1789–1897* (Washington, 1907), II, 640 ff.

to be endured, but on the strange position
that any one State may not only declare an
act of Congress void, but prohibit its execution; that they may do this consistently
with the Constitution; that the true construction of that instrument permits a State
to retain its place in the Union and yet be
bound by no other of its laws than those it
may choose to consider as unconstitutional.
It is true, they add, that to justify this abro-
gation of a law it must be palpably contrary
to the Constitution; but it is evident that to
give the right of resisting laws of that description, coupled with the uncontrolled
right to decide what laws deserve that character, is to give the power of resisting all
laws; for as by the theory there is no appeal,
the reasons alleged by the State, good or
bad, must prevail. If it should be said that
public opinion is a sufficient check against
the abuse of this power, it may be asked why
it is not deemed a sufficient guard against
the passage of an unconstitutional act by
Congress? . . . There is no appeal from the
State decision in theory, and the practical
illustration shows that the courts are closed
against an application to review it, both
judges and jurors being sworn to decide in
its favor. But reasoning on this subject is
superfluous when our social compact, in express terms, declares that the laws of the
United States, its Constitution, and treaties
made under it are the supreme law of the
land, and, for greater caution, adds "that the
judges in every State shall be bound thereby,
anything in the constitution or laws of any
State to the contrary notwithstanding." And
it may be asserted without fear of refutation
that no federative government could exist
without a similar provision. . . .

If this doctrine had been established at an
earlier day, the Union would have been dissolved in its infancy. The excise law in Pennsylvania, the embargo and nonintercourse
law in the Eastern States, the carriage tax in
Virginia, were all deemed unconstitutional,
and were more unequal in their operation
than any of the laws now complained of;
but, fortunately, none of those States discovered that they had the right now claimed
by South Carolina. The war into which we
were forced to support the dignity of the
nation and the rights of our citizens might
have ended in defeat and disgrace, instead
of victory and honor, if the States who supposed it a ruinous and unconstitutional measure had thought they possessed the right
of nullifying the act by which it was declared
and denying supplies for its prosecution.
Hardly and unequally as those measures bore
upon several members of the Union, to the
legislatures of none did this efficient and
peaceable remedy, as it is called, suggest itself. The discovery of this important feature
in our Constitution was reserved to the
present day. To the statesmen of South Carolina belongs the invention, and upon the citizens of that State will unfortunately fall the
evils of reducing it to practice.

If the doctrine of a State veto upon the
laws of the Union carries with it internal
evidence of its impracticable absurdity, our
constitutional history will also afford abundant proof that it would have been repudiated with indignation had it been proposed
to form a feature in our Government.

Our present Constitution was formed . . .
in vain if this fatal doctrine prevails. . . .

I consider, then, the power to annul a law
of the United States, assumed by one State,
*incompatible with the existence of the Union,
contradicted expressly by the letter of the
Constitution, unauthorized by its spirit, inconsistent with every principle on which it
was founded, and destructive of the great object for which it was formed. . . .*

This, then, is the position in which we
stand: A small majority of the citizens of one
State in the Union have elected delegates to
a State convention; that convention has ordained that all the revenue laws of the
United States must be repealed, or that they
are no longer a member of the Union. The
governor of that State has recommended to
the legislature the raising of an army to
carry the secession into effect, and that he

may be empowered to give clearances to vessels in the name of the State. No act of violent opposition to the laws has yet been committed, but such a state of things is hourly apprehended. And it is the intent of this instrument to *proclaim*, not only that the duty imposed on me by the Constitution "to take care that the laws be faithfully executed" shall be performed to the extent of the powers already vested in me by law, or of such others as the wisdom of Congress shall devise and intrust to me for that purpose, but to warn the citizens of South Carolina who have been deluded into an opposition to the laws of the danger they will incur by obedience to the illegal and disorganizing ordinance of the convention; to exhort those who have refused to support it to persevere in their determination to uphold the Constitution and laws of their country; and to point out to all the perilous situation into which the good people of that State have been led, and that the course they are urged to pursue is one of ruin and disgrace to the very State whose rights they affect to support. . . .

If your leaders could succeed in establishing a separation, what would be your situation? Are you united at home? Are you free from the apprehension of civil discord, with all its fearful consequences? Do our neighboring republics, every day suffering some new revolution or contending with some new insurrection, do they excite your envy? But the dictates of a high duty oblige me solemnly to announce that you can not succeed. The laws of the United States must be executed. I have no discretionary power on the subject; my duty is emphatically pronounced in the Constitution. Those who told you that you might peaceably prevent their execution deceived you; they could not have been deceived themselves. They know that a forcible opposition could alone prevent the execution of the laws, and they know that such opposition must be repelled. Their object is disunion. But be not deceived by names. Disunion by armed force is *treason*. Are you really ready to incur its guilt?

GOVERNMENT AND THE ECONOMY

13

The South Carolina nullification controversy vastly widened a gulf already forming between two factions of the National Republican party. On one side were Jackson, Martin Van Buren of New York, and other representatives of the small farmer-workingman-small planter groups. On the other side were Henry Clay of Kentucky, Daniel Webster of Massachusetts, and, after 1832 when he broke with Jackson over nullification, John C. Calhoun. Their constituents were members of the manufacturer-merchant-great planter groups who had controlled the nation until the rise of Jacksonian democracy. The open break between these factions was occasioned by the attempts of the Second Bank of the United States to obtain congressional recharter on the eve of the election of 1832. Congress passed the bill but Jackson, who considered the bank an "octopus of finance" that oppressed the majority for the benefit of the few, vetoed the measure in one of his most forceful messages:[13]

TO THE SENATE:

The bill "to modify and continue" the act entitled "An act to incorporate the subscribers to the Bank of the United States" was presented to me on the 4th July instant. Having . . . come to the conclusion that it ought not to become a law, I herewith return it to the Senate, in which it originated, with my objections.

A bank of the United States is in many respects convenient for the Government and useful to the people. Entertaining this opinion, and deeply impressed with the belief that some of the powers and privileges possessed by the existing bank are unauthorized by the Constitution, subversive of the rights of the States, and dangerous to the liberties of the people, I felt it my duty at an early period of my Administration to call the attention of Congress to the practicability of organizing an institution combining all its advantages and obviating these objections. I sincerely regret that in the act before me I can perceive none of those modifications of the bank charter which are necessary, in my

---

[13] *Ibid.*, II, 576–581, 583–590.

opinion, to make it compatible with justice, with sound policy, or with the Constitution of our country.

The present corporate body . . . enjoys an exclusive privilege of banking under the authority of the General Government, a monopoly of its favor and support, and, as a necessary consequence, almost a monopoly of the foreign and domestic exchange. The powers, privileges, and favors bestowed upon it in the original charter, by increasing the value of the stock far above its par value, operated as a gratuity of many millions to the stockholders. . . .

The act before me proposes another gratuity to the holders of the same stock, . . . On all hands it is conceded that its passage will increase at least 20 to 30 per cent more the market price of the stock, subject to the payment of the annuity of $200,000 per year secured by the act, thus adding in a moment one-fourth to its par value. It is not our own citizens only who are to receive the bounty of our Government. More than eight millions of the stock of this bank are held by foreigners. By this act the American Republic proposes virtually to make them a present of some millions of dollars. For these gratuities to foreigners and to some of our own opulent citizens the act secures no equivalent whatever. . . .

Every monopoly and all exclusive privileges are granted at the expense of the public, which ought to receive a fair equivalent. The many millions which this act proposes to bestow on the stockholders of the existing bank must come directly or indirectly out of the earnings of the American people. It is due to them, therefore, if their Government sell monopolies and exclusive privileges, that they should at least exact for them as much as they are worth in open market. The value of the monopoly in this case may be correctly ascertained. The twenty-eight millions of stock would probably be at an advance of 50 per cent, and command in market at least $42,000,000, subject to the payment of the present bonus. The present value of the monopoly, there-

fore, is $17,000,000, and this the act proposes to sell for three millions, payable in fifteen annual installments of $200,000 each.

It is not conceivable how the present stockholders can have any claim to the special favor of the Government. The present corporation has enjoyed its monopoly during the period stipulated in the original contract. If we must have such a corporation, why should not the Government sell out the whole stock and thus secure to the people the full market value of the privileges granted? Why should not Congress create and sell twenty-eight millions of stock, incorporating the purchasers with all the powers and privileges secured in this act and putting the premium upon the sales into the Treasury? . . .

The modifications of the existing charter proposed by this act are not such, in my view, as make it consistent with the rights of the States or the liberties of the people. The qualification of the right of the bank to hold real estate, the limitation of its power to establish branches, and the power reserved to Congress to forbid the circulation of small notes are restrictions comparatively of little value or importance. All the objectionable principles of the existing corporation, and most of its odious features, are retained without alleviation. . . .

Is there no danger to our liberty and independence in a bank that in its nature has so little to bind it to our country? The president of the bank has told us that most of the State banks exist by its forbearance. Should its influence become concentered, as it may under the operation of such an act as this, in the hands of a self-elected directory whose interests are identified with those of the foreign stockholders, will there not be cause to tremble for the purity of our elections in peace and for the independence of our country in war? Their power would be great whenever they might choose to exert it; but if this monopoly were regularly renewed every fifteen or twenty years on terms proposed by themselves, they might seldom in peace put forth their strength to influence elections or control the affairs of the nation. But if any private citizen or public functionary should interpose to curtail its powers or prevent a renewal of its privileges, it can not be doubted that he would be made to feel its influence. . . .

If we must have a bank with private stockholders, every consideration of sound policy and every impulse of American feeling admonishes that it should be *purely American.* Its stockholders should be composed exclusively of our own citizens, who at least ought to be friendly to our Government and willing to support it in times of difficulty and danger. . . . To a bank exclusively of American stockholders, possessing the powers and privileges granted by this act, subscriptions for $200,000,000 could be readily obtained. . . . Let us examine the details of this act in accordance with the rule of legislative action which they have laid down. It will be found that many of the powers and privileges conferred on it can not be supposed necessary for the purpose for which it is proposed to be created, and are not, therefore, means necessary to attain the end in view, and consequently not justified by the Constitution. . . .

The Constitution declares that "the Congress shall have power to exercise exclusive legislation in all cases whatsoever" over the District of Columbia. Its constitutional power, therefore, to establish banks in the district of Columbia and increase their capital at will is unlimited and uncontrollable by any other power than that which gave authority to the Constitution. Yet this act declares that Congress shall *not* increase the capital of existing banks, nor create other banks with capital exceeding in the whole $6,000,000. The Constitution declares that Congress *shall* have power to exercise exclusive legislation over this District *"in all cases whatsoever,"* and this act declares they shall not. Which is the supreme law of the land? This provision can not be *"necessary"* or *"proper"* or *constitutional* unless the absurdity be admitted that whenever it be "necessary and proper" in the opinion of

Congress they have a right to barter away one portion of the powers vested in them by the Constitution as a means of executing the rest. . . .

The Government is the only *"proper"* judge where its agents should reside and keep their offices, because it best knows where their presence will be *"necessary."* It can not, therefore, be *"necessary"* or *"proper"* to authorize the bank to locate branches where it pleases to perform the public service, without consulting the Government, and contrary to its will. The principle laid down by the Supreme Court concedes that Congress can not establish a bank for purposes of private speculation and gain, but only as a means of executing the delegated powers of the General Government. By the same principle a branch bank can not constitutionally be established for other than public purposes. The power which this act gives to establish two branches in any State, without the injunction or request of the Government and for other than public purposes, is not *"necessary"* to the due *execution* of the powers delegated to Congress. . . .

The principle is conceded that the States can not rightfully tax the operations of the General Government. They can not tax the money of the Government deposited in the State banks, nor the agency of those banks in remitting it; but will any man maintain that their mere selection to perform this public service for the General Government would exempt the State banks and their ordinary business from State taxation? Had the United States, instead of establishing a bank at Philadelphia, employed a private banker to keep and transmit their funds, would it have deprived Pennsylvania of the right to tax his bank and his usual banking operations? . . .

It can not be *necessary* to the character of the bank as a fiscal agent of the Government that its private business should be exempted from that taxation to which all the State banks are liable, nor can I conceive it *"proper"* that the substantive and most essential powers reserved by the States shall be thus attacked and annihilated as a means of executing the powers delegated to the General Government. It may be safely assumed that none of those sages who had an agency in forming or adopting our Constitution ever imagined that any portion of the taxing power of the States not prohibited to them nor delegated to Congress was to be swept away and annihilated as a means of executing certain powers delegated to Congress.

If our power over means is so absolute that the Supreme Court will not call in question the constitutionality of an act of Congress the subject of which "is not prohibited, and is really calculated to effect any of the objects intrusted to the Government," although, as in the case before me, it takes away powers expressly granted to Congress and rights scrupulously reserved to the States, it becomes us to proceed in our legislation with the utmost caution. Though not directly, our own powers and the rights of the States may be indirectly legislated away in the use of means to execute substantive powers. We may not enact that Congress shall not have the power of exclusive legislation over the District of Columbia, but we may pledge the faith of the United States that as a means of executing other powers it shall not be exercised for twenty years or forever. We may not pass an act prohibiting the States to tax the banking business carried on within their limits, but we may, as a means of executing our powers over other objects, place that business in the hands of our agents and then declare it exempt from State taxation in their hands. Thus may our own powers and the rights of the States, which we can not directly curtail or invade, be frittered away and extinguished in the use of means employed by us to execute other powers. That a bank of the United States, competent to all the duties which may be required by the Government, might be so organized as not to infringe on our own delegated powers or

the reserved rights of the States I do not entertain a doubt. . . .

Under such circumstances the bank comes forward and asks a renewal of its charter for a term of fifteen years upon conditions which not only operate as a gratuity to the stockholders of many millions of dollars, but will sanction any abuses and legalize any encroachments. . . .

The bank is professedly established as an agent of the executive branch of the Government, and its constitutionality is maintained on that ground. Neither upon the propriety of present action nor upon the provisions of this act was the Executive consulted. It has had no opportunity to say that it neither needs nor wants an agent clothed with such powers and favored by such exemptions. There is nothing in its legitimate functions which makes it necessary or proper. Whatever interest or influence, whether public or private, has given birth to this act, it can not be found either in the wishes or necessities of the executive department, by which present action is deemed premature, and the powers conferred upon its agent not only unnecessary, but dangerous to the Government and country. . . .

There are no necessary evils in government. Its evils exist only in its abuses. If it would confine itself to equal protection, and, as Heaven does its rains, shower its favors alike on the high and the low, the rich and the poor, it would be an unqualified blessing. In the act before me there seems to be a wide and unnecessary departure from these just principles. . . .

Experience should teach us wisdom. Most of the difficulties our Government now encounters and most of the dangers which impend over our Union have sprung from an abandonment of the legitimate objects of Government by our national legislation, and the adoption of such principles as are embodied in this act. Many of our rich men have not been content with equal protection and equal benefits, but have besought us to make them richer by act of Congress. By attempting to gratify their desires we have in the results of our legislation arrayed section against section, interest against interest, and man against man, in a fearful commotion which threatens to shake the foundations of our Union. It is time to pause in our career to review our principles, and if possible revive that devoted patriotism and spirit of compromise which distinguished the sages of the Revolution and the fathers of our Union.

14

Marvin Meyers, a thoughtful modern student of Jacksonian Democracy, finds the essence of the entire movement in Jackson's war on privilege, as exemplified in the Second Bank of the United States:[14]

The great specific mission of Jacksonian Democracy was the war against the Monster Bank. Here the party formed, or found, it character. Here was the issue which stood for all issues. Broad popular fear and hatred of the Second Bank, evoked by Jacksonian appeals, cannot be understood simply as a matter-of-fact reaction to material injuries. The economic operations of the institution conferred some manifest general benefits, directly crossed the interests of only a limited group: its hand was not found upon men's throats or in their pockets. The Bank was called a Monster by Jacksonians. A monster is an unnatural thing, its acts are out of reason, and its threat cannot be estimated in ordinary practical terms. The effort to destroy the Monster Bank and its vicious brood —privilege corporations, paper money—enlisted moral passions in a drama of social justice and self-justification.

Broadly speaking, the Jacksonians blamed the Bank for the transgressions committed by the people of their era against the political, social and economic values of the Old Republic. The Bank carried the bad seed of

Hamilton's first Monster, matured all the old evils, and created some new ones. To the Bank's influence, Jacksonians traced constitutional impiety, consolidated national power, aristocratic privilege, and plutocratic corruption. Social inequality, impersonal and intangible business relations, economic instability, perpetual debt and taxes, all issued from the same source.

Jefferson had brought into temporary equilibrium the formal ideal of a dynamic liberal society and the concrete image of a stable, virtuous yeoman republic. "It is," he wrote, "the manners and spirit of a people which preserve a republic in vigor." And God had made the independent citizen farmer "His peculiar deposit for substantial and genuine virtue." Nothing is more revealing than Jefferson's later concession of the need for domestic manufacturing, under the pressures of war: "Our enemy has indeed the consolation of Satan on removing our first parents from Paradise: from a peaceful agricultural nation he makes us a military and manufacturing one." Now Jacksonian society was caught between the elements—the liberal principle and the yeoman image—and tried again to harmonize them. Americans were boldly liberal in economic affairs, out of conviction and appetite combined, and moved their world in the direction of modern capitalism. But they were not inwardly prepared for the grinding uncertainties, the shocking changes, the complexity and indirection of the new economic ways. Their image of the good life had not altered: somehow, as men and as a society, they hoped to have their brave adventures, their provocative rewards, their open-ended progress, and remain essentially the same. The practical outcomes of the free pursuit of economic interest had never been legitimated, or even fully associated with the abstract liberal principle. Yet the ideological and material attachment to the liberal code was too deep to be severed, even in considerable distress.

Thus many found in the anti-Bank crusade, and in the Jacksonian appeal generally,

---

[14] Reprinted from *The Jacksonian Persuasion: Politics and Belief* by Marvin Meyers, pp. 6–10, with the permission of the publishers, Stanford University Press. Copyright 1957 by the Board of Trustees of the Leland Stanford Junior University.

a way to damn the unfamiliar, threatening, sometimes punishing elements in the changing order by fixing guilt upon a single protean agent. A laissez-faire society with this source of corruptions cut out would re-establish continuity with that golden age in which liberty and progress were joined inseparably with simple yeoman virtues. Under the Jacksonian persuasion men could follow their desires, protest their injuries, affirm their innocence. In this direction one can begin to meet the Jacksonian paradox: the fact that the movement which helped to clear the path for laissez-faire capitalism and its culture in America, and the public which in its daily life eagerly entered on that path, held nevertheless in their political conscience an ideal of a chaste republican order, resisting the seductions of risk and novelty, greed and extravagance, rapid motion and complex dealings.

The Jacksonian movement was forged in the Bank War. Its new machine carried its influence throughout American society; its Old Hero, at once the voice and the exemplar of Jacksonian values, linked the machine to the essential cause. However far Jacksonians went in adapting policies to the practical requirements of local conditions, special interests, and effective party operation, the movement continually returned to its core appeal: death to the Monster; life and health to the old republican virtues. However carefully the knowledgeable voter looked to his immediate interests—when they could be linked plausibly to party policies—he would always see the moral choice proposed by Jacksonian Democracy.

If the Jacksonian persuasion gained relevance and force from common social experience, common tradition, how then did the Whigs develop a distinct voice and a substantial following? Reducing a complex matter to the utmost simplicity: the Whig party spoke to the explicit hopes of Americans as Jacksonians addressed their diffuse fears and resentments. To say this is to reverse a common historical appraisal. The Federalists had been, at the end, a party of fear and resentment. There is some loose justice in deriving Whiggery from Federalism; but only if one recognizes that the language of mob terror and elite guidance had gone out of general use before Jacksonians and Whigs assumed political leadership. Some unregenerate Federalists who worried openly about the dangers of extreme democracy still survived; Whig party leaders tapped them for campaign funds and otherwise wished them out of sight.

What the Whigs deliberately maintained in the inheritance was the ambitious scheme for economic progress through banks, tariffs, and public promotion of internal improvements. Clay's American System, the nearest approach to a coherent Whig policy, was a popularization of Hamiltonian economic designs and John Marshall's flexible interpretation of national authority. Whigs, too, fully associated themselves with the Old Republican idyll—Webster wept in memory of his father's forest hut; zealous clerks helped to clutter city streets with Harrison log cabins —but they felt no serious tension between past and present. Their cabin was a nostalgic prop, a publicity gimmick without focused moral content. The fulfillment of liberal premises in capitalist progress was for them entirely natural and unproblematic.

The Whigs distinctively affirmed the material promise of American life as it was going; and they promised to make it go faster. They were inclined to see the corporation not as a nameless monster but as an engine of progress; public debt not as a curse on honest labor but as a sound gamble on a richer future. Ironically, depression gave them their greatest popular success; yet they did not take depression as an omen of profound social maladjustment. They could see only that an imperious demagogue with primitive economic notions had thrown society into crisis by his spiteful war against the Bank. Indeed the Whigs were so markedly an anti-Jackson coalition that often their positive message was obscured in mere personal invective. To some degree, perhaps, the Whigs did succeed in spreading the con-

viction that Jacksonian dictatorship menaced
the integrity of the republic. Principally,
however, the party appealed to interested
hopes, offering concrete advantages to groups
and sections and a quickening of economic
progress for society as a whole.

SLAVERY AND SECTIONALISM

15

*The panic of 1837 sharpened the sectional
antagonisms that had been developing since the
end of the "era of good feeling" that had
characterized the early 1820s. With hard times
each of the three sections—the industrial Northeast, the agricultural West, and the cotton South
—demanded national legislation beneficial to
its own distinctive economy, leaving Congress
unable to legislate except by compromise and
sectional juggling. To make matters far worse,
the growing conflict over slavery provided an
emotional basis for ill feeling. By this time the
South was so wedded to cotton culture that the
slave system seemed essential to its economy.
Abandoning the mild attitude of the past, when
they had apologized for slaves as a necessary
evil, Southerners now defended their labor system as a positive good. John C. Calhoun voices
the new spirit of his section in a speech to the
Senate on February 6, 1837:[15]*

But let me not be understood as admitting,
even by implication, that the existing relation between the two races in the slaveholding States is an evil—far otherwise; I
hold it to be a good, as it has thus far proved
itself to be to both, and will continue to
prove so if not disturbed by the fell spirit of
abolition. I appeal to facts. Never before has
the black race of Central Africa, from the
dawn of history to the present day, attained
a condition so civilized and so improved,
not only physically, but morally and intellectually. It came among us in a low, degraded,
and savage condition; and in the course of a
few generations it has grown up under the
fostering care of our institutions, reviled as
they have been, to its present comparatively
civilized condition. This, with the rapid in-

---

[15] *The Works of John C. Calhoun* (New York,
1853), pp. 630–633.

crease of numbers, is conclusive proof of the
general happiness of the race, in spite of all
the exaggerated tales to the contrary.

In the meantime, the white or European
race has not degenerated. It has kept pace
with its brethren in other sections of the
Union where slavery does not exist. It is
odious to make comparison; but I appeal
to all sides whether the South is not equal
in virtue, intelligence, patriotism, courage,
disinterestedness, and all the high qualities
which adorn our nature. I ask whether we
have not contributed our full share of talents and political wisdom in forming and
sustaining this political fabric; and whether
we have not constantly inclined most strongly
to the side of liberty, and been the first to see
and first to resist the encroachments of power.
In one thing only are we inferior—the arts of
gain; we acknowledge that we are less wealthy
than the Northern section of this Union, but
I trace this mainly to the fiscal action of this
government, which has extracted much from,
and spent little among us. Had it been the
reverse,—if the exaction had been from the
other section, and the expenditure with us,
this point of superiority would not be against
us now, as it was not at the formation of this
government.

But I take higher ground. I hold that in
the present state of civilization, where two
races of different origin, and distinguished
by color, and other physical differences, as
well as intellectual, are brought together, the
relation now existing in the slaveholding
States between the two, is, instead of an evil,
a good—a positive good. I feel myself called
upon to speak freely upon the subject where
the honor and interests of those I represent
are involved. I hold, then, that there never
has yet existed a wealthy and civilized society in which one portion of the community
did not, in point of fact, live on the labor of
the other. Broad and general as is this assertion, it is fully borne out by history. This is
not the proper occasion, but if it were it
would not be difficult to trace the various
devices by which the wealth of all civilized
communities has been so unequally divided,

and to show by what means so small a share has been allotted to those by whose labor it was produced, and so large a share given to the non-producing class. The devices are almost innumerable, from the brute force and gross superstition of ancient times, to the subtle and artful fiscal contrivances of modern. I might well challenge a comparison between them and the more direct, simple, and patriarchal mode by which the labor of the African race is, among us, commanded by the European. I may say with truth, that in few countries so much is left to the share of the laborer, and so little exacted from him, or where there is more kind attention paid to him in sickness or infirmities of age. Compare his condition with the tenants of the poor-houses in the more civilized portions of Europe—look at the sick and the old and infirm slave, on one hand, in the midst of his family and friends, under the kind superintending care of his master and mistress; and compare it with the forlorn and wretched condition of the pauper in the poorhouse.

But I will not dwell on this aspect of the question; I turn to the political; and here I fearlessly assert that the existing relation between the two races in the South, against which these blind fanatics are waging war, forms the most solid and durable foundation on which to rear free and stable political institutions. It is useless to disguise the fact. There is, and always has been in an advanced stage of wealth and civilization, a conflict between labor and capital. The condition of society in the South exempts us from the disorders and dangers resulting from this conflict; and which explains why it is that the political condition of the slaveholding States has been so much more stable and quiet than that of the North. The advantages of the former in this respect will become more and more manifest, if left undisturbed by interference from without, as the country advances in wealth and numbers. We have, in fact, but just entered that condition of society where the strength and durability of our political institutions are to be tested; and I venture nothing in predicting

that the experience of the next generation will fully test how vastly more favorable our condition of society is to that of other sections for free and stable institutions, provided we are not disturbed by the interference of others, or shall have sufficient intelligence and spirit to resist promptly and successfully such interference. It rests with ourselves to meet and repel them. I look not for aid to this government, or to the other States: not but there are kind feelings towards us on the part of the great body of the non-slaveholding States; but as kind as their feelings may be, we may rest assured that no political party in those States will risk their ascendency for our safety. If we do not defend ourselves, none will defend us; if we yield, we will be more and more pressed as we recede; and if we submit, we will be trampled under foot. Be assured that emancipation itself would not satisfy these fanatics; that gained, the next step would be to raise the negroes to a social and political equality with the whites; and that being effected, we would soon find the present condition of the two races reversed. They and their Northern allies would be the masters, and we the slaves; the condition of the white race in the British West India islands, bad as it was, would be happiness to ours. There the mother country is interested in sustaining the supremacy of the European race. It is true that the authority of the former master is destroyed, but the African will there still be a slave, not to individuals but to the community,—forced to labor, not by the authority of the overseer, but by the bayonet of the soldiery and the rod of the civil magistrate.

Surrounded as the slaveholding States are with such imminent perils, I rejoice to think that our means of defense are ample, if we shall prove to have intelligence and spirit and to see and apply them before it is too late. All we want is concert, to lay aside all party differences, and unite with zeal and energy in repelling approaching dangers. Let there be concert of action, and we shall find ample means of security without resorting to secession or disunion. I speak with full knowledge and a thorough examination of the subject, and for one see my way clearly. One thing alarms me—the eager pursuit of gain which overspreads the land, and which absorbs every faculty of the mind and every feeling of the heart. Of all passions avarice is the most blind and compromising—the last to see and the first to yield to danger. I dare not hope that anything I can say will arouse the South to a due sense of danger; I fear it is beyond the power of mortal voice to awaken it in time from the fatal security into which it has fallen.

16

At the same time, northern opinion shifted in the opposite direction. Always prone to look disapprovingly on slavery, certain Northerners developed a positive fanaticism on the subject under the prodding of abolitionists who made themselves heard during the 1830s. The violence of these outspoken reformers is evidenced by the following statement in the first issue of William Lloyd Garrison's abolitionist newspaper, The Liberator, *published in Boston January 1, 1831:*[16]

In the month of August, I issued proposals for publishing "THE LIBERATOR" in Washington City; but the enterprise, though hailed in different sections of the country, was palsied by public indifference. Since that time, the removal of the *Genius of Universal Emancipation* to the Seat of Government has rendered less imperious the establishment of a similar periodical in that quarter.

During my recent tour for the purpose of exciting the minds of the people by a series of discourses on the subject of slavery, every place that I visited gave fresh evidence of the fact, that a greater revolution in public sentiment was to be effected in the free states —*and particularly in New England*—than at the south. I found contempt more bitter, opposition more active, detraction more relentless, prejudice more stubborn, and apathy

more frozen, than among slave owners themselves. Of course, there were individual exceptions to the contrary. This state of things afflicted, but did not dishearten me. I determined, at every hazard, to lift up the standard of emancipation in the eyes of the nation, *within sight of Bunker Hill and in the birth place of liberty.* That standard is now unfurled; and long may it float, unhurt by the spoliations of time or the missiles of a desperate foe—yea, till every chain be broken, and every bondman set free! Let Southern oppressors tremble—let their secret abettors tremble—let their Northern apologists tremble—let all the enemies of the persecuted blacks tremble.

I deem the publication of my original Prospectus unnecessary, as it has obtained a wide circulation. The principles therein inculcated will be steadily pursued in this paper, excepting that I shall not array myself as the political partisan of any man. In defending the great cause of human rights, I wish to derive the assistance of all religions and of all parties.

Assenting to the "self evident truth" maintained in the American Declaration of Independence, "that all men are created equal, and endowed by their Creator with certain inalienable rights—among which are life, liberty and the pursuit of happiness," I shall strenuously contend for the immediate enfranchisement of our slave population. In Park-Street Church, on the Fourth of July, 1829, in an address on slavery, I unreflectingly assented to the popular but pernicious doctrine of *gradual* abolition. I seize this opportunity to make a full and unequivocal recantation, and thus publicly to ask pardon of my God, of my country, and of my brethren the poor slaves, for having uttered a sentiment so full of timidity, injustice and absurdity. A similar recantation, from my pen, was published in the *Genius of Universal Emancipation* at Baltimore, in September, 1829. My conscience is now satisfied.

I am aware, that many object to the severity of my language; but is there not cause for severity? I *will be* as harsh as truth, and

---

[16] Wendell Phillips Garrison and Francis Jackson Garrison, *William Lloyd Garrison, 1805–1879: The Story of His Life Told by His Children* (New York, 1885), I, 224–225.

as uncompromising as justice. On this subject, I do not wish to think, or speak, or write, with moderation. No! no! Tell a man whose house is on fire, to give a moderate alarm; tell him to moderately rescue his wife from the hands of the ravisher; tell the mother to gradually extricate her babe from the fire into which it has fallen;—but urge me not to use moderation in a cause like the present. I am in earnest—I will not equivocate—I will not excuse—I will not retreat a single inch—*AND I WILL BE HEARD.* The apathy of the people is enough to make every statue leap from its pedestal, and to hasten the resurrection of the dead.

It is pretended, that I am retarding the cause of emancipation by the coarseness of my invective and the precipitancy of my measures. *The charge is not true.* On this question my influence,—humble as it is,— is felt at this moment to a considerable extent, and shall be felt in coming years—not perniciously, but beneficially—not as a curse, but as a blessing; and posterity will bear testimony that I was right. I desire to thank God, that he enables me to disregard "the fear of man which bringeth a snare," and to speak his truth in its simplicity and power.

17

The French observer Alexis de Tocqueville was impressed with the gravity of the conflict between slavery and antislavery partisans:[17]

The first Negroes were imported into Virginia about the year 1621. In America, therefore, as well as in the rest of the globe, slavery originated in the South. Thence it spread from one settlement to another; but the number of slaves diminished towards the Northern states, and the Negro population was always very limited in New England.

A century had scarcely elapsed since the foundation of the colonies when the attention of the planters was struck by the extraordinary fact that the provinces which were comparatively destitute of slaves increased in population, in wealth, and in prosperity more rapidly than those which contained many of them. In the former, however, the inhabitants were obliged to cultivate the soil themselves or by hired laborers; in the latter they were furnished with hands for which they paid no wages. Yet though labor and expense were on the one side and ease with economy on the other, the former had the more advantageous system. This result seemed the more difficult to explain since the settlers, who all belonged to the same European race, had the same habits, the same civilization, the same laws, and their shades of difference were extremely slight.

Time, however, continued to advance, and the Anglo-Americans, spreading beyond the coasts of the Atlantic Ocean, penetrated farther and farther into the solitudes of the West. They met there with a new soil and an unwonted climate; they had to overcome obstacles of the most various character; their races intermingled, the inhabitants of the South going up towards the North, those of the North descending to the South. But in the midst of all these causes the same result occurred at every step; in general, the colonies in which there were no slaves became more populous and more prosperous than those in which slavery flourished. The farther they went, the more was it shown that slavery, which is so cruel to the slave, is prejudicial to the master.

But this truth was most satisfactorily demonstrated when civilization reached the banks of the Ohio. The stream that the Indians had distinguished by the name of Ohio, of the Beautiful River, waters one of the most magnificent valleys which have ever been made the abode of man. Undulating lands extend upon both shores of the Ohio, whose soil affords inexhaustible treasures to the laborer; on either bank the air is equally wholesome and the climate mild; and each of them forms the extreme frontier of a vast state: that which follows the numerous windings of the Ohio upon the left is called Kentucky; that upon the right bears the name of the river. These two states differ only in

[17] Alexis de Tocqueville, *Democracy in America* (Cambridge, 1862), I, 462–467.

a single respect: Kentucky has admitted slavery, but the state of Ohio has prohibited the existence of slaves within its borders. Thus the traveler who floats down the current of the Ohio to the spot where that river falls into the Mississippi may be said to sail between liberty and servitude; and a transient inspection of surrounding objects will convince him which of the two is more favorable to humanity.

Upon the left bank of the stream the population is sparse; from time to time one descries a troop of slaves loitering in the half-desert fields; the primeval forest reappears at every turn; society seems to be asleep, man to be idle, and nature alone offers a scene of activity and life.

From the right bank, on the contrary, a confused hum is heard, which proclaims afar the presence of industry; the fields are covered with abundant harvests; the elegance of the dwellings announces the taste and activity of the laborers; and man appears to be in the enjoyment of that wealth and contentment which is the reward of labor.

The state of Kentucky was founded in 1775, the state of Ohio only twelve years later; but twelve years are more in America than half a century in Europe; and at the present day the population of Ohio exceeds that of Kentucky by two hundred and fifty thousand souls. These different effects of slavery and freedom may readily be understood; and they suffice to explain many of the differences which we notice between the civilization of antiquity and that of our own time.

Upon the left bank of the Ohio labor is confounded with the idea of slavery, while upon the right bank it is identified with that of prosperity and improvement; on the one side it is degraded, on the other it is honored. On the former territory no white laborers can be found, for they would be afraid of assimilating themselves to the Negroes; all the work is done by slaves; on the latter no one is idle, for the white population extend their activity and intelligence to every kind of employment. Thus the men whose task it is to cultivate the rich soil of Kentucky are ignorant and apathetic, while those who are active and enlightened either do nothing or pass over into Ohio, where they may work without shame.

It is true that in Kentucky the planters are not obliged to pay the slaves whom they employ, but they derive small profits from their labor, while the wages paid to free workmen would be returned with interest in the value of their services. The free workman is paid, but he does his work quicker than the slave; and rapidity of execution is one of the great elements of economy. The white sells his services, but they are purchased only when they may be useful; the black can claim no remuneration for his toil, but the expense of his maintenance is perpetual; he must be supported in his old age as well as in manhood, in his profitless infancy as well as in the productive years of youth, in sickness as well as in health. Payment must equally be made in order to obtain the services of either class of men; the free workman receives his wages in money; the slave in education, in food, in care, and in clothing. The money which a master spends in the maintenance of his slaves goes gradually and in detail, so that it is scarcely perceived; the salary of the free workman is paid in a round sum and appears to enrich only him who receives it; but in the end the slave has cost more than the free servant, and his labor is less productive.

The influence of slavery extends still further: it affects the character of the master and imparts a peculiar tendency to his ideas and tastes. Upon both banks of the Ohio the character of the inhabitants is enterprising and energetic, but this vigor is very differently exercised in the two states. The white inhabitant of Ohio, obliged to subsist by his own exertions, regards temporal prosperity as the chief aim of his existence; and as the country which he occupies presents inexhaustible resources to his industry, and ever varying lures to his activity, his acquisitive ardor surpasses the ordinary limits of human cupidity; he is tormented by the desire of wealth, and he boldly enters upon every path that fortune opens to him; he becomes a sailor, a pioneer, an artisan, or a cultivator with the same indifference, and supports with equal constancy the fatigues and the dangers incidental to these various professions; the resources of his intelligence are astonishing, and his avidity in the pursuit of gain amounts to a species of heroism.

But the Kentuckian scorns not only labor but all the undertakings that labor promotes; as he lives in an idle independence, his tastes are those of an idle man; money has lost a portion of its value in his eyes; he covets wealth much less than pleasure and excitement; and the energy which his neighbor devotes to gain turns with him to a passionate love of field sports and military exercises; he delights in violent bodily exertions, he is familiar with the use of arms, and is accustomed from a very early age to expose his life in single combat. Thus slavery prevents the whites not only from becoming opulent, but even from desiring to become so.

18

The continuing impact of sectionalism has been one of the principal forces in American politics, although seldom have antagonisms reached the height of the 1840s and 1850s. A thoughtful student of America's past, Frederick Jackson Turner, assesses the relationship between sectional loyalties and party allegiance in one of his most stimulating essays, written in 1914:[18]

In this country there is an interesting geography of party preponderance. Too complicated for statement in brief, in general the situation may be described, geographically, as regional conflicts within such different sections or larger groups of states as the South, or the North Central States. The rough country, the least valuable farm lands, the illiterate counties, tend, by and large, to be Democratic, as do the principal immigrant populations of the greater cities. The favored-soil regions, the least illiterate areas, the most highly capitalized and industrial dis-

tricts, tend to be anti-Democratic, Federal, Whig, Republican, according to the era. Where there are important exceptions, as along the foothills and ridges of the Carolina mountains, which have been Whig and Republican often, the explanation is usually traceable to historic factors, such as the conflict of the slaveholding Whig coast against the upcountry over legislative apportionment, taxation, internal improvements, and slavery. It was a contest of regions, of economic and social ideals. Physical geography, taken simply, was far from dictating the precise way in which the region acted. The Black Belt in central Georgia and Alabama, and western Mississippi, was strongly Whig, with a small degree of white illiteracy, the abode of wealthy aristocrats. But in the mountain countries of the Carolinas, among the illiterate poor whites, they found political companions in arms. As a rule there were, and are, within each section as classified in the Census Atlas, divergent subdivisions, geographic regions, sometimes running to neighboring sections, or finding allies in similar though isolated regions in other sections. These sections usually show political preponderances (taking the county as the unit) of one or the other party. This is a check upon purely sectional parties, or upon exploitive and ruthless action by the section which controls a major political party. Within each section, moreover, partly due to the regional factor, and partly due to the factors of migration and inherited political faiths, the parties are closely divided. To this, the South since the Civil War is an exception; but the Northern industrial wedge pushed down along the mines, the mills, the hydroelectric powers of the Alleghenies and their foothills, constitutes a menace to Southern solidarity. With these regional varieties, with these close party majorities, there are checks to sectional particularism. Its political power is in a state of unstable equilibrium. It stands in danger of disintegration itself, unless its cause overwhelmingly appeals to its people.

National party, then, has been in America a flexible bond, yielding in extreme cases

[18] From *The Significance of Sections in American History* by Frederick Jackson Turner, pp. 203–205. Copyright 1932 by Holt, Rinehart and Winston, Inc.

to sectional insurgency, yielding often, in the construction of bills, to sectional demands and to sectional threats, but always tending to draw sections together toward national adjustments by compromise and bargain. A common language, law, and institutions, absence of sectional concentration of religions and races, absence of historical hatreds, have helped to prevent America from splitting apart and falling into European conditions; but regional geography, quasi-continental parties, and a national, that is, intersectional (our equivalent of international), congressional organization by which sectionalism could express itself in voting instead of by war—these are important factors in the contrast between European and American ways of settling difficulties, and are important explanations of our continued unity.

The Triumph of Democratic Reform

Jacksonian democracy promised social gains for the underprivileged. Americans sought to abolish outmoded institutions that blocked the way toward a democratic utopia. They set out to eliminate political and economic inequalities, stamp out sin, and assuage social evils. Their vision was a hopeful one: a society modeled on the Declaration of Independence, one where all men had a right to "life, liberty, and the pursuit of happiness." Sectional conflict and civil war temporarily halted the democratic movement that had already gained such momentum.

THE GOALS OF SOCIAL REFORM

1

The Jacksonian era was one of infinite optimism. From the concept of equalitarianism stemmed another basic proposition of the Age of the Common Man: the concept of the unlimited perfectibility of mankind. Alexis de Tocqueville records the optimism of the people:[1]

Equality suggests to the human mind several ideas which would not have originated from any other source, and it modifies almost all those previously entertained. I take as an example the idea of human perfectibility, because it is one of the principal notions that the intellect can conceive, and because it constitutes of itself a great philosophical theory, which is every instant to be traced by its consequences in the practice of human affairs.

Although man has many points of resemblance with the brute creation, one characteristic is peculiar to himself,—he improves: they are incapable of improvement. Mankind could not fail to discover this difference from its earliest period. The idea of perfectibility is therefore as old as the world; equality did not give birth to it, although it has imparted to it a novel character.

[1] Alexis de Tocqueville, *Democracy in America* (London, 1862 ed.), II, 37–39, 118–120.

When the citizens of a community are classed according to their rank, their profession, or their birth, and when all men are constrained to follow the career which happens to open before them, everyone thinks that the utmost limits of human power are to be discerned in proximity to himself, and none seeks any longer to resist the inevitable law of his destiny. Not indeed that an aristocratic people absolutely contests man's faculty of self-improvement, but they do not hold it to be indefinite; amelioration they conceive, but not change; they imagine that the future condition of society may be better, but not essentially different; and whilst they admit that mankind has made vast strides in improvement, and may still have some to make, they assign to it beforehand certain impassable limits.

Thus they do not presume that they have arrived at the supreme good or at absolute truth (what people or what man was ever wild enough to imagine it?) but they cherish a persuasion that they have pretty nearly reached that degree of greatness and knowledge which our imperfect nature admits of; and as nothing moves about them they are willing to fancy that everything is in its fit place. Then it is that the legislator affects to lay down eternal laws; that kings and nations will raise none but imperishable monuments;

and that the present generation undertakes to spare generations to come the care of regulating their destinies.

In proportion as castes disappear and the classes of society approximate,—as manners, customs, and laws vary, from the tumultuous intercourse of men,—as new facts arise,—as new truths are brought to light,—as ancient opinions are dissipated and others take their place,—the image of an ideal perfection, forever on the wing, presents itself to the human mind. Continual changes are then every instant occurring under the observation of every man: the position of some is rendered worse; and he learns but too well, that no people and no individual, how enlightened soever they may be, can lay claim to infallibility;—the condition of others is improved; whence he infers that man is endowed with an indefinite faculty of improvement. His reverses teach him that none may hope to have discovered absolute good,—his success stimulates him to the never-ending pursuit of it. Thus, forever seeking—forever falling, to rise again—often disappointed, but not discouraged,—he tends unceasingly towards that unmeasured greatness so indistinctly visible at the end of the long track which humanity has yet to tread.

It can hardly be believed how many facts naturally flow from the philosophical theory of the indefinite perfectibility of man, or how strong an influence it exercises even on men who, living entirely for the purposes of action and not of thought, seem to conform their actions to it, without knowing anything about it.

I accost an American sailor, and I inquire why the ships of his country are built so as to last but for a short time; he answers without hesitation that the art of navigation is every day making such rapid progress that the finest vessel would become almost useless if it lasted beyond a certain number of years. In these words, which fell accidentally and on a particular subject from a man of rude attainments, I recognize the general and systematic idea upon which a great people directs all its concerns.

Aristocratic nations are naturally too apt to narrow the scope of human perfectibility; democratic nations to expand it beyond compass. . . .

I have shown how it is that in ages of equality every man seeks for his opinions within himself: I am now about to show how it is that, in the same ages, all his feelings are turned towards himself alone. *Individualism* is a novel expression, to which a novel idea has given birth. Our fathers were only acquainted with egotism. Egotism is a passionate and exaggerated love of self, which leads a man to connect everything with his own person, and to prefer himself to everything in the world. Individualism is a mature and calm feeling, which disposes each member of the community to sever himself from the mass of his fellow-creatures; and to draw apart with his family and his friends; so that, after he has thus formed a little circle of his own, he willingly leaves society at large to itself. Egotism originates in blind instinct: individualism proceeds from erroneous judgment more than from depraved feelings; it originates as much in the deficiencies of the mind as in the perversity of the heart.

Egotism blights the germ of all virtue: individualism, at first, only saps the virtues of public life; but, in the long run, it attacks and destroys all others, and is at length absorbed in downright egotism. Egotism is a vice as old as the world, which does not belong to one form of society more than to another: individualism is of democratic origin, and it threatens to spread in the same ratio as the equality of conditions.

Amongst aristocratic nations, as families remain for centuries in the same condition, often on the same spot, all generations become as it were contemporaneous. A man almost always knows his forefathers, and respects them: he thinks he already sees his remote descendants, and he loves them. He willingly imposes duties on himself towards the former and the latter; and he will frequently sacrifice his personal gratifications to those who went before and to those who will come after him.

Aristocratic institutions have, moreover, the effect of closely binding every man to several of his fellow-citizens. As the classes of an aristocratic people are strongly marked and permanent, each of them is regarded by its own members as a sort of lesser country, more tangible and more cherished than the country at large. As in aristocratic communities all the citizens occupy fixed positions, one above the other, the result is that each of them always sees a man above himself whose patronage is necessary to him, and below himself another man whose co-operation he may claim.

Men living in aristocratic ages are therefore almost always closely attached to something placed out of their own sphere, and they are often disposed to forget themselves. It is true that in those ages the notion of human fellowship is faint, and that men seldom think of sacrificing themselves for mankind; but they often sacrifice themselves for other men. In democratic ages, on the contrary, when the duties of each individual to the race are much more clear, devoted service to any one man becomes more rare; the bond of human affection is extended, but it is relaxed.

Amongst democratic nations new families are constantly springing up, others are constantly falling away, and all that remain change their condition; the woof of time is every instant broken, and the track of generations effaced. Those who went before are soon forgotten; of those who will come after no one has any idea: the interest of man is confined to those in close propinquity to himself.

As each class approximates to other classes, and intermingles with them, its members become indifferent and as strangers to one another. Aristocracy had made a chain of all the members of the community, from the peasant to the king: democracy breaks that chain, and severs every link of it.

As social conditions become more equal, the number of persons increases who, al-though they are neither rich enough nor powerful enough to exercise any great influence over their fellow-creatures, have nevertheless acquired or retained sufficient education and fortune to satisfy their own wants. They owe nothing to any man, they expect nothing from any man; they acquire the habit of always considering themselves as standing alone, and they are apt to imagine that their whole destiny is in their own hands. Thus not only does democracy make every man forget his ancestors, but it hides his descendants, and separates his contemporaries from him; it throws him back forever upon himself alone, and threatens in the end to confine him entirely within the solitude of his own heart.

2

The imperative need for reform was brought home to humanitarians by the intolerable condition of the Northeast's working class. Wages, particularly after the panic of 1837, were pitifully low, hours of work cruelly long, and working conditions scandalous. The situation in Lowell, Massachusetts, a newly built textile city where employers were reputedly more humane than elsewhere, is described by a traveler in 1846:[2]

We have lately visited the cities of Lowell and Manchester, and have had an opportunity of examining the factory system more closely than before. We had distrusted the accounts, which we had heard from persons engaged in the Labor Reform, now beginning to agitate New England; we could scarcely credit the statements made in relation to the exhausting nature of the labor in the mills, and to the manner in which the young women, the operatives, lived in their boarding-houses, six sleeping in a room, poorly ventilated.

We went through many of the mills, talked particularly to a large number of the operatives, and ate at their boarding-houses, on purpose to ascertain by personal inspec-

---

[2] *The Harbinger* (Boston), November 14, 1846, pp. 366–367.

tion the facts of the case. We assure our readers that very little information is possessed, and no correct judgments formed, by the public at large, of our factory system, which is the first germ of the Industrial or Commercial Feudalism, that is to spread over our land. . . .

The operatives work *thirteen hours* a day in the summer time, and *from daylight to dark* in the winter. At half past four in the morning the factory bell rings, and at five the girls must be in the mills. A clerk, placed as a watch, observes those who are a few minutes behind the time, and effectual means are taken to stimulate to punctuality. This is the morning commencement of the industrial discipline—(should we not rather say industrial tyranny?) which is established in these Associations of this moral and Christian community. At seven the girls are allowed thirty minutes for breakfast, and at noon thirty minutes more for dinner, except during the first quarter of the year, when the time is extended to forty-five minutes. But within this time they must hurry to their boarding-houses and return to the factory, and that through the hot sun, or the rain and cold. A meal eaten under such circumstances must be quite unfavorable to digestion and health, as any medical man will inform us. At seven o'clock in the evening the factory bell sounds the close of the day's work.

Thus thirteen hours per day of close attention and monotonous labor are exacted from the young women in these manufactories. . . . So fatigued,—we should say, exhausted and worn out, but we wish to speak of the system in the simplest language,— are numbers of the girls, that they go to bed soon after their evening meal, and endeavor by a comparatively long sleep to resuscitate their weakened frames for the toils of the coming day. When Capital has got thirteen hours of labor daily out of a being, it can get nothing more. It would be a poor speculation in an industrial point of view to *own* the operative; for the trouble and expense of providing for times of sickness and old

age would more than counterbalance the difference between the price of wages and the expense of board and clothing. The far greater number of fortunes, accumulated by the North in comparison with the South, shows that hireling labor is more profitable for Capital than slave labor.

Now let us examine the nature of the labor itself, and the conditions under which it is performed. Enter with us into the large rooms, when the looms are at work. The largest that we saw is in the Amoskeag Mills at Manchester. It is four hundred feet long, and about seventy broad; there are five hundred looms, and twenty-one thousand spindles in it. The din and clatter of these five hundred looms under full operation, struck us on first entering as something frightful and infernal, for it seemed such an atrocious violation of one of the faculties of the human soul, the sense of hearing. After a while we became somewhat inured to it, and by speaking quite close to the ear of an operative and quite loud, we could hold a conversation, and make the inquiries we wished.

The girls attend upon an average three looms; many attend four, but this requires a very active person, and the most unremitting care. However, a great many do it. Attention to two is as much as should be demanded of an operative. This gives us some idea of the application required during the thirteen hours of daily labor. The atmosphere of such a room cannot of course be pure; on the contrary it is charged with cotton filaments and dust, which, we were told, are very injurious to the lungs. On entering the room, although the day was warm, we remarked that the windows were down; we asked the reason, and a young woman answered very *naïvely*, and without seeming to be in the least aware that this privation of fresh air was anything else than perfectly natural, that "when the wind blew, the threads did not work so well." After we had been in the room for fifteen or twenty minutes, we found ourselves, as did the persons who accompanied us, in quite a perspiration, produced by a certain moisture which we observed in the air, as well as by the heat. . . .

The young women sleep upon an average six in a room; three beds to a room. There is no privacy, no retirement here; it is almost impossible to read or write alone, as the parlor is full and so many sleep in the same chamber. A young woman remarked to us, that if she had a letter to write, she did it on the head of a band-box, sitting on a trunk, as there was not space for a table. So live and toil the young women of our country in the boarding-houses and manufactories, which the rich and influential of our land have built for them.

3

Many workers who escaped the tyranny of the textile mills were still bound to the operations of the industrial machine. Crowded together in unhealthful tenements, always ill-clothed and ill-fed, they managed to maintain existence only by constant toil. The life of New York shoemakers who did piecework for factories is described by the New York Daily Tribune *in 1845:[3]*

There is no class of mechanics in New York who average so great an amount of work for so little money as the journeymen shoemakers. The number of journeymen out of employment is also large. . . . There are hundreds of them in the city constantly wandering from shop to shop in search of work, while many of them have families in a state of absolute want. . . . We have been in more than fifty cellars in different parts of the city, each inhabited by a shoemaker and his family. The floor is made of rough plank laid loosely down, the ceiling is not quite so high as a tall man. The walls are dark and damp, and a wide, desolate fireplace yawns in the center to the right of the entrance. There is no outlet back and of course no yard privileges of any kind. The miserable room is lighted only by a shallow sash, partly projecting above the surface of the ground and

by the little light that struggles down the steep and rotting stairs. In this . . . often live the man with his work-bench, his wife and five or six children of all ages, and perhaps a palsied grandfather or grandmother and often both. In one corner is a squalid bed and the room elsewhere is occupied by the work-bench, a cradle made from a dry-goods box, two or three broken, seatless chairs, a stew-pan and a kettle.

4

But even a marginal existence was far from certain. Workers were completely dependent upon employers, who could discharge their employees without cause, lower their wages without excuse, or discard them without mercy if their efficiency faltered. Work contracts, a precondition to employment, demonstrated the utter helplessness of employees. One, used by the Cocheco Manufacturing Company of Dover, New Hampshire, is typical:[4]

We, the subscribers, do hereby agree to enter the service of the *Cocheco Manufacturing Company*, and conform, in all respects, to the REGULATIONS which are now, or may hereafter be adopted, for the good government of the Institution.

We further agree, *to work for such wages per week, and prices by the Job, as the Company may see fit to pay*, AND BE SUBJECT TO THE FINES as well as entitled to the premiums paid by the Company.

We further agree to allow two cents each week, to be deducted from our wages, for the benefit of the SICK FUND.

☞ We also agree not to leave the service of the Company, without giving two weeks notice of our intentions, without permission of an agent; and if we do, we agree to forfeit to the use of the Company, two weeks' pay.

We also agree not to be engaged in any combination, whereby the work may be impeded, or the Company's interest in any work injured; if we do, we agree to forfeit

---

[3] New York *Daily Tribune*, September 9, 1845. Reprinted in Norman Ware, *The Industrial Worker, 1840–1860* (Boston, 1924), p. 45.

[4] Quoted in Seth Luther, *An Address to the Working-Men of New-England* (Boston, 1832), p. 36.

to the use of the Company, the amount of wages that may be due to us at the time.

We also agree that in case we are discharged from the service of the Company for any fault, we will not consider ourselves entitled to be settled with, in less than two weeks from the time of such discharge.

Payments for labor performed are to be made monthly.

5

These conditions degraded the men and women who worked, and left deep scars on the whole social structure. Children who were forced either to labor long hours in mills or to roam the streets while their parents worked touched the heart of Theodore Parker, a Unitarian clergyman who devoted much of his life to righting social wrongs:[5]

If you could know the life of one of those poor lepers of Boston, you would wonder, and weep. Let me take one of them at random out of the mass. He was born, unwelcome, amid wretchedness and want. His coming increased both. Miserably he struggles through his infancy, less tended than the lion's whelp. He becomes a boy. He is covered only with rags, and those squalid with long accumulated filth. He wanders about your streets, too low even to seek employment, now snatching from a gutter half-rotten fruit which the owner flings away. He is ignorant; he has never entered a school-house; to him even the alphabet is a mystery. He is young in years, yet old in misery. There is no hope in his face. He herds with others like himself,—low, ragged, hungry and idle. If misery loves company, he finds that satisfaction. Follow him to his home at night; he herds in a cellar; in the same sty with father, mother, brothers, sisters, and perhaps yet other families of like degree. What served him for dress by day, is his only bed by night.

Well, this boy steals some trifle, a biscuit, a bit of rope, or a knife from a shop-window; he is seized and carried to jail. The day

comes for trial. He is marched through the streets in handcuffs, the companion of drunkards and thieves, thus deadening the little self-respect which Nature left even in an outcast's bosom. He sits there chained like a beast; a boy in irons! the sport and mockery of men vulgar as the common sewer. His trial comes. Of course he is convicted. The show of his countenance is witness against him. His rags and dirt, his ignorance, his vagrant habits, his idleness, all testify against him. That face so young, and yet so impudent, so sly, so writ all over with embryo villainy, is evidence enough. The jury are soon convinced, for they see his temptations in his look, and surely know that in such a condition men will steal: yes, they themselves would steal. The judge represents the law, and that practically regards it a crime even for a boy to be weak and poor. Much of our common law, it seems to me, is based on might, not right. So he is hurried off to jail at a tender age, and made legally the companion of felons. Now the State has him wholly in her power; by that rough adoption, has made him her own child, and sealed the indenture with the jailer's key. His handcuffs are the symbol of his sonship to the State. She shuts him in her college for the Little. What does that teach him; science, letters,—even morals and religion? Little enough of this, even in Boston, and in most counties of Massachusetts, I think nothing at all, not even a trade which he can practice when his term expires! I have been told a story, and I wish it might be falsely told, of a boy, in this city, of sixteen, sent to the house of correction for five years because he stole a bunch of keys, and coming out of that jail at twenty-one, unable to write, or read, or calculate, and with no trade but that of picking oakum. Yet he had been five years the child of the State, and in that college for the Poor! Who would employ such a youth; with such a reputation; with the smell of the jail in his very breath? Not your shrewd men of business, they know the risk; not your respectable men, members of churches and all that; not they! Why it

[5] Theodore Parker, *Social Classes in a Republic* (Boston, n.d.), pp. 107–110.

would hurt a man's reputation for piety to do good in that way. Besides, the risk is great, and it argues a great deal more Christianity than it is popular to have, for a respectable man to employ such a youth. He is forced back into crime again. I say forced, for honest men will not employ him when the State shoves him out of the jail. Soon you will have him in the court again, to be punished more severely. Then he goes to the State prison, and then again, till death mercifully ends his career!

Who is to blame for all that? I will ask the best man among the best of you, what he would have become, if thus abandoned, turned out in childhood, and with no culture, into the streets, to herd with the wickedest of men. Somebody says, there are "organic sins" in society which nobody is to blame for. But by this sin organized in society, these vagrant children are training up to become thieves, pirates, and murderers. I cannot blame them. But there is a terrible blame somewhere, for it is not the will of God that one of these little ones should perish. Who is it that organizes the sin of society?

6

Against these conditions, Jacksonian reformers launched a sustained attack. They employed both possible weapons—government intervention and labor solidarity—but the role of the government was inhibited by theories of laissez faire and constitutional limitations. The most obvious sphere of action was that designed to limit hours of labor. After two decades of agitation, New Hampshire in 1847 became the first state to limit the working day to ten hours:[6]

SECTION 1. Be it enacted by the Senate and House of Representatives in General Court convened, that in all contracts for or relating to labor, ten hours of actual labor shall be taken to be a day's work, unless otherwise agreed by the parties; and no per-

son shall be required or holden to perform more than ten hours labor in one day, except in pursuance of an express contract requiring greater time.

SEC. 2. No minor under the age of 15 shall be employed in any manufacturing establishment more than 10 hours the day, in any labor, without the written consent of the parent or guardian of such minor first obtained. If any manufacturer, or any corporation, or the agent of any manufacturer or corporation, shall employ any such minor in violation of the provisions of this section, he or they shall be punished by a fine not exceeding one hundred dollars. Approved July 3, 1847.

7

That other states belatedly followed this example was due largely to the reception accorded the ten-hour law. The enthusiasm with which workingmen of Manchester, New Hampshire, greeted the measure is set forth in resolutions adopted at a mass meeting in August 1847:[7]

Resolved, That we hold these truths self-evident, that man is endowed by his creator with certain inalienable rights; among which is life, liberty, the pursuit of happiness, a home on the earth, a right to labor, and the power to limit for himself, his hours of labor.

Resolved, That agreeable to the laws of New Hampshire, Ten Hours constitutes a legal day's work.

Resolved, That ten hours' labor in each day is all that man's constitution is able to bear.

Resolved, That on and after the 15th of September next, we will not work more than the legal number of hours in each day.

Resolved, That we will sign no contracts to work more than ten hours per day.

Resolved, That, to the support of these Resolutions we pledge our lives and our sacred honor.

Resolved, That a copy of these Resolutions be sent to each of the manufacturing towns in the State.

---

[6] Reprinted by permission of the publishers, The Arthur H. Clark Company, from *A Documentary History of American Industrial Society,* edited by John R. Commons and others (Cleveland, 1910), VIII, 192.

---

[7] *Ibid.*

Resolved, That a copy of these Resolutions be published in the Manchester *Democrat and American,* and the *Voice of Industry,* published in Lowell, Mass.

8

Slow as was the process of achieving economic equalitarianism through government action, the other possible course open to reformers—the more equitable distribution of wealth through labor solidarity—was no less difficult to attain. Trade unions were defined as "conspiracies" under the English common law followed in most states; members who organized to raise wages or to regulate terms of employment were arrested and imprisoned. Not until 1842 did a state discard this archaic definition. The Massachusetts courts, in the case of Commonwealth v. Hunt, *boldly proclaimed the right of laborers to unite for their own protection:*[8]

We have no doubt, that by the operation of the constitution of this Commonwealth, the general rules of the common law, making conspiracy an indictable offence, are in force here, . . . Still it is proper in this connexion to remark, that although the common law in regard to conspiracy in this Commonwealth is in force, yet it will not necessarily follow that every indictment at common law for this offence is a precedent for a similar indictment in this State. The general rule of the common law is, that it is a criminal and indictable offence, for two or more to confederate and combine together, by concerted means, to do that which is unlawful or criminal, to the injury of the public, or portions or classes of the community, or even to the rights of an individual. This rule of law may be equally in force as a rule of the common law, in England and in this Commonwealth; and yet it must depend upon the local laws of each country to determine, whether the purpose to be accomplished by the combination, or the concerted means of accomplishing it, be unlawful or criminal in the respective countries. All those laws of the parent country, whether rules of the common law, or early English

statutes, which were made for the purpose of regulating the wages of laborers, the settlement of paupers, and making it penal for anyone to use a trade or handicraft to which he had not served a full apprenticeship—not being adapted to the circumstances of our colonial condition—were not adopted, used or approved, and therefore do not come within the description of the laws adopted and confirmed by the provision of the constitution already cited. . . .

Stripped then of these introductory recitals and alleged injurious consequences, and of the qualifying epithets attached to the facts, the averment is this; that the defendents and others formed themselves into a society, and agreed not to work for any person who should employ any journeymen or other person, not a member of such society, after notice given him to discharge such workman. The manifest intent of the association is, to induce all those engaged in the same occupation to become members of it. Such a purpose is not unlawful. It would give them a power which might be exerted for useful and honorable purposes, or for dangerous and pernicious ones. If the latter were the real and actual object, and susceptible of proof, it should have been specially charged. Such an association might be used to afford each other assistance in times of poverty, sickness and distress; or to raise their intellectual, moral and social condition; or to make improvement in their art; or for other proper purposes. Or the association might be designed for purposes of oppression and injustice. . . .

Nor can we perceive that the objects of this association, whatever they may have been, were to be attained by criminal means. The means which they proposed to employ, as averred in this count, and which, as we are now to presume, were established by the proof, were, that they would not work for a person, who, after due notice, should employ a journeyman not a member of their society. Supposing the object of the association to be laudable and lawful, or at least not unlawful, are these means criminal? The case sup-

---

[8] *Massachusetts Reports,* 4 METCALF 45–50.

poses that these persons are not bound by contract, but free to work for whom they please, or not to work, if they so prefer. In this state of things, we cannot perceive, that it is criminal for men to agree together to exercise their own acknowledged rights, in such a manner as best to subserve their own interests. One way to test this is, to consider the effect of such an agreement, where the object of the association is acknowledged on all hands to be a laudable one. Suppose a class of workmen, impressed with the manifold evils of intemperance, should agree with each other not to work in a shop in which ardent spirit was furnished, or not to work in a shop with any one who used it, or not to work for an employer, who should, after notice, employ a journeyman who habitually used it. The consequences might be the same. A workman, who should still persist in the use of ardent spirit, would find it more difficult to get employment; a master employing such an one might, at times, experience inconvenience in his work, in losing the services of a skilful but intemperate workman. Still it seems to us, that as the object would be lawful, and the means not unlawful, such an agreement could not be pronounced a criminal conspiracy. . . .

We think, therefore, that associations may be entered into, the object of which is to adopt measures that may have a tendency to impoverish another, that is, to diminish his gains and profits, and yet so far from being criminal or unlawful, the object may be highly meritorious and public spirited. The legality of such an association will therefore depend upon the means to be used for its accomplishment.

IDEALS OF ECONOMIC DEMOCRACY

9

Many reformers were irked by what they considered creeping progress toward economic democracy made by the workers themselves. Fearful lest the widening gulf between the earnings of capital and labor lead to industrial feudalism before the trend could be checked, humanitarians adopted various panaceas designed to restore equality among men. What stimulated their attitude is described by Parke Godwin, a middle-class lawyer and editor, whose Democracy, Constructive and Pacific *(1844) expresses serious concern for the future:*[9]

A striking phenomenon is beginning to show itself in these days, even to the eyes of those least observant of such things. We refer to the rapid and powerful constitution of a new Aristocracy, of a commercial and financial Feudality, which is taking the place of the ancient aristocracy of nobles and warriors, by the annihilation and impoverishment of the lower and middling classes.

After the grand explosions of the American and French Revolutions, after the overturn of the ancient political system, after the abolition of feudal property, of laws of primogeniture, of trading guilds and commercial corporations, and the bold proclamation of the great doctrine of free-trade, society has believed itself forever emancipated from the domination of aristocratic and exclusive powers. It has supposed that it had achieved the enfranchisement of every individual, that it had bequeathed to the universal race of man the opportunity for a full development of all its faculties.

There never was a greater mistake, as the result most abundantly proves.

An essential element in the calculation has been overlooked. Now that the agitation caused by the first onset of destruction has somewhat subsided, when matters begin to assume their regular places, it is found that individuals indeed enter upon the new race of life, with perfect *freedom* to use themselves and their natural powers as they please; but upon what very different conditions have they entered? They are free to run the same race, but on most unequal and disadvantageous terms. The same course is open to all, but each one, to continue our sporting metaphor, carries different weights. Nay, they cannot be said to have been started

---

[9] Parke Godwin, *Democracy, Constructive and Pacific* (New York, 1844), pp. 10–12.

at the same starting-place. Some were already provided with facilities to carry them swiftly and surely along their way,—they had fortune, talents, education, high and influential positions,—and the accumulated experience of ages; others, and these are the most numerous, had none of these things; they had, nor fortune, nor rank, nor talents developed by anterior education, none of the aids and spurs by which the more favored rise; they are banished to the outer borders of civilized existence, they welter in the lowest pools of corrupt and stagnant companionships.

What must result in such a state of things, from that industrial liberty on which we reckoned so much—from that famous doctrine of free-trade, which was the peculiar glory of the new science of political economy, and which we fondly thought the last best expression of the democratic theory? What result? Let facts answer the question! They will point us to the general subjection of the masses—of the class without wealth, talent or education—to the class which is well-provisioned and equipped!

"The lists are open," say you, "all men are called to the combat, the terms are equal for all capacities." Hold! you have forgotten one thing! It is, that on this great field of battle, some are trained, disciplined, caparisoned, armed to the teeth an impenetrable hauberk and shield is round their bodies, swords and spears are in their hands—and they hold the advantageous places for assault or for flight; while others, despoiled, naked, ignorant, famished, are compelled to live from day to day, and support their wives and children, on the meagre pittance extorted from their adversaries or picked by piecemeals from the streets. Oh! most benevolent free-trader, what sort of equality is this? What fight, what resistance even, are we of the many-headed multitude to make? Your absolute liberty is only an absolute abandonment of the unarmed and destitute masses to the charity of the well-fed and well-armed few. Your democratic civilization, which began in aristocratic feudalism—the progress of which

has emancipated the working-classes from direct and personal servitude only—will end in a moneyed aristocracy, will lead to a collective and indirect servitude just as oppressive as that from which we have been so lately relieved.

10

The solutions for the problems of society were almost as numerous as the reformers who espoused them. One was the brain child of George Henry Evans, an English-born labor leader, who thought he found the answer in the unused lands of the West. The National Reform Association, formed in 1844, was devoted to opening the public domain to actual settlers, for Evans was convinced that the magnet of free lands would drain enough workers westward to raise the wages of those left behind. Typical of the Association's propaganda was a handbill, "Vote Yourself a Farm," circulated in 1846:[10]

Are you an American citizen? Then you are a joint-owner of the public lands. Why not take enough of your property to provide yourself a home? Why not vote yourself a farm?

Remember poor Richard's saying: "Now I have a sheep and a cow, every one bids me 'good morrow.'" If a man have a house and a home of his own, though it be a thousand miles off, he is well received in other people's houses; while the homeless wretch is turned away. The bare right to a farm, though you should never go near it, would save you from many an insult. Therefore, Vote yourself a farm.

Are you a party follower? Then you have long enough employed your vote to benefit scheming office-seekers; use it for once to benefit yourself—Vote yourself a farm.

Are you tired of slavery—of drudging for others—of poverty and its attendant miseries? Then, Vote yourself a farm.

Are you endowed with reason? Then you

[10] *True Workingman,* January 24, 1846. Reprinted by permission of the publishers, The Arthur H. Clark Company, from *A Documentary History of American Industrial Society,* edited by John R. Commons and others (Cleveland, 1910), VII, 305–306.

must know that your right to life hereby includes the right to a place to live in—the right to a home. Assert this right, so long denied mankind by feudal robbers and their attorneys. Vote yourself a farm.

Are you a believer in the scriptures? Then assert that the land is the Lord's, because He made it. Resist then the blasphemers who exact money for His work, even as you would resist them should they claim to be worshipped for His holiness. Emancipate the poor from the necessity of encouraging such blasphemy—Vote the freedom of the public lands.

Are you a man? Then assert the sacred rights of man—especially your right to stand upon God's earth, and to till it for your own profit. Vote yourself a farm.

Would you free your country, and the sons of toil everywhere, from the heartless, irresponsible mastery of the aristocracy of avarice? Would you disarm this aristocracy of its chief weapon, the fearful power of banishment from God's earth? Then join with your neighbors to form a true American party, having for its guidance the principles of the American revolution, and whose chief measures shall be—1. To limit the quantity of land that any one man may henceforth monopolize or inherit; and 2. To make the public lands free to actual settlers only, each having the right to sell his improvements to any man not possessed of other land. These great measures once carried, wealth would become a changed social element; it would then consist of the accumulated products of human labor, instead of a hoggish monopoly of the products of God's labor; and the antagonism of capital and labor would forever cease. Capital could no longer grasp the largest share of the laborer's earnings, as a reward for not doing him all the injury the laws of the feudal aristocracy authorize, viz: the denial of all stock to work upon and all place to live in. To derive any profit from the laborer, it must first give him work; for it could no longer wax fat by levying a dead tax upon his existence. The hoary iniquities of Norman land pirates would cease to pass

current as American law. Capital, with its power for good undiminished, would lose the power to oppress; and a new era would dawn upon the earth, and rejoice the souls of a thousand generations. Therefore forget not to Vote yourself a farm.

11

Other reformers sought to restore economic equilibrium between the classes by founding communal experiments where all could live together in harmony. One leader was Albert Brisbane, a well-to-do New Yorker, whose self-appointed mission was popularizing the views of Charles Fourier, a French social philosopher. Fourier insisted that men could enjoy peace and plenty only when they lived in small self-sufficient groups called phalanxes, far from the tumult of industrialism. Brisbane's principal work, The Social Destiny of Man (1840), not only expounded the Fourier thesis but castigated the social order:[11]

Riches are the leading wish of man, and in this country wealth has become the all absorbing object of desire. In this strife after wealth, in which millions are engaged, why has it not been perceived, that not one-twentieth can succeed? If but one-third of the population are producers, if production is the only source of riches, and if our system of consumption in isolated households is so complicated, that the small amount produced by the third does not go one-half as far as it would in a system of Combination and Association (or in other words, if one-half of the small product created by the producing third of society is wasted), how is it possible that even the common wants of the entire population, setting aside all superfluity, can be satisfied?

Let us draw a comparison, which will explain this clearly. Suppose that, out of three persons living together, one alone was engaged in producing, while the other two were idle: it is very evident that the active laborer could not alone produce enough to maintain himself and the other two comfort-

---

[11] Albert Brisbane, *Social Destiny of Man: Or Association and Reorganization of Industry* (Philadelphia, 1840), pp. 78–83.

ably. But if we suppose in addition, that each has a separate house, has his meals prepared separately in his own dwelling, the small product of the producer would not go near as far as possible, the most excessive complimized their means; to the loss caused by the idleness of two inactive persons, is to be added the waste of separate and complicated preparations. This is a perfect illustration of the present state of things. One-third of the population produce; two-thirds are non-producers. Instead of uniting and associating for the purpose of making the insufficient product of the labor of the active third go as far as possible, the most excessive complication and waste takes place, there being as many separate houses, kitchens, cooks, fires, &c., as there are families. The result is that the population of all countries, except this, are removed but one degree from starvation. . . . If we accept and approve of the system which allots to each family a separate house, we must approve of the effects which result from such a system. With four hundred families and four hundred separate dwellings, all the cares and duties attendant upon providing for a household, must be gone through with four hundred times, until the complication becomes frightful. Four hundred persons must be sent to market, to make four hundred separate purchases, who lose time enough in selecting articles wanted and in bargaining, to produce them nearly. The four hundred houses imply that there are four hundred *dark holes,* called kitchens, in which four hundred *poor creatures* must pass their time over a hot fire in the middle of summer. Four hundred monotonous meals are prepared, three-fourths of them badly so, which give rise to many discords as there are dishes. As neither mistresses nor servants are satisfied in this system, the former scold, and the latter are indifferent or faithless. If an ox is killed, it is cut up and disposed of in an infinite number of little lots; every hogshead of sugar, every box of tea has to be retailed out pound by pound; this excess of complication increases ten-times the number of butchers and dealers necessary, whose

intermediate profits are a heavy indirect tax upon the consumer. The more we go into these details, the more we shall be convinced, that with this waste and want of system, individual economies are illusive, and that the mass must suffer poverty and privation under the best of governments. . . .

Nine permanent evils characterize the course of our societies; let the mass call upon those leaders to discover the principles of a society which will produce nine results directly opposed to them, will guarantee social happiness, and give us the standard of a true social organization.

NINE PERMANENT SCOURGES OF CIVILIZATION.

Indigence;
Fraud;
Oppression;
War;
Derangement of climate;
Diseases artificially produced; plague; yellow fever; cholera; small pox, &c.;
Vicious circle, without any opening for improvement;
UNIVERSAL SELFISHNESS;
DUPLICITY OF SOCIAL ACTIONS.

NINE PERMANENT BENEFITS TO BE ATTAINED.

General riches;
Practical truth in all relations of life;
Effective liberty in the same;
Constant peace;
Equilibrium of temperature and climate;
System of preventive medicine and extirpation of artificial diseases;
Opening offered to all improvements and ameliorations;
COLLECTIVE AND INDIVIDUAL PHILANTHROPY;
UNITY OF SOCIAL ACTION.

Such are the benefits Association would realize; but can we look for co-operation from men whose interests, as we said, are concentrated in personal success? The circle of our civilized politics is very narrow, but it insures the successful individual, often without merit or great effort, applause for the day, and frequently pecuniary reward with it. Immediate and personal advantage only stimulates the great majority; the idea of a social reform which would change the destiny of mankind, although vast and sublime, is too far off, too severed from all personal advantages, to find many adherents and enthusiasts. There must be, however, some characters so constituted as to feel the want of an object, high and lasting, with which to connect their efforts, so that something may remain to show that they lived upon this earth, and that their intellectual was not as fleeting as their material existence. It is among such temperaments, that we must seek for the advocates of the great social reform, which the present age may have the glory of achieving!

12

This propaganda was effective. Three years after Brisbane's book, forty phalanxes appeared in the United States. Although most suffered from poor management or inadequate finances, a few endured long enough to arouse conservative alarm. A description of one, the Integral Phalanx at Lick Creek, Illinois, comes from a traveler's account in 1846:[12]

Since the first effort here, under the name of the Sangamon Association, we have aimed to make no "blow," but to preserve the even tenor of our way, with one eye fixed upon a scientific development of Association as the great ultimatum of our desires. In pecuniary affairs we have pursued a safe plan. Our members are honest, industrious and moral; 23 of them being members of the Campbellite Baptists, 7 of the Methodist, and 9 of the Swedenborgian or New Church, 51 (including children) are not members of any church. Our members are from every State in the Union.

---

[12] New York *Daily Tribune*, July 4, 1846. Reprinted by permission of the publishers, The Arthur H. Clark Company, from *A Documentary History of American Industrial Society*, edited by John R. Commons and others (Cleveland, 1910), VII, 281–282.

We have now 555 acres of land—412 in cultivation—250 in Corn, 30 in Wheat, 25 in Oats, 15 in Garden and vegetables, the balance in Meadow and for Fall Wheat—our crops all look well—our corn crop is 75 per cent better than that of the farmers around us. We have 80 feet of frame building up and occupied by 5 families, some dozen isolated frames and cabins scattered about the Domain occupied by families. The lumber for a frame two story building is sawed. We will have fruit this season to make us comfortable; milk between 30 and 40 cows, have 18 work horses, besides young horses, cattle, sheep and hogs. But with all these advantages, added to as rich a soil and healthy a climate as is to be found in the States, yet we do not say our ultimate success is sure. Success has thus far crowned our efforts, and we can now see no reason why we may not succeed to the extent of our desires, but at the same time shall not blaze forth to the world that "our permanency as an Association is no longer a matter of doubt" and tomorrow publish our downfall. Success with us is sure so long as we perform our duty to God and man.

13

Most famous of all the communistic experiments was Brook Farm, in Massachusetts, organized by George Ripley. Between 1841 and 1844 this was a co-operative agricultural society supported by such intellectual giants as Hawthorne, Alcott, and Parker. It was later reorganized as a Fourier phalanx. The high idealism of its founders is recorded in the constitution of 1841:[13]

In order more effectually to promote the great purposes of human culture; to establish the external relations of life on a basis of wisdom and purity; to apply the principles of justice and love to our social organization in accordance with the laws of Divine Providence; to substitute a system of brotherly coöperation for one of selfish competition; to secure to our children and those

---

[13] John T. Codman, *Brook Farm, Historic and Personal Memoirs* (Boston, 1894), pp. 11–15.

who may be entrusted to our care, the benefits of the highest physical, intellectual and moral education in the present state of human knowledge, the resources at our command will permit; to institute an attractive, efficient, and productive system of industry; to prevent the exercise of worldly anxiety by the competent supply of our necessary wants; to diminish the desire of excessive accumulation by making the acquisition of individual property subservient to upright and disinterested uses; to guarantee to each other the means of physical support, and of spiritual progress, and thus to impart a greater freedom, simplicity, truthfulness, refinement, and moral dignity, to our mode of life,—

We, the undersigned, do unite in a Voluntary Association, to wit:

ARTICLE 1. The name and style of the Association shall be "(The Brook Farm) Institute of Agriculture and Education." All persons who shall hold one or more shares in the stock of the Association, and shall sign the articles of agreement, or who shall hereafter be admitted by the pleasure of the Association, shall be members thereof.

ART. 2. No religious test shall ever be required of any member of the Association; no authority assumed over individual freedom of opinion by the Association, nor by any member over another; nor shall anyone be held accountable to the Association except for such acts as violate rights of the members, and the essential principles on which the Association is founded; and in such cases the relation of any member may be suspended, or discontinued, at the pleasure of the Association.

ART. 3. The members of this Association shall own and manage such real and personal estate, in joint-stock proprietorship, as may, from time to time, be agreed on, and establish branches of industry as may be deemed expedient and desirable.

ART. 4. The Association shall provide such employment for all of its members as shall be adapted to their capacities, habits and tastes, and each member shall select and perform such operation of labor, whether corporal or mental, as he shall deem best suited to his own endowments, and the benefit of the Association.

ART. 5. The members of this Association shall be paid for all labor performed under its direction and for its advantage, at a fixed and equal rate, both for men and women. This rate shall not exceed one dollar per day, nor shall more than ten hours in the day be paid for as a day's labor.

ART. 6. The Association shall furnish to all its members, their children and family dependents, house-rent, fuel, food and clothing, and all other comforts and advantages possible, at the actual cost, as nearly as the same can be ascertained; but no charge shall be made for education, medical or nursing attendance, or the use of the library, public rooms or baths to the members; nor shall any charge be paid for food, rent or fuel by those deprived of labor by sickness, nor for food of children under ten years of age, unless at the special request of the individual by whom the charges are paid, or unless the credits in his favor exceed, or equal, the amount of such charges.

ART. 7. All labor performed for the Association shall be duly credited, and all articles furnished shall be charged, and a full settlement made with every member once every year.

ART. 8. Every child over ten years of age shall be charged for food, clothing, and articles furnished at cost, and shall be credited for his labor, not exceeding fifty cents per day, and on the completion of his education in the Association at the age of twenty, shall be entitled to a certificate of stock, to the amount of credits in his favor, and may be admitted a member of the Association.

ART. 9. Every share-holder in the joint-stock proprietorship of the Association, shall be paid on such stock, at the rate of five per cent, annually.

ART. 10. The net profits of the Association remaining in the treasury after the payments of all demands for interest on stock, labor performed, and necessary repairs, and improvements, shall be divided into a number of shares corresponding with the number of days' labor, and every member shall be entitled to one share for every day's labor performed by him.

ART. 11. All payments may be made in certificates of stock at the option of the Association; but in any case of need, to be decided by himself, every member may be permitted to draw on the funds of the treasury to an amount not exceeding the credits in his favor.

ART. 12. The Association shall hold an annual meeting for the choice of officers, and such other necessary business as shall come before them.

ART. 13. The officers of the Association shall be twelve directors, divided into four departments, as follows: first, General Direction; second, Direction of Agriculture; third, Direction of Education; fourth, Direction of Finance; consisting of three persons each, provided that the same persons may be a member of each Direction at the pleasure of the Association.

ART. 14. The Chairman of the General Direction shall be presiding officer in the Association, and together with the Director of Finance, shall constitute a Board of Trustees, by whom the property of the Association shall be managed.

ART. 15. The General Direction shall oversee and manage the affairs of the Association so that every department shall be carried on in an orderly and efficient manner. Each department shall be under the general supervision of its own Direction, which shall select, and, in accordance with the General Direction, shall appoint, all such overseers, directors and agents, as shall be necessary to the complete and systematic organization of the department, and shall have full authority to appoint such persons to these stations as they shall judge best qualified for the same.

ART. 16. No Directors shall be deemed to possess any rank superior to the other members of the Association, nor shall be chosen in reference to any other consideration than their capacity to serve the Association; nor shall they be paid for their official service

except at the rate of one dollar for ten hours in a day, actually employed in official duties.

ART. 17. The Association may, from time to time, adopt such rules and regulations, not inconsistent with the spirit and purpose of the Articles of Agreement, as shall be found expedient and necessary.

THE CRUSADE FOR THE EQUALITY OF WOMEN

14

Economic democracy was only one Jacksonian goal. The extension of democratic privileges to segments of society hitherto neglected was another. One group denied rights in the past was made up of women. Agitation for women's rights began in 1841, after delegates from an American female antislavery society were denied admittance to the 1840 World Antislavery Convention in London; the crusade reached a climax in 1848, when the first Women's Rights Convention in the history of the world met at Seneca Falls, New York, and issued a ringing Declaration of Independence:[14]

1. *Declaration of Sentiments*

When, in the course of human events, it becomes necessary for one portion of the family of man to assume among the people of the earth a position different from that which they have hitherto occupied, but one to which the laws of nature and of nature's God entitle them, a decent respect to the opinions of mankind requires that they should declare the causes that impel them to such a course.

We hold these truths to be self-evident: that all men and women are created equal; that they are endowed by their Creator with certain inalienable rights; that among these are life, liberty, and the pursuit of happiness; that to secure these rights governments are instituted, deriving their just powers from the consent of the governed. Whenever any form of government becomes destructive of

---

[14] Elizabeth Cady Stanton, Susan B. Anthony, and M. J. Gage (eds.), *The History of Woman Suffrage* (New York, 1881), I, 70–73.

these ends, it is the right of those who suffer from it to refuse allegiance to it, and to insist upon the institution of a new government, laying its foundation on such principles, and organizing its powers in such form, as to them shall seem most likely to effect their safety and happiness. Prudence, indeed, will dictate that governments long established should not be changed for light and transient causes; and accordingly all experience hath shown that mankind are more disposed to suffer, while evils are sufferable, than to right themselves by abolishing the forms to which they are accustomed. But when a long train of abuses and usurpations, pursuing invariably the same object, evinces a design to reduce them under absolute despotism, it is their duty to throw off such government, and to provide new guards for their future security. Such has been the patient sufferance of the women under this government, and such is now the necessity which constrains them to demand the equal station to which they are entitled.

The history of mankind is a history of repeated injuries and usurpations on the part of man toward woman, having in direct object the establishment of an absolute tyranny over her. To prove this, let facts be submitted to a candid world.

He has never permitted her to exercise her inalienable right to the elective franchise.

He has compelled her to submit to laws, in the formation of which she had no voice.

He has withheld from her rights which are given to the most ignorant and degraded men—both natives and foreigners.

Having deprived her of this first right of a citizen, the elective franchise, thereby leaving her without representation in the halls of legislation, he has oppressed her on all sides.

He has made her, if married, in the eye of the law, civilly dead.

He has taken from her all right in property, even to the wages she earns.

He has made her, morally, an irresponsible being, as she can commit many crimes with impunity, provided they be done in the presence of her husband. In the covenant of marriage, she is compelled to promise obedience to her husband, he becoming, to all intents and purposes, her master—the law giving him power to deprive her of her liberty, and to administer chastisement.

He has so framed the laws of divorce, as to what shall be the proper causes, and in case of separation, to whom the guardianship of the children shall be given, as to be wholly regardless of the happiness of women —the law, in all cases, going upon a false supposition of the supremacy of man, and giving all power into his hands.

After depriving her of all rights as a married woman, if single, and the owner of property, he has taxed her to support a government which recognizes her only when her property can be made profitable to it.

He has monopolized nearly all the profitable employments, and from those she is permitted to follow, she receives but a scanty remuneration. He closes against her all the avenues to wealth and distinction which he considers most honorable to himself. As a teacher of theology, medicine, or law, she is not known.

He has denied her the facilities for obtaining a thorough education, all colleges being closed against her.

He allows her in Church, as well as State, but a subordinate position, claiming Apostolic authority for her exclusion from the ministry, and, with some exceptions, from any public participation in the affairs of the Church.

He has created a false public sentiment by giving to the world a different code of morals for men and women, by which moral delinquencies which exclude women from society, are not only tolerated, but deemed of little account in man.

He has usurped the prerogative of Jehovah himself, claiming it as his right to assign for her a sphere of action, when that belongs to her conscience and to her God.

He has endeavored, in every way that he could, to destroy her confidence in her own powers, to lessen her self-respect and to make her willing to lead a dependent and abject life.

Now, in view of this entire disfranchisement of one-half the people of this country, their social and religious degradation—in view of the unjust laws above mentioned, and because women do feel themselves aggrieved, oppressed, and fraudulently deprived of their most sacred rights, we insist that they have immediate admission to all the rights and privileges which belong to them as citizens of the United States.

In entering upon the great work before us, we anticipate no small amount of misconception, misrepresentation, and ridicule; but we shall use every instrumentality within our power to effect our object. We shall employ agents, circulate tracts, petition the State and National legislatures, and endeavor to enlist the pulpit and the press in our behalf. We hope this Convention will be followed by a series of Conventions embracing every part of the country.

2. Resolutions

WHEREAS, The great precept of nature is conceded to be, that "man shall pursue his own true and substantial happiness." Blackstone in his Commentaries remarks, that this law of Nature being coeval with mankind, and dictated by God himself, is of course superior in obligation to any other. It is binding over all the globe, in all countries and at all times; no human laws are of any validity if contrary to this, and such of them as are valid, derive all their force, and all their validity, and all their authority, mediately and immediately, from this original; therefore,

Resolved, That such laws as conflict, in any way with the true and substantial happiness of woman, are contrary to the great precept of nature and of no validity, for this is "superior in obligation to any other."

Resolved, That all laws which prevent woman from occupying such a station in society as her conscience shall dictate, or which place her in a position inferior to that of man, are contrary to the great precept of

nature, and therefore of no force or authority.

Resolved, That woman is man's equal—was intended to be so by the Creator, and the highest good of the race demands that she should be recognized as such.

Resolved, That the women of this country ought to be enlightened in regard to the laws under which they live, that they may no longer publish their degradation by declaring themselves satisfied with their present position, nor their ignorance, by asserting that they have all the rights they want.

Resolved, That inasmuch as man, while claiming for himself intellectual superiority, does accord to woman moral superiority, it is pre-eminently his duty to encourage her to speak and teach, as she has an opportunity, in all religious assemblies.

Resolved, That the same amount of virtue, delicacy, and refinement of behavior that is required of woman in the social state, should also be required of man, and the same transgressions should be visited with equal severity on both man and woman.

Resolved, That the objection of indelicacy and impropriety, which is so often brought against woman when she addresses a public audience, comes with a very ill-grace from those who encourage, by their attendance, her appearance on the stage, in the concert, or in feats of the circus.

Resolved, That woman has too long rested satisfied in the circumscribed limits which corrupt customs and a perverted application of the Scriptures have marked out for her, and that it is time she should move in the enlarged sphere which her great Creator has assigned her.

Resolved, That it is the duty of the women of this country to secure to themselves their sacred right to the elective franchise.

Resolved, That the equality of human rights results necessarily from the fact of the identity of the race in capabilities and responsibilities.

Resolved, therefore, That, being invested by the creator with the same capabilities, and the same consciousness of responsibility for their exercise, it is demonstrably the right and duty of woman, equally with man, to promote every righteous cause by every righteous means; and especially in regard to the great subjects of morals and religion, it is self-evidently her right to participate with her brother in teaching them, both in private and in public, by writing and by speaking, by any instrumentalities proper to be used, and in any assemblies proper to be held; and this being a self-evident truth growing out of the divinely implanted principles of human nature, any custom or authority adverse to it, whether modern or wearing the hoary sanction of antiquity, is to be regarded as a self-evident falsehood, and at war with mankind.

Resolved, That the speedy success of our cause depends upon the zealous and untiring efforts of both men and women, for the overthrow of the monopoly of the pulpit, and for the securing to women an equal participation with men in the various trades, professions, and commerce.

THE RELIGIOUS SEARCH FOR UTOPIA

15

To Jacksonian humanitarians, the connection between religion and reform was intimate. Reform promised the continuing improvement of institutions; religion the continuing improvement of man. Man had only to accept salvation, evangelists insisted, to achieve that moral and spiritual perfectibility which was necessary for utopia on earth and bliss in afterlife. Americans set out to better themselves, just as they labored to better the society in which they lived. The affinity between social and individual perfection was frequently stressed by religious writers, exemplified in an article appearing in The Home Missionary *for June 1829:*[15]

The influence of the old world has been frittered away from the fact that it never has had UNITY. It is an aggregate of nations of different usages, languages, laws, religions,

---

[15] *The Home Missionary,* II (June 1, 1829), 18–19.

and modes of thinking. Besides this evil, its institutions have been such as to depress the mass of its population, and consequently to diminish its power. The fact that the little island of Great Britain, with her ten or twenty millions of inhabitants, has probably already had, and will yet have, greater influence on the human race, than all Europe besides, has resulted from her having freer institutions, a more generally enlightened population, from her protestant religion, and her peculiar local advantages. European power in passing into our hands comes to *one people*—the hundreds of millions which must one day inhabit this vast country will be one—having one language, one literature, essentially, one religion, and one common soul. This is a unity which mere political divisions, should they unhappily occur, cannot destroy. That a country thus situated must exert a dominant influence in the world is unavoidable. . . .

If we are to have this controlling influence on the destinies of other nations, it is a question of unutterable importance, what is to be the nature of this influence? If this country is to be the hot-bed of infidelity and vice, then will it be the widest and most desolating curse the world has ever known; but if the Gospel is to form our character, and guide our power, we shall be a fountain of life to all nations. The decision of this question, involving not only the temporal and eternal welfare of our own children, and of the countless millions who are to come after us, but the welfare of all the millions over whom the direct or indirect influence of this country is hereafter to extend, depends, under God, mainly on the men of this generation. It depends on us. We live at the forming period of this great nation. We are now in our infancy. Now, if ever, our national character must be formed for God. Neglect the intellectual and moral culture of an individual in youth, and you find it exceedingly difficult to mould his riper years. His character is fixed. The difficulty is far greater in nations, because the field of operation is so much larger, and because they must themselves be brought to engage in the work for which, under the circumstances supposed, they will have no disposition. The population of this country is increasing with so much rapidity, there are now so many of our new settlements, and extended districts, growing up in ignorance, that the work which we have to do is appallingly great, and if neglected now, its accomplishments will be next to impossible in the generation which is to follow us. Living, then, as we do, at this crisis of our country's history, the formation of her future character being to such an extent thrown on us, and this character being of such unutterable importance to the world, it may be questioned whether a generation ever lived on whose fidelity so much depended.

This is a responsibility which we cannot throw off. In other countries it rests with the government to supply the means of moral and religious instruction to the people. Here it rests with individual Christians. Jesus Christ has here called his people to a work most gloriously difficult. They have to support the gospel among themselves, and send it to the rising millions who must perish without it. This constitutes the great peculiarity of our situation. It is here to be determined whether the religion of Christ has power enough to sustain and extend itself, unaided by legislative interference. This is an experiment on which the eyes of the world are fixed, and in the result of which, the destinies of generations are involved.

16

The desire for individual perfection explained the success of the dozens of new religious cults that sprang up during the restless thirties and forties. Thousands of Americans were ready to follow any self-proclaimed messiah who promised them salvation for their souls and betterment for their bodies. One prophet was John Humphrey Noyes who, in 1848, organized a communal society at Oneida, New York. Inspired by the belief that God and man could work together, these Perfectionists, as they called themselves, were soon successfully engaged in farming, fruit growing, and making silverware. The community is described by Noyes:[16]

The Oneida Community has two hundred and two members, and two affiliated societies, one of forty members at Wallingford, Connecticut, and one of thirty-five members at Willow Place, on a detached part of the Oneida domain. This domain consists of six hundred and sixty-four acres of choice land, and three excellent water-powers. The manufacturing interest here created is valued at over $200,000. The Wallingford domain consists of two hundred and twenty-eight acres, with a water-power, a printing-office and a silk-factory. The three Community families (in all two hundred and seventy-seven persons) are financially and socially a unit.

The main dwelling of the Community is a brick structure consisting of a center and two wings, the whole one hundred and eighty-seven feet in length, by seventy in breadth. It has towers at either end and irregular extensions reaching one hundred feet in the rear. This is the Community Home. It contains the chapel, library, reception-room, museum, principal drawing-rooms, and many private apartments. The other buildings of the group are the "old mansion," containing the kitchen and dining-room, the Tontine, which is a work-building, the fruit-house, the store, etc. The manufacturing buildings in connection with the water-powers are large, and mostly of brick. The organic principle of Communism in industry and domestic life, is seen in the common roof, the common table, and the daily meetings of all the members.

The extent and variety of industrial operations at the Oneida Community may be seen in part by the following statistics from the report of last year, . . .

No. of steel traps manufactured during the year,	278,000.
" " packages of preserved fruits,	104,458.

---

[16] John Humphrey Noyes, *History of American Socialisms* (Philadelphia, 1870), pp. 641–643.

Amount of raw silk manufac-
tured,   4,664 lbs.
Iron cast at the foundry,   227,000 do.
Lumber manufactured at
sawmill,   305,000 feet.
Product of milk from the
dairy,   31,143 gallons.
"   " hay on the domain,   300 tons.
"   " potatoes,   800 bushels.
"   " strawberries,   740 do.
"   " apples,   1,450 do.
"   " grapes,   9,631 lbs.

Stock on the farm, 93 cattle and 25 horses. Amount of teaming done, valued at $6,260.

In addition to these, many branches of industry necessary for the convenience of the family are pursued, such as shoemaking, tailoring, dentistry, etc. The cash business of the Community during the year, as represented by its receipts and disbursements, was about $575,000. Amount paid for hired labor, $34,000. Family expenses (exclusive of domestic labor by the members, teaching, and work in the printing office), $41,533.43.

The amount of labor performed by the Community members during the year, was found to be approximately as follows:

	Number
Able-bodied men	80
" women	84
Invalid and aged men	6
Boys	4
Invalid and aged women	9
Girls	2

Amount of labor per day
7 hours
6   "   40 min
3   "   40   "
3   "   40   "
1   "   20   "
1   "   20   "

This is exclusive of care of children, schoolteaching, printing and editing the *Circular,* and much head-work in all departments.

Taking 304 days for the working year, we have, as a product of the above figures, a total of 35,568 days' work at ten hours each. Supposing this labor to be paid at the rate of $1.50 per day, the aggregate sum for the year would be $53,352.00. By comparing this with the amount of family expenses, $41,533.43, we find, at the given rate of wages, a surplus profit amounting to $11,818.57, or 33 cents profit for each person per day. This represents the saving which ordinary unskilled labor would make by means of the mere economy of Association. Were it possible for a skillful mechanic to live in cooperation with others, so that his wife and elder children could spend some time at productive labor, and his family could secure the economies of combined households, their wages at present rates would be more than double the cost of living. Labor in the Community being principally of the higher class, is proportionately rewarded, and in fact earns much more than $1.50 per day.

17

Other cults placed less emphasis on earthly perfection than on spiritual salvation. One of the most successful of this sort was inspired by the preaching of William Miller, a farmer from Low Hampton, New York, whose study of the Scriptures revealed that the end of the earth was to come in 1843. Father Miller announced the approaching calamity in 1831; when the time arrived, he had almost a million followers, all impatiently awaiting the millennium—when they would be drawn heavenward before the world and unbelievers consumed in flames. The final preparations for the catastrophe in Philadelphia are described by a local historian:[17]

The excitement in Philadelphia had been growing for two or more years, and by the summer of 1844 it was indescribable. The Millerite Church was on Julianna Street, between Wood and Callowhill, and there Miller's followers met night and day, and watched the stars and sun, and prayed and warned the unrepentant that the "Day of Judgment was at hand."

[17] J. Thomas Scharf and Thompson Westcott, *History of Philadelphia* (Philadelphia, 1884), II, 1448–1449.

Many of them began to sell their houses at prices which were merely nominal. Others gave away their personal effects, shut up their business, or vacated their houses. On a store on Fifth Street, above Chestnut, was a placard which read thus:

"This shop is closed in honor of the King of Kings who will appear about the 20th of October. Get ready friends to crown Him Lord of all." . . . People laboring under the excitement went mad.

On one occasion all the windows of a meeting-house were surrounded at night by a crowd of young fellows, and at a given signal the darkness and gloom were made lurid by flaming torches, and the air resounded with the roar of firecrackers. The Saints inside went wild with terror, for they thought the fiery whirlwind was come.

The Sunday before the final day was an eventful one. The Julianna Street Chapel was crowded. A mob of unbelievers on the pavements stoned the windows and hooted at the worshippers. The police of Northern Liberties, and Spring Garden, and a sheriff's posse, headed by Morton McMichael, were on hand to quell the threatened disturbance. The members of the congregation repaired to their homes, and after, in many cases, leaving their doors and windows open, and giving away their furniture, set out for the suburban districts. A large number went over into New Jersey, but their chief party assembled in Isaac Yocomb's field on the Darby Road, three miles and a half from the Market Street bridge. While here a furious hurricane strengthened the faith of the Millerites and struck awful terror to the souls of the timid. It swept over the city, destroying shipping and demolishing houses. . . .

The crowd at Darby was gathered in two tents, but so great was it that the children for two days were obliged to run about the fields, exposed to the pelting of a pitiless storm, and crying for their parents. The parents, clad in their white ascension robes, were almost exhausted for want of food, slept on the cold wet ground, and prayed and hymned and groaned incessantly.

At midnight on the 22d, the Bridegroom was to come, and a rain of fire was to descend from the heavens, and the Saints were to be gathered up in a whirlwind. There they stood on that black, tempestuous October night, shivering with cold and fear—their faces upturned, and every eye strained to catch a beam of the awful light piercing the clouds. The morning broke, and with it came the end of the delusion. The assemblage dispersed in despair, and slunk away silently and downcast to their houses.

18

The Millerites lost most of their followers when the prophesied last judgment failed to occur. More enduring was the faith revealed through another prophet of the Jacksonian period, Joseph Smith. According to Smith's own testimony, divine guidance directed him to the spot where a number of golden plates were buried near his Palmyra, New York, home. Engraved on them was the revelation of God's true faith. This was translated and published in 1830 as the Book of Mormon. In the same year, the Church of Jesus Christ of Latter-Day Saints was organized and the Mormons began the wanderings that eventually carried them to Utah. Joseph Smith records his own experiences on that day in September 1823 when the golden plates were first revealed to him: [18]

After I had retired to my bed for the night, I betook myself to prayer and supplication to Almighty God for forgiveness of all my sins and follies, and also for a manifestation to me, that I might know of my state and standing before Him; for I had full confidence in obtaining a divine manifestation, as I previously had one. While I was thus in the act of calling upon God, I discovered a light appearing in my room, which continued to increase until the room was lighter than at noonday, when immediately a personage appeared at my bedside, standing in the air, for his feet did not touch the floor. He had on a loose robe of most exquisite whiteness. It was a whiteness beyond anything earthly I had ever seen; nor do I believe

---

[18] Joseph Smith, *The Prophet Joseph Smith Tells His Own Story* (New York, n.d.), pp. 8–14.

that any earthly thing could be made to appear so exceedingly white and brilliant. His hands were naked, and his arms, also, a little above the wrist; so, also, were his feet naked, as were his legs, a little above the ankles. His head and neck were also bare. I could discover that he had no other clothing on but this robe, as it was open, so that I could see into his bosom. Not only was his robe exceedingly white, but his whole person was glorious beyond description, and his countenance truly like lightning. The room was exceedingly light, but not so very bright as immediately around his person.

When I first looked upon him, I was afraid; but the fear soon left me. He called me by name, and said unto me that he was a messenger sent from the presence of God to me, and that his name was Moroni; that God had a work for me to do; and that my name should be had for good and evil among all nations, kindreds, and tongues, or that it should be both good and evil spoken of among all people. He said there was a book deposited, written upon gold plates, giving an account of the former inhabitants of this continent, and the source from whence they sprang. He also said that the fulness of the everlasting Gospel was contained in it, as delivered by the Savior to the ancient inhabitants; also, that there were two stones in silver bows—and these stones, fastened to a breastplate, constituted what is called the Urim and Thummim—deposited with the plates; and the possession and use of these stones were what constituted "Seers" in ancient or former times; and that God had prepared them for the purpose of translating the book.

After telling me these things, he commenced quoting the prophecies of the Old Testament. . . .

Again, he told me, that when I got those plates of which he had spoken—for the time that they should be obtained was not yet fulfilled—I should not show them to any person; neither the breast plate with the Urim and Thummim; only to those to whom I should be commanded to show them; if I did I should be destroyed. While he was conversing with me about the plates, the vision was opened to my mind that I could see the place where the plates were deposited, and that so clearly and distinctly that I knew the place again when I visited it. . . .

I shortly after arose from my bed, and, as usual, went to the necessary labors of the day; but in attempting to work as at other times, I found my strength so exhausted as to render me entirely unable. My father, who was laboring along with me, discovered something to be wrong with me, and told me to go home. I started with the intention of going to the house; but, in attempting to cross the fence out of the field where we were, my strength entirely failed me, and I fell helpless on the ground, and for a time was quite unconscious of anything. The first thing that I can recollect was a voice speaking unto me, calling me by name. I looked up, and beheld the same messenger standing over my head, surrounded by light as before. . . . I returned to my father in the field, and rehearsed the whole matter to him. He replied to me that it was of God, and told me to go and do as commanded by the messenger. I left the field, and went to the place where the messenger had told me the plates were deposited; and owing to the distinctness of the vision which I had had concerning it, I knew the place the instant that I arrived there.

Convenient to the village of Manchester, Ontario county, New York, stands a hill of considerable size, and the most elevated of any in the neighborhood. On the west side of this hill, not far from the top, under a stone of considerable size, lay the plates, deposited in a stone box. This stone was thick and rounding in the middle on the upper side, and thinner towards the edges, so that the middle part of it was visible above the ground, but the edge all round was covered with earth.

Having removed the earth, I obtained a lever, which I got fixed under the edge of the stone, and with a little exertion raised it up. I looked in, and there indeed did I behold the plates, the Urim and Thummim, and the breastplate, as stated by the messenger. The box in which they lay was formed by laying stones together in some kind of cement. In the bottom of the box were laid two stones crossways of the box, and on these stones lay the plates and the other things with them.

I made an attempt to take them out, but was forbidden by the messenger, and was again informed that the time for bringing them forth had not yet arrived, neither would it, until four years from that time; but he told me that I should come to that place precisely in one year from that time, and that he would there meet with me, and that I should continue to do so until the time should come for obtaining the plates. Accordingly, as I had been commanded, I went at the end of each year, and at each time I found the same messenger there, and received instruction and intelligence from him at each of our interviews, respecting what the Lord was going to do, and how and in what manner His kingdom was to be conducted in the last days.

BLUEPRINTS FOR SOCIAL REFORM

19

The striving for perfection, the faith in human brotherhood, and the zeal for salvation that characterized the religious activities of Jacksonian days were easily transferred to the social realm. If souls could be saved by positive action, so too could mankind. If sin could be stamped out, so could the sins of society. Inspired by the example of churchmen, and impelled by a desire to mold a perfect world for the newly risen common man, dozens of humanitarians joined the reform movements. One of the most effective was Dorothea Dix, a Massachusetts Quaker, whose personal crusade was directed toward improving the lot of the insane. For two years Miss Dix investigated the barbarous treatment of the mentally unbalanced in the jails of her own state before preparing her classic Memorial to the Legislature of Massa-chusetts (1843), which first awakened men to the plight of those unfortunates:[19]

I come to present the strong claims of suffering humanity. I come to place before the Legislature of Massachusetts the condition of the miserable, the desolate, the outcast. I come as the advocate of helpless, forgotten, insane, and idiotic men and women; of beings sunk to a condition from which the most unconcerned would start with real horror; of beings wretched in our prisons, and more wretched in our almshouses. And I cannot suppose it needful to employ earnest persuasion, or stubborn argument, in order to arrest and fix attention upon a subject only the more strongly pressing in its claims because it is revolting and disgusting in its details.

I must confine myself to few examples, but am ready to furnish other and more complete details, if required. If my pictures are displeasing, coarse, and severe, my subjects, it must be recollected, offer no tranquil, refined, or composing features. The condition of human beings, reduced to the extremest states of degradation and misery, cannot be exhibited in softened language, or adorn a polished page.

I proceed, gentlemen, briefly to call your attention to the *present* state of insane persons confined within this Commonwealth, in *cages, closets, cellars, stalls, pens! Chained, naked, beaten with rods,* and *lashed* into obedience.

As I state cold, severe *facts,* I feel obliged to refer to persons, and definitely to indicate localities. But it is upon my subject, not upon localities or individuals, I desire to fix attention; and I would speak as kindly as possible of all wardens, keepers, and other responsible officers, believing that *most* of these have erred not through hardness of heart and wilful cruelty so much as want of skill and knowledge, and want of consideration.

---

[19] Dorothea L. Dix, *Memorial to the Legislature of Massachusetts* (1843). Reprinted in *Old South Leaflets,* VI, no. 148 (Boston, n.d.), pp. 2–6, 31.

Familiarity with suffering, it is said, blunts the sensibilities, and where neglect once finds a footing other injuries are multiplied. This is not all, for it may justly and strongly be added that, from the deficiency of adequate means to meet the wants of these cases, it has been an absolute impossibility to do justice in this matter. Prisons are not constructed in view of being converted into county hospitals, and almshouses are not founded as receptacles for the insane. And yet, in the face of justice and common sense, wardens are by law compelled to receive, and the masters of almshouses not to refuse, insane and idiotic subjects in all stages of mental disease and privation.

It is the Commonwealth, not its integral parts, that is accountable for most of the abuses which have lately and do still exist. I repeat it, it is defective legislation which perpetuates and multiplies these abuses. In illustration of my subject, I offer the following extracts from my Note-book and Journal:—. . . .

. . . I have seen many who, part of the year, are chained or caged. The use of cages all but universal. Hardly a town but can refer to some not distant period of using them; chains are less common; negligences frequent; wilful abuse less frequent than sufferings proceeding from ignorance, or want of consideration. I encountered during the last three months many poor creatures wandering reckless and unprotected through the country. Innumerable accounts have been sent me of persons who had roved away unwatched and unsearched after; and I have heard that responsible persons, controlling the almshouses, have not thought themselves culpable in sending away from their shelter, to cast upon the chances of remote relief, insane men and women. These, left on the highways, unfriended and incompetent to control or direct their own movements, sometimes have found refuge in the hospital, and others have not been traced. But I cannot particularize. In traversing the State, I have found hundreds of insane persons in every variety of circumstance and condition, many whose situation could not and need not be improved; a less number, but that very large, whose lives are the saddest pictures of human suffering and degradation. I give a few illustrations; but description fades before reality.

Danvers. November. Visited the almshouse. A large building, much out of repair. Understand a new one is in contemplation. Here are from fifty-six to sixty inmates, one idiotic, three insane; one of the latter in close confinement at all times.

Long before reaching the house, wild shouts, snatches of rude songs, imprecations and obscene language, fell upon the ear, proceeding from the occupant of a low building, rather remote from the principal building to which my course was directed. Found the mistress, and was conducted to the place which was called *"the home"* of the *forlorn* maniac, a young woman, exhibiting a condition of neglect and misery blotting out the faintest idea of comfort, and outraging every sentiment of decency. She had been, I learnt, "a respectable person, industrious and worthy. Disappointments and trials shook her mind, and, finally, laid prostrate reason and self-control. She became a maniac for life. She had been at Worcester Hospital for a considerable time, and had been returned as incurable." The mistress told me she understood that, "while there, she was comfortable and decent." Alas, what a change was here exhibited! She had passed from one degree of violence to another, in swift progress. There she stood, clinging to or beating upon the bars of her caged apartment, the contracted size of which afforded space only for increasing accumulations of filth, a *foul* spectacle. There she stood with naked arms and dishevelled hair, the unwashed frame invested with fragments of unclean garments, the air so extremely offensive, though ventilation was afforded on all sides save one, that it was not possible to remain beyond a few moments without retreating for recovery to the out-

ward air. Irritation of body, produced by
utter filth and exposure, incited her to the
horrid process of tearing off her skin by
inches. Her face, neck, and person were thus
disfigured to hideousness. She held up a
fragment just rent off. To my exclamation of
horror, the mistress replied: "Oh, we can't
help it. Half the skin is off sometimes. We
can do nothing with her; and it makes no
difference what she eats, for she consumes
her own filth as readily as the food which
is brought her." . . . .

It is not few, but many, it is not a part,
but the whole, who bear unqualified testimony to this evil. A voice strong and deep
comes up from every almshouse and prison
in Massachusetts where the insane are or
have been protesting against such evils as
have been illustrated in the preceding pages.

Gentlemen, I commit to you this sacred
cause. Your action upon this subject will affect the present and future condition of
hundreds and of thousands.

In this legislation, as in all things, may
you exercise that "wisdom which is the
breath of the power of God."

Respectfully submitted,

D. L. Dix

20

*Miss Dix's disclosures forced some states to
separate the mentally ill from criminals, but
progress was slow. By the 1850s she and her
co-workers were besieging Congress for aid. Because of their influence, a measure was passed
in 1854 which would have set aside ten million
acres of the public domain to support the indigent insane. President Franklin Pierce's veto
of this bill illustrates the conflict between concepts of laissez-faire and the views of humanitarian reformers:*[20]

This bill therefore proposes that the Federal Government shall make provision to the
amount of the value of 10,000,000 acres of
land for an eleemosynary object within the
several States, to be administered by the

political authority of the same; and it presents at the threshold the question whether
any such act on the part of the Federal Government is warranted and sanctioned by the
Constitution, the provisions and principles
of which are to be protected and sustained
as a first and paramount duty.

It can not be questioned that if Congress
has power to make provision for the indigent insane without the limits of this District
it has the same power to provide for the indigent who are not insane, and thus to transfer
to the Federal Government the charge of all
the poor in all the States. It has the same
power to provide hospitals and other local
establishments for the care and cure of every
species of human infirmity, and thus to assume all that duty of either public philanthropy or public necessity to the dependent,
the orphan, the sick, or the needy which is
now discharged by the States themselves or
by corporate institutions or private endowments existing under the legislation of the
States. The whole field of public beneficence
is thrown open to the care and culture of the
Federal Government. Generous impulses no
longer encounter the limitations and control
of our imperious fundamental law; for however worthy may be the present object in
itself, it is only one of a class. It is not exclusively worthy of benevolent regard. Whatever considerations dictate sympathy for this
particular object apply in like manner, if not
in the same degree, to idiocy, to physical
disease, to extreme destitution. If Congress
may and ought to provide for any one of
these objects, it may and ought to provide
for them all. And if it be done in this case,
what answer shall be given when Congress
shall be called upon, as it doubtless will be,
to pursue a similar course of legislation in
the others? It will obviously be vain to reply
that the object is worthy, but that the application has taken a wrong direction. The
power will have been deliberately assumed,
the general obligation will by this act have
been acknowledged, and the question of
means and expediency will alone be left for
consideration. The decision upon the prin-

[20] J. D. Richardson (comp.), *A Compilation of
the Messages and Papers of the Presidents, 1789–
1897* (Washington, 1897), V, 249–250.

ciple in any one case determines it for the whole class. The question presented, therefore, clearly is upon the constitutionality and propriety of the Federal Government assuming to enter into a novel and vast field of legislation, namely, that of providing for the care and support of all those among the people of the United States who by any form of calamity become fit objects of public philanthropy.

I readily and, I trust, feelingly acknowledge the duty incumbent on us all as men and citizens, and as among the highest and holiest of our duties, to provide for those who, in the mysterious order of Providence, are subject to want and to disease of body or mind; but I can not find any authority in the Constitution for making the Federal Government the great almoner of public charity throughout the United States. To do so would, in my judgment, be contrary to the letter and spirit of the Constitution and subversive of the whole theory upon which the Union of these States is founded. And if it were admissible to contemplate the exercise of this power for any object whatever, I can not avoid the belief that it would in the end be prejudicial rather than beneficial in the noble offices of charity to have the charge of them transferred from the States to the Federal Government. Are we not too prone to forget that the Federal Union is the creature of the States, not they of the Federal Union? We were the inhabitants of colonies distinct in local government one from the other before the Revolution. By that Revolution the colonies each became an independent State. They achieved that independence and secured its recognition by the agency of a consulting body, which, from being an assembly of the ministers of distinct sovereignties instructed to agree to no form of government which did not leave the domestic concerns of each State to itself, was appropriately denominated a Congress. When, having tried the experiment of the Confederation, they resolved to change that for the present Federal Union, and thus to confer on the Federal Government more ample authority, they

scrupulously measured such of the functions of their cherished sovereignty as they chose to delegate to the General Government. With this aim and to this end the fathers of the Republic framed the Constitution, in and by which the independent and sovereign States united themselves for certain specified objects and purposes, and for those only, leaving all powers not therein set forth as conferred on one or another of the three great departments—the legislative, the executive, and the judicial—indubitably with the States. And when the people of the several States had in their State conventions, and thus alone, given effect and force to the Constitution, not content that any doubt should in future arise as to the scope and character of this act, they ingrafted thereon the explicit declaration that "the powers not delegated to the United States by the Constitution nor prohibited by it to the States are reserved to the States respectively or to the people." Can it be controverted that the great mass of the business of Government—that involved in the social relations, the internal arrangements of the body politic, the mental and moral culture of men, the development of local resources of wealth, the punishment of crimes in general, the preservation of order, the relief of the needy or otherwise unfortunate members of society—did in practice remain with the States; that none of these objects of local concern are by the Constitution expressly or impliedly prohibited to the States, and that none of them are by any express language of the Constitution transferred to the United States? Can it be claimed that any of these functions of local administration and legislation are vested in the Federal Government by any implication? I have never found anything in the Constitution which is susceptible of such a construction. No one of the enumerated powers touches the subject or has even a remote analogy to it. The powers conferred upon the United States have reference to federal relations, or to the means of accomplishing or executing things of federal relation. So also of the same character are the powers taken away from the States by enumeration. In either case the powers granted and the powers restricted were so granted or so restricted only where it was requisite for the maintenance of peace and harmony between the States or for the purpose of protecting their common interests and defending their common sovereignty against aggression from abroad or insurrection at home.

21

Another evil that attracted the attention of reformers was alcoholic overindulgence. After the American Temperance Union was formed in 1836, a great amount of propaganda appeared to demonstrate the baleful consequences of strong drink. During parades of the Cold Water Army, or at meetings of the Washingtonian Temperance Societies, songs like the following were sung with exuberant piety:[21]

COME HOME, FATHER

Father, dear father, come home with me
    now!
  The clock in the steeple strikes one,—
You said you were coming right home from
    the shop,
  As soon as your day's work was done.—
Our fire has gone out, our house is all dark,
  And mother's been watching since tea,—
With poor brother Benny so sick in her arms,
  And no one to help her but me.—
Come home, come home, come home!—
  Please,—father, dear father, come home!—

Hear the sweet voice of the child,—
  Which the night-winds repeat as they
    roam!
Oh, who could resist this most plaintive of
    pray'rs?
  Please, father, dear father, come home!

Father, dear father, come home with me
    now!

---

21 Henry Clay Work, *Come Home, Father* (Chicago, 1864). "Jonathan's Declaration," *Washington Teetotaler's Minstrel* (1845). Reprinted in John A. Krout, *The Origin of Prohibition* (New York, 1925), p. 253.

  The clock in the steeple strikes two;
The night has grown colder, and Benny is
    worse—
  But he has been calling for you.
Indeed he is worse—Ma says he will die—
  Perhaps before morning shall dawn;
And this is the message she sent me to
    bring—
  "Come quickly, or he will be gone."
Come home! come home! come home!
  Please, father, dear father, come home.

Father, dear father, come home with me
    now!
  The clock in the steeple strikes three;
The house is so lonely!—the hours are so long
  For poor weeping mother and me.
Yes, we are alone—poor Benny is dead,
  And gone with the angels of light;
And these were the very last words that he
    said—
  "I want to kiss Papa good night."
Come home! come home! come home!
  Please, father, dear father, come home.

JONATHAN'S DECLARATION OF INDEPENDENCE

Says Jonathan, says he, today
  I will be independent,
And so my grog I'll throw away,
  And that shall be the end on't.

Clear the house, the tarnal stuff,
  Shan't be here so handy,
Wife has given the winds her snuff,
  So now here goes my brandy.

And now, says Jonathan, towards rum
  I'm desperate unforgiving,
The tyrant never more shall come
  Into the house I live in.

Kindred spirits, too, shall in-
  To utter darkness go forth,
Whiskey, Toddy, Julep, Gin,
  Brandy, Beer, and so forth.

22

Reformist energy was also enlisted against war, which conflicted with the concept of universal brotherhood, a concept shared by all faiths. Local peace societies dating from the 1820s were united in 1828 as the American Peace Society under the leadership of William Ladd, a Maine humanitarian. Among Ladd's prominent disciples was the "Learned Blacksmith" of New Britain, Connecticut, Elihu Burritt, a humble man whose self-taught knowledge of thirty languages convinced him of their common origin and hence of the common origin of mankind. His Thoughts and Things at Home and Abroad *(1854) is a powerful plea for peace through universal benevolence:*[22]

We have considered the power and dignity of passive resistance, when opposed to assaults from without, or oppression from within. We have tried to show that necessity does not make it a virtue in any case; but that its inherent virtue always makes it a necessity. We now proceed to demonstrate its patriotism. We deem it due to the principles and advocates of peace, to rebut the charge that is often brought against them, that they are "the complacent allies of despotism—that they would stand by and see, without concern or remonstrance, communities, peoples, and nations manacled hand and foot, by tyrants; their rights, liberties, hopes, and aspirations, trodden out of existence by the iron heel of oppression." The imputation of cowardice, unmanly imbecility, a crouching, abject spirit, is involved in this charge. "What! would you have us lie down in the dust, and be trampled upon by these despotic powers and governments! Would you have us permit them to enslave us, and hold out our arms and feet to the fettering without a struggle or a murmur?" And then, having filled their bosoms to bursting with patriotic indignation at the course and disposition described interrogatively by these triumphant questions, they exclaim, "No! we would spill the last drop of our blood;—we would see our cities burned with fire;—we would per-

ish with arms in our hands on the battle-field, or pine in exile in Siberia or Botany Bay, before we would tamely submit to be slaves! Liberty or death!" These are the most striking and usual terms of comparison in the vocabulary of martial patriotism. Frequently the sentiments they express take a figurative form more fearful still. We recollect one employed by the editor of an American journal, pending the Oregon controversy, to this effect: "Sooner than relinquish our just rights to the disputed territory, we would shed every drop of blood in the heart of the nation!" Mr. Borrow, agent of the Bible Society, records "a broken prayer for my native land, which, after my usual thankgiving, I breathed forth to the Almighty, ere retiring to rest that Sunday night at Gibraltar"; a prayer *for* his native country which contains this passage—"May'st thou sink, if thou dost sink, amidst blood and flame, with a mighty noise, causing more than one nation to participate in thy downfall!" And these are regarded as the outbursts of a patriotic feeling —of a love of country so intense that they would see it engulfed in fire and blood, and even the last vein of the nation's heart pierced, and its existence extinguished, rather than endure insult, injury, or oppression! They measure their attachment and devotion to their country and its institutions by the awful calamities which they would bring upon it, in defending its honor and rights. What a fearful antithesis of alternatives! How many peoples and nations have "sunk, amidst blood and flame, and with a mighty noise," in the abyss which yawns between these alternative conditions! How many patriots of this order have seen their country a smoking sea of ruin, without finding a bulrush ark in which to float "the immediate jewel of its soul"—the charter of its existence as a nation!

We wish no one to accept or share the responsibility of our convictions, or of the views we wish to express in reference to this aspect of the subject. If peace has its victories no less than war, it has its heroism and its patriotism. The men of peace can find no

---

[22] Elihu Burritt, *Thoughts and Things at Home and Abroad, with a Memoir by Mary Howitt* (Boston, 1854), pp. 277–280.

attribute, in the great Gospel principles of their faith, that can side with despotism, or wink with indifference at oppression. They are not cowards. They counsel no tame, unmanly submission to wrong; but to oppose to wrong a courage of the human will that shall never faint or waver at any extremity of endurance;—aye, to "resist unto blood," if it be unavoidable,—to give their own necks to the axe or to the halter, on the block or the scaffold, but never to shed themselves a single drop, or perpetrate a single act of malevolent injury on any human being, un-

der the severest pressure of despotic rule. Peace has its heroism, serene and dauntless, that neither trembles nor pales before the guillotine, the halter, or the knout. Peace has its patriotism; deep, earnest, unselfish, self-sacrificing, and sensitive,—a love of country that would bleed to the last vein, but never wound, for its rights, honor, and prosperity. Peace has its battle-fields; bloodless, but brave to a degree of heroic endurance of wrong and outrage to which martial courage could never attain.

Sectionalism and Expansion

The American people were on the march during the 1840s. They surged west-ward to fill the Oregon country, added Texas to their domain, and acquired California and the southwestern territories from Mexico. When, in the midst of their conquests, they paused to ask themselves whether the new-won lands would be slave or free, they posed a question answered only after another ten years of sectional controversy culminating in a bloody civil war.

"MANIFEST DESTINY"

1

Driving the pioneers westward were the hard times that followed the panic of 1837; luring them onward were the agricultural riches prom-ised by the black soil of Texas and the fertile valleys of the Willamette and Sacramento rivers. Yet something more than economic gain inspired these migrations: a powerful psychological force known as "manifest destiny." American demo-cratic institutions, they believed, were too per-fect to be confined within narrow borders; a kindly God manifestly intended them to move ever onward until the unfortunates of other lands could enjoy the blessings of liberty and democracy. John L. O'Sullivan, the jingoistic editor of the Democratic Review, *expresses the philosophy of "manifest destiny" in an article that not only bristled with expansionist demands but first introduced the term into the national vocabulary:[1]*

Why, were other reasoning wanting, in favor of now elevating this question of the reception of Texas into the Union, out of the lower region of our past party dissen-sions, up to its proper level of a high and broad nationality, it surely is to be found, found abundantly, in the manner in which other nations have undertaken to intrude themselves into it, between us and the

[1] *Democratic Review,* XVII (July–August 1845), 5–6, 9–10.

proper parties to the case, in a spirit of hos-tile interference against us, for the avowed object of thwarting our policy and hamper-ing our power, limiting our greatness and checking the fulfilment of our manifest des-tiny to overspread the continent allotted by Providence for the free development of our yearly multiplying millions. This we have seen done by England, our old rival and en-emy; and by France, strangely coupled with her against us, under the influence of the Anglicism strongly tinging the policy of her present prime minister, Guizot. The zealous activity with which this effort to defeat us was pushed by the representatives of those governments, together with the character of intrigue accompanying it, fully constituted that case of foreign interference, which Mr. Clay himself declared should, and would unite us all in maintaining the common cause of our country against the foreigner and the foe. We are only astonished that this effect has not been more fully and strongly produced, and that the burst of in-dignation against this unauthorized, insolent and hostile interference against us, has not been more general even among the party be-fore opposed to Annexation, and has not ral-lied the national spirit and national pride unanimously upon that policy. We are very sure that if Mr. Clay himself were now to add another letter to his former Texas correspondence, he would express this sentiment, and carry out the idea already strongly stated in one of them, in a manner which would tax all the powers of blushing belonging to some of his party adherents.

It is wholly untrue, and unjust to ourselves, the pretence that the Annexation has been a measure of spoliation, unrightful and unrighteous—of military conquest under forms of peace and law—of territorial aggrandizement at the expense of justice, and justice due by a double sanctity to the weak. This view of the question is wholly unfounded, and has been before so amply refuted in these pages, as well as in a thousand other modes, that we shall not again dwell upon it. The independence of Texas was complete and absolute. It was an independence, not only in fact but of right. No obligation of duty towards Mexico tended in the least degree to restrain our right to effect the desired recovery of the fair province once our own—whatever motives of policy might have prompted a more deferential consideration of her feelings and her pride, as involved in the question. If Texas became peopled with an American population, it was by no contrivance of our government, but on the express invitation of that of Mexico herself; accompanied with such guaranties of State independence, and the maintenance of a federal system analogous to our own, as constituted a compact fully justifying the strongest measures of redress on the part of those afterwards deceived in this guaranty, and sought to be enslaved under the yoke imposed by its violation. She was released, rightfully and absolutely released, from all Mexican allegiance, or duty of cohesion to the Mexican political body, by the acts and fault of Mexico herself, and Mexico alone. There never was a clearer case. It was not revolution; it was resistance to revolution; and resistance under such circumstances as left independence the necessary resulting state, caused by the abandonment of those with whom her former federal association had existed. What then can be more preposterous

than all this clamor by Mexico and the Mexican interest, against Annexation, as a violation of any rights of hers, any duties of ours? . . .

California will, probably, next fall away from the loose adhesion which, in such a country as Mexico, holds a remote province in a slight equivocal kind of dependence on the metropolis. Imbecile and distracted, Mexico never can exert any real governmental authority over such a country. The impotence of the one and the distance of the other, must make the relation one of virtual independence; unless, by stunting the province of all natural growth, and forbidding that immigration which can alone develop its capabilities and fulfil the purposes of its creation, tyranny may retain a military dominion which is no government in the legitimate sense of the term. In the case of California this is now impossible. The Anglo-Saxon foot is already on its borders. Already the advance guard of the irresistible army of Anglo-Saxon emigration has begun to pour down upon it, armed with the plough and the rifle, and marking its trail with schools and colleges, courts and representative halls, mills and meeting-houses. A population will soon be in actual occupation of California, over which it will be idle for Mexico to dream of dominion. They will necessarily become independent. All this without agency of our government, without responsibility of our people—in the natural flow of events, the spontaneous working of principles, and the adaptation of the tendencies and wants of the human race to the elemental circumstances in the midst of which they find themselves placed. And they will have a right to independence—to self-government—to the possession of the homes conquered from the wilderness by their own labors and dangers, sufferings and sacrifices—a better and a truer right than the artificial title of sovereignty in Mexico a thousand miles distant, inheriting from Spain a title good only against those who have none better. Their right to independence will be the natural right of self-government belonging to any community

strong enough to maintain it—distinct in position, origin and character, and free from
any mutual obligations of membership of a
common political body, binding it to others
by the duty of loyalty and compact of public faith. This will be their title to independence; and by this title, there can be no
doubt that the population now fast streaming down upon California will both assert
and maintain that independence. Whether
they will then attach themselves to our Union
or not, is not to be predicted with any certainty. Unless the projected railroad across
the continent to the Pacific be carried into
effect, perhaps they may not; though even in
that case, the day is not distant when the
Empires of the Atlantic and Pacific would
again flow together into one, as soon as their
inland border should approach each other.
But that great work, colossal as appears the
plan on its first suggestion, cannot remain
long unbuilt. Its necessity for this very purpose of binding and holding together in its
iron clasp our fast settling Pacific region with
that of the Mississippi valley—the natural
facility of the route—the ease with which
any amount of labor for the construction can
be drawn in from the overcrowded populations of Europe, to be paid in the lands made
valuable by the progress of the work itself—
and its immense utility to the commerce of
the world with the whole eastern coast of
Asia, alone almost sufficient for the support
of such a road—these considerations give assurance that the day cannot be distant which
shall witness the conveyance of the representatives from Oregon and California to
Washington within less time than a few
years ago was devoted to a similar journey
by those from Ohio; while the magnetic tele-
graph will enable the editors of the "San
Francisco Union," the "Astoria Evening
Post," or the "Nootka Morning News" to set
up in type the first half of the President's Inaugural, before the echoes of the latter half
shall have died away beneath the lofty porch
of the Capitol, as spoken from his lips.

Away, then, with all idle French talk of
balances of power on the American Conti-

nent. There is no growth in Spanish America!
Whatever progress of population there may
be in the British Canadas, is only for their
own early severance of their present colonial
relation to the little island three thousand
miles across the Atlantic; soon to be followed by Annexation, and destined to swell
the still accumulating momentum of our
progress. And whosoever may hold the balance, though they should cast into the opposite scale all the bayonets and cannon, not
only of France and England, but of Europe
entire, how would it kick the beam against
the simple solid weight of the two hundred
and fifty or three hundred millions—and
American millions—destined to gather beneath the flutter of the stripes and stars, in
the fast hastening year of the Lord 1945!

2

*Thereafter American publications radiated be-
lief in American superiority and proclaimed it
as the nation's destiny to enlighten benighted
creatures in autocratic lands. The despot-ridden
masses of Canada must be free from the yoke
of kingship; Mexico and South America must
be added to the United States to save their mis-
treated serfs from tyranny! This was the theme
of the editor of the prominent southern journal,*
DeBow's Commercial Review, *as he surveyed
the state of the Latin-American republics in
1848:*[2]

We have frequently had occasion to advert to the absurd and cruel restrictions
which are put, by the Spanish Colonial System, now greatly moderated, upon the commerce of all its dependencies. From this
South America was a principal sufferer, and
they have had much influence in paralyzing
its industry and arresting its progress. That
other causes may be assigned for the rela-
tively-unimportant position of the republics
which have been established there, and their
slow advances in population and wealth,
made even under a system of freedom, is
not denied. With equal advantages of soil
and climate, the inferiority of the Spanish

---

[2] "The South American States," *DeBow's Commercial Review*, VI (July 1848), 8–9.

and Creole character tend to place the countries inhabited and administered by them, even under the best possible systems, far, very far behind those in which the Anglo-Saxon element is allowed to operate. Industry and unlimited enterprise are the inheritance of the latter. Indolence and pride hang like an incubus upon the former. The law of one is progress, the other decay. The Anglo-Saxons have been sweeping everything before them on the North American continent, and establishing an empire which is felt, respected and feared, in every quarter of the globe. Their arts, their policy, and their institutions, find imitators where, but a few years ago, it was fashionable to revile. The old thrones of Europe are being shaken down by the young Hercules of America. It is impossible to foresee the ends which are to be ultimately worked out. Will the knowledge of power and resources be followed by their abuse? Will the love of enterprise, and the desire of more extended territory, already so plainly manifested among us, lead to excursions upon the impotent neighbors that surround us upon every hand? Have not results in Mexico taught the *invincibility* of the American arms? What power on this continent is there that can arrest their progress? What army that would not be shattered to pieces in the encounter? What state whose capital would not be occupied? We are not vaunting our prowess in haughty pride, but adducing sentiments and facts *universally* admitted. The time has even passed when Europe can interfere in the movements of the western world. The powers have enough to do in looking after each other, and preventing the overshadowing importance of any particular one. Mr. Calhoun, the other day in the Senate, scoffed, with great propriety, at the apprehension of English power being unduly exercised upon this continent again. There is no European army that could be brought to this country and landed, large enough to withstand the force that could be brought against it. It is but too evident that the destinies of America are in *our* hands. Wisdom and moderation should induce us

to attend to our own peculiar affairs, and leave other American powers to do the same. The Mexican war was in many respects unfortunate, and we hail the peace with gratification. We have territories enough to be peopled for a generation to come. We have states enough formed and in embryo to govern. Let us leave events to take their own course. The North Americans *will* spread out far beyond their present bounds. They *will* encroach again and again upon their neighbors. New territories *will* be planted, declare their independence, and be annexed! We have New Mexico and California! We *will* have Old Mexico and Cuba! The isthmus cannot arrest—nor even the Saint Lawrence! Time has all of this in her womb. *A hundred states* will grow up where now exists but thirty. Let us not anticipate. The end of all this shall come, and God only can tell what it will be and when.

3

Another journalist was even less restrained as he poured forth in a Boston newspaper, a year later, his concept of American destiny:[3]

An American has said of his countrymen that the genuine Yankee would not be able to repose in Heaven itself if he could travel farther westward. He MUST go ahead. Prophecy looks forward to the time when the valley of the Mississippi shall overflow with this restless population, and Europe be subjected to a new migration. "What do I consider the boundaries of my country, sir," exclaimed a Kentuckian. "Why, sir, on the east we are bounded by the rising sun, on the north by the aurora borealis, on the west by the precession of the equinoxes, and on the south by the Day of Judgment."

4

So buoyant an attitude was certain to affect the public conduct of American statesmen. They assumed an attitude of condescending superiority when dealing with other nations, especially those of autocratic Eastern Europe. When

---

[3] *American Union* (Boston), October 13, 1849.

Austria rightly protested official meddling by the United States in one of its internal conflicts (the Hungarian revolution), Daniel Webster, secretary of state in 1850, replied to Chevalier J. G. Hulsemann, the chargé d'affaires in Washington, in a note that is a model of gallus-snapping, stump-speaking diplomacy:[4]

The power of this republic, at the present moment, is spread over a region one of the richest and most fertile on the globe, and of an extent in comparison with which the possessions of the house of Hapsburg are but as a patch on the earth's surface. Its population, already twenty-five millions, will exceed that of the Austrian empire within the period during which it may be hoped that Mr. Hülsemann may yet remain in the honorable discharge of his duties to his government. Its navigation and commerce are hardly exceeded by the oldest and most commercial nations; its maritime means and its maritime power may be seen by Austria herself, in all seas where she has ports, as well as they may be seen, also, in all other quarters of the globe. Life, liberty, property, and all personal rights, are amply secured to all citizens, and protected by just and stable laws; and credit, public and private, is as well established as in any government of Continental Europe; and the country, in all its interests and concerns, partakes most largely in all the improvements and progress which distinguish the age. Certainly, the United States may be pardoned, even by those who profess adherence to the principles of absolute government, if they entertain an ardent affection for those popular forms of political organization which have so rapidly advanced their own prosperity and happiness, and enabled them, in so short a period, to bring their country, and the hemisphere to which it belongs, to the notice and respectful regard, not to say the admiration, of the civilized world. Nevertheless, the United States have abstained, at all times, from acts of interference with the political changes of Europe. They cannot, however, fail to cher-

ish always a lively interest in the fortunes of nations struggling for institutions like their own. But this sympathy, so far from being necessarily a hostile feeling toward any of the parties to these great national struggles, is quite consistent with amicable relations with them all. The Hungarian people are three or four times as numerous as the inhabitants of these United States were when the American Revolution broke out. They possess, in a distinct language, and in other respects, important elements of a separate nationality, which the Anglo-Saxon race in this country did not possess; and if the United States wish success to countries contending for popular constitutions and national independence, it is only because they regard such constitutions and such national independence, not as imaginary, but as real blessings. They claim no right, however, to take part in the struggles of foreign powers in order to promote these ends. It is only in defence of his own government, and its principles and character, that the undersigned has now expressed himself on this subject. But when the people of the United States behold the people of foreign countries, without any such interference, spontaneously moving toward the adoption of institutions like their own, it surely cannot be expected of them to remain wholly indifferent spectators.

5

Many historians of America have wondered why, since all the elements of "manifest destiny" were present long before they combined in the 1840s, only then did they combine to give both a rationale and a stimulus to American expansionism. A modern historian, A. K. Weinberg, offers a solution as part of his larger work on the philosophy of "manifest destiny":[5]

In the "roaring 'forties," a decade thus designated because the spirit of American life rose into high and turbulent flame, there was

---

[4] Daniel Webster, *The Writings and Speeches of Daniel Webster* (Boston, 1903), VII, 170–171.

[5] Albert K. Weinberg, *Manifest Destiny: A Study of Nationalist Expansionism in American History* (Baltimore, 1935), pp. 100–129, *passim*. Reprinted with the permission of the publishers, The Johns Hopkins Press.

welded an association of two ideals which gave a new integration to the American's consciousness of national destiny. One of these ideals was territorial expansion. After several decades of relative quiescence, expansionism was rekindled by the issues of Texas and Oregon and was fanned to white heat by the oratory of Democrats in the presidential election of 1844. For the first time the wish of numerous American fathered the thought that their eventual possession of no less a domain than the entire North American continent was "manifest destiny" —a phrase which now passed into the national vocabulary.

The central implication of "manifest destiny" in the 'forties, however, was less a matter of the scope of expansion than of its purpose. The conception of expansion as a destiny meant primarily that it was a means to the fulfillment of a certain social ideal the preservation and perfection of which was America's providential mission or destiny. This ideal, conceived as "the last best revelation of human thought," was democracy— a theory of mass sovereignty but in a more important aspect a complex of individualistic values which, despite Fisher Ames's observation that America was too democratic for liberty, Americans most frequently summarized by the inspiring word "freedom." It was because of the association of expansion and freedom in a means-end relationship that expansion now came to seem most manifestly a destiny.

While the championship of the rights of man appeared from the beginning of national life to be America's special destiny, expansion had not seemed in general to be a necessary element in this preeminent national purpose. It is true that expansionists of the Revolution and the War of 1812 tendered "liberty" to the "oppressed" Canadians, and that Jefferson once included not only Canada but Cuba and Florida as well in America's "empire for liberty." Yet in all these instances . . . the extension of democracy was probably neither a primary motive of any expansionists nor even a secondary motive of

many of them. It was not until the 'forties that the popular ideology of expansionism centered in democracy. The new importance of this ideal to the expansionist was shown by the words which rang through the land as his slogan, "extension of the area of freedom."

It was because of its infusion with this ideal that American expansionism of the middle 'forties became possessed, as Professor Adams says in his valuable essay on "Manifest Destiny," of a "spiritual exaltation" in contemplation of the assumed superiority of American institutions. . . .

When Representative Severance urged in the 'forties that Americans "rather extend the 'area of freedom' by . . . our bright and shining example as a pattern republic," he was reverting to the conception which had been held by the founders of the nation. Originally "the extension of the area of freedom" signified extension of freedom regardless of political connection. Moreover the chief method chosen for extending freedom was the purely passive one of radiating democratic influence through impressive example. Thus Joel Barlow said in 1787 that "the example of political wisdom and felicity, here to be displayed, will excite emulation throughout the kingdoms of the earth, and meliorate the condition of the human race." Thomas Jefferson spoke of America as "a standing monument and example" which would "ameliorate the condition of man over a great portion of the globe." Jefferson also suggested another non-expansionist method of extending freedom. It was the pioneer migration covering even the Western Coast "with free and independent Americans, unconnected with us but by the ties of blood and interest, and employing like us the rights of self-government." It is clear from many such utterances that Americans at first perceived no necessary logical relationship between the extension of democracy and the extension of America's boundaries.

Why did early Americans see no logical nexus between the two ideals which were firmly associated by their descendants? One reason for the original disassociation of democracy and expansion was the internationalist orientation of many of the founders of the Republic. Early idealists, as the nationalistic Gouverneur Morris complained, had a *penchant* for referring to themselves as "citizens of the world." Associated with this internationalism was a devotion to democracy for its own sake. If only the offshoots of the American Republic blossomed into freedom, the retention of political connection seemed to Jefferson "not very important to the happiness of either part. ...."

The idea of individualism perhaps did more than anything else to cement the association between democracy and expansion. For the sturdiest element in democracy was its valuation of individualism—the thesis of the individual's right not only to exemption from undue interference by government but also to the most abundant opportunity for self-development. Those entirely misread its spirit who believe that the enthusiasm for democracy was merely enthusiasm over a form of government as such. Fundamentally, indeed, the Jeffersonian American rather disliked government; though recognizing the necessity of giving some power to the State, he at least verged on anarchism in his belief that "the best government is that which governs least." Whereas individualism in its negative phase meant restraint from undue interference with individual rights, in its positive phase it signified that "care of human life and happiness" which Jefferson called the only legitimate object of government.

Although both individualism and the pioneer spirit had prevailed from the beginning, it was not until the 'forties that the enterprise of the pioneer seemed the most perfect expression of American individualism. The coming of the pioneer movement to self-consciousness in this decade was due to various factors: the popular interest aroused by the accelerating trek to Oregon and the Southwest; the fact that the pioneer movement now became involved with territorial issues of national concern; and above all,

perhaps, the general land-hunger which caused the pioneer to seem now not a deviation from but the very expression of Americanism. It was in the fervent appreciation of the pioneer movement that there were forged all the links uniting individualism and expansionism. ...

Enshrined in expansionism, then, was this dogma of the special mission. Moral idealism divested of all intent of sacrilege the half-belief that God, who walked with Noah, rode with the American pioneer in his journeys over the continent. Even theological literature was scarcely more abundant in references to Providence than was the literature of expansionism. For it seemed that especially in expanding our territory, as a poet wrote upon the prospect of annexing Texas, "we do but follow out our destiny, as did the ancient Israelite." The expansionist conception of destiny was essentially ethical in its assumption that "Providence had given to the American people a great and important mission . . . to spread the blessings of Christian liberty." It was ambitiously ethical in its further assumption that "Providence" had a "design in extending our free institutions as far and as wide as the American continent." But the primary providential end was no more the elevation of the Latin-American heathen than was the elevation of the adjacent Philistines the end of the Israelite's journey to the Promised Land. The end in view was, as stated by John L. O'Sullivan in his first passage on manifest destiny, "the free development of our yearly multiplying millions." But in a second reference to manifest destiny he implied the moral significance of this free development of Americans. Americans were destined to develop themselves as subjects in "the great experiment of liberty and federated self-government entrusted to us."

Such was the credo which encouraged American expansionists to conceive that the free rather than the meek would inherit the earth. Its logic harmonized Calvinistic pride and equalitarianism. Still greater was its service in permitting the harmonization of the American's two deepest impulses—the expansionism oriented toward the good earth, and the democratic idealism oriented toward "Fair freedom's star." Believing like the Crusader that "God wills it," the expansionist had the joyful illusion of hitching his pioneer wagon to a star.

THE EXPANSION WESTWARD

6

Although destiny-minded Americans looked covetously on Latin America or blustered in their dealings with Europe, their immediate goal was the conquest of their own West. Lying beyond the Louisiana Purchase were good lands peopled only by "inferior" Spaniards, British traders, or Indians. Surely a benevolent Deity did not intend that garden spot to be occupied forever by such backward races! Attention was first directed to this frontier by the fur traders of the Rocky Mountain country and the Santa Fe traders. But just as influential in advertising the West were the missionaries. Their role was particularly prominent in the Oregon country, then jointly claimed by England and the United States. Missionary attention was directed to this region by William Walker, a Christianized Indian who visited the Missouri River country in 1832, seeking a reservation site for his own eastern tribe. While there, he recorded an incident that, when published in The Christian Advocate *and Journal and Zion's Herald March 1, 1833, aroused great interest, largely because of its description of the manner in which the Flathead Indians mutilated their children:*[6]

The country we explored is truly a land of savages. It is wild and romantic; it is a champaign, but beautifully undulated country. You can travel in some parts for whole days and not find timber enough to afford a riding switch, especially after you get off the Missouri and her principal tributary streams. The soil is generally a dark loam, but not of a durable kind for agriculture. As a country for agricultural pursuits, it is far inferior to what it has been represented to be. It is de-

plorably defective in timber. There are millions of acres on which you cannot procure timber enough to make a chicken coop. Those parts that are timbered are on some of the principal streams emptying into the great Missouri, and are very broken, rough, and cut up with deep ravines; and the timber, what there is of it, is of an inferior quality, generally a small growth of white, black, and bur oaks; hickory, ash, buckeye, mulberry, linwood, coffee bean, a low scrubby kind of birch, red and slippy elm, and a few scattering walnut trees. It is remarkable, in all our travels west of the Mississippi river, we never found even one solitary poplar, beech, pine, or sassafras tree, though we were informed that higher up the Missouri river, above Council Bluffs, pine trees abound to a great extent, especially the nearer you approach the Rocky mountains. The immense country embraced between the western line of the State of Missouri, and the territory of Arkansas, and the eastern base of the Rocky mountains on the west, and Texas and Santa Fe on the south, is inhabited by the Osage, Sioux (pronounced Sooz), Pawnees, Comanches, Panchas, Arrapohoes, Assinaboins, Riccarees, Yanktons, Omahaws, Blackfeet, Ottoes, Crow Indians, Sacs, Foxes, and Iowas: all a wild, fierce, and war-like people. West of the mountains reside the Fatheads, and many other tribes, whose names I do not now recollect.

I will here relate an anecdote, if I may so call it. Immediately after we landed in St. Louis, on our way to the West, I proceeded to Gen. Clark's, superintendent of Indian affairs, to present our letters of introduction from the Secretary of War, and to receive the same from him to the different Indian agents in the upper country. While in his office and transacting business with him, he informed me that three chiefs from the Flathead nation were in his house, and were quite sick, and that one (the fourth) had died a few days ago. They were from the west of the Rocky mountains. Curiosity prompted me to step into the adjoining room to see them, having never seen any, but often

---

[6] *The Christian Advocate and Journal and Zion's Herald,* March 1, 1833. Reprinted in Hiram M. Chittenden, *The American Fur Trade of the Far West* (New York, 1902), III, 914–918.

heard of them. I was struck with their appearance. They differ in appearance from any tribe of Indians I have ever seen: small in size, delicately formed, small limbs, and the most exact symmetry throughout, except the head. I had always supposed from their being called "Flatheads," that the head was actually flat on top; but this is not the case. The head is flattened thus:

From the point of the nose to the apex of the head, there is a perfect straight line, the protuberance of the forehead is flattened or leveled. . . . This is produced by a pressure upon the cranium while in infancy. The distance they had traveled on foot was nearly three thousand miles to see General Clark, their great father, as they called him, he being the first American officer they ever became acquainted with, and having much confidence in him, they had come to consult him as they said, upon very important matters. Gen. Clark related to me the object of their mission, and, my dear friend, it is impossible for me to describe to you my feelings while listening to his narrative. I will here relate it as briefly as I well can. It appeared that some white man had penetrated into their country, and happened to be a spectator at one of their religious ceremonies, which they scrupulously perform at stated periods. He informed them that their mode of worshipping the Supreme Being was radically wrong, and instead of being acceptable and pleasing, it was displeasing to him; he also informed them that the white people away toward the rising of the sun had been put in possession of the true mode of worshipping the great Spirit. They had a book containing directions how to conduct themselves in order to enjoy his favor and hold converse with him; and with this guide, no one need go astray; but every one that would follow the directions laid down there could enjoy, in this, his favor, and after death would be received into the country where the great Spirit resides, and live for ever with him.

Upon receiving this information, they called a national council to take this sub-

ject into consideration. Some said, if this be true, it is certainly high time we were put in possession of this mode, and if *our* mode of worshipping be wrong and displeasing to the great Spirit, it is time we had laid it aside. We must know something about this; it is a matter that cannot be put off; the sooner we know it the better. They accordingly deputed four of the chiefs to proceed to St. Louis to see their great father, General Clark, to inquire of him, having no doubt but he would tell them the whole truth about it.

They arrived at St. Louis, and presented themselves to Gen. C. The latter was somewhat puzzled being sensible of the responsibility that rested on him; he, however, proceeded by informing them that what they had been told by the white man in their own country was true. Then he went into a succinct history of man, from his creation down to the advent of the Saviour; explained to them all the moral precepts contained in the Bible, expounded to them the decalogue; informed them of the advent of the Saviour, his life, precepts, his death, resurrection, ascension, and the relation he now stands to man as a mediator—that he will judge the world, etc.

Poor fellows, they were not all permitted to return home to their people with the intelligence. Two died in St. Louis, and the remaining two, though somewhat indisposed, set out for their native land. Whether they reached home or not is not known. The change of climate and diet operated very severely upon their health. Their diet when at home is chiefly vegetables and fish.

If they died on their way home, peace be to their manes! They died inquirers after the truth. . . .

Yours in haste,
WM. WALKER

7

The missionaries who trekked to the Oregon country in response to this public interest proved good advertisers; their letters and speeches pictured the Willamette Valley in such glowing terms that by 1841 a mass movement of farmers was under way. One of the largest migrations occurred in 1843, when more than a thousand pioneers gathered at Independence, Missouri, the jumping-off place for the Oregon Trail. Dividing into two parties they set out, those without livestock moving ahead rapidly, those with cattle following more slowly. The leader of the group, Jesse Applegate, left a vivid description of his charges as they moved across the plains:[7]

The caravan has been about two hours in motion and is now extended as widely as a prudent regard for safety will permit. First, near the bank of the shining river, is a company of horsemen; they seem to have found an obstruction, for the main body has halted while three or four ride rapidly along the bank of the creek or slough. They are hunting a favorable crossing for the wagons; while we look they have succeeded; it has apparently required no work to make it passable, for all but one of the party have passed on and he has raised a flag, no doubt a signal to the wagons to steer their course to where he stands. The leading teamster sees him though he is yet two miles off, and steers his course directly towards him, all the wagons following in his track. They (the wagons) form a line three quarters of a mile in length; some of the teamsters ride upon the front of their wagons, some walk beside their teams; scattered along the line companies of women and children are taking exercise on foot; they gather bouquets of rare and beautiful flowers that line the way; near them stalks a stately greyhound or an Irish wolf dog, apparently proud of keeping watch and ward over his master's wife and children.

Next comes a band of horses; two or three men or boys follow them, the docile and sagacious animals scarce needing this attention, for they have learned to follow in the rear of the wagons, and know that at noon they will be allowed to graze and rest. Their knowledge of time seems as accurate as of the place they are to occupy in the line, and even a full-blown thistle will scarcely tempt them to straggle or halt until the dinner hour has arrived. Not so with the large herd of horned beasts that bring up the rear; lazy, selfish and unsocial, it has been a task to get them in motion, the strong always ready to domineer over the weak, halt in the front and forbid the weaker to pass them. They seem to move only in fear of the driver's whip; though in the morning full to repletion, they have not been driven an hour before their hunger and thirst seem to indicate a fast of days' duration. Through all the long day their greed is never sated nor their thirst quenched, nor is there a moment of relaxation of the tedious and vexatious labors of their drivers, although to all others the march furnishes some season of relaxation or enjoyment. For the cow-drivers there is none.

8

The pioneers who blazed the Oregon Trail were followed by hordes of land-hungry farmers. By 1846, several thousand Americans lived in the Willamette Valley of Oregon, all of them insistent that the United States provide them with an orderly government. This could never be done as long as the region was held jointly with England, whose powerful Hudson's Bay Company occupied the area north of the Columbia River. The pioneers' discontent was infectious; all the nation was soon demanding that Britain be forced to give up its claims. Typical of the American martial spirit was a Senate speech of Thomas Hart Benton, senator from Missouri and an ardent spokesman for the frontiersmen:[8]

The value of the country—I mean the Columbia River and its valley—(I must repeat the limitation every time, lest I be carried up to 54° 40′)—has been questioned on this floor and elsewhere. It has been supposed to be of little value—hardly worth the possession, much less the acquisition; and treated rather as a burden to be got rid of,

---

[7] Jesse Applegate, *A Day with the Cow Column in 1843* (Chicago, 1934), pp. 10–11. Reprinted from the *Transactions of the Oregon Pioneer Association for 1876.*

[8] Speech of May 28, 1846. *Congressional Globe,* 29th Cong., 1st Sess. 914.

than as a benefit to be preserved. This is a great error, and one that only prevails on this side of the water: the British know better; and if they held the tithe of our title, they would fight the world for what we depreciate. It is not a worthless country, but one of immense value, and that under many respects, and will be occupied by others, to our injury and annoyance, if not by ourselves for our own benefit and protection. Forty years ago it was written by Humboldt, that the banks of the Columbia presented the only situation on the northwest coast of America fit for the residence of a civilized people. Experience has confirmed the truth of this wise remark. All the rest of the coast, from the Straits of Fuca out to New Archangel, (and nothing but a fur trading post there,) remains a vacant waste, abandoned since the quarrel of Nootka Sound, and become the derelict of nations. The Columbia only invites a possessor; and for that possession, sagacious British diplomacy has been weaving its web. It is not a worthless possession; but valuable under many and large aspects; to the consideration of some of which I now proceed.

It is valuable, both as a country to be inhabited, and as a position to be held and defended. I speak of it, first, as a position, commanding the North Pacific ocean, and overlooking the eastern coast of Asia. The North Pacific is a rich sea, and is already the seat of a great commerce: British, French, American, Russian, and ships of other nations, frequent it. Our whaling ships cover it: our ships of war go there to protect our interest; and, great as that interest now is, it is only the beginning. Futurity will develop an immense, and various, commerce on that sea, of which the far greater part will be American. That commerce, neither in the merchant ships which carry it on, nor in the military marine which protects it, can find a port, to call its own, within twenty thousand miles of the field of its operations. The double length of the two Americas has to be run—a stormy and tempestuous cape to be doubled—to find itself in a port of its own country: while here lies one in the very edge of its field, ours by right, ready for use, and ample for every purpose of refuge and repair, protection and domination. Can we turn our back upon it? and, in turning the back, deliver it up to the British? Insane, and suicidal would be the fatal act!

To say nothing of the daily want of such a port in time of peace, its want, in time of war, becomes ruinous. Commodore Porter has often told me that, with protection from batteries in the mouth of the Columbia, he never would have put himself in a condition to be attacked under the weak, or collusive guns of a neutral port. He has told me that, with such a port for the reception of his prizes, he would not have sunk in the ocean, or hid in islands where it was often found, the three millions of British property captured in his three years daring and dauntless cruise. Often has he told me, that, with such a port at his hand, he would never have been driven to spill upon the waters, that oil, for want of which, as a member of the British Parliament said, London had burnt darkly— had been in the dark—for a whole year. What happened to Commodore Porter and his prizes—what happened to all our merchant ships, driven from the North Pacific during the war—all this to happen again, and upon a far larger scale, is but half the evil of turning our backs now upon this commanding position; for, to do so, is to deliver it into the hands of a Power that knows the value of positions—the four quarters of the globe, and our own coasts attest that—and has her eye on this one. The very year after the renewal of the delusive convention of 1818—in the year 1819—a master ship-carpenter was despatched from London to Fort Vancouver, to begin there the repair of vessels, and even the construction of small ones; and this work has been going on ever since. She resists our possession now! If we abandon, she will retain! And her wooden walls, bristling with cannon, and issuing from the mouth of the Columbia, will give the law to the North Pacific, permitting our ships to sneak about in time of peace—sinking, seizing, or chasing them away, in time of war. As a position, then, and if nothing but a rock, or desert point, the possession of the Columbia is invaluable to us; and it becomes our duty to maintain it at all hazards.

9

Oregon passed into American hands in 1846, when the British government surrendered an apparently useless territory as a gesture toward international peace. A year earlier, "manifest destiny" had added another vast region to the United States. Texas, overrun with American pioneers during the 1820s and early 1830s, won its independence from Mexico in 1836, then sought annexation. For a time this was not forthcoming, partly because Northerners objected to the addition of more slave territory, partly because of fear that a war with Mexico would follow. But by the spring of 1845, after President James K. Polk had been elected on a platform calling for the "reannexation of Texas," even war seemed preferable to the prospect of losing so rich a prize. Realizing this, but fearful lest northern votes in the Senate prevent the two-thirds majority needed to ratify a treaty, President Tyler in the waning months of his administration proposed annexation by joint resolution:[9]

Resolved . . . , That Congress doth consent that the territory properly included within, and rightfully belonging to the Republic of Texas, may be erected into a new State, to be called the State of Texas, with a republican form of government, to be adopted by the people of said republic, by deputies in convention assembled, with the consent of the existing government, in order that the same may be admitted as one of the States of this Union.

2. . . . That the foregoing consent of Congress is given upon the following conditions, and with the following guarantees, to wit: *First,* Said State to be formed, subject to the adjustment by this government of all questions of boundary that may arise with other governments; and the constitution thereof, with the proper evidence of its adoption by the people of said Republic of

Texas, shall be transmitted to the President of the United States, to be laid before Congress for its final action, on or before the first day of January, one thousand eight hundred and forty-six. *Second,* Said State, when admitted into the Union, after ceding to the United States, all public edifices, fortifications, barracks, ports and harbors, navy and navy-yards, docks, magazines, arms, armaments, and all other property and means pertaining to the public defence belonging to said Republic of Texas, shall retain all the public funds, debts, taxes, and dues of every kind, which may belong to or be due and owing said republic; and shall also retain all the vacant and unappropriated lands lying within its limits, to be applied to the payment of the debts and liabilities of said Republic of Texas, and the residue of said lands, after discharging said debts and liabilities, to be disposed of as said State may direct; but in no event are said debts and liabilities to become a charge upon the Government of the United States. *Third,* New States, of convenient size, not exceeding four in number, in addition to said State of Texas, and having sufficient population, may hereafter, by the consent of said State, be formed out of the territory thereof, which shall be entitled to admission under the provisions of the federal constitution. And such States as may be formed out of that portion of said territory lying south of thirty-six degrees thirty minutes north latitude, commonly known as the Missouri compromise line, shall be admitted into the Union with or without slavery, as the people of each State asking admission may desire. And in such State or States as shall be formed out of said territory north of said Missouri compromise line, slavery, or involuntary servitude, (except for crime,) shall be prohibited.

3. . . . That if the President of the United States shall in his judgment and discretion deem it most advisable, instead of proceeding to submit the foregoing resolution to the Republic of Texas, as an overture on the part of the United States for admission, to negotiate with that Republic; then,

---

[9] U. S., *Statutes at Large,* V, 797–798.

Be it resolved, That a State, to be formed out of the present Republic of Texas, with suitable extent and boundaries, and with two representatives in Congress, until the next apportionment of representation, shall be admitted into the Union, by virtue of this act, on an equal footing with the existing States, as soon as the terms and conditions of such admission, and the cession of the remaining Texan territory to the United States shall be agreed upon by the Governments of Texas and the United States: And that the sum of one hundred thousand dollars be, and the same is hereby, appropriated to defray the expenses of missions and negotiations, to agree upon the terms of said admission and cession, either by treaty to be submitted to the Senate, or by articles to be submitted to the two houses of Congress, as the President may direct.

THE MEXICAN CAMPAIGN

10

That such an ardent expansionist as Polk could long remain in office without adding more territory to the United States was unlikely. His objective was the northern Mexican provinces, already being peopled by Americans who followed the California Trail westward in the 1840s. Polk's acquisitive attitude, combined with Mexican anger at the annexation of Texas, rapidly brought the two nations to the point of war. Neither was completely at fault; Mexico was justly outraged at the American interest in its northern provinces; the United States was equally annoyed by Mexico's failure to pay its debts or meet its international obligations. President Polk decided to use these grievances as justification for war. He discloses his intentions to his Cabinet on May 9, 1846, and confides its reaction to his diary:[10]

SATURDAY, *9th May, 1846.*—The Cabinet held a regular meeting to-day; all the members present. I brought up the Mexican question, and the question of what was the duty of the administration in the present state

---

[10] Milo M. Quaife (ed.), *The Diary of James K. Polk* (Chicago, 1910), I, 384–386. Reprinted by permission of Milo M. Quaife.

of our relations with that country. The subject was very fully discussed. All agreed that if the Mexican forces at Matamoras committed any act of hostility on Gen'l Taylor's forces I should immediately send a message to Congress recommending an immediate declaration of War. I stated to the Cabinet that up to this time, as they knew, we had heard of no open act of aggression by the Mexican army, but that the danger was imminent that such acts would be committed. I said that in my opinion we had ample cause of war, and that it was impossible that we could stand in *statu quo*, or that I could remain silent much longer; that I thought it was my duty to send a message to Congress very soon & recommend definitive measures. I told them that I thought I ought to make such a message by Tuesday next, that the country was excited and impatient on the subject, and if I failed to do so I would not be doing my duty. I then propounded the distinct question to the Cabinet and took their opinions individually, whether I should make a message to Congress on Tuesday, and whether in that message I should recommend a declaration of War against Mexico. All except the Secretary of the Navy gave their advice in the affirmative. Mr. Bancroft dissented but said if any act of hostility should be committed by the Mexican forces he was then in favour of immediate war. Mr. Buchanan said he would feel better satisfied in his course if the Mexican forces had or should commit any act of hostility, but that as matters stood we had ample cause of war against Mexico, & he gave his assent to the measure. It was agreed that the message should be prepared and submitted to the Cabinet in their meeting on Tuesday. A history of our causes of complaint against Mexico had been at my request previously drawn up by Mr. Buchanan. I stated that what was said in my annual message in December gave that history as succinctly and satisfactorily as Mr. Buchanan's statement, that in truth it was the same history in both, expressed in different language, and that if I repeated that history in [a] message to Congress now I had better employ the precise language used in my message of December last. without deciding this point the Cabinet passed to the consideration of some other subjects of minor importance. . . .

About 6 o'clock P.M. Gen'l R. Jones, the Adjutant General of the army, called and handed to me despatches received from Gen'l Taylor by the Southern mail which had just arrived, giving information that a part of [the] Mexican army had crossed . . . the Del Norte, and attacked and killed and captured two companies of dragoons of Gen'l Taylor's army consisting of 63 officers & men. The despatch also stated that he had on that day (26th April) made a requisition on the Governors of Texas & Louisiana for four Regiments each, to be sent to his relief at the earliest practicable period. Before I had finished reading the despatch, the Secretary of War called. I immediately summoned the Cabinet to meet at 7½ O'Clock this evening. The Cabinet accordingly assembled at that hour; all the members present. The subject of the despatch received this evening from Gen'l Taylor, as well as the state of our relations with Mexico, were fully considered. The Cabinet were unanimously of opinion, and it was so agreed, that a message should be sent to Congress on Monday laying all the information in my possession before them and recommending vigorous & prompt measure[s] to enable the Executive to prosecute the War.

11

The dispatches reporting the skirmish between troops under General Zachary Taylor, who had been sent into the region between the Rio del Norte [Rio Grande] and the Nueces rivers then in dispute between the two nations, and the Mexican army caused Polk to change his plans at once. The message that he rushed to Congress on May 11, 1846, called for war on the basis of that skirmish:[11]

---

[11] James D. Richardson (comp.), *A Compilation of the Messages and Papers of the Presidents, 1789–1897* (Washington, 1897), IV, 440–443.

In my message at the commencement of the present session I informed you that upon the earnest appeal both of the Congress and convention of Texas I had ordered an efficient military force to take a position "between the Nueces and the Del Norte." This had become necessary to meet a threatened invasion of Texas by the Mexican forces, for which extensive military preparations had been made. The invasion was threatened solely because Texas had determined, in accordance with a solemn resolution of the Congress of the United States, to annex herself to our Union, and under these circumstances it was plainly our duty to extend our protection over her citizens and soil.

This force was concentrated at Corpus Christi, and remained there until after I had received such information from Mexico as rendered it probable, if not certain, that the Mexican Government would refuse to receive our envoy.

Meantime Texas, by the final action of our Congress, had become an integral part of our Union. The Congress of Texas, by its act of December 19, 1836, had declared the Rio del Norte to be the boundary of that Republic. Its jurisdiction had been extended and exercised beyond the Nueces. The country between that river and the Del Norte had been represented in the Congress and in the convention of Texas, had thus taken part in the act of annexation itself, and is now included within one of our Congressional districts. Our own Congress had, moreover, with great unanimity, by the act approved December 31, 1845, recognized the country beyond the Nueces as a part of our territory by including it within our own revenue system, and a revenue officer to reside within that district has been appointed by and with the advice and consent of the Senate. It became, therefore, of urgent necessity to provide for the defense of that portion of our country. Accordingly, on the 13th of January last instructions were issued to the general in command of these troops to occupy the left bank of the Del Norte. This river, which is the southwestern boundary of the State of Texas, is an exposed frontier. From this quarter invasion was threatened; upon it and in its immediate vicinity, in the judgment of high military experience, are the proper stations for the protecting forces of the Government. In addition to this important consideration, several other occurred to induce this movement. Among these are the facilities afforded by the ports at Brajor Santiago and the mouth of the Del Norte for the reception of supplies by sea, the stronger and more healthful military positions, the convenience for obtaining a ready and more abundant supply of provisions, water, fuel, and forage, and the advantages which are afforded by the Del Norte in forwarding supplies to such posts as may be established in the interior and upon the Indian frontier.

The movement of the troops to the Del Norte was made by the commanding general under positive instructions to abstain from all aggressive acts toward Mexico or Mexican citizens and to regard the relations between that Republic and the United States as peaceful unless she should declare war or commit acts of hostility indicative of a state of war. . . .

The Mexican forces at Matamoras assumed a belligerent attitude, and on the 12th of April General Ampudia, then in command, notified General Taylor to break up his camp within twenty-four hours and to retire beyond the Nueces River, and in the event of his failure to comply with these demands announced that arms, and arms alone, must decide the question. But no open act of hostility was committed until the 24th of April. On that day General Arista, who had succeeded to the command of the Mexican forces, communicated to General Taylor that "he considered hostilities commenced and should prosecute them." A party of dragoons of 63 men and officers were on the same day dispatched from the American camp up the Rio del Norte, on its left bank, to ascertain whether the Mexican troops had crossed or were preparing to cross the river, "became engaged with a large body of these

troops, and after a short affair, in which some 16 were killed and wounded, appear to have been surrounded and compelled to surrender." . . .

The cup of forbearance had been exhausted even before the recent information from the frontier of the Del Norte. But now, after reiterated menaces, Mexico has passed the boundary of the United States, has invaded our territory and shed American blood upon American soil. She has proclaimed that hostilities have commenced, and that the two nations are now at war.

As war exists, and, notwithstanding all our efforts to avoid it, exists by the act of Mexico herself, we are called upon by every consideration of duty and patriotism to vindicate with decision the honor, the rights, and the interests of our country. . . .

In further vindication of our rights and defense of our territory, I invoke the prompt action of Congress to recognize the existence of the war, and to place at the disposition of the Executive the means of prosecuting the war with vigor, and thus hastening the restoration of peace.

12

Sincere friends of freedom were outraged by Polk's flagrant distortion of the truth. One, an Illinois member of the House of Representatives named Abraham Lincoln, gained momentary fame in the North by introducing his "Spot Resolutions," December 22, 1847:[12]

Resolved, by the House of Representatives, That the President of the United States be respectfully requested to inform this House—

First. Whether the spot on which the blood of our citizens was shed, as in his message declared, was or was not within the territory of Spain, at least after the treaty of 1819 until the Mexican revolution.

Second. Whether that spot is or is not within the territory which was wrested from

---

[12] John G. Nicolay and John Hay (eds.), *Complete Works of Abraham Lincoln* (New York, 1894), I, 319–320.

Spain by the revolutionary Government of Mexico.

Third. Whether that spot is or is not within a settlement of people, which settlement has existed ever since long before the Texas revolution, and until its inhabitants fled before the approach of the United States army.

Fourth. Whether that settlement is or is not isolated from any and all other settlements by the Gulf and the Rio Grande on the south and west, and by wide uninhabited regions on the north and east.

Fifth. Whether the people of that settlement, or a majority of them, or any of them, have ever submitted themselves to the government or laws of Texas or of the United States, by consent or by compulsion, either by accepting office, or voting at elections, or paying tax, or serving on juries, or having process served upon them, or in any other way.

Sixth. Whether the people of that settlement did or did not flee from the approach of the United States army, leaving unprotected their homes and their growing crops, *before* the blood was shed, as in the message stated; and whether the first blood, so shed, was or was not shed within the inclosure of one of the people who had thus fled from it.

Seventh. Whether our citizens, whose blood was shed, as in his message declared, were or were not, at that time, armed officers and soldiers, sent into that settlement by the military order of the President, through the Secretary of War.

Eighth. Whether the military force of the United States was or was not so sent into that settlement after General Taylor had more than once intimated to the War Department that, in his opinion, no such movement was necessary to the defense or protection of Texas.

EXPANSION AND SLAVERY

13

The triumph of victory recorded in the Treaty of Guadalupe Hidalgo cost the United States

heavily. Long before the clash of arms died away, the whole nation was asking a question that none seemingly could answer: should the conquered lands be slave or free? Northerners were particularly aroused, aware that the Mexican provinces lay squarely in the path of the advancing cotton frontier and would probably become slave states. Determined to prevent this, James Russell Lowell, the Massachusetts poet, sums up the sentiments of his section in the Biglow Papers *(1846):*[13]

Thet air flag's a leetle rotten,
    Hope it aint your Sunday's best;
Fact! it takes a sight o' cotton
    To stuff out a soger's chest:
Sence we farmers hev to pay fer 't,
    Ef you must wear humps like these,
Sposin' you should try salt hay fer 't,
    It would du ez slick ez grease.

'Twould n't suit them Southun fellers,
    They're a dreffle graspin' set,
We must ollers blow the bellers
    Wen they want their irons het;
May be it 's all right ez preachin',
    But *my* narves it kind o' grates,
Wen I see the overreachin'
    O' them nigger-drivin' States.

Them thet rule us, them slave-traders,
    Haint they cut a thunderin' swarth
(Helped by Yankee renegaders),
    Thru the vartu o' the North!
We begin to think it 's nater
    To take sarse an' not be riled;—
Who 'd expect to see a tater
    All on eend at bein' biled?

Ez fer war, I call it murder,—
    There you hev it plain an' flat;
I don't want to go no furder
    Than my Testyment fer that;
God hez sed so plump an' fairly,
    It 's ez long ez it is broad,
An' you 've gut to git up airly
    Ef you want to take in God.

[13] James Russell Lowell, *The Complete Writings of James Russell Lowell* (Boston, 1904), X, 61–64.

'Taint your eppyletts an' feathers
  Make the thing a grain more right;
'Taint afollerin' your bell-wethers
  Will excuse ye in His sight;
Ef you take a sword an' dror it,
  An' go stick a feller thru,
Guv'ment aint to answer for it,
  God 'll send the bill to you.

Wut 's the use o' meetin'-goin'
  Every Sabbath, wet or dry,
Ef it 's right to go amowin'
  Feller-men like oats an' rye?
I dunno but wut it 's pooty
  Trainin' round in bobtail coats,—
But it 's curus Christian dooty
  This 'ere cuttin' folks's throats.

They may talk o' Freedom's airy
  Tell they 're pupple in the face,—
It's a grand gret cemetary
  Fer the barthrights of our race;
They jest want this Californy
  So 's to lug new slave-states in
To abuse ye, an' to scorn ye,
  An' to plunder ye like sin.

Aint it cute to see a Yankee
  Take sech everlastin' pains,
All to git the Devil's thankee
  Helpin' on 'em weld their chains?
Wy, it 's jest ez clear ez figgers,
  Clear ez one an' one make two,
Chaps thet make black slaves o' niggers
  Want to make wite slaves o' you.

Tell ye jest the eend I've come to
  Arter cipherin' plaguy smart,
An' it makes a handy sum, tu,
  Any gump could larn by heart;
Laborin' man an' laborin' woman
  Hev one glory an' one shame.
Ev'y thin' thet 's done inhuman
  Injers all on 'em the same.

'Taint by turnin' out to hack folks
  You're agoin' to git your right,
Nor by lookin' down on black folks
  Coz you 're put upon by wite;

Slavery aint o' nary color,
  'Taint the hide thet makes it wus,
All it keers fer in a feller
  'S jest to make him fill its pus.

14

*Northern insistence on freedom for the South-
west was translated into political form by the
Wilmot Proviso. This famous measure was introduced into Congress on August 8, 1846, by
David Wilmot, an antislavery representative
from Pennsylvania, as an amendment to a bill
appropriating funds for the prosecution of the
Mexican War:*[14]

The Committee of the Whole on the state
of the Union resumed its session, (Mr.
NORRIS in the chair).

Message—Foreign Intercourse

On motion of Mr. McKAY the committee
proceeded . . . to the consideration of the
President's message, and of the following
bill, introduced this morning by Mr. McKAY:

*Be it enacted by the Senate and House of
Representatives of the United States of America in Congress assembled,* That a sum of
$2,000,000, in addition to the provision here-
tofore made, be, and the same is hereby, appropriated, for the purpose of defraying any
extraordinary expenses which may be incurred in the intercourse between the United
States and foreign nations, to be paid out of
any money in the treasury not otherwise appropriated, and to be applied under the direction of the President of the United States,
who shall cause an account of the expenditure thereof to be laid before Congress as
soon as may be. . . .

Mr. WILMOT regretted that the President
had not disclosed his views. He disliked to
act in the dark on this or any subject. If
this had been done, and it had been inexpedient to have received and deliberated
upon it publicly, they might have gone into

---

[14] *Congressional Globe,* 29th Cong., 1st Sess.
1213–1217.

secret session. He would vote for this appropriation in case the amendment he intended to offer was adopted. He disagreed with some of his friends that this was an unnecessary war; he believed it a necessary and proper war. He believed it not to be a war of conquest; if so, he was opposed to it now and hereafter. If this country was now to be forced into such a war, he pronounced it against the spirit of the age, against the holy precepts of our religion; he was opposed to it in every form and shape. But he trusted it was not to be a war of conquest. He trusted that the President was sincerely ready to negotiate for an honorable peace.

But the President asked for two millions of dollars for concessions which Mexico was to make. We claim the Rio Grande as our boundary—that was the main cause of the war. Are we now to purchase what we claim as a matter of right? Certainly she was not to be paid for the debts she owes our citizens.

Mr. W. took it, therefore, that the President looked to the acquisition of territory in that quarter. To this he had no objection, provided it were done on proper conditions. On the contrary, he was most earnestly desirous that a portion of territory on the Pacific, including the bay of San Francisco, should come into our possession by fair and honorable means, by purchase or negotiation—not by conquest.

But whatever territory might be acquired, he declared himself opposed, now and forever, to the extension of this "peculiar institution" that belongs to the South. He referred to the annexation of Texas, and to his affirmative vote on the proposition connected with it at this session; he was for taking it as it was; slavery had already been established there. But if free territory comes in, God forbid that he should be the means of planting this institution upon it. . . .

Mr. WILMOT moved an amendment, to add at the end of Mr. McKAY's . . . bill the following:

Provided, That, as an express and fundamental condition to the acquisition of any territory from the Republic of Mexico by the United States, by virtue of any treaty which may be negotiated between them, and to the use by the Executive of the moneys herein appropriated, neither slavery nor involuntary servitude shall ever exist in any part of said territory, except for crime, whereof the party shall first be duly convicted.

15

Seldom has a congressional resolution thrown the nation into such a turmoil. Forgotten were party loyalties or national allegiance; overnight, men became conscious that they were Northerners or Southerners, and spoke accordingly. For months Congress angrily debated whether California and the Southwest should be slave or free. The House, more representative of the national majority than the Senate, favored the principle of the Wilmot Proviso. The bitterness of the controversy is shown in a speech delivered by Representative Robert Toombs of Georgia, December 13, 1849:[15]

Mr. TOOMBS said the difficulties in the way of the organization of this House are apparent and well understood here, and should be understood by the country. A great sectional question lies at the foundation of all these troubles. . . . We have just listened to strong appeals upon the necessity of organizing the House. I confess I do not feel that necessity. From the best lights before me, I cannot see that my constituents have anything to hope from your legislation, but everything to fear. We are not impatient to have the doors of your Treasury thrown open, and forty millions of the common taxes of the whole nation thrown into the lap of one half of it. We ask for none of it; we expect none of it; therefore gentlemen must pardon my want of sympathy for their impatience. By giving you the control of the Treasury, we increase your ability to oppress. I want grievances redressed, and security against their future perpetration, before I am willing to give you power over the supplies. Sir, I do not regret this state of things in the House. It is time we understood one another; that we should speak out, and carry our principles in our foreheads.

---

[15] *Ibid.,* 31st Cong., 1st Sess. 27–28.

It seems, from the remarks of the gentleman from New York, that we are to be intimidated by eulogies upon the Union, and denunciations of those who are not ready to sacrifice national honor, essential interests, and constitutional rights, upon its altar. Sir, I have as much attachment to the Union of these States, under the Constitution of our fathers, as any freeman ought to have, I am ready to concede and sacrifice for it whatever a just and honorable man ought to sacrifice—I will do no more. I have not heeded the aspersions of those who did not understand, or desired to misrepresent, my conduct or opinions in relation to these questions, which, in my judgment, so vitally affect it. The time has come when I shall not only utter them, but make them the basis of my political action here. I do not, then, hesitate to avow before this House and the country, and in the presence of the living God, that if by your legislation you seek to drive us from the territories of California and New Mexico, purchased by the common blood and treasure of the whole people, and to abolish slavery in this District, thereby attempting to fix a national degradation upon half the States of this Confederacy, *I am for disunion;* and if my physical courage be equal to the maintenance of my convictions of right and duty, I will devote all I am and all I have on earth to its consummation. From 1787 to this hour the people of the South have asked nothing but justice—nothing but the maintenance of the principles and the spirit which controlled our fathers in the formation of the Constitution. Unless we are unworthy of our ancestors, we will never accept less as a condition of union. . . . The Territories are the common property of the people of the United States, purchased by their common blood and treasure. You are their common agents; it is your duty, while they are in a territorial state, to remove all impediments to their free enjoyment by all sections and people of the Union, the slaveholder and the non-slaveholder. You have given the strongest indications that you will not perform this trust—that you will appropriate to your-

selves all of this Territory, perpetrate all these wrongs which I have enumerated; yet with these declarations on your lips, when southern men refused to act in party caucuses with you, in which you have a controlling majority—when we ask the simplest guarantee for the future—we are denounced out of doors as recusants and factionists, and indoors we are met with the cry of "Union, Union."

16

As the debate raged, both in the halls of Congress and throughout the nation, the need for a solution became more pressing, especially after the California gold rush of 1849 peopled the territory and required an orderly government. Faced by possible southern rebellion, cautious Senate leaders looked for a means of keeping slavery out of politics and avoiding the moral issue. Chief among these were Henry Clay of Kentucky and Stephen A. Douglas of Illinois. They sought a solution through compromise, and they fashioned a series of resolutions designed to treat slavery so far as possible as though it were a local question:[16]

It being desirable, for the peace, concord, and harmony of the Union of these States, to settle and adjust amicably all existing questions of controversy between them arising out of the institution of slavery upon a fair, equitable and just basis: therefore,

1. *Resolved,* That California, with suitable boundaries, ought, upon her application to be admitted as one of the States of this Union, without the imposition by Congress of any restriction in respect to the exclusion or introduction of slavery within these boundaries.

2. *Resolved,* That as slavery does not exist by law, and is not likely to be introduced into any of the territory acquired by the United States from the republic of Mexico, it is inexpedient for Congress to provide by law either for its introduction into, or exclusion from, any part of the said territory; and that appropriate territorial governments ought to be established by Congress in all

---

[16] The resolutions were introduced on January 29, 1850. *Senate Journal,* 31st Cong., 1st Sess. 118–119.

of the said territory, not assigned as the boundaries of the proposed State of California, without the adoption of any restriction or condition on the subject of slavery.

3. *Resolved,* That the western boundary of the State of Texas ought to be fixed on the Rio del Norte, commencing one marine league from its mouth, and running up that river to the southern line of New Mexico; thence with that line eastwardly, and so continuing in the same direction to the line as established between the United States and Spain, excluding any portion of New Mexico, whether lying on the east or west of that river.

4. *Resolved,* That it be proposed to the State of Texas, that the United States will provide for the payment of all that portion of the legitimate and bona fide public debt of that State contracted prior to its annexation to the United States, and for which the duties on foreign imports were pledged by the said State to its creditors, not exceeding the sum of —— dollars, in consideration of the said duties so pledged having been no longer applicable to that object after the said annexation, but having thenceforward become payable to the United States; and upon the condition, also, that the said State of Texas shall, by some solemn and authentic act of her legislature or of a convention, relinquish to the United States any claim which it has to any part of New Mexico.

5. *Resolved,* That it is inexpedient to abolish slavery in the District of Columbia whilst that institution continues to exist in the State of Maryland, without the consent of that State, without the consent of the people of the District, and without just compensation to the owners of slaves within the District.

6. *But, resolved,* That it is expedient to prohibit, within the District, the slave trade in slaves brought into it from States or places beyond the limits of the District, either to be sold therein as merchandise, or to be transported to other markets without the District of Columbia.

7. *Resolved,* That more effectual provision ought to be made by law, according to the requirement of the constitution, for the restitution and delivery of persons bound to service or labor in any State, who may escape into any other State or Territory in the Union. And,

8. *Resolved,* That Congress has no power to promote or obstruct the trade in slaves between the slaveholding States; but that the admission or exclusion of slaves brought from one into another of them, depends exclusively upon their own particular laws.

17

Henry Clay supported these compromise proposals in one of his most magnificent speeches:[17]

Such, Mr. President, is the series of resolutions which, in an earnest and anxious desire to present the olive branch to both parts of this distracted, and at the present moment, unhappy country, I have thought it my duty to offer. Of all men upon earth I am the least attached to any productions of my own mind. No man upon earth is more ready than I am to surrender anything which I have proposed, and to accept in lieu of it anything that is better; but I put it to the candor of honorable Senators on the other side and upon all sides of the House, whether their duty will be performed by simply limiting themselves to objections to any one or to all of the series of resolutions that I have offered. If my plan of peace, and accommodation, and harmony, is not right, present us your plan. Let us see the counter project. Let us see how all the questions that have arisen out of this unhappy subject of slavery can be better settled, more fairly and justly settled to all quarters of the Union, than on the plan proposed in the resolutions which I have offered. Present me such a scheme, and I will hail it with pleasure, and will accept it without the slightest feeling of regret that my own was abandoned. . . .

Now, sir, when I came to consider the

----

[17] Speech to the Senate, February 5 and 6, 1850. *Congressional Globe,* 31st Cong., 1st Sess. 115–116, 127.

subject and to compare the provisions of
the line of 36 degrees 30 minutes—the Missouri Compromise line—with the plan which
I propose for the accommodation of this
question, what said I to myself? Why, sir, if
I offer the line of 36 degrees 30 minutes,
interdicting slavery north of it, and leaving
the question open south of that line, I offer
that which is illusory to the South; I offer
that which will deceive them, if they suppose that slavery will be introduced south
of that line. It is better for them, I said to
myself—it is better for the whole South, that
there should be non-action on both sides,
than that there should be action interdicting
slavery on one side, without action for admission of slavery on the other side of the
line. Is it not so? What, then, is gained by
the South, if the Missouri line is extended
to the Pacific, with an interdiction of slavery
north of it? Why, sir, one of the very arguments which have been most often and most
seriously urged by the South has been this,
that we do not want you to legislate upon
the subject at all; you ought not to touch it;
you have no power over it. I do not concur,
as is well known from what I have said upon
this occasion, in this view of the subject.
But that is the Southern argument. We do
not want you to legislate at all on the subject of slavery. But if you adopt the Missouri
line and extend it to the Pacific, and interdict
slavery north of that line, you do legislate
upon the subject of slavery, and you legislate without a corresponding equivalent of
legislation on the subject south of the line.
For, if there be legislation interdicting slavery north of the line, the principle of equality would require that there should be legislation admitting slavery south of the line.

Sir, I have said that I never could vote
for it, and I repeat that I never can, and
never will vote for it; and no earthly power
shall ever make me vote to plant slavery
where slavery does not exist. Still, if there
be a majority—and there ought to be such
a majority—for interdicting slavery north
of the line, there ought to be an equal majority—if equality and justice be done to

the South—to admit slavery south of the
line. And if there be a majority ready to
accomplish both of these purposes, though
I can not concur in the action, yet I would
be one of the last to create any disturbance,
I would be one of the first to acquiesce in
such legislation, though it is contrary to my
own judgment and my own conscience. I
think, then, it would be better to keep the
whole of these territories untouched by any
legislation by Congress on the subject of
slavery, leaving it open, undecided, without
any action of Congress in relation to it; that
it would be best for the South, and best for
all the views which the South has, from time
to time, disclosed to us as correspondent with
her wishes. . . .

And, sir, I must take occasion here to say
that in my opinion there is no right on the
part of any one or more of the States to secede from the Union. War and dissolution of
the Union are identical and inevitable, in my
opinion. There can be a dissolution of the
Union only by consent or by war. Consent
no one can anticipate, from any existing state
of things, is likely to be given; and war is
the only alternative by which a dissolution
could be accomplished. If consent were
given—if it were possible that we were to
be separated by one great line—in less than
sixty days after such consent was given war
would break out between the slaveholding
and non-slaveholding portions of this Union
—between the two independent parts into
which it would be erected in virtue of the
act of separation. In less than sixty days, I
believe, our slaves from Kentucky, flock-
ing over in numbers to the other side of the
river, would be pursued by their owners.
Our hot and ardent spirits would be restrained by no sense of the right which appertains to the independence of the other
side of the river, should that be the line of
separation. They would pursue their slaves
into the adjacent free States; they would be
repelled; and the consequence would be
that, in less than sixty days, war would be
blazing in every part of this now happy and
peaceful land.

And, sir, how are you going to separate the States of this confederacy? In my humble opinion, Mr. President, we should begin with at least three separate confederacies. There would be a confederacy of the North, a confederacy of the Southern Atlantic slave-holding States, and a confederacy of the valley of the Mississippi. My life upon it, that the vast population which has already concentrated and will concentrate on the head-waters and the tributaries of the Mississippi will never give their consent that the mouth of that river shall be held subject to the power of any foreign State or community whatever. Such, I believe, would be the consequences of a dissolution of the Union, immediately ensuing; but other confederacies would spring up from time to time, as dissatisfaction and discontent were disseminated throughout the country—the confederacy of the lakes, perhaps the confederacy of New England, or of the middle States. Ah, sir, the veil which covers these sad and disastrous events that lie beyond it, is too thick to be penetrated or lifted by any mortal eye or hand. . . .

Mr. President, I have said, what I solemnly believe, that dissolution of the Union and war are identical and inevitable; and they are convertible terms; and such a war as it would be, following a dissolution of the *Union!* Sir, we may search the pages of history, and none so ferocious, so bloody, so implacable, so exterminating—not even the wars of Greece, including those of the Commoners of England and the revolutions of France—none, none of them all would rage with such violence, or be characterized with such bloodshed and enormities as would be the war which must succeed, if that ever happens, the dissolution of the Union. And what would be its termination? Standing armies, and navies, to an extent stretching the revenues of each portion of the dissevered members, would take place. An exterminating war would follow—not sir, a war of two or three years' duration, but a war of interminable duration—and exterminating wars would ensue, until, after the

struggles and exhaustion of both parties, some Philip or Alexander, some Caesar or Napoleon, would arise and cut the Gordian knot, and solve the problem of the capacity of man for self-government, and crush the liberties of both the severed portions of this common empire. Can you doubt it?

Look at all history—consult her pages, ancient or modern—look at human nature; look at the contest in which you would be engaged in the supposition of war following upon the dissolution of the Union, such as I have suggested; and I ask you if it is possible for you to doubt that the final disposition of the whole would be some despot treading down the liberties of the people—the final result would be the extinction of this last and glorious light which is leading all mankind, who are gazing upon it, in the hope and anxious expectation that the liberty which prevails here will sooner or later be diffused throughout the whole of the civilized world. Sir, can you lightly contemplate these consequences? Can you yield yourself to the tyranny of passion, amid dangers which I have depicted, in colors far too tame, of what the result would be if that direful event to which I have referred should ever occur? Sir, I implore gentlemen, I adjure them, whether from the South or the North, by all that they hold dear in this world—by all their love of liberty—by all their veneration for their ancestors—by all their regard for posterity—by all their gratitude to Him who has bestowed on them such unnumbered and countless blessings—by all the duties which they owe to mankind—and by all the duties which they owe to themselves, to pause, solemnly to pause at the edge of the precipice, before the fearful and dangerous leap be taken into the yawning abyss below, from which none who ever take it shall return in safety.

Finally, Mr. President, and in conclusion, I implore, as the best blessing which Heaven can bestow upon me upon earth, that if the direful event of the dissolution of this Union is to happen, I shall not survive to behold the sad and heart-rending spectacle.

18

Many from both North and South refused to accept Clay's sober advice. Northerners, concerned for the moral issue and insisting upon majority rule, wanted nothing less than open recognition of the power of Congress to bar slavery from the territories. Their principal spokesman was William H. Seward of New York, whose penetrating remarks disclose the democratic issues involved:[18]

It is now avowed by the honorable senator from South Carolina . . . that nothing will satisfy the slave states but a compromise that will convince them that they can remain in the Union consistently with their honor and their safety. And what are the concessions which will have that effect? Here they are, in the words of that senator:

"The north must do justice by conceding to the south an equal right in the acquired territory, and do her duty by causing the stipulations relative to fugitive slaves to be faithfully fulfilled—cease the agitation of the slave question, and provide for the insertion of a provision in the Constitution, by an amendment, which will restore to the south in substance the power she possessed, of protecting herself, before the equilibrium between the sections was destroyed by the action of this government."

These terms amount to this: that the free States having already, or although they may hereafter have, majorities of population, and majorities in both houses of Congress, shall concede to the slave States, being in a minority in both, the unequal advantage of an equality. That is, that we shall alter the Constitution so as to convert the Government from a national democracy, operating by a constitutional majority of voices, into a federal alliance, in which the minority shall have a veto against the majority. And this would be nothing less than to return to the original Articles of Confederation! . . .

The next of this class of arguments is, that the inhibition of slavery in the new territories is unnecessary; . . . But why is it unneces-

[18] Speech to the Senate, March 11, 1850. *Ibid.*, 263, 266.

sary? It is said, *first*, by reason of *climate*. I answer, if this be so, why do not the representatives of the slave States concede the proviso? They deny that the climate prevents the introduction of slavery. Then I will leave nothing to a contingency. But, in truth, I think the weight of argument is against the proposition. Is there any climate where slavery has not existed? It has prevailed all over Europe, from sunny Italy to bleak England, and is existing now, stronger than in any other land, in ice-bound Russia. But it will be replied, that this is not African slavery. I rejoin, that only makes the case the stronger. If this vigorous Saxon race of ours was reduced to slavery, while it retained the courage of semi-barbarism in its own high northern latitude, what security does climate afford against the transplantation of the more gentle, more docile, and already enslaved and debased African to the genial climate of New Mexico and Eastern California?

Sir, there is no climate uncongenial to slavery. It is true it is less productive than free labor in many northern countries; but so it is less productive than free white labor in even tropical climates. Labor is in demand quick in all new countries. Slave labor is cheaper than free labor, and it would go first into new regions; and wherever it goes it brings labor into dishonor, and therefore free white labor avoids competition with it. Sir, I might rely on climate if I had not been born in a land where slavery existed—and this land was all of it north of the fortieth parallel of latitude—and if I did not know the struggle it has cost, and which is yet going on, to get complete relief from the institution and its baleful consequences. I desire to propound this question to those who are now in favor of dispensing with the Wilmot proviso: Was the ordinance of 1787 necessary or not? Necessary, we all agree. It has received too many eulogiums to be now decried as an idle and superfluous thing. And yet that ordinance extended the inhibition of slavery from the 37th to the 40th parallel of north latitude; and now we are told that the inhibition named is unnecessary anywhere north of 36° 30′! We are told that we may rely upon the laws of God, which prohibit slave labor north of that line, and that it is absurd to re-enact the laws of God. Sir, there is no human enactment which is just, that is not a re-enactment of the law of God.

19

Southerners, on the other hand, were so concerned for property rights that they insisted on constitutional limitations upon majority rule. This undemocratic cause was upheld by John C. Calhoun of South Carolina, whose fiery words concealed the weakness of a body fast succumbing to a fatal illness. The closing sections of his great speech of March 4, 1850, were tinged with defiance and sadness—sadness that the Union he loved seemed on the point of dissolution:[19]

The strongest of those [broken ties of Union] of a spiritual and ecclesiastical nature, consisted in the unity of the great religious denominations, all of which originally embraced the whole Union. All these denominations, with the exception, perhaps, of the Catholics, were organized very much upon the principle of our political institutions. Beginning with smaller meetings, corresponding with the political divisions of the country, their organization terminated in one great central assemblage, corresponding very much with the character of Congress. At these meetings the principal clergymen and lay members of the respective denominations, from all parts of the Union, met to transact business relating to their common concerns. It was not confined to what appertained to the doctrines and discipline of the respective denominations, but extended to plans for disseminating the Bible, establishing missionaries, distributing tracts, and of establishing presses for the publication of tracts, newspapers, and periodicals, with a view of diffusing religious information, and for the support of the doctrines and creeds of the denomination. All this combined, contributed greatly to strengthen the bonds of the Union. The ties which held each denomination together formed a strong cord to hold the whole Union together; but, powerful as they were, they have not been able to resist the explosive effect of slavery agitation.

The first of these cords which snapped, under its explosive force, was that of the powerful Methodist Episcopal Church. The numerous and strong ties which held it together, are all broken, and its unity gone. They now form separate churches, and, instead of that feeling of attachment and devotion to the interests of the whole church which was formerly felt, they are now arrayed into two hostile bodies, engaged in litigation about what was formerly their common property.

The next cord that snapped was that of the Baptists, one of the largest and most respectable of the denominations. That of the Presbyterian is not entirely snapped, but some of its strands have given way. That of the Episcopal Church is the only one of the four great Protestant denominations which remains unbroken and entire.

The strongest cord, of a political character consists of the many and powerful ties that have held together the two great parties which have, with some modifications, existed from the beginning of the Government. They both extended to every portion of the Union, and strongly contributed to hold all its parts together. But this powerful cord has fared no better than the spiritual. It resisted, for a long time, the explosive tendency of the agitation, but has finally snapped under its force—if not entirely, in a great measure. Nor is there one of the remaining cords which has not been greatly weakened. To this extent the Union has already been destroyed by agitation, in the only way it can be, by snapping asunder and weakening the cords which bind it together.

If the agitation goes on, the same force, acting with increased intensity, as has been shown, will finally snap every cord, when nothing will be left to hold the States together except force. But, surely that can,

[19] *Ibid.*, 453–455.

with no propriety of language, be called a Union, when the only means by which the weaker is held connected with the stronger portion is *force*. It may, indeed, keep them connected; but the connection will partake much more of the character of subjugation, on the part of the weaker to the stronger, than the union of free, independent, and sovereign States, in one confederation, as they stood in the early stages of the Government, and which only is worthy of the sacred name of Union.

Having now, Senators, explained what it is that endangers the Union, and traced it to its cause, and explained its nature and character, the question again recurs, How can the Union be saved? To this I answer, there is but one way by which it can be, and that is, by adopting such measures as will satisfy the States belonging to the southern section that they can remain in the Union consistently with their honor and their safety. There is, again, only one way by which this can be effected, and that is, by removing the causes by which this belief has been produced. *Do that* and discontent will cease, harmony and kind feelings between the sections be restored, and every apprehension of danger to the Union removed. The question, then, is, By what can this be done? But, before I undertake to answer this question, I propose to show by what the Union cannot be saved.

It cannot, then, be saved by eulogies on the Union, however splendid or numerous. The cry of "Union, Union, the glorious Union!" can no more prevent disunion than the cry of "Health, health, glorious health!" on the part of the physician, can save a patient lying dangerously ill. So long as the Union, instead of being regarded as a protector, is regarded in the opposite character, by not much less than a majority of the States, it will be in vain to attempt to conciliate them by pronouncing eulogies on it.

Besides this cry of Union comes commonly from those whom we cannot believe to be sincere. It usually comes from our assailants. But we cannot believe them to be sincere;

for, if they loved the Union, they would necessarily be devoted to the constitution. It made the Union, and to destroy the constitution would be to destroy the Union. But the only reliable and certain evidence of devotion to the Constitution is, to abstain, on the one hand, from violating it, and to repel, on the other, all attempts to violate it. It is only by faithfully performing these high duties that the Constitution can be preserved, and with it the Union.

But how stands the profession of devotion to the Union by our assailants, when brought to this test? Have they abstained from violating the Constitution? Let the many acts passed by the Northern States to set aside and annul the clause of the Constitution providing for the delivery up of fugitive slaves answer. I cite this, not that it is the only instance (for there are many others,) but because the violation in this particular is too notorious and palpable to be denied. Again, have they stood forth faithfully to repel violations of the Constitution? Let their course in reference to the agitation of the slavery question, which was commenced and has been carried on for fifteen years, avowedly for the purpose of abolishing slavery in the States—an object all acknowledged to be unconstitutional—answer. Let them show a single instance, during this long period, in which they have denounced the agitators of their attempts to effect what is admitted to be unconstitutional, or a single measure which they have brought forward for that purpose. How can we, with all these facts before us, believe that they are sincere in their profession of devotion to the Union, or avoid believing their profession is but intended to increase the vigor of their assaults and to weaken the force of our resistance?

Nor can we regard the profession of devotion to the Union, on the part of those who are not our assailants, as sincere, when they pronounce eulogies upon the Union, evidently with the intent of charging us with disunion, without uttering one word of denunciation against our assailants. If friends of the Union, their course should be to unite with us in repelling these assaults, and denouncing the authors as enemies of the Union. Why they avoid this, and pursue the course they do, it is for them to explain.

Nor can the Union be saved by invoking the name of the illustrious Southerner whose mortal remains repose on the western bank of the Potomac. He was one of us—a slaveholder and a planter. We have studied his history, and find nothing in it to justify submission to wrong. On the contrary, his great fame rests on the solid foundation, that, while he was careful to avoid doing wrong to others, he was prompt and decided in repelling wrong. I trust that, in this respect, we profited by his example.

Nor can we find any thing in his history to deter us from seceding from the Union, should it fail to fulfil the objects for which it was instituted, by being permanently and hopelessly converted into the means of oppressing instead of protecting us. On the contrary, we find much in his example to encourage us, should we be forced to the extremity of deciding between submission and disunion.

There existed then, as well as now, a Union —that between the parent country and her then colonies. It was a union that had much to endear it to the people of the colonies. Under its protecting and superintending care, the colonies were planted and grew up and prospered, through a long course of years, until they became populous and wealthy. Its benefits were not limited to them. Their extensive agricultural and other productions, gave birth to a flourishing commerce, which richly rewarded the parent country for the trouble and expense of establishing and protecting them. Washington was born and grew up to manhood under that union. He acquired his early distinction in its service, and there is every reason to believe that he was devotedly attached to it. But his devotion was a rational one. He was attached to it, not as an end, but as a means to an end. When it failed to fulfil its end, and, instead of affording protection, was converted into the means of oppressing the colonies, he did not hesitate to draw his sword, and head the great movement by which that union was for ever severed, and the independence of these States established. This was the great and crowning glory of his life, which has spread his fame over the whole globe, and will transmit it to the latest posterity.

Nor can the plan proposed by the distinguished Senator from Kentucky, nor that of the administration save the Union. I shall pass by, without remark, the plan proposed by the Senator, and proceed directly to the consideration of that of the Administration. I however assure the distinguished and able Senator, that, in taking this course, no disrespect whatever is intended to him or his plan. I have adopted it, because so many Senators of distinguished abilities, who were present when he delivered his speech, and explained his plan, and who were fully capable to do justice to the side they support, have replied to him.

The plan of the administration cannot save the Union, because it can have no effect whatever, towards satisfying the States composing the Southern section of the Union, that they can, consistently with safety and honor, remain in the Union. It is, in fact, but a modification of the Wilmot proviso. It proposes to effect the same object, to exclude the South from all territory acquired by the Mexican treaty. It is well known that the South is united against the Wilmot proviso, and has committed itself by solemn resolutions, to resist, should it be adopted. Its opposition *is not to the name,* but that which it *proposes to effect.* That, the southern States hold to be unconstitutional, unjust, inconsistent with their equality as members of the common Union, and calculated to destroy irretrievably the equilibrium between the two sections. These objections equally apply to what, for brevity, I will call the Executive proviso. There is no difference between it and the Wilmot, except in the mode of effecting the object, and in that respect I must say that the latter is much the least objectionable. It goes to its object openly, boldly, and distinctly. It claims for Congress unlimited power over the territories, and proposes to assert it over the territories acquired from Mexico, by a positive prohibition of slavery. Not so the Executive Proviso. It takes an indirect course, and in order to elude the Wilmot Proviso, and thereby avoid encountering the united and determined resistance of the South, it denies, by implication, the authority of Congress to legislate for the territories, and claims the right as belonging exclusively to the inhabitants of the territories. But to effect the object of excluding the South, it takes care, in the mean time, to let in emigrants freely from the Northern States and all other quarters, except from the South, which it takes special care to exclude, by holding up to them the danger of having their slaves liberated under the Mexican laws. The necessary consequence is to exclude the South from the territory, just as effectually as would the Wilmot proviso. The only difference in this respect is, that what one proposes to effect directly and openly, the other proposes to effect indirectly and covertly.

But the Executive Proviso is more objectionable than the Wilmot, in another and more important particular. The latter, to effect its object, inflicts a dangerous wound upon the Constitution, by depriving the southern States, as joint partners and owners of the territories, of their rights in them; but it inflicts no greater wound than is absolutely necessary to effect its object. The former, on the contrary, while it inflicts the same wound, inflicts others equally great, and, if possible, greater, as I shall next proceed to explain.

In claiming the right for the inhabitants, instead of Congress, to legislate for the territories, in the Executive proviso, it assumes that the sovereignty over the territories is vested in the former; or, to express it in the language used in a resolution offered by one of the Senators from Texas, (General Houston, now absent,) they have "the same inherent right of self-government as the people

in the States." The assumption is utterly unfounded, unconstitutional, without example, and contrary to the entire practice of the Government, from its commencement to the present time. . . .

Having now shown what cannot save the Union, I return to the question with which I commenced, How can the Union be saved? There is but one way by which it can with any certainty; and that is, by a full and final settlement, on the principle of justice, of all the questions at issue between the two sections. The South asks for justice, simple justice, and less she ought not to take. She has no compromise to offer, but the Constitution; and no concession or surrender to make. She has already surrendered so much that she has little left to surrender. Such a settlement would go to the root of the evil, and remove all cause of discontent, by satisfying the South, that she could remain honorably and safely in the Union, and thereby restore the harmony and fraternal feelings between the sections which existed anterior to the Missouri agitation. Nothing else can, with any certainty, finally and for ever settle the questions at issue, terminate agitation, and save the Union.

But can this be done? Yes, easily; not by the weaker party, for it can of itself do nothing—not even protect itself—but by the stronger. The North has only to will it to accomplish it—to do justice by conceding to the South an equal right in the acquired territory, and to do her duty by causing the stipulations relative to fugitive slaves to be faithfully fulfilled—to cease the agitation of the slave question, and to provide for the insertion of a provision in the Constitution, by an amendment, which will restore to the South, in substance, the power she possessed of protecting herself, before the equilibrium between the sections was destroyed by the action of this Government. There will be no difficulty in devising such a provision—one that will protect the South, and which, at the same time, will improve and strengthen the Government, instead of impairing and weakening it.

But will the North agree to this? It is for her to answer the question. But, I will say, she cannot refuse, if she has half the love of the Union which she professes to have, or without justly exposing herself to the charge that her love of power and aggrandizement is far greater than her love of the Union. At all events, the responsibility of saving the Union rests on the North, and not on the South. The South cannot save it by any act of hers, and the North may save it without any sacrifice whatever, unless to do justice, and to perform her duties under the Constitution, should be regarded by her as a sacrifice.

It is time, Senators, that there should be an open and manly avowal on all sides, as to what is intended to be done. If the question is not now settled, it is uncertain whether it ever can hereafter be; and we, as the representatives of the States of this Union, regarded as governments, should come to a distinct understanding as to our respective views, in order to ascertain whether the great questions at issue can be settled or not. If you, who represent the stronger portion, cannot agree to settle them on the broad principle of justice and duty, say so; and let the States we both represent agree to separate and part in peace. If you are unwilling we should part in peace, tell us so; and we shall know what to do, when you reduce the question to submission or resistance. If you remain silent, you will compel us to infer by your acts what you intend. In that case, California will become the test question. If you admit her, under all the difficulties that oppose her admission, you compel us to infer that you intend to exclude us from the whole of the acquired territories, with the intention of destroying, irretrievably, the equilibrium between the two sections. We would be blind not to perceive, in that case, that your real objects are power and aggrandizement, and infatuated not to act accordingly.

I have now, Senators, done my duty in expressing my opinions fully, freely, and candidly, on this solemn occasion. In doing so, I have been governed by the motives which have governed me in all the stages of the agitation of the slavery question since its commencement. I have exerted myself, during the whole period, to arrest it, with the intention of saving the Union, if it could be done; and if it could not, to save the section where it has pleased Providence to cast my lot, and which I sincerely believe has justice and the Constitution on its side. Having faithfully done my duty to the best of my ability, both to the Union and my section, throughout this agitation, I shall have the consolation, let what will come, that I am free from all responsibility.

20

Daniel Webster, the grand old statesman from Massachusetts, delivered his most famous speech in support of Clay's resolutions on March 7, 1850:[20]

MR. PRESIDENT,—I wish to speak to-day, not as a Massachusetts man, nor as a northern man, but as an American, and a member of the Senate of the United States. It is fortunate that there is a Senate of the United States; a body not yet moved from propriety, not lost to a just sense of its own dignity and its own high responsibilities, and a body to which the country looks, with confidence, for wise, moderate, patriotic, and healing counsels. It is not to be denied that we live in the midst of strong agitations, and are surrounded by very considerable dangers to our institutions and government. The imprisoned winds are let loose. The East, the West, the North, and the stormy South, all combine to throw the whole sea into commotion, to toss its billows to the skies, and disclose its profoundest depths. I do not affect to regard myself, Mr. President, as holding, or as fit to hold, the helm in this combat with the political elements; but I have a duty to perform, and I mean to perform it with fidelity—not without a sense of existing dangers, but not without hope. I have a part to act, not for my own security or safety, for I am looking out for no fragment upon which

20 *Ibid.*, 269, 276.

to float away from the wreck, if wreck there must be, but for the good of the whole, and the preservation of the whole; and there is that which will keep me to my duty during this struggle, whether the sun and the stars shall appear, or shall not appear for many days. I speak to-day for the preservation of the Union. "Hear me for my cause." I speak to-day, out of a solicitous and anxious heart, for the restoration to the country of that quiet and that harmony which make the blessings of this Union so rich and so dear to us all. These are the topics that I propose to myself to discuss; these are the motives, and the sole motives, that influence me in the wish to communicate my opinions to the Senate and the country; and if I can do anything, however little, for the promotion of these ends, I shall have accomplished all that I desire. . . .

Mr. President, I should much prefer to have heard, from every member on this floor, declarations of opinion that this Union could never be dissolved, than the declaration of opinion that in any case, under the pressure of circumstances, such a dissolution was possible. I hear with pain, and anguish, and distress, the word secession, especially when it falls from the lips of those who are eminently patriotic, and known to the country, and known all over the world, for their political services. Secession! Peaceable secession! Sir, your eyes and mine are never destined to see that miracle. The dismemberment of this vast country without convulsion! The breaking up of the fountains of the great deep without ruffling the surface! Who is so foolish—I beg every body's pardon—as to expect to see any such thing? Sir, he who sees these States, now revolving in harmony around a common centre, and expects to see them quit their places and fly off without convulsion, may look the next hour to see the heavenly bodies rush from their spheres, and jostle against each other in the realms of space, without producing the crush of the universe. There can be no such thing as a peaceable secession. Peaceable secession is an utter impossibility. Is the great Constitu-

tion under which we live—covering this whole country—is it to be thawed and melted away by secession, as the snows on the mountain melt under the influence of a vernal sun—disappear almost unobserved, and die off? No, sir! No, sir! I will not state what might produce the disruption of the states; but, sir, I see it as plainly as I see the sun in heaven—I see that disruption must produce such a war as I will not describe, in its twofold characters.

Peaceable secession! peaceable secession! The concurrent agreement of all the members of this great Republic to separate! A voluntary separation, with alimony on one side and on the other! Why, what would be the result? Where is the line to be drawn? What States are to secede?—What is to remain American? What am I to be?—an American no longer? Where is the flag of the republic to remain? Where is the eagle still to tower? or is he to cower, and shrink, and fall to the ground? Why, Sir, our ancestors—our fathers and our grandfathers, those of them that are yet living amongst us with prolonged lives—would rebuke and reproach us; and our children and our grandchildren would cry out, Shame on us! if we of this generation, should dishonor those ensigns of the power of the Government, and the harmony of the Union, which is every day felt among us with so much joy and gratitude. What is to become of the army? What is to become of the navy? What is to become of the public lands? How is each of the thirty States to defend itself? I know, although the idea has not been stated distinctly, there is to be a southern Confederacy. I do not mean, when I allude to this statement, that any one seriously contemplates such a state of things. I do not mean to say that it is true, but I have heard it suggested elsewhere, that idea has originated in a design to separate. I am sorry, sir, that it has ever been thought of, talked of, or dreamed of, in the wildest flights of human imagination. But the idea must be of a separation, including the slave States upon one side and the free States on the other. Sir, I may express myself too strongly, perhaps—but some things, some moral things, are almost as impossible, as other natural or physical things; and I hold the idea of a separation of these States—those that are free to form one government, and those that are slaveholding to form another—as a moral impossibility. We could not separate the States by any such line, if we were to draw it. We could not sit down here today and draw a line of separation, that would satisfy any five men in the country. There are natural causes that would keep and tie us together, and there are social and domestic relations which we could not break if we would, and which we should not, if we could. Sir, nobody can look over the face of this country at the present moment—nobody can see where its population is the most dense and growing—without being ready to admit, and compelled to admit, that ere long, America will be in the valley of the Mississippi. . . .

And now, Mr. President, instead of speaking of the possibility or utility of secession, instead of dwelling in these caverns of darkness, instead of groping with those ideas so full of all that is horrid and horrible, let us come out into the light of day; let us enjoy the fresh air of liberty and union; let us cherish those hopes which belong to us; let us devote ourselves to those great objects that are fit for our consideration and our action; let us raise our conceptions to the magnitude and the importance of the duties that devolve upon us; let our comprehension be as broad as the country for which we act, our aspirations as high as its certain destiny; let us not be pigmies in a case that calls for men. Never did there devolve, on any generation of men, higher trusts than now devolve upon us for the preservation of this Constitution and the harmony and peace of all who are destined to live under it. Let us make our generation one of the strongest and brightest links in that golden chain which is destined, I fully believe, to grapple the people of all the States to this Constitution, for ages to come. It is a great popular constitutional Government, guarded by leg-

islation, law, and by judicature, and defended by the affections of the whole people. No monarchical throne presses the States together; no iron chain of military power encircles them; they live and stand upon a Government popular in its form, representative in its character, founded upon principles of equality, and calculated, we hope, as to last forever. In all its history, it has been beneficent; it has trodden down no man's liberty; it has crushed no State. Its daily respiration is liberty and patriotism; its yet youthful veins are full of enterprise, courage, and honorable love of glory and renown. Large before, the country has now, by recent events, become vastly larger. This republic now extends, with a vast breadth, across the whole continent. The two great seas of the world wash the one and the other shore. We realize on a mighty scale, the beautiful description of the ornamental border of the buckler of Achilles—

"Now the broad shield complete the artist
    crowned,
With his last band, and poured the ocean
    round;
In living silver seemed the waves to roll,
And beat the buckler's verge, and bound the
    whole."

21

Webster's motives were severely criticized by his countrymen of the Northeast. Certain that he had deserted his principles and his section to win southern votes in the presidential race of 1852, they turned solidly against him. John Greenleaf Whittier, the Massachusetts poet of abolitionism, saved some of his most vitriolic words for Webster in his poem "Ichabod":[21]

So fallen! so lost! the light withdrawn
    Which once he wore!
The glory from his gray hairs gone
    Forevermore!

Revile him not, the Tempter hath
    A snare for all;

---

[21] *The Complete Poetical Works of John Greenleaf Whittier* (Boston, 1895), pp. 186–187.

And pitying tears, not scorn and wrath,
    Befit his fall!

Oh, dumb be passion's stormy rage,
    When he who might
Have lifted up and led his age,
    Falls back in night.

Scorn! would the angels laugh, to mark
    A bright soul driven,
Fiend-goaded, down the endless dark,
    From hope and heaven!

Let not the land once proud of him
    Insult him now,
Nor brand with deeper shame his dim,
    Dishonored brow.

But let its humbled sons, instead,
    From sea to lake,
A long lament, as for the dead,
    In sadness make.

Of all we loved and honored, naught
    Save power remains;
A fallen angel's pride of thought,
    Still strong in chains.

All else is gone; from those great eyes
    The soul has fled:
When faith is lost, when honor dies,
    The man is dead!

Then pay the reverence of old days
    To his dead fame;
Walk backward, with averted gaze,
    And hide the shame!

Drifting Toward Disunion

If the Compromise of 1850 held the nation together, it was only because time was not yet ripe for disunion. The conflict over the Wilmot Proviso might easily have driven the Northeast and South to arms, but the West was not ready. Tied to the older sections by commercial and ideological bonds, it hung in the balance, making civil war impossible. During the 1850s the tenuous equilibrium was upset. The increasing dependence of the West on northeastern industry, the construction of east-west railroads, and the growth of abolitionism in the trans-Appalachian country, gradually merged Northeast and West. By 1860 two antagonistic sections —North and South—faced each other across Mason and Dixon's line.

THE DEBATE IS RENEWED

1

While both the North and South accepted the Compromise of 1850, both sections had substantial reservations. Those of the North centered on the provisions of the new Fugitive Slave Act, which made private persons liable for assistance in recapturing fugitives, even in the free states. It was this provision that led Ralph Waldo Emerson to exclaim, "This filthy enactment was made in the nineteenth century, by people who could read and write. I will not obey it, by God!" Pertinent provisions of the Fugitive Slave Act of 1850 are presented below:[1]

Sec. 5. That it shall be the duty of all marshals and deputy marshals to obey and execute all warrants and precepts issued under the provisions of this act, when to them directed; and should any marshal or deputy marshal refuse to receive such warrant, or other process, when tendered, or to use all proper means diligently to execute the same, he shall, on conviction thereof, be fined in the sum of one thousand dollars, to the use of such claimant, . . . and after arrest of such fugitive, by such marshal or his deputy, or whilst at any time in his custody under the provisions of this act, should such fugitive escape, whether with or without the assent

of such marshal or his deputy, such marshal shall be liable, on his official bond, to be prosecuted for the benefit of such claimant, for the full value of the service or labor of said fugitive in the State, Territory, or District whence he escaped: and the better to enable the said commissioners, when thus appointed, to execute their duties faithfully and efficiently, in conformity with the requirements of the Constitution of the United States and of this act, they are hereby authorized and empowered, within their counties respectively, to appoint, . . . any one or more suitable persons, from time to time, to execute all such warrants and other process as may be issued by them in the lawful performance of their respective duties; with authority to such commissioners, or the persons to be appointed by them, to execute process as aforesaid, to summon and call to their aid the bystanders, or *posse comitatus* of the proper county, when necessary to ensure a faithful observance of the clause of the Constitution referred to, in conformity with the provisions of this act; and all good citizens are hereby commanded to aid and assist in the prompt and efficient execution of this law, whenever their services may be required, as aforesaid, for that purpose; and said warrants shall run, and be executed by said officers, any-

---

[1] U. S., *Statutes at Large*, IX, 462ff.

where in the State within which they are issued.

Sec. 7. That any persons who shall knowingly and willingly obstruct, hinder, or prevent such claimant, his agent or attorney, or any person or persons lawfully assisting him, her, or them, from arresting such a fugitive from service or labor, either with or without process as aforesaid, or shall rescue, or attempt to rescue, such fugitive from service or labor, from the custody of such claimant, ... or other person or persons lawfully assisting as aforesaid, when so arrested, ... or shall aid, abet, or assist such person so owing service or labor as aforesaid, directly or indirectly, to escape from such claimant, ... or shall harbor or conceal such fugitive so as to prevent the discovery and arrest of such person, after notice or knowledge of the fact that such person was a fugitive from service or labor ... shall, for either of said offences, be subject to a fine not exceeding one thousand dollars, and imprisonment not exceeding six months . . . ; and shall moreover forfeit and pay, by way of civil damages to the party injured by such illegal conduct, the sum of one thousand dollars, for each fugitive so lost as aforesaid.

2

During the 1850s, the rising tide of abolitionism crossed the Appalachians, convincing thousands that slavery was a sin in the eyes of God and man. The most effective instruments in this conversion were the hundreds of propaganda works published yearly, and of these none was more persuasive than Harriet Beecher Stowe's novel Uncle Tom's Cabin *(1852). The description of the first meeting between the two leading characters, Simon Legree and Uncle Tom— who became stereotypes in northern eyes for all Southerners and all slaves—typifies the emotional tone of the book:*[2]

Mr. Simon Legree, Tom's master, had purchased slaves at one place and another, in New Orleans, to the number of eight, and driven them, handcuffed, in couples of two and two, down to the good steamer Pirate,

which lay at the levee, ready for a trip up the Red River.

Having got them fairly on board, and the boat being off, he came round, with that air of efficiency which ever characterized him, to take a review of them. Stopping opposite to Tom, who had been attired for sale in his best broadcloth suit, with well-starched linen and shining boots, he briefly expressed himself as follows:—

"Stand up."

Tom stood up.

"Take off that stock!" and, as Tom, encumbered by his fetters, proceeded to do it, he assisted him, by pulling it, with no gentle hand, from his neck, and putting it in his pocket.

Legree now turned to Tom's trunk, which, previous to this, he had been ransacking, and, taking from it a pair of old pantaloons and a dilapidated coat, which Tom had been wont to put on about his stable-work, he said, liberating Tom's hands from the handcuffs, and pointing to a recess in among the boxes,—

"You go there, and put these on."

Tom obeyed, and in a few moments returned.

"Take off your boots," said Mr. Legree.

Tom did so.

"There," said the former, throwing him a pair of coarse stout shoes, such as were common among the slaves, "put these on."

In Tom's hurried exchange, he had not forgotten to transfer his cherished Bible to his pocket. It was well he did so; for Mr. Legree, having refitted Tom's handcuffs, proceeded deliberately to investigate the contents of his pockets. He drew out a silk handkerchief, and put it into his own pocket. Several little trifles, which Tom had treasured, chiefly because they had amused Eva, he looked upon with a contemptuous grunt, and tossed them over his shoulder into the river.

Tom's Methodist hymn-book, which, in his hurry, he had forgotten, he now held up and turned over.

"Humph! pious, to be sure. So, what's yer name,—you belong to the church, eh?"

---

[2] Harriet Beecher Stowe, *Uncle Tom's Cabin* (Boston, 1889 ed.), pp. 376–379.

"Yes, Mas'r," said Tom, firmly.

"Well, I'll soon have *that* out of you. I have none o' yer bawling, praying, singing niggers on my place; so remember. Now, mind yourself," he said, with a stamp and a fierce glance of his gray eye, directed at Tom, "*I'm* your church now! You understand,—you've got to be as I say."

Something within the silent black man answered *No!* and, as if repeated by an invisible voice, came the words of an old prophetic scroll, as Eva had often read them to him,—"Fear not! for I have redeemed thee. I have called thee by my name. Thou art MINE!"

But Simon Legree heard no voice. That voice is one he never shall hear. He only glared for a moment on the downcast face of Tom, and walked off. He took Tom's trunk, which contained a very neat and abundant wardrobe, to the forecastle, where it was soon surrounded by various hands of the boat. With much laughing, at the expense of niggers who tried to be gentlemen, the articles very readily were sold to one and another, and the empty trunk finally put up at auction. It was a good joke, they all thought, especially to see how Tom looked after his things, as they were going this way and that; and then the auction of the trunk, that was funnier than all, and occasioned abundant witticisms.

This little affair being over, Simon sauntered up again to his property.

"Now, Tom, I've relieved you of any extra baggage, you see. Take mighty good care of them clothes. It'll be long enough 'fore you get more. I go in for making niggers careful; one suit has to do for one year, on my place."

Simon next walked up to the place where Emmeline was sitting, chained to another woman.

"Well, my dear," he said, chucking her under the chin, "keep up your spirits."

The involuntary look of horror, fright, and aversion with which the girl regarded him, did not escape his eye. He frowned fiercely.

"None o' your shines, gal! you's got to keep a pleasant face, when I speak to ye, —d' ye hear? And you, you old yellow poco moonshine!" he said, giving a shove to the mulatto woman to whom Emmeline was chained, "don't you carry that sort of face! You's got to look chipper, I tell ye!"

"I say, all on ye," he said, retreating a pace or two back, "look at me,—look at me, —look me right in the eye,—*straight*, now!" said he, stamping his foot at every pause.

As by a fascination, every eye was now directed to the glaring greenish-gray eye of Simon.

"Now," said he, doubling his great, heavy fist into something resembling a blacksmith's hammer, "d' ye see this fist? Heft it!" he said, bringing it down on Tom's hand. "Look at these yer bones! Well, I tell ye this yer fist has got as hard as iron *knocking down niggers*. I never see the nigger, yet, I couldn't bring down with one crack," said he, bringing his fist down so near to the face of Tom that he winked and drew back. "I don't keep none o' yer cussed overseers; I does my own overseeing; and I tell you things *is* seen to. You's every one on ye got to toe the mark, I tell ye; quick,—straight,—the moment I speak. That's the way to keep in with me. Ye won't find no soft spot in me, nowhere. So, now, mind yerselves; for I don't show no mercy!"

The women involuntarily drew in their breath, and the whole gang sat with downcast, dejected faces. Meanwhile, Simon turned on his heel, and marched up to the bar of the boat for a dram.

3

Many of Mrs. Stowe's strictures on slavery seemed less extravagant after an incident involving the fugitive slave Anthony Burns made news in the early summer of 1854. Anthony Burns was a Virginia slave who had fled to Boston and found work in a clothing store. The account of his apprehension and return to slavery is by an eyewitness, Charles E. Stevens:[3]

[3] Charles Emory Stevens, *Anthony Burns, A History* (Boston, 1856), pp. 15–19, 143–150.

In the evening of the twenty-fourth of May, 1854, Anthony Burns was arrested as a fugitive slave in the heart of Boston. He had been employed, during the day, in a clothing store situated in Brattle street, and belonging to Coffin Pitts, a respectable colored trader. . . .

The arrest was made under a warrant issued on the same day, by Edward G. Loring, a United States Commissioner. The person charged with its immediate execution was a man who had already become infamous by making the hunting of fugitive slaves his special vocation. The name of this man was Asa O. Butman. He had been observed in the store of Mr. Pitts during the day; but, although he was seen more than once to fix his eyes upon Burns, no suspicion had been excited by his appearance. Not dreaming of danger, Burns kept about his business until the hour of closing the shop arrived, when he locked the door and departed. It had been his constant custom to accompany his employer, with whom he boarded, directly home; but on the evening in question he took it into his head, from mere caprice, to stroll down the street in an opposite direction. Mr. Pitts meanwhile pursued his way homeward. After going on aimlessly for a few rods, Burns retraced his steps, intending to overtake his employer, who, at that moment, was disappearing round the corner of Brattle and Court streets. Apprehending nothing, he went leisurely along until, just as he had reached the corner of Hanover and Court streets, a hand was roughly laid on his shoulder, and an exclamation of, "Stop, old boy!" arrested his steps. On turning, he found himself in the grasp of Butman. Still unsuspicious of the real state of the case, and supposing that he had been beset only by a street brawler, he demanded to know why he was detained. Butman informed him that he was arrested on a charge of having broken into and robbed a jewelry-store. Conscious of innocence, and feeling assured that he could easily clear himself of the charge, Burns made no resistance, and did not even alarm his employer, who was then only two or three rods in advance. The spot where the arrest was made, was hard by Peter B. Brigham's drinking-saloon, the most noted establishment of the kind in Boston. From that, or from some other lurking-place in the vicinity, six or seven men immediately rushed forth to the assistance of the officer. Encircling the prisoner, they in a moment had him off his feet, took him in their arms horizontally as they would a dead person, and, avoiding the side-walk, rapidly bore him down the middle of the street to the Court House. At the entrance, they were received by the United States Marshal, who stood with a drawn sword upon the outer steps, manifestly awaiting their appearance. Without pause, or being set down upon his feet, the prisoner was hurried up several flights of stairs to the United States jury-room, near the top of the building. He had been informed, on being arrested, that he was to be conducted into the presence of the person whom he was accused of robbing. Finding no such person present, he now demanded to know why the jeweller did not come. Butman and his associates professed wonder at his non-appearance. The delay continued. Suddenly, the truth flashed upon the unhappy prisoner—he was an arrested fugitive slave! Then, with the quickness of thought, the whole dismal future opened up before his mental vision. As in a dissolving view, the land of freedom faded out, and the dark land of slavery usurped its place. He saw himself again a slave; far worse than that, a slave disgraced; pointed at as a runaway; punished; perhaps punished unto death. Overpowered by the prospect, he, in his own simple but expressive phrase, "gave all up." Fast confined within granite walls, and closely guarded by eight armed men, he saw the full hopelessness of his situation, and did not for a moment indulge any thought of escape.

Twenty minutes had elapsed, when the door was thrown open, and the Marshal, accompanied by two men, entered the room. The men were Charles F. Suttle, the claimant of Burns, and his agent, William Brent; Virginians both. Immediately stepping toward the prisoner, Mr. Suttle, with mock politeness, took off his hat, saluted the latter with a low bow, and said, with emphasis on the appellation:

"How do you do, *Mr.* Burns?"

The prisoner had no reply for this unseemly triumph over his blasted hopes.

"Why did you run away from me?" pursued Suttle.

"I fell asleep on board the vessel where I worked, and, before I woke up, she set sail and carried me off."

"Haven't I always treated you well, Tony?"

To this question Burns made no answer.

"Haven't I always given you money when you needed?"

"You have always given me twelve and a half-cents once a year."

Nothing further passed between the two, but in this brief colloquy Burns had already made admissions decisive of his fate. While it was going on, Brent stood gazing steadily in the prisoner's face, but exchanged no words, not even salutations with him. The object of the wily slaveholder had been accomplished, and with his friend he now took his departure. As he passed out, the Marshal put the inquiry, "Well, that's the man, is it?" to which Suttle responded, "Yes." [Editor's note: Abolitionists in Boston promptly organized an assault on the prison in an effort to free Burns. The assault failed. In the subsequent trial Burns was adjudged a fugitive slave, a fact he had never denied, and was remanded to the custody of his master. Boston abolitionists saw a new opportunity to rescue Burns, and a substantial number of moderate Bostonians proved ready to join them. Word of the planned rescue attempt spread, but great precautions were taken to forestall it. Those precautions are described below.]

At eleven o'clock, Court Square presented a spectacle that became indelibly engraved upon the memories of men. The people had been swept out of the Square, and stood crowded together in Court street, presenting to the eye a solid rampart of living beings. At the eastern door of the Court House, stood the cannon, loaded, with its mouth pointed full upon the compact mass. By its side stood the officer commanding the detachment of United States troops, gazing with steady composure in the same direction. It was the first time that the armed power of the United States had ever been arrayed against the people of Massachusetts. Men who witnessed the sight, and reflected upon its cause, were made painfully to recognize the fact, before unfelt, that they were the subjects of two governments. . . .

At length, about two o'clock, the column was formed in the Square. First came a detachment of United States Artillery, followed by a platoon of United States Marines. After these followed the armed civil posse of the Marshal, to which succeeded two platoons of Marines. The cannon, guarded by another platoon of Marines, brought up the rear. When this arrangement was completed, Burns, accompanied by an officer on each side with arms interlocked, was conducted from his prison through a passage lined with soldiers, and placed in the centre of the armed posse. Immediately after the decision, Mr. Dana and Mr. Grimes had asked permision to walk with Burns arm in arm, from the Court House to the vessel at the wharf; and the Marshal had given them his consent. At the last moment, he sought them out and requested that they would not insist upon the performance of his promise, because, in the opinion of some of the military officers, such a spectacle would add to the excitement. Mr. Dana declined to release the Marshal from his promise. The latter persisted in urging the abandonment of the purpose.

"Do I understand you," asked Mr. Dana, "to say distinctly that we *shall not* accompany Burns, after having given your promise that we might?"

The Marshal winced under the pressure of this pointed question, but after a momentary reluctance answered firmly, "Yes."

Accordingly, without a single friend at his side, and hemmed in by a thick-set hedge of gleaming blades, Burns took his departure.

The route from the Court House to the wharf had by this time become thronged with a countless multitude. It seemed as if the whole population of the city had been concentrated upon this narrow space. In vain the military and police had attempted to clear the streets; the carriage-way alone was kept vacant. On the sidewalks in Court and State streets, every available spot was occupied; all the passages, windows, and balconies, from basement to attic, over-flowed with gazers, while the roofs of the buildings were black with human beings. It was computed that not less than fifty thousand people had gathered to witness the spectacle.

At different points along the route, were displayed symbols significant of the pre-vailing sentiment. A distinguished member of the Suffolk Bar, whose office was directly opposite the courtroom, and who was, at the time, commander of the Ancient and Honorable Artillery, draped his windows in mourning. The example was quickly fol-lowed by others. From a window opposite the Old State House, was suspended a black coffin, upon which was the legend, *The Funeral of Liberty*. At a point farther on toward the wharf, a venerable merchant had caused a rope to be stretched from his own warehouse across State street to an opposite point, and the American flag, draped in mourning, to be suspended therefrom with the union down. . . .

Along this Via Dolorosa, with its cloud of witnesses, the column now began to move. No music enlivened its march; the dull tramp of soldiers on the rocky pavements, and the groans and hisses of the bystanders, were the only sounds. As it proceeded, its numbers were swelled by unexpected addi-tions. Unauthorized, the zealous commander of the mounted Dragoons joined in with his corps. The Lancers, jealous of their rivals, hastened to follow the example: thus vanguard and rear-guard consisted of Mas-sachusetts troops. In its progress, it went past the Old State House, . . . Just below, it passed over the ground where, in the Massacre of 1770, fell Attucks, the first negro martyr in the cause of American liberty.

Opposite the Custom House, the column turned at a right angle into another street. This cross movement suddenly checked the long line of spectators which had been pressing down State street, parallel with the other body; but the rear portion, not under-standing the nature of the obstruction, con-tinued to press forward, and forced the front from the sidewalk into the middle of the Street. To the chafed and watchful mili-tary, this movement wore the aspect of an assault on the *cortege;* instantly some Lan-cers, stationed near, rode their horses furi-ously at the surging crowd, and hacked with their sabres upon the defenceless heads within their reach. Immediately after, a de-tachment of infantry charged upon the dense mass, at a run, with fixed bayonets. Some were pitched headlong down the cellar-ways, some were forced into the pas-sages, and up flights of stairs, and others were overthrown upon the pavement, bruised and wounded.

While this was passing, the procession moved on and reached the wharf. A breach of trust had secured to the Federal authori-ties the use of this wharf for their present purpose. It was the property of a company, by whom it had been committed in charge to an agent. Without their knowledge and against their wishes, he had granted to the Marshal its use on this occasion. When ar-raigned afterward by his employers for such betrayal of trust, he replied that he had since been rewarded by an appointment to a place in the Custom House.

At the end of the wharf lay a small steamer which had been chartered by the United States Government. On board this vessel Burns was conducted by the Marshal, and immediately withdrawn from the sight of the gazing thousands into the cabin be-low. The United States troops followed, and, after an hour's delay, the cannon was also shipped. At twenty minutes past three o'clock, the steamer left the wharf, and went down the harbor.

4

Additional evidence of the breakup of the Compromise of 1850 came in 1854, when southern hopes for the expansion of slave territory were proclaimed in the Ostend Manifesto. This was a remarkable document drawn up at Ostend, Belgium, August 1854, by the American ministers to Spain, France, and England. In it, these three southern Democrats proclaimed the right to annex Cuba and insisted that the island be acquired at once:[4]

1. The United States ought, if practicable, to purchase Cuba with as little delay as possible.

2. The probability is great that the government and cortes of Spain will prove willing to sell it, because this would essentially promote the highest and best interests of the Spanish people.

Then, 1. It must be clear to every reflecting mind that, from the peculiarity of its geographical position, and the considerations attendant on it, Cuba is as necessary to the North American republic as any of its present members, and that it belongs naturally to that great family of States of which the Union is the providential nursery. . . .

The natural and main outlet to the products of this entire population, the highway of their direct intercourse with the Atlantic and the Pacific States, can never be secure, but must ever be endangered whilst Cuba is a dependency of a distant power in whose possession it has proved to be a source of constant annoyance and embarrassment to their interests.

Indeed, the Union can never enjoy repose, nor possess reliable security, as long as Cuba is not embraced within its boundaries.

Its immediate acquisition by our government is of paramount importance, and we cannot doubt but that it is a consummation devoutly wished for by its inhabitants.

The intercourse which its proximity to our coasts begets and encourages between them and the citizens of the United States, has, in the progress of time, so united their interests and blended their fortunes that they now look upon each other as if they were one people and had but one destiny.

Considerations exist which render delay in the acquisition of this island exceedingly dangerous to the United States. . . .

Cuba has thus become to us an unceasing danger, and a permanent cause of anxiety and alarm.

But we need not enlarge on these topics. It can scarcely be apprehended that foreign powers, in violation of international law, would interpose their influence with Spain to prevent our acquisition of the island. . . .

Besides, the commercial nations of the world cannot fail to perceive and appreciate the great advantages which would result to their people from a dissolution of the forced and unnatural connexion between Spain and Cuba, and the annexation of the latter to the United States. The trade of England and France with Cuba would, in that event, assume at once an important and profitable character, and rapidly extend with the increasing population and prosperity of the island.

2. But if the United States and every commercial nation would be benefited by this transfer, the interests of Spain would also be greatly and essentially promoted.

She cannot but see what such a sum of money as we are willing to pay for the island would effect in the development of her vast natural resources. . . .

Should Spain reject the present golden opportunity for developing her resources, and removing her financial embarrassments, it may never again return. . . .

After we shall have offered Spain a price for Cuba far beyond its present value, and this shall have been refused, it will then

---

[4] *H. R. Exec. Doc. No. 93, 33d Cong., 2d Sess., X, 128–132.*

be time to consider the question, does Cuba, in the possession of Spain, seriously endanger our internal peace and existence of our cherished Union?

Should this question be answered in the affirmative, then, by every law, human and divine, we shall be justified in wresting it from Spain if we possess the power; and this upon the very same principle that would justify an individual in tearing down the burning house of his neighbor if there were no other means of preventing the flames from destroying his own home.

Under such circumstances we ought neither to count the cost nor regard the odds which Spain might enlist against us. We forbear to enter into the question, whether the present condition of the island would justify such a measure? We should, however, be recreant to our duty, be unworthy of our gallant forefathers, and commit base treason against our posterity, should we permit Cuba to be Africanized and become a second St. Domingo, with all its attendant horrors to the white race, and suffer the flames to extend to our own neighboring shores, seriously to endanger or actually to consume the fair fabric of our Union.

We fear that the course and current of events are rapidly tending towards such a catastrophe. We, however, hope for the best, though we ought certainly to be prepared for the worst. . . .

Yours, very respectfully,

JAMES BUCHANAN
J. Y. MASON
PIERRE SOULÉ

5

Northern strength and hostile world opinion frustrated the southern ambitions expressed in the Ostend Manifesto, but the South's drive to secure more slave territory within the United States was more successful. Its unwitting agent was the senator from Illinois Stephen A. Douglas, who sought to promote a railroad to the Pacific by opening the unorganized territory west of Missouri. Sincerely believing that the people of the West should determine whether or not they wanted slavery, and convinced that local control of the institution would remove a troublesome question from national politics, Douglas drew up the Kansas-Nebraska Act, adopted after furious debate May 30, 1854:[5]

Be it enacted . . . , That all that part of the territory of the United States included within the following limits, except such portions thereof as are hereinafter expressly exempted from the operations of this act, to wit: beginning at a point in the Missouri River where the fortieth parallel of north latitude crosses the same; thence west on said parallel to the east boundary of the Territory of Utah, on the summit of the Rocky Mountains; thence on said summit northward to the forty-ninth parallel of north latitude; thence east on said parallel to the western boundary of the territory of Minnesota; thence southward on said boundary to the Missouri River; thence down the main channel of said river to the place of beginning, be, and the same is hereby, created into a temporary government by the name of the Territory of Nebraska; and when admitted as a State or States, the said Territory, or any portion of the same, shall be received into the Union with or without slavery, as their constitution may prescribe at the time of their admission: . . .

SECTION 14. *And be it further enacted,* . . . That the Constitution, and all laws of the United States which are not locally inapplicable, shall have the same force and effect within the said Territory of Nebraska as elsewhere within the United States, except the eighth section of the act preparatory to the admission of Missouri into the Union, approved March sixth, eighteen hundred and twenty, which, being inconsistent with the principle of non-intervention by Congress with slavery in the States and Territories, as recognized by the legislation of eighteen hundred and fifty, commonly called the Compromise Measures, is hereby declared inoperative and void; it being the true intent and meaning of this act not to

---

[5] U. S., *Statutes at Large*, X, 277, 282–284.

legislate slavery into any Territory or State, nor to exclude it therefrom, but to leave the people thereof perfectly free to form and regulate their domestic institutions in their own way, subject only to the Constitution of the United States: *Provided,* that nothing herein contained shall be construed to revive or put in force any law or regulation which may have existed prior to the act of sixth March, eighteen hundred and twenty, either protecting, establishing, prohibiting, or abolishing slavery. . . .

SEC. 19. *And be it further enacted,* That all that part of the Territory of the United States included within the following limits, except such portions thereof as are hereinafter expressly exempted from the operations of this act, to wit, beginning at a point on the western boundary of the State of Missouri, where the thirty-seventh parallel of north latitude crosses the same; thence west on said parallel to the eastern boundary of New Mexico; thence north on said boundary to latitude thirty-eight; thence following said boundary westward to the east boundary of the Territory of Utah, on the summit of the Rocky Mountains; thence northward on said summit to the fortieth parallel of latitude; thence east on said parallel to the western boundary of the State of Missouri; thence south with the western boundary of said State to the place of beginning, be, and the same is hereby, created into a temporary government by the name of the Territory of Kansas; and when admitted as a State or States, the said Territory, or any portion of the same, shall be received into the Union with or without slavery, as their constitution may prescribe at the time of their admission.

THE DIVISION DEEPENS

6

With Northeast and Northwest united by commercial and ideological ties, Southern leaders cried down majority rule and cried up minority rights. The South, now more than ever a minority section, was ready to succumb to what

a modern psychologist might call a sectional inferiority complex. One manifestation of this was the heightened aggressive manner adopted by Southerners in defending their peculiar labor system and the stratified social order that stemmed from the plantation economy. Instead of apologizing for a society that allowed human bondage and the exploitation of the many by the few, they insisted that slavery and inequality were essential to progress. This philosophy was expressed by George Fitzhugh, a Virginia lawyer, whose Sociology for the South *(1854) argued that all men are not created equal, that the few should command the many, and that the untrained masses should be bound as serfs to planters or manufacturers:*[6]

But far the worst feature of modern civilization, which is the civilization of free society, remains to be exposed. Whilst labor-saving processes have probably lessened by one half, in the last century, the amount of work needed for comfortable support, the free laborer is compelled by capital and competition to work more than he ever did before, and is less comfortable. The organization of society cheats him of his earnings, and those earnings go to swell the vulgar pomp and pageantry of the ignorant millionaires, who are the only great of the present day. These reflections might seem, at first view, to have little connexion with negro slavery; but it is well for us of the South not to be deceived by the tinsel glare and glitter of free society, and to employ ourselves in doing our duty at home, and studying the past, rather than in insidious rivalry of the expensive pleasures and pursuits of men whose sentiments and whose aims are low, sensual and grovelling.

Human progress, consisting in moral and intellectual improvement, and there being no agreed and conventional standard weights or measures of moral and intellectual qualities and quantities, the question of progress can never be accurately decided. We maintain that man has not improved, because in all save the mechanic

---

[6] George Fitzhugh, *Sociology for the South or the Failure of Free Slavery* (Richmond, 1854), pp. 92–95.

arts he reverts to the distant past for models to imitate, and he never imitates what he can excel.

We need never have white slaves in the South, because we have black ones. Our citizens, like those of Rome and Athens, are a privileged class. We should train and educate them to deserve the privileges and to perform the duties which society confers on them. Instead, by a low demagoguism depressing their self-respect by discourses on the equality of man, we had better excite their pride by reminding them that they do not fulfil the menial offices which white men do in other countries. Society does not feel the burden of providing for the few helpless paupers in the South. And we should recollect that here we have but half the people to educate, for half are negroes; whilst at the North they profess to educate all. It is in our power to spike this last gun of the abolitionists. We should educate all the poor. The abolitionists say that it is one of the necessary consequences of slavery that the poor are neglected. It was not so in Athens, and in Rome, and should not be so in the South. If we had less trade with and less dependence on the North, all our poor might be profitably and honorably employed in trades, professions and manufactures. Then we should have a rich and denser population. Yet we but marshal her in the way that she was going. The South is already aware of the necessity of a new policy, and has begun to act on it. Every day more and more is done for education, the mechanic arts, manufactures and internal improvements. We will soon be independent of the North.

We deem this peculiar question of negro slavery of very little importance. The issue is made throughout the world on the general subject of slavery in the abstract. The argument has commenced. One set of ideas will govern and control after awhile the civilized world. Slavery will every where be abolished, or every where be re-instituted. We think the opponents of practical, existing slavery, are estopped by their own admission; nay, that unconsciously, as socialists, they are the defenders and propagandists of slavery, and have furnished the only sound arguments on which its defence and justification can be rested. We have introduced the subject of negro slavery to afford us a better opportunity to disclaim the purpose of reducing the white man any where to the condition of negro slaves here. It would be very unwise and unscientific to govern white men as you would negroes. Every shade and variety of slavery has existed in the world. In some cases there has been much of legal regulation, much restraint of the master's authority; in others, none at all. The character of slavery necessary to protect the whites in Europe should be much milder than negro slavery, for slavery is only needed to protect the white man, whilst it is more necessary for the government of the negro even than for his protection. But even negro slavery should not be outlawed. We might and should have laws in Virginia, as in Louisiana, to make the master subject to presentment by the grand jury and to punishment, for any inhuman or improper treatment or neglect of his slave.

We abhor the doctrine of the "Types of Mankind"; first, because it is at war with scripture, which teaches us that the whole human race is descended from a common parentage; and, secondly, because it encourages and incites brutal masters to treat negroes, not as weak, ignorant and dependent brethren, but as wicked beasts, without the pale of humanity. The Southerner is the negro's friend, his only friend. Let no intermeddling abolitionist, no refined philosophy, dissolve this friendship.

7

Sentiments such as these found ready acceptance among those prepared emotionally to defy the principles of the Declaration of Independence as a final defense of a minority way of life. Hence others took up the cry. One was William J. Grayson, a South Carolina politician, whose lengthy poem The Hireling and the Slave (1854) *attempted to show that the* *bond slave of the South was infinitely better* *off than the wage slave of the North:*[7]

There, unconcerned, the philanthropic
    eye
Beholds each phase of human misery;
Sees the worn child compelled in mines to
    slave
Through narrow seams of coal, a living
    slave,
Driven from the breezy hill, the sunny
    glade,
By ruthless hearts, the drudge of labour
    made,
Unknown the boyish sport, the hour of play,
Stript of the common boon, the light of
    day,
Harnessed like brutes, like brutes to tug,
    and strain,
And drag, on hands and knees, the loaded
    wain:
There crammed in huts, in reeking masses
    thrown,
All moral sense and decency unknown,
With no restraint, but what the felon knows,
With the sole joy, that beer or gin bestows,
To gross excess and brutalizing strife,
The drunken Hireling dedicates his life:
There women prostitute themselves for
    bread,
And mothers, rioting with savage glee,
For murder'd infants spend the funeral fee;
Childhood bestows no childish sports or
    toys,
Age neither reverence nor repose enjoys,
Labor with hunger wages ceaseless strife,
And want and suffering only end with life;
Dull typhus lurks, and deadlier plagues
    assail,
In crowded huts contagious ills prevail,
Gaunt Famine prowls around his pauper
    prey,
And daily sweeps his ghastly hosts away;
Unburied corses taint the summer air,
And crime and outrage revel with despair.

---

[7] William J. Grayson, *The Hireling and the Slave,* *Chicora, and other Poems* (Charleston, S. C., 1856), pp. 24–26, 50–53.

Torn from the cottage, conscript peasants
    go
To distant wars, against an unknown foe,
On fields of carnage, at ambition's call,
Perish—the warrior's tool, the monarch's
    thrall;
Wasted by plagues, unhonored their re-
    mains,
They fill a ditch on Danube's marshy plains;
In the night trench of mingled mire and
    blood,
Swept by cold winds and rains, a ceaseless
    flood,
Half fed, half clad, the tentless earth their
    bed,
Reeking with gore in mutual slaughter shed,
Scourged by disease, at every dreary post,
They fall in myriads on Crimea's coast,
Or whelmed in snows on Beresina's shore,
Sleep the long treacherous sleep that wakes
    no more;
Worn by the toilsome march, the sleety sky,
Crouching in groups, the sinking squadrons
    lie;

No longer fly the fierce barbarian bands,
But, rapt in visions of far-distant lands,
In their last wild delirious fancies see
The sunny hills—the haunts of infancy,
Green summer meadows, warm unclouded
    skies,
Welcome of homely joy and glad surprise,
Till the stern frost-king stops the crimson
    stream
Of life, and breaks the dying soldier's
    dream;
Home, friends, recede before his icy sway,
The dream of bliss and reamer fade away,
With frozen hosts, the snowy waste is
    spread,
And howling wolves feast on the unburied
    dead.

Far from their humble homes and native
    land,
Forced by a landlord's pitiless command,
In uncongenial climes condemned to roam,
That sheep may batten in the peasant's
    home,

The pauper exiles, from the hill that yields
One parting look on their abandoned fields,
Behold with tears no manhood can restrain,
Their ancient hamlet level'd with the plain:
They go in crowded ships, new ills to find,
More hideous still than those they left be-
    hind;
Grim Chol'ra thins their ranks, ship fevers
    sweep
Their livid tithes of victims to the deep;
The sad survivors, on a foreign shore,
The double loss of homes and friends de-
    plore,
And beg a stranger's bounty to supply
The food and shelter that their homes
    deny. . . .

And yet the life, so unassailed by care,
So blest with moderate work, with ample
    fare,
With all the good the starving pauper
    needs,
The happier slave on each plantation leads:
Safe from harassing doubts and annual
    fears,
He dreads no famine in unfruitful years;
If harvest fail from inauspicious skies,
The master's providence his food supplies;
No paupers perish here for want of bread,
Or lingering live, by foreign bounty fed;
No exiled trains of homeless peasants go,
In distant climes, to tell their tales of woe;
Far other fortune, free from care and strife,
For work, or bread, attends the Negro's life,
And Christian slaves may challenge as their
    own,
The blessings claimed in fabled states
    alone—
The cabin home, not comfortless, though
    rude,
Light daily labor, and abundant food,
The sturdy health that temperate habits
    yield,
The cheerful song that rings in every field,
The long loud laugh, that freemen seldom
    share,
Heaven's boon to bosoms unapproached by
    care,
And boisterous jest and humour unrefined

That leave, though rough, no painful sting
    behind;
While, nestling near, to bless their humble
    lot,
Warm social joys surround the Negro's cot,
The evening dance its merriment imparts,
Love, with his rapture, fills their youthful
    hearts,
And placid age, the task of labor done,
Enjoys the summer shade, the winter sun,
And, as through life no pauper want he
    knows,
Laments no poorhouse penance at its close.

Safe in Ambition's trumpet call to strife,
No conscript fears harass his quiet life,
While the crushed peasant bleeds—a worth-
    less thing,
The broken toy of emperor or king;
Calm in his peaceful home, the slave pre-
    pares
His garden-spot, and plies his rustic cares;
The comb and honey that his bees afford,
The eggs in ample gourd compactly stored,
The pig, the poultry, with a chapman's art,
He sells or barters at the village mart,
Or, at the master's mansion, never fails
An ampler price to find and readier sales.

There, when December's welcome frosts
    recall
The friends and inmates of the crowded
    hall,
To each glad nursling of the master's race
He brings his present, with a cheerful face
And offered hand—of warm, unfeigning
    heart,
In all his master's joys he claims a part,
And, true as clansman to the Highland
    chief,
Mourns every loss, and grieves in all his
    grief;
When Christmas now, with its abundant
    cheer
And thornless pleasure, speeds the parting
    year,
He shares the common joy—the early morn
Wakes hunter, clamorous hound, and echo-
    ing horn,

Quick steps are heard, the merry season
named,
The loiterers caught, the wonted forfeit
claimed,
In feasts maturing busy hands appear,
And jest and laugh and assail the ready
ear;
Whose voice, than his, more gayly greets
the dawn,
Whose foot so lightly treads the frosty lawn,
Whose heart as merrily, where mirth pre-
vails,
On every side the joyous season hails?
Around the slaughtered ox—a Christmas
prize,
The slaves assembling stand with eager
eyes—
Rouse, with their dogs, the porker's pierc-
ing cry,
Or drag its squealing tenant from the sty;
With smile and bow receive their winter
dues,
The strong, warm clothing and substantial
shoes,
Blankets adorned with stripes of border red,
And caps of wool that warm the woolier
head;
Then clear the barn, the ample area fill,
In the gay jig display their vigorous skill;
No dainty steps, no mincing measures
here—
Ellsler's trained graces—seem to float in air,
But hearts of joy and nerves of living steel,
On floors that spring beneath the bounding
reel;
Proud on his chair, with magisterial glance
And stamping foot, the fiddler rules the
dance;
Draws, if he nods, the still unwearied bow,
And gives a joy no bearded hands bestow;
The triple holiday, on angel wings,
With every fleeting hour a pleasure brings;
No ennui clouds, no coming cares annoy,
Nor wants nor sorrows check the Negro's
joy.

His too the Christian privilege to share
The weekly festival of praise and prayer;
For him the Sabbath shines with holier light,

The air grows balmier, and the sky more
bright;
Winter's brief suns with warmer radiance
glow,
With softer breath the gales of autumn
blow,
Spring with new flowers more richly strews
the ground,
And summer spreads a fresher verdure
round;
The early shower is past; the joyous breeze
Shakes patt'ring rain-drops from the rustling
trees,
And with the sun, the fragrant offerings rise,
From Nature's censers to the bounteous
skies;
With cheerful aspect, in his best array,
To the far forest church he takes his way;
With kind salute the passing neighbor
meets,
With awkward grace the morning traveller
greets,
And joined by crowds, that gather as he
goes,
Seeks the calm joy the Sabbath morn be-
stows.

8

*Few Southerners were willing to admit that
a sectional inferiority complex inspired such
aggressive outbursts as those of Grayson or
Fitzhugh, but none could deny that the South's
position within the nation became daily subject
to increasing pressures. Each year, northern
political strength increased as immigrants added
to the population and free-state men filled the
western territories; each year, northern economic
supremacy became more clear as new factories
multiplied their produce. Identifying capitalism
in the North as the enemy, planters conceived
of themselves as reduced to a state of complete
subserviency. With their economy mortgaged to
cotton growing, they were forced to buy everything they needed from hated Yankee merchants, going regularly into debt in the process.
From a poor white came still another indication
of internal pressures. Southern dependence on
the North was pictured by Hinton R. Helper,
a nonslaveholder from North Carolina, whose
The Impending Crisis of the South (1857) in-
dicted slavery for its effect on white men:[8]*

---

[8] Hinton R. Helper, *The Impending Crisis of the
South* (New York, 1857), pp. 355–356.

Reader! would you understand how abjectly slaveholders themselves are enslaved to the products of Northern industry? If you would, fix your mind on a Southern "gentleman"—a slave-breeder and human-flesh monger, who professes to be a Christian! Observe the routine of his daily life. See him rise in the morning from a Northern bed, and clothe himself in Northern apparel; see him walk across the floor on a Northern carpet, and perform his ablutions out of a Northern ewer and basin. See him uncover a box of Northern powders, and cleanse his teeth with a Northern brush; see him reflecting his physiognomy in a Northern mirror, and arranging his hair with a Northern comb. See him dosing himself with the medicaments of Northern quacks, and perfuming his handkerchief with Northern cologne. See him referring to the time in a Northern watch, and glancing at the news in a Northern gazette. See him and his family sitting in Northern chairs, and singing and praying out of Northern books. See him at the breakfast table, saying grace over a Northern plate, eating with Northern cutlery, and drinking from Northern utensils. See him charmed with the melody of a Northern piano, or musing over the pages of a Northern novel. See him riding to his neighbor's in a Northern carriage, or furrowing his lands with a Northern plow. See him lighting his segar with a Northern match, and flogging his negroes with a Northern lash. See him with Northern pen and ink, writing letters on Northern paper, and sending them away in Northern envelopes, sealed with Northern wax, and impressed with a Northern stamp. Perhaps our Southern "gentleman" is a merchant; if so, see him at his store, making an unpatriotic use of his time in the miserable traffic of Northern gimcracks and haberdashery; see him when you will, where you will, he is ever surrounded with the industrial products of those whom, in the criminal inconsistency of his heart, he execrates as enemies, yet treats as friends. His labors, his talents, his influence, are all for the North, and not

for the South; for the stability of slavery, and for the sake of his own personal aggrandizement, he is willing to sacrifice the dearest interests of his country.

As we see our ruinous system of commerce exemplified in the family of our Southern "gentleman," so we may see it exemplified, to a greater or less degree, in almost every other family throughout the length and breadth of the slaveholding States. We are all constantly buying, and selling, and wearing, and using Northern merchandise, at a double expense to both ourselves and our neighbors. If we but look at ourselves attentively, we shall find that we are all clothed *cap-a-pié* in Northern habiliments. Our hats, our caps, our cravats, our coats, our vests, our pants, our gloves, our boots, our shoes, our undergarments—all come from the North; whence, too, Southern ladies procure all their bonnets, plumes, and flowers; dresses, shawls, and scarfs; frills, ribbons, and ruffles; cuffs, capes, and collars.

9

The yawning economic gulf between Northeast and South—one industrial, the other agricultural—focused attention on the intellectual chasm that separated their people. By the middle of the 1850s, Southerners and Northerners not only lived different lives; their thought patterns had little in common. Amidst the stimulating atmosphere of the North, cultural progress was rapid; there the new wealth supported schools and libraries which trained a whole generation to enjoy the arts and literature. This appreciative audience, together with the atmosphere of progress prevailing, inspired New England's Golden Age of literature. The self-assured optimism of readers and writers alike was reflected by one of the greatest of them all, Walt Whitman, in the preface to his Leaves of Grass *(1855):*[9]

America does not repel the past or what it has produced under its forms or amid other politics or the idea of castes or the old religions . . . accepts the lesson with calm-

[9] Reprinted in Floyd Stovall (ed.), *Walt Whitman, Representative Selections* (New York, 1934), pp. 314–318.

ness . . . is not so impatient as has been supposed that the slough still sticks to opinions and manners and literature while the life which served its requirements has passed into the new life of the new forms . . . perceives that the corpse is slowly borne from the eating and sleeping rooms of the house . . . perceives that it waits a little while in the door . . . that it was fittest for its days . . . that its action has descended to the stalwart and well-shaped heir who approaches . . . and that he shall be fittest for his days.

The Americans of all nations at any time upon the earth have probably the fullest poetical nature. The United States themselves are essentially the greatest poem. In the history of the earth hitherto the largest and most stirring appear tame and orderly to their ampler largeness and stir. Here at last is something in the doings of man that corresponds with the broadcast doings of the day and night. Here is not merely a nation but a teeming nation of nations. Here is action untied from strings necessarily blind to particulars and details magnificently moving in vast masses. Here is the hospitality which forever indicates heroes. . . . Here are the roughs and beards and space and ruggedness and nonchalance that the soul loves. Here the performance disdaining the trivial unapproached in the tremendous audacity of its crowds and groupings and the push of its perspective spreads with crampless and flowing breadth and showers its prolific and splendid extravagance. One sees it must indeed own the riches of the summer and winter, and need never be bankrupt while corn grows from the ground or the orchards drop apples or the bays contain fish or men beget children upon women.

Other states indicate themselves in their deputies . . . but the genius of the United States is not best or more in its executives or legislatures, nor in its ambassadors or authors or colleges or churches or parlors, nor even in its newspapers or inventors , , , but always most in the common people. Their manners, speech, dress, friendships—the freshness and candor of their physiognomy— the picturesque looseness of their carriage . . . their deathless attachment to freedom— their aversion to anything indecorous or soft or mean—the practical acknowledgment of the citizens of one state by the citizens of all other states—the fierceness of their roused resentment—their curiosity and susceptibility to a slight—the air they have of persons who never knew how it felt to stand in the presence of superiors—the fluency of their speech —their delight in music, the sure symptom of manly tenderness and native elegance of soul . . . their good temper and openhandedness —the terrible significance of their elections— the President's taking off his hat to them not they to him—these too are unrhymed poetry. It awaits the gigantic and generous treatment worthy of it.

The largeness of nature or the nation were monstrous without a corresponding largeness and generosity of the spirit of the citizen. Not nature nor swarming states nor streets and steamships nor prosperous business nor farms nor capital nor learning may suffice for the ideal of man . . . nor suffice the poet. No reminiscences may suffice either. A live nation can always cut a deep mark and can have the best authority the cheapest . . . namely from its own souls. This is the sum of the profitable uses of individuals or states and of present action and grandeur and of the subjects of poets.—As if it were necessary to trot back generation after generation to the eastern records! As if the beauty and sacredness of the demonstrable must fall behind that of the mythical! As if men do not make their mark out of any times! As if the opening of the western continent by discovery and what has transpired since in North and South America were less than the small theatre of the antique or the aimless sleepwalking of the middle ages! The pride of the United States leaves the wealth, the finesse of the cities and all returns of commerce and agriculture and all the magnitude of geography or shows of exterior victory to enjoy the breed of full sized men or one full sized man unconquerable and simple.

The American poets are to enclose old and new for America is the race of races. Of them a bard is to be commensurate with a people. To him the other continents arrive as contributions . . . he gives them reception for their sake and his own sake. His spirit responds to his country's spirit . . . he incarnates its geography and natural life and rivers and lakes. Mississippi with annual freshets and changing chutes, Missouri and Columbia and Ohio and Saint Lawrence with the falls and beautiful masculine Hudson, do not embouchure where they spend themselves more than they embouchure into him. The blue breadth over the inland sea of Virginia and Maryland and the sea off Massachusetts and Maine and over Manhattan bay and over Champlain and Erie and over Ontario and Huron and Michigan and Superior, and over the Texan and Mexican and Floridian and Cuban seas and over the seas off California and Oregon, is not tallied by the blue breadth of the waters below more than the breadth of above and below is tallied by him. When the long Atlantic coast stretches longer and the Pacific coast stretches longer he easily stretches with them north or south. He spans between them also from east to west and reflects what is between them. On him rise solid growths that offset the growths of pine and cedar and hemlock and liveoak and locust and chestnut and cypress and hickory and limetree and cottonwood and tuliptree and cactus and wildvine and tamarind and persimmon . . . and tangles as tangled as any canebrake or swamp . . . and forests coated with transparent ice and icicles hanging from the boughs and crackling in the wind . . . and sides and peaks of mountains . . . and pasturage sweet and free as savannah or upland or prairie . . . with flights and songs and screams that answer those of the wildpigeon and highhold and orchard-oriole and coot and surf-duck and red-shouldered-hawk and fishhawk and white-ibis and indian-hen and cat-owl and water-pheasant and qua-bird and pied sheldrake and blackbird and mockingbird and buzzard and condor and night-heron and eagle. To him the hereditary countenance descends both mother's and father's. To him enter the essences of the real things and past and present events—of the enormous diversity of temperature and agriculture and mines—the tribes of red aborigines—the weatherbeaten vessels entering new ports or making landings on rocky coasts—the first settlements north or south—the rapid stature and muscle—the haughty defiance of '76, and the war and peace and formation of the constitution . . . the union always surrounded by blatherers and always calm and impregnable—the perpetual coming of immigrants—the wharf-hem'd cities and superior marine—the unsurveyed interior—the loghouses and clearings and wild animals and hunters and trappers . . . the free commerce—the fisheries and whaling and gold-digging—the endless gestation of new states—the convening of Congress every December, the members duly coming up from all climates and the uttermost parts . . . the noble character of the young mechanics and of all free American workmen and workwomen . . . the general ardor and friendliness and enterprise—the perfect equality of the female with the male . . . the large amativeness—the fluid movement of the population—the factories and mercantile life and labor-saving machinery—the Yankee swap—the New-York firemen and the target excursion—the southern plantation life—the character of the northeast and of the northwest and southwest—slavery and the tremulous spreading of hands to protect it, and the stern opposition to it which shall never cease till it ceases or the speaking of tongues and the moving of lips cease. For such the expression of the American poet is to be transcendant and new. It is to be indirect and not direct or descriptive or epic. Its quality goes through these to much more. Let the age and wars of other nations be chanted and their eras and characters be illustrated and that finish the verse. Not so the great psalm of the republic. Here the theme is creative and has vista. Here comes one among the well-beloved stone-cutters and plans with decision and science and the solid and beautiful forms of the future where there are now no solid forms.

10

Another writer whose pen contributed to the greatness of New England's Golden Age was James Russell Lowell. A Boston Brahmin, with little sympathy for the nationalism of the West or the provincialism of the South, Lowell viewed American literature with the eyes of a cultured cosmopolitan. His opinions, which were as typical of his class as were those of Whitman, were expressed in a review of Longfellow's "Kavanaugh," written for the North American Review *in 1849:*[10]

The feeling that it was absolutely necessary to our respectability that we should have a literature, has been a material injury to such as we have had. Our criticism has oscillated between the two extremes of depreciation and overpraise. On the one hand, it has not allowed for the variations of the magnetic needle of taste, and on the other, it has estimated merit by the number of degrees west from Greenwich. It seems never to have occurred to either sect of critics, that there were such things as principles of judgment immutable as those of mathematics. One party has been afraid to commend lest an English Reviewer might afterward laugh; the other has eulogized because it considered so terrible a catastrophe probable. The Stamp Act and the Boston Port Bill scarcely produced a greater excitement in America than the appalling question, *Who reads an American book?* It is perfectly true, that the amount of enlightenment which a reader will receive from a book depends upon the breadth of surface which he brings within its influence, for we never get *something* for *nothing;* but we would deferentially suggest for the relief of many a still trembling soul, repeating to itself the *quid sum miser tunc dicturus* to that

awful question from the Edinburgh judgment-seat, that it is barely possible that the *power* of a book resides in the book itself, and that real books somehow compel an audience without extraneous intervention. From the first, it was impossible that Art should show here the successive stages of growth which have characterized it in the Old World. It is only geographically that we can call ourselves a new nation. However else our literature may avoid the payment of its liabilities, it can surely never be by a plea of infancy. Intellectually, we were full-grown at the start. Shakespeare had been dead five years, and Milton was eleven years old, when Mary Chilton leaped ashore on Plymouth Rock.

In looking backward or forward mentally, we seem to be infected with a Chinese incapacity of perspective. We forget the natural foreshortening, taking objects as they are reflected upon our retina, and neglecting to supply the proper interstices of time. This is equally true whether we are haruspicating the growth of desired opinions and arts, or are contemplating those which are already historical. Thus, we know statistically the amount which any race or nation has stored in its intellectual granaries, but made no account of the years of scarcity, of downright famine even, which have intervened between every full harvest. There is an analogy between the successive stages of a literature and those of a plant. There is, first of all, the seed, then the stalk, and then the seed again. What a length of stalk between Chaucer and Spenser, and again between Milton and Wordsworth! Except in India, perhaps, it would be impossible to affirm confidently an indigenous literature. The seed has been imported, accidentally or otherwise, as the whiteweed and Hessian fly into America. Difference of soil, climate, and exposure will have their legitimate influence, but characteristics enough ordinarily remain for the tracing of the pedigree. The locality of its original production is as disputable as that of the garden of Eden. Only this is certain, that our search carries us farther and farther eastward.

---

[10] *North American Review,* CXLIV (July 1849), 200–202, 207–210.

No literature, of which we have authentic record or remains, can be called national in this limited and strict sense. Nor, if one could be found, would the calling it so be commendation. The best parts of the best authors in all languages can be translated; but, had they this element of exclusive nationality, the idea would demand a lexicon as well as the language which enveloped it. This shell within a shell would give more trouble in the cracking than any author can safely demand of his readers. Only a Dante can compel us to take an interest in the petty local politics of his day. No grubs were ever preserved in such amber. No Smiths and Browns were ever elevated upon so sublime and time-defying pinnacles of love, horror, and pity. The key by which we unlock the great galleries of Art is their common human interest. Nature supplies us with lexicon, commentary, and glossary to the great poems of all ages.

It would be hard to estimate the immediate indebtedness of Grecian literature; easier to reckon how much must have been due to the indirect influence of a religion and philosophy, whose esoteric ideas were of Egyptian derivation. Aristophanes is perhaps the only Grecian poet who is characterized by that quality of nationality of which we are speaking. Nay, it is something intenser than mere nationality in which his comedy is steeped. It is not the spirit of Greece, not even of Attica, but of Athens. It is cockneyism, not nationality. But his humor is more than Athenian. Were it not so, it would be dreary work enough deciphering jokes, as it were, in a mummypit, by the dim light of the scholiast's taper, too choked with dust and smoke to do any thing but cough when we are solemnly assured that we have come to the point.

There is a confusion in men's minds upon this subject. Nationality and locality are not distinguished from one another; and, were this jumble fairly cleared up, it would appear that there was a still farther confounding of truth to nature with fidelity of local coloring. Mere nationality is no more nor less than so much provincialism, and will be found but a treacherous antiseptic for any poem. It is because they are men and women, that we are interested in the characters of Homer. The squabbles of a score of petty barbarian chiefs, and the siege of a city which never existed, would have been as barren and fruitless to us as a Welsh genealogy, had the foundations of the Iliad had been laid no wider and deeper than the Troad. In truth, the only literature which can be called purely national is the Egyptian. What poetry, what philosophy, the torch of the Arab has fruitlessly lighted up for European eyes, we as yet know not; but that any ideas valuable to mankind are buried there, we do not believe. These are not at the mercy of sand, or earthquake, or overflow. No race perishes without intellectual heirs, but whatever was locally peculiar in their literature, their art, or their religious symbols, becomes in time hieroglyphical to the rest of the world, to be, perhaps, painfully deciphered for the verification of useless history, but incapable of giving an impulse to productive thought. Literature survives, not because of its nationality, but in spite of it. . . . .

Nationality, then, is only a less narrow form of provincialism, a sublimer sort of clownishness and ill-manners. It deals in jokes, anecdotes, and allusions of such purely local character that a majority of the company are shut out from all approach to an understanding of them. Yet so universal a demand must have for its basis a more or less solid substratum of truth. There are undoubtedly national, as truly as family, idiosyncrasies, though we think that these will get displayed without any special schooling for that end. The substances with which a nation is compelled to work will modify its results, as well intellectual as material. The still renewing struggle with the unstable desert sands gave to the idea of durability in the Egyptian imagination a preponderance still further increased by the necessity of using granite, whose toughness of fibre and vagueness of coloring yielded unwillingly to fineness of outline, but seemed the natural helpmates of massiveness and repose. The out-of-door life of the Greeks, conducing at once to health and an unconscious education of the eye, and the perfection of physical development resulting from their palaestral exercises and constantly displayed in them, made the Greeks the first to perceive the noble symmetry of the human figure, for embodying the highest types of which Pentelicus supplied the fittest material. Corporeal beauty and strength, therefore, entered largely into their idea of the heroic, and perhaps it was rather policy than dandyism which hindered Alcibiades from learning to play the flute. With us, on the other hand, clothed to the chin in the least graceful costume ever invented by man, and baked half the year with stoves and furnaces, beauty of person has gradually receded from view, and wealth or brain is the essential of the modern novelist's hero. It may not be fanciful to seek in climate, and its resultant effects upon art, the remote cause of that fate-element which entered so largely into the Greek drama. In proportion as sculpture became more perfect, the images of the gods became less and less merely symbolical, and at last presented to the popular mind nothing more than actual representations of an idealized humanity. Before this degradation had taken place, and the divinities had been vulgarized in marble to the common eye, the ideas of the unseen and supernatural came to the assistance of the poet in giving interest to the struggles or connivances between heroes and gods. But presently a new and deeper chord of the imagination must be touched, and the unembodiable shadow of Destiny was summoned up, to move awe and pity as long as the human mind is incapable of familiarizing by precise definition the fearful and the vague. In that more purely objective age, the conflict must be with something external, and the struggles of the mind with itself afforded no sufficient theme for the poet. With us introspection has become a disease, and a poem is a self-dissection.

That Art in America will be modified by circumstances, we have no doubt, though it is impossible to predict the precise form of the moulds into which it will run. New conditions of life will stimulate thought and give new forms to its expression. It may not be our destiny to produce a great literature, as, indeed, our genius seems to find its kindliest development in practicalizing simpler the more perfect forms of social organization. We have yet many problems of this kind to work out, and a continent to subdue with the plough and the railroad, before we are at leisure for aesthetics. Our spirit of adventure will take first a material and practical direction, but will gradually be forced to seek outlet and scope in unoccupied territories of the intellect. In the meantime we may fairly demand our literature that it should be national to the extent of being as free from outworn conventionalities, and as thoroughly impregnated with humane and manly sentiment, as is the idea on which our political fabric rests. Let it give a true reflection of our social, political, and household life. The "Poems on Man in the Republic," by Cornelius Mathews, disfigured as they were by gross faults of dialect and metre, had the great merit of presenting the prominent features of our civilization in an American light. The story of "Margaret" is the most emphatically *American* book ever written. The want of plan and slovenliness of construction are characteristic of a new country. The scenery, character, dialect, and incidents mirror New England life as truly as Fresh Pond reflects the sky. The moral, also, pointing forward to a new social order, is the intellectual antitype of that restlessness of disposition, and facility of migration which are among our chief idiosyncrasies. The mistake of our imaginative writers generally is that, though they may take an American subject, they *costume* it in a foreign or antique fashion. The consequence is a painful vagueness and unreality. It is like putting Roman drapery upon a statue of Washington, the absurdity of which does not strike us so forcibly because we are accustomed to it, but which we should recognize at once were the same treatment applied to Franklin. The old masters did exactly the reverse of this. They took ancient or foreign subjects, but selected their models from their own immediate neighborhood.

11

Southern culture contrasted sadly with that of the Northeast. Some great planters, always a minority, were men of intelligence and gentility, but the great mass of the people endured bleak lives without ever tasting the joys of civilization. Goaded on by unrelenting ambition, they devoted their days and nights to eternal toil, hoping always to attain that coveted pinnacle at the peak of the highly stratified society: membership in the great planter class. A northern traveler, Frederick L. Olmsted, wrote a damning indictment of the slave system merely by describing southern life:[11]

A different standard of comfort is used by most persons at the South from that known at the North, and that used by Northern writers. People at the South are content and happy with a condition which few accept at the North unless with great complaint, or with expressions of resignation such as are the peculiar property of slaves at the South. If, reader, you had been travelling all day through a country of the highest agricultural capability, settled more than twenty years ago, and toward nightfall should be advised by a considerate stranger to ride five miles further, in order to reach the residence of Mr. Brown, because Mr. Brown, being a well-to-do man, and a right good fellow, had built an uncommonly good house, and got it well furnished, had a score of servants, and being at a distance from neighbours, was always glad to entertain a respectable stranger—after hearing this, as you continued your ride somewhat impatiently in the evening chill, what consolations would your imagination find in the prospect before you? My New England and New York experience would not forbid the hope of a private room, where I could, in the first place, wash off the dust of the road, and make some change of clothing before being admitted to

a family apartment. This family room would be curtained and carpeted, and glowing softly with the light of sperm candles or a shaded lamp. When I entered it, I could expect that a couch or an arm-chair, and a fragrant cup of tea, with refined sugar, and wholesome bread of wheaten flour, leavened, would be offered me. I should think it likely that I could then have the snatch of Tannhäuser or Trovatore, which had been running faintly in my head all day, fingered clearly out to my entire satisfaction upon a pianoforte. I should then look with perfect confidence to being able to refer to Shakespeare, or Longfellow, or Dickens, if anything I had seen or thought during the day had haply led me to wish to do so. I should expect, as a matter of course, a clean, sweet, bed, where I could sleep alone and undisturbed, until possibly in the morning a jug of hot water should be placed at my door, to aid the removal of a traveller's rigid beard. I should expect to draw a curtain from before a window, to lift the sash without effort, to look into a garden and fill my lungs with fragrant air; and I should be certain when I came down of a royal breakfast. A man of these circumstances in this rich country, he will be asking my opinion of his fruits. A man of his disposition cannot exist in the country without ladies, and ladies cannot exist in the country without flowers; and might I not hope for the refinement which decks even the table with them? and that the breakfast would be a meal as well as a feed—an institution of mental and moral sustenance as well as of palatable nourishment to the body? My horse I need hardly look after, if he be a sound brute;—good stables, litter, oats, hay, and water, grooming, and discretion in their use, will never be wanting in such a man's house in the country.

In what civilized region, after such advice, would such thoughts be preposterous, unless in the Slave States? Not but that such men and such houses, such family and home comforts may be found in the South. I have found them—a dozen of them, delightful

[11] Frederick L. Olmsted, *The Cotton Kingdom* (London, 1861), II, 283–286.

homes. But then in a hundred cases where I received such advice, and heard houses and men so described, I did not find one of the things imagined above, nor anything ranging with them. In my last journey of nearly three months between the Mississippi and the Upper James River, I saw not only none of those things, received none of those attentions, but I saw and met nothing of the kind. Nine times out of ten, at least, after such a promise, I slept in a room with others, in a bed which stank, supplied with but one sheet, if with any; I washed with utensils common to the whole household; I found no garden, no flowers, no fruit, no tea, no cream, no sugar, no bread; (for corn pone— let me assert, in parenthesis, though possibly, as tastes differ, a very good thing of its kind for ostriches—is not bread: neither does even flour, salt, fat, and water, stirred together and warmed, constitute bread;) no curtains, no lifting windows (three times out of four absolutely no windows), no couch—if one reclined in the family room it was on the bare floor—for there were no carpets or mats. For all that, the house swarmed with vermin. There was no hay, no straw, no oats (but mouldy corn and leaves of maize), no discretion, no care, no honesty, at the ——— there was no stable, but a log-pen; and besides this, no other out-house but a smoke-house, a corn-house, and a range of nigger houses.

In nine-tenths of the houses south of Virginia, in which I was obliged, making all reasonable endeavour to find the best, to spend the night, there were none of these things. And most of these had been recommended to me by disinterested persons on the road as being better than ordinary—houses where they "sot up for travellers and had things." From the banks of the Mississippi to the banks of James, I did not (that I remember) see, except perhaps in one or two towns, a thermometer, nor a book of Shakespeare, nor a pianoforte or sheet of music; nor the light of a carcel or other good centre-table or reading-lamp, nor an engraving or copy of any kind, of a work of art of the slightest merit. I am not speaking of what

are commonly called "poor whites"; a large majority of all these houses were the residences of share-holders, a considerable proportion cotton-planters.

A HOUSE DIVIDED

12

Northern furor at news of the Kansas-Nebraska Act was beyond belief. Democrats by the thousands deserted the party that had repealed the Missouri Compromise, joining now with ex-Whigs to form the Republican party, pledged to ban slavery from the territories. More radical Northerners decided to block southern designs on Kansas by sending free-state men there in such numbers that popular sovereignty would win the area for freedom. Feverishly they organized "emigrant aid societies," enlisted immigrants, and sent them west. The most energetic of these organizations was the New England Emigrant Aid Society, a product of the enthusiasm of Eli Thayer, a Worcester, Massachusetts, abolitionist. Thayer describes the purpose of his society to a congressional committee in 1856:[12]

I am familiar with the purposes and history of this company. We sent, first, men to explore the Territory of Kansas, that being the first Territory opened for settlement, to ascertain the character and resources of that Territory. This and other information we published and furnished gratuitously to all who applied for it. We then opened an office in Boston, where application could be made by those who wished to emigrate to Kansas. The secretary kept a book in which the names of these applicants were recorded. When a party of sufficient number was formed, the day was fixed for their departure, tickets were purchased by the company, at a reduced price, on various lines of transportation, and were furnished to the emigrants at cost. A conductor was furnished by the company for each party. His duty was to provide for their safe, expeditious,

[12] *H. R. Rep. No. 200*, 34th Cong., 1st and 2d Sess. II, 884–885.

and economical conveyance to Kansas. We established local agents in the Territory, whose duty it was to receive these colonists, and to inform them of the best locations open to settlement. The company, in no instance, paid the passage of any emigrant. It was not doubted that the great body of emigrants were in favor of making Kansas a free State. The company furnished these emigrants with no articles of personal property, and never, directly or indirectly, furnished them with any arms or munitions of war of any kind, and never invested a dollar for any such purpose. . . .

. . . The moment they arrive at the place named in their ticket all connexion between them and the society ceases. . . . The company built a hotel in Lawrence, at an expense of about $20,000. At that time there was no hotel worthy of the name in the Territory, there being but little capital in the Territory at the time, as is usual among all pioneers in a new country. This hotel the company leased to Mr. Eldridge, who furnished it, and it was destroyed on the 21st of May last.

We also erected, and prepared to erect, mills in the Territory at different places, some eight or ten of them. The company, I think, had one other building in Lawrence, but I do not now recollect what it is. Some temporary sheds were also erected by the company for the accommodation of emigrants there until they could erect buildings of their own. These were the only buildings that the Emigrant Aid Society ever were interested in. The total expenditures of the company, for all purposes, since its organization have been less than $100,000. . . .

The company laid out no towns, and had no interest in laying out any. The towns were laid out by the settlers themselves, in some cases, the settlers making some arrangements to give the company certain lots to induce us to make investments there and thus aid in building up the place. This was the case with the town association of Lawrence. The town association would have given similar advantages to any person or company of men who would have made improvements.

13

Such efforts accomplished little; Kansas was filled with frontiersmen from adjacent states, rather than with idealists from the Northeast. Yet rabid partisans from both sections were sufficiently numerous to turn the territory into a battleground between 1854 and 1858. Some fought with guns and faggots; other with orations and ballots. Northerners among the latter group drew up their own constitution barring slavery from Kansas, and adopted it in an election in which Southerners refused to participate. Proslavery men countered by framing the "Lecompton Constitution" of September 4, 1857. This document not only defended slavery but gave voters no chance to bar the institution from the territory:[13]

ARTICLE VII
Slavery

SECTION 1. The right of property is before and higher than any constitutional sanction, and the right of the owner of a slave to such slave and its increase is the same, and as inviolable as the right of the owner of any property whatever.

SEC. 2. The legislature shall have no power to pass laws for the emancipation of slaves without the consent of the owners, or without paying the owners previous to their emancipation a full equivalent in money for the slaves so emancipated. They shall have no power to prevent emigrants to the State from bringing with them such persons as are deemed slaves by the laws of any one of the United States or Territories, so long as any person of the same age or description shall be continued in slavery by the laws of this State: *Provided,* That such person or slave be the *bona-fide* property of such emigrants: And *provided also,* That laws may be passed to prohibit the introduction into this State of slaves who have committed high crimes in other States or Territories. They shall have power to pass laws to permit the owners of slaves to emancipate them, saving

---

[13] Francis N. Thorpe (ed.), *The Federal and State Constitutions, Colonial Charters, and other organic laws of the States, Territories, and Colonies now or heretofore forming the United States of America* (Washington, 1909), II, 1210–1218.

the rights of creditors, and preventing them from becoming a public charge. They shall have power to oblige the owners of slaves to treat them with humanity, to provide for them necessary food and clothing, to abstain from all injuries to them extending to life or limb, and, in case of their neglect or refusal to comply with the direction of such laws, to have such slave or slaves sold for the benefit of the owner or owners.

Sec. 3. In the prosecution of slaves for crimes of higher grade than petit larceny, the legislature shall have no power to deprive them of an impartial trial by a petit jury.

Sec. 4. Any person who shall maliciously dismember or deprive a slave of life shall suffer such punishment as would be inflicted in case the like offence had been committed on a free white person, and on the like proof, except in case of insurrection of such slave. . . .

Schedule

Before this constitution shall be sent to Congress, asking for admission into the Union as a State, it shall be submitted to all the white male inhabitants of this Territory, for approval or disapproval, as follows: The president of this convention shall, by proclamation, declare that on the twenty-first day of December, one thousand eight hundred and fifty seven, at the different election-precincts now established by law, or which may be established as herein provided, in the Territory of Kansas, an election shall be held, . . . at which election the constitution framed by this convention shall be submitted to all the white male inhabitants of the Territory of Kansas in the said Territory upon that day, and over the age of twenty-one years, for ratification or rejection, in the following manner and form: The voting shall be by ballot. The judges of said election shall cause to be kept two poll-books by two clerks, by them appointed. The ballots cast at said election shall be endorsed, "Constitution with slavery," and "Constitution with no slavery." One of said poll-books shall be returned within eight days to the president

of this convention, and the other shall be retained by the judges of election and kept open for inspection. The president, with two or more members of this convention, shall examine said poll-books, and if it shall appear upon said examination that a majority of the legal votes cast at said election be in favor of the "Constitution with slavery," he shall immediately have the same transmitted to the Congress of the United States, as hereinbefore provided; but if, upon such examination of said poll-books, it shall appear that a majority of the legal votes cast at said election be in favor of the "Constitution with no slavery," then the article providing for slavery shall be stricken from this constitution by the president of this convention, and slavery shall no longer exist in the State of Kansas, except that the right of property in slaves now in this Territory shall in no manner be interfered with, and shall have transmitted the constitution, so ratified, . . . to the Congress of the United States, as hereinbefore provided.

14

The heat engendered by the struggle in "Bleeding Kansas" had one important national effect. Outraged Northerners, reading distorted accounts of the warfare in their newspapers, flocked by the thousands into the Republican party, convinced that the time for appeasement was past. In 1856, that political infant came within five hundred thousand votes of electing a president. Yet, only a year later the party's whole future was imperiled by one of the Supreme Court's most controversial decisions. The case of Dred Scott v. Sandford (1857) *arose when Scott, a Missouri slave, sued for his freedom on the ground that an earlier residence in the free state of Illinois and the free territory of Minnesota released him from bondage. The immediate problem facing the court was one of jurisdiction; Scott's owner was a citizen of New York, and Scott had to prove that he himself was a citizen of Missouri before the Court could accept the case. Chief Justice Roger B. Taney held that Scott was not a citizen, both because he was a Negro and because he was still a slave. The section of the opinion which ruled that his residence in Minnesota Territory did not make him free was all-important:*[14]

14 19 Howard 430–432, 439–440, 449–450, 454.

We proceed, therefore, to inquire whether the facts relied on by the plaintiff entitled him to his freedom. . . .

In considering this part of the controversy, two questions arise: 1. Was he, together with his family, free in Missouri by reason of the stay in the territory of the United States hereinbefore mentioned? And 2. If they were not, is Scott himself free by reason of his removal to Rock Island, in the State of Illinois, as stated in the above admissions?

We proceed to examine the first question.

The Act of Congress, upon which the plaintiff relies, declares that slavery and involuntary servitude, except as a punishment for crime, shall be forever prohibited in all that part of the territory ceded by France, under the name of Louisiana, which lies north of thirty-six degrees thirty minutes north latitude, and not included within the limits of Missouri. And the difficulty which meets us at the threshold of this part of the inquiry is, whether Congress was authorized to pass this law under any of the powers granted to it by the Constitution; for if the authority is not given by that instrument, it is the duty of this court to declare it void and inoperative, and incapable of conferring freedom upon any one who is held as a slave under the laws of any one of the States.

The counsel for the plaintiff has laid much stress upon that article in the Constitution which confers on Congress the power "to dispose of and make all needful rules and regulations respecting the territory or other property belonging to the United States"; but, in the judgment of the court, that provision has no bearing on the present controversy, and the power there given, whatever it may be, is confined, and was intended to be confined, to the territory which at that time belonged to, or was claimed by, the United States, and was within their boundaries as settled by the treaty with Great Britain, and can have no influence upon a territory afterwards acquired from a foreign Government. It was a special provision for a known and particular territory, and to meet a present emergency, and nothing more. . . .

But if this clause is construed to extend to territory acquired by the present Government from a foreign nation, outside of the limits of any charter from the British Government to a colony, it would be difficult to say, why it was deemed necessary to give the Government the power to sell any vacant lands belonging to the sovereignty which might be found within it; and if this was necessary, why the grant of this power should precede the power to legislate over it and establish a Government there; and still more difficult to say, why it was deemed necessary so specially and particularly to grant the power to make needful rules and regulations in relation to any personal or movable property it might acquire there. For the words, *other property* necessarily, by every known rule of interpretation, must mean property of a different description from territory or land. And the difficulty would perhaps be insurmountable in endeavoring to account for the last member of the sentence, which provides that "nothing in this Constitution shall be so construed as to prejudice any claims of the United States or any particular State," or to say how any particular State could have claims in or to a territory ceded by a foreign Government, or to account for associating this provision with the preceding provisions of the clause, with which it would appear to have no connection. . . .

But the power of Congress over the person or property of a citizen can never be a mere discretionary power under our Constitution and form of Government. The powers of the Government and the rights and privileges of the citizen are regulated and plainly defined by the Constitution itself. And when the Territory becomes a part of the United States, the Federal Government enters into possession in the character impressed upon it by those who created it. It enters upon it with its powers over the citizen strictly defined, and limited by the Constitution, from which it derives its own existence, and by virtue of which alone it continues to exist and act as a Government and sovereignty. It has no power of any kind beyond it; and it cannot, when it enters a Territory of the

United States, put off its character, and assume discretionary or despotic powers which the Constitution has denied to it. It cannot create for itself a new character separated from the citizens of the United States, and the duties it owes them under the provisions of the Constitution. The Territory being a part of the United States, the Government and the citizen both enter it under the authority of the Constitution, with their respective rights defined and marked out; and the Federal Government can exercise no power over his person or property, beyond what that instrument confers, nor lawfully deny any right which it has reserved. . . .

The rights of private property have been guarded with equal care. Thus the rights of property are united with the rights of person, and placed on the same ground by the fifth amendment to the Constitution. . . . An Act of Congress which deprives a person of the United States of his liberty or property merely because he came himself or brought his property into a particular Territory of the United States, and who had committed no offense against the laws, could hardly be dignified with the name of due process of law. . . .

And this prohibition is not confined to the States, but the words are general, and extend to the whole territory over which the Constitution gives it power to legislate, including those portions of it remaining under Territorial Government, as well as that covered by States. It is a total absence of power everywhere within the dominion of the United States, and places the citizens of a territory, so far as these rights are concerned, on the same footing with citizens of the States, and guards them as firmly and plainly against any inroads which the general government might attempt, under the plea of implied or incidental powers. And if Congress itself cannot do this—if it is beyond the powers conferred on the Federal Government—it will be admitted, we presume, that it could not authorize a Territorial Government to exercise them. It could confer no power on any local government, established

by its authority, to violate the provisions of the Constitution.

It seems, however, to be supposed, that there is a difference between property in a slave and other property, and that different rules may be applied to it in expounding the Constitution of the United States. And the laws and usages of nations, and the writings of eminent jurists upon the relation of master and slave and their mutual rights and duties, and the powers which governments may exercise over it, have been dwelt upon in the argument.

But . . . if the Constitution recognizes the right of property of the master in a slave, and makes no distinction between that description of property and other property owned by a citizen, no tribunal, acting under the authority of the United States, whether it be legislative, executive, or judicial, has a right to draw such a distinction, or deny to it the benefit of the provisions and guarantees which have been provided for the protection of private property against the encroachments of the Government.

Now . . . the right of property in a slave is distinctly and expressly affirmed in the Constitution. The right to traffic in it, like an ordinary article of merchandise and property, was guaranteed to the citizens of the United States, in every State that might desire it, for twenty years. And the Government in express terms is pledged to protect it in all future time, if the slave escapes from his owner. . . . And no word can be found in the Constitution which gives Congress a greater power over slave property, or which entitles property of that kind to less protection than property of any other description. The only power conferred is the power coupled with the duty of guarding and protecting the owner in his rights.

Upon these considerations, it is the opinion of the court that the act of Congress which prohibited a citizen from holding and owning property of this kind in the territory of the United States north of the line therein mentioned, is not warranted by the Constitution, and is therefore void; and that neither Dred Scott himself, nor any of his family, were made free by being carried into this territory; even if they had been carried there by the owner, with the intention of becoming a permanent resident. . . .

Upon the whole, therefore, it is the judgment of this court, that it appears by the record before us that the plaintiff in error is not a citizen of Missouri, in the sense in which that word is used in the Constitution; and that the Circuit Court of the United States, for that reason, had no jurisdiction in the case, and could give no judgment in it.

Its judgment for the defendant must, consequently, be reversed, and a mandate issued directing the suit to be dismissed for want of jurisdiction.

15

The Dred Scott decision illustrated the power of the Supreme Court to frustrate the popular will. Why, Northerners asked themselves, should seven men (for two northern justices wrote dissenting opinions) have the right to open the territories to slavery when the majority of the nation was opposed? Was "judicial review" becoming "judicial tyranny"? One who asked these questions was an Illinois lawyer, Abraham Lincoln, who summed up his thinking on the subject by warning an Illinois audience in 1857 that tyranny would be the national fate if America acquiesced in another Dred Scott decision:[15]

What constitutes the bulwark of our own liberty and independence? It is not our frowning battlements, our bristling sea coasts, our army and our navy. These are not our reliance against tyranny. All of those may be turned against us without making us weaker for the struggle. Our reliance is in the love of liberty which God has planted in us. Our defence is in the spirit which prized liberty as the heritage of all men, in all lands everywhere. Destroy this spirit and you have planted the seeds of despotism at your own doors. Familiarize yourself with the chains of bondage and you prepare your own limbs to wear them. Accustomed to trample on the

rights of others, you have lost the genius of your own independence and become the fit subjects of the first cunning tyrant who rises among you. And let me tell you, that all these things are prepared for you by the teachings of history, if the elections shall promise that the next Dred Scott decision and all future decisions will be quietly acquiesced in by the people.

16

The Dred Scott decision damaged the Republican party by denying Congress the right to bar slavery from the territories, but its impact on the Democratic party was even more disastrous. Until that time the Democrats had maintained a dubious unity, for northern adherents had accepted popular sovereignty. Now they were left in a quandary: would the party accept the Dred Scott decision as its new platform, or would it cling to the compromising principles of Douglas' doctrine? The supreme importance of the answer to this question was realized by Abraham Lincoln: if the Democrats clung to popular sovereignty the southern faction would rebel; if not, the northern wing would split away. During his debates with Stephen A. Douglas, as the two men campaigned for the Illinois senatorial seat in 1858, Lincoln forced his opponent to grasp the nettle. How, he asked his Democratic rival, can you reconcile popular sovereignty with the Dred Scott decision? Douglas's answer was delivered at Freeport, Illinois:[16]

I will answer his question. In reference to Kansas, it is my opinion that as she has population enough to constitute a slave State, she has people enough for a free State. I will not make Kansas an exceptional case to the other States of the Union. I hold it to be a sound rule, of universal application, to require a Territory to contain the requisite population for a member of Congress before it is admitted as a State into the Union. I made that proposition in the Senate in 1856, and I renewed it during the last session, in a bill providing that no Territory of the United States should form a constitution and apply for admission until it had the requisite population. On another occasion I proposed

[15] John G. Nicolay and John Hay (eds.), *Complete Works of Abraham Lincoln* (New York, 1894), XI, 110–111.

[16] *Ibid.*, III, 295–298.

that neither Kansas nor any other Territory should be admitted until it had the requisite population. Congress did not adopt any of my propositions containing this general rule, but did make an exception of Kansas. I will stand by that exception. Either Kansas must come in as a free State, with whatever population she may have, or the rule must be applied to all the other Territories alike. I therefore answer at once, that, it having been decided that Kansas has people enough for a slave State, I hold that she has enough for a free State. I hope Mr. Lincoln is satisfied with my answer; ...

The next question propounded to me by Mr. Lincoln is: Can the people of a Territory in any lawful way, against the wishes of any citizen of the United States, exclude slavery from their limits prior to the formation of a State constitution? I answer emphatically, as Mr. Lincoln has heard me answer a hundred times from every stump in Illinois, that in my opinion the people of a Territory can, by lawful means, exclude slavery from their limits prior to the formation of a State constitution. Mr. Lincoln knew that I had answered that question over and over again. He heard me argue the Nebraska Bill on that principle all over the State in 1854, in 1855, and in 1856, and he has no excuse for pretending to be in doubt as to my position on that question. It matters not what way the Supreme Court may hereafter decide as to the abstract question whether slavery may or may not go into a Territory under the Constitution, the people have the lawful means to introduce it or exclude it as they please, for the reason that slavery cannot exist a day or an hour anywhere, unless it is supported by local police regulations. Those police regulations can only be established by the local legislature, and if the people are opposed to slavery they will elect representatives to that body who will by unfriendly legislation effectually prevent the introduction of it into their midst. If, on the contrary, they are for it, their legislation will favor its extension. Hence, no matter what the decision of the Supreme Court may be

on that abstract question, still the right of the people to make a slave Territory or a free Territory is perfect and complete under the Nebraska Bill. I hope Mr. Lincoln deems my answer satisfactory on the point.

17

Northerners and Southerners had lost the capacity to communicate. The same words took on different meanings in each section. And when the elected congressmen and senators went about their business in the houses of Congress armed with knives and guns, it was only a matter of time before less responsible men would take the law into their own hands. In late 1859, John Brown, a northern fanatic, swooped down on the Federal Arsenal at Harper's Ferry, Virginia, with the avowed purpose of creating a haven for fugitive slaves. Federal marines, under Colonel Robert E. Lee, and Virginia militia were hurried to the scene. John Brown was captured and tried for treason against the state of Virginia, as well as for criminal conspiracy to incite a slave insurrection. Upon his conviction in the court at Charles Town, Virginia, Brown asked, and was given permission, to make the following speech to the Court on November 2, 1859. A month later he was hanged:[17]

I have, may it please the Court, a few words to say.

In the first place, I deny everything but what I have all along admitted, of the design on my part to free the slaves. I intended certainly to have made a clean thing of that matter, as I did last Winter, when I went into Missouri and there took slaves without the snapping of a gun on either side, moving them through the country, and finally left them in Canada. I designed to have done the same thing again, on a larger scale. That was all I intended. I never did intend murder, or treason, or the destruction of property, or to excite or incite slaves to rebellion, or to make insurrection.

I have another objection; and that is, it is unjust that I should suffer such a penalty. Had I interfered in the manner which I admit, and which I admit has been fairly proved (for I admire the truthfulness and

---

[17] New York *Daily Tribune,* November 3, 1859, p. 5.

candor of the greater portion of the witnesses who have testified in this case),—had I so interfered in behalf of the rich, the powerful, the intelligent, the so-called great, or in behalf of any of their friends,—either father, mother, brother, sister, wife, or children, or any of that class,—and suffered and sacrificed what I have in this interference, it would have been all right; and every man in this court would have deemed it an act worthy of reward rather than punishment.

This court acknowledges, as I suppose, the validity of the law of God. I see a book kissed here which I suppose to be the Bible, or at least the New Testament which teaches me that all things whatsoever I would that men should do to me, I should do even so to them. It teaches me, further, to "remember them that are in bonds, as bound with them." I endeavored to act up to that instruction. I say, I am yet too young to understand that God is any respecter of persons. I believe that to have interfered as I have done—as I have always freely admitted I have done in behalf of His despised poor is no wrong, but right. Now, if it is deemed necessary that I should forfeit my life for the furtherance of the ends of justice, and mingle my blood further with the blood of my children and with the blood of millions in this slave country whose rights are disregarded by wicked, cruel, and unjust enactments, I say so let it be done!

Let me say one word further.

I feel entirely satisfied with the treatment I have received on my trial. Considering all the circumstances, it has been more generous than I expected. But I feel no consciousness of guilt, I have stated from the first what was my intention, and what was not. I never had any design against the life of any person, nor any disposition to commit treason, or excite slaves to rebel, or make any general insurrection. I never encouraged any man to do so, but always discouraged any idea of that kind.

Let me say, also, a word in regard to the statements made by some of those connected with me. I hear it has been stated by some of them that I have induced them to join me. But the contrary is true. I do not say this to injure them, but as regretting their weakness. There is not one of them but joined me of his own accord, and the greater part of them at their own expense. A number of them I never saw, and never had a word of conversation with, till the day they came to me; and that was for the purpose I have stated.

Now I have done.

18

The author of the letter below, James A. Seddon, was a prominent planter and lawyer of Fredericksburg, Virginia, who subsequently became secretary of war to President Jefferson Davis of the Confederate States of America. His correspondent was Robert M. T. Hunter, United States Senator from Virginia:[18]

ST. JAMES PARISH, LOUISIANA,
December 26th, 1859.

I left Virginia with great reluctance just as the Harper's Ferry Raid had occurred for I knew it to be a crisis of great moment to our State and Country and of deep interest to your political fortunes in which as a sincere friend I always cherished a lively concern. It was too early however to judge the effects of the events occurring or of the feelings they would excite, and since, I have been so engaged in affairs and so removed from sources of correct information, rarely ever seeing a paper from V[irgini]a or the North, I feel real diffidence in forming or expressing opinions on the aspect of public affairs. I must venture however to say that in my humble opinion the train of events and the course of public conduct and opinion upon them, as especially in V[irgini]a have been injudiciously and alarmingly mismanaged and misdirected, and I hold the unsound judgment, insatiate vanity and selfish policy of our fussy Governor mainly responsible for them. The Harper's Ferry affair ought

[18] American Historical Association, *Annual Report*, 1916, II, "Correspondence of Robert M. T. Hunter, 1826–1876," edited by Charles H. Ambler (Washington, 1918), 281–282. Reprinted with the kind permission of the American Historical Association.

to have been treated and represented either in its best light as the mad folly of a few deluded cranks branded fanatics, or, more truly, as the vulgar crime and outrage of a squad of reckless desperate Ruffians, ripe for any scheme of repaine [*sic*] and murder, and they should have been accordingly tried and executed as execrable criminals in the simplest and most summary manner. There should not have been the chance offered of elevating them to *political* offenders or making them representatives and champions of Northern Sentiment. Indeed, our Honorable Governor, seduced by the passion of oratorical display, commenced by a picturesque description of them as heroes and martyrs, and, by insisting on holding them as the chiefs of an organized conspiracy at the North, has provoked and in a measure invoked the sympathy and approbation of large masses and of established organs of public opinion at the North (who might otherwise have been frowned and rebuked through a correct estimate of public opinion as to the base criminality of the fanatics and their deeds into shame and silence) to them as veritable heroes and martyrs, exponents and champions of the North immolated for their love of liberty and aid to the oppressed to the Molach for Southern Slavery.

In V[irgini]a and throughout the South with corresponding policy, all possible representations have been made and agencies adopted to make these infamous felons grand political criminals—to hold the whole North or at least the whole Republican party identified with them and to spread the greatest excitement and indignation against that whole section and its people. In short, for I can't dwell, with his favorite policy of swaggering and bullying, Wise has *exploited* this whole affair to his own selfish aggrandizement, to aid his vain hopes for the Presidency and to strengthen the fragment of a Southern party he heads. And as the result, has conjured a Devil neither he nor perhaps any other can lay, and, arraying the roused pride and animosities of both sections against each other, has brought on a *real* crisis of imminent peril to both.

19

Whether the crisis had been brought on by ambitious politicians like John Wise working on the deeds of fanatics like John Brown, or whether these men were victims of historic forces beyond their power to direct remains a moot question. The ties that bound the nation together were breaking. Even the national church organizations were splitting in two. One of the national parties, the Whigs, had all but disappeared, and the Democratic party was on the verge of disintegration. Filling the political vacuum left by the breakup of the old parties was the Republican party. Born out of the Kansas-Nebraska controversy, it had diligently sought to avoid identification as an abolitionist, or antislavery, party. At its 1860 Chicago convention, the Republicans passed over likely radical candidates to select the moderate Lincoln as their standard-bearer. They wrote a moderate platform designed to win the entire North on both ideological and material grounds:[19]

Resolved, That we, the delegated representatives of the Republican electors of the United States, in Convention assembled, in discharge of the duty we owe to our constituents and our country, unite in the following declarations:—

1. That the history of the nation, during the last four years, has fully established the propriety and necessity of the organization and perpetuation of the Republican party, and that the causes which called it into existence are permanent in their nature, and now, more than ever before, demand its peaceful and constitutional triumph.

2. That the maintenance of the principles promulgated in the Declaration of Independence and embodied in the Federal Constitution,—"that all men are created equal; that they are endowed by their Creator with certain inalienable rights; that among these are life, liberty and the pursuit of happiness; that, to secure these rights, governments are instituted among men, deriving their just powers from the consent of the governed,"—is essential to the preservation of our republican institutions; and that the Federal Constitution, the rights of the States, and the

---

[19] Edward Stanwood, *A History of Presidential Elections* (Boston, 1892), pp. 228–231.

Union of the States, must and shall be preserved.

3. That to the union of the States this nation owes its unprecedented increase in population, its surprising development of material resources, its rapid augmentation of wealth, its happiness at home and its honor abroad; and we hold in abhorrence all schemes for disunion, come from whatever source they may; And we congratulate the country that no Republican member of Congress has uttered or countenanced the threats of disunion so often made by Democratic members, without rebuke and with applause from their political associates; and we denounce those threats of disunion, in case of a popular overthrow of their ascendency, as denying the vital principles of a free government, and as an avowal of contemplated treason, which it is the imperative duty of an indignant people sternly to rebuke and forever silence.

4. That the maintenance inviolate of the rights of the States, and especially the right of each State to order and control its own domestic institutions according to its own judgment exclusively, is essential to that balance of powers on which the perfection and endurance of our political fabric depends; and we denounce the lawless invasion by armed force of the soil of any State or Territory, no matter under what pretext, as among the gravest of crimes.

5. That the present Democratic administration has far exceeded our worst apprehensions, in its measureless subserviency to the exactions of a sectional interest, as especially evinced in its desperate exertions to force the infamous Lecompton Constitution upon the protesting people of Kansas; in construing the personal relation between master and servant to involve an unqualified property in person; in its attempted enforcement, everywhere, on land and sea, through the intervention of Congress and of the Federal Courts of the extreme pretensions of a purely local interest; and in its general and unvarying abuse of the power intrusted to it by a confiding people. . . .

7. That the new dogma that the Consti-

tution, of its own force, carries slavery into any or all of the Territories of the United States, is a dangerous political heresy, at variance with the explicit provisions of that instrument itself, with contemporaneous exposition, and with legislative and judicial precedent; is revolutionary in its tendency, and subversive of the peace and harmony of the country.

8. That the normal condition of all the territory of the United States is that of freedom; That as our Republican fathers, when they had abolished slavery in all our national territory, ordained that no person should be deprived of life, liberty, or property, without due process of law, it becomes our duty, by legislation, whenever such legislation is necessary, to maintain this provision of the Constitution against all attempts to violate it; and we deny the authority of Congress, of a territorial legislature, or of any individuals, to give legal existence to slavery in any Territory of the United States.

9. That we brand the recent reopening of the African slave-trade, under the cover of our national flag, aided by perversions of judicial power, as a crime against humanity and a burning shame to our country and age; and we call upon Congress to take prompt and efficient measures for the total and final suppression of that execrable traffic.

10. That in the recent vetoes, by their Federal Governors, of the acts of the Legislatures of Kansas and Nebraska, prohibiting Slavery in those Territories, we find a practical illustration of the boasted Democratic principle of non-intervention and popular Sovereignty embodied in the Kansas-Nebraska Bill, and a demonstration of the deception and fraud involved therein.

11. That Kansas should of right be immediately admitted as a State under the Constitution recently formed and adopted by her people, and accepted by the House of Representatives.

12. That, while providing revenue for the support of the General Government by duties upon imports, sound policy requires such an adjustment of these imposts as to encourage the development of the indus-

trial interests of the whole country; and we commend that policy of national exchanges which secures to the working men liberal wages, to agriculture remunerating prices, to mechanics and manufacturers an adequate reward for their skill, labor, and enterprise, and to the nation commercial prosperity and independence.

13. That we protest against any sale or alienation to others of the public lands held by actual settlers, and against any view of the free homestead policy which regards the settlers as paupers or supplicants for public bounty; and we demand the passage by Congress of the complete and satisfactory Homestead measure which has already passed the house.

14. That the Republican Party is opposed to any change in our naturalization laws or any State legislation by which the rights of our citizenship hitherto accorded to immigrants from foreign lands shall be abridged or impaired; and in favor of giving a full and efficient protection to the rights of all classes of citizens, whether native or naturalized, both at home and abroad.

15. That appropriations by Congress for river and harbor improvements of a national character, required for the accommodation and security of an existing commerce, are authorized by the Constitution, and justified by the obligations of Government to protect the lives and property of its citizens.

16. That a railroad to the Pacific Ocean is imperatively demanded by the interests of the whole country; that the Federal Government ought to render immediate and efficient aid in its construction; and that, as preliminary thereto, a daily overland mail should be promptly established.

Civil War

Republican triumph in the election of 1860 posed the most serious problem in the South's history. Should Southerners sever the bonds of union? Moderates knew that secession was no answer; independence would free the section from neither economic dependence on the North nor world-wide criticism of slavery. Yet even the most lukewarm southern partisan realized that continued alliance with the hostile Yankees presented an equally unpleasant alternative. Sooner or later northern political triumph would be translated into an economic control that meant high tariffs, a homestead act, subsidies to railroads, and other laws beneficial to industry rather than to agriculture. Preferring not to face so uncertain a future, the South decided to withdraw at once, thus plunging the nation into four years of bloody warfare.

THE BREAKDOWN OF THE DEMOCRATIC PROCESS

1

The first step was taken by South Carolina. On December 20, 1860, a convention at Charleston unanimously adopted an Ordinance of Secession:[1]

We, the people of the State of South Carolina, in Convention assembled, do declare and ordain, and it is hereby declared and ordained, that the ordinance adopted by us in Convention, on the 23d day of May, in the year of our Lord 1788, whereby the Constitution of the United States of America was ratified, and also all Acts and parts of Acts of the General Assembly of this State ratifying the amendments of the said Constitution, are hereby repealed, and that the union now subsisting between South Carolina and other States under the name of the United States of America is hereby dissolved.

[1] Frank Moore (ed.), *The Rebellion Record: A Diary of American Events* (New York, 1869), I, 2. (Pages not numbered consecutively.)

2

One of the cornerstones of the new Confederacy was the concept of white supremacy. Alexander H. Stephens made this clear in a speech on the new Confederate Constitution at Atlanta, Georgia, in March of 1861:[2]

But not to be tedious in enumerating the numerous changes for the better, allow me to allude to one other—though last, not least: The new constitution has put to rest, *forever,* all agitating questions relating to our peculiar institution, African slavery as it exists among us,—the proper status of the negro in our form of civilization. This was the immediate cause of the late rupture and present revolution. Jefferson, in his forecast, had anticipated this as the "rock upon which the old Union would split." He was right. What was conjecture with him is now a realized fact. But whether he fully comprehended the great truth upon which that rock *stood* and *stands* may be doubted. The prevailing ideas entertained by him and most of the leading statesmen at the time of the

[2] *Ibid.*, I, 44–45.

formation of the old Constitution were that the enslavement of the African was in violation of the laws of nature; that it was wrong in *principle*, socially, morally, and politically. It was an evil they knew not well how to deal with, but the general opinion of the men of that day was that somehow or other, in the order of Providence, the institution would be evanescent and pass away. This idea, though not incorporated in the Constitution, was the prevailing idea at the time. The Constitution, it is true, secured every essential guaranty to the institution while it should last, and hence no argument can be justly used against the constitutional guaranties thus secured, because of the common sentiment of the day. Those ideas, however, were fundamentally wrong. They rested upon the assumption of the equality of races. This was an error. It was a sandy foundation, and the idea of the government built upon it; when the "storm came and the wind blew, it *fell*."

Our new government is founded upon exactly the opposite idea; its foundations are laid, its corner-stone rests, upon the great truth that the negro is not equal to the white man; that slavery—subordination to the superior race—is his natural and normal condition.

3

Much the same point was made by President Jefferson Davis in his message to the Confederate Congress April 29, 1861:[3]

In addition to the long-continued and deep-seated resentment felt by the Southern States at the persistent abuse of the powers they had delegated to the Congress for the purpose of enriching the manufacturing and shipping classes of the North at the expense of the South, there has existed for nearly half a century another subject of discord, involving interests of such transcendent magnitude as at all times to create the apprehension in the minds of many devoted lovers of the Union that its permanence was impossible.

When the several States delegated certain powers to the United States Congress, a large portion of the laboring population were imported into the colonies by the mother country. In twelve out of the fifteen States, negro slavery existed, and the right of property existing in slaves was protected by law; this property was recognized in the Constitution, and provision was made against its loss by the escape of the slave. . . .

As soon, however, as the Northern States, that prohibited African slavery within their limits, had reached a number sufficient to give their representation a controlling vote in the Congress, a persistent and organized system of hostile measures against the rights of the owners of slaves in the Southern States was inaugurated and gradually extended. A series of measures was devised and prosecuted for the purpose of rendering insecure the tenure of property in slaves.

Fanatical organizations, supplied with money by voluntary subscriptions, were assiduously engaged in exciting amongst the slaves a spirit of discontent and revolt. Means were furnished for their escape from their owners, and agents secretly employed to entice them to abscond. . . .

The transactions of public affairs was impeded by repeated efforts to usurp powers not delegated by the Constitution, for the purpose of impairing the security of property in slaves, and reducing those States which held slaves to a condition of inferiority. . . .

In the meantime, under the mild and genial climate of the Southern States, and the increasing care for the well-being and comfort of the laboring classes, dictated alike by interest and humanity, the African slaves had augmented in number from about six hundred thousand, at the date of the adoption of the constitutional compact, to upwards of four millions.

In moral and social condition they had been elevated from brutal savages into docile, intelligent, and civilized agricultural laborers, and supplied not only with bodily comforts, but with careful religious instruction, under the supervision of a superior race. Their labor had been so directed as not only to allow a gradual and marked amelioration

_____
[3] *Ibid.,* I, 168–169.

of their own condition, but to convert hundreds of thousands of square miles of the wilderness into cultivated lands covered with a prosperous people. Towns and cities had sprung into existence, and had rapidly increased in wealth and population under the social system of the South.

The white population of the Southern slave-holding States had augmented from about 1,250,000, at the date of the adoption of the Constitution, to more than 8,500,000 in 1860, and the productions of the South in cotton, rice, sugar and tobacco, for the full development and continuance of which the labor of African slaves was and is indispensable, had swollen to an amount which formed nearly three-fourths of the export of the whole United States, and had become absolutely necessary to the wants of civilized man.

With interests of such overwhelming magnitude imperiled, the people of the Southern States were driven by the conduct of the North to the adoption of some course of action to avoid the dangers with which they were openly menaced. With this view, the Legislatures of the several States invited the people to select delegates to conventions to be held for the purpose of determining for themselves what measures were best to be adopted to meet so alarming a crisis in their history.

4

Avery O. Craven, one of the most perceptive students of the causes of the Civil War, summarizing years of research and thought, blames the war on the breakdown of the democratic process:[4]

The most significant thing about the American Civil War is that it represents a complete breakdown of the democratic process. After years of strain, men ceased to discuss their problems, dropped the effort to compromise their differences, refused to abide

---

[4] Avery O. Craven, "The 1840's and the Democratic Process," *The Journal of Southern History*, XVI (1950), 161–176, *passim*. Reprinted with the permission of publishers, *The Journal of Southern History*.

by the results of a national election, and resorted to the use of force. After four years of bloody civil strife, one side was beaten into submission and the other had its way in national affairs. The emergence of modern America was largely the product of that outcome.

If the breakdown of the democratic process is the significant thing about the coming of the Civil War, then the important question is not *what* the North and South were quarreling about half as much as it is *how* their differences got into such shape that they could not be handled by the process of rational discussion, compromise, or the tolerant acceptance of majority decisions. The question is not "What caused the Civil War?" but rather "How did it come about?" The two questions are quite different, yet hopelessly tangled. The effort to distinguish between them, however, is important and needs to be stressed.

If one were to discuss the *causes* of the Civil War, he might begin with geography, move on to historical developments in time and place, trace the growth of economic and social rivalries, outline differences in moral values, and then show the way in which personalities and psychological factors operated. The part which slavery played would loom large. It might even become the symbol of all differences and of all conflicts. State rights, territorial expansion, tariffs, lands, internal improvements, and a host of other things, real and imagined, would enter the picture. There would be economic causes, constitutional causes, social causes, moral causes, political causes involving the breaking of old parties and the rise of sectional ones, and psychological causes which ultimately permitted emotion to take the place of reason. There would be remote or background causes, and immediate causes, and causes resting on other causes, until the most eager pedagogue would be thoroughly satisfied.

The matter of how issues got beyond the abilities of the democratic process is, on the other hand, a bit less complex and extended. It has to do with the way in which concrete issues were reduced to abstract principles and the conflicts between interests simplified to basic levels where men feel more than they reason, and where compromise or yielding is impossible because issues appear in the form of right and wrong and involve the fundamental structure of society. This is not saying, as some have charged, that great moral issues were not involved. They certainly were, and it is a matter of choice with historians as to whether or not they take sides, praise or condemn, become partisans in this departed quarrel, or use past events for present-day purposes.

As an approach to this second more modest problem, a correspondence which took place between Abraham Lincoln and Alexander H. Stephens between November 30 and December 22, 1860, is highly revealing. On November 14, Stephens had delivered one of the great speeches of his life before the legislature of Georgia. It was a Union speech. He had begged his fellow Southerners not to give up the ship, to wait for some violation of the Constitution before they attempted secession. Equality might yet be possible inside the Union. At least, the will of the whole people should be obtained before any action was taken.

Abraham Lincoln, still unconvinced that there was real danger, wrote Stephens, as an old friend, for a revised copy of his speech. Stephens complied, and he ended his letter with a warning about the great peril which threatened the country and a reminder of the heavy responsibility now resting on the president-elect's shoulders. Lincoln answered with assurance that he would not "*directly,* or *indirectly,* interfere with the slaves" or with the southern people about their slaves, and then closed with this significant statement: "I suppose, however, this does not meet the case. You think slavery is right and ought to be extended, while we think it is wrong and ought to be restricted. That I suppose is the rub. It certainly is the only substantial difference between us."

The reduction of "the only substantial difference" between North and South to a simple question of *right and wrong* is the im-

portant thing about Lincoln's statement. It revealed the extent to which the sectional controversy had, by 1860, been simplified and reduced to a conflict of principles in the minds of the northern people.

Stephens' answer to Lincoln's letter is equally revealing. He expressed "an earnest desire to preserve and maintain the Union of the States, if it can be done upon the principles and in furtherance of the objects for which it was formed." He insisted, however, that private opinion on the question of "African Slavery" was not a matter over which "the Government under the Constitution" had any control. "But now," he said, "this subject, which is confessedly on all sides outside of the Constitutional action of the Government so far as the States are concerned, is made the 'central idea' in the Platform of principles announced by the triumphant Party." It was this total disregard of the Constitution and the rights guaranteed under it that lay back of southern fears. It was the introduction into party politics of issues which projected action by Congress outside its constitutional powers that had made all the trouble. Stephens used the word "Constitution" seven times in his letter.

The significant thing here is Stephens' reduction of sectional differences to the simple matter of southern rights under the Constitution. He too showed how completely the sectional controversy had been simplified into a conflict of principles. And he with Lincoln, speaking for North and South, emphasized the fact that after years of strife the complex issues between the sections had assumed the form of a conflict between *right* and *rights.*

To the scholar it must be perfectly clear that this drastic simplification of sectional differences did not mean that either Lincoln or Stephens thought that all the bitter economic, social, and political questions could be ignored. It simply meant that *right* and *rights* had become the symbols or carriers of all those interests and values. Yet it is equally clear that as symbols they carried an emotional force and moral power in themselves that was far greater than the sum total of all the material issues involved. They suggested things which cannot be compromised—things for which men willingly fight and die. Their use, in 1860, showed that an irrepressible conflict existed. . . .

The [sectional conflict] had certainly shown the weakness of the democratic process in dealing with issues cast as moral conflicts or having to do with the fundamental structure of society. It seemed to show, as Carl Becker has said, that "government by discussion works best when there is nothing of profound importance to discuss, and when there is plenty of time to discuss it. The party system works best when the rival programs involve the superficial aspects rather than the fundamental structure of the social system, and majority rule works best when the minority can meet defeat at the polls in good temper because they need not regard the decision as either a permanent or a fatal surrender of their vital interests."

That, however, was only half of the difficulty. The [sectional conflict] had also shown that a democratic society cannot stand still. The conservative urge to hold fast to that which has been established may prove as fatal as the fanatic's prod to constant change. Those who profess a belief in democracy must ever remember that alongside the Constitution of the United States stands that other troublesome document, the Declaration of Independence, with its promise of greater freedom and equality. If politicians and parties do not sometimes give it heed, they may learn to their sorrow that the great document was written to justify revolt. That too may be a fatal weakness in the democratic process.

THE LINES ARE DRAWN

5

One of the first of the great war correspondents was William Howard Russell of the London Times. *He had learned his trade in the Crimean War, and during the winter of 1860–1861 he was in America watching the mounting crisis. Because of the desire on the part of both North and South to win the support of the English, Russell was given ready access to both governments. His word portraits of Lincoln and Davis were made just a few weeks apart, one in Washington, the other in Montgomery, Alabama:*[5]

[LINCOLN]

Soon afterward there entered, with a shambling, loose, irregular, almost unsteady gait, a tall, lank, lean man, considerably over six feet in height, with stooping shoulders, long pendulous arms, terminating in hands of extraordinary dimensions, which, however, were far exceeded in proportion by his feet. He was dressed in an ill-fitting, wrinkled suit of black, which put one in mind of an undertaker's uniform at a funeral; round his neck a rope of black silk was knotted in a large bulb, with flying ends projecting beyond the collar of his coat; his turned-down shirt-collar disclosed a sinewy muscular yellow neck, and above that, nestling in a great black mass of hair, bristling and compact like a riff of mourning pins, rose the strange quaint face and head, covered with its thatch of wild republican hair, of President Lincoln. The impression produced by the size of his extremities, and by his flapping and wide projecting ears, may be removed by the appearance of kindliness, sagacity, and the awkward bonhommie of his face; the mouth is absolutely prodigious; the lips, straggling and extending almost from one line of black beard to the other, are only kept in order by two deep furrows from the nostril to the chin; the nose itself—a prominent organ—stands out from the face with an inquiring, anxious air, as though it were sniffing for some good thing in the wind; the eyes dark, full, and deeply set, are penetrating, but full of an expression which almost amounts to tenderness; and above them projects the shaggy brow, running into the small hard frontal space, the development of which can scarcely be estimated accurately, owing to the irregular flocks of thick hair carelessly brushed across it. One would say that, although the mouth was made to enjoy a joke, it could also utter the severest sentence which

[5] William H. Russell, *My Diary North and South* (London, 1863), pp. 54–55; 249–250.

the head could dictate, but that Mr. Lincoln would be ever more willing to temper justice with mercy, and to enjoy what he considers the amenities of life, than to take a harsh view of men's nature and of the world. . . .

[DAVIS]

I had an opportunity of observing the President very closely: he did not impress me as favorably as I had expected, though he is certainly a very different looking man from Mr. Lincoln. He is like a gentleman— has a slight, light figure, little exceeding middle height, and holds himself erect and straight. He was dressed in a rustic suit of slate-coloured stuff, with a black silk handkerchief round his neck; his manner is plain, and rather reserved and drastic; his head is well-formed, with a fine full forehead, square and high, covered with innumerable fine lines and wrinkles, features regular, though the cheek-bones are too high, and the jaws too hollow to be handsome; the lips are thin, flexible, and curved, the chin square, well-defined; the nose very regular, with wide nostrils; and the eyes deep set, large and full —one seems nearly blind, and is partly covered with a film, owing to excruciating attacks of neuralgia and tic. Wonderful to relate, he does not chew, and is neat and clean-looking, with hair trimmed and boots brushed. The expression of his face is anxious, he has a very haggard, care-worn, and pain-drawn look, though no trace of anything but the utmost confidence and greatest decision could be detected in his conversation.

6

One by one, the states of the deep South followed South Carolina's example, until by February 1, 1861, all states bordering the Gulf of Mexico were out of the Union. With secession every Southerner had to ask himself: will I fight, and for what? Was he taking up arms for slavery, or states' rights, or a vague southern nationalism? Were these things worth bleeding, and dying, for? Most found the answer to these questions, not in the stratosphere of theory, but in their love for their homeland. The poetic

imagination of Stephen Vincent Benét recaptures these emotions in that section of John Brown's Body *in which "Wingate takes his stand for Dixie":[6]*

Wingate put his book on the shelf
And went to the window. It was good
To walk in the ghost through a silver wood
And set one's mettle against the far
Bayonet-point of the fixed North Star.
He stood there a moment, wondering.
North Star, wasp with the silver sting
Blue-nosed star on the Yankee banners,
We are coming against you to teach you manners!
With crumbs of thunder and wreaths of myrtle
And cannon that dance to a Dixie chorus,
With a song that bites like a snapping-turtle
And the tiger-lily of Summer before us,
To pull you down like a torn bandanna,
And drown you deeper than the Savannah!

And still, while his arrogance made its cry,
He shivered a little, wondering why.

There was his uniform, grey as ash,
The boots that shone like a well-rubbed table,
The tassels of silk on the colored sash
And sleek Black Whistle down in the stable,
The housewife, stitched from a beauty's fan,
The pocket-Bible with Mother's writing,
The sabre never yet fleshed in man,
And all the crisp new toys of fighting.
He gloated at them with a boyish pride,
But still he wondered, Monmouth-eyed.
The Black Horse Troop was a cavalier
And gallant name for a lady's ear.
He liked the sound and the ringing brag
And the girls who stitched on the county flag,
The smell of horses and saddle-leather
And the feel of the squadron riding together,
From the loose-reined canter of colts at large,

---

[6] From *John Brown's Body* in *Selected Works of Stephen Vincent Benét*, I, 63–66, published by Holt, Rinehart, and Winston, Inc. Copyright, 1927, 1928, by Stephen Vincent Benét.

To the crammed, tense second before the
    charge:
He liked it all with the young, keen zest
Of a hound unleashed and a hawk unjessed.
And yet—what happened to men in war?
Why were they all going out to war?
He brooded a moment. It wasn't slavery,
That stale red-herring of Yankee knavery
Nor even states-rights, at least not solely,
But something so dim that it must be holy.
A voice, a fragrance, a taste of wine,
A face half-seen in old candleshine,
A yellow river, a blowing dust,
Something beyond you that you must trust,
Something so shrouded it must be great,
The dead men building the living State
From 'simmon-seed on a sandy bottom,
The woman South in her rivers laving
That body whiter than new-blown cotton
And savage and sweet as wild-orange-blos-
    som,
The dark hair streams on the barbarous
    bosom,
If there ever has been a land worth saving—
In Dixie land, I'll take my stand,
And live and die for Dixie! . . . .

So Wingate pondered in Wingate Hall,
And hated and loved in a single breath,
As he tried to unriddle the doubtful scrawl
Of war and courage and love and death,
And then was suddenly nothing but sleep—
And tomorrow they marched—to a two
    months chasing
Of Yankees running away like sheep
And peace in time for the Macon racing.
He got in his bed. Where the moonlight
    poured,
It lay like frost on a sleeping sword.

7

*The firing on Fort Sumter echoed in villages
and towns all across the land. An Indiana farm
boy, not yet sixteen, confides to his journal how
the news had come to prairie farmers:*[7]

---

[7] Oscar O. Winthur (ed.), Theodore F. Upson,
*With Sherman to the Sea, the Civil War Letters,
Diaries & Reminiscences of Theodore F. Upson*
(Bloomington, 1958), pp. 9–12. Reprinted by per-
mission of the publishers, Indiana University Press.

April, 1861

Father and I were husking out some corn.
We could not finish it before it wintered up.
When William Cory came across the field
(he had been down after the Mail) he was
excited and said, "Jonathan the Rebels have
fired upon Fort Sumpter." Father got white
and couldn't say a word.

William said, "The President will soon fix
them. He has called for 75,000 men and is
going to blocade thier ports, and just as soon
as those fellows find out that the North
means business they will get down off thier
high horse."

Father said little. We did not finish the
corn and drove to the barn. Father left me
to unload and put out the team and went to
the house. After I had finished I went in to
dinner. Mother said, "What is the matter
with Father?" He had gone right upstairs.
I told her what we had heard. She went to
him. After a while they came down. Father
looked ten years older. We sat down to the
table. Grandma wanted to know what was
the trouble. Father told her and she began
to cry. "Oh my poor children in the South!
Now they will suffer! God knows how they
will suffer! I knew it would come! Jonathan
I told you it would come!"

"They can come here and stay," said
Father.

"No they will not do that. There is thier
home. There they will stay. Oh to think
I should have lived to see the day when
Brother should rise against Brother."

She and Mother were crying and I lit
out for the barn. I do hate to see women cry.

We had another meeting at the school
house last night; we are raising money to
take care of the families of those who enlist.
A good many gave money, others subscribed.
The Hulper boys have enlisted and Steve
Lampman and some others. I said I would
go but they laughed at me and said they
wanted men not boys for this job; that it
would all be over soon; that those fellows
down South are big bluffers and would rather
talk than fight. I am not so sure about that.
I know the Hale boys would fight with thier

fists at any rate and I believe they would fight with guns too if needs be. I remember how Charlie would get on our Dick and ride on a galop across our south field cutting off mullin heads with his wooden sword playing they were Indians or Mexicans (his Father was in the Mexican War), and he looked fine. To be sure there was no danger but I feel pretty certain he could fight. May be it wont be such a picnic as some say it will. There has been a fight down in Virginia at Big Bethel. Al Beechers Nephew was in it and wrote to his Uncle and he read the letter in his store. I could not make out which side whipped but from the papers I think the Rebels had the best of it. Mother had a letter from the Hales. Charlie and his Father are in thier army and Dayton wanted to go but was too young. I wonder if I were in our army and they should meet me would they shoot me. I suppose they would.

Steve Lampman has been in a battle and was wounded. He wrote home & they read his letter in the Methodist Church last Sunday (he was a Methodist). He said it was auful to see men shot down like cattle. I guess some of these folks will think its not a picnic after all. We had a great celebration here the Fourth of July. The military Company from Sturgis was here and a band. Some of us boys had a fife and drum and a flag and marched behind them. There was a speaker from away off some place and he told what the government was going to do to the Rebels and a lot of such talk and finally grabbed the flag from Johnny Woodruff, waved it around and shouted, "On to Richmond." No one started but the people cheered and cheered.

We have just heard about the Battle of Bull Run; we got whipped all right and no mistake. Some folks feel pretty blue.

We had a war meeting (they call them war meetings now) in the school house. Some talked one thing, some another. Mr. Van Orman said the President had no power to coerce a soverign State. I think he soon found out he was on the wrong side when Mr John B Howe got up and said this was

no time for quarreling, that the integrity of the government was assailed, that there was nothing to do but to stand by the President regardless of party, and he proposed that a vote be taken so we would know who were our friends. It was done and those who wouldent vote soon left. Then it got quiet.

A lot more have enlisted. Some went to Michigan. Our folks dont like that; they say we will not get our proper credit. I dont understand it. They are getting up a Company here and at Lagrange. Captain Dawson is doing it. I have enlisted. When I told Father about it he only laughed and said it would not hurt me to play soldier a while. I drill with them and Captain Dawson says I pick it up quickly. The Company all fell in yesterday morning and Miss Reb[e]cca Williams gave each one a Testament and they were given blouses and a Company flag. I did not get a Testament or anything else for Captain Dawson says I must get my Fathers consent before he can take me (as if that would make any difference). Well the Company went away in wagons—started for Ft Wayne. I went to Lagrange with them, then Capt Dawson called me to one side and said he could not take me without my Fathers consent and he would not give it. I was so mad I bawled. Then some of them said "You would make a pretty soldier." That made me madder than ever and I walked home though I could have rode as well as not. Well if they dont want me they can fight their old war for all of me. I dont care.

8

How the northern armies were raised is described by Michael Fitch of the 6th Wisconsin Volunteers. Many a southern regiment was recruited in exactly the same fashion:[8]

The region in northwestern Wisconsin, bounded on the west and northwest by the Mississippi and the St. Croix rivers, and contiguous thereto, in 1861 was sparsely settled. There was no railroad. Transportation was

---

[8] Michael H. Fitch, *Echoes of the Civil War as I hear Them* (New York, 1905), pp. 17–20.

made either by steamboat on the water or by horses on the land. These factors made the raising of a volunteer company for service, an arduous task. When Mr. Lincoln made the first call for seventy-five thousand volunteers, the quota of Wisconsin was one regiment. At least, only one regiment of three months' men left the state under that call. That regiment, I believe, was largely made up of militia companies that had been previously organized and equipped. Yet active recruiting commenced at once all over the state in the latter part of April, 1861. I presume every company that was recruited in any part of the state at that time, made effort to get into that three months' regiment. The sentiment then was quite universal that three months would close the war. Hence, whoever failed to become a part of the first regiment would see no service and receive no military glory.

A mass meeting was held at once in our town, Prescott, Pierce County. Several addresses were made. Patriotism was effervescent, and thirty young men signed the roll of the Prescott Guards. We at once notified the Governor that we would like to be a part of the troops about to be called. But at that time, as we were informed, enough companies had been offered to fill four regiments. As only one regiment was called for three months, our little squad out on the northwestern border had very little show. This did not discourage this little patriotic band. They began drilling every day, studied the tactics, erected a liberty pole mounted by a bayonet, pointing south, with the stars and stripes floating from its top. The fiery spirit of '76, as we understood it, was thoroughly aroused. By April 30th, a full company was enlisted. Daniel J. Dill, a prominent merchant who had military tastes and who afterwards became captain of the company, went up the river to Hastings, Minnesota, and down the river to various towns, in pursuit of recruits. Rollin P. Converse and myself took a pair of horses and a buggy and started into the back country. That ride across the prairie and through the woods for

several days, was novel and exceedingly interesting. We visited, not only the towns, but every farm. At one town, I think River Falls, we met recruiting officers from Hudson, the county seat of the adjoining county of St. Croix, on the same errand. We held a joint meeting at night at which several addresses were made. We found western pioneer hospitality everywhere. Every rugged backswoodsman, whether American, German or Norwegian, was full of patriotism. Indignation at the firing on Fort Sumter was genuine and universal. The roads, especially through the woods, were in a wretched condition. It rained, and the mud was frightful. One evening in a lonely spot in the primeval forest, a singletree of the buggy broke. But there stood, by the side of the road, a sturdy pioneer with an axe on his shoulder. In five minutes he had cut a hickory withe, twisted it into a pliable rope, tied it around the broken tree in the most skillful manner, and sent us on our way rejoicing, with a buggy stronger than it was before. Wherever we stopped over night the host would refuse pay for our entertainment. The mother and daughters would look after our comfort, even drying our apparel when wet with rain. Everywhere we were bidden Godspeed in our patriotic efforts. How many recruits we procured on this trip, I have now forgotten. But some walked to Prescott for miles to enlist. The muster rolls of the company show that almost every township in Pierce County was represented among its members. There were no better soldiers in the army than many of these backwoods farmer boys. A number of them never returned. We had some enlistments from far up the St. Croix River among the lumbermen and loggers. Captain Dill was successful in getting recruits from Hastings, Menominee and other towns. A. C. Ellis, a bright-eyed boy with curly black hair brought quite a number from Menominee. Before the first of May, between ninety and one hundred had taken the oath of service and allegiance to the United States. I administered the oath to each one who signed the enlistment. D. J. Dill was elected captain. Two alleged Mexican war veterans were made lieutenants. I was appointed first sergeant. The Governor was notified that we were ready for service. But, not only the first, but the second, third, fourth and fifth regiments of volunteer infantry were organized at Madison without our company being assigned. There was great uncertainty for some time after this about being called into service. The men went back to their homes, and some of them enlisted in other companies. We thought the rebellion would be over before our chance would come. However, by May 10th, we were informed that we were the sixth company in the sixth regiment.

9

George Eggleston, a transplanted Hoosier who had gone, before the war, to live with relatives in Virginia, was loyal to his adopted state and to the Confederacy. Retaining his sense of humor, he was able to see and describe the efforts of his friends and neighbors to prepare for war with considerable sympathy and only a touch of sarcasm:[9]

A newspaper correspondent has told us that the great leader of the German armies, Count Von Moltke, has never read anything —even a history—of our war, and that when questioned on the subject, he has said he could not afford to spend time over "the wrangling of two armed mobs." If he ever said anything of the kind, which is doubtful, his characterization of the two armies had reference, probably, to their condition during the first year or two of the struggle, when they could lay very little claim indeed to any more distinctively military title. The Southern army, at any rate, was simply a vast mob of rather ill-armed young gentlemen from the country. As I have said . . . every gentleman in Virginia, not wholly incapable of rendering service, enlisted at the beginning of the war, and the companies, unarmed, untrained, and hardly even organized, were sent at once to camps of

[9] George Cary Eggleston, *A Rebel's Recollections* (New York, 1875), pp. 29–55, *passim.*

instruction. Here they were in theory drilled and disciplined and made into soldiers, by the little handful of available West-Pointers and the lads from the Military Institute at Lexington. In point of fact, they were only organized and taught the rudiments of the drill before being sent to the front as full-fledged soldiers; and it was only after a year or more of active service in the field that they began to suspect what the real work and the real character of the modern soldier is.

Our ideas of the life and business of a soldier were drawn chiefly from the adventures of Ivanhoe and Charles O'Malley, two worthies with whose personal history almost every man in the army was familiar. The men who volunteered went to war of their own accord, and were wholly unaccustomed to acting on any other than their own motion. They were hardy lovers of field sports, accustomed to out-door life, and in all physical respects excellent material of which to make an army. But they were not used to control of any sort, and were not disposed to obey anybody except for good and sufficient reason given. While actually on drill they obeyed the word of command, not so much by reason of its being proper to obey a command, as because obedience was in that case necessary to the successful issue of a pretty performance in which they were interested. Off drill they did as they pleased, holding themselves gentlemen, and as such bound to consult only their own wills. Their officers were of themselves, chosen by election, and subject, by custom, to enforced resignation upon petition of the men. Only corporals cared sufficiently little for their position to risk any magnifying of their office by the enforcement of discipline. I make of them an honorable exception, out of regard for the sturdy corporal who, at Ashland, marched six of us (a guard detail) through the very middle of a puddle, assigning as his reason for doing so the fact that "It's plagued little authority they give us corporals, and I mean to use that little, any how." Even corporals were elected, however, and until December, 1861, I never knew a single instance in which a captain dared offend his men by breaking a noncommissioned officer, or appointing one, without submitting the matter to a vote of the company. . . .

With troops of this kind, the reader will readily understand, a feeling of very democratic equality prevailed, so far at least as military rank had anything to do with it. . . . The theory was that the officers were the creatures of the men, chosen by election to represent their constituency in the performance of certain duties, and that only during good behavior. And to this theory the officers themselves gave in their adhesion in a hundred ways. Indeed, they could do nothing else, inasmuch as they knew no way of quelling a mutiny.

There was one sort of rank, however, which was both maintained and respected from the first, namely, that of social life. The line of demarkation between gentry and common people is not more sharply drawn anywhere than in Virginia. It rests there upon an indeterminate something or other, known as family. To come of a good family, is a patent of nobility, and there is no other way whatever by which any man or any woman can find a passage into the charmed circle of Virginia's peerage. . . . The man of good family felt himself superior, as in most cases he unquestionably was, to his fellow-soldier of less excellent birth; and this distinction was sufficient, during the early years of the war, to override everything like military rank. In one instance which I remember, a young private asserted his superiority of social standing so effectually as to extort from the lieutenant commanding his company a public apology for an insult offered in the subjection of the private to double duty, as a punishment for absence from roll-call. . . .

In the camp of instruction at Ashland, where the various cavalry companies existing in Virginia were sent to be made into soldiers, it was a very common thing indeed for men who grew tired of camp fare to take their meals at the hotel, and one or two of them rented cottages and brought their families there, excusing themselves from attendance upon unreasonably early roll-calls, by pleading the distance from their cottages to the parade-ground. Whenever a detail was made for the purpose of cleaning the camp-ground, the men detailed regarded themselves as responsible for the proper performance of the task by their servants, and uncomplainingly took upon themselves the duty of sitting on the fence and superintending the work. The two or three men of the overseer class who were to be found in nearly every company turned some nimble quarters by standing other men's turns of guard-duty at twenty-five cents an hour. . . .

It was in this undisciplined state that the men who afterwards made up the army under Lee were sent to the field to meet the enemy at Bull Run and elsewhere, and the only wonder is that they were ever able to fight at all. They were certainly not soldiers. They were as ignorant of the alphabet of obedience as their officers were of the art of commanding. And yet they acquitted themselves reasonably well, a fact which can be explained only by reference to the causes of their insubordination in camp. These men were the people of the South, and the war was their own; wherefore they fought to win it of their own accord, and not at all because their officers commanded them to do so. Their personal spirit and their intelligence were their sole elements of strength. Death has few terrors for such men, as compared with dishonor, and so they needed no officers at all, and no discipline, to insure their personal good conduct on the field of battle. The same elements of character, too, made them accept hardship with the utmost cheerfulness, as soon as hardship became a necessary condition to the successful prosecution of a war that every man of them regarded as his own. In camp, at Richmond or Ashland, they had shunned all unnecessary privation and all distasteful duty, because they then saw no occasion to endure avoidable discomfort. But in the field they showed themselves great, stalwart men in spirit as well as in bodily frame, and endured cheerfully the hardships of campaigning precisely as they would have borne the fatigues of a hunt, as incidents encountered in the prosecution of their purposes.

THE SOUND OF BATTLE

10

John Hampden Chamberlayne was a native Virginian who gloried in fighting under the immortal "Stonewall" Jackson. The action he describes in the following letter to his mother was the fighting that preceded and comprised the battle of Second Manassas, August 28 and 29, 1862. On that occasion, Jackson made one of his famous end runs around the Union right flank and landed on General Pope's base of operations:[10]

FREDERICK CITY, MD., *Saturday Sept. 6*
[1862]

MY DEAR MOTHER:

I am brimful of matter as an egg of meat. Let me try to outline our progress since my last letter—date not remembered—from Raccoon Ford—you bearing in mind that I am in A. P. Hill's division, in Jackson's corps—that corps consisting of Jackson's own division, Ewell's and Hill's. You will not think me egotistical for speaking of this corps and of the corps of Hill's division, for of them I know most, and in truth their share was, to me at least, the most memorable in the almost incredible campaign of the last fortnight.

Crossing Raccoon Ford, Jackson in front —remember, Jackson, so used, includes Hill, Ewell, and the Stonewall division—General Lee, without much opposition, reached Rappahannock River, a few miles above Rappahannock station, where a part of Longstreet's troops had a sharp fight. On Friday Evening, August twenty-second, Jackson bivouacked in Culpeper, opposite Warrenton Springs, and the same evening threw over two of Ewell's

brigades. The river rose and destroyed the bridge. Saturday the bridge was rebuilt, and that night the two brigades, after some sharp fighting, were withdrawn.

On Monday morning the enemy appeared in heavy force, and the batteries of Hill's division were put in position and shelled their infantry. They retired the infantry, and bringing up a large number of batteries, threw a storm of shot and shell at us—we not replying. They must have exploded several thousand rounds, and in all, so well sheltered were we, our killed did not reach twenty. That evening Jackson's whole force moved up to Jefferson, in Culpeper County, Longstreet close to him. The enemy was completely deceived, and concluded that we had given the thing up.

Now comes the great wonder. Starting up the bank of the river on Monday, the twenty-fifth, we marched through Amosville, in Rappahannock County—still further up, crossed the Rappahannock within ten miles of the Blue Ridge, marched across open fields, by strange country paths and comfortable homesteads, by a little town in Fauquier, called Orleans, on and on, as if we would never cease—to Salem, on the Manassas Gap Railroad, reaching there after midnight. Up again by day—dawn, and still on, along the Manassas Gap road, meeting crowds—all welcoming, cheering, staring with blank amazement. So all day Tuesday, through White Plains, Haymarket, Thoroughfare Gap, in Bull Run Mountains, Gainesville, to Bristow station, on the Orange and Alexandria Railroad—making the difference from Amosville to Bristow (between forty-five and fifty miles) within the forty-eight hours. We burned up at Bristow two or three railway-trains, and moved up to Manassas Junction on Wednesday, taking our prisoners with us. Ewell's division brought up the rear, fighting all the way a force Pope had sent up from Warrenton, supposing us a cavalry party.

Upon reaching Manassas Junction, we met a brigade—the First New-Jersey—which had been sent from Alexandria on the same

---

[10] John H. Chamberlayne, "Narrative by a Rebel Lieutenant," in Frank Moore (ed.), *The Rebellion Record: A Diary of American Events* (New York, 1869), V, 402–404.

supposition. They were fools enough to send a flag demanding our surrender at once. Of course we scattered the brigade, killing and wounding many, and among them the Brigadier-General (Taylor,) who has since died. At the Junction was a large dépôt of stores, five or six pieces of artillery, two trains containing probably two hundred large cars loaded down with many millions of quartermaster and commissary stores. Besides these, there were very large sutlers' dépôts, full of every thing; in short, there was collected there, in the space of a square mile, an amount and variety of property such as I had never conceived of, (I speak soberly.) 'Twas a curious sight to see our ragged and famished men helping themselves to every imaginable article of luxury or necessity, whether of clothing, food, or what not. For my part, I got a tooth-brush, a box of candles, a quantity of lobster salad, a barrel of coffee, and other things which I forget. But I must hurry on, for I have not time to tell the hundredth part, and the scene utterly beggars description.

A part of us hunted that New-Jersey brigade like scattered partridges over the hills just to the right of the battle-field of the eighteenth of July, 1861, while the rest were partly plundering, partly fighting the forces coming on us from Warrenton. Our men had been living on roasted corn since crossing the Rappahannock, and we had brought no wagons, so we could carry little away of the riches before us. But the men could eat for one meal at least. So they were marched up, and as much of every thing eatable served out as they could carry. To see a starving man eating lobster-salad and drinking Rhine wine, barefooted and in tatters, was curious; the whole thing was incredible.

Our situation now was very critical. We were between Alexandria and Warrenton— between the hosts of McClellan and Pope with over eighteen thousand jaded men, for the corps had not more than that. At nightfall, fire was set to the dépôt, storehouses, the loaded trains, several, empty trains, sutlers' houses, restaurants, every thing. As

the magnificent conflagration began to subside, the Stonewall or First division of Jackson's corps moved off toward the battlefield of Manassas, the other two divisions to Centreville, six miles distant.

As day broke, we came in sight of Centreville, rested a few hours, and toward evening the rear-guard of the corps crossed Bull Run at Stone Bridge—the scene of the great slaughter of last year—closely pursued by the enemy. A part of the force came up the Warrenton turnpike, and in a furious action of two hours—the last two daylight hours of Thursday, August twenty-eighth—disputed the possession of a ridge running from Sudley Church Ford to the Warrenton turnpike. We drove them off, and on Friday morning we held the ridge, in front of which runs an incomplete railroad-cut and embankment. Now, we had made a circuit from the Gap in Bull Run Mountains around to the Junction and Centreville, breaking up the railroad and destroying their stores, and returned to within six miles of the Gap, through which Longstreet must come. The enemy disputed his passage and delayed him till late in the day, and, meanwhile, they threw against our corps, all day long, vast masses of troops—Sigel's, Bank's, and Pope's own division. We got out of ammunition; we collected more from cartridge-boxes of fallen friend and foe; that gave out, and we charged with never-failing yell and steel. All day long they threw their masses on us; all day they fell back shattered and shrieking. When the sun went down, their dead were heaped in front of the incomplete railway, and we sighed with relief, for Longstreet could be seen coming into position on our right. The crisis was over; Longstreet never failed yet; but the sun went down so slowly. . . .

I am proud to have borne my humble part in these great operations—to have helped, even so little, to consummate the grand plan, whose history will be a text-book to all young soldiers, and whose magnificent success places Lee at the side of the greatest captains, Hannibal, Caesar, Eugene, Napoleon. I hope you have preserved my letters in which I have spoken of my faith in Lee. He and his round-table of generals are worthy the immortality of Napoleon and his Marshals. He moves his agencies like a god —secret, complicated, vast, resistless, complete.

11

Walt Whitman could not enlist in the Union army, but he could not stay away from the scenes of carnage in which the nation he loved so well was being tested. He spent most of his time in the hospitals that sprang up about Washington, with an occasional expedition to the field hospitals at nearby battle sites:[11]

A NIGHT BATTLE, OVER A WEEK SINCE. MAY 12, 1863

There was part of the battle at Chancellorsville (Second Fredericksburg) a little over a week ago, Saturday, Saturday night, and Sunday, under General Joe Hooker, I would like to give you just a glimpse of (a moment's look in a terrible storm at sea, of which a few suggestions are enough, and full details impossible).

The fighting had been very hot during the day, and, after an intermission, the latter part was resumed at night and kept up with furious energy till three o'clock in the morning. That afternoon (Saturday) an attack sudden and strong by Stonewall Jackson had gained a great advantage to the Southern Army and broken our lines, entering us like a wedge and leaving things in that position at dark. But Hooker at 11 at night made a desperate push, drove the Secesh forces back, restored his original lines, and resumed his plans.

This night scrimmage was very exciting, and afforded countless strange and fearful pictures. The fighting had been general both at Chancellorsville and northeast at Fredericksburg. (We hear of some poor fighting, episodes, skedaddling on our part—I think

not of it. I think of the fierce bravery, the general rule.)

One corps, the 6th, Sedgwick's, fights four dashing and bloody battles in thirty-six hours, retreating in great jeopardy, losing largely, but maintaining itself, fighting with the sternest desperation under all circumstances, getting over the Rappahannock only by the skin of its teeth, yet getting over. It lost many, many brave men, yet it took vengeance, ample vengeance.

But it was the tug of Saturday evening and through the night and Sunday morning I wanted to make a special note of. It was largely in the woods and quite a general engagement. The night was very pleasant; at times the moon shining out full and clear, all Nature so calm in itself, the early summer grass so rich and foliage of the trees— yet there was the battle raging and many good fellows lying helpless, with new accessions to them; and every minute, amid the rattle of muskets and crash of cannon (for there was an artillery contest, too), the red lifeblood oozing out from heads or trunks or limbs upon that green and dewy earth.

Patches of the woods take fire, and several of the wounded, unable to move, are consumed; quite large spaces are swept over, burning the dead also. Some of the men have their hair and beards singed; some, burns on their faces and hands; others, with holes burnt in their clothing.

The flashes of fire from the cannon, the quick-flaring flames and smoke, and the immense roar; the musketry so general; the light nearly bright enough for each side to see the other; the crashing, tramping of men; the yellow, close quarters. We hear the Secesh yells; our men cheer loudly back, especially if Hooker is in sight; hand-to-hand conflicts; each side stands up to it— brave, determined as demons, they often charge upon us; a thousand deeds are done worth to write newer, greater poems on— and still the woods on fire; still many are not only scorched; too many, unable to move, are burned to death.

---

[11] Walter Lowenfels (ed.), *Walt Whitman's Civil War* (New York, 1960), pp. 44–47. Reprinted with the permission of the publishers, Alfred A. Knopf, Inc.

Then the camps of the wounded—O heavens! what scene is this? Is this indeed *humanity*—these butchers' shambles? There are several of them. There they lie in the largest, in an open space in the woods, from two hundred to three hundred poor fellows; the groans and screams, the odor of blood mixed with the fresh scent of the night, the grass, the trees; that slaughter house!

O well is it their mothers, their sisters, cannot see them; cannot conceive and never conceived these things. One man is shot by a shell, both in the arm and leg; both are amputated—there lie the rejected members. Some of them have their legs blown off; some bullets through the breast; some indescribably horrid wounds in the face or head. All mutilated, sickening, torn, gouged out—some in the abdomen—some mere boys, many Rebels (they take their regular turns with the rest, just the same as any; the surgeons use them just the same).

Such is the camp of the wounded; such a fragment, a reflection afar off of the bloody scene; while over all the clear, large moon comes out at times softly, quietly shining. Amid the woods—that scene of flitting souls; amid the crack and crash and yelling sounds —the impalpable perfume of the woods and yet the pungent stifling smoke; the radiance of the moon looking from the heaven at intervals, so placid; the sky so heavenly; the clear-obscure up there, those buoyant upper oceans; a few large placid stars beyond, coming silently and languidly out and then disappearing; the melancholy, draperied night above, around.

And there, upon the roads, the fields, and in those woods, that contest, never one more desperate in any age or land; both parties now in force—masses—no fancy battle, no semi-play, but fierce and savage demons fighting there; courage and scorn of death the rule, exceptions almost none.

What history, I say, can ever give—for who can know?—the mad, determined tussle of the armies in all their separate large and little squads—as this—each steeped from crown to toe in desperate, mortal pur-

ports? Who know the conflict, hand-to-hand, the many conflicts in the dark, those shadowy-tangled, flashing-moonbeamed woods, the writhing groups and squads, the cries, the din, the cracking guns and pistols, the distant cannon, the cheers and calls and threats and awful music of the oaths; the indescribable mix—the officers' orders, persuasions, encouragements—the devils fully roused in human hearts; the strong shout: "charge, men, charge," the flash of the naked sword—and rolling flame and smoke?

And still the broken clear and clouded heaven; and still again the moonlight pouring silvery soft its radiant patches over all.

12

One of the famed battle descriptions in the English language is by Frank A. Haskell. A Union soldier, he wrote of the repulse of Pickett's charge at Gettysburg in a book-length letter to his brother. No excerpt can do it justice, but any part of it bears the stamp of a minor classic:[12]

Who can describe such a conflict as is raging around us? To say that it was like a summer storm, with the crash of thunder, the glare of lightning, the shrieking of the wind, and the clatter of hailstones, would be weak. The thunder and lightning of these two hundred and fifty guns and their shells, whose smoke darkens the sky, are incessant, all pervading, in the air above our heads, on the ground at our feet, remote, near, deafening, ear-piercing, astounding; and these hailstones are massy iron, charged with exploding fire. And there is little of human interest in a storm; it is an absorbing element of this. You may see flame and smoke, and hurrying men, and human passion at a great conflagration; but they are all earthly and nothing more. These guns are great infuriate demons, not of the earth, whose mouths blaze with smoky tongues of living fire, and whose murky breath, sulphur-laden, rolls around them and along the ground, the smoke of Hades. These grimy men, rushing, shouting, their souls in

---

[12] Frank A. Haskell, *The Battle of Gettysburg* (1863), in *The Harvard Classics*, edited by Charles W. Eliot (New York, 1910), XLIII, 396–399.

frenzy, plying the dusky globes and the igniting spark, are in their league, and but their willing ministers. We thought that at the second Bull Run, at the Antietam and at Fredericksburg on the 11th of December, we had heard heavy cannonading; they were but holiday salutes compared with this. Besides the great ceaseless roar of the guns, which was but the background of the others, a million various minor sounds engaged the ear. The projectiles shriek long and sharp. They hiss, they scream, they growl, they sputter; all sounds of life and rage; and each has its different note, and all are discordant. Was ever such a chorus of sound before? We note the effect of the enemies' fire among the batteries and along the crest. We see the solid shot strike axle, or pole, or wheel, and the tough iron and heart of oak snap and fly like straws. The great oaks there by Woodruff's guns heave down their massy branches with a crash, as if the lightning smote them. The shells swoop down among the battery horses standing there apart. A half a dozen horses start, they tumble, their legs stiffen, their vitals and blood smear the ground. And these shot and shells have no respect for men either. We see the poor fellows hobbling back from the crest, or unable to do so, pale and weak, lying on the ground with the mangled stump of an arm or leg, dripping their lifeblood away; or with a cheek torn open or a shoulder mashed. And many, alas! hear not the roar as they stretch upon the ground with upturned faces and open eyes, though a shell should burst at their very ears. Their ears and their bodies this instant are only mud. We saw them but a moment since there among the flame, with brawny arms and muscles of iron, wielding the rammer and pushing home the cannon's plethoric load.

Strange freaks these round shot play! We saw a man coming up from the rear with his full knapsack on, and some canteens of water held by the straps in his hands. He was walking slowly and with apparent unconcern, though the iron hailed around him. A shot struck the knapsack, and it and its contents flew thirty yards in every direction, the knapsack disappearing like an egg thrown spitefully against a rock. The soldier stopped and turned about in a puzzled surprise, put up one hand to his back to assure himself that the knapsack was not there, and then walked slowly on again unharmed, with not even his coat torn. Near us was a man crouching behind a small disintegrated stone, which was about the size of a common water bucket. He was bent up, with his face to the ground, in the attitude of a Pagan worshipper before his idol. It looked so absurd to see him thus, that I went and said to him, "Do not lie there like a toad. Why not go to your regiment and be a man?" He turned up his face with a stupid, terrified look upon me, and then without a word turned his nose again to the ground. An orderly that was with me at the time told me a few moments later, that a shot struck the stone, smashing it in a thousand fragments, but did not touch the man, though his head was not six inches from the stone.

All the projectiles that came near us were not so harmless. Not ten yards away from us a shell burst among some small bushes, where sat three or four orderlies holding horses. Two of the men and one horse were killed. Only a few yards off a shell exploded over an open limber box in Cushing's battery, and at the same instant, another shell over a neighboring box. In both the boxes the ammunition blew up with an explosion that shook the ground, throwing fire and splinters and shells far into the air and all around, and destroying several men. We watched the shells bursting in the air, as they came hissing in all directions. Their flash was a bright gleam of lightning radiating from a point, giving place in the thousandth part of a second to a small, white puffy cloud, like a fleece of the lightest, whitest wool. These clouds were very numerous. We could not often see the shell before it burst; but sometimes, as we faced toward the enemy, and looked above our heads, the approach would be heralded by a prolonged hiss, which always seemed to me to be a line of something tangible, terminating in a black globe, distinct to the eye, as the sound had been to the ear. The shell would seem to stop, and hang suspended in the air an instant, and then vanish in fire and smoke and noise.

We saw the missiles tear and plow the ground. All in rear of the crest for a thousand yards, as well as among the batteries, was the field of their blind fury. Ambulances, passing down the Taneytown road, with wounded men, were struck. The hospitals near this road were riddled. The house which was General Meade's headquarters was shot through several times, and a great many horses of officers and orderlies were lying dead around it. Riderless horses, galloping madly through the fields, were brought up, or down rather, by these invisible horse-tamers, and they would not run any more. Mules with ammunition, pigs wallowing about, cows in the pastures, whatever was animate or inanimate, in all this broad range, were no exception to their blind havoc. The percussion shells would strike, and thunder, and scatter the earth and their whistling fragments; the Whitworth bolts would pound and ricochet, and bowl far away sputtering, with the sound of a mass of hot iron plunged in water; and the great solid shot would smite the unresisting ground with a sounding "thud," as the strong boxer crashes his iron fist into the jaws of his unguarded adversary. Such were some of the sights and sounds of this great iron battle of missiles. Our artillerymen upon the crest budged not an inch, nor intermitted, but, though caisson and limber were smashed, and guns dismantled, and men and horses killed, there amidst smoke and sweat, they gave back, without grudge, or loss of time in the sending, in kind whatever the enemy sent, globe, and cone, and bolt, hollow or solid, an iron greeting to the rebellion, the compliments of the wrathful Republic.

13

A very different view of combat comes from the pen of Major James A. Connolly, a Union

soldier who fought with Rosecrans, Thomas, and Sherman through the central South. The following incident took place as the Union army dogged the retreating footsteps of General Bragg. When Connolly wrote this letter to his wife, he could not have known that Bragg would turn in his tracks and inflict a stunning defeat upon the Union army along nearby Chickamauga Creek:[13]

ACROSS THE RIVER FROM CHATTANOOGA,
Sept. 5, 1863.

DEAR WIFE:

I have deferred writing you for a very long time, you will say. Well I have indeed, but I couldn't help it. I wrote you from Tracy City, on the mountains, about the 16th or 18th of August, then I wrote you another from Dunlap in the Sequatchee Valley, in a couple of days afterwards. The next morning after writing you the last letter we started across the last range of mountains which separated us from the Tennessee River, leaving our baggage behind us. Since that morning we have been marching, fighting, bushwhacking, reconnoitering, living on hard crackers and talking across the river and exchanging papers with the rebel pickets of Chattanooga. Our wagons reached us day before yesterday and this is about the first chance I have had at pen, ink and paper for many a day. I was in command of the regiment for several days while crossing the mountains, and on the morning of the day we reached Chattanooga, or rather the river bank opposite Chattanooga, I was in command of the advance guard, and the men under my command were the first to open the fight and fire into the stronghold. Just as we dashed up to the river bank a ferry boat, which had just unloaded a lot of mules and a dozen rebel soldiers on our side of the river, was preparing to return to the Chattanooga side; we began firing into the boat, and, as we have since learned, killed 6 and wounded several more, while the boat

[13] Major James A. Connolly to his wife, September 5, 1863, in Illinois State Historical Society, *Transactions*, 1928 (Springfield, 1929), pp. 278–280. Reprinted with the kind permission of the Illinois State Historical Society.

drifted off down the river out of our range, and left us sitting there on our horses, drinking out of the river, and we looking up the main street of the city. I had started from Poe's tavern, 12 miles up the valley that morning, in advance of every thing, had moved briskly, and it was very early when we reached the river. They were completely thunderstruck at our sudden appearance and audacity, and so great was their surprise that, if it were not for the river over which there was no bridge we could have ridden clear through the city without being molested by its garrison. I sent a courier back to inform the brigade commander where I was, and withdrew my men under cover of the timber, but it was nearly half an hour before they had their guns manned so as to open their batteries on us. Soon after that the balance of the brigade and our battery came up on the gallop, our rifled guns were unlimbered on the hill top opposite the city, and then we had an artillery duel from that time (about 9 A. M.) until near dark with a loss of one man and 4 horses on our side but we don't know the loss in the city. Since then we have been lying here on the hills opposite the city, watching the soldiers and citizens, moving about the streets, shelling the railroad depot every few days, skirmishing along the river bank with soldiers in the streets of the city, and picking up deserters as they swim across the river.

We are the *extreme front*, and have remained here at Chattanooga longer than any portion of the Federal army since the war began. I know where the balance of our army is and what doing but it would not be prudent for me to write it here, for this letter may fall into rebel hands, yet I may say that I have the fullest confidence in the success of Rosecrans' present movement. From our present position we can look down into the streets of Chattanooga and even read the sign-boards. We could lay the place in ruins in one day if we chose to do so. Colonel [Monroe] and myself have crossed the river several times in a canoe and spent several hours talking and playing cards with rebel officers under the shadow of Lookout mountain, and they have as often crossed to our side and talked and played with us. We find them intelligent gentlemen and good fellows.

I doubt very much whether you have received any of my letters since I left Decherd, for mail communication has been largely interdicted, and I suppose you are somewhat uneasy about me, but you never need feel so, for I am getting along finely and am having an experience that will be a treasure to me in the future. I am like a vegetable, ripening rapidly under the intense artificial light of this war. I am very anxious to get home, but here we are in the face of the enemy, sleeping at night under the very shadow of the hills whose tops bristle with rebel cannon; in momentary expectation of an attack. Last night the enemy built a pontoon bridge, and this morning it is lying on the bank on the opposite side of the river, only about 650 yards from us, but too low for our guns on the hills to reach it; we expect them to attempt to launch it tonight and cross over a body of troops to this side. If they attempt it we must prevent them if possible, otherwise we shall be compelled to burn our baggage and fall back to a supporting force which is a good way off, so you see, under such circumstances, it would be considered an exhibition of the "white feather" to ask for leave of absence, and I must defer it until matters are more settled.

I would write you more details now but that confounded pontoon bridge is on my mind so much that I can hardly think of anything else, besides I have very slender hope that this will ever reach you and therefore feel very little like spending much time in writing, possibly for the amusement of some Johnnie who may get this. If you should get it though, let me again impress you with the fact that probably for the next three months our mail communication may be very much interrupted and you may hear from me but seldom and you must not, therefore, feel disappointed because you don't hear from me regularly as before.

Commending you to the same Providence that has protected me in my rough pathway, and hoping that a *restored union,* in a double sense, may soon dawn upon us. . . .

YOUR HUSBAND.

14

Thomas Wentworth Higginson was a New England clergyman who had been active in abolitionist circles. His convictions were put to an acid test when he was offered the command of a Negro regiment, the First South Carolina Volunteers. No wild-eyed dreamer, Higginson accepted the command and found much to praise, as well as to deplore, among the troops he led:[14]

Their courage I had before seen tested; their docile and lovable qualities I had known; and the only real surprise that experience brought me was in finding them so little demoralized. I had not allowed for the extreme remoteness and seclusion of their lives, especially among the Sea Islands. Many of them had literally spent their whole existence on some lonely island or remote plantation, where the master never came, and the overseer only once or twice a week. With these exceptions, such persons had never seen a white face, and of the excitements or sins of large communities they had not a conception. My friend Colonel Hallowell, of the Fifty-Fourth Massachusetts, told me that he had among his men some of the worst reprobates of Northern cities. While I had some men who were unprincipled and troublesome, there was not one whom I could call a hardened villain. I was constantly expecting to find male Topsies, with no notions of good and plenty of evil. But I never found one. Among the most ignorant there was very often a childlike absence of vices, which was rather to be classed as inexperience than as innocence, but which had some of the advantages of both.

Apart from this, they were very much like other men. General Saxton, examining with

some impatience a long list of questions from some philanthropic Commission at the North, respecting the traits and habits of the freedmen, bade some staff-officer answer them all in two words,—"Intensely human." We all admitted that it was a striking and comprehensive description.

For instance, as to courage. So far as I have seen, the mass of men are naturally courageous up to a certain point. A man seldom runs away from danger which he ought to face, unless others run; and each is apt to keep with the mass, and colored soldiers have more than usual of this gregariousness. In almost every regiment, black or white, there are a score or two of men who are naturally daring, who really hunger after dangerous adventures, and are happiest when allowed to seek them. Every commander gradually finds out who these men are, and habitually uses them; certainly I had such, and I remember with delight their bearing, their coolness and their dash. Some of them were negroes, some mulattoes. One of them would have passed for white, with brown hair and blue eyes, while others were so black you could hardly see their features. These picked men varied in other respects too; some were neat and well-drilled soldiers, while others were slovenly, heedless fellows— the despair of their officers at inspection, their pride on a raid. They were the natural scouts and rangers of the regiments; they had the two-o'clock-in-the-morning courage, which Napoleon thought so rare. The mass of the regiment rose to the same level under excitement, and were more excitable, I think, than whites, but neither more or less courageous. . . .

I often asked myself why it was that, with the capacity of daring and endurance, they had not kept the land in a perpetual flame of insurrection; why, especially since the opening of the war, they had kept so still. The answer was to be found in the peculiar temperament of the races, in their religious faith, and in the habit of patience that centuries had fortified. The shrewder men all said substantially the same thing. What

---

[14] Thomas W. Higginson, *Army Life in a Black Regiment* (New York, 1870), pp. 263–267.

was the use of insurrection, where everything was against them? They had no knowledge, no money, no arms, no drill, no organization,—above all, no mutual confidence. It was the tradition among them that all insurrections were always betrayed by somebody. They had no mountain passes to defend like the Maroons of Jamaica,—no impenetrable swamps, like the Maroons of Surinam. Where they had these, even on a small scale, they had used them—as in certain swamps round Savannah and in the everglades of Florida, where they united with the Indians, and would stand fire—so I was told by General Saxton, who had fought them there—when the Indians would retreat.

It always seemed to me that, had I been a slave, my life would have been one long scheme of insurrection. But I learned to respect the patient self-control of those who had waited till the course of events should open a better way. When it came they accepted it. Insurrection on their part would at once have divided the Northern sentiment; and a large part of our army would have joined with the Southern army to hunt them down. By their waiting till we needed them, their freedom was secured.

Two things chiefly surprised me in their feeling toward their former masters,—the absence of affection and the absence of revenge. I expected to find a great deal of the patriarchal feeling. It always seemed to me a very ill-applied emotion, as connected with the facts and laws of American slavery, —still I expected to find it. I suppose that my men and their families and visitors may have had as much of it as the mass of freed slaves; but certainly they had not a particle. I never could cajole one of them, in his most discontented moments, into regretting "ole mas'r time" for a single instant. I never heard one speak of the masters except as natural enemies. Yet they were perfectly discriminating as to individuals; many of them claimed to have had kind owners, and some expressed great gratitude to them for particular favors received. It was not the

individuals, but the ownership, of which they complained. That they saw to be a wrong which no special kindnesses could right. On this, as on all points connected with slavery, they understood the matter as clearly as Garrison or Phillips; the wisest philosophy could teach them nothing as to that, nor could any false philosophy befog them. After all, personal experience is the best logician.

Certainly this indifference did not proceed from any want of personal affection, for they were the most affectionate people among whom I had ever lived. They attached themselves to every officer who deserved love, and to some who did not; and if they failed to show it to their masters, it proved the wrongfulness of the mastery. On the other hand, they rarely showed one gleam of revenge, and I shall never forget the self-control with which one of our best sergeants pointed out to me, at Jacksonville, the very place where one of his brothers had been hanged by the whites for leading a party of fugitive slaves. He spoke of it as a historic matter, without any bearing on the present issue.

But side by side with this faculty of patience, there was a certain tropical element in the men, a sort of fiery ectasy when aroused, which seemed to link them by blood with the French Turcos, and made them really resemble their natural enemies, the Celts, far more than the Anglo-Saxon temperament. To balance this there were great individual resources when alone,—a sort of Indian wiliness and subtlety of resource. Their gregariousness and love of drill made them more easy to keep in hand than white American troops, who rather like to straggle or go in little squads, looking out for themselves, without being bothered with officers. The blacks prefer organization.

The point of inferiority that I always feared, though I never had occasion to prove it, was that they might show less fibre, less tough and dogged resistance, than whites, during a prolonged trial,—a long, disastrous march, for instance, or the hopeless defence of a besieged town. I should not be afraid of their mutinying or running away, but of their dropping and dying. It might not turn out so; but I mention it for the sake of fairness, and to avoid overstating the merits of these troops. As to the simple general fact of courage and reliability I think no officer in our camp ever thought of there being any difference between black and white. And certainly the opinions of these officers, who for years risked their lives every moment on the fidelity of their men, were worth more than those of all the world beside.

No doubt there were reasons why this particular war was an especially favorable test of the colored soldiers. They had more to fight for than the whites. Besides the flag and the Union, they had home and wife and child. They fought with ropes round their necks, and when orders were issued that the officers of colored troops should be put to death on capture, they took a grim satisfaction. It helped their *esprit de corps* immensely. With us, at least, there was to be no play-soldier. Though they had begun with a slight feeling of inferiority to the white troops, this compliment substituted a peculiar sense of self-respect. And even when the new colored regiments began to arrive from the North my men still pointed out this difference,—that in case of ultimate defeat, the Northern troops, black or white, would go home, while the First South Carolina must fight it out or be re-enslaved.

15

While the war raged on land from the trans-Mississippi West to the shores of the Chesapeake, a second, and strategically critical, contest was being waged at sea. At the outset of the war, the Union had proclaimed a blockade of the Confederate coast. The resulting game of cat-and-mouse gave adventuresome masters like John Wilkinson a splendid opportunity to achieve wealth and fame. Wilkinson's ship, the Robert E. Lee, *ran the Union blockade some twenty-one times before it was captured:*[15]

[15] John Wilkinson, *The Narrative of a Blockade Runner* (New York, 1877), pp. 162–168.

The *Lee* continued to make her regular trips either to Nassau or Bermuda, as circumstances required, during the summer of 1863; carrying abroad cotton and naval stores, and bringing in "hardware," as munitions of war were then invoiced. Usually the time selected for sailing was during the "dark of the moon," but upon one occasion, a new pilot had been detailed for duty on board, who failed in many efforts to get the ship over the "rip," a shifting sand bar a mile or more inside the true bar. More than a week of valuable time had thus been lost, but the exigencies of the army being at that time more than usually urgent, I determined to run what appeared to be a very great risk.

The tide serving at ten o'clock, we succeeded in crossing the rip at that hour, and as we passed over New Inlet bar, the moon rose in a cloudless sky. It was a calm night too, and the regular beat of our paddles through the smooth water sounded to our ears ominously loud. As we closely skirted the shore, the blockading vessels were plainly visible to us, some at anchor, some them so near to us that we saw, or fancied we saw, with our night glasses, the men on watch on their forecastles; but as we were inside of them all, and invisible against the background of the land, we passed beyond them undiscovered. The roar of the surf breaking upon the beach, prevented the noise of our paddles from being heard. The *Lee*'s head was not pointed seaward, however, until we had run ten or twelve miles along the land so close to the breakers that we could almost have tossed a biscuit into them, and no vessel was to be seen in any direction.

Discovery of us by the fleet would probably have been fatal to us, but the risk was not really so great as it appeared; for, as I had been informed by a blockade-runner who had once been captured and released, being a British subject, the vigilance on board the blockading fleet was much relaxed during the moonlit nights. The vessels were sent to Beaufort to coal at these times.

My informant was an officer of the British Navy, and was the guest, for a few days after his capture, of Captain Patterson then commanding the blockading fleet off Cape Fear. Speaking of the arduous service, P. remarked to him, that he never undressed nor retired to bed, during the dark nights; but could enjoy those luxuries when the moon was shining. On this hint I acted.

It was about this time that I adopted an expedient which proved of great service on several occasions. A blockade-runner did not often pass through the fleet without receiving one or more shots, but these were always preceded by the flash of a calcium light, or by a blue light; and immediately followed by two rockets thrown in the direction of the blockade-runner. The signals were probably concerted each day for the ensuing night, as they appeared to be constantly changed; but the rockets were invariably sent up. I ordered a lot of rockets from New York. Whenever all hands were called to run through the fleet, an officer was stationed alongside of me on the bridge with the rockets. One or two minutes after our immediate pursuer had sent his rockets, I would direct ours to be discharged at a right angle to our course. The whole fleet would be misled, for even if the vessel which had discovered us were not deceived, the rest of the fleet would be baffled. . . .

We were ready to sail for Nassau on the 15th of August, 1863, and had on board, as usual, several passengers. . . .

We passed safely through the blockading fleet off the New Inlet Bar, receiving no damage from the few shots fired at us, and gained an offing from the coast of thirty miles by daylight. By this time our supply of English coal had been exhausted, and we were obliged to commence upon North Carolina coal of very inferior quality, and which smoked terribly. We commenced on this fuel a little after daylight. Very soon afterwards the vigilant lookout at the mast-head called out "Sail ho!" and in reply to the "where away" from the deck, sang out "Right astern, sir, and in chase."

The morning was very clear. Going to the mast-head I could just discern the royal of the chaser; and before I left there, say in half an hour, her top-gallant sail showed above the horizon. By this time the sun had risen in a cloudless sky. It was evident our pursuer would be alongside of us by mid-day at the rate we were then going. The first orders were given to throw overboard the deck-load of cotton and to make more steam. The latter proved to be more easily given than executed; the chief engineer reporting that it was impossible to make steam with the wretched stuff filled with slate and dirt. A moderate breeze from the north and east had been blowing ever since daylight and every stitch of canvas on board the square-rigged steamer in our wake was drawing.

We were steering east by south, and it was clear that the chaser's advantages could only be neutralized either by bringing the *Lee* gradually head to wind or edging away to bring the wind aft. The former course would be running toward the land, besides incurring the additional risk of being intercepted and captured by some of the inshore cruisers. I began to edge away, therefore, and in two or three hours enjoyed the satisfaction of seeing our pursuer clew up and furl his sails. The breeze was still blowing as fresh as in the morning, but we were now running directly away from it, and the cruiser was going literally as fast as the wind, causing the sails to be rather a hindrance than a help. But she was still gaining on us.

A happy inspiration occurred to me when the case seemed hopeless. Sending for the chief engineer I said "Mr. S., let us try cotton, saturated with spirits of turpentine." There were on board, as part of the deck-load, thirty or forty barrels of "spirits." In a very few moments, a bale of cotton was ripped open, a barrel tapped, and buckets full of the saturated material passed down into the fire-room. The result exceeded our expectations. The chief engineer, an excitable little Frenchman from Charleston, very soon made his appearance on the bridge, his eyes sparkling with triumph, and reported a full head of steam. Curious to see the effect upon our speed, I directed him to wait until the log was hove. I threw it myself, nine and a half knots. "Let her go now sir!" I said. Five minutes afterwards, I hove the log again, *thirteen and a quarter*. We now began to hold our own, and even to gain a little upon the chaser; but she was fearfully near, and I began to have visions of another residence at Fort Warren, as I saw the "big bone in the mouth" of our pertinacious friend, for she was near enough us at one time for us to see distinctly the white curl of foam under her bows, called by that name among seamen. I wonder if they could have screwed another turn of speed out of her if they had known that the *Lee* had on board, in addition to her cargo of cotton, a large amount of gold shipped by the Confederate Government?

There continued to be a very slight change in our relative positions till about six o'clock in the afternoon, when the chief engineer again made his appearance, with a very ominous expression of countenance. He came to report that the burnt cotton had choked the flues, and that the steam was running down. "Only keep her going till dark, sir," I replied, "and we will give our pursuer the slip yet." A heavy bank was lying along the horizon to the south and east; and I saw a possible means of escape.

At sunset the chaser was about four miles astern and gaining upon us. Calling two of my most reliable officers, I stationed one of them on each wheel-house, with glasses, directing them to let me know the instant they lost sight of the chaser in the growing darkness. At the same time, I ordered the chief engineer to make as black a smoke as possible, and to be in readiness to cut off the smoke by closing the dampers instantly, when ordered. The twilight was soon succeeded by darkness. Both of the officers on the wheel house called out at the same moment, "We have lost sight of her," while a dense column of smoke was streaming far

in our wake. "Close the dampers," I called out through the speaking tube, and at the same moment ordered the helm "hard a starboard." Our course was altered eight points, at a right angle to the previous one. I remained on deck an hour, and then retired to my state-room with a comfortable sense of security.

WAR ECHOES

16

Many Civil War soldiers achieved fame and glory; many others suffered only pain and death. A few earned dishonor. A cryptic record of the dishonor comes from the diary of General Marsena R. Patrick. Patrick was the provost marshal general of the Army of the Potomac—its chief of police—and the incident described here took place while the Union army was lying in the trenches before Petersburg, Virginia, in the final year of the war:[16]

Friday Night, 24 June. . . .
Tonight I am sending off an expedition to get another man, who has been raping—
Saturday Night, 9'30", 25' June, '64. . . .
I have had a Mrs. Stiles here, who identified a man named Gordon, of the 72' New York, as the man who had committed the outrage upon her person last Saturday—He will be tried tomorrow. . . .
Sunday Night 26' June. . . .
A Court Martial has been in Session all day, trying the Rape Case on the person of Mrs. Stiles—Tonight we have caught the other culprit & he will be tried tomorrow. . . .
Tuesday, 28' June. . . .
We had on Sunday & yesterday a Court Martial in Session in my Office Tent, for the trial of two men who had committed a crime upon the body of a Mrs. Stiles living near Prince George's Court House. There seemed to be no clew to the perpetrators, at first, but the leader could not keep away from the Spot, after the crime, & was the *first* to speak of it as an outrage, before *any* other

---

[16] Diary of Marsena R. Patrick, Manuscripts Division, Library of Congress.

person knew of it—He was arrested & to make his own story good, he had to tell of his comrade—They were identified by the woman & her cousin & both have been tried; with what results is not yet known—The woman feels terribly and has been here to see me. . . .

Wednesday Night, 13' July. . . .

The day has been hot and dusty so that I did not go, as I thought of doing, to see Mrs. Stiles & read to her the Sentence of the Court, that Gordon & Geary be hanged on Friday. There is some feeling expressed by some of the Troops in regard to the Sentence. . . .

Thursday Night 14' July. . . .

Slept well & rose in tolerably good season —Breakfast late—That over & morning matters disposed of, I took Chaplain Rammell with me & started off over to see Mrs. Stiles & the Robertson family—I read the Order to her & Rammell had quite a long conversation with her—At their request we had prayers & then left—The Chaplain came back, perfectly satisfied of the truth of her Statement—He & a Catholic priest have both been very anxious & diligent in behalf of their two patients—Arrangements have been made for their execution near the Waggon Camp, as being a public place and also near the Teamsters, who, to a large extent, are the persons committing these outrages. . . .

Friday 15' July, 9 P.M. . . .

Up in good season & found work enough to be done until it was about time to move to the place of Execution—Was there by 9 o'clock & the Cavalry holding the ground— The 68'[N.Y.] & 114' [Penn.] soon came into position & then the Guard, with the condemned in a Waggon, with their Ministers— They mounted the Scaffold & there I read the Order of the Court & Sentence—The Clergy talked with them a few moments & at their request, Rammel Said for them, that they died hoping for mercy thro' Jesus Christ & acknowledging the justice of the sentence about to be executed—Rammell made a short prayer & both clergymen took leave of the condemned & left the Scaffold—The

feet were tied, the eyes bandaged, the ropes adjusted, the tap upon the drum & the drop fell! Scarcely a convulsion, both being killed instantly—They hung, perhaps, 5 minutes, when I remounted the Scaffold & said such words of warning, of reproof & of correction as seemed proper in the presence of Such a Mass of life as stood before & around me, with the dead hanging beneath my feet— My words will not soon be forgotten by those who stood before me—Leaving the Scaffold I turned over the whole to Col. Collis, who afterwards had them cut down, put in their boxes & sent down to me, to City Point, where I had ridden from the place of execution, with Col. Gates—Arrangements were made, by me, to have them embalmed tonight & sent off with the Brother, Geary, by the morning Boat.

17

Carl Schurz, a German-born politician who had come to the United States after the failure of the 1848 revolts, was a general in the Union army, by 1863 commanding the XI Corps at Gettysburg:[17]

To look after the wounded of my command, I visited the places where the surgeons were at work. At Bull Run, I had seen only on a very small scale what I was now to behold. At Gettysburg the wounded—many thousands of them—were carried to the farmsteads behind our lines. The houses, the barns, the sheds, and the open barnyards were crowded with the moaning and wailing human beings, and still an unceasing procession of stretchers and ambulances was coming in from all sides to augment the number of the sufferers. A heavy rain set in during the day—the usual rain after a battle— and large numbers had to remain unprotected in the open, there being no room left under roof. I saw long rows of men lying under the eaves of the buildings, the water pouring down upon their bodies in streams. Most of

---

[17] F. Bancroft and W. A. Dunning, *The Reminiscences of Carl Schurz, with a Sketch of his Life and Public Services from 1869 to 1906* (New York, 1908), III, 38–40.

the operating tables were placed in the open where the light was best, some of them partially protected against the rain by tarpaulins or blankets stretched upon poles.

There stood the surgeons, their sleeves rolled up to the elbows, their bare arms as well as their linen aprons smeared with blood, their knives not seldom held between their teeth, while they were helping a patient on or off the table, or had their hands otherwise occupied; around them pools of blood and amputated arms or legs in heaps, sometimes more than man-high. Antiseptic methods were still unknown at that time. As a wounded man was lifted on the table, often shrieking with pain as the attendants handled him, the surgeon quickly examined the wound and resolved upon cutting off the injured limb. Some ether was administered and the body put in position in a moment. The surgeon snatched his knife from between his teeth, where it had been while his hands were busy, wiped it rapidly once or twice across his blood-stained apron, and the cutting began. The operation accomplished, the surgeon would look around with a deep sigh, and then—"Next!"

And so it went on, hour after hour, while the number of expectant patients seemed hardly to diminish. Now and then one of the wounded men would call attention to the fact that his neighbor lying on the ground had given up the ghost while waiting for his turn, and the dead body was then quietly removed. Or a surgeon, having been long at work, would put down his knife, exclaiming that his hand had grown unsteady, and that this was too much for human endurance —not seldom hysterical tears streaming down his face. Many of the wounded men suffered with silent fortitude, fierce determination in the knitting of their brows and the steady gaze of their bloodshot eyes. Some would even force themselves to a grim jest about their situation or about the "skedaddling of the rebels." But there were, too, heart-rending groans and shrill cries of pain piercing the air, and despairing exclamations, "Oh, Lord! Oh, Lord;" or "Let me die!" or softer

murmurings in which the words "mother" or "father" or "home" were often heard.

I saw many of my command among the sufferers, whose faces I well remembered, and who greeted me with a look or even a painful smile of recognition, and usually with the question what I thought of their chances of life, or whether I could do anything for them, sometimes, also, whether I thought the enemy were well beaten. I was sadly conscious that many of the words of cheer and encouragement I gave them were mere hollow sounds, but they might be at least some solace for the moment.

18

Far from the scenes of mass murder, the war made itself felt in a thousand little ways. Emma Le Conte, the seventeen-year-old daughter of a chemistry professor at South Carolina College in Columbia, kept a diary in which she records her impressions of the southern home front:[18]

JANUARY 23RD [1865]. No more news from Father. I begin to think he has stayed to get the negroes out. We hear so many rumors of the movements of the Yankees and of our own troops, but they are not worth noting. Mother has packed up the clothing and bed-linen that we may save those at least. All the books are packed, too. I have not been in the library since they were taken down. It would make me too sad to look at the empty shelves.

It may be of interest some day to recall the poor style in which we lived during the war, so I shall make a few notes. My underclothing is of coarse unbleached homespun, such as we gave the negroes formerly, only much coarser. My stockings I knit myself, and my shoes are of heavy calfskin. My dresses are two calicoes (the last one bought cost sixteen dollars a yard), a homespun of black and white plaid, and an old delaine of prewar times that hangs on in a dilapidated condition, a reminiscence of better days. We have

---

[18] Earl S. Miers (ed.), *When the World Ended, the Diary of Emma LeConte* (New York, 1957), pp. 16–17. Reprinted with the permission of the publishers, the Oxford University Press.

a couple of old silks, carefully preserved for great occasions and which do not look shabby for the simple reason that all the other old silks that still survive the war are in the same state of decay. The homespun cost about eight or ten dollars a yard—calico is twenty to thirty dollars a yard now, and going higher from week to week. My shoes are one hundred and fifty dollars a pair. In two or three months these prices will be doubled.

We live tolerably poorly. Two meals a day. Two plates of bread for breakfast, one of wheat flour as five bags of flour were recently made a present to us else we would only have corn bread. Corn itself is forty dollars a bushel. Dinner consists of a very small piece of meat, generally beef, a few potatoes and a dish of hominy and a pone of corn bread. We have no reason to complain, so many families are so much worse off. Many have not tasted meat for months, and we, too, having a cow, are able to have butter. Wood is hard to get at one hundred dollars a load. We keep but one fire in the dining room where we sit. We have been fortunate in having gas thus far (at eighty dollars a thousand), but since the freshet, the supply of rosin has been deficient and now and then it is cut off and we burn tallow candles at two dollars apiece. We never have sweet things now, and even molasses candy is a rarity seldom to be thought of.

19

The notorious Andersonville prison camp was to produce one of the horror stories of American Civil War history. Nearly as bad, and with much less excuse, was the Union prison camp at Point Lookout, Maryland. Situated on the promontory between the Potomac River and the Chesapeake Bay, it was on low and swampy land. Luther Hopkins, a Virginia boy captured while riding with Jeb Stuart, describes it:[19]

The steamer on which we were placed and given such a good, substantial dinner,

---

[19] Luther W. Hopkins, *From Bull Run to Appomattox, a Boy's View* (Baltimore, 1908), pp. 169–180.

soon after this took its departure down the James and landed us at Fortress Monroe. . . . After remaining there a few days the Confederates were again marched aboard a steamer and taken to "Point Lookout," where a regular prison-camp had been established. I think there were about 15,000 prisoners at this camp guarded by Negro troops, which made our Southern blood boil. As the darkies used to say, "The bottom rail had got on top."

The camp was on a point of land formed by the junction of the Potomac river and Chesapeake Bay on the north side of the river. I imagine there were about 20 acres of ground, surrounded by a high board fence, probably about 14 feet high. Just below the top was built a platform about three feet wide, and on this platform the guards walked to and fro with their guns on their shoulders. From their position they could overlook the whole camp, as the ground was perfectly level. There was also a strong guard inside the camp, while artillery and regiments of infantry were stationed near the camp to guard it from outside attack, and one or more gunboats patrolled the waters that nearly surrounded the camp.

Notwithstanding this precaution, occasionally prisoners made their escape. One ingenious method that baffled our guards for a long time was the following:

The prisoners were allowed to go outside of the enclosure on the beach to bathe. And if an empty barrel or box happened to be floating on the water, a prisoner in bathing would watch his opportunity, slip his head under the barrel or box, and then as the tide drifted up the river, would follow it, keeping as near the shore as necessary until he got beyond the reach of the guard, and then take to the woods.

The punishment for trying to escape was cruel. Those who were caught at it were strung up to a pole by the thumbs, with the tips of their toes just touching the ground. Sometimes men would faint, and had to be cut down.

Upon the whole, prison life was very monotonous. It was such an unhealthy camp that the prisoners considered that they had a better chance for their lives fighting in the army.

The water was brackish and unpleasant to the taste. The only water we had was from pumps scattered about over the camps, and during the four months that I was there the pumps were always surrounded by a thirsty crowd of from 40 to 50 prisoners, each with his tin cup, trying to wedge his way in, that he might quench his thirst.

The food, while good, was very scant. Breakfast consisted of coffee and a loaf of bread, the latter under ordinary circumstances, with vegetables and other food, would probably suffice for two meals. This loaf was given us at breakfast, and if we ate it all then we went without bread for dinner. If there was any left over we took it to our tents, laid it on the ground, and saved it for the next meal.

The dinners consisted of a tin cup of soup (generally bean or other vegetable), a small piece of meat on a tin plate, on which a little vinegar was poured to prevent scurvy. My recollection is we had no other meal, but my mind is not perfectly clear on this point. I do know, however, that we were always hungry, and the chief topic of conversation was the sumptuous meals we had sat down to in other days. . . .

We were told that the short rations were given us in retaliation for the scanty food supplied to their soldiers in Southern prisons.

The hospitals were crowded all the time, and there were many sick in the camp waiting their opportunity to go into hospitals.

We lived in what is known as Sibley tents, shaped like a bell, with an opening in the top about 15 inches in diameter.

There were 12 men to a tent, who, when they slept, arranged themselves in a circle, like the spokes of a wagon, with their feet toward the center. These tents were as close as they could stand on the ground, with wide avenues between every two rows of tents, thus allowing every tent to front on an avenue.

Every day the prisoners were called out of their tents and formed in line; roll was called and the prisoners searched. And while they were being searched, the guards were searching the tents. For just what purpose this search was done I do not know, unless it was for fear that arms might be smuggled in to be used by the prisoners for making their escape.

Many of the prisoners had a peculiar affection of the eyes, caused, perhaps, by the glare from the white tents, the sand, and the reflection from the water. There was nothing green to be seen anywhere, consequently many of the prisoners became blind for a portion of the 24 hours. Just as the sun was sinking behind the fence they would become totally blind, and had to be led by someone. As morning light came the blindness would disappear.

Some of the prisoners who were mechanics or artisans got work outside, but I believe they got no pay except full rations and the privilege of bringing things into camp, such as blocks of wood and pieces of metal. Out of these were manufactured a great many interesting little articles—small steam locomotives, wooden fans, rings from rubber buttons set with gold and silver, and sometimes gems. One ingenious fellow built a small distillery and made whiskey from potato rinds or whatever refuse he could pick up, and got drunk on the product.

All about the camp were boards on which these manufactured articles were exposed for sale. A cracker would buy a chew of tobacco. The tobacco was cut up into chews and half chews. The crackers were brought in by the men who went out to work. I cannot recall all the curious things that were exposed for sale within the camp. . . .

The nurses were all men, chosen from among the prisoners. I never saw a woman the whole time I was in prison.

The hospitals were long tents, each holding about 30 cots. As soon as a patient died, he was taken out to the dead-house, the sheets changed, and another brought in.

When I was first taken there I remarked to my neighbor that I did not think that was very prudent (meaning the placing of a new patient at once on a bed that was still warm from the body that had just been removed). He replied that the bed that I was on had been occupied by a smallpox patient and I was put on it a few minutes after the patient was taken out.

However, there was a separate hospital for contagious diseases, and the patient had been removed as soon as the disease developed.

Most of those who went into the hospital died. The dead were all carried at once to the dead-house on stretchers, and once a day a two-horse wagon came in, and their bodies were laid in it like so much cord wood, uncoffined, taken out and buried in long trenches. The trenches were seven feet wide and three feet deep, and the bodies were laid across the trench side by side and covered with earth.

I had been in prison about four months when news came that the two Governments had agreed upon an exchange of prisoners; it only included the sick in the hospitals. Of course, every patient in the hospital was on the anxious bench, wondering whether he would be included among the fortunate ones. Some days afterwards a corps of physicians came to the hospital tents to examine the different patients who lay on the cots, taking the name of one and leaving another. I happened to be among those who were selected for exchange. The object seemed to be to take only those who were not liable to be fit for service soon.

THE GREATER CONFLICT

20

Despite the North's faith in democracy and Lincoln's unflagging zeal, military victories were dismally few during the first years of fighting. To make matters far worse, most of Europe openly sided with the Confederacy. This was especially the case with England, where upper-class industrialists, hungry for tariff-free southern markets, favored immediate recognition of the rebellious government. Liberals and workers in England were less sure; they were inclined to favor any revolutionary struggle for democratic

freedom and hesitated to support a slave power. Lincoln realized he could swing the English masses to the North only by going on record as an avowed opponent of slavery. Yet he was aware that this move would alienate the border states and perhaps be taken by foreign diplomats as a sign of weakness. Hence he resolved to use emancipation as a tool rather than an ideal, freeing the slaves only when the step would do the most good. His attitude was explained in a letter to Horace Greeley, editor of the New York Tribune, *in reply to an editorial in 1861 favoring immediate abolition:*[20]

Hon. Horace Greeley:

DEAR SIR: I have just read yours of the nineteenth, addressed to myself through the New-York *Tribune.* If there be in it any statements or assumptions of fact which I may know to be erroneous, I do not now and here controvert them. If there be in it any inferences which I may believe to be falsely drawn, I do not now and here argue against them. If there be perceptible in it an impatient and dictatorial tone, I waive it in deference to an old friend, whose heart I have always supposed to be right.

As to the policy I "seem to be pursuing," as you say, I have not meant to leave any one in doubt.

I would save the Union. I would save it the shortest way under the Constitution. The sooner the National authority can be restored, the nearer the Union will be "the Union as it was." If there be those who would not save the Union unless they could at the same time *save* Slavery, I do not agree with them. If there be those who would not save the Union unless they could at the same time *destroy* Slavery, I do not agree with them. My paramount object in this struggle *is* to save the Union, and is *not* either to save or destroy Slavery. If I could save the Union without freeing *any* slave, I would do it; and if I could save it by freeing *all* the slaves, I would do it; and if I could do it by freeing some and leaving others alone, I would also do that. What I do about Slavery and the

[20] Frank Moore (ed.), *The Rebellion Record: A Diary of American Events* (New York, 1861–1869), XII, 482–483.

colored race, I do because I believe it helps to save this Union; and what I forbear, I forbear because I do *not* believe it would help to save the Union. I shall do *less* whenever I shall believe what I am doing hurts the cause, and I shall do *more* whenever I shall believe doing more will help the cause. I shall try to correct errors when shown to be errors; and I shall adopt new views so fast as they shall appear to be true views. I have here stated my purpose according to my view of *official* duty, and I intend no modification of my oft-expressed *personal* wish that all men, everywhere, could be free.

Yours,

A. LINCOLN

21

By the fall of 1862, the President knew that the time to act had arrived. England was dangerously close to recognizing the Confederacy; France would go further, favoring international intervention. A decisive northern victory at the battle of Antietam stifled suspicion that emancipation was a defeatist gesture. On September 22, 1862, Lincoln issued the Preliminary Emancipation Proclamation:[21]

I, Abraham Lincoln, President of the United States of America and Commander in Chief of the Army and Navy thereof, do hereby proclaim and declare that hereafter, as heretofore, the war will be prosecuted for the object of practically restoring the constitutional relation between the United States and each of the States and the people thereof in which States that relation is or may be suspended or disturbed.

That it is my purpose, upon the next meeting of Congress, to again recommend the adoption of a practical measure tendering pecuniary aid to the free acceptance or rejection of all slave States, so called, the people whereof may not then be in rebellion against the United States, and which States may then have voluntarily adopted, or thereafter may voluntarily adopt, immediate or gradual abolishment of slavery within their

respective limits; and that the effort to colonize persons of African descent with their consent upon this continent or elsewhere, with the previously obtained consent of the governments existing there, will be continued.

That on the 1st day of January, A.D. 1863, all persons held as slaves within any State or designated part of a State the people whereof shall then be in rebellion against the United States shall be then, thenceforward, and forever free; and the executive government of the United States, including the military and naval authority thereof, will recognize and maintain the freedom of such persons and will do no act or acts to repress such persons, or any of them, in any efforts they may make for their actual freedom.

That the Executive will on the 1st day of January aforesaid, by proclamation, designate the States and parts of States, if any, in which the people thereof, respectively, shall then be in rebellion against the United States; and the fact that any State or the people thereof shall on that day be in good faith represented in the Congress of the United States by members chosen thereto at elections wherein a majority of the qualified voters of such State shall have participated shall, in the absence of strong countervailing testimony, be deemed conclusive evidence that such State and the people thereof are not then in rebellion against the United States.

22

Too often overlooked in assessing Lincoln's role in emancipation is his essential conservatism. Nearly three months after the issuance of the preliminary Emancipation Proclamation, Lincoln, in his annual message to Congress, attempted to persuade his listeners of the wisdom of a series of amendments to the Constitution which would have brought freedom to the slaves over a thirty-seven year period, and which would have sought to colonize the freedmen outside the United States. It was in support of these measures that Lincoln wrote some of the most moving prose ever to appear in an American state paper:[22]

---

[21] James D. Richardson (comp.), *A Compilation of the Messages and Papers of the Presidents, 1789–1897* (Washington, 1897), VI, 96–97.

[22] *Ibid.*, VI, 126–142, *passim*.

Among the friends of the Union there is great diversity, of sentiment, and of policy, in regard to slavery, and the African race amongst us. Some would perpetuate slavery; some would abolish it suddenly, and without compensation; some would abolish it gradually, and with compensation; some would remove the freed people from us, and some would retain them with us; and there are yet other minor diversities. Because of these diversities, we waste much strength in struggles among ourselves. By mutual concession we should harmonize, and act together. This would be compromise; but it would be compromise among the friends, and not with the enemies of the Union. These articles are intended to embody a plan of such mutual concessions. If the plan shall be adopted, it is assumed that emancipation will follow, at least, in several of the States.

As to the first article, the main points are: first, the emancipation; secondly, the length of time for consummating it—thirty-seven years; and thirdly, the compensation.

The emancipation will be unsatisfactory to the advocates of perpetual slavery; but the length of time should greatly mitigate their dissatisfaction. The time spares both races from the evils of sudden derangement—in fact, from the necessity of any derangement —while most of those whose habitual course of thought will be disturbed by the measure will have passed away before its consummation. They will never see it. Another class will hail the prospect of emancipation, but will deprecate the length of time. They will feel that it gives too little to the now living slaves. But it really gives them much. It saves them from the vagrant destitution which must largely attend immediate emancipation in localities where their numbers are very great; and it gives the inspiring assurance that their posterity shall be free forever. The plan leaves to each State, choosing to act under it, to abolish slavery now, or at the end of the century, or at any intermediate time, or by degrees, extending over the whole or any part of the period; and it obliges no two states to proceed alike. It also provides for compensation, and generally the mode of making it. This, it would seem, must further mitigate the dissatisfaction of those who favor perpetual slavery, and especially of those who are to receive the compensation. Doubtless some of those who are to pay, and not to receive will object. Yet the measure is both just and economical. In a certain sense the liberation of slaves is the destruction of property—property acquired by descent, or by purchase, the same as any other property. It is no less true for having been often said, that the people of the south are not more responsible for the original introduction of this property, than are the people of the north; and when it is remembered how unhesitatingly we all use cotton and sugar, and share the profits of dealing in them, it may not be quite safe to say, that the south has been more responsible than the north for its continuance. If then, for a common object, this property is to be sacrificed is it not just that it be done at a common charge? . . .

The third article relates to the future of the freed people. It does not oblige, but merely authorizes, Congress to aid in colonizing such as may consent. This ought not to be regarded as objectionable, on the one hand, or on the other, in so much as it comes to nothing, unless by the mutual consent of the people to be deported, and the American voters, through their representatives in Congress.

I cannot make it better known than it already is, that I strongly favor colonization. And yet I wish to say there is an objection urged against free colored persons remaining in this country, which is largely imaginary, if not sometimes malicious.

It is insisted that their presence would injure, and displace white labor and white laborers. If there ever could be a proper time for mere catch arguments, that time surely is not now. In times like the present, men should utter nothing for which they would not willingly be responsible through time and in eternity. Is it true, then, that colored people can displace any more white labor, by being free, than by remaining slaves? If they stay in their old places, they jostle no white laborers; if they leave their old places, they leave them open to white laborers. Logically, there is neither more nor less of it. Emancipation, even without deportation, would probably enhance the wages of white labor, and, very surely, would not reduce them. Thus, the customary amount of labor would still have to be performed; the freed people would surely not do more than their old proportion of it, and very probably, for a time, would do less, leaving an increased part to white laborers, bringing their labor into greater demand, and, consequently, enhancing the wages of it. With deportation, even to a limited extent, enhanced wages to white labor is mathematically certain. Labor is like any other commodity in the market—increase the demand for it, and you increase the price of it. Reduce the supply of black labor, by colonizing the black laborer out of the country, and, by precisely so much, you increase the demand for, and wages of, white labor.

Is it doubted, then, that the plan I propose, if adopted, would shorten the war, and thus lessen its expenditure of money and of blood? Is it doubted that it would restore the national authority and national prosperity, and perpetuate both indefinitely? Is it doubted that we here—Congress and Executive—can secure its adoption? Will not the good people respond to a united, and earnest appeal from us? Can we, can they, by any other means, so certainly, or so speedily, assure these vital objects? We can succeed only by concert. It is not "can any of us imagine better?" but "can we all do better?" Object whatsoever is possible, still the question recurs "can we do better?" The dogmas of the quiet past, are inadequate to the stormy present. The occasion is piled high with difficulty, and we must rise with the occasion. As our case is new, so we must think anew, and act anew. We must disenthrall our selves, and then we shall save our country.

Fellow-citizens, *we* cannot escape history.

We of this Congress and this administration, will be remembered in spite of ourselves. No personal significance, or insignificance, can spare one or another of us. The fiery trial through which we pass, will light us down, in honor or dishonor, to the latest generation. We *say* we are for the Union. The world will not forget that we say this. We know how to save the Union. The world knows we do know how to save it. We—even *we here*—hold the power, and bear the responsibility. In *giving* freedom to the *slave*, we *assure* freedom to the *free*—honorable alike in what we give, and what we preserve. We shall nobly save, or meanly lose, the last, best, hope of earth. Other means may succeed; this could not fail. The way is plain, peaceful, generous, just—a way which, if followed, the world will forever applaud, and God must forever bless.

December 1, 1862   ABRAHAM LINCOLN

23

Of the final outcome of the war there could be little doubt. The North had the man power, and the industrial might, and something else even more valuable. This was a boundless faith in democracy, a realization that the war was not simply a contest between slavery and freedom but a struggle to determine whether the American experiment in popular rule could survive. Here, indeed, was a cause worth striving for. Abraham Lincoln's finest contribution to victory was his undying belief in government of the people, by the people, and for the people. His repeated expressions of faith in democratic principles reached classic heights in his Gettysburg Address, delivered at the Pennsylvania battlefield November 19, 1863:[23]

Fourscore and seven years ago our fathers brought forth on this continent a new nation, conceived in liberty, and dedicated to the proposition that all men are created equal.

Now we are engaged in a great civil war, testing whether that nation, or any nation so conceived and so dedicated, can long en-

---

[23] John G. Nicolay and John Hay (eds.), *Complete Works of Abraham Lincoln* (New York, 1894), IX, 209–210.

dure. We are met on a great battlefield of that war. We have come to dedicate a portion of that field as a final resting-place for those who here gave their lives that that nation might live. It is altogether fitting and proper that we should do this.

But, in a larger sense, we cannot dedicate —we cannot consecrate—we cannot hallow— this ground. The brave men, living and dead, who struggled here, have consecrated it far above our poor power to add or detract. The world will little note nor long remember what we say here, but it can never forget what they did here. It is for us, the living, rather, to be dedicated here to the unfinished work which they who fought here have thus far so nobly advanced. It is rather for us to be here dedicated to the great task remaining before us—that from these honored dead we take increased devotion to that cause for which they gave the last full measure of devotion; that we here highly resolve that these dead shall not have died in vain; that this nation, under God, shall have a new birth of freedom; and that government of the people, by the people, for the people, shall not perish from the earth.

24

By the time Lincoln appeared on the steps of the Capitol to take the oath of office for the second time, it was obvious that the war was almost over. Unquestionably, Lincoln's greatness as a wartime leader lay in his refusal to permit extraneous matters to interfere with his primary objective—that of saving the Union. His greatness as a statesman surely came, in no small measure, from his ability to sense and express the deepest longings of plain people. The yearning for a just and generous peace, which Lincoln put into words on the occasion of his second inaugural, was deep in the hearts of a vast number of Americans, North and South:[24]

March 4, 1865

[FELLOW COUNTRYMEN:]

At this second appearing to take the oath of the presidential office, there is less occasion for an extended address than there was

---

[24] James D. Richardson (comp.), *A Compilation of the Messages and Papers of the Presidents, 1789–1897* (Washington, 1903), VI, 276–277.

at the first. Then a statement, somewhat in detail, of a course to be pursued, seemed fitting and proper. Now, at the expiration of four years, during which public declarations have been constantly called forth on every point and phase of the great contest which still absorbs the attention, and engrosses the enerergies [*sic*] of the nation, little that is new could be presented. The progress of our arms, upon which all else chiefly depends, is as well known to the public as to myself; and it is, I trust, reasonably satisfactory and encouraging to all. With high hope for the future, no prediction in regard to it is ventured.

On the occasion corresponding to this four years ago, all thoughts were anxiously directed to an impending civil-war. All dreaded it—all sought to avert it. While the inaugural address was being delivered from this place, devoted altogether to *saving* the Union without war, insurgent agents were in the city seeking to *destroy* it without war—seeking to dissol[v]e the Union, and divide effects, by negotiation. Both parties deprecated war; but one of them would *make* war rather than let the nation survive; and the other would *accept* war rather than let it perish. And the war came.

One eighth of the whole population were colored slaves, not distributed generally over the Union, but localized in the Southern part of it. These slaves constituted a peculiar and powerful interest. All knew that this interest was, somehow, the cause of the war. To strengthen, perpetuate, and extend this interest was the object for which the insurgents would rend the Union, even by war; while the government claimed no right to do more than to restrict the territorial enlargement of it. Neither party expected for the war, the magnitude, or the duration, which it has already attained. Neither anticipated that the *cause* of the conflict might cease with, or even before, the conflict itself should cease. Each looked for an easier triumph, and a result less fundamental and astounding. Both read the same Bible, and pray to the same God; and each invokes His aid against the

other. It may seem strange that any men
should dare to ask a just God's assistance
in wringing their bread from the sweat of
other men's faces; but let us judge not that
we be not judged. The prayers of both could
not be answered; that of neither has been
answered fully. The Almighty has His own
purposes. "Woe unto the world because of
offences! for it must needs be that offences
come; but woe to that man by whom the
offence cometh!" If we shall suppose that
American Slavery is one of those offences,
which, in the providence of God, must needs
come, but which, having continued through
His appointed time, He now wills to remove,
and that He gives to both North and South,
this terrible war, as the woe due to those by
whom the offence came, shall we discern
therein any departure from those divine attributes which the believers in a Living God
always ascribe to Him? Fondly do we hope
—fervently do we pray—that this mighty
scourge of war may speedily pass away. Yet,
if God wills that it continue, until all the
wealth piled by the bond-man's two hundred
and fifty years of unrequited toil shall be
sunk, and until every drop of blood drawn
with the lash, shall be paid by another drawn
with the sword, as was said three thousand
years ago, so still it must be said "the judgments of the Lord, are true and righteous
altogether."

With malice toward none; with charity
for all; with firmness in the right, as God
gives us to see the right, let us strive on to
finish the work we are in; to bind up the
nation's wounds; to care for him who shall
have borne the battle, and for his widow,
and his orphan—to all which may achieve
and cherish a just, and a lasting peace,
among ourselves, and with all nations.

THE FALLING CURTAIN

25

*One of the reasons General Robert E. Lee
has become a symbol of which all Americans
are proud is the manner in which he conducted
himself when the last battle had been fought*

*and he was forced to part company with the
men whom he had led for three years:*[25]

HEADQUARTERS, ARMY OF NORTHERN
VIRGINIA
April 10, 1865

After four years of arduous service,
marked by unsurpassed courage and fortitude, the Army of Northern Virginia has
been compelled to yield to overwhelming
numbers and resources. I need not tell the
survivors of so many hard-fought battles,
who have remained steadfast to the last, that
I have consented to this result from no distrust of them; but, feeling that valour and
devotion could accomplish nothing that
could compensate for the loss that would
have attended the continuation of the contest, I have determined to avoid the useless
sacrifice of those whose past services have
endeared them to their countrymen. By the
terms of the agreement, officers and men can
return to their homes and remain there until
exchanged. You will take with you the satisfaction that proceeds from the consciousness
of duty faithfully performed; and I earnestly
pray that a merciful God will extend to you
His blessing and protection. With an increasing admiration of your constancy and
devotion to your country, and a grateful
remembrance of your kind and generous
consideration of myself, I bid you an affectionate farewell.

R. E. LEE, General

26

*In after years, as the ranks of the Blue and
the Gray grew thin, many an old soldier sought
to establish for himself the significance of what
he had felt, thought, seen, and done during the
bitter years of the Civil War. Supreme Court
Justice Oliver Wendell Holmes, Jr., a thrice-
wounded veteran of that war, makes the attempt:*[26]

25 Robert E. Lee, *Recollections and Letters of
General Robert E. Lee* (New York, 1905), pp. 153–
154.
26 Oliver W. Holmes, Jr., "Dead, Yet Living,"
Memorial Day Address, Keene, New Hampshire,
May 30, 1884 (Boston, 1884), pp. 11–12.

But, nevertheless, the generation that carried on the war has been set apart by its experience. Through our great good fortune, in our youth our hearts were touched with fire. It was given us to learn at the outset that life is a profound and passionate thing. While we are permitted to scorn nothing but indifference, and do not pretend to undervalue the worldly rewards of ambition, we have seen with our own eyes beyond and above the gold fields, the snowy heights of honor, and it is for us to bear the report to those who come after us.

The Road to Reunion

Appomattox failed to bring peace to the United States. The guns were silenced, but, as in all wars, peace could not simply be declared; it had to be made. The times called for long-range plans and strong leadership. Instead, after Lincoln's death, lesser men sat in the White House, and the long-range plans of Radical Republicans in Congress proved more suggestive for a remote future than for the critical years that followed the war. Political support from the North for reform of the South dwindled in less than a decade. Adequate internal support for reform from southern farmers and workers did not materialize. Despite the promise shown by individual Negroes, the freedmen were not yet an emergent class with the dedication and leadership that was to mark the movement for higher status a century later. Nor were white reformers in the South disposed to make common cause with freedmen against the system of class and caste. Radical Republicans contributed a vital constitutional heritage; but the years between 1865 and 1876 were not truly years of reconstruction. Economic currents were, in fact, remaking society, North and South, and the politics of business contributed to the decline of the movement to extend an equality of rights.

THE UNRESOLVED CONFLICT

1

Thaddeus Stevens of Pennsylvania was a thorough-going radical. He believed that the Civil War had prepared the ground for a just and necessary revolution in the South. Opposed to all caste and aristocracy, Stevens was sincerely concerned with the welfare of the freedman. He felt that the mild reconstruction policy outlined by Lincoln would only delay the inevitable readjustment in the relations between the two races. He regarded military rule as necessary: the confiscation of plantation estates, the punishment of unreconstructed rebels, and the rehabilitation of unprotected freedmen required the supervision of federal troops. Stevens reveals his hatred of southern aristocracy in an address delivered at Lancaster, Pennsylvania, September 7, 1865:[1]

[1] Thaddeus Stevens, "Reconstruction." Printed by the Lancaster (Pa.) *Examiner and Herald,* 1865. In collection of speeches and documents bound by the New York Public Library, entitled *U. S. History, 1866–1908* (Ford Collection), pp. 2–6. (Pages not numbered consecutively.)

We hold it to be the duty of the Government to inflict condign punishment on the rebel belligerents, and so weaken their hands that they can never again endanger the Union; and so reform their municipal institutions as to make them republican in spirit as well as in name.

We especially insist that the property of the chief rebels should be seized and appropriated to the payment of the National debt, caused by the unjust and wicked war which they instigated.

How can such punishments be inflicted and such forfeitures produced without doing violence to established principles?

Two positions have been suggested.

1st—To treat those States as never having been out of the Union, because the Constitution forbids secession, and, therefore, a fact forbidden by law could not exist.

2nd—To accept the position in which they placed themselves as severed from the union; an independent government *de facto,* and an alien enemy to be dealt with according to the laws of war.

It seems to me that while we do not aver that the United States are bound to treat them as an alien enemy, yet they have a right to elect so to do if it be for the interest of the nation; and that the "Confederate States" are estopped from denying that position. . . . The Confederate States were for four years what they claimed to be, an alien enemy in all their rights and liabilities. To say that they were states under the protection of that constitution which they were assaulting with bloody defeats, simply because they became belligerents through crime, is making theory over-rule fact to an absurd degree. It will I suppose at least be conceded that the United States if not obliged so to do, have a right to treat them as an alien enemy now conquered, and subject to all the liabilities of a vanquished foe. . . .

All writers agree that the victor may inflict punishment upon the vanquished enemy even to the taking of his life, liberty, or the confiscation of all his property; but that this extreme right is never exercised, except upon a cruel, barbarous, obstinate, or dangerous foe who has waged an unjust war.

Upon the character of the belligerent, and the justice of the war, and the manner of conducting it, depends our right to take the lives, liberty, and property of the belligerent. This war had its origin in treason without one spark of justice. It was prosecuted before notice of it, by robbing our forts and armories, and our navy-yards; by stealing our money from the mints and depositories, and by surrendering our forts and navies by perjurers who had sworn to support the Constitution. In its progress our prisoners, by the authority of their government were slaughtered in cold blood. Ask Fort Pillow and Fort Wagner. Sixty thousand of our prisoners have been deliberately starved to death because they would not enlist in the rebel armies. The graves at Andersonville have each an accusing tongue. The purpose and avowed object of the enemy "to found an empire whose corner-stone should be slavery," render its perpetuity or revival dangerous to human liberty.

Surely, these things are sufficient to justify the exercise of the extreme rights of war—"to execute, to imprison, to confiscate." How many captive enemies it would be proper to execute, as an example to nations, I leave others to judge. I am not fond of sanguinary punishments, but surely some victims must propitiate the *manes* of our starved, murdered, slaughtered martyrs. A court martial could do justice according to law.

But we propose to confiscate all the estate of every rebel belligerent whose estate was worth $10,000, or whose land exceeded two hundred acres in quantity. Policy if not justice would require that the poor, the ignorant, and the coerced should be forgiven. They followed the example and teachings of their wealthy and intelligent neighbors. The rebellion would never have originated with them. Fortunately those who would thus escape form a large majority of the people though possessing but a small portion of the wealth. The proportion of those exempt compared with the punished would be I believe about nine tenths.

There are about six millions of freemen in the South. The number of acres of land is 465,000,000. Of this those who own above two hundred acres each, number about 70,000 persons, holding in the aggregate (together with the States) about 394,000,000 acres, leaving for all the others below 200 each about 71,000,000 of acres. By thus forfeiting the estates of the leading rebels, the Government would have 394,000,000 of acres beside their town property, and yet nine tenths of the people would remain untouched. Divide this land into convenient farms. Give if you please forty acres to each adult male freedman. Suppose there are one million of them. That would require 40,000-

000 of acres, which deducted from 394,000-
000 leaves three hundred and fifty-four
millions of acres for sale. Divide it into
suitable farms and sell it to the highest
bidders. I think it, including town property,
would average at least ten dollars per
acre. That would produce $3,540,000,000,—
Three billions, five hundred and forty millions of dollars.

Let that be applied as follows to wit:

1. Invest $300,000,000 in six per cent.
government bonds, and add the interest
semi-annually to the pensions of those who
have become entitled by this villanous war.

2. Appropriate $200,000,000 to pay the
damages done to loyal men North and
South by the rebellion.

3. Pay the residue being $3,040,000,000
towards the payment of the National debt.

What loyal man can object to this? Look
around you, and everywhere behold your
neighbors, some with an arm, some with a
leg, some with an eye carried away by rebel
bullets. Others horribly mutilated in every
form. And yet numerous others wearing
the weeds which mark the death of those
on whom they leaned for support. Contemplate these monuments of rebel perfidy, and
of patriotic suffering, and then say if too
much is asked for our valiant soldiers. . . .

The whole fabric of southern society
must be changed and never can it be done
if this opportunity is lost. Without this, this
Government can never be, as it never has
been, a true republic. Heretofore, it had
more the features of aristocracy than of
democracy.—The Southern States have
been despotisms, not governments of the
people. It is impossible that any practical
equality of rights can exist where a few
thousand men monopolize the whole landed
property. The larger the number of small
proprietors the more safe and stable the
government. As the landed interest must
govern, the more it is subdivided and held
by independent owners, the better. What
would be the condition of the State of New
York if it were not for her independent yeo-
manry? She would be overwhelmed and
demoralized by the Jews, Milesians and
vagabonds of licentious cities. How can republican institutions, free schools, free
churches, free social intercourse exist in a
mingled community of nabobs and serfs; of
the owners of twenty thousand acre manors
with lordly palaces, and the occupants of
narrow huts inhabited by "low white trash?"
—If the south is ever to be made a safe
republic let her lands be cultivated by the
toil of the owners or the free labor of intelligent citizens. This must be done even
though it drive her nobility into exile. If
they go, all the better.

It will be hard to persuade the owner of
ten thousand acres of land, who drives a
coach and four, that he is not degraded by
sitting at the same table, or in the same
pew, with the embrowned and hard-handed
farmer who has himself cultivated his own
thriving homestead of 150 acres. This sub-
division of the lands will yield ten bales of
cotton to one that is made now, and he
who produced it will own it and *feel himself a man.*

It is far easier and more beneficial to
exile 70,000 proud, bloated, and defiant
rebels, than to expatriate four millions of
laborers, native to the soil and loyal to the
Government. . . .

Let us forget all parties, and build on
the broad platform of "reconstructing the
Government out of the conquered territory, converted into new and free States,
and admitted into the Union by the sovereign power of Congress, with another
plank,"—THE PROPERTY OF THE REBELS SHALL
PAY OUR NATIONAL DEBT, *and indemnify
freed-men and loyal sufferers.*—and that
under no circumstances will we suffer the
National debt to be repudiated, or the
interest scaled below the contract rates; nor
permit any part of the rebel debt to be assumed by the nation.

Let all who approve of these principles
tarry with us. Let all others go with Cop-
perheads and rebels. Those will be the
opposing parties. Young men, this duty de-
volves on you. Would to God, if only for

that, I were still in the prime of life, that I might aid you to fight through this last and greatest battle of Freedom.

2

Had Abraham Lincoln lived, his great popularity and his remarkable political insight might have altered the plans of congressional Republicans. But Lincoln's assassination was a national tragedy. Andrew Johnson, the Tennessee Democrat who ascended to the presidency, had no love for the southern planter class, but he lacked Lincoln's faith in the future of the former slaves. He appealed neither to Republicans, who advocated immediate social equality for Negroes, nor to Democrats, who urged mildness in the treatment of southern whites. Moreover, he lacked both the humility and the political skill that made Lincoln a master of men. Taking advantage of the fact that Congress was not in session during the summer, President Johnson applied his Reconstruction Plan so successfully that by December 4, 1865, all the ex-slave states save Texas, Kentucky, and Delaware were ready to take their accustomed places in the Union. When Congressmen reassembled in December, they refused to seat the representatives of the southern states and began work on a reconstruction plan of their own. Their first step was an act of February 1866, extending the life of the wartime Freedmen's Bureau and at the same time authorizing the agency to use troops in protecting Negro rights. Johnson's veto reveals the gulf between Congress and the President:[2]

I have examined with care the bill, which originated in the Senate and has been passed by the two Houses of Congress, to amend an act entitled "An act to establish a bureau for the relief of freedmen and refugees," and for other purposes. Having with much regret come to the conclusion that it would not be consistent with the public welfare to give my approval to the measure, I return the bill to the Senate with my objections. . . .

I share with Congress the strongest desire to secure to the freedmen the full enjoyment of their freedom and property and their entire independence and equality in making contracts for their labor, but the bill before me contains provisions which in my opinion are not warranted by the Constitution and are not well suited to accomplish the end in view.

The bill proposes to establish by authority of Congress military jurisdiction over all parts of the United States containing refugees and freedmen. It would by its very nature apply with most force to those parts of the United States in which the freedmen most abound, and it expressly extends the existing temporary jurisdiction of the Freedmen's Bureau, with greatly enlarged powers, over those States "in which the ordinary course of judicial proceedings has been interrupted by the rebellion." The source from which this military jurisdiction is to emanate is none other than the President . . . acting through the War Department and the Commissioner of the Freedmen's Bureau. The agents to carry out this military jurisdiction are to be selected either from the Army or from civil life; the country is to be divided into districts and sub-districts, and the number of salaried agents to be employed may be equal to the number of counties or parishes in all the United States where freedmen and refugees are to be found.

The subjects over which this military jurisdiction is to extend in every part of the United States include protection to "all employees, agents, and officers of this bureau in the exercise of the duties imposed" upon them by the bill. In eleven States it is further to extend over all cases affecting freedmen and refugees discriminated against "by local law, custom, or prejudice." In those eleven States the bill subjects any white person who may be charged with depriving a freedman of "any civil rights or immunities belonging to white persons" to imprisonment or fine, or both, without, however, defining the "civil rights and immunities" which are thus to be secured to the freedmen by military law. This military jurisdiction also extends to all questions that may arise respecting contracts. The agent who is thus to exercise the office

[2] James D. Richardson (comp.), *A Compilation of the Messages and Papers of the Presidents, 1789–1897* (Washington, 1897, 1909; taken from the 1909 vol.), VI, 312.

of a military judge may be a stranger, entirely ignorant of the laws of the place, and exposed to the errors of judgment to which all men are liable. The exercise of power over which there is no legal supervision by so vast a number of agents as is contemplated by the bill must, by the very nature of man, be attended by acts of caprice, injustice, and passion.

The trials having their origin under this bill are to take place without the intervention of a jury and without any fixed rules of law or evidence. The rules on which offenses are to be "heard and determined" by the numerous agents are such rules and regulations as the President, through the War Department, shall prescribe. No previous presentment is required nor any indictment charging the commission of a crime against the laws; but the trial must proceed on charges and specifications. The punishment will be, not what the law declares, but such as a court-martial may think proper; and from these arbitrary tribunals there lies no appeal, no writ of error to any of the courts in which the Constitution . . . vests exclusively the judicial power of the country.

While the territory and the classes of actions and offenses that are made subject to this measure are so extensive, the bill itself, should it become a law, will have no limitation in point of time, but will form a part of the permanent legislation of the country. I can not reconcile a system of military jurisdiction of this kind with the words of the Constitution which declare that "no person shall be held to answer for a capital or otherwise infamous crime unless on a presentment or indictment of a grand jury, except in cases arising in the land or naval forces, or in the militia when in actual service in time of war or public danger," and that "in all criminal prosecutions the accused shall enjoy the right to a speedy and public trial by an impartial jury of the State and district wherein the crime shall have been committed." The safeguards which the experience and wisdom of ages

taught our fathers to establish as securities for the protection of the innocent, the punishment of the guilty, and the equal administration of justice are to be set aside, and for the sake of a more vigorous interposition in behalf of justice we are to take the risks of the many acts of injustice that would necessarily follow from an almost countless number of agents established in every parish or county in nearly a third of the States of the Union, over whose decisions there is to be no supervision or control by the Federal courts. The power that would be thus placed in the hands of the President is such as in time of peace certainly ought never to be intrusted to any one man.

If it be asked whether the creation of such a tribunal within a State is warranted as a measure of war, the question immediately presents itself whether we are still engaged in war. Let us not unnecessarily disturb the commerce and credit and industry of the country by declaring to the American people and to the world that the United States are still in a condition of civil war. At present there is no part of our country in which the authority of the United States is disputed. Offenses that may be committed by individuals should not work a forfeiture of the rights of whole communities. The country has returned, or is returning, to a state of peace and industry, and the rebellion is in fact at an end. The measure, therefore, seems to be as inconsistent with the actual condition of the country as it is at variance with the Constitution of the United States. . . .

I can not but add another very grave objection to this bill. The Constitution imperatively declares, in connection with taxation, that each State *shall* have at least one Representative, and fixes the rule for the number to which, in future times, each State shall be entitled. It also provides that the Senate . . . *shall* be composed of two Senators from each State, and adds with peculiar force "that no State, without its consent, shall be deprived of its equal suffrage in the Senate." The original act was necessarily passed in the absence of the States chiefly to be affected, because their people were then contumaciously engaged in the rebellion. Now the case is changed, and some, at least, of those States are attending Congress by loyal representatives, soliciting the allowance of the constitutional right for representation. At the time, however, of the consideration and the passing of this bill there was no Senator or Representative in Congress from the eleven States which are to be mainly affected by its provisions. The very fact that reports were and are made against the good disposition of the people of that portion of the country is an additional reason why they need and should have representatives of their own in Congress to explain their condition, reply to accusations, and assist by their local knowledge in the perfecting of measures immediately affecting themselves. While the liberty of deliberation would then be free and Congress would have full power to decide according to its judgment, there could be no objection urged that the States most interested had not been permitted to be heard. The principle is firmly fixed in the minds of the American people that there should be no taxation without representation. Great burdens have now to be borne by all the country, and we may best demand that they shall be borne without murmur when they are voted by a majority of the representatives of all the people. I would not interfere with the unquestionable right of Congress to judge, each House for itself, "of the elections, returns, and qualifications of its own members"; but that authority can not be construed as including the right to shut out in time of peace any State from the representation to which it is entitled by the Constitution. . . .

In accordance with the Constitution, I return the bill to the Senate, in the earnest hope that a measure involving questions and interests so important to the country will not become a law, unless upon deliberate consideration by the people it shall receive the sanction of an enlightened public judgment.

3

The conflicting aims of President Johnson and the congressional radicals stemmed from differing views of the southern mind and heart. Few men, on either side, realized that the complexity of the issues, and the intensity of the hatreds, ruled out simple solutions. Carl Schurz, a liberal Republican, was an exception. His report to Congress in 1866 shows the difficulties facing those who were attempting to reconstruct the South:[3]

I regret to say that views and intentions so reasonable I found confined to a small minority. Aside from the assumption that the negro will not work without physical compulsion, there appears to be another popular notion prevalent in the south, which stands as no less serious an obstacle in the way of a successful solution of the problem. It is that the negro exists for the special object of raising cotton, rice and sugar *for the whites,* and that it is illegitimate for him to indulge, like other people, in the pursuit of his own happiness in his own way. Although it is admitted that he has ceased to be the property of a master, it is not admitted that he has a right to become his own master. . . . An ingrained feeling like this is apt to bring forth that sort of class legislation which produces laws to govern one class with no other view than to benefit another. This tendency can be distinctly traced in the various schemes for regulating labor which here and there see the light. . . .

In seeking remedies for such disorders we ought to keep in view, above all, the nature of the problem to be solved. As to what is commonly termed "reconstruction," it is not only the political machinery of the States and their constitutional relations to the general government, but the whole organism of southern society that must be reconstructed, or rather constructed anew, so as to bring it in harmony with the rest of American society. The difficulties of this task are not be considered overcome when the people of the south take the oath of alle-

[3] Carl Schurz, "An Impartial View," U. S., S. *Exec. Doc. No. 2,* 39th Cong., 1st Sess., 20–40.

giance and elect governors and legislatures and members of Congress, and militia captains. . . .

The true nature of the difficulties of the situation is this: The general government of the republic has, by proclaiming the emancipation of the slaves, commenced a great social revolution in the south, but has, as yet, not completed it. Only the negative part of it is accomplished. The slaves are emancipated in point of form, but free labor has not yet been put in the place of slavery in point of fact. . . .

In my despatches from the south I repeatedly expressed the opinion that the people were not yet in a frame of mind to legislate calmly and understandingly upon the subject of free negro labor. . . . When the rebellion was put down they found themselves not only conquered in a political and military sense, but economically ruined. The planters, who represented the wealth of the southern country, are partly laboring under the severest embarrassments, partly reduced to absolute poverty. Many who are stripped of all available means, and have nothing but their land, cross their arms in gloomy despondency, incapable of rising to a manly resolution. Others, who still possess means, are at a loss how to use them, as their old way of doing things is, by the abolition of slavery, rendered impracticable, at least where the military arm of the government has enforced emancipation. Others are still trying to go on in the old way, and that old way is in fact the only one they understand, and in which they have any confidence. Only a minority is trying to adopt the new order of things. A large number of the plantations, probably a considerable majority of the more valuable estates, is under heavy mortgages, and the owners know that, unless they retrieve their fortunes in a comparatively short space of time, their property will pass out of their hands. Almost all are, to some extent, embarrassed. The nervous anxiety which such a state of things produces extends also to those classes of society which, although not composed of planters, were always in close business con-

nexion with the planting interest, and there was hardly a branch of commerce or industry in the south which was not directly or indirectly so connected. Besides, the southern soldiers, when returning from the war, did not, like the northern soldiers, find a prosperous community which merely waited for their arrival to give them remunerative employment. They found, many of them, their homesteads destroyed, their farms devastated, their families in distress; and those that were less unfortunate found, at all events, an impoverished and exhausted community which had but little to offer them. Thus a great many have been thrown upon the world to shift as best they can. They must do something honest or dishonest, and must do it soon, to make a living, and their prospects are, at present, not very bright. Thus that nervous anxiety to hastily repair broken fortunes, and to prevent still greater ruin and distress, embraces nearly all classes, and imprints upon all the movements of the social body a morbid character.

In which direction will these people be most apt to turn their eyes? Leaving the prejudice of race out of the question, from early youth they have been acquainted with but one system of labor, and with that one system they have been in the habit of identifying all their interests. They know of no way to help themselves but the one they are accustomed to. Another system of labor is presented to them, which, however, owing to circumstances which they do not appreciate, appears at first in an unpromising light. To try it they consider an experiment which they cannot afford to make while their wants are urgent. They have not reasoned calmly enough to convince themselves that the trial must be made. It is, indeed, not wonderful that, under such circumstances, they should study, not how to introduce and develop free labor, but how to avoid its introduction, and how to return as much and as quickly as possible to something like the old order of things. Nor is it wonderful that such studies should find an expression in their attempts at legislation.

But the circumstance that this tendency is natural does not render it less dangerous and objectionable. The practical question presents itself: Is the immediate restoration of the late rebel States to absolute self-control so necessary that it must be done even at the risk of endangering one of the great results of the war, and of bringing on in those States insurrection or anarchy, or would it not be better to postpone that restoration until such dangers are past? If, as long as the change from slavery to free labor is known to the southern people only by its destructive results, these people must be expected to throw obstacles in its way, would it not seem necessary that the movement of social "reconstruction" be kept in the right channel by the hand of the power which originated the change, until that change can have disclosed some of its beneficial results? . . .

One reason why the southern people are slow in accommodating themselves to the new order of things is, that they confidently expect soon to be permitted to regulate matters according to their own notions. Every concession made to them by the government has been taken as an encouragement to persevere in this hope, and, unfortunately for them, this hope is nourished by influences from other parts of the country. Hence their anxiety to have their State governments restored *at once,* to have the troops withdrawn, and the Freedmen's Bureau abolished, although a good many discerning men know well that, in view of the lawless spirit still prevailing, it would be far better for them to have the general order of society firmly maintained by the federal power until things have arrived at a final settlement. . . . If, therefore, the national government firmly and unequivocally announces its policy not to give up the control of the free-labor reform until it is finally accomplished, the progress of that reform will undoubtedly be far more rapid and far less difficult than it will be if the attitude of the government is such as to permit contrary hopes to be indulged in.

THE FOURTEENTH AMENDMENT

4

No sooner was the Civil Rights Act adopted than Republican leaders, fearful that this was not enough, began casting about for additional means to assure permanent protection for Negroes. A constitutional amendment was the obvious device. The Fourteenth Amendment, ratified in July 1868, not only defined citizenship but granted federal protection against an invasion of individual rights by the states—a historic reversal in federal relations:[4]

SECTION 1. All persons born or naturalized in the United States, and subject to the jurisdiction thereof, are citizens of the United States and of the State wherein they reside. No State shall make or enforce any law which shall abridge the privileges or immunities of citizens of the United States; nor shall any State deprive any person of life, liberty, or property, without due process of law; nor deny to any person within its jurisdiction the equal protection of the laws.

SEC. 2. Representatives shall be apportioned among the several States according to their respective numbers, counting the whole number of persons in each State, excluding Indians not taxed. But when the right to vote at any election for the choice of electors for President and Vice-President of the United States, Representatives in Congress, the Executive and Judicial officers of a State, or the members of the Legislature thereof, is denied to any of the male inhabitants of such State, being twenty-one years of age, and citizens of the United States, or in any way abridged, except for participation in rebellion, or other crime, the basis of representation therein shall be reduced in the proportion which the number of such male citizens shall bear to the whole number of male citizens twenty-one years of age in such State.

SEC. 3. No person shall be a Senator or Representative in Congress, or elector of

---

[4] U. S., *Statutes at Large,* XV, 708–709.

President and Vice-President, or hold any office, civil or military, under the United States, or under any State, who, having previously taken an oath, as a member of Congress, or as an officer of the United States, or as a member of any State legislature, or as an executive or judicial officer of any State, to support the Constitution of the United States, shall have engaged in insurrection or rebellion against the same, or given aid or comfort to the enemies thereof. But Congress may by a vote of two-thirds of each House, remove such disability.

SEC. 4. The validity of the public debt of the United States, authorized by law, including debts incurred for payment of pensions and bounties for services in suppressing insurrection or rebellion, shall not be questioned. But neither the United States nor any State shall assume or pay any debt or obligation incurred in aid of insurrection or rebellion against the United States, or any claim for the loss or emancipation of any slave; but all such debts, obligations and claims shall be held illegal and void.

SEC. 5. The Congress shall have power to enforce, by appropriate legislation, the provisions of this article.

5

The motives governing the framers of the Fourteenth Amendment are admirably summarized by Representative Thaddeus Stevens, one of the chief architects of the measure, in a speech to Congress May 8, 1866:[5]

This proposition is not all that the committee desired. It falls far short of my wishes, but it fulfills my hopes. I believe it is all that can be obtained in the present state of public opinion. Not only Congress but the several States are to be consulted. Upon a careful survey of the whole ground, we did not believe that nineteen of the loyal States could be induced to ratify any proposition more stringent than this. I say

[5] Thaddeus Stevens, "The Fourteenth Amendment," *Congressional Globe*, 39th Cong., 1st Sess., XXXVI, Pt. 3, 2459–2460.

nineteen, for I utterly repudiate and scorn the idea that any State not acting in the Union is to be counted on the question of ratification. It is absurd to suppose that any more than three fourths of the States that propose the amendment are required to make it valid; that States not here are to be counted as present. Believing then, that this is the best proposition that can be made effectual, I accept it. . . .

The first section prohibits the States from abridging the privileges and immunities of citizens of the United States, or unlawfully depriving them of life, liberty, or property, or of denying to any person within their jurisdiction the "equal" protection of the laws.

I can hardly believe that any person can be found who will not admit that every one of these provisions is just. They are all asserted, in some form or other, in our DECLARATION or organic law. But the Constitution limits only the action of Congress, and is not a limitation on the States. This amendment supplies that defect, and allows Congress to correct the unjust legislation of the States, so far that the law which operates upon one man shall operate *equally* upon all. Whatever law punishes a white man for a crime shall punish the black man precisely in the same way and to the same degree. Whatever law protects the white man shall afford "equal" protection to the black man. Whatever means of redress is afforded to one shall be afforded to all. Whatever law allows the white man to testify in court shall allow the man of color to do the same. These are great advantages over their present codes. Now different degrees of punishment are inflicted, not on account of the magnitude of the crime, but according to the color of the skin. Now color disqualifies a man from testifying in courts, or being tried in the same way as white men. I need not enumerate these partial and oppressive laws. Unless the Constitution should restrain them, those States will all, I fear, keep up this discrimination, and crush to death the hated freedmen. Some answer, "Your civil rights bill secures the same things." That is partly true, but a law is repealable by a majority. And I need hardly say that the first time that the South with their copperhead allies obtain the command of Congress it will be repealed. The veto of the President and their votes on the bill are conclusive evidence of that. And yet I am amazed and alarmed at the impatience of certain well-meaning Republicans at the exclusion of the rebel States until the Constitution shall be so amended as to restrain their despotic desires. This amendent once adopted cannot be annulled without two thirds of Congress. That they will hardly get. And yet certain of our distinguished friends propose to admit State after State before this becomes a part of the Constitution. What madness! Is their judgment misled by their kindness; or are they unconsciously drifting into the haven of power at the other end of the avenue? I do not suspect it, but others will.

The second section I consider the most important in the article. It fixes the basis of representation in Congress. If any State shall exclude any of her adult male citizens from the elective franchise, or abridge that right, she shall forfeit her right to representation in the same proportion. The effect of this provision will be either to compel the States to grant universal suffrage or so to shear them of their power as to keep them forever in a hopeless minority in the national Government, both legislative and executive. If they do not enfranchise the freedmen, it would give to the rebel States but thirty-seven Representatives. Thus shorn of their power, they would soon become restive. Southern pride would not long brook a hopeless minority. True, it will take two, three, possibly five years before they conquer their prejudices sufficiently to allow their late slaves to become their equals at the polls. That short delay would not be injurious. In the mean time the freedmen would become more enlightened, and more fit to discharge the high duties of their new condition. In that time, too, the loyal Con-

gress could mature their laws and so amend the Constitution as to secure the rights of every human being, and render disunion impossible. Heaven forbid that the southern States, or *any one of them,* should be represented on this floor until such muniments of freedom are built high and firm. Against our will they have been absent for four bloody years; against our will they must not come back until we are ready to receive them. Do not tell me that there are loyal representatives waiting for admission —until their States are loyal they can have no standing here. They would merely *misrepresent* their constituents.

I admit that this article is not as good as the one we sent to death in the Senate. In my judgment, we shall not approach the measure of justice until we have given every adult freedman a homestead on the land where he was born and toiled and suffered. Forty acres of land and a hut would be more valuable to him than the immediate right to vote. Unless we give them this we shall receive the censure of mankind and the curse of Heaven. That article referred to provided that if *one* of the injured race was excluded the State should forfeit the right to have any of them represented. That would have hastened their full enfranchisement. This section allows the States to discriminate among the same class, and receive proportionate credit in representation. This I dislike. But it is a short step forward. The large stride which we in vain proposed is dead; the murderers must answer to the suffering race. I would not have been the perpetrator. A load of misery must sit heavy on their souls.

The third section may encounter more difference of opinion here. Among the people I believe it will be the most popular of all the provisions; it prohibits rebels from voting for members of Congress and electors of President until 1870. My only objection to it is that it is too lenient. I know that there is a morbid sensibility, sometimes called mercy, which affects a few of all classes, from the priest to the clown, which has more sympathy for the murderer on the gallows than for his victim. I hope I have a heart as capable of feeling for human woe as others. I have long since wished that capital punishment were abolished. But I never dreamed that all punishment could be dispensed with in human society. Anarchy, *treason,* and violence would reign triumphant. Here is the mildest of all punishments ever inflicted on traitors. I might not consent to the extreme severity denounced upon them by a provisional governor of Tennessee—I mean the late lamented Andrew Johnson of blessed memory—but I would have increased the severity of this section. I would be glad to see it extended to 1876, and to include all State and municipal as well as national elections. In my judgment we do not sufficiently protect the loyal men of the rebel States from the vindictive persecutions of their victorious rebel neighbors. Still I will move no amendment, nor vote for any, lest the whole fabric should tumble to pieces.

I need say nothing of the fourth section, for none dare object to it who is not himself a rebel. To the friend of justice, the friend of the Union, of the perpetuity of liberty, and the final triumph of the rights of man and their extension to every human being, let me say, sacrifice as we have done your peculiar views, and instead of vainly insisting upon the instantaneous operation of all that is right accept what is possible, and "all these things shall be added unto you."

6

A modern scholar, Joseph B. James, makes an intensive analysis of the intent of the congressional framers of the Fourteenth Amendment:[6]

In brief recapitulation, several general conclusions may be indicated. Despite an apparent difference of opinion in Congress,

[6] Joseph B. James, *The Framing of the Fourteenth Amendment* (Urbana, 1956), pp. 179–181. Reprinted with the kind permission of the University of Illinois Press.

statements of congressmen before their constituents definitely identify the provisions of the first section of the amendment with those of the Civil Rights Bill. Though some of the opposition pointed out the dangers of centralization concealed within its broad terminology, not even these critics indicated the possibility of its becoming a legal loophole through which corporations might escape unpleasant state regulation. It should be emphasized here that, if any framer or framers had any such purpose, it was not even hinted at openly in 1866 and no available private records substantiate the idea. Contemporary records indicate a general understanding that citizens and unnaturalized aliens were meant by the term "persons." These were to be protected in the fundamental rights of life, liberty, and property. The definition of citizenship contained in the first clause was generally regarded as declaratory of what already was law. Some thought the only need for such clarification arose from Taney's opinion in the Dred Scott case. The citizens thus defined were to be protected in their privileges and immunities as citizens of the United States in whatever state they might reside. Statements of framers indicate that these broad terms, "privileges and immunities," were to embrace those guaranteed by the first eight amendments and other basic liberties recognized in the common law. Discriminatory state legislation was forbidden.

Contemporary evidence seems to indicate that the second section was a rather clumsy substitute for an outright grant of Negro suffrage. Politicians believed that the direct issue could not be carried in the North at that time. Part of the opposition apparently was expected to arise from a natural prejudice, and part from a fear of too much power in the hands of the federal government. The regulation of suffrage was regarded as one of those rights reserved to the states which should not be touched. To avoid these difficulties and to exert political pressure for Negro suffrage in the South, the measure was constructed. Though its impracticability was seen by some congressional leaders, it was intended to reduce Southern representation until the Negro would be in a position to divide, if not dominate, the political power of the South.

The third section was not what Radicals desired, but it was the best that they could get. The original aim had been to disfranchise a large part of those who had participated in insurrection. By this means, the influence of the formerly dominant group could be weakened if not destroyed. Popular opinion in the North was ready to support some penalty for leaders of the Confederacy, but many politicians feared that disfranchisement of almost the entire population in some areas was too much for their constituents to accept. Then, too, the adoption of such a measure would make it obvious that Congress did not want the South to approve the amendment. A number of Republicans, no doubt, opposed the measure for more statesmanlike reasons. Disqualification for office-holding was far less drastic, and might tend toward the desired result of perpetuating Republican control. In comparison with some punishments that were discussed, the section was mild. Some apparently anticipated rejection of the amendment by Southern legislatures because of this section. Others seemed to believe that, despite objections, it would be ratified in order to restore normal conditions.

The fourth section was important only politically. In its earlier form, repudiation of the rebel debt, nobody opposed it except on the grounds of its uselessness. When the guarantee of national obligations was added, the only opposition came from fear that it was intended to block Democratic moves to tax bonds or to pay part of the debt in new issues of greenbacks. Indeed, such possible action was termed "repudiation" by many Republicans. No real purpose can be definitely ascertained in that respect. Probably such an idea was fostered to gain support of moneyed interests. The inclusion of pensions and bounties in the guarantee was so skillfully used that one can hardly doubt that the winning of votes was its purpose.

The fifth section was designed as an important part of the whole. To realize what many must have contemplated, one has only to examine the many bills, granting everything from civil rights to suffrage, that were framed under the alleged authority of such a clause in the Thirteenth Amendment. The Civil Rights legislation of the "seventies," based on the authority that congressmen claimed existed in this amendment, bears out that theory. These laws were later declared unconstitutional.

Several purposes can be clearly seen in early proposals for a fourteenth amendment. The finished product, however, found most of these compromised or lost in the necessity of framing something which all could approve. The most important purpose in the minds of most framers and members of the Republican party in the summer of 1866 was undoubtedly that the amendment might furnish a popular platform in the political campaign. That was the immediate aim, and politicians traditionally have been willing to sacrifice ultimate hopes for present success.

THE ISSUE OF WHITE SUPREMACY

7

Had the militant leaders of conservative southern opinion shown moderation, they might have swung the North to Johnson's reconstruction policy. Instead, each state seeking readmittance under the Presidential Reconstruction Plan insisted on two steps that caused great indignation in the North. One was the return of prominent Confederates to important governmental office; the other was the adoption of a "Black Code" that virtually returned Negroes to slavery. Of the latter, the code adopted by Alabama December 15, 1865 is typical:[7]

[7] *Acts of the Session of 1865–1866 of the General Assembly of Alabama* (Montgomery, 1866), pp. 119–121.

SECTION 1. . . . That the commissioners' court of any county in this State may purchase, rent, or provide such lands, buildings and other property as may be necessary for a poor-house, or house of correction for any such county, and may appoint suitable officers for the management thereof, and make all necessary bylaws, rules and regulations for the government of the inmates thereof, and cause the same to be enforced; but in no case shall the punishment inflicted exceed hard labor, either in or out of said house; the use of chain-gangs, putting in stocks, if necessary, to prevent escapes; such reasonable correction as a parent may inflict upon a stubborn, refractory child; and solitary confinement for not longer than one week, on bread and water; and may cause to be hired out such as are vagrants, to work in chain-gangs or otherwise, for the length of time for which they are sentenced; and the proceeds of such hiring must be paid into the county treasury, for the benefits of the helpless in said poor-house, or house of correction.

SEC. 2. . . . That the following persons are vagrants in addition to those already declared to be vagrants by law, or that may hereafter be so declared by law; a stubborn or refractory servant; a laborer or servant who loiters away his time, or refuses to comply with any contract for a term of service, without just cause; and such person may be sent to the house of correction in the county in which such offense is committed; and for want of such house of correction, the common jail of the county may be used for that purpose.

SEC. 3. . . . That when a vagrant is found, any justice of the peace of the county must, upon complaint made upon oath, or on his own knowledge, issue his warrant to the sheriff or any constable of the county, to bring such person before him; and if, upon examination and hearing of testimony, it appears to the justice, that such person is a vagrant, he shall assess a fine of fifty dollars and costs against such vagrant; and in default of payment, he must commit such vagrant to the house of correction; or if no

such house, to the common jail of the county, for a term not exceeding six months, and until such fine, costs and charges are paid, or such party is otherwise discharged by law; *Provided,* That when committed to jail under this section, the commissioners' court may cause him to be hired out in like manner as in section one of this act.

SEC. 4. . . . That when any person shall be convicted of vagrancy, as provided for in this act, the justice of the peace, before whom such conviction is had, may, at his discretion, either commit such person to jail, to the house of correction, or hire such person to any person who will hire the same, for a period not longer than six months, for cash, giving three days' notice of the time and place of hiring; and the proceeds of such hiring, after paying all costs and charges, shall be paid into the county treasury for the benefit of the helpless in the poor-house.

SEC. 5. . . . That all fines received by any justice of the peace under the provisions of this act, shall be paid into the county treasury for the purposes as set forth in section one of this act.

SEC. 6. . . . That it shall be the duty of the justice of the peace to settle with the county treasurer at least once a month, for all fines received by him under this act, and for a willful default so to do, he shall be guilty of a misdemeanor; and upon conviction in any court having jurisdiction, shall be fined in double the amount so received or collected by him, and all costs of suit.

SEC. 7. . . . That the court of county commissioners of each county shall have full and complete control of the public works and public highways therein, and shall make all contracts in relation thereto; and shall have power to appoint a superintendent of said public works and highways, under such rules and regulations as said court shall determine; and any justice of the peace trying any cause under this act, on conviction, shall have power to sentence such vagrant to work on said public works and highways, under the supervision of such superintendent, for not more than forty days.

8

When Congress passed the First Reconstruction Act (March 2, 1867), Andrew Johnson once more accepted the challenge. Undaunted by defeat at the polls and undismayed by the prospect of a hostile congressional majority capable of overriding his veto, he vetoed the law. The lengthy veto message emphasizes the disparity between the two reconstruction plans:[8]

The bill places all the people of the ten States therein named under the absolute domination of military rulers; and the preamble undertakes to give . . . the ground upon which it is justified. It declares that there exists in those States no legal governments and no adequate protection for life or property, and asserts the necessity of enforcing peace and good order within their limits. Is this true as matter of fact?

It is not denied that the States in question have each of them an actual government, with all the powers—executive, judicial, and legislative—which properly belong to a free state. They are organized like the other States of the Union, and, like them, they make, administer, and execute the laws which concern their domestic affairs. An existing *de facto* government, exercising such functions as these, is itself the law of the state upon all matters within its jurisdiction. To pronounce the supreme law-making power of an established state illegal is to say that law itself is unlawful.

The provisions which these governments have made for the preservation of order, the suppression of crime, and the redress of private injuries are in substance and principle the same as those which prevail in the Northern States. . . .

The bill, however, would seem to show upon its face that the establishment of peace and good order is not its real object. . . .

The ten States named in the bill are divided into five districts. For each district an officer of the Army, not below the rank of a brigadier-general, is to be appointed to

rule over the people; and he is to be supported with an efficient military force to enable him to perform his duties and enforce his authority. Those duties and that authority, as defined by the third section of the bill, are "to protect all persons in their rights of person and property, to suppress insurrection, disorder, and violence, and to punish or cause to be punished all disturbers of the public peace or criminals." The power thus given to the commanding officer over all the people of each district is that of an absolute monarch. His mere will is to take the place of all law. The law of the States is now the only rule applicable to the subjects placed under his control, and that is completely displaced by the clause which declares all interference of State authority to be null and void. He alone is permitted to determine what are rights of person or property, and he may protect them in such way as in his discretion may seem proper. It places at his free disposal all the lands and goods in his district, and he may distribute them without let or hindrance to whom he pleases. Being bound by no State law, and there being no other law to regulate the subject, he may make a criminal code of his own; and he can make it as bloody as any recorded in history, or he can reserve the privilege of acting upon the impulse of his private passions in each case that arises. He is bound by no rules of evidence; there is, indeed, no provision by which he is authorized or required to take any evidence at all. Everything is a crime which he chooses to call so, and all persons are condemned whom he pronounces to be guilty. He is not bound to keep and record or make any report of his proceedings. He may arrest his victims wherever he finds them, without warrant, accusation, or proof of probable cause. If he gives them a trial before he inflicts the punishment, he gives it of his grace and mercy, not because he is commanded so to do. . . .

I come now to a question which is, if possible, still more important. Have we the power to establish and carry into execution a measure like this? I answer, certainly not,

[8] James D. Richardson (comp.), *A Compilation of the Messages and Papers of the Presidents, 1789–1897* (Washington, 1909), VI, 498–511.

if we derive our authority from the Constitution and if we are bound by the limitations which it imposes.

This proposition is perfectly clear, that no branch of the Federal Government—executive, legislative, or judicial—can have any just powers except those which it derives through and exercises under the organic law of the Union. Outside of the Constitution we have no legal authority more than private citizens, and within it we have only so much as that instrument gives us. This broad principle limits all our functions and applies to all subjects. It protects not only the citizens of States which are within the Union, but it shields every human being who comes or is brought under our jurisdiction. . . . If, therefore, the Southern States were in truth out of the Union, we could not treat their people in a way which the fundamental law forbids.

Some persons assume that the success of our arms in crushing the opposition which was made in some of the States to the execution of the Federal laws reduced those States and all their people—the innocent as well as the guilty—to the condition of vassalage and gave us a power over them which the Constitution does not bestow or define or limit. No fallacy can be more transparent than this. Our victories subjected the insurgents to legal obedience, not to the yoke of an arbitrary despotism. . . .

The United States are bound to guarantee to each State a republican form of government. Can it be pretended that this obligation is not probably broken if we carry out a measure like this, which wipes away every vestige of republican government in ten States and puts the life, property, liberty, and honor of all the people in each of them under the domination of a single person clothed with unlimited authority?

The purpose and object of the bill—the general intent which pervades it from beginning to end—is to change the entire structure and character of the State governments and to compel them by force to the adoption of organic laws and regulations which they are unwilling to accept if left to themselves.

The negroes have not asked for the privilege of voting; the vast majority of them have no idea what it means. This bill not only thrusts it into their hands, but compels them, as well as the whites, to use it in a particular way. If they do not form a constitution with prescribed articles in it and afterwards elect a legislature which will act upon certain measures in a prescribed way, neither blacks nor whites can be relieved from the slavery which the bill imposes upon them. Without pausing here to consider the policy or impolicy of Africanizing the southern part of our territory, I would simply ask the attention of Congress to that manifest, well-known, and universally acknowledged rule of constitutional law which declares that the Federal Government has no jurisdiction, authority, or power to regulate such subjects for any State. To force the right of suffrage out of the hands of the white people and into the hands of the negroes is an arbitrary violation of this principle. . . .

The bill also denies the legality of the governments of ten of the States which participated in the ratification of the amendment to the Federal Constitution abolishing slavery forever within the jurisdiction of the United States and practically excludes them from the Union. If this assumption of the bill be correct, their concurrence can not be considered as having been legally given, and the important fact is made to appear that the consent of three-fourths of the States—the requisite number—has not been constitutionally obtained to the ratification of that amendment, thus leaving the question of slavery where it stood before the amendment was officially declared to have become a part of the Constitution.

9

While Congress and President battled for power in Washington, reconstruction in the South went slowly on. By the spring of 1868 seven of the ten southern states had re-entered the Union under the congressional formula and were operating efficiently with legislatures composed of Negroes, northern carpetbaggers, and southern Republicans—or Scalawags. Historians have sometimes ridiculed the conduct of the Negro legislators, picturing them as reckless spenders whose fradulent acts set a new standard in corruption. Such a judgment ignores the significant social progress to which Negro legislators contributed. In every state educational systems were installed, public works were begun, roads were built, sanitation was improved, and life made better for rich and poor alike. The nature of the reform laws passed by the so-called black-and-tan legislatures is illustrated by the South Carolina Constitution of 1868:[9]

ARTICLE VIII: RIGHT OF SUFFRAGE

SECTION 1. In all elections by the people the electors shall vote by ballot.

SEC. 2. Every male citizen of the United States, of the age of twenty-one years and upwards, not laboring under the disabilities named in this Constitution, without distinction of race, color, or former condition, who shall be a resident of this State at the time of the adoption of this Constitution, or who shall thereafter reside in this State one year, and in the County in which he offers to vote, sixty days next preceding any election, shall be entitled to vote for all officers that are now, or hereafter may be, elected by the people, and upon all questions submitted to the electors at any elections; *Provided,* That no person shall be allowed to vote or hold office who is now or hereafter may be disqualified therefor by the Constitution of the United States, until such disqualification shall be removed by the Congress of the United States; *Provided further,* That no person, while kept in any alms house or asylum, or of unsound mind, or confined in any public prison, shall be allowed to vote or hold office.

SEC. 3. It shall be the duty of the General Assembly to provide from time to time for the registration of all electors.

SEC. 4. For the purpose of voting no person shall be deemed to have lost his residence by reason of absence while employed in the service of the United States, nor while engaged upon the waters of this State or the United States, or of the high seas, nor while temporarily absent from the State.

SEC. 5. No soldier, seaman or marine in the army or navy of the United States shall be deemed a resident of this State in consequence of having been stationed therein.

SEC. 6. Electors shall, in all cases, except treason, felony or breach of the peace, be privileged from arrest and civil process during their attendance at elections, and in going to and returning from the same.

SEC. 7. Every person entitled to vote at any election shall be eligible to any office which now is or hereafter shall be elective by the people in the County where he shall have resided sixty days previous to such election, except as otherwise provided in this Constitution or the Constitution and laws of the United States.

SEC. 8. The General Assembly shall never pass any law that will deprive any of the citizens of this State of the right of suffrage except for treason, murder, robbery, or duelling, whereof the persons shall have been duly tried and convicted.

SEC. 9. Presidential electors shall be elected by the people.

SEC. 10. In all elections held by the people under this Constitution, the person or persons who shall receive the highest number of votes shall be declared elected.

SEC. 11. The provision of this Constitution concerning the term of residence necessary to enable persons to hold certain offices therein mentioned, shall not be held to apply to officers chosen by the people at the first election, or by the General Assembly at its first session.

SEC. 12. No person shall be disfranchised for felony, or other crimes committed while such person was a slave.

10

Negro scholars, such as W. E. B. DuBois, have protested that many books on American history tend to slight or ignore the life and contributions of the Negro population. In his own slashing account of the era, Black Reconstruction, DuBois

---

[9] *The Constitution of South Carolina* (Charleston, 1868), pp. 2–6. (Pages not numbered consecutively.) Collection entitled *State Constitutions,* collected and bound by the New York Public Library.

seeks to right the balance by discussing gains that were made under carpetbag regimes:[10]

It is fair to say that the Negro carpetbag governments established the public schools of the South. Although recent researches have shown many germs of a public school system in the South before the war, there can be no reasonable doubt that common school instruction in the South . . . was founded by the Freedmen's Bureau and missionary societies, and that the state public school system was formed mainly by Negro Reconstruction governments. . . .

From the beginning of the public school system under Reconstruction, and after, the fight between local and state control and supervision has been bitter. Local control meant the control of property and racial particularism. It stood for reaction and prejudice; and wherever there was retrogression, particularly in Negro schools, it can be traced to the increased power of the county and district administrators. . . .

For the first success of the Negro schools, the South deserved little praise. From the beginning, most of the Southern states made the Negro schools just as bad as they dared to in the face of national public opinion, and every cent spent on them was taken from Negro rents and wages, and came back to the property-holders tenfold in increased opportunities for exploitation.

It is said, for instance, in one state: "There were to be free public schools. The blacks were to be the chief beneficiaries of the new system, but the whites would pay the taxes. Whites considered such education either useless or positively dangerous to society." Of free, self-sacrificing gifts for the sake of Negro uplift and intelligence, the vast majority of Southern white people contributed almost nothing. . . .

Finally, the movement that saved the Negro public school system was not enlightened Southern opinion, but rather that Northern

philanthropy which at the very beginning of the Negro education movement contributed toward the establishment of Negro colleges. The reason for them at first was to supply the growing demand for teachers, and was also a concession to Southern prejudice, which so violently disliked the white teacher in the Negro school.

This led to the establishment by 1879 of eighty-four normal and high schools and sixteen colleges, with over twelve thousand students. But these institutions soon saw a higher misson. In the midst of reaction and disfranchisement, of poverty and growing caste, they became the centers of a training in leadership and ideals for the whole Negro race, and the only fine and natural field of contact between white and black culture. . . .

Howard University and Freedmen's Hospital are survivals of the Freedmen's Bureau. Howard University was chartered in 1867 and General O. O. Howard, head of the Freedmen's Bureau, was made its first president. Succeeding as presidents were W. W. Patton, J. E. Rankin, who wrote "God Be with You Until We Meet Again," and John Gordon, a lineal descendant of Jonathan Edwards. On its governing board have been Douglass, Langston and Bruce; it has the largest Negro medical center in the United State, and has furnished about half of the Negro lawyers.

Berea College was started by John G. Fee, a Kentuckian, who became an abolitionist. After the war, colored students were admitted, and a brother of the President of Oberlin was at the head of the school. For forty years, colored students attended Berea, but finally, in 1904, the institution was by law closed to Negroes.

Hampton Institute was founded by General S. C. Armstrong, near where the Negroes were first made "contraband of war," and where a colored woman founded the first colored school. Among its trustees were Mark Hopkins, Phillips Brooks, and John G. Whittier.

Atlanta University was founded by Ed-

---

10 From *Black Reconstruction* by W. E. Burghardt DuBois, pp. 664–667. Copyright 1935, by Harcourt, Brace and Company, Inc.

mund Ware in 1867. "To have gone on as President Ware did during those early years there must have been in his heart deathless love and pity for men who needed what he could give them—a faith in the gospel and eternal righteousness that never wavered, and a love for God that made work easy and suffering joy."

Add to this the picture of DeForrest at Talladega, Cravath at Fisk, and others at Biddle, Knoxville, New Orleans, and Central Tennessee. There were those two influential schools at the edge of the South, Lincoln in Pennsylvania, and Wilberforce in Ohio.

Nearly all of these educational leaders were either nominated by Howard, head of the Freedmen's Bureau, as in the case of General S. C. Armstrong, or received from him the most thorough-going co-operation. There is no greater tribute to the Freedmen's Bureau than this.

Propaganda has centered the attention of the world upon these Northerners who took part in . . . political reconstruction . . . and particularly upon those who were charged with dishonesty, while of the history of this astonishing movement to plant the New England college in the South, and to give the Southern black man a leadership based on scholarship and character, almost nothing has been said. And yet this was the salvation of the South and the Negro. These "carpetbaggers" deserve to be remembered and honored. Without them there can be no doubt that the Negro would have rushed into revolt and vengeance and played into the hands of those determined to crush him. As it was, when reaction triumphed in 1876, there was already present a little group of trained leadership which grew by leaps and bounds until it gripped and held the mass of Negroes at the beginning of the twentieth century.

Had it not been for the Negro school and college, the Negro would, to all intents and purposes, have been driven back to slavery. His economic foothold in land and capital was too slight in ten years of turmoil to effect any defense or stability. His reconstruc-tion leadership had come from Negroes educated in the North, and white politicans, capitalists and philanthropic teachers. The counter-revolution of 1876 drove most of these, save the teachers, away. But already, through establishing public schools and private colleges, and by organizing the Negro church, the Negro had acquired enough leadership and knowledge to thwart the worst designs of the new slave drivers. They avoided the mistake of trying to meet force by force. They bent to the storm of beating, lynching and murder, and kept their souls in spite of public and private insult of every description; they built an inner culture which the world recognizes in spite of the fact that it is still half-strangled and inarticulate.

11

Although Republican architects planned their reconstruction policy well, they faced an insurmountable obstacle. The justices of the Supreme Court held that the wartime amendments gave Congress no power over southern whites, who were still free, as individual citizens, to deprive Negroes of civil rights. The new constitutional restrictions, the Court maintained, applied only to the states, which could make no laws denying freedmen the privileges guaranteed them in the amendments. This doctrine, on which the "Jim Crow" civilization of the South was to rest, was advanced in the Civil Rights Cases (1883), which arose when Negroes were denied access to accommodations solely on the grounds of color:[11]

It is true that slavery cannot exist without law any more than property in lands and goods can exist without law, and therefore the Thirteenth Amendment may be regarded as nullifying all state laws which establish or uphold slavery. But it has a reflex character also, establishing and decreeing universal civil and political freedom throughout the United States; and it is assumed that the power in Congress to enforce the articles by appropriate legislation, clothes Congress with power to pass all laws necessary and proper for abolishing all badges and incidents of slavery in the United States; and

11 *United States Reports,* 109 U. S. 20–25.

upon this assumption it is claimed that this is sufficient authority for declaring by law that all persons shall have equal accommodations and privileges in all inns, public conveyances, and places of public amusement; the argument being that the denial of such equal accommodations and privileges is in itself a subjection to a species of servitude within the meaning of the amendment. Conceding the major proposition to be true, that Congress has a right to enact all necessary and proper laws for the obliteration and prevention of slavery with all its badges and incidents, is the minor proposition also true, that the denial to any person of admission to the accommodations and privileges of an inn, a public conveyance, or a theatre, does subject that person to any form of servitude, or tend to fasten upon him any badge of slavery? If it does not, then power to pass the law is not found in the Thirteenth Amendment. . . .

But is there any similarity between such servitudes and a denial by the owner of an inn, a public conveyance, or a theatre, of its accommodations and privileges to an individual, even though the denial be founded on the race or color of that individual? Where does any slavery or servitude, or badge of either, arise from such an act of denial? Whether it might not be a denial of a right which, if sanctioned by the state law, would be obnoxious to the prohibitions of the Fourteenth Amendment, is another question. But what has it to do with the question of slavery? . . .

The long existence of African slavery in this country gave us very distinct notions of what it was, and what were its necessary incidents. Compulsory service of the slave for the benefit of the master, restraint of his movements except by the master's will, disability to hold property, to make contracts, to have a standing in court, to be a witness against a white person, and such like burdens and incapacities were the inseparable incidents of the institution. . . . Can the act of a mere individual, the owner of the inn, the public conveyance, or place of amuse-

ment, refusing the accommodation, be justly regarded as imposing any badge of slavery or servitude upon the applicant, or only as inflicting an ordinary civil injury, properly cognizable by the laws of the State, and presumably subject to redress by those laws until the contrary appears?

After giving to these questions all the consideration which their importance demands, we are forced to the conclusion that such an act of refusal has nothing to do with slavery or involuntary servitude, and that if it is violative of any right of the party, his redress is to be sought under the laws of the State; or, if those laws are adverse to his rights and do not protect him, his remedy will be found in the corrective legislation which Congress has adopted, or may adopt, for counteracting the effect of state laws, or state action, prohibited by the Fourteenth Amendment. It would be running the slavery argument into the ground to make it apply to every act of discrimination which a person may see fit to make as to the guests he will entertain, or as to the people he will take into his coach or cab or car, or admit to his concert or theatre, or deal with in other matters of intercourse or business. . . .

When a man has emerged from slavery, and by the aid of beneficent legislation has shaken off the inseparable concomitants of that state, there must be some stage in the progress of his elevation when he takes the rank of a mere citizen, and ceases to be the special favorite of the laws, and when his rights as a citizen, or a man, are to be protected in the ordinary modes by which other men's rights are protected. There were thousands of free colored people in this country before the abolition of slavery, enjoying all the essential rights of life, liberty and property the same as white citizens; yet no one, at that time, thought that it was any invasion of his personal status as a freeman because he was not admitted to all the privileges enjoyed by white citizens, or because he was subjected to discriminations in the enjoyment of accommodations in inns, public conveyances and places of amusement.

Mere discriminations on account of race or color were not regarded as badges of slavery. If, since that time, the enjoyment of equal rights in all these respects has become established by constitutional enactment, it is not by force of the Thirteenth Amendment (which merely abolishes slavery), but by force of the Fourteenth and Fifteenth Amendments.

On the whole we are of the opinion that no countenance of authority for the passage of the law in question can be found in either the Thirteenth or Fourteenth Amendment of the Constitution; and no other ground of authority for its passage being suggested, it must necessarily be declared void, at least so far as its operation in the several States is concerned.

12

Thirty years after the close of the Civil War, the former bondsmen were still engaged in a struggle for equal rights before the law. One phase of their struggle ended in defeat when the Supreme Court handed down its decision in the case of Plessy v. Ferguson *in 1896. Plessy appeared to be white but he was one-eighth Negro. On a trip in Louisiana he occupied a vacant seat in a railroad coach reserved for white passengers. He refused to move to the coach set aside for Negro passengers when ordered to do so by the conductor. He was then arrested and charged with violating a Louisiana law prohibiting any one from "insisting" on sitting in the "wrong" car. The Supreme Court affirmed the decision of the lower courts, which had upheld the state's right to provide "separate but equal" facilities for the two races:*[12]

Mr. Justice Brown, after stating the case, delivered the opinion of the Court:

This case turns upon the constitutionality of an act of the General Assembly of the state of Louisiana, passed in 1890, providing for separate railway carriages for the white and colored races. . . .

The constitutionality of this act is attacked upon the ground that it conflicts both with the Thirteenth Amendment of the Constitution, abolishing slavery, and the Four-

teenth Amendment, which prohibits certain restrictive legislation on the part of the states.

1. That it does not conflict with the Thirteenth Amendment, which abolished slavery and involuntary servitude, except as a punishment for a crime, is too clear for argument. Slavery implies involuntary servitude —a state of bondage; the ownership of mankind as a chattel, or at least the control of the labor and services of one man for the benefit of another, and the absence of a legal right to the disposal of his own person, property, and service. . . .

A statute which implies merely a legal distinction between the white and colored races—a distinction which is founded in the color of the two races, and which must always exist so long as white men are distinguished from the other race by color— has no tendency to destroy the legal equality of the two races, or re-establish a state of involuntary servitude. Indeed, we do not understand that the Thirteenth Amendment is strenuously relied upon by the plaintiff in error in this connection.

2. By the Fourteenth Amendment, all persons born or naturalized in the United States, and subject to the jurisdiction thereof, are made citizens of the United States and of the state wherein they reside; and the states are forbidden from making or enforcing any law which shall abridge the privileges or immunities of citizens of the United States, or shall deprive any person of life, liberty, or property without due process of law, or deny to any person within their jurisdiction the equal protection of the laws. . . .

The object of the amendment was undoubtedly to enforce the absolute equality of the two races before the law, but in the nature of things it could not have been intended to abolish distinctions based upon color, or to enforce social, as distinguished from political, equality, or a commingling of the two races upon terms unsatisfactory to either. Laws permitting, and even requiring, their separation in places where

---

[12] 163 U. S. 537 (1896), 540, 542–544, 550–552, 554–564.

they are liable to be brought into contact do not necessarily imply the inferiority of either race to the other, and have been generally, if not universally, recognized as within the competency of the state legislatures in the exercise of their police powers. The most common instance of this is connected with the establishment of separate schools for white and colored children, which has been held to be a valid exercise of the legislative power even by courts of states where the political rights of the colored race have been longest and most earnestly enforced. . . .

So far, then, as a conflict with the Fourteenth Amendment is concerned, the case reduces itself to the question whether the statute of Louisiana is a reasonable regulation, and with respect to this there must necessarily be a large discretion on the part of the legislature. In determining the question of reasonableness it is at liberty to act with reference to the established usages, customs, and traditions of the people, and with a view to the promotion of their comfort, and the preservation of the public peace and good order. Gauged by this standard, we cannot say that a law which authorizes or even requires the separation of the two races in public conveyances is unreasonable or more obnoxious to the Fourteenth Amendment than the acts of Congress requiring separate schools for colored children in the District of Columbia, the constitutionality of which does not seem to have been questioned, or the corresponding acts of state legislatures.

We consider the underlying fallacy of the plaintiff's argument to consist in the assumption that the enforced separation of the two races stamps the colored race with a badge of inferiority. If this be so, it is not by reason of anything found in the act, but solely because the colored race chooses to put that construction upon it. The argument necessarily assumes that if, as has been more than once the case, and is not unlikely to be so again, the colored race should become the dominant power in the state legislature, and should enact a law in precisely similar terms, it would thereby relegate the white race, to an inferior position. We imagine that the white race, at least, would not acquiesce in this assumption. The argument also assumes that social prejudices may be overcome by legislation and that equal rights cannot be secured to the Negro except by an enforced commingling of the two races. We cannot accept this proposition. If the two races are to meet upon terms of social equality, it must be the result of natural affinities, a mutual appreciation of each other's merits, and a voluntary consent of individuals. . . . Legislation is powerless to eradicate racial instincts or to abolish distinctions based upon physical differences, and the attempt to do so can only result in accentuating the difficulties of the present situation. If the civil and political rights of both races be equal, one cannot be inferior to the other civilly or politically. If one race be inferior to the other socially, the Constitution of the United States cannot put them upon the same plane. . . .

The judgment of the court below is, therefore, Affirmed.

Mr. Justice Harlan dissenting: . . .

In respect of civil rights, common to all citizens, the Constitution of the United States does not, I think, permit any public authority to know the race of those entitled to be protected in the enjoyment of such rights. Every true man has pride of race, and under appropriate circumstances when the rights of others, his equals before the law, are not to be affected, it is his privilege to express such pride and to take such action based upon it as to him seems proper. But I deny that any legislative body or judicial tribunal may have regard to the race of citizens when the civil rights of those citizens are involved. Indeed, such legislation, as that here in question, is inconsistent not only with that equality of rights which pertains to citizenship, national and state, but with the personal liberty enjoyed by everyone within the United States. . . .

It was said in argument that the statute of Louisiana does not discriminate against either race but prescribes a rule applicable alike to white and colored citizens. But this argument does not meet the difficulty. Everyone knows that the statute in question had its origin in the purpose, not so much to exclude white persons from railroad cars occupied by blacks, as to exclude colored people from coaches occupied by or assigned to white persons. Railroad corporations of Louisiana did not make discrimination among whites in the matter of accommodation for travelers. The thing to accomplish was, under the guise of giving equal accommodation for whites and blacks, to compel the latter to keep to themselves while traveling in railroad passenger coaches. No one would be so wanting in candor as to assert the contrary. The fundamental objection, therefore, to the statute is that it interferes with the personal freedom of citizens. . . . If a white man and a black man choose to occupy the same public conveyance on a public highway, it is their right to do so, and no government, proceeding alone on grounds of race, can prevent it without infringing the personal liberty of each.

It is one thing for railroad carriers to furnish, or to be required by law to furnish, equal accommodations for all whom they are under a legal duty to carry. It is quite another thing for government to forbid citizens of the white and black races from traveling in the same public conveyance, and to punish officers of railroad companies for permitting persons of the two races to occupy the same passenger coach. If a state can prescribe, as a rule of civil conduct, that whites and blacks shall not travel as passengers in the same railroad coach, why may it not so regulate the use of the streets of its cities and towns as to compel white citizens to keep on one side of a street and black citizens to keep on the other? Why may it not, upon like grounds, punish whites and blacks who ride together in streetcars or in open vehicles on a public road or street?

Why may it not require sheriffs to assign whites to one side of a courtroom and blacks to the other? And why may it not also prohibit the commingling of the two races in the galleries of legislative halls or in public assemblages convened for the consideration of the political questions of the day? Further, if this statute of Louisiana is consistent with the personal liberty of citizens, why may not the state require the separation in railroad coaches of native and naturalized citizens of the United States, or of Protestants and Roman Catholics? . . .

The white race deems itself to be the dominant race in this country. And so it is, in prestige, in achievements, in education, in wealth, and in power. So, I doubt not, it will continue to be for all time, if it remains true to its great heritage and holds fast to the principles of constitutional liberty. But in view of the Constitution, in the eye of the law, there is in this country no superior, dominant, ruling class of citizens. There is no caste here. Our Constitution is colorblind and neither knows nor tolerates classes among citizens. In respect of civil rights, all citizens are equal before the law. The humblest is the peer of the most powerful. The law regards man as man and takes no account of his surroundings or of his color when his civil rights as guaranteed by the supreme law of the land are involved. It is, therefore, to be regretted that this high tribunal, the final expositor of the fundamental law of the land, has reached the conclusion that it is competent for a state to regulate the enjoyment by citizens of their civil rights solely upon the basis of race. . . .

The arbitrary separation of citizens, on the basis of race, while they are on a public highway, is a badge of servitude wholly inconsistent with the civil freedom and the equality before the law established by the Constitution. It cannot be justified upon any legal grounds.

If evils will result from the commingling of the two races upon public highways established for the benefit of all, they will be infinitely less than those that will surely come from state legislation regulating the enjoyment of civil rights upon the basis of race. We boast of the freedom enjoyed by our people above all other peoples. But it is difficult to reconcile that boast with a state of the law which, practically, puts the brand of servitude and degradation upon a large class of our fellow-citizens, our equals before the law. The thin disguise of "equal" accommodations for passengers in railroad coaches will not mislead anyone, nor atone for the wrong this day done.

THE LEGACY OF RECONSTRUCTION

13

Reconstruction bequeathed a legacy of hatred, fear, and bigotry to America. The brief period of Republican rule in the South convinced Bourbons—the name for the new southern industrial aristocracy that succeeded the planter—that Negroes must be perpetually repressed if white rule was to be re-established below the Mason and Dixon line. This could be done only by voting for the party of the whites—the Democratic party—and systematically stripping away the political privileges of Negroes who might vote the Republican ticket. The tragic result was the emergence of the Solid South, which for generations never strayed from the Democratic column. The effects are assessed by a modern student of politics, Arthur N. Holcombe, in his study of The Political Parties of Today:[13]

The extent of this advantage which the South and the Democratic party gained through the failure of negro suffrage is reflected in the figures showing the distribution of the Congressmen between the sections under the successive apportionments. By the apportionment based on the census of 1850, New England and the three Middle Atlantic states had 92 representatives in the Congress of the United States and the Northeast was the leading section of the country. The fifteen slave states . . . came next with 90 representatives. The old Northwest, comprising the present Central

---

[13] *The Political Parties of Today* by Arthur N. Holcombe, pp. 190–195. Copyright, 1929, by Harper & Brothers.

and North Central sections, followed with 52 representatives. The Far West had two representatives. During the succeeding forty years the Central, North Central, and West Central sections grew more rapidly than any other part of the country and steadily advanced in population until in 1890, if the Fifteenth Amendment had not been adopted, it would have been easily in first place, on the basis of representation in Congress, and the South would have been in third place. But actually the South jumped into first place after 1870 and in 1890 had 127 representatives, while the Northeast had only 99 and the Central, North Central, and West Central sections had 113. The Mountain and Pacific sections had 18 representatives. The additional representation which the Southern states received under the Fifteenth Amendment fell largely to the Lower South. There were between 25 and 30 of these additional representatives under the apportionment based on the census of 1870, and probably as many as 35 under the apportionment based on the census of 1890. At least two-thirds of these additional representatives went to the eight states of the Lower South, the balance to the other states in which slavery had formerly existed. The corresponding increase of Southern representation in the electoral college did not affect the result of any presidential election during this period, but without these additional Congressmen the Democrats more than once would have had to yield the control of the Congress to the Republicans.

The indirect effects of the failure of negro suffrage in the South were more important to the Republicans than the direct. The solidification of the South in support of the Democratic party compelled the Republican leaders to fall back on sectional appeals such as had been the original justification of the party before the Civil War. But now the war was over, and the conscience of the North and West responded to Grant's magnanimous plea, "Let us have peace." People wearied of "waving the bloody shirt". . . . Though freely indulged in by Republican politicians during the political campaigns of this period, it was discountenanced by the better elements of the party. At Republican national conventions, too, Southern delegates demanded that something be done to protect the political rights of the freedmen, and, despite the reluctance of prudent politicians to stir up old animosities, it was difficult to resist these appeals. In 1890, when for the first time since 1875 the Republicans had a working majority in both branches of Congress and also controlled the Presidency, a so-called Force Bill was introduced into the Congress for the purpose of establishing effective federal supervision of presidential and congressional elections. The popular outcry against this measure throughout the country doubtless contributed to the Republican defeat in the congressional elections of that year, the worst the party has ever suffered. Despite the popular criticism, the measure passed the House, but failed in the Senate through the defection of eight Silver Republicans from the Far West. Since that time the Republican party has made no further attempt to use the authority of the federal government to secure the right to vote for negroes in the Southern states.

The most far-sighted Republican leaders had foreseen the failure of negro suffrage in the South unless something more were done for the freedmen than merely to give them the franchise. They recognized that without economic independence and political intelligence the vote alone is worth little. The expression, "forty acres and a mule," indicates the kind of foundation some of them deemed essential for the free development of the negro. But nothing substantial was done by the federal government during the period of reconstruction to set the negro upon his feet. He was left to find his way for himself as best he could. Later, wise leaders advocated federal aid to education in the South with a view to encouraging the intellectual development of the negro. President Garfield was especially interested in such plans. . . . One of the unfortunate results of his assassination was the loss of his leadership in this promising enterprise. Doubtless it will be a great advantage to this country in the long run that no state can ever make any civil or political discrimination against any class of citizens on account of their race, or color, or previous condition. In a country like ours, where racial differences are great and racial animosities can be easily aroused by unscrupulous politicians, it is well that racial discrimination should be made as difficult as possible. The individual must be dealt with as far as possible on his individual merits. Hence the adoption of the Fifteenth Amendment should prove in the end a great service to the American people. But the immediate consequences were disappointing, both to the Southern negro and to the Republican party. It did not secure the vote for the former, and it did not secure political supremacy for the latter.

Although the Fifteenth Amendment failed to accomplish what had been expected from it at the elections which followed the period of reconstruction, it was not without important effects upon the internal organization of the party itself. The suppression of most of the negro vote in the South threw the party organization in the Southern states into the hands of a few local leaders and bosses, who found ways of turning their partisan activities to account, even if they could not hope to win public elections. When the Republicans controlled the Presidency, these Southern politicians enjoyed the federal patronage and other perquisites in their section of the country. Whether the Republicans were in or out of power at Washington, the federal officeholders and would-be officeholders at the South controlled the delegations from that section to the national nominating conventions. They held the balance of power in all contests among Northern Republicans for the presidential nominations and had little incentive to consult any interests but their own in the disposition of their votes. At every national convention since 1876 the struggle for the votes of the Southern delegates has exercised a demoralizing influence. When the party has been in power at Washington, the administration candidate has always had an advantage over his competitors. That advantage was not great enough to enable Secretary Sherman to win over Grant and Blaine in 1880, nor to enable President Arthur to renominate himself against the opposition of powerful Blaine delegations from the big Republican states of the North in 1884. But it was a very disturbing factor in the convention of 1888, and it enabled President Harrison to defeat Blaine and McKinley in 1892. The greatest mischief, however, did not arise until a later period in the history of the party.

The creation of the Solid South had an unfortunate effect also on the Democratic party. Since there was no substantial opposition to the Democratic party in the eight states of the Lower South, and not enough in the eight other states, where slavery had formerly existed, to make the success of Democratic candidates very doubtful, there was little need for the Democratic party to consider the opinions of the people in those sections on questions of national concern. The national policy of the Democratic party, as defined by the national conventions, was determined by the Northern Democrats. But when the party got into power, the execution of the policy, so far as it was dependent on Acts of Congress, was largely in the hands of the Senators and Representatives from the South who under the rule of seniority generally dominated the important committees and controlled the course of business. The Democrats who wrote the party platforms were not the ones who would carry them into effect. Moreover, since the electoral votes of sixteen states were almost certain to be cast for the Democratic presidential candidate, whoever he might be, it was not necessary to give much consideration to the aspirations of Democratic leaders from that part of the country. No man of Southern birth received the Democratic nomination for the Presidency until 1912, and no active politician from a Southern state has yet been nomi-

nated. Doubtless much of the unavailability of Southern politicians was the result of the sectional jealousies caused by the Civil War, but the complete exclusion of Southern Democrats from the lists of candidates considered by the national conventions would have been much less likely if the South had been less solid in its support of the Democratic party. The attempt to establish negro suffrage, and the concentration of the white voters in one party in order to maintain white supremacy in local politics, were the direct causes of the practical abdication by Southern leaders of their legitimate authority in national politics. In effect they traded their influence in the councils of the party at Washington for the privilege of unrestricted home rule in the state and local governments.

14

But the tragedy of reconstruction can be found in the souls of men as well as in columns of election figures. For these Langston Hughes, poet of equality, speaks in "I, Too, Sing America":[14]

I, TOO, SING AMERICA

I am the darker brother.
They send me to eat in the kitchen
When company comes,
But I laugh,
And eat well,
And grow strong.

Tomorrow,
I'll sit at the table
When company comes.
Nobody'll dare
Say to me,
"Eat in the kitchen,"
Then.

Besides,
They'll see how beautiful I am
And be ashamed,—

I, too, am America.

[14] From *The Dream Keeper and Other Poems* by Langston Hughes, by permission of Alfred A. Knopf, Inc. Copyright 1932 by Alfred A. Knopf, Inc.

RULE OF THE STALWARTS

15

Henry Adams was the grandson of one President and the great-grandson of another. A peculiarly sensitive young man, Adams watched the antics of the politicians of the era of President Grant with a particularly mordant eye:[15]

At least four-fifths of the American people —Adams among the rest—had united in the election of General Grant to the Presidency, and probably had been more or less affected in their choice by the parallel they felt between Grant and Washington. Nothing could be more obvious. Grant represented order. He was a great soldier, and the soldier always represented order. He might be as partisan as he pleased, but a general who had organized and commanded half a million or a million men in the field, must know how to administer. Even Washington, who was, in education and experience, a mere cave-dweller, had known how to organize a government, and had found Jeffersons and Hamiltons to organize his departments. The task of bringing the Government back to regular practices, and of restoring moral and mechanical order to administration, was not very difficult; it was ready to do it itself, with a little encouragement. No doubt the confusion, especially in the old slave States and in the currency, was considerable, but the general disposition was good, and every one had echoed the famous phrase: "Let us have peace."

. . . Had Grant been a Congressman one would have been on one's guard, for one knew the type. One never expected from a Congressman more than good intentions and public spirit. Newspaper-men as a rule had no great respect for the lower House; Senators had less; and Cabinet officers had none at all. Indeed, one day when Adams was pleading with a Cabinet officer for patience and tact in dealing with Representatives, the Secretary impatiently broke out: "You can't use tact with a Congressman! A Congressman is a hog! You must take a stick and hit him on the snout!" Adams knew far too little, compared with the Secretary, to contradict him, though he thought the phrase somewhat harsh even as applied to the average Congressman of 1869—he saw little or nothing of later ones— but he knew a shorter way of silencing criticism. He had but to ask: "If a Congressman is a hog, what is a Senator?" This innocent question, put in a candid spirit, petrified any executive officer that ever sat a week in his office. Even Adams admitted that Senators passed belief. The comic side of their egotism partly disguised its extravagance, but faction had gone so far under Andrew Johnson that at times the whole Senate seemed to catch hysterics of nervous bucking without apparent reason. Great leaders, like Sumner and Conkling, could not be burlesqued; they were more grotesque than ridicule could make them; even Grant, who rarely sparkled in epigram, became witty on their account; but their egotism and factiousness were no laughing matter. They did permanent and terrible mischief, as Garfield and Blaine, and even McKinley and John Hay, were to feel. The most troublesome task of a reform President was that of bringing the Senate back to decency.

Therefore no one, and Henry Adams less than most, felt hope that any President chosen from the ranks of politics or politicians would raise the character of government; and by instinct if not by reason, all the world united on Grant. The Senate understood what the world expected, and waited in silence for a struggle with Grant more serious than that with Andrew Johnson. Newspaper-men were alive with eagerness to support the President against the Senate. The newspaper-man is, more than most men, a double personality; and his person feels best satisfied in its double instincts when writing in one sense and thinking in another. All newspaper-men, whatever they wrote, felt alike about the Senate. Adams floated with the stream. He was eager to join

---

[15] Henry Adams, *The Education of Henry Adams, an Autobiography* (Boston, 1918), pp. 260–262. Reprinted by permission of the publishers, Houghton Mifflin Company.

in the fight which he foresaw as sooner or later inevitable. He meant to support the executive in attacking the Senate and taking away its two-thirds vote and power of confirmation, or did he much care how it should be done, for he thought it safer to effect the revolution in 1870 than to wait till 1920.

With this thought in mind, he went to the Capitol to hear the names announced which should reveal the carefully guarded secret of Grant's Cabinet. To the end of his life, he wondered at the suddenness of the revolution which actually, within five minutes, changed his intended future into an absurdity so laughable as to make him ashamed of it. He was to hear a long list of Cabinet announcements not much weaker or more futile than that of Grant, and none of them made him blush, while Grant's nominations had the singular effect of making the hearer ashamed, not so much of Grant, as of himself. He had made another total misconception of life—another inconceivable false start. Yet, unlikely as it seemed, he had missed his motive narrowly, and his intention had been more than sound, for the Senators made no secret of saying with senatorial frankness that Grant's nominations betrayed his intent as plainly as they betrayed his incompetence. A great soldier might be a baby politician.

16

Excessive tariffs, the rape of the public domain, and a currency system tailored to the needs of investors evoked political protest and popular complaint. But the scandals which came to light during the Grant administrations produced a furor. An unholy alliance of corrupt business leaders and Republican "Stalwarts" in both state and national governments plundered the public treasury with such uninhibited flagrancy that the nation and the world were staggered. Of these enterprises, the Crédit Mobilier —a construction company organized by the backers of the Union Pacific Railroad to take advantage both of private investors and of government aid to transcontinental railways so as to divert an undue share of the building profits into their own pockets—was the most nefarious. The company succeeded, for the Mobilier's first dividend almost equaled the sum invested in it;

subsequent dividends climbed to nearly 350 percent a year. Fearful that Congress might investigate their profitable enterprise, its backers distributed stock judiciously among members of that body. These fradulent practices were exposed by a congressional committee headed by Luke P. Poland of Vermont, which reported in February, 1873. Particularly startling are its revelations concerning Oakes Ames, a Republican member of Congress from Massachusetts:[16]

On the 16th day of August, 1867, a contract was executed between the Union Pacific Railroad Company and Oakes Ames, by which Mr. Ames contracted to build six hundred and sixty-seven miles of the Union Pacific road at prices ranging from $42,000 to $96,000 per mile, amounting in the aggregate to $47,000,000. Before the contract was entered into it was understood that Mr. Ames was to transfer it to seven trustees, who were to execute it, and the profits of the contract were to be divided among the stockholders in the Crédit Mobilier Company, who should comply with certain conditions set out in the instrument transferring the contract to the trustees. The Ames contract and the transfer to trustees are incorporated in the evidence submitted, and therefore further recital of their terms is not deemed necessary.

Substantially, all the stockholders of the Crédit Mobilier complied with the conditions named in the transfer, and thus became entitled to share in any profits said trustees might make in executing the contract.

All the large stockholders in the Union Pacific were also stockholders in the Crédit Mobilier, and the Ames contract and its transfer to trustees were ratified by the Union Pacific, and received the assent of the great body of stockholders, but not of all.

After the Ames contract had been executed, it was expected by those interested that by reason of the enormous prices agreed to be paid for the work very large profits would be derived from building the road, and very soon the stock of the Crédit Mo-

---

[16] H. R. Rep. Doc. No. 77, 42nd Cong., 33d Sess., ii–iv.

bilier was understood by those holding it to be worth much more than its par value. The stock was not in the market and had no fixed market value, but the holders of it, in December, 1867, considered it worth at least double the par value, and in January and February, 1868, three or four times the par value, but it does not appear that these facts were generally or publicly known, or that the holders of the stock desired they should be.

The foregoing statement the committee think gives enough of the historic details, and condition and value of the stock, to make the following detailed facts intelligible.

Mr. Oakes Ames was then a member of the House of Representatives, and came to Washington at the commencement of the session, about the beginning of December, 1867. During that month Mr. Ames entered into contracts with a considerable number of members of Congress, both Senators and Representatives, to let them have shares of stock in the Crédit Mobilier Company at par, with interest thereon from the first day of the previous July. It does not appear that in any instance he asked any of these persons to pay a higher price than the par value and interest, nor that Mr. Ames used any special effort or urgency to get these persons to take it. In all these negotiations Mr. Ames did not enter into any details as to the value of the stock or the amount of dividend that might be expected upon it, but stated generally that it would be good stock, and in several instances said he would guarantee that they should get at least 10 per cent. on their money.

Some of these gentlemen, in their conversations with Mr. Ames, raised the question whether becoming holders of this stock would bring them into any embarrassment as members of Congress in their legislative action. Mr. Ames quieted such suggestions by saying it could not, for the Union Pacific had received from Congress all the grants and legislation it wanted, and they should ask for nothing more. In some instances those members who contracted for stock

paid to Mr. Ames the money for the price of the stock, par and interest; in others, where they had not the money, Mr. Ames agreed to carry the stock for them until they could get the money or it should be met by the dividends.

Mr. Ames was at this time a large stockholder in the Crédit Mobilier, but he did not intend any of these transactions to be sales of his own stock, but intended to fulfill all these contracts from stock belonging to the company.

At this time there were about six hundred and fifty shares of the stock of the company, which had for some reason been placed in the name of Mr. T. C. Durant, one of the leading and active men of the concern.

Mr. Ames claimed that a portion of this stock should be assigned to him to enable him to fulfill engagements he had made for stock. Mr. Durant claimed that he had made similar engagements that he should be allowed stock to fulfill. Mr. McComb, who was present at the time, claimed that he had also made engagements for stock which he should have stock given him to carry out. This claim of McComb was refused, but after the stock was assigned to Mr. Ames, McComb insisted that Ames should distribute some of the stock to his (McComb's) friends, and named Senators Bayard and Fowler, and Representatives Allison and Wilson, of Iowa.

It was finally arranged that three hundred and forty-three shares of the stock of the company should be transferred to Mr. Ames to enable him to perform his engagements, and that number of shares were set over on the books of the company to Oakes Ames, trustee, to distinguish it from the stock held by him before. Mr. Ames at the time paid to the company the par of the stock and interest from the July previous, and this stock still stands on the books in the name of Oakes Ames, trustee, except thirteen shares which have been transferred to parties in no way connected with Congress. The committee do not find that Mr. Ames had any negotiation whatever with any of these members of Congress on the subject of this stock prior to the commencement of the session of December, 1867, except Mr. Scofield, of Pennsylvania, and it was not claimed that any obligation existed from Mr. Ames to him as the result of it.

In relation to the purpose and motives of Mr. Ames in contracting to let members of Congress have Crédit Mobilier stock at par, which he and all other owners of it considered worth at least double that sum, the committee, upon the evidence taken by them and submitted to the House, cannot entertain doubt. When he said he did not suppose the Union Pacific Company would ask or need further legislation, he stated what he believed to be true. But he feared the interests of the road might suffer by adverse legislation, and what he desired to accomplish was to enlist strength and friends in Congress who would resist any encroachment upon or interference with the rights and privileges already secured, and to that end wished to create in them an interest identical with his own. This purpose is clearly avowed in his letters to McComb, copied in the evidence. He says he intends to place the stock "where it will do most good to us." And again, "we want more friends in this Congress." In his letter to McComb, and also in his statement prepared by counsel, he gives the philosophy of his action, to wit, "That he has found there is no difficulty in getting men to look after their own property." The committee are also satisfied that Mr. Ames entertained a fear that, when the true relations between the Crédit Mobilier Company and the Union Pacific became generally known, and the means by which the great profits expected to be made were fully understood, there was danger that congressional investigation and action would be invoked.

The members of Congress with whom he dealt were generally those who had been friendly and favorable to a Pacific Railroad, and Mr. Ames did not fear or expect to find them favorable to movements hostile to it; but he desired to stimulate their activity and watchfulness in opposition to any unfavor-

able action by giving them a personal interest in the success of the enterprise, especially so far as it affected the interest of the Crédit Mobilier Company. On the 9th day of December, 1867, Mr. C. C. Washburn, of Wisconsin, introduced in the House a bill to regulate by law the rates of transportation over the Pacific Railroad.

Mr. Ames, as well as others interested in the Union Pacific road, was opposed to this, and desired to defeat it. Other measures apparently hostile to that company were subsequently introduced into the House by Mr. Washburn of Wisconsin, and Mr. Washburne of Illinois. The committee believe that Mr. Ames, in his distributions of stock, had specially in mind the hostile efforts of the Messrs. Washburn, and desired to gain strength to secure their defeat. The reference in one of his letters to "Washburn's move" makes this quite apparent.

17

Revelations of plunder during Grant's first administration led Liberal Republicans to rebel. They rebelled against the corruption of northern Stalwarts and against corruption and force in southern reconstruction policies. The American Free Trade League induced liberals to support the program of tariff reform; exposure of the Tweed Ring and other scandals convinced Carl Schurz and like-minded Republicans of the need for higher standards in public life. The Liberal Republicans called a convention in 1872, and placed their own candidate in the field. A split on the tariff resulted in the nomination of Horace Greeley, venerable editor of the New York Tribune *and a high-tariff man, to run against Grant; but in other respects the platform echoes the old democratic spirit of the days before the Civil War:*[17]

We, the Liberal Republicans of the United States, in National Convention assembled at Cincinnati, proclaim the following principles as essential to just government:

1. We recognize the equality of all men before the law, and hold that it is the duty of Government, in its dealings with the peo-

---

[17] Edward Stanwood, *A History of Presidential Elections* (Boston, 1892), pp. 287–288.

ple to mete out equal and exact justice to all, of whatever nativity, race, color, or persuasion, religious or political.

2. We pledge ourselves to maintain the union of these States, emancipation and enfranchisement, and to oppose any reopening of the questions settled by the Thirteenth, Fourteenth, and Fifteenth Amendments to the Constitution.

3. We demand the immediate and absolute removal of all disabilities imposed on account of the Rebellion, which was finally subdued seven years ago, believing that universal amnesty will result in complete pacification in all sections of the country.

4. Local self-government, with impartial suffrage, will guard the rights of all citizens more securely than any centralized power. The public welfare requires the supremacy of the civil over the military authority, and freedom of person under the protection of the *habeas corpus.* We demand for the individual the largest liberty consistent with public order; for the State self-government, and for the nation a return to the methods of peace and the constitutional limitations of power.

5. The Civil Service of the Government has become a mere instrument of partisan tyranny and personal ambition, and an object of selfish greed. It is a scandal and reproach upon free institutions, and breeds a demoralization dangerous to the perpetuity of republican government. We therefore regard such thorough reforms of the Civil Service as one of the most pressing necessities of the hour; that honesty, capacity, and fidelity, constitute the only valid claims to public employment; that the offices of the Government cease to be a matter of arbitrary favoritism and patronage, and that public station become again a post of honor. To this end it is imperatively required that no President shall be a candidate for re-election.

6. We demand a system of Federal taxation which shall not unnecessarily interfere with the industry of the people, and which shall provide the means necessary to pay the expenses of the Government economically administered, the pensions, the interest on the public debt, and a moderate reduction annually of the principal thereof; and, recognizing that there are in our midst honest but irreconcilable differences of opinion with regard to the respective systems of Protection and Free Trade, we remit the discussion of the subject to the people in their Congressional Districts, and to the decision of Congress thereon, wholly free of Executive interference or dictation.

7. The public credit must be sacredly maintained, and we denounce repudiation in every form and guise.

8. A speedy return to specie payment is demanded alike by the highest considerations of commercial morality and honest government.

9. We remember with gratitude the heroism and sacrifices of the soldiers and sailors of the republic, and no act of ours shall ever detract from their justly-earned fame, or the full reward of their patriotism.

10. We are opposed to all further grants of land to railroads or other corporations. The public domain should be held sacred to actual settlers.

11. We hold that it is the duty of the Government, in its intercourse with foreign nations, to cultivate the friendship of peace, by treating with all on fair and equal terms, regarding it alike dishonorable either to demand what is not right, or to submit to what is wrong.

12. For the promotion and success of these vital principles, and the support of the candidates nominated by this convention we invite and cordially welcome the cooperation of all patriotic citizens, without regard to previous affiliations.

18

After Greeley's futile campaign, the Liberal Republican movement died swiftly; but its liberalism lived in the Republican left wing that cooperated with liberal Democrats. Meanwhile popular insistence upon reform obviously increased during the second Grant administration, as fresh evidence of fraud was presented to the nation. Indignation was so apparent that the President himself felt called upon to apologize; his last annual message to Congress, December 5, 1876, is a document remarkable for its admissions as well as for its naïveté:[18]

In submitting my eighth and last annual message to Congress it seems proper that I should refer to and in some degree recapitulate the events and official acts of the past eight years.

It was my fortune, or misfortune, to be called to the office of Chief Executive without any previous political training. From the age of 17 I had never even witnessed the excitement attending a Presidential campaign but twice antecedent to my own candidacy, and at but one of them was I eligible as a voter.

Under such circumstances it is but reasonable to suppose that errors of judgment must have occurred. Even had they not, differences of opinion between the Executive, bound by an oath to the strict performance of his duties, and writers and debaters must have arisen. It is not necessarily evidence of blunder on the part of the Executive because there are these differences of views. Mistakes have been made, as all can see and I admit, but it seems to me oftener in the selections made of the assistants appointed to aid in carrying out the various duties of administering the Government—in nearly every case selected without a personal acquaintance with the appointee, but upon recommendations of the representatives chosen directly by the people. It is impossible, where so many trusts are to be allotted, that the right parties should be chosen in every instance. History shows that no Administration from the time of Washington to the present has been free from these mistakes. But I leave comparisons to history, claiming only that I have acted in every instance from a conscientous desire to do what was right, constitutional, within the law, and for the very

best interests of the whole people. Failures have been errors of judgment, not of intent.

19

A modern student of the South, historian C. Vann Woodward, attempts to find in the history of the Reconstruction years some attitudes and values that might prove useful in the "cold war" days of the twentieth century:[19]

In a time when nationalism sweeps everything else before it, as it does at present, the regional historian is likely to be oppressed by a sense of his unimportance. America is the all-important subject, and national ideas, national institutions, and national policies are the themes that compel attention. Foreign peoples, eager to know what this New World colossus means to them and their immediate future, are impatient with details of regional variations, and Americans, intent on the need for national unity, tend to minimize their importance. New England, the West, and other regions are occasionally permitted to speak for the nation. But the South is thought to be hedged about with peculiarities that set apart as unique. As a standpoint from which to write American history it is regarded as eccentric and as a background for a historian something of a handicap to be overcome.

Of the eccentric position of the South in the nation there are admittedly many remaining indications. I do not think, however, that this eccentricity need be regarded as entirely a handicap. In fact, I think it could possibly be turned to advantage by the southern historian both in understanding American history and in interpreting it to non-Americans. For from a broader point of view it is not the South but America that is unique among the peoples of the world. This eccentricity arises out of the American legend of success and victory, a legend that is not shared by any other people of the

---

[18] James D. Richardson (comp.), *A Compilation of the Messages and Papers of the Presidents, 1789–1897* (Washington, 1909), VII, 399–400.

[19] C. Vann Woodward, "The Irony of Southern History," *The Journal of Southern History,* XIX (February, 1953), 1–7, 15–16, 18–19. Reprinted with the permission of the publishers, *The Journal of Southern History.*

civilized world. The collective will of this country has simply never known what it means to be confronted by complete frustration. Whether by luck, by abundant resources, by ingenuity, by technology, by organizing cleverness, or by sheer force of arms America has been able to overcome every major historic crisis—economic, political, or foreign—with which it has had to cope. This remarkable record has naturally left a deep imprint upon the American mind. It explains in large part the national faith in unlimited progress, in the efficacy of material means, in the importance of mass and speed, the worship of success, and the unquestioning belief in the invincibility of American arms.

The legend had been supported by an unbroken succession of victorious wars. Battles have been lost, and whole campaigns —but not wars. In the course of their national history the Americans, who have been called a bellicose though unmartial people, have fought eight wars. And among them there has not been so much as one South African fiasco such as England encountered in the heyday of her power. This unique good fortune has isolated America, I think rather dangerously, from the common experience of the rest of mankind, all the great peoples of which have without exception known the bitter taste of defeat and humiliation. It has fostered the tacit conviction that American ideals, values, and principles inevitably prevail in the end. That conviction has never received a name, nor even so much explicit formulation as the old concept of Manifest Destiny. It is assumed, not discussed. And the assumption exposes us to the temptation of believing that we are somehow immune from the forces of history.

The country that has come nearest to approximating the American legend of success and victory is England. The nearness of continental rivals and the precariousness of the balance of power, however, bred in the English an historical sophistication that prevented the legend from flourishing as luxuriantly as it has in the American climate.

Only briefly toward the end of the Victorian period did the legend threaten to get out of hand in England. Arnold J. Toynbee has recalled those piping days in a reminiscent passage. "I remember watching the Diamond Jubilee procession myself as a small boy," he writes. "I remember the atmosphere. It was: well, here we are on the top of the world, and we have arrived at this peak to stay there—forever! There is, of course, a thing called history, but history is something unpleasant that happens to other people. We are comfortably outside all that. I am sure, if I had been a small boy in New York in 1897 I should have felt the same. Of course, if I had been a small boy in 1897 in the Southern part of the United States, I should not have felt the same; I should then have known from my parents that history had happened to my people in my part of the world."

The South has had its full share of illusions, fantasies, and pretensions, and it has continued to cling to some of them with an astonishing tenacity that defies explanation. But the illusion that "history is something unpleasant that happens to other people" is certainly not one of them—not in the face of accumulated evidence and memory to the contrary. It is true that there have been many southern converts to the gospel of progress and success, and there was even a period following Reconstruction when it seemed possible that these converts might carry a reluctant region with them. But the conversion was never anywhere near complete. Full participation in the legend of irresistible progress, success, and victory could, after all, only be vicarious at best. For the inescapable facts of history were that the South had repeatedly met with frustration and failure. It had learned what it was to be faced with economic, social, and political problems that refused to yield to all the ingenuity, patience, and intelligence that a people could bring to bear upon them. It had learned to accommodate itself to conditions that it swore it would never accept and it had learned the taste left in the mouth by the swallowing of one's own words. It had learned to live for long decades in quite un-American poverty, and it had learned the equally un-American lesson of submission. For the South had undergone an experience that it could share with no other part of America—though it is shared by nearly all the peoples of Europe and Asia—the experience of military defeat, occupation, and reconstruction. Nothing about this history was conducive to the theory that the South was the darling of divine providence.

II

In his recent book, *The Irony of American History*, Reinhold Niebuhr conducts an astute analysis of national character and destiny that emphasizes another set of American pretensions which he calls the illusions of innocence and virtue. These illusions have their origins in both North and South, though at a period before there was any distinct regional consciousness. They were fostered by the two great moral traditions of early national life, New England Calvinism and Virginia humanism of the Jeffersonian school. While they differed upon theology, theocrats and humanists were agreed that their country was "God's American Israel," called out of a wicked and corrupt Old World and set apart by providence to create a new humanity and restore man's lost innocence. I believe that Niebuhr would agree that what I have described as the American legend of success and victory has assisted in fostering and perpetuating these illusions of innocence and virtue. At any rate he demonstrates that these illusions have been preserved past infancy and into national adulthood. Arriving at man's estate, we have suddenly found ourselves in possession of immense and undreamed of power and compelled to use this power in ways that are not innocent and that cover us with guilt. In clinging to our infant illusions of innocence along with our new power, writes the theologian, we are "involved in ironic perils which compound the

experiences of Babylon and Israel"—the perils of overweening power and overweening virtue.

Our opposite numbers in the world crisis, the Russian Communists, are bred on illusions that parallel our own with ironic fidelity, even though they are of very different origin and have been used to disguise (perhaps even from themselves) what seems to us much greater guilt of oppression and cruelty. They combine these illusions with Messianic passions that find a paler reflection in one layer of American conscience. Looking upon their own nation as the embodiment of innocence and justice, the Russians take it for granted that America is the symbol of the worst form of capitalistic injustice. Both America and Russia find it almost impossible to believe that anyone could think ill of them and are persuaded that only malice could prompt suspicions of motives so obviously virtuous. Each tends to regard the other as the only force willfully thwarting its dream of bringing happiness to all mankind.

There are many perils, both for our nation and for the world, inherent in this situation —and they do not all come from abroad. We are exasperated by the ironic incongruities of our position. Having more power than ever before, America enjoys less security than in the days of her weakness. Convinced of her virtue, she finds that even her allies accuse her of domestic vices invented by her enemies. The liberated prove ungrateful for their liberation, the reconstructed for their reconstruction, and the late colonial peoples vent their resentment upon our nation—the most innocent, we believe, of the imperial powers. Driven by these provocations and frustrations, there is the danger that America may be tempted to exert all the terrible power she possesses to compel history to conform to her own illusions. The extreme, but by no means the only expression, would be the so-called preventive war. This would be to commit the worst impiety of the Marxists, with whom it is dogma that they can compel history to conform to the pattern of their dreams by the ruthless use of force. . . .

In the field of diplomacy and foreign relations modern America suffers from a divided mind, torn between one policy that is reminiscent of the way of the South and another more suggestive of the way of the North in the Civil War crisis. On the one hand are those who would meet the foreign challenge by withdrawing from a critical community of nations teeming with heresies and, by erecting an impregnable barricade, forcibly keep out all alien ways, influences, and ideas. Another modern group that has a counterpart in at least one school of Southerners in the 1850's are those who in the 1950's, heedless of world opinion, would brook no opposition, would not co-operate with, nor consult other people's views, but insist that America must be strong enough to carry her way by economic coercion or by force. Suggestive also of the southern way are those who, in competing with our opponents for the favor of uncommitted peoples, would urge upon them institutions and abstract ideas of our own that have little or no relevance to their real needs and circumstances. And there are those also who resent as evidence of disloyalty any defection on the part of our allies from the particular economic faith upon which we have decided to take our stand.

More reminiscent of the way of the North, on the other hand, are those who hold that this is an irrepressible conflict, that a world divided against itself cannot stand, that the issue is essentially a moral one, that we are morally obligated to liberate the enslaved peoples of the earth, punish the wicked oppressors, and convert the liberated peoples to our way of thought. The true American mission, according to those who support this view, is a moral crusade on a world-wide scale. Such people are likely to concede no validity whatever and grant no hearing to the opposing point of view, and to appeal to a higher law to justify bloody and revolting means in the name of a noble end. For what end could be nobler, they ask, than the liberation of man? Fortunately wiser counsel prevails at the moment, counsel which charts a course of foreign policy between the perilous extremes of isolationism and world crusade. But each of the extreme courses still has powerful advocates and neither yet be regarded as a dead issue.

We have been admonished lately to heed the ironic consequences of the characteristic American approach to international affairs since the beginning of the present century. The main deficiencies of our policy of the last fifty years, we are told, are our legalistic and moralistic approaches to foreign relations. It is possible and even desirable, I believe, to accept the validity of this critical insight without embracing the strictly amoral, pragmatic, power-conscious policy of national self-interest that has been proposed as an alternative by those who criticize the moralistic approach. It is all too apparent that the association of the legalistic with the moralistic concept results in a torrent of indignation and bitterness against the lawbreaker and a blinding conviction of moral superiority to the enemy. Expressed in military policy and war aims these passions overwhelm reason and find no bounds short of the complete submission, unconditional surrender, and total domination of the defeated people. The irony of the moralistic approach, when exploited by nationalism, is that the high motive to end injustice and immorality actually results in making war more amoral and horrible than ever and in shattering the foundations of the political and moral order upon which peace has to be built.

With all her terrible power and new responsibilities combined with her illusions of innocence and her legends of immunity from frustration and defeat, America stands in greater need than she ever did of understanding her own history. Our European friends, appalled by the impetuosity and naïveté of some of our deeds and assumptions, have attributed our lack of historical sophistication to our lack of a history—in their sense of the word. America's apparent immunity to the tragic and ironic aspects of man's fate—that charmed and fabled immunity that once made America the Utopia of both the common men and the philosophers of Europe—has come to be pictured as Europe's curse. For the fear that haunts Europeans is the fear that America's lack of a common basis of experience and suffering will blind her to the true nature of their dilemmas and end by plunging them into catastrophe. But the Europeans are not entirely right. America has a history. It is only that the tragic aspects and the ironic implications of that history have been obscured by the national legend of success and victory and by the perpetuation of infant illusions of innocence and virtue.

CONSTITUTION OF THE UNITED STATES[1]

We the people of the United States in order to form a more perfect union, establish justice, insure domestic tranquillity, provide for the common defence, promote the general welfare and secure the blessings of liberty to ourselves and our posterity, do ordain and establish this CONSTITUTION for the United States of America.

Article I

Section 1. All legislative powers herein granted shall be vested in a Congress of the United States, which shall consist of a Senate and House of Representatives.

Section 2. The House of Representatives shall be composed of members chosen every second year by the people of the several States, and the electors in each State shall have the qualifications requisite for electors of the most numerous branch of the State Legislature.

No person shall be a Representative who shall not have attained to the age of twenty-five years, and been seven years a citizen of the United States, and who shall not when elected, be an inhabitant of that State in which he shall be chosen.

Representatives and direct taxes shall be apportioned among the several States which may be included within this Union, according to their respective numbers, which shall be determined by adding to the whole number of free persons, including those bound to service for a term of years, and excluding Indians not taxed, three fifths of all other persons. The actual enumeration shall be made within three years after the first meeting of the Congress of the United States, and

within every subsequent term of ten years, in such manner as they shall by law direct. The number of Representatives shall not exceed one for every thirty thousand, but each State shall have at least one Representative; and until such enumeration shall be made, the State of *New Hampshire* shall be entitled to choose three, *Massachusetts* eight, *Rhode Island* and *Providence Plantations* one, *Connecticut* five, *New York* six, *New Jersey* four, *Pennsylvania* eight, *Delaware* one, *Maryland* six, *Virginia* ten, *North Carolina* five, *South Carolina* five, and *Georgia* three.

When vacancies happen in the representation from any State, the Executive authority thereof shall issue writs of election to fill such vacancies.

The House of Representatives shall choose their Speaker and other officers; and shall have the sole power of impeachment.

Section 3. The Senate of the United States shall be composed of two Senators from each State, chosen by the Legislature thereof, for six years; and each Senator shall have one vote.

Immediately after they shall be assembled in consequence of the first election, they shall be divided as equally as may be, into three classes. The seats of the Senators of the first class shall be vacated at the expiration of the second year, of the second class at the expiration of the fourth year, and of the third class at the expiration of the sixth year, so that one third may be chosen every second year; and if vacancies happen by resignation or otherwise, during the recess of the Legislature of any State, the executive thereof may make temporary appointments, until the next meeting of the Legislature, which shall then fill such vacancies.

No person shall be a Senator who shall not have attained to the age of thirty years,

---

[1] Jonathan Elliot, *The Debates in the Several Conventions on the Adoption of the Federal Constitution* (1836), 1–21, "copied and carefully compared with the original in the Department of State. Punctuation, paragraphs, and capital letters, same as said original," p. 1.

and been nine years a citizen of the United States, and who shall not, when elected, be an inhabitant of that State for which he shall be chosen.

The Vice President of the United States shall be President of the Senate, but shall have no vote unless they be equally divided.

The Senate shall choose their other officers, and also a President protempore, in the absence of the Vice President or when he shall exercise the office of President of the United States.

The Senate shall have the sole power to try all impeachments: when sitting for that purpose, they shall be on oath or affirmation. When the President of the United States is tried the Chief Justice shall preside: and no person shall be convicted without the concurrence of two-thirds of the members present.

Judgment in cases of impeachment shall not extend farther than to removal from office, and disqualification to hold and enjoy any office of honor, trust, or profit under the United States: but the party convicted shall nevertheless be liable and subject to indictment, trial, judgment and punishment, according to law.

Section 4. The times, places and manner of holding elections for Senators and Representatives, shall be prescribed in each State by the legislature thereof; but the Congress may at any time by law make or alter such regulations, except as to the places of choosing Senators.

The Congress shall assemble at least once in every year, and such meeting shall be on the first Monday in December unless they shall by law appoint a different day.

Section 5. Each House shall be the judge of the elections, returns and qualifications of its own members, and a majority of each shall constitute a quorum to do business; but a smaller number may adjourn from day to day, and may be authorized to compel the attendance of absent members, in such manner, and under such penalties as each House may provide.

Each House may determine the rules of its proceedings, punish its members for disorderly behavior, and, with the concurrence of two thirds, expel a member.

Each House shall keep a journal of its proceedings, and from time to time publish the same, excepting such parts as may in their judgment require Secrecy; and the yeas and nays of the members of either House on any question shall, at the desire of one-fifth of those present, be entered on the journal.

Neither House, during the Session of Congress, shall, without the consent of the other, adjourn for more than three days, nor to any other place than that in which the two Houses shall be sitting.

Section 6. The Senators and Representatives shall receive a compensation for their services, to be ascertained by law, and paid out of the Treasury of the United States. They shall in all cases except treason, felony and breach of the peace, be privileged from arrest during their attendance at the session of their respective Houses, and in going to and returning from the same; and for any speech or debate in either House, they shall not be questioned in any other place.

No Senator or Representative shall, during the time for which he was elected, be appointed to any civil office under the authority of the United States, which shall have been created, or the emoluments whereof shall have been increased during such time: and no person holding any office under the United States shall be a member of either House during his continuance in office.

Section 7. All bills for raising revenue shall originate in the House of Representatives; but the Senate may propose, or concur with; amendments, as on other bills.

Every bill which shall have passed the House of Representatives, and the Senate, shall, before it becomes a law, be presented to the President of the United States; if he approve he shall sign it, but if not he shall return it, with his objections to that House in which it shall have originated, who shall enter the objections at large on their journal, and proceed to reconsider it. If after such reconsideration two thirds of that House shall agree to pass the bill, it shall be sent, together with the objections, to the other House, by which it shall likewise be reconsidered, and if approved by two thirds of that House, it shall become a law. But in all such cases the votes of both Houses shall be determined by yeas and nays, and the names of the persons voting for and against the bill shall be entered on the journal of each House respectively. If any bill shall not be returned by the President within ten days (Sundays excepted), after it shall have been presented to him, the same shall be a law, in like manner as if he had signed it, unless the Congress by their adjournment prevent its return, in which case it shall not be a law.

Every order, resolution, or vote to which the concurrence of the Senate and House of Representatives may be necessary (except on a question of adjournment) shall be presented to the President of the United States; and before the same shall take effect, shall be approved by him, or, being disapproved by him, shall be repassed by two-thirds of the Senate and House of Representatives, according to the rules and limitations prescribed in the case of a bill.

Section 8. The Congress shall have power To lay and collect taxes, duties, imposts and excises, to pay the debts and provide for the common defence and general welfare of the United States; but all duties, imposts and excises shall be uniform throughout the United States;

To borrow money on the credit of the United States;

To regulate commerce with foreign nations, and among the several States, and with the Indian tribes;

To establish an uniform rule of naturalization, and uniform laws on the subject of bankruptcies throughout the United States;

To coin money, regulate the value thereof, and of foreign coin, and fix the standard of weights and measures;

To provide for the punishment of counterfeiting the securities and current coin of the United States;

To establish post offices and post roads;

To promote the progress of science and useful arts, by securing for limited times to authors and inventors the exclusive right to their respective writings and discoveries;

To constitute tribunals inferior to the supreme court;

To define and punish piracies and felonies committed on the high seas and offences against the law of nations;

To declare war, grant letters of marque and reprisal, and make rules concerning captures on land and water;

To raise and support armies, but no appropriation of money to that use shall be for a longer term than two years;

To provide and maintain a navy;

To make rules for the government and regulation of the land and naval forces;

To provide for calling forth the militia to execute the laws of the Union, suppress insurrections and repel invasions;

To provide for organizing, arming and disciplining, the militia, and for governing such part of them as may be employed in the service of the United States, reserving to the States respectively, the appointment of the officers, and the authority of training the militia according to the discipline prescribed by Congress;

To exercise exclusive legislation in all cases whatsoever over such district (not exceeding ten miles square) as may, by cession of particular States, and the acceptance of Congress, become the seat of the government of the United States, and to exercise like authority over all places purchased by the consent of the Legislature of the State in which the same shall be, for the erection of forts, magazines, arsenals, dockyards, and other needful buildings;— And

To make all laws which shall be necessary and proper for carrying into execution the foregoing powers, and all other powers vested by this constitution in the government of the United States, or in any department or officer thereof.

Section 9. The migration or importation of such persons as any of the States now existing shall think proper to admit, shall not be prohibited by the Congress prior to the year eighteen hundred and eight, but a tax or duty may be imposed on such importation, not exceeding ten dollars for each person.

The privilege of the writ of *Habeas Corpus* shall not be suspended, unless when in cases of rebellion or invasion the public safety may require it.

No bill of attainder or ex post facto law shall be passed.

No capitation, or other direct, tax shall be laid, unless in proportion to the census or enumeration herein before directed to be taken.

No tax or duty shall be laid on articles exported from any State.

No preference shall be given by any regulation of commerce or revenue to the ports of one State over those of another: nor shall vessels bound to, or from, one State, be obliged to enter, clear, or pay duties in another.

No money shall be drawn from the Treasury, but in consequence of appropriations made by law; and a regular statement and account of the receipts and expenditures of all public money shall be published from time to time.

No title of nobility shall be granted by the United States and no person holding any office of profit or trust under them, shall, without the consent of the Congress, accept of any present, emolument, office, or title, of any kind whatever, from any king, prince, or foreign State.

Section 10. No State shall enter into any treaty, alliance, or confederation; grant letters of marque and reprisal; coin money, emit bills of credit; make any thing but gold and silver coin a tender in payment of debts; pass any bill of attainder, ex post facto law; or law impairing the obligation of contracts; or grant any title of nobility.

No State shall, without the consent of the Congress, lay any imposts or duties on imports or exports, except what may be absolutely necessary for executing its inspection laws: and the net produce of all duties and imposts, laid by any State on imports or ex-

ports, shall be for the use of the Treasury of the United States; and all such laws shall be subject to the revision and control of the Congress.

No State shall, without the consent of Congress, lay any duty of tonnage, keep troops, or ships of war in time of peace, enter into any agreement or compact with another State, or with a foreign power, or engage in war, unless actually invaded, or in such imminent danger as will not admit of delay.

Article II

Section 1. The executive power shall be vested in a President of the United States of America. He shall hold his office during the term of four years, and, together with the Vice-President, chosen for the same term, be elected as follows:

Each State shall appoint, in such manner as the Legislature thereof may direct, a number of electors equal to the whole number of Senators and Representatives to which the State may be entitled in the Congress; but no Senator or Representative, or person holding an office of trust or profit under the United States, shall be appointed an elector.

The electors shall meet in their respective States, and vote by ballot for two persons, of whom one at least shall not be an inhabitant of the same State with themselves. And they shall make a list of all the persons voted for, and of the number of votes for each; which list they shall sign and certify, and transmit sealed to the seat of the government of the United States, directed to the President of the Senate. The President of the Senate shall, in the presence of the Senate and House of Representatives, open all the certificates, and the votes shall then be counted. The person having the greatest number of votes shall be the President, if such number be a majority of the whole number of electors appointed; and if there be more than one who have such majority, and have an equal number of votes, then the House of Representatives shall immediately choose by ballot one of them for President; and if no person have a majority, then from the five highest on the list the said House shall, in like manner, choose the President. But in choosing the President, the votes shall be taken by States, the representation from each State having one vote; a quorum for this purpose shall consist of a member or members from two-thirds of the States, and a majority of all the States shall be necessary to a choice. In every case, after the choice of the President, the person having the greatest number of votes of the electors shall be the Vice-President. But if there should remain two or more who have equal votes, the Senate shall choose from them by ballot the Vice-President.

The Congress may determine the time of choosing the electors, and the day on which they shall give their votes; which day shall be the same throughout the United States.

No person except a natural born citizen, or a citizen of the United States, at the time of the adoption of this constitution, shall be eligible to the office of President; neither shall any person be eligible to that office who shall not have attained to the age of thirty-five years, and been fourteen years a resident within the United States.

In case of the removal of the President from office, or of his death, resignation or inability to discharge the powers and duties of the said office, the same shall devolve on the Vice-President, and the Congress may by law provide for the case of removal, death, resignation or inability, both of the President and Vice-President, declaring what officer shall then act as President, and such officer shall act accordingly, until the disability be removed, or a President shall be elected.

The President shall, at stated times, receive for his services, a compensation, which shall neither be increased nor diminished during the period for which he shall have been elected, and he shall not receive within that period any other emolument from the United States, or any of them.

Before he enter on the execution of his office, he shall take the following oath or affirmation: *"I do solemnly swear (or affirm)* *that I will faithfully execute the office of President of the United States, and will, to the best of my ability, preserve, protect, and defend the Constitution of the United States."*

Section 2. The President shall be commander in chief of the army and navy of the United States, and of the militia of the several States, when called into the actual service of the United States; he may require the opinion, in writing, of the principal officer in each of the executive departments, upon any subject relating to the duties of their respective offices; and he shall have power to grant reprieves and pardons for offences against the United States, except in cases of impeachment.

He shall have power, by and with the advice and consent of the Senate, to make treaties, provided two-thirds of the Senators present concur; and he shall nominate, and by and with the advice and consent of the Senate, shall appoint ambassadors, other public ministers and consuls, judges of the supreme court, and all other officers of the United States, whose appointments are not herein otherwise provided for, and which shall be established by law: But the Congress may by law vest the appointment of such inferior officers as they think proper, in the President alone, in the courts of law, or in the heads of departments.

The President shall have power to fill up all vacancies that may happen during the recess of the Senate, by granting commissions which shall expire at the end of their next session.

Section 3. He shall from time to time give to the Congress information of the state of the Union, and recommend to their consideration such measures as he shall judge necessary and expedient; he may, on extraordinary occasions, convene both Houses, or either of them, and, in case of disagreement between them, with respect to the time of adjournment, he may adjourn them to such time as he shall think proper; he shall receive ambassadors and other public ministers; he shall take care that the laws be faithfully executed, and shall commission all the officers of the United States.

Section 4. The President, Vice-President and all civil officers of the United States, shall be removed from office on impeachment for, and conviction of, treason, bribery, or other high crimes and misdemeanors.

Article III

Section 1. The judicial power of the United States shall be vested in one Supreme Court, and in such inferior courts as the Congress may from time to time ordain and establish. The judges, both of the supreme and inferior courts, shall hold their offices during good behaviour, and shall, at stated times, receive for their services, a compensation, which shall not be diminished during their continuance in office.

Section 2. The judicial power shall extend to all cases in law and equity, arising under this constitution, the laws of the United States, and the treaties made, or which shall be made, under their authority; to all cases —affecting ambassadors, other public ministers, and consuls;—to all cases of admiralty and maritime jurisdiction;—to controversies to which the United States shall be a party; —to controversies between two or more States;—between a State and citizens of another State;—between citizens of different States;—between citizens of the same State, claiming lands under grants of different States, and between a State or the citizens thereof, and foreign States, citizens or subjects.

In all cases affecting ambassadors, other public ministers and consuls, and those in which a State shall be party, the supreme court shall have original jurisdiction. In all the other cases before-mentioned, the supreme court shall have appellate jurisdiction, both as to law and fact, with such exceptions, and under such regulations, as the Congress shall make.

The trial of all crimes, except in cases of impeachment, shall be by jury; and such trial shall be held in the State where the said crimes shall have been committed; but when not committed within any State, the trial shall be at such place or places as the Congress may by law have directed.

Section 3. Treason against the United States, shall consist only in levying war against them, or in adhering to their enemies, giving them aid and comfort. No person shall be convicted of treason, unless on the testimony of two witnesses to the same overt act, or on confession in open court.

The Congress shall have power to declare the punishment of treason, but no attainder of treason shall work corruption of blood, or forfeiture except during the life of the person attainted.

Article IV

Section 1. Full faith and credit shall be given in each State to the public acts, records, and judicial proceedings of every other State. And the Congress may by general laws prescribe the manner in which such acts, records, and proceedings shall be proved, and the effect thereof.

Section 2. The citizens of each State shall be entitled to all the privileges and immunities of citizens in the several States.

A person charged in any State with treason, felony, or other crime, who shall flee from justice, and be found in another State, shall on demand of the executive authority of the State from which he fled, be delivered up, to be removed to the State having jurisdiction of the crime.

No person held to service or labor in one State, under the laws thereof, escaping into another, shall, in consequence of any law or regulation therein, be discharged from such service or labor, but shall be delivered up on claim of the party to whom such service or labor may be due.

Section 3. New States may be admitted by the Congress into this Union; but no new State shall be formed or erected within the jurisdiction of any other State; nor any State be formed by the junction of two or more States, or parts of States, without the consent of the Legislature of the States concerned as well as of the Congress.

The Congress shall have power to dispose of and make all needful rules and regulations respecting the territory or other property belonging to the United States; and nothing in this constitution shall be so construed as to prejudice any claims of the United States, or of any particular State.

Section 4. The United States shall guaranty to every State in this Union a republican form of government, and shall protect each of them against invasion; and on application of the legislature, or of the executive (when the legislature cannot be convened) against domestic violence.

Article V

The Congress whenever two-thirds of both Houses shall deem it necessary, shall propose amendments to this constitution, or, on the application of the legislatures of two-thirds of the several States, shall call a convention for proposing amendments, which in either case, shall be valid to all intents and purposes, as part of this constitution, when ratified by the legislatures of three-fourths of the several States, or by conventions in three-fourths thereof, as the one or the other mode of ratification may be proposed by the Congress; provided, that no amendment, which may be made prior to the year one thousand eight hundred and eight, shall in any manner affect the first and fourth clauses in the ninth section of the first article; and that no State, without its consent, shall be deprived of its equal suffrage in the Senate.

Article VI

All debts contracted and engagements entered into, before the adoption of this constitution, shall be as valid against the United States under this constitution as under the confederation.

This constitution, and the laws of the United States which shall be made in pursuance thereof; and all treaties made, or which shall be made, under the authority of the United States, shall be the supreme law of the land; and the judges in every state shall be bound thereby, any thing in the constitution or laws of any State to the contrary notwithstanding.

The Senators and Representatives before mentioned, and the members of the several State legislatures, and all executive and judicial officers, both of the United States and of the several States shall be bound by oath or affirmation, to support this constitution: but no religious test shall ever be required as a qualification to any office or public trust under the United States.

Article VII

The ratification of the conventions of nine states, shall be sufficient for the establishment of this constitution between the States so ratifying the same.

Done in convention by the unanimous consent of the States present the seventeenth day of September in the year of our Lord one thousand seven hundred and eighty-seven and of the independence of the United States of America the twelfth.

THE BILL OF RIGHTS:
1791

Amendments[2]
Article I

Congress shall make no law respecting an establishment of religion, or prohibiting the free exercise thereof; or abridging the freedom of speech, or of the press; or the right of the people peaceably to assemble, and to petition the government for a redress of grievances.

Article II

A well-regulated militia being necessary to the security of a free State, the right of the people to keep and bear arms shall not be infringed.

Article III

No soldier shall, in time of peace, be quartered in any house without the consent of the owner, nor in time of war but in a manner to be prescribed by law.

Article IV

The right of the people to be secure in their persons, houses, papers, and effects,

---

[2] The first ten Articles declared in force December 15, 1791.

against unreasonable searches and seizures, shall not be violated; and no warrants shall issue but upon probable cause, supported by oath or affirmation, and particularly describing the place to be searched and the persons or things to be seized.

Article V

No person shall be held to answer for a capital or otherwise infamous crime, unless on a presentment or indictment of a grand jury, except in cases arising in the land or naval forces, or in the militia when in actual service, in time of war or public danger; nor shall any person be subject, for the same offence, to be twice put in jeopardy of life or limb, nor shall be compelled in any criminal case to be a witness against himself; nor be deprived of life, liberty, or property, without due process of law; nor shall private property be taken for public use without just compensation.

Article VI

In all criminal prosecutions the accused shall enjoy the right to a speedy and public trial, by an impartial jury of the State and district wherein the crime shall have been committed, which district shall have been previously ascertained by law; and to be informed of the nature and cause of the accusation; to be confronted with the witnesses against him; to have compulsory process for obtaining witnesses in his favor; and to have the assistance of counsel for his defence.

Article VII

In suits at common law, where the value in controversy shall exceed twenty dollars, the right of trial by jury shall be preserved; and no fact tried by a jury shall be otherwise reëxamined in any court of the United States, than according to the rules of the common law.

Article VIII

Excessive bail shall not be required, nor excessive fines imposed, nor cruel and unusual punishments inflicted.

Article IX

The enumeration in the Constitution of certain rights shall not be construed to deny or disparage others retained by the people.

Article X

The powers not delegated to the United States by the Constitution, nor prohibited by it to the States, are reserved to the States respectively, or to the people.

LATER CONSTITUTIONAL AMENDMENTS

Article XI[3]

The judicial power of the United States shall not be construed to extend to any suit in law or equity commenced or prosecuted against any one of the United States by citizens of another state, or by citizens or subjects of any foreign State.

Article XII[4]

The electors shall meet in their respective States, and vote by ballot for President and Vice-President, one of whom, at least, shall not be an inhabitant of the same State with themselves; they shall name in their ballots the person voted for as President, and in distinct ballots the person voted for as Vice-President; and they shall make distinct lists of all persons voted for as President, and of all persons voted for as Vice-President, and of the number of votes for each; which lists they shall sign and certify, and transmit sealed to the seat of the government of the United States, directed to the President of the Senate; the President of the Senate shall, in the presence of the Senate and House of Representatives, open all the certificates, and the votes shall then be counted: the person having the greatest number of votes for President shall be the President, if such number be a majority of the whole number of electors appointed; and if no person have such majority, then, from the persons

---

[3] January 8, 1798.
[4] September 25, 1804.

having the highest numbers, not exceeding three, on the list of those voted for as President, the House of Representatives shall choose, immediately, by ballot, the President. But, in choosing the President, the votes shall be taken by States, the representation from each State having one vote; a quorum for this purpose shall consist of a member or members from two-thirds of the States, and a majority of all the States shall be necessary to a choice. And if the House of Representatives shall not choose a President whenever the right of choice shall devolve upon them, before the fourth day of March next following, then the Vice-President shall act as President, as in the case of the death or other constitutional disability of the President. The person having the greatest number of votes as Vice-President shall be the Vice-President, if such number be a majority of the whole number of electors appointed; and if no person have a majority, then, from the two highest numbers on the list, the Senate shall choose the Vice-President: a quorum for the purpose shall consist of two-thirds of the whole number of Senators, and a majority of the whole number shall be necessary to a choice. But no person constitutionally ineligible to the office of President, shall be eligible to that of Vice-President of the United States.

Article XIII[5]

Section 1. Neither slavery nor involuntary servitude, except as a punishment for crime whereof the party shall have been duly convicted, shall exist within the United States, or any place subject to their jurisdiction.

Section 2. Congress shall have power to enforce this article by appropriate legislation.

Article XIV[6]

Section 1. All persons born or naturalized in the United States, and subject to the jurisdiction thereof, are citizens of the United States and of the State wherein they reside.

---

[5] December 18, 1865.
[6] July 23, 1868.

No State shall make or enforce any law which shall abridge the privileges or immunities of citizens of the United States; nor shall any State deprive any person of life, liberty, or property, without due process of law; nor deny to any person within its jurisdiction the equal protection of the laws.

Section 2. Representatives shall be apportioned among the several States according to their respective numbers, counting the whole number of persons in each State, excluding Indians not taxed. But when the right to vote at any election for the choice of electors for President and Vice-President of the United States, Representatives in Congress, the Executive and Judicial officers of a State, or the members of the Legislature thereof, is denied to any of the male inhabitants of such State, being twenty-one years of age, and citizens of the United States, or in any way abridged, except for participation in rebellion, or other crime, the basis of representation therein shall be reduced in the proportion which the number of such male citizens shall bear to the whole number of male citizens twenty-one years of age in such State.

Section 3. No person shall be a Senator or Representative in Congress, or elector of President and Vice President, or hold any office, civil or military, under the United States, or under any State, who, having previously taken an oath, as a member of Congress, or as an officer of the United States, or as a member of any State legislature, or as an executive or judicial officer of any State, to support the Constitution of the United States, shall have engaged in insurrection or rebellion against the same, or given aid or comfort to the enemies thereof. But Congress may by a vote of two-thirds of each House, remove such disability.

Section 4. The validity of the public debt of the United States, authorized by law, including debts incurred for payment of pensions and bounties for services in suppressing insurrection or rebellion, shall not be questioned. But neither the United States nor any State shall assume or pay any debt or obligation incurred in aid of insurrection or rebellion against the United States, or any claim for the loss or emancipation of any slave; but all such debts, obligations and claims shall be held illegal and void.

Section 5. The Congress shall have power to enforce, by appropriate legislation, the provisions of this article.

Article XV[7]

Section 1. The right of citizens of the United States to vote shall not be denied or abridged by the United States or by any State on account of race, color, or previous condition of servitude.

Section 2. The Congress shall have power to enforce this article by appropriate legislation.

Article XVI[8]

The Congress shall have power to lay and collect taxes on incomes, from whatever source derived, without apportionment among the several States, and without regard to any census or enumeration.

Article XVII[9]

The Senate of the United States shall be composed of two senators from each State, elected by the people thereof, for six years; and each Senator shall have one vote. The electors in each State shall have the qualifications requisite for electors of the most numerous branch of the State legislature.

When vacancies happen in the representation of any State in the Senate, the executive authority of such State shall issue writs of election to fill such vacancies: *Provided,* That the legislature of any State may empower the executive thereof to make temporary appointments until the people fill the vacancies by election as the legislature may direct.

This amendment shall not be so construed as to affect the election or term of any Senator chosen before it becomes valid as part of the Constitution.

Article XVIII[10]

Section I. After one year from the ratification of this article the manufacture, sale, or transportation of intoxicating liquors within, the importation thereof into, or the exportation thereof from the United States and all territory subject to the jurisdiction thereof for beverage purposes is hereby prohibited.

Section 2. The Congress and the several States shall have concurrent power to enforce this article by appropriate legislation.

This article shall be inoperative unless it shall have been ratified as an amendment to the Constitution by the legislatures of the several States, as provided in the Constitution, within seven years from the date of the submission hereof to the States by the Congress.

Article XIX[11]

The right of citizens of the United States to vote shall not be denied or abridged by the United States or by any State on account of sex.

Congress shall have power to enforce this article by appropriate legislation.

Article XX[12]

Section 1. The terms of the President and Vice-President shall end at noon on the 20th day of January, and the terms of Senators and Representatives at noon on the 3d day of January, of the years in which such terms would have ended if this article had not been ratified; and the terms of their successors shall then begin.

Section 2. The Congress shall assemble at least once in every year, and such meeting shall begin at noon on the 3d day of January, unless they shall by law appoint a different day.

Section 3. If, at the time fixed for the beginning of the term of the President, the President elect shall have died, the Vice-President elect shall become President. If a President shall not have been chosen before

---

[7] March 30, 1870.
[8] February 25, 1913.
[9] May 31, 1913.

[10] January 29, 1919.
[11] August 26, 1920.
[12] February 6, 1933.

the time fixed for the beginning of his term, or if the President elect shall have failed to qualify, then the Vice-President elect shall act as President until a President shall have qualified; and the Congress may by law provide for the case wherein neither a President elect nor a Vice-President elect shall have qualified, declaring who shall then act as President, or the manner in which one who is to act shall be selected, and such person shall act accordingly until a President or Vice-President shall have qualified.

Section 4. The Congress may by law provide for the case of the death of any of the persons from whom the House of Representatives may choose a President whenever the right of choice shall have devolved upon them, and for the case of the death of any of the persons from whom the Senate may choose a Vice-President whenever the right of choice shall have devolved upon them.

Section 5. Sections 1 and 2 shall take effect on the 15th day of October following the ratification of this article.

Section 6. This article shall be inoperative unless it shall have been ratified as an amendment to the Constitution by the legislatures of three-fourths of the several States within seven years from the date of its submission.

Article XXI[13]

Section 1. The eighteenth article of amendment to the Constitution of the United States is hereby repealed.

Section 2. The transportation or importation into any State, Territory or possession of the United States for delivery or use therein of intoxicating liquors, in violation of the laws thereof, is hereby prohibited.

Section 3. This article shall be inoperative unless it shall have been ratified as an amendment to the Constitution by conventions in the several States, as provided in the Constitution, within seven years from the date of the submission hereof to the States by the Congress.

Article XXII[14]

No person shall be elected to the office of the President more than twice, and no person who has held the office of President, or acted as President, for more than two years of a term to which some other person was elected President shall be elected President more than once. But this article shall not apply to any person holding the office of President when this Article was proposed by the Congress, and shall not prevent any person who may be holding the office of President, or acting as President, during the term within which this Article becomes operative from holding the office of President or acting as President during the remainder of such term.

This article shall be inoperative unless it shall have been ratified as an amendment to the Constitution by the legislatures of three fourths of the several States within seven years from the date of its submission to the States by the Congress.

Article XXIII[15]

Section 1. The District constituting the seat of Government of the United States shall appoint in such manner as the Congress may direct:

A number of electors of President and Vice President equal to the whole number of Senators and Representatives in Congress to which the District would be entitled if it were a State, but in no event more than the least populous State; they shall be in addition to those appointed by the States, but they shall be considered, for the purposes of the election of President and Vice President, to be electors appointed by a State; and they shall meet in the District and perform such duties as provided by the twelfth article of amendment.

Section 2. The Congress shall have power to enforce this article by appropriate legislation.

---

[13] December 5, 1933.

[14] February 26, 1951,
[15] March 25, 1961,

Index